THE POLITICS
OF
UNITED STATES
FOREIGN POLICY

THE POLITICS
OF
UNITED STATES
FOREIGN POLICY

SIXTH EDITION

Jerel A. Rosati
University of South Carolina

James M. Scott
Texas Christian University

 WADSWORTH
CENGAGE Learning·

Australia • Brazil • Japan • Korea • Mexico • Singapore • Spain • United Kingdom • United States

WADSWORTH
CENGAGE Learning®

**The Politics of United States Foreign Policy,
Sixth Edition**
Jerel A. Rosati and James M. Scott

Publisher: Suzanne Jeans

Executive Editor: Carolyn Merrill

Development Editor: Michael B. Kopf,
S4Carlisle Publishing Services

Assistant Editor: Scott Greenan

Marketing Manager: Michael Ledesma

Editorial Assistant: Eireann Aspell

Rights Acquisitions Specialist:
Jennifer Meyer Dare

Manufacturing Planner: Fola Orekoya

Art and Design Direction, Production
Management, and Composition:
PreMediaGlobal

Cover Image:

Flag Image: Statue of Liberty
© Andrew Howe/iStockphoto

Wrench Image: Wrench turning 'world' bolt
© Roy Wiemann, The Image Bank/Getty
Images

For product information and technology assistance, contact us at
Cengage Learning Customer & Sales Support, 1-800-354-9706

For permission to use material from this text or product,
submit all requests online at **www.cengage.com/permissions.**
Further permissions questions can be emailed to
permissionrequest@cengage.com.

Library of Congress Control Number: 2012955610

ISBN-13: 978-1-133-60215-6

ISBN-10: 1-133-60215-0

Wadsworth
20 Channel Center Street
Boston, MA 02210
USA

Cengage Learning is a leading provider of customized learning solutions
with office locations around the globe, including Singapore, the United
Kingdom, Australia, Mexico, Brazil and Japan. Locate your local office at
international.cengage.com/region

Cengage Learning products are represented in Canada by
Nelson Education, Ltd.

For your course and learning solutions, visit **www.cengage.com.**

Purchase any of our products at your local college store or at our preferred
online store **www.cengagebrain.com.**

Instructors: Please visit login.cengage.com and log in to access instructor-
specific resources.

Printed in the United States of America
1 2 3 4 5 6 7 16 15 14 13

*To our students and all those
who strive to learn and understand*

PREFACE TO THE SIXTH EDITION

Welcome to the 6th edition of *The Politics of United States Foreign Policy*. As in each of our previous five editions, our newest edition of this text engages students of American foreign policy to consider the players, processes, and politics that drive U.S. decisions and involvement in the global political system. This emphasis on the "politics" of U.S. foreign policy springs from our collective experiences in academia and the policy arena, and we believe we bring a focus that many other textbooks on this subject do not have. The struggle to define problems, formulate options, choose policies, and implement them is a highly political process in which a variety of players play a role, and in which the struggle over competing values, purposes, meanings, and interests is never far from the surface—and more important than ever in a world of globalization and constant technological change. Although politics can be seen as boring, we believe it is interesting and sometimes fascinating, and it is central to understanding foreign policy.

In this respect, we have written this newest edition of *The Politics of United States Foreign Policy* with five general goals in mind:

1. *To provide information and knowledge that is accessible, interesting, and useful to readers.* Throughout our text, we have tried to emphasize relevant information while stressing significant patterns, and their explanations in the foreign policymaking process. We have tried to convey this information clearly and with ample examples of the concepts, ideas, and patterns we discuss.

2. *To be comprehensive in topical and analytical coverage.* We have organized our text around three levels of analysis—the historical-global environment, the government, and the society—how they interact and impact the real world of politics and the policymaking process.

3. *To unify our text by emphasizing and integrating three central questions or themes in U.S. foreign policy throughout the book.* (1) To what extent has the president been able to manage and govern foreign policy? (2) What have been the dominant historical patterns of continuity and change in the foreign policy process over time, including the impact of the end of the cold war, the September 11, 2001 terrorist attacks, and the global economic recession after 2007? (3) How has the constant tension between the demands of democracy and national security evolved?

4. *To provide a strong sense of the actual workings of politics.* We believe that very few textbooks capture the "reality" and dynamic nature of politics, and this focus helps set us apart. We are convinced that students benefit from learning who the players are; how they operate, interact, conflict, win, compromise, and lose; and how the competing and complementary beliefs and the personalities of these players within and outside government shape foreign policy decisions.

5. *To integrate theory and practice throughout so as to encourage students to think analytically and theoretically.* We introduce and apply different concepts and theoretical approaches throughout our text to integrate and make sense of the material covered, as well as to emphasize the importance of conceptual thinking to further understanding. As a consequence, we encourage our readers to formulate answers to the questions of "how" and "why?"

Overall, substantive knowledge, historical knowledge, and theoretical knowledge are woven together throughout the book to maximize understanding and critical thinking.

NEW TO THIS EDITION

We have been gratified by the warm reception our text has received from students, instructors, and practitioners since its inception, and we have made every effort to strengthen and improve this most recent edition. While our overall approach and outline remain consistent, we have revised this edition substantially to ensure its continued relevance and success.

- *We have made considerable effort to streamline and focus the text, and make it even more readable.* The result is a leaner, more accessible book that is more tightly presented even as it maintains breadth and depth of coverage. Our text now consists of twelve substantive chapters (down from thirteen), sandwiched between an introduction and a conclusion. Throughout the text we have revised the writing to improve its accessibility.

- *We have included complete and timely updates to cover the developments since Barack Obama's election in 2008 through the elections of 2012.* Not only does this include the consequences for the presidency, but also Congress, the global economic crisis, the Iraq and Afghanistan wars, and much more. These substantial updates are woven throughout every chapter, making this revised version as up-to-date as possible.

- *New boxed features and incorporated throughout the book.* Each chapter now contains the following:

    o *A Closer Look* box to consider significant issues or developments in more detail;

    o *A Different Perspective* box to explore competing or alternative viewpoints on policy or conceptual matters;

    o *A Liberty–Security Dilemma* box to highlight the importance of civil liberties and the tension between the demands of national security and democracy in specific, real-world situations.

Each box also ends by posing one or more critical thinking questions to spur analysis and discussion.

- *We have added and updated figures, tables, maps, and other supporting material throughout.* While some older, important material remains, much more is new or updated for this sixth edition.

- *We have updated suggested sources for more information in each chapter.* These recommended books and articles provide sources for additional information and knowledge to guide students and instructors through the labyrinth of available resources.

- *We have updated the list of recommended websites* of the most significant "governmental and societal sources" that appears on the inside front and back covers.

HELPFUL SUPPLEMENTS (FOR INSTRUCTORS)

- **PowerLecture DVD with ExamView® for *The Politics of United States Foreign Policy*, 6e** (*Contact your Cengage representative to receive a copy upon adoption*)

ISBN-13: 978-1-133-93907-8

An all-in-one multimedia resource for class preparation, presentation, and testing, this DVD includes (1) Microsoft® PowerPoint® slides, (2) a test bank in both Microsoft® Word and ExamView® formats, and (3) an instructor's manual. The book-specific slides of lecture outlines, as well as photos, figures, and tables from the text, make it easy for you to assemble lectures for your course. The test bank, offered in Microsoft Word® and ExamView® formats, includes thirty multiple-choice questions with answers and page references along with five essay questions for each chapter. ExamView® features a user-friendly testing environment that allows you to publish not only traditional paper and computer based tests, but also Web-deliverable exams. The Instructor's Manual includes learning objectives, chapter outlines, summaries, discussion questions, class activities and lecture launchers, key concepts, Web links, and other instructor resources. *Contact your Cengage representative to receive a copy upon adoption.*

- **Free Companion Website for Cengage Advantage:** *The Politics of United States Foreign Policy*, 6e

ISBN-13: 978-1-133-93867-5

This password-protected website for instructors features all of the free student assets plus an instructor's manual, book-specific PowerPoint® presentations, and a test bank. *Access your resources by logging into your account at www.cengage.com/login.*

- **CourseReader 0-30: International Relations** (*Please contact your Cengage sales representative for details*)

ISBN-13 PAC: 978-1-111-48060-8
ISBN-13 IAC: 978-1-111-48059-2

CourseReader for International Relations allows you to create your reader, your way, in just minutes. This affordable, fully customizable online reader provides access to thousands of permissions-cleared readings, articles, primary sources, and audio and video selections from the regularly updated Gale research library database. This easy-to-use solution allows you to search for and select just the material you want for your courses. Each selection opens with a descriptive introduction to provide context, and concludes with critical-thinking and multiple-choice questions to reinforce key points. CourseReader is loaded with convenient tools like highlighting, printing, note-taking, and downloadable MP3 audio files for each reading. CourseReader is the perfect complement to any Political Science course. It can be bundled with your current textbook, sold alone, or integrated into your learning management system. CourseReader 0-30 allows access to up to thirty selections in the reader. *Please contact your Cengage sales representative for details.*

CONTINUING PEDAGOGICAL FEATURES (FOR INSTRUCTORS AND STUDENTS)

This book continues to rely on a variety of pedagogical features:

- *Examples and historical context* aid students in understanding the nature of the institutions involved, the dynamics of the process, and the larger themes addressed.

- *Overviews and summaries* are provided in the introduction and concluding section of each chapter. Chapters 1–3 provide broad context and perspectives on U.S. foreign policy, while grand syntheses can be found in Chapters 9 and 14.

- *Each chapter begins with a list of key questions* that guide students through the text and ends with a brief summary as well as key assessments, questions, and issues for consideration about the future.

- *Theory and practice are integrated and discussed* throughout the book.

- *Photographs and brief narratives* are placed at the beginning of each chapter, linking it to the essence of the topic of the chapter.

- *Major points* are highlighted within each chapter through use of *italicized boldfacing.*

- *Key terms* have been streamlined and **boldfaced** in the text and listed at the end of each chapter under the headings Key Concepts and Other Key Terms, which divide the terms into those concerned with theory and those with practice.

- *International and foreign economic policymaking* is addressed in a full chapter and integrated throughout the textbook.

- *Student (and instructor) reviews and summaries* of each chapter are aided considerably by the use of key questions, key terms, major points, and subheadings for each chapter—helping preparation for exams, papers, and other exercises.

- *Each chapter can stand on its own* and be assigned out of order to reflect each instructor's organization preferences (although linked together by addressing the three themes throughout).

A FINAL NOTE

All told, this major revision not only brings the text up to date, but it also delivers a more readable, better focused, and pedagogically helpful book. It draws on our many years of collective experience in the classroom and the success we have enjoyed working together with our students to examine the nature and consequences of the U.S. foreign policymaking process. We hope that you find it helpful in your classes and that it contributes to your efforts to engage your students on this subject as well.

ABOUT THE AUTHORS

Jerel Rosati is a *Professor* of International Studies and Political Science at the University of South Carolina since 1982. His area of specialization is the theory and practice of foreign policy, focusing on the United States policymaking process. He has been a *Fulbright Senior Specialist* in Argentina and Colombia, and a *Visiting Scholar* in Argentina, Armenia, China, and Somalia (in 1984). He also has been a *Research Associate* in the Foreign Affairs and National Defense Division (FAND) of the Library of Congress's Congressional Research Service (CRS) in Washington DC., *President* of the International Studies Association's (ISA) Foreign Policy Analysis Section, and *President* of the Southern region of ISA. He was the *PI (Principal Investigator), Program Director, and Academic Director* of a six-week *U.S. Department of State Fulbright American Studies Institute on U.S. Foreign Policy* for six years for 108 scholars-practitioners from over sixty countries. He is the author of over seventy articles and chapters, as well as five books. He has been the *Director* and *Reader* of over fifty Ph.D. Dissertations and over fifty Master's Theses, mentored many more individuals in promoting both their academic and professional careers within the United States and throughout the world, and the recipient of numerous outstanding teaching awards.

James M. Scott is the *Herman Brown Chair and Professor* of Political Science at Texas Christian University. His primary research and teaching interests are in international relations and foreign policy analysis and he has special interests in U.S. foreign policymaking, the role of Congress, and U.S. democracy promotion. He has authored/co-authored seven books and more than hundred journal articles, book chapters, other nonrefereed publications, review essays, and conference papers. To date, he has been awarded nearly $1,000,000 in external funding from various agencies, including the National Science Foundation and the Dirksen Congressional Center, and another $18,500 in internal awards from the universities at which he has served. Dr. Scott is the recipient of the 2012 Quincy Wright Distinguished Scholar Award from the International Studies Association-Midwest. During his career, he has earned over two dozen teaching awards from students, faculty, administration, and professional associations, including his university's highest awards for research (2000, 2001), teaching (2002), and research mentoring (2002). Dr. Scott has been active in professional associations, serving on the governing boards, as conference *Program Chair*, and as *President* of both the International Studies Association-midwest (2000) and the Foreign Policy Analysis Section (2001) of the International Studies Association. He began a five-year term as *Co-editor* of the International Studies Association journal *Foreign Policy Analysis* in Fall 2009. Since 2004, he has been the *Director* of the annual NSF-funded Democracy and World Politics Summer Research Experience for Undergraduates Program.

ACKNOWLEDGMENTS

We are indebted to a large number of people who inspired us, from whom we have learned, and who took the time and effort to directly assist and support us in the writing of this book. We would like to thank the following professors for having a large impact on our education: Bernard Brodie, Lawrence Finkelstein, David Sears, Steven Spiegel, Martin Weil, Sheldon Simon, Stephen Walker, Matt Bonham, Duncan Clarke, Stephen Cohen, Theodore Coloumbis, Nicholas Onuf, and Burton Sapin. We also very much appreciate the comments of the outside reviewers, including Philip Brenner, American University; Samuel B. Hoff, Delaware State University; John Creed, College of Charleston; Dan Caldwell, Pepperdine University; David Houghton, University of Central Florida; and Renato Corbetta, University of Alabama at Birmingham. Reviewers of previous editions include J. Joseph Hewitt, Christopher M. Jones, Andrew L. Oros, Steve Twing, Matthew C. Zierler, Andrew Bennett, Douglas Borer, Steve Chan, Larry Elowitz, John Gilbert, George Kieh, Martin Kyre, J. Patrice McSherry, Dean Minix, B. David Myers, Martin Sampson, David Skidmore, Donald Sylvan, Larry Taulbee, David W. Thornton, Lane Van Tassell, and Walter F. Weiker. We remain grateful to our academic colleagues for providing valuable feedback: Earl Black, Ralph Carter, Ken Clements, Roger Coate, Cooper Drury, Betty Glad, Mal Hyman, Joe Hagan, Don Puchala, Zhou Qipeng, Dan Sabia, and Laura Woliver. And we remain grateful to numerous professional colleagues, including: Hal Birch (U.S. Army), James Davidson (U.S. Navy), Paul Kattenburg (Department of State), and Frank Sloan (Department of Defense).

Graduate students provided tremendous and valuable assistance, including Patrick Anderson (U.S. Army), Tony Bell, Jane Berthusen, John Cass (U.S. Army), Tyra Blew, Kemp Chester (U.S. Army), Dave Cohen, John Creed, Janine Davidson (former U.S. Air Force), Scott Davis (U.S. Army), G. Scott Dewitt (U.S. Army), Lisa Flick, Dwayne Fulmer,

Mark Germano (U.S. Army), Rick Haeuber, Greg Haskamp, Byongok Han, Steve Hook, Pamela Howard, Shyam Kulkarni, Jack Lechelt, Jikuo (Jeffrey) Lu, Bobby Phillips, Jason Simons, Bret Traw, Steve Twing, Art Vanden Houten, KristinVanden Belt, Darin Van Tassell, Jennifer Willand, and Li Xinyu. We also have been fortunate enough to have had critical assistance from undergraduates: Teresa Brazell, Julie Close, Jeff Hall, Anne Harvey, Cody Lidge, Tina Morgan, Gwyn Pauley, Katherine Ray, Elliott Robinson, Peter Shooner, Adinal Sigal, Samuel Snideman, Juli Sproules, Kathleen Tenant, and Kathryn Ware.

Our book has benefited from the excellent editors with whom we have been fortunate to work. These include David Tatom, who guided the text through its first four editions, and Carolyn Merrill, our current editor at Cengage, whose excellent advice and efforts have helped us through the last two revisions. We are deeply appreciative of the patience, guidance, support, and professionalism they have offered. We also thank the many fine folks involved at Holt, Rinehart & Winston, Harcourt Brace Jovanovich, Harcourt Brace, and Wadsworth Cengage Learning. Finally, crucial psychological support has been essential and provided by our families and our friends. Altogether, it has been an incredibly satisfying and taxing experience involving the help of many people that has produced a book on the politics of U.S. foreign policy for which we alone take complete responsibility.

Jerel Rosati
University of South Carolina

James Scott
Texas Christian University

BRIEF CONTENTS

CONTENTS

CHAPTER 5

UNDERSTANDING BUREAUCRACY: THE STATE DEPARTMENT AT HOME AND ABROAD   130

CHAPTER 6

THE MILITARY ESTABLISHMENT   160

CHAPTER 7

THE INTELLIGENCE COMMUNITY 199

CHAPTER 8

FOREIGN ECONOMICS, THE NATIONAL ECONOMIC COUNCIL, AND THE GREAT RECESSION   237

CHAPTER 9

DECISIONMAKING THEORY
AND FOREIGN POLICYMAKING   268

CHAPTER 10

CONGRESS AND
INTERBRANCH POLITICS   302

PART III

THE SOCIETY AND
DOMESTIC POLITICS   339

CHAPTER 11

THE PUBLIC AND ITS BELIEFS   340

CHAPTER 12

POLITICAL PARTICIPATION
AND GROUP POLITICS   374

PART I

INTRODUCTION

Chapter 1 discusses why understanding U.S. foreign policy is significant, introduces the concept of foreign policy, and describes the underlying analytical framework used throughout this book for studying the complex politics of U.S. foreign policy. Chapter 2 provides the historical and global-power context, and describes the major patterns in the history of U.S. foreign policy from its roots to the present, ending with a discussion of whether the twenty-first century is an American century.

. . .

THE POLITICS OF U.S. FOREIGN POLICY

The foreign policy of the United States has experienced important continuities and changes over time. After World War I, U.S. foreign policy reflected a strong isolationist sentiment against Wilsonian involvement in the international political economy. Following World War II and with the rise of the cold war, the United States emerged as the global leader during the 1950s and 1960s, shaping its foreign policy around the containment of Soviet and communist expansion throughout the world. The cold war years were also a time when the power of the presidency was preeminent in the making of U.S. foreign policy and the American economy was the engine for the global economy. Yet, over the last few decades numerous developments have occurred throughout the world and American society that have affected the conduct of U.S. foreign policy. Events such as the Vietnam War, Watergate, and the breakdown of the Bretton Woods system in the 1960s and 1970s challenged the power of the presidency and America's postwar containment policy, while intensifying a relative economic decline. The collapse of the Soviet Union and communism in Eastern Europe in the late 1980s brought an end to the cold war, the September 11th 2001, terrorist attacks, the Afghanistan and Iraq Wars, and the global economic crisis that resulted in the Great Recession of 2008–2009, each opened up new opportunities, challenges, and questions about U.S. foreign policy in the two critical areas of national security and economics. In what ways has U.S. foreign policy remained the same? In what ways has it changed? What is its likely future? Answers to these crucial questions can be found only by examining the politics of U.S. foreign policy.

This chapter provides a basic guide to the politics of U.S. foreign policy and an overview of the rest of the book. *It addresses the following questions:* What is foreign policy and the nature of the foreign policy process, and why does it matter? How is U.S. foreign policy commonly studied? What basic perspectives (or levels of analysis) and central themes (or questions) will be utilized as an analytical framework to organize, discuss, and make sense of the politics of U.S. foreign policy?

THE RELEVANCE AND SIGNIFICANCE OF FOREIGN POLICY

Why should people care about the politics of U.S. foreign policy? Very simply, because *U.S. foreign policy has profound significance for the lives of people, both Americans and people abroad, in a variety of ways.* Americans, in particular, may be unaware of the important consequences that U.S. foreign policy has because the impact on their everyday lives appears so distant, indirect, and is often taken for granted.

For example, the American standard of living is heavily affected by the state of the economy and America's role throughout the world economy, which is affected by foreign economic policies involving trade in goods and services, investment in companies and capital, monetary policies and currency fluctuations, and access to raw materials and energy. In fact, the American economy has become more integral to, and dependent upon, the international political economy. Over the first decade of the twenty-first century, the United States has exported more than $1 trillion a year and imported much more than $1 trillion of goods and services. American investment abroad is approaching $10 trillion a year, while foreign investment is even larger within the United States. Monetary transactions valued at trillions of dollars are made almost every day in American and global markets, which has a significant impact on the value of the American dollar and affects investment and trade. The United States imports over 60 percent of its oil, much of it from the Middle East, making it a vital area of the world, as demonstrated by the Persian Gulf War of 1991 and the Iraq War. The U.S. government also spends almost $1 trillion a year (which is about one-third of the federal government's budget) on the military and a scientific-industrial infrastructure which heavily impacts the economy and the standard of living of people throughout American society. Such economic transactions as these have significant implications for the level of growth, inflation, debt, and unemployment within the American economy (and for the global economy in general), as well as for the jobs and incomes of individuals, including interest rates and taxes. All this is clearly illustrated by the Great Recession that began in 2008.

More direct and obvious is the impact of U.S. foreign policy on the security and health of the nation's citizens. Since the 1930s, the United States has been engaged in numerous conflicts, including five major wars, which required millions of personnel to serve in the military and potentially place their lives at risk. World War II resulted in over 400,000 U.S. battle deaths, over 35,000 Americans died during the Korean War, over 55,000 died during the Vietnam War, and over 7,000 Americans have died in the Afghan and Iraqi Wars. In addition to those who died, many casualties suffered from physical and psychological injuries in each of these major wars. In fact, since the Korean War, the United States has maintained a large permanent military in times of peace as well as war, deployed both at home and throughout the world.

Times of war and national emergency are also times of greater presidential power and political tension at home when the demands of democracy are usually in conflict with the demands of national security. This impacts American individual freedom, liberties, and civil rights guaranteed in the Constitution of the United States. Despite the end of the cold war and the collapse of the Soviet Union, such concerns about security, physical well-being, and individual freedom are not likely to disappear. Events such as the tragedy surrounding the events of September 11, 2001, and the war on terrorism, bring all these issues very close to the lives of all Americans.

There are other important areas of foreign policy that impact Americans beyond economics and individual livelihood, security, and individual health and freedom. Some that come to mind involve immigration and population dynamics, the drug trade, the spread of AIDS, travel and tourism, and issues such as environmental protection, deforestation, and global warming. The point is that U.S. foreign policy involves many activities and issues throughout the world that have implications—sometimes more immediate and direct, sometimes more indirect and underlying—for the everyday lives and futures of Americans.

Not only does U.S. foreign policy have significance for Americans, but it also impacts the lives of people throughout the world. Because the United States is much more powerful and wealthy than most other societies and peoples, Americans must understand that U.S. foreign policy can affect societies and lives all around the world—sometimes for the better, sometimes for the worse. In fact, the impact can be quite profound on the lives as well as the "perceptions and attitudes" of others, including Americans. Certainly the September 11th terrorist attacks; the subsequent war on terrorism; the wars in Afghanistan and Iraq; and the Great Recession, which began in 2008 and spread globally, clearly highlight the importance of America's connection to and policies toward the world, neither of which is likely to decline any time soon. Thus, studying how and why the United States does what it does in foreign policy—the politics of U.S. foreign policy—is important for Americans and the world.

THE CONCEPT AND NATURE OF FOREIGN POLICY

But what is meant by foreign policy? This term is used all the time, and we probably know foreign policy when we see it. But the concept is rarely, if ever, defined, and this lack of clarity contributes to ambiguity, confusion, and unnecessary disagreement. Very simply, **foreign policy**, or foreign relations, refers to the scope of involvement abroad and the collection of goals, strategies, and instruments that are selected by governmental policymakers (see Rosenau 1976).

In order to understand the foreign policy of a country, one needs to recognize who decides and acts. To say "the United States intervened" is part of our everyday language. But what do people mean when they use this phrase? In reality, countries do not act, people act. What the phrase usually means is that certain governmental officials, representing the state—that is, the United States—acted. A **state** is a legal concept that refers to the governmental institutions through which policymakers act in the name of the people of a given territory. The **foreign policy process**, or the politics of foreign policy, therefore, refers to how governmental decisions and policies get on the agenda, are formulated, and are implemented—the focus of this book. Nevertheless, while we stress process and politics, the substance of policy is woven throughout.

With this in mind, let us begin with *two simple, but very important, points about the nature of the U.S. foreign policy process:*

1. it is a very complex process, and

2. it is a very political process.

First, the U.S. foreign policy process is complex and extremely messy, not simply dominated by the president. Many Americans initially tend to hold a very simple view of the foreign policy process: that U.S. foreign policy is made and defined basically at the top of the political hierarchy, especially by the president. According to Roger Hilsman (1964:5), former assistant secretary of state for Far Eastern affairs in the Kennedy administration, "As Americans, we think it only reasonable that the procedures for making national decisions should be orderly, with clear lines of responsibility and authority." We expect decisions to be made by "the proper, official, and authorized persons, and to know that the really big decisions will be made at the top . . . with each of the participants having roles and powers so well and precisely defined that they can be held accountable for their actions by their superiors and eventually by the electorate."

Clearly, the president and his beliefs play a crucial role in the making of U.S. foreign policy. However, the president does not make U.S. foreign policy alone. According to Charles Maechling, Jr. (1976:1), "In propagating the delusion of a master hand and only one tiller, both the executive branch and the news media have collaborated as if in a silent conspiracy—the executive branch in order to enhance the prestige and image of its political leadership, and the news media to simplify the task of reporting and enlarge their audience by dramatizing a few personalities."

The reality is that many other individuals and institutions are involved within the government and throughout society in the foreign policy process: presidential advisors, high-level officials within the executive branch, the foreign policy bureaucracies, Congress, the courts, state and local governments, the public, political parties, interest groups and social movements, the media, and international actors. It is in this sense that the making of U.S. foreign policy is a complex process. It is also a messy process, for the variety of individuals and institutions that affect U.S. foreign policy do not stand still but constantly interact with and have an impact on one another. In other words, the policymaking process is not static but, as the word "process" implies, it is dynamic. If the process initially sounds confusing, don't be dismayed; given its overall complexity, the foreign policy process can easily be confusing.

Second, the foreign policy process in the United States is also a very political process. What is politics? In the minds of many Americans, politics is a dirty word that implies unsavory behavior in the political arena. Given such a negative connotation, there appears to be a widespread set of expectations and hopes that American politics should result in a rational process that is somehow "above politics." Let's turn to Roger Hilsman (1964:4–5) once again: "As Americans, with our flair for the mechanical and love of efficiency combined with a moralistic Puritan heritage, we would like to think not only that policymaking is a conscious and deliberate act, one of analyzing problems and systematically examining grand alternatives in all their implications, but also that the alternative chosen is aimed at achieving overarching ends that serve a high moral purpose. . . . And we feel that the entire decisionmaking process ought to be a dignified, even majestic [process]." This, unfortunately, is a rather simple, unrealistic view of the nature of politics.

One common definition of **politics** is "who gets what, when, and how" (Lasswell 1938). This definition emphasizes that politics is, as Hedrick Smith (1988:xvi) says in *The Power Game*, a "serious game with high stakes, one in which the winners and losers affect many lives—yours, mine, those of the people down the street, and of people all over the world." Another definition of politics is the "competition for power and shared meaning." This simple but meaningful definition emphasizes the importance that ideas and symbolism play in the policy process. A final definition describes politics as "competition between different individuals and groups for support of the public and influence throughout society in order to control the government and policymaking process for certain ends." This is the broadest of the three definitions, emphasizing the role of different goal-oriented individuals and groups and the various arenas in which the political process takes place.

The three definitions are complementary and contribute to an understanding of what politics is all about. Together they illustrate that the politics of U.S. foreign policy involves competition among differently motivated individuals and groups, that politics involves the flow of power and symbolism throughout government and society, and that it involves winners and losers. Such politics defines the **national interest**—a concept that is supposed to represent what is best for the country. However, it is a very subjective concept, for different people will define what is best for the country differently. Not surprisingly, the term national interest is often invoked behind a particular policy view to garner support from government and society. Ultimately, U.S. foreign policy (and the so-called national interest) tends to reflect the goals and priorities of those individuals and groups who are the most successful in influencing the political process within government and throughout society. Such a foreign policy process may be more or less moral depending on the type of value judgment made (Rosenau 1980).

Clearly, the making of U.S. foreign policy is a complex process inseparable from politics. This has been a dominant theme that most of the early theorists—including Gabriel Almond (1950), Richard Snyder (1958), Charles Lindblom (1959), Richard Neustadt (1960), Paul Hammond, Warner Schilling and Glenn Snyder (1962), Roger Hilsman (1964), and Stanley Hoffmann (1968)—emphasized throughout their work on the U.S. foreign policymaking process during the "high cold war" period of the 1950s and 1960s, when the world seemed simpler, a time when presidential power and the cold war consensus were at their apex.

Since the Vietnam War, the policy process has become increasingly complex, political, and visible. One consequence is that it has become very difficult for a president to govern successfully and lead the country in foreign policy. In the words of I. M. Destler, Leslie H. Gelb, and Anthony Lake (1984:20), in *Our Own Worst Enemy: The Unmaking of American Foreign Policy*, "The making of American foreign policy [has] entered a new and far more ideological and political phase." Or as Hedrick Smith (1988:xvi) likewise observed, "Presidents now have much greater difficulty marshaling governing coalitions" for "it is a much looser power game now, more wide open, harder to manage and manipulate than it was a quarter of a century ago when I came to town." The complex politics of U.S. foreign policy, if anything, has been heightened with the collapse of the cold war, the war on terrorism, and the global economic crisis with which both presidents George W. Bush and Barack Obama have had to contend (see also Scott, 1998; Hook and Scott 2012).

THE STUDY OF U.S. FOREIGN POLICY

The purpose of this book is to foster understanding of the complex politics inherent in U.S. foreign policy. Clearly, most Americans, as indicated earlier, and most non-Americans and observers of the American scene from abroad, tend to simplify the American political process—often equating "the president" with "U.S. foreign policy." Even the most educated and, as Hedrick Smith (1988:xx) found, "some of the most sophisticated people around the country often fail to understand the rules of the Washington power game."

How does one study and understand the complex politics of U.S. foreign policy? *Three different approaches to the study of U.S. foreign policy have predominated* over the years: (1) the policy approach, (2) the historical approach, and (3) the social science approach. Although these approaches are not mutually exclusive, Alexander George (1993:3) has argued over the years that different approaches to the study of U.S. foreign policy have produced different cultures, or communities, of individuals who have been "socialized in quite different professional and intellectual worlds." This has created a gap in communication and understanding not only between academic scholars and practitioners but also among academic scholars who take different approaches to the study of U.S. foreign policy (see also Herspring 1992; Nye 2009).

The "policy approach" predominates among practitioners and those involved in politics and the policy world. Policy analysts tend to concern themselves primarily with contemporary affairs, emphasize the present and the near future, make policy recommendations, and write for policymakers and a broad, general audience. Policy analysts may use the tools of the historian or the social scientist. The "historical approach" to U.S. foreign policy comes out of the scholarly tradition of diplomatic history and the humanities within academia. It tends to emphasize a historical understanding of U.S. foreign policy, attempts to recapture the specifics of the times, recognizes a wealth of factors influencing foreign policy, relies heavily on primary source documentation (such as government documents and private papers), and results often in well-written narratives for a scholarly and more general audience. Finally, the "social science" approach to U.S. foreign policy reflects the rise of science within academia, as found in the disciplines of anthropology, economics, psychology, sociology, and, in particular, political science. Social scientists tend to be concerned with explaining more limited facets of foreign policy decisions and outcomes in order to identify basic patterns. They attempt to understand these patterns through the use of concepts and the development of theory, employ more systematic research tools for collecting and analyzing information, and communicate their conclusions predominantly to fellow social scientists.

Each approach or orientation has something important to contribute, yet each cannot stand alone in furnishing a comprehensive understanding of the politics of U.S. foreign policy. Synthesizing the three approaches so they complement each other is key to acquiring breadth and depth of knowledge and understanding (see Hermann and Woyach 1994). Consequently, this work is sensitive to broad patterns and specific information about the politics of U.S. foreign policy, contemporary and past politics, a theoretical and historical understanding, competing policy views and recommendations, and a reliance on a variety of sources of information and studies from all three approaches. In other words, our orientation to the study of foreign policy is that of a social scientist sensitive to the importance of history and practice, thereby better realizing a full understanding of the politics of U.S. foreign policy.

THE ANALYTICAL FRAMEWORK

How will we make sense of the complex politics of U.S. foreign policy? We will use a general **analytical framework** that provides the basic structure or frame of reference for organizing and thinking about (i.e., analyzing, conceptualizing, and synthesizing) the information and knowledge available in order to understand the politics of U.S. foreign policy. In other words, it lays out the key factors that are the basis for analysis and understanding.

The analytical framework consists of two key elements. First, we will examine the policy process from three different perspectives or levels. Second, we will address three central themes that have been integral to the study of U.S. foreign policy since World War II.

The Three Perspectives

To make the complex politics of U.S. foreign policy fully understandable, we utilize the following *three theoretical perspectives or levels of analysis:*

1. the historical and global-power context (briefly in Chapter 2),

2. the government and the policymaking process (in Part II), and

3. society and domestic politics (in Part III).

Each perspective or **level of analysis,** especially governmental and domestic politics, examines the key actors and forces involved and how they interact and impact the politics of U.S. foreign policy. As Burton Sapin (1966:1) argued over forty years ago in his classic work, *The Making of United States Foreign Policy*, "While the characteristics of the contemporary international scene are of fundamental importance in shaping the contours of American foreign policy, they are not completely determining . . . An important part of the explanation for American foreign policy actions lies in the nature of American society and the functioning of its political system and its national governmental machinery." Such a multicausal framework is consistent with Kenneth Waltz's (1959) classic argument in *Man, State and War*. It is only by examining all three elements—the context, but especially the government and the society—that one can arrive at a comprehensive understanding of how and why American foreign policy is made (see **Figure 1.1**).

Figure 1.1   The Theoretical Foundation for Explaining Foreign Policy

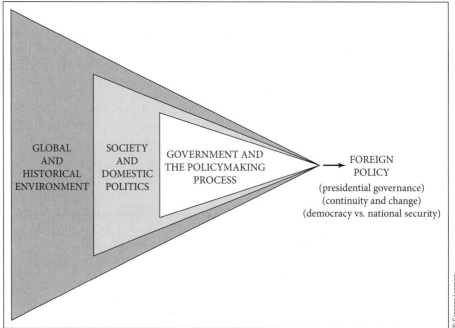

GLOBAL AND HISTORICAL ENVIRONMENT

SOCIETY AND DOMESTIC POLITICS

GOVERNMENT AND THE POLICYMAKING PROCESS

FOREIGN POLICY
(presidential governance)
(continuity and change)
(democracy vs. national security)

© Cengage Learning

HISTORICAL AND GLOBAL-POWER CONTEXT We begin with the historical and global contexts, which set the stage and provide the foundation for the politics of U.S. foreign policy throughout government and society. Chapter 2 briefly provides the historical context, an overview of the major patterns in the history of U.S. foreign policy from its beginning to the present, and a discussion of the future of American global power throughout the world.

GOVERNMENT AND THE POLICYMAKING PROCESS In Part II, we delve into the center of the policymaking process with the government—beginning with the president, who has the most immediate and direct impact on policy, and then expanding to include other important players. Chapter 3 examines presidential power and the president's ability to direct U.S. foreign policy, providing an overview of the politics of U.S. foreign policy for the rest of the book. Chapter 4 discusses how the president attempts to manage foreign policy and makes use of the National Security Council within the executive branch. This sets the stage for examination of the major institutions of the foreign policy bureaucracy and their input in the policy process: the State Department in Chapter 5, the military establishment in Chapter 6, the intelligence community in Chapter 7, and foreign economic policymaking in Chapter 8. After this substantive foundation has been established, Chapter 9 provides a summary overview and theoretical synthesis of presidential and bureaucratic power and employs different decisionmaking models to discuss the interaction of these actors to explain the dynamics of the policymaking process within the executive branch. Following coverage of the executive branch, Chapter 10 examines the role of Congress in foreign policy and the nature of interbranch politics. Hence, these eight chapters form the core of the book, since a comprehensive understanding of the foreign policy process requires considerable knowledge of the major governmental institutions and players involved in U.S. foreign policy.

SOCIETY AND DOMESTIC POLITICS Part III examines how the larger society and domestic politics affect the government and the foreign policymaking process, topics that do not always receive the level of attention they deserve. We begin in Chapter 11 with the significant and often underestimated role of the public and its beliefs—public opinion, political ideology, and American national style—in the making of U.S. foreign policy. Then we examine the most common and important form of active participation that affects foreign policy: group politics in Chapter 12. The powerful effect of the media and the role of communications on the domestic and governmental political process are examined in Chapter 13.

The book concludes in Part IV with Chapter 14, which provides a summary of all that we have covered, including a synthesis of how global, governmental, and societal factors interact, with a discussion of the implications for the three central themes in the politics of U.S. foreign policy in the twenty-first century.

The Three Themes

The information and knowledge presented in the following chapters is *integrated around three themes that address three major questions:*

1. To what extent has the president been able to manage and govern foreign policy?

2. What have been the dominant patterns of continuity and change over time in the foreign policy process, including the impact of the end of the cold war, the war on terrorism, and the Great Recession?

3. How have the tensions between the demands of democracy and national security evolved?

These questions have attracted the interest of scholars and are integral to understanding the foreign policy process, especially since World War II.

PRESIDENTIAL GOVERNANCE OF FOREIGN POLICY When most Americans consider who makes foreign policy, they immediately think of the president as the commander in chief. As we have already tried to suggest, the story is much more complex than this. In brief, prior to World War II the continuous struggle for power between the president and Congress in making U.S. foreign policy usually resulted in Congress dominating in times of peace and the president dominating in times of war. It was only with American involvement in World War II and, subsequently, the dawning of the cold war that power seemed to shift to the president in foreign affairs, laying the basis for this popular perception.

Two major patterns have prevailed since World War II with regard to the president's role in foreign policy. During the cold war years from Harry Truman to Lyndon Johnson, the president and the executive branch dominated U.S. foreign policymaking. However, in the post–Vietnam War years, the president's power declined within government and in society, making it more difficult for the president to manage and govern foreign policy effectively. In other words, presidents are no longer as powerful as they once were in leading the country in foreign policy. With the end of the cold war in 1989 and the global economic crisis two decades later, this post–Vietnam pattern has continued, but presidents now face the paradox of both greater opportunities to lead but also considerable political risks in attempting to govern foreign policy, as experienced by former presidents George H. W. Bush, Bill Clinton, George W. Bush, and Barack Obama.

CONTINUITY AND CHANGE Some analysts emphasize the prevalence of continuity—that is, little or incremental change over time—in the foreign policy process since World War II, while other analysts emphasize change. In fact, *three major patterns involving both continuity and change have predominated since World War II.* First, World War II and the rise of the cold war resulted in major changes in the context and making of U.S. foreign policy, such as the dominance of American power throughout the world, an increase in presidential power, the establishment of a national security bureaucracy, and the rise of an anticommunist consensus in government and society. These developments continued to affect foreign policy throughout the 1950s and 1960s until America's failure in Vietnam and the breakdown of the Bretton Woods economic system resulted in a second pattern of changes, including the decline of presidential power, the collapse of the anticommunist consensus, the rise of foreign economic issues and policymaking, and the relative decline of American power abroad. Not all has changed since the 1950s, however, and this is reflected in a third pattern: the continuation, for example, of a major American global presence and of a large and significant national security and foreign economic bureaucracy within government tied closely to society since World War II.

What has been the impact of the end of the cold war on national security and economic policymaking? To what extent have the terrorist strikes of September 11, 2001—the 9/11 attacks—and the subsequent U.S. war on terrorism changed things? And how will the wars in Afghanistan and Iraq and the worst economic downturn in decades play out in the future? It appears that many of the changes and continuities prevailing since the Vietnam War have intensified for the most part, though this will be explored throughout the book, given differences of opinion and the uncertainty of the future.

TENSIONS BETWEEN DEMOCRACY AND NATIONAL SECURITY Another major theme that has confronted Americans, especially since World War II, is the constant tension between the demand (or requirements) for democracy and for national security. The democratic foundation of the United States, embodied in the Declaration of Independence and Bill of Rights, is premised on individual rights and the need to protect individual freedom and civil liberties from the central government. However, World War II and the cold war resulted in a massive expansion of the national security apparatus within the U.S. government. This has resulted in a classic contradiction. Democracy demands an informed and active citizenry, individual access to information, an open dialogue about the ends and means of society, and governmental accountability—often a cumbersome process. The demands of national security traditionally are quite the opposite: secrecy, distrust of enemies from without and within, unquestioning mass support, and an efficient process allowing quick responses to events abroad. Therefore, democracy and national security are in constant tension with each other.

Three patterns have prevailed in the tension between national security and democracy since World War II. During the cold war years, when most Americans perceived a major threat posed by Soviet communism, national security gained undisputed priority over democratic practice in the politics of U.S. foreign policy. However, in the wake of the Vietnam War, democratic considerations and the promotion of civil liberties grew in importance due to changes in the foreign policy process. Therefore, the tension between democracy and national security also grew because both orientations lack sufficient political support from government and society to be ascendant. The Iran-Contra affair during the Reagan Administration is symptomatic of the difficulty of balancing these contradictory demands. Third, these tensions intensified after the September 11 attacks on the World Trade Center towers and the Pentagon and the subsequent start of the war on terrorism. At the same time, increased governmental involvement to promote economic stability and recovery and the incredible developments and constant change in **information communications technology (ICT)** may result in new and unforeseen consequences in the future.

POLITICS AND UNCERTAINTY
IN THE TWENTY-FIRST CENTURY

This book is organized in terms of these three perspectives, while the three themes will be discussed throughout the book. The analytical framework thus provides a meaningful way to make sense of the complexity and politics of U.S. foreign policy. We hope the net result will be your acquisition of better insights into and understanding of how and why the United States engages in foreign policy as it does.

This is a particularly interesting time to examine the complex politics of U.S. foreign policy because the cold war has come to an end, the United States has entered the twenty-first century, and the nation has experienced the September 11 terrorist attacks and Great Recession. George W. Bush and Barack Obama entered office at a particularly difficult and challenging time, as will be the case for future presidents. What is the future of the politics of U.S. foreign policy? How has the historical development of U.S. foreign policy shaped and affected its current politics and policies? How will the interaction of context, government, and society affect presidential governance, continuity and change, and the tension between national security and democracy in the making of U.S. foreign policy? We take up these questions throughout this book.

SUGGESTED SOURCES FOR MORE INFORMATION

Art, Robert. (1973) "Bureaucratic Politics and American Foreign Policy: A Critique," *Policy Sciences* 4:467–490. On the first wave of foreign policymaking theorists.

Destler, I. M., Leslie H. Gelb, and Anthony Lake. (1984) *Our Own Worst Enemy: The Unmaking of American Foreign Policy*. New York: Simon and Schuster. On the difficulty for a president to govern successfully and lead the country in foreign policy since the Vietnam War.

George, Alexander L. (1994) "The Two Cultures of Academia and Policymaking: Bridging the Gap," *Political Psychology* 15:143–172. On the differences between the academic and policymaking subcultures.

Hermann, Margaret G. and Robert B. Woyach. (1994) "Toward Reflection, Evaluation, and Integration in International Studies: An Editorial Perspective," *Mershon International Studies Review* 38(1):1–10. On the importance of integration and synthesis.

Herspring, Dale R. (1992) "Practitioners and Political Scientists," *PS: Political Science & Politics* (September):554–558. On the differences between the academic and policymaking subcultures.

Hilsman, Roger. (1964) *To Move a Nation: The Politics of Foreign Policy in the Administration of John F. Kennedy.* New York: Delta. A classic on the complexity and politics of U.S. foreign policy as far back as the early 1960s, see especially Chapters 1 and 35.

Hoffmann, Stanley. (1968) *Gulliver's Troubles, or the Setting of American Foreign Policy*. New York: McGraw-Hill. Provides a strong sense of the complexity and politics of U.S. foreign policy, especially Part III.

Rosenau, James N. (1976) "The Study of Foreign Policy," in James N. Rosenau, Gavin Boyd, and Kenneth W. Thompson, eds., *World Politics,* pp. 15–35. New York: Free Press. Helpful work that clarifies the meaning of foreign policy, the difference between process and policy, and its determinants.

Scott, James M., ed. (1998) *After the End: Making U.S. Foreign Policy in the Post–Cold War World*. Durham, NC: Duke University Press. An excellent overview and collection of chapters on the post–cold war era.

Smith, Hedrick. (1988, 1996) *The Power Game: How Washington Works*. New York: Ballantine. Provides a strong sense of the complexity and politics of U.S. foreign policy.

KEY CONCEPTS

analytical framework
foreign policy
foreign policy process
information communications technology (ICT)
level of analysis
national interest
politics
state

LEWIS AND CLARK WEST TO THE PACIFIC BY *FRANK R. "BOB" DAVENPORT.*
WHO FUNDED THE LEWIS AND CLARK EXPEDITION? WHY?
WHY DID THEY GO TO THE PACIFIC? WHAT WERE THE FUTURE
IMPLICATIONS FOR AMERICAN POWER?

HISTORICAL CONTEXT AND THE FUTURE OF U.S. GLOBAL POWER

In *The Tempest*, Shakespeare writes "What's past is prologue." The present and future of U.S. foreign policy is shaped by past decisions and actions, as well as the evolution of American power in a global context. How do most Americans describe the history of U.S. foreign policy? Typically, most use the label "isolationist" to describe U.S. foreign policy until World War II, when it became a global power—despite plenty of evidence to the contrary. The reality is that U.S. foreign policy has had a long and rich history since gaining independence over two hundred years ago, and understanding that history and the rise of American power is important to understanding where we are today.

This chapter addresses the following questions: Has U.S. foreign policy been isolationist as many Americans are raised to believe? What were the European and colonial roots of U.S. foreign policy? How and why did U.S. foreign policy—in national security and economics—evolve after independence as the United States became a global power in the twentieth century? And how has the global environment and globalization affected American power from the cold war into the future of the twenty-first century? Such historical and global context will help set the stage for better understanding the politics of U.S. foreign policy in the past and present and into the future.

THE HISTORICAL MYTH OF ISOLATIONISM

Many Americans have the perception that U.S. foreign policy was isolationist before World War II and internationalist after. However, as any U.S. diplomatic historian knows, this simple breakdown of U.S. foreign policy over time distorts much more than it enlightens. If one defines **isolationism** to mean noninvolvement abroad, clearly the United States has never been isolationist during its history. Even if one defines isolationism more narrowly to mean noninvolvement in European political affairs, it would still be stretching reality to conclude that U.S. foreign policy was isolationist. In fact, the United States was never uninvolved with Europe, whether in North America or across the Atlantic. As A. J. Bacevich (1994:75) stated, "Only by the loosest conceivable definition of the term, however, could 'isolation' be said to represent the reality of United States policy during the first century-and-a-half of American independence. A nation that by 1900 had quadrupled its land mass at the expense of other claimants, engaged in multiple wars of conquest, vigorously pursued access to markets in every quarter of the globe, and acquired by force an overseas empire could hardly be said to have been 'isolated' in any meaningful sense."

For example, a study by the U.S. Congress makes clear the *long history of the use of U.S. armed force throughout the world since 1798* (see **Table 2.1**). Before World War II, U.S. armed forces were used abroad 163 times. Before the Spanish-American War of 1898, there were 98 uses of U.S. armed forces abroad. Overall, the frequency of U.S. armed intervention has remained pretty much the same over time—an average of about one "armed intervention" per year for over 140 years. Although many of the cases might be considered "minor" incidents, especially from a twenty-first-century perspective, they all involved the "official" use of U.S. armed forces in conflicts with other states while pursuing American interests. Moreover, this list does not include the use of U.S. armed forces against Native American people as the United States expanded westward during the nineteenth century.

The extent of the use of military force throughout the world by the U.S. government since independence may come as a surprise to many Americans. Nevertheless, it demonstrates the United States' internationalist orientation from the beginning. Although the scope of armed intervention tended to be concentrated in the Western Hemisphere and Asia, Table 2.1 shows that the United States clearly intervened in other parts of the world as well. Not only does such interventionist behavior indicate that the United States was quite active internationally and behaved similarly to other European powers abroad, it inevitably made the United States a part of the evolving international political economy that was dominated by European states. In short, throughout its history the United States has been anything but isolationist in its foreign policy (see Braumoeller 2010).

Table 2.1 U.S. Military Interventions Before World War II

1798–1801—Undeclared naval war with France	1844—Mexico	1882—Egypt	1912–1941—China
1801–1805—Tripoli	1846–1848—Mexico	1885—Panama	1913—Mexico
1806—Mexico	1849—Smyrna	1888—Korea	1914—Haiti
1806–1810—Gulf of Mexico	1851—Turkey	1888—Haiti	1914—Dominican Republic
1810—West Florida (Spanish Territory)	1851—Johanna Island	1888–1889—Samoa	1914–1917—Mexico
1812—East Florida (Spanish Territory)	1852–1853—Argentina	1889—Hawaiian Islands	1915–1934—Haiti
1812–1815—Great Britain	1853—Nicaragua	1890—Argentina	1916—China
1813—West Florida (Spain)	1853–1854—Japan	1891—Haiti	1916–1924—Dominican Republic
1813–1815—Marquesas Islands	1853–1854—Ryukyu and Bonin Islands	1891—Bering Sea	1917—China
1815—Tripoli	1854—China	1891—Chile	1917–1918—WWI
1816—Spanish Florida	1854—Nicaragua	1893—Hawaii	1917–1922—Cuba
1816–1818—Spanish Florida (First Seminole War)	1855—China	1894—Brazil	1918–1919—Mexico
1817—Amelia Island (Spanish Territory)	1855—Fiji Islands	1894—Nicaragua	1918–1920—Panama
1818—Oregon	1855—Uruguay	1894–1895—China	1918–1920—Soviet Russia
1820–1823—Africa	1856—Panama	1894–1896—Korea	1919—Dalmatia
1822—Cuba	1856—China	1895—Colombia	1919—Turkey
1823—Cuba	1857—Nicaragua	1896—Nicaragua	1919—Honduras
1824—Cuba	1858—Uruguay	1898—Spain	1920—China
1824—Puerto Rico	1858—Fiji Islands	1898–1899—China	1920—Guatemala
1825—Cuba	1858–1859—Turkey	1899—Nicaragua	1920–1922—Russia
1827—Greece	1859—Paraguay	1899—Samoa	1921—Panama, Costa Rica
1831–1832—Falkland Islands	1859—Mexico	1899–1901—Philippines	1922—Turkey
1832—Sumatra	1859—China	1900—China	1922–1923—China
1833—Argentina	1860—Angola, Portuguese West Africa	1901–1902—Colombia	1924—Honduras
1835–1836—Peru	1860—Colombia	1903—Honduras	1924—China
1836—Mexico	1863—Japan	1903—Dominican Republic	1925—Honduras
1838–1839—Sumatra	1864—Japan	1903—Syria	1925—Panama
1840—Fiji Islands	1864—Japan	1903–1904—Abyssinia	1926—China
1841—Drummond Islands	1865—Panama	1903–1914—Panama	1926–1933—Nicaragua
1841—Samoa	1866—Mexico	1904—Dominican Republic	1927—China
1842—Mexico	1866—China	1904—Tangier, Morocco	1932—China
1843—China	1867—Nicaragua	1904—Panama	1933—Cuba
1843—Africa	1868—Japan	1904–1905—Korea	1934—China
	1868—Uruguay	1906–1909—Cuba	1940—Newfoundland, Bermuda, St. Lucia, Bahamas, Jamaica, Antigua, Trinidad, and British Guiana
	1868—Colombia	1907—Honduras	1941—Greenland
	1870—Mexico	1910—Nicaragua	1941—Dutch Guiana
	1870—Hawaiian Islands	1911—Honduras	1941—Iceland
	1871—Korea	1911—China	1941—Germany
	1873—Colombia	1912—Honduras	1941–1945—WWII
	1873—Mexico	1912—Panama	
	1874—Hawaiian Islands	1912—Cuba	
	1876—Mexico	1912—China	
		1912—Turkey	

SOURCE: U.S. Congress, House, Committee on Foreign Relations, *Background Information on the Use of U.S. Armed Forces in Foreign Countries*, 1975 Revision, Committee Print (94th Cong., 1st Sess., 1975).

European and English Colonial Roots

The original thirteen colonies were created as a result of European expansion in the world. During the fifteenth and sixteenth centuries, Europe was emerging from a feudal age and becoming a dynamic global force, starting the age of European discovery and expansion that would last into the twentieth century. The rise of Europe, and so-called European great powers—initially by the rise of Spain and Portugal, followed by the Dutch, and then the English and the French—would forever change the map of the world. By the seventeenth century, following Christopher Columbus's historic (and mistaken) voyage, most of present-day South America, Central America, and the Caribbean were colonized by Portugal and Spain (including the southern part of North America as far north as St. Augustine on the East Coast in present-day Florida). By this time, though, the power of Spain and Portugal were in decline, while that of England and France were on the rise.

England and France aggressively expanded and colonized throughout much of the world in search of power and wealth, including the "new world" of North America. The founding of Jamestown (in present-day Virginia) in 1607 and Plymouth (in present-day Massachusetts) in 1620 represented the beginnings of what was to become the thirteen English colonies. As Gregory Nobles (1997:54) writes, "Europeans did not come to North America just to explore, convert, and trade, of course; they came to stay. From their first footholds they extended their reach into the interior and planted permanent settlements. As they did so, the eastern half of North America became a patchwork of power bases, with European enclaves interspersed among traditional tribal territories."

From a global and European perspective, such settlements resulted in the extension of the British Empire into the eastern seaboard of North America and intensified European rivalry, especially between the French and British, for imperial control of the continent. Hence, the United States' historical roots can be found in the expansion and rivalry by which the fate of European empires was being determined in various parts of the world, including North America (see also Wolfe 1982).

By the latter part of the eighteenth century, what eventually resulted in the **American Revolution** involved Englishmen fighting Englishmen for the future destiny of the eastern seaboard and, in hindsight, much of the continent of North America. The issues that over time incited the American revolutionaries, formerly loyal British subjects, involved the nature of the imperial relationship with the "mother" country. From the perspective of the British crown, the thirteen colonies were an integral part of the British colonial and mercantile empire that increasingly spanned the globe. Therefore, the colonists rightfully were subjects of British imperial rule. From the perspective of the colonists, who increasingly saw themselves as possessing the rights of Englishmen, the British increasingly were abusing their power as they denied representation, taxed the colonies, and controlled trade with the rest of the world.

Eventually the political and economic conflicts escalated to the point of a formal **Declaration of Independence** in 1776. The document began by describing certain "truths" and natural rights (with which most Americans are familiar) and then listed the "history of repeated injuries and usurpations" by the king of Great Britain (with which most Americans are less familiar). It ended by declaring

> that these United Colonies are, and of right ought to be, FREE AND INDEPEN-
> DENT STATES; that they are absolved from all allegiance to the British Crown,
> and that all political connection between them and the state of Great Britain is,

and ought to be, totally dissolved; and that, as free and independent states, they have full power to levy war, conclude peace, contract alliances, establish commerce, and do all other acts and things which independent states may of right do.

The British attempted unsuccessfully to put down the unlawful "rebellion," while the colonialists fought a "war of independence" for five long years. The outcome was far from preordained. With significant French assistance, the former colonists finally won American independence when British General Cornwallis surrendered at Yorktown in 1781, and the United States was officially recognized with the signing of the **Treaty of Paris of 1783** (by England, France, Spain, and the United States). Ironically, in addition to independence for the thirteen former colonies, the Treaty of Paris also "gave the new American nation what England had fought for over a century to obtain: the vast interior region that reached westward to the Mississippi and ran from the upper Great Lakes almost to the Gulf of Mexico (Spain obtained all of Florida, which included the coastal region as far west as the Mississippi)" (Nobles 1997:91).

Significantly, in addition to the hard-fought efforts of American troops under General George Washington (and other American colonists who supported the independence effort), *other European powers were heavily involved in the war because of its implications for the European balance-of-power system and for the world.* German (Hessian) troops fought alongside British troops, and the Americans (through the Continental Congress—the governing institution at the time) entered into a critical formal alliance with France, which supplied badly needed money and supplies (including arms) and a French fleet that was able to penetrate the British blockade and prevent General Cornwallis's escape. Furthermore, American merchants and traders secured guns and other essential items from other Europeans, especially the Dutch.

As Barbara Tuchman (1988) details, such European support and commerce, though typically underplayed in American history books, were vital to the success of the American war effort. The creation of the United States, then, was a function of European power politics and expansion. And Europe and the larger global environment would continue to play an integral role in U.S. foreign policy after independence.

One way to think about the development and trajectory of U.S. foreign policy after independence is to divide it into *three major periods or eras since independence:* (1) The Continental Era, 1776–1860s; (2) The Regional Era, 1860s–1940s; and (3) The Global Era, 1940s–present. Although this division runs the risk of simplifying the complex history of U.S. foreign relations, it helps to reveal the general patterns of continuity and change that run through U.S. foreign policy (see **A Closer Look** on the historiography and differing interpretations of the history of U.S. foreign relations).

THE CONTINENTAL ERA

From its earliest days as an independent state, the United States had an active foreign policy. In **George Washington's "Farewell Address,"** the first president of the United States argued in favor of a foreign policy, not of isolationism, but of "nonalignment"—whereby the United States should avoid permanent alliances and entanglements. U.S. government officials followed his advice throughout this era, though most U.S. actions focused on the surrounding North American continent until the latter half of the nineteenth century. During this time, *two general goals preoccupied most American leaders:* nation-building and continental expansion.

A CLOSER LOOK

Historiography and Competing Interpretations of U.S. Foreign Relations

The study of the conduct of U.S. foreign policy has always been characterized by disagreement and differing interpretations, or schools of thought. As reflected in *American Diplomatic History*, an overview by Jerald Combs (1985), there have been two centuries of changing interpretations in American diplomatic history. Basically, a popular or orthodox interpretation prevails, is eventually challenged by revisionist interpretations, which often leads to a new postrevisionist synthesis.

With regard to an overview of the larger history of U.S. foreign policy, there have been three competing interpretations since World War II. By the 1950s and the height of the cold war, one interpretation initially dominated among scholars of U.S. foreign policy—commonly referred to as the "traditional" or **orthodox interpretation**. This interpretation usually depicted the Spanish-American War of 1898 as "the" breaking point in U.S. foreign policy, where the United States was characterized as more isolationist before the war and then emerged as a world power with the war. This interpretation of "discontinuity" in U.S. foreign policy is best represented by Dexter Perkins (1968) in *The American Approach to Foreign Policy*. Despite the use of a language of isolationism and the description of the growth among the mass public of isolationist sentiment toward European wars, U.S. foreign policy was still depicted as quite active abroad, though limited in geographic scope. Nevertheless, such an interpretation helped to propagate among the general public the notion that U.S. foreign policy was "isolationist" throughout much of its history, including after World War I—that is, until the cataclysmic events of World War II forced U.S. international involvement.

With time and new sources, other interpretations—known as **revisionism**—emerged that revised and challenged this orthodoxy. By the 1960s and 1970s, revisionist interpretations grew in popularity and importance among diplomatic historians, challenging the conventional understanding and its isolationist implications for U.S. foreign policy. Revisionists rejected the isolationist thesis and tended to depict the history of U.S. foreign policy as being much more "continuous" and globally expansive since its beginnings, as reflected in such classic works as William Appleman Williams's *The Tragedy of American Diplomacy* (1959) and Richard Van Alstyne's *The Rising American Empire* (1974).

Usually a melding of orthodox and revisionist interpretations eventually occurs, producing a postrevisionist synthesis, or **postrevisionism**, the third interpretation (as reflected in this chapter). According to this view, although U.S. foreign policy was never isolationist, it did experience both continuity and change over time. On the one hand, the United States steadily grew in power and expanded throughout North America and the world over 200 years. On the other hand, the United States experienced changes in its foreign policy; most important, the scope of its involvement abroad grew overtime. As Thomas Bailey (1961), one of America's preeminent diplomatic historians, basically confessed, "The embarrassing truth is that for eighteen years I further misled the youth of this land [about U.S. isolationism]. . . . By the time I became a graduate student I should have realized that cataclysmic changes, especially in the power position of a nation, seldom or never occur overnight. I should also have known that the very first obligation of the scholar is to examine critically all basic assumptions—the more basic the more critically."

Which interpretation (or combination of interpretations) do you think best explains the historical patterns of U.S. foreign policy?

Nation-building was critical since the United States was a new and relatively weak (emerging) country at the turn of the nineteenth century. It had won its national independence from the global superpower of its time, England, but it faced many of the problems that any new country with a colonial history faces upon gaining independence. Although far from Europe, the former thirteen colonies were surrounded by territories that England, France, Spain, and Russia coveted and fought over. As Walter LaFeber (1994:11) has stated, "From the beginning of their history, Americans lived not in any splendid isolation, far from the turmoil and corruption of Europe many had hoped to escape. They instead had to live in settlements that were surrounded by great and ambitious European powers."

The economy of the North American colonies also was dependent on the English economy. In addition, the new country was attempting to implement the first democratic experiment in the modern world. Given this environment, a priority for most Americans was nation-building: to build an independent country safe from its neighbors, construct a strong national economy, and establish a stable democratic polity. Therefore, much of the focus was on strengthening the internal situation in the United States.

The second goal, **continental expansion,** was closely linked to nation-building. What better way to protect the nation from potentially hostile neighbors than to expand its territory and push the British, French, Spanish, and Russians (as well as the Mexicans and Native Americans) farther and farther away from the eastern seaboard, preferably off the North American continent and out of the Western Hemisphere? What better way to build a strong economy than through the acquisition of more land that could be put to work? Strengthening national security and the national economy also contributed to political stability. But this meant that "Americans—whether they liked it or not—were part of European power politics even as they moved into the forests and fertile lands beyond the Appalachian Mountains. They could not separate their destiny from the destiny of those they had left behind in Europe" (LaFeber 1994:12; see also Weeks 1996).

Up to and including the purchase of Alaska from Russia in 1867, U.S. foreign policy was responsible for acquiring and eventually annexing increasing amounts of territory throughout the North American continent. Such *continental territory was inhabited predominantly by Native Americans and claimed by European states, but was acquired by the United States* from England in the North and Northwest, such as northern Maine and the Oregon territories; from France in the Louisiana Territory to the west; from Spain in the Florida territories to the south; from Mexico in the Southwest, such as Texas and the southwestern territories (including California); and from Russia in the farthest reaches of the Northwest, with Alaska (see **Figure 2.1**).

Ultimately, much of the land, in fact, was sold to the United States by the weaker countries in response to ongoing European power struggles or was literally taken by force. Americans, for example, during colonial times and after independence, repeatedly attacked Canada, then a dominion of the British Empire, in attempting to expand northward. *Native American peoples, naturally, suffered the most* from Western expansion. According to Walter LaFeber (1994:10), "a central theme of American diplomatic history must be the clash between the European settlers and the Native Americans"—a population estimated to be between eight million and ten million inhabitants throughout North America by the time Christopher Columbus first arrived. Clashes were constant with Native Americans— misnamed "Indians"—as Americans expanded westward."

Shortly after independence, in fact, the U.S. government devised a plan to annex new territory to the United States—thereby allowing new states into the Union. The **Northwest Ordinance of 1787,** originally devised by a committee of the Continental Congress

Figure 2.1   U.S. Territorial and Continental Expansion by the Mid-Nineteenth Century

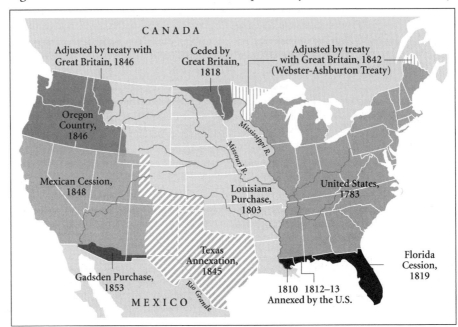

SOURCE: Walter LaFeber, *The American Age: United States Foreign Policy at Home and Abroad*, 2nd ed. (New York: W.W. Norton, 1994), p. 132.

in New York (the first capital under the Articles of Confederation, the first constitution), chaired by Thomas Jefferson, called for dividing territory into a gridwork of townships. "Once the land had been surveyed, it could be sold to land companies or individuals, thus creating not just a source of revenue for the government but also a pattern of orderly settlement in the territory." Eventually, when the population reached sixty thousand, the territory could enter the Union "on an equal footing with the original states in all respects whatsoever." Hence, "while the delegates to the Constitutional Convention in Philadelphia were hammering out a plan for a new national government, members of the Congress in New York [laid] out a plan for national expansion" (Nobles 1997:93).

The agents of U.S. continental expansion were not only the government, especially the army, but also thousands of private and entrepreneurial Americans spilling westward in search of land, gold, profit, and freedom. "To be sure, the relationship between settlers and the state was often a troubled, even tumultuous one, and the desires of independent-minded people often clashed with the designs of government officials for 'orderly' settlement. Still, whatever the underlying uneasiness, common people and policymakers ultimately became allies in a process of conquest" (Nobles 1997:15). The net result was that by the 1860s the United States had grown from thirteen colonies on the eastern seaboard to a country that spanned the continent. In the words of diplomatic historian Thomas Bailey (1961:3), "The point is often missed that during the nineteenth century the United States practiced internal colonialism and imperialism on a continental scale."

According to Van Alstyne (1974), the United States was a creature of the British tradition and was conceived by American leaders in terms of **empire**—as an **imperial republic,** more similar to European states than different. Thomas Jefferson, author of the *Declaration of Independence* and the third president of the United States—who dramatically increased the size of the United States with the Louisiana Purchase 1803 and sponsored the Lewis and Clark expedition to discover the West and search for a northwest passage to the Pacific (and the rich markets of the Orient; see photo at beginning of chapter)—communicated his expansive vision of an "empire of liberty" to James Monroe in 1801:

> However our present interests may restrain us within our limits, it is impossible not to look forward to distant times, when our rapid multiplication will expand it beyond those limits, and cover the whole northern if not the southern continent, with people speaking the same language, governed in similar forms, and by similar laws. (quoted in Van Alstyne 1974:87)

The United States was "active beyond the continent" as well, but this activity was more sporadic in nature. ***American commerce and merchants were active in all areas of the globe,*** especially Europe, the West Indies (i.e., the Caribbean), the Orient, and the slave trade of Africa. As Van Alstyne (1974:100) states:

> As a coastal country of the eighteenth century, the United States looked seaward as well as landward, and the paths of its growing empire in the nineteenth century stretched out to sea as well as across the continent. The United States was a commercial and seafaring state, as well as an agrarian state; and its mercantile and seafaring population was busily active in extending and developing long-distance sea routes even while the physical handicaps to transcontinental migration remained unsolved.

In the tradition of European expansion and the search for wealth abroad, "China was the magnet which accounted for the path of empire into the Pacific broken by Yankee shipping in the 1780s. . . . From Portsmouth, New Hampshire, to Charleston, South Carolina, there was hardly a port on the Atlantic seaboard that did not have its China merchants." As Van Alstyne (1974:170) further explains:

> Sealskins from the Falkland Islands, sea-otter pelts from the Pacific Northwest, natural sandalwood from the Sandwich Islands [i.e., Hawaiian Islands], ginseng from the Pacific southwest, opium from Turkey and India, kegs of Spanish silver dollars, and finally cotton-piece goods from the new New England mill towns furnished the bulk of the cargoes with which the American China merchants maintained a balance of payments for their purchases [of such commodities as spices, silk, porcelain, and tea] in China.

"During the eighteenth and nineteenth centuries," according to Alfred Eckes (1995:1), "the founders of U.S. foreign policy pressed to open markets and attacked mercantilistic barriers abroad in order to bolster the domestic economy and secure independence." Interruption of American commerce by the British during the Napoleonic War, for example, was a major cause of the War of 1812 between the United States and England.

Despite the "spirit of commerce" since colonial times, American merchants were unable to open up the mercantilist control of trade by the European powers and increasingly adopted a policy of economic nationalism, including the use of tariffs to encourage (and protect) the growth of domestic manufactures. Increasingly, tariff policy became trade policy in the nineteenth century. As Eckes (1995:23) found, "In practice the high-tariff position generally carried the day. Over a forty-year period from 1821 to 1861, the ratio of duties to total imports ranged from a low of 14.21 percent in 1861 to over 57 percent in 1832 under the Tariff of Abominations" (see also Kindleberger 1977).

The U.S. government, especially through the Navy, was also politically and militarily active beyond the continent (review Table 2.1). The first diplomatic consulate established overseas by the new government was in Canton, China, in 1789—one year after the approval of the (second) Constitution of the United States. As early as 1821 "the navy began operating a squadron off the west coast of South America; and by 1835 intercourse with China and the East Indies reached the point where it justified the establishment of a separate East India squadron" (Van Alstyne 1974:126).

Regarding Latin America, in 1823 the **Monroe Doctrine** was declared, stating that the Western Hemisphere was not open to colonization by Europeans. As early as 1850, the United States negotiated the Clayton-Bulwer Treaty for rights to build an interoceanic canal. And attempts also were made to annex Cuba and Santo Domingo (now known as the Dominican Republic) to the U.S. republic. In Asia, the United States, led by Daniel Webster, negotiated the 1844 Treaty of Wangxia, giving Americans "most favored nation" status (like other European countries) in trade and extraterritorial rights with China; Americans, led by Commodore Matthew C. Perry, forced Japan to open its ports to foreigners and commerce in 1854; and the Hawaiian and Midway Islands were occupied as transit points for American commerce with the Orient.

Unlike the thrust across the North American continent, these foreign national security and economic policies beyond the continent were less integral and much more sporadic, lacking any consistent pattern over time. Thus, it is most helpful to view this era as a period of continentalism in U.S. foreign policy.

THE REGIONAL ERA

By the latter half of the nineteenth century, the United States had been quite successful in building an independent and transcontinental country that was growing more powerful. By the end of the Civil War, the United States no longer faced any immediate threats from its neighbors in the hemisphere. The Civil War also settled the divisions between the North and the South, allowing political stability at the national level. The national economy was vibrant and growing, and the transcontinental railroad was completed in 1869. In the words of Van Alstyne (1960:10), "By all tests of pragmatism the United States emerged from that war more than ever an imperial state. It entered its period of consolidation and centralization, it began developing its internal economy intensively, and abroad it soon joined in the international scramble for material wealth and power," best exemplified by the **Spanish-American War** of 1898 in which Cuba and the Philippines became U.S. colonies.

As the United States reached the limits of continental expansion, more and more Americans during the latter half of the nineteenth century were beginning to speak of the future of the United States in terms of a **manifest destiny**. According to William Weeks (1996:61), "Manifest Destiny was founded on the a priori conviction of the uniqueness of the American nation and the necessity of an American empire." Such an orientation reflected three key themes: "the special virtues of the American people and their institutions; their mission to redeem and remake the world in the image of America; and the American destiny under God to accomplish this sublime task. Under the aegis of virtue, mission, and destiny evolved a powerful nationalist mythology that was virtually impossible to oppose" (see also Stephanson 1995).

In fact, the foundation for ideas of United States' special virtue, mission, and destiny had existed from the time of the Puritan settlements in New England. They were popularized by John Winthrop's sermon in 1631 that the Puritan colony in Massachusetts Bay represented a "city upon a hill" from which the regeneration of the world might proceed. Many Americans came to characterize the United States as a special place where human society might begin anew, uncorrupted by Old World institutions and ideas, giving it a special mission and role in the world.

William H. Seward, a U.S. senator from New York and later a prominent secretary of state under presidents Lincoln, Johnson, and Grant, captured this nationalistic and expansive vision in 1850, declaring:

> The world contains no seat of empire so magnificent as this, which, while it embraces all the varying climates of the temperate zone, and is traversed by the wide-expanding lakes and long branching rivers, offers supplies on the Atlantic shores to the over-crowded nations of Europe, while on the Pacific coast it intercepts the commerce of the Indies. The nation thus situated, and enjoying forest, mineral, and agricultural resources unequalled . . . must command the empire of the seas, which alone is real empire. . . .
>
> The Atlantic States, through their commercial, social, and political affinities and sympathies, are steadily renovating the Governments and social constitutions of Europe and Africa; the Pacific States must necessarily perform the same sublime and beneficent functions in Asia. If, then, the American people shall remain an undivided nation, the ripening civilization of the West, after a separation growing wider and wider for four thousand years, will in its circuit of the world, meet again, and mingle with the declining civilization of the East on our own free soil, and a new and more perfect civilization will arise to bless the earth, under the sway of our own cherished and beneficent democratic institutions. (Quoted in Van Alstyne 1974:146)

Following the Civil War, in fact, *U.S. foreign policy actively promoted political stability and economic expansion abroad, especially in two regions of the world,* Latin America and Asia. U.S. foreign policy became increasingly a presence on the global stage, as best symbolized by the Spanish-American War, fought in 1898. "The Spanish-American War was an expression of two powerful historic drives: the pull to the south, and the pull across the Pacific toward Asia" (Van Alstyne 1974:166).

The U.S. government and American business dramatically increased their "presence in Latin America," especially throughout Central America and the Caribbean. The presence of American business intensified with the rapid expansion of American trade, loans, and investment in the region. The U.S. government was also active in promoting friendly political regimes in the region that would be unresponsive to European involvement, open to American trade and investment, and stable enough to pay back their American bank loans.

Involvement of the U.S. government and American business in Latin America—a region that was experiencing decolonization, nation-building by independent states, and considerable political instability—resulted in constant American military intervention and occupation, especially after the turn of the century. As Secretary of State Richard Olney proclaimed in 1895, "the United States is practically sovereign on this continent, and its fiat is law upon the subjects to which it confines its interposition." The **Olney Proclamation** reinforced the original purpose of the Monroe Doctrine, that the United States had the right, and now the power, to intervene and dominate its "own backyard"—foreshadowing what was to come with the Spanish-American War and after.

From President Theodore Roosevelt's "Big Stick" policies to William Howard Taft's "Dollar Diplomacy" and Woodrow Wilson's "New Freedom," through the Warren Harding, Calvin Coolidge, and Herbert Hoover administrations, the United States regularly sent the Marines to crush local rebellions, prop up old or new regimes, and restore political stability in virtually every major state in Central America and the Caribbean, often only to return again and again. Military intervention usually meant that the local "customs houses" were subsequently run by U.S. government (usually Treasury Department) officials to guarantee that revenues from tariffs and duties were collected to repay American loans. Financial supervision, for example, lasted thirteen years in Nicaragua (1911–1924), twenty-five years in Haiti (1916–1941), thirty-six years in the Dominican Republic (1905–1941), and sixty years in America's colony of Cuba (1898–1958). American leaders so badly wanted a canal to connect the Atlantic and Pacific oceans that in 1903 President Roosevelt actively instigated and supported Panamanian secession from Colombia. He then immediately recognized the new country and signed a treaty giving Panama $10 million, plus $250,000 a year for rights "in perpetuity" for a ten-mile-wide strip—which became the Panama Canal Zone—that cut the new country literally in half.

Clearly, American involvement and power had carved out a regional **sphere of influence**. This was the period during which the United States acquired its earliest colonial possessions (and "protectorates") in the area, including Cuba, Puerto Rico, and the Virgin Islands. It was the 1920s and 1930s, with Herbert Hoover and then Franklin Roosevelt's "Good Neighbor" policy, before direct intervention of American troops into the domestic affairs of U.S. neighbors was temporarily abandoned.

American foreign policy was in search of political stability and U.S. economic expansion in Asia as well, with China being the major prize. "Merchants, missionaries, adventurers, sea captains, naval officers, and consular officers crowded into the Pacific during the nineteenth century and spun a web whose strands extended to every part of the ocean" (Van Alstyne 1974:125). Unlike Latin America, which was Christianized by the Spanish, there was a large American missionary presence in Asia, particularly in Japan and in China (over three thousand by 1905). And during the crisis with Spain over Cuba, the U.S. Navy, just before the Spanish-American War began, attacked the remnants of the Spanish empire in Asia, producing American Samoa, Guam, Wake Island, and, most important, the Philippines as colonies of the United States (see also Rosenberg 1982).

American involvement in Asia and the Pacific, however, (unlike that in Latin America) resulted in a much more limited use of force because of the region's distance from American shores and the strong military presence of England, France, Russia, and Japan. U.S. foreign policy in China, for example, emphasized an **"Open Door"** approach in order to maximize American involvement and trade (Williams 1959). Therefore, America's military and commercial involvement resulted in fewer costs as well as fewer gains. The United States, nevertheless, sent more than 120,000 American troops from 1899 to 1902 to fight its first non-continental counterinsurgency war, eventually defeating a national independence movement in the Philippines to preserve its new colonial control.

Even though U.S. foreign policy was oriented toward the regions to its immediate south and distant west, it became *increasingly active in European affairs and on the world scene* in general. While officially neutral during the early part of World War I, the United States eventually became a major participant in bringing about the war's outcome. Woodrow Wilson was, in fact, highly instrumental in influencing the Treaty of Versailles, which officially ended the war and attempted to create a new liberal world order through the League of Nations. During 1918–1919, the United States even sent fourteen thousand troops—along with the British, Canadians, French, Czechs, and Japanese—to occupy part of the newly declared Soviet Union in an effort to aid the anti-Bolsheviks and reestablish a Russian front against Germany.

The 1920s and 1930s are popularly thought of as the **height of isolationism** in U.S. foreign policy. There is some truth to this, evidenced by the U.S. rejection of American participation in the League of Nations, the rise of isolationist sentiment among the American public and a strong peace movement, and American reluctance to become actively involved in European conflicts (especially during the Great Depression and the early years of World War II). As diplomatic historian William Cohen (1987:xii) has argued, "rejection of the Treaty of Versailles and lack of membership in the League had little impact, however, on American involvement in world affairs in the decade that followed. In the 1920s the United States was more profoundly engaged in international matters than in any peacetime era in its history."

Not only was U.S. foreign policy active in Latin America and Asia, but the United States also took a number of important diplomatic initiatives with the Europeans and Japanese. From November 1921 to February 1922, the United States hosted and actively promoted a major naval disarmament conference in Washington, D.C., that resulted in the first major arms control treaty in modern times (in addition, the same conference produced a Four Power Treaty and a Nine Power Treaty involving Pacific island possessions and the rivalry in China, signed by the United States). In 1928, the United States and France jointly sponsored the Kellogg-Briand Pact in an effort to outlaw war. The United States also began to play an active, though unofficial, role relative to League activities.

Also, the United States became increasingly important to the international political economy following World War I, which was still dominated by the Europeans. As a result of the debts and damage incurred by the war, European economies became increasingly dependent on the U.S. government and on American business as a source of trade and finance. "Demand for American capital was intense throughout the [1920s] despite high interest rates. Europeans needed dollars to purchase American goods needed for reconstruction, and they borrowed regardless of cost. The rest of the world, which traditionally turned to European bankers, had no alternative in the 1920s but to queue up in Wall Street" (Cohen 1987:28).

This foreshadowed the global leadership role that the United States would soon fully occupy but was reluctant to take until Europe once again rebuilt and launched a second world war. As Cohen (1987:41) has asserted, "Clearly, the impact of American trade, investments, and tourism on the world economy in the 1920s was enormous. No other nation even approximated the United States in economic importance. The British, who kept first place among importing nations, lost their preeminent investment role in Latin America and Canada, and were being challenged throughout Europe and the rest of the world, including their colonies, by American capitalists." Nevertheless, the United States continued promotion of protectionism in trade and unwillingness to take a strong leadership position with a declining Great Britain, which contributed to the world falling into a great depression (Kindleberger 1977).

In summary, during the 1920s and 1930s the United States had become a great power and acquired a "formal" and "informal" empire. As Cohen (1987:xii) stated in *Empire Without Tears:*

It controlled an empire that included not only the Caribbean basin, but stretched across the Pacific, north and south, through Hawaii and Alaska, Midway, Wake,

Guam, Samoa, and the Aleutians, to East Asia and the Philippines. Manufacturers nurtured markets and sired multinational corporations in Europe, while mining and lumber interests scoured North and South America. American entrepreneurs and missionaries wandered across the Middle East, South Asia, and Africa. It was the dawning of what Henry Luce would later call the "American century."

Clearly, the United States was growing into a formidable power on the world stage while at the same time trying to maintain considerable unilateral and independence of action. Outside of Latin America and Asia, U.S. foreign policy lacked coherence and consistent involvement. Therefore, this era of U.S. foreign policy is best remembered as predominantly regionalist in orientation.

THE GLOBAL ERA

The Japanese attack on Pearl Harbor, on December 7, 1941, abruptly ended the regional era in U.S. foreign policy. The next four years saw the beginning of a third era of global involvement in which the United States, along with the Soviets, British, Chinese, French, and other allies, fought the Axis powers of Germany and Japan over the destiny of the globe. With the end of World War II, the United States became an active global power in the world and developed foreign policies of global consequence while the president was increasingly able to govern the making of foreign policy and lead the country.

World War II and Immediate Postwar Foreign Policy

Consistent with U.S. foreign policy throughout its history, *the Roosevelt administration's postwar aims revolved around two broad key issues:* economics and national security. But now the United States took an active leadership role in world affairs. The first goal involved the need to *restore economic stability and prosperity* in the United States, as well as in Western Europe and throughout the world. This was deemed essential because the U.S. economy was heavily intertwined with the larger global capitalist economy, particularly the Western European economies—which were the core of the global economy and shattered by the Great Depression and World War II. Many Americans also feared that the end of the war would produce a massive recession in the U.S. economy.

The original strategy, arrived at in Bretton Woods, New Hampshire, in 1944, was to promote multilateral efforts with American allies to restore and manage an increasingly liberal, global market economy, based on a new system of fixed exchange rates and open, free trade. What came to be called the **Bretton Woods system** would provide necessary assistance and rules for economic transactions principally through the creation of three multilateral international organizations: the International Bank for Reconstruction and Development (IBRD, known as the World Bank) to make loans for economic recovery and development, the International Monetary Fund (IMF) to support the stability of national currencies based on gold, and the General Agreement on Tariffs and Trade (GATT) to promote and govern open trade (originally the ITO, International Trade Organization, was to be created but was opposed by the U.S. Senate). Success on the economic front in promoting a liberal capitalist world order was thought to be crucial for ensuring peace and minimizing threats to international stability, as had occurred when the Great Depression led to the rise of Adolf Hitler (Gardner 1980; Ikenberry 1992).

The second goal involved U.S. attempts to *construct a new international political order* that was stable and promoted the national security of the United States and its wartime allies, thereby preventing the outbreak of further wars. U.S. postwar involvement was deemed vital because of the collapse of Europe, which had dominated world politics for over two hundred years until the impact of the two world wars. In an effort to protect national security, President Franklin Roosevelt relied on a strategy of multilateral cooperation based on a sphere-of-influence approach and the creation of a new international organization to replace the League of Nations—the United Nations.

Roosevelt's strategy depended on global cooperation among members of the "Grand Alliance" during the war: the United States, Soviet Union, Great Britain, France, and China. The instrument for maintaining cooperation among the "big five" and preventing a challenge to the status quo, which could lead to the outbreak of a new war, was the high-level diplomacy and creation of the United Nations, and especially the operation of the United Nations Security Council (a body in which each of the big five held veto power). Roosevelt also assumed that each of the five so-called great powers would exercise power over its regional sphere of influence: the United States in Latin America, the Soviet Union in Eastern Europe, Great Britain and France in Europe and their colonial possessions, and China in East Asia. This multilateral strategy of promoting global peace complemented the strategy of promoting global economic recovery and prosperity.

Admittedly, there is little scholarly consensus on the particular nature of the Roosevelt administration's postwar goals and strategy. Some scholars highlight President Roosevelt, and the foreign policy that emanated from his administration, as very complex and at times contradictory. In fact, it could be argued that he was both hopeful and pragmatic (see Stoler 1981). Whether Roosevelt was an idealist committed to democracy, human rights, and social welfare, and the establishment of the United Nations and other international organizations, or a pragmatist concentrating on the role of power and spheres of influence to restore political and economic stability is hotly debated.

Whatever the case, Roosevelt's overall strategy for restoring economic prosperity and national security quickly unraveled during the latter part of the 1940s. Before the war even came to an end, Roosevelt died and was succeeded by Harry Truman, who was unfamiliar with Roosevelt's postwar plans and lacked Roosevelt's considerable experience. The European economies were in much worse shape than most people had thought and were in need of assistance beyond that which the Bretton Woods–devised multilateral international organizations were capable of providing. Finally, any hope for lasting cooperation among members of the Grand Alliance to achieve national security quickly eroded as distrust, fear, and conflict between the United States and the Soviet Union escalated.

With the collapse of Roosevelt's grand strategy, U.S. foreign policy took a new course and can be seen as going through three periods (or eras) since World War II: (1) the cold war era, late 1940s–1960s; (2) the post–Vietnam War era, late 1960s–1980s; and (3) the post–cold war era, 1990s–present (see Ambrose and Brinkley 1998; Barnet 1983; Gaddis 1982; LaFeber 2006).

The Cold War Era

For roughly twenty years, *through the administrations of President Truman and President Johnson, U.S. foreign policy experienced considerable continuity based upon the twin goals of national security and economic prosperity.* The twin goals were based

on the quest for global security and stability from a perception of the rising "threat" of Soviet communist expansionism and the promotion of a liberal international market economy
based upon the principles of free, open trade and fixed exchange rates. The cold war era also
represented the height of the president's power to lead the country in foreign policy, as we
discuss further in subsequent chapters.

The development and **origins of the cold war** are a topic of unending interest and
debate to scholars. The orthodox and popular interpretation throughout the 1950s was that
Soviet-communist expansionism caused the cold war; revisionist accounts grew in the 1960s
to emphasize U.S. postwar ambitions in contributing to the cold war; and during the 1970s
postrevisionist accounts combining both orthodox and especially revisionist explanations
became quite popular (see Melanson 1983; Walker 1981; Yergin 1983).

Following the war, for the first time since independence and the period of continentalism, Americans began to perceive an external threat to their national security: the advance
of Soviet communism. *Because the new fear of Soviet communism became the key problem for most Americans, national security concerns drove U.S. foreign policy during the
cold war.* U.S. national security was defined in terms of global security and stability, for the
threat was perceived to be global and American leaders believed that, with the collapse of
the British and French empires, only the United States had the power to respond. Although
the United States and the Soviet Union never engaged in a "hot war" (i.e., a direct military
clash), the United States prepared for a direct military confrontation with the Soviet Union
and engaged in a global **cold war**. Under American leadership a **containment strategy** was
developed that aimed to deter, by the threat of coercion, the spread of Soviet communism,
first in Europe, then in Asia with the Korean War, and eventually throughout the world.

The containment strategy was initially embodied in the **Truman Doctrine**, announced
in 1947 and directed at containing Soviet expansion in the eastern Mediterranean countries
of Greece and Turkey. In the words of one analyst, its future implications for U.S. foreign
policy were to be global and quite profound:

> The Truman Doctrine contained the seeds of American aid, economic or military,
> to more than one hundred countries; of mutual defense treaties with more than
> forty of them; of the great regional pacts, alliances, and unilateral commitments:
> to NATO, to the Middle East, to the Western Hemisphere, and to Southeast Asia.
> It justified fleets of carriers patrolling the Mediterranean and the South China Sea,
> nuclear submarines under the polar icecap, air bases in the Thai jungle, and police
> advisers in Uruguay and Bolivia. In support of it, an average of a million sol-
> diers were deployed for twenty-five years in some four thousand bases in thirty
> countries. It contained the seeds of a habit of intervention: clandestine in Iran,
> Guatemala, Cuba, the Philippines, Chile, and the CIA alone knows where else;
> overt in Korea, Lebanon, the Dominican Republic, Laos, Cambodia and Vietnam.
> (Hodgson 1976:32)

The U.S. global strategy that developed during the late 1940s and 1950s involved
two interrelated, and mutually supporting, but distinguishable strands: a "containment
order" and a "liberal economic order." The focus of the first strand was to surround the
Soviet Union and its allies in Eastern Europe and mainland Asia with American allies, alliances, and military (conventional and nuclear) forces in order to deter the Soviet Union
from initiating a military strike and possibly triggering a World War III—which came to
be known as "deterrence theory." In the Third World, where the U.S.-Soviet confrontation

tended to be fought more indirectly over the "hearts and minds" of local elites and peoples, the United States relied on foreign assistance, counterinsurgency, and the use of covert paramilitary operations to promote friendly regimes. Containment of the Soviet Union was also pursued through the use of broad economic sanctions (i.e., boycott) by the United States against it and its allies (such as in Eastern Europe and Cuba). Diplomacy and other less coercive instruments of policy were put aside by the United States in East–West relations and superseded by the threat and use of coercion to deter and contain what American leaders saw as major challenges to American national security commitments and national interests (see George and Smoke 1974; Jentleson 1987; Mastanduno 1985).

In the second strand, as Western European economies struggled to recover from the Depression and the war, the United States also took the lead in unilaterally sustaining the Bretton Woods system to promote a stable and prosperous international market economy built around economic openness and multilateral management. This was really **Bretton Woods II**. The original Bretton Woods system was to be based on a multilateral effort by the Europeans and Americans. However, the war-torn European economies were in need of recovery, which prevented the Bretton Woods system from operating as originally agreed. Instead, the strength of the American economy allowed the United States to unilaterally support the Bretton Woods system and focus on European economic recovery—hence Bretton Woods II.

The revival of the European economies was to be accomplished by providing massive capital outlays (of dollars) in the form of American assistance (such as the Marshall Plan), private investment and loans by U.S. multinational corporations, and trade based on opening the U.S. domestic market to foreign imports. Therefore, the Bretton Woods international economic system based on free trade and fixed exchange rates became dependent on the United States acting as the world's banker. Although primarily European-oriented, and later also Japanese-oriented, U.S. foreign economic policy was also active in promoting a market system in the Third World through its support of private investment and development abroad (see Kuttner 1991; Spero and Hart 2002).

With European economic recovery under way and America's growing prosperity during the 1950s, national security policy became the predominant concern of most American leaders, especially after the Korean War globalized and institutionalized the containment policy (Halberstam 2007). Foreign economic policy often came to be referred to as **low policy,** while national security policy was usually referred to as **high policy**—an indication of their level of significance for those engaged in making U.S. foreign policy during the cold war years (see Morse 1973; Yergin 1983). One of the unfortunate consequences of the distinction between high policy and low policy is that most scholars of U.S. foreign policy and world politics since World War II have tended to emphasize American national security over economic policy despite the latter's obvious importance.

For twenty years American leaders, preoccupied with promoting national security throughout the globe, relied on a strategy of global containment and deterrence, trying to prevent Soviet communism from expanding its empire. American policymakers believed that protecting other countries from the Soviet threat indirectly protected the United States and enhanced its national security. Hence, the United States drew lines, labeled countries as friend or foe, and made national commitments to friendly regimes. And when foreign threats were perceived, the United States responded.

This policy of global containment inevitably led to American interventionism abroad and its tragic involvement in the Vietnam War. Over four different presidential administrations from the late 1940s to the mid-1960s, the steady and increasing American commitment to South Vietnam was never seriously challenged within the executive branch or by members of Congress. American policymakers were operating within the cold war consensus in which South Vietnam was seen as an independent state threatened by the expansionist designs of a communist monolith (North Vietnam, China, and the Soviet Union). Therefore, the United States could not afford to appease the so-called expansion anywhere in the world for fear that this would feed the appetite of the aggressor and allow other countries to fall (like dominoes) to communism.

The Post–Vietnam War Era

The Vietnam War was the first time in its history that the United States lost a war. Simply put, after investing as much as $30 billion a year and over 500,000 troops during the height of American involvement in a war that lasted at least fifteen years, the United States' containment strategy was unsuccessful in keeping South Vietnam an independent, noncommunist country. As a result of America's failure in Vietnam, the policy of global containment of Soviet communism, which had prevailed since World War II, was challenged by competing foreign policy perspectives.

U.S. foreign economic policy also changed in 1971 when President Richard Nixon responded to increasing international pressure on the U.S. economy by discarding the convertibility of the U.S. dollar to gold and placing a 10 percent surcharge on Japanese imports. In doing so, he violated the principles of fixed exchange rates and free trade, contributing to a situation in which the Bretton Woods system could no longer be sustained. This reflected a "relative" decline in the U.S. economy, the economic recovery of Europe and Japan, and the rise of OPEC (Organization of Petroleum Exporting Countries). Currencies would now float: the German Deutschmark, the British pound, the French franc, and the Japanese yen increased in value relative to the dominance of the U.S. dollar (the Euro did not exist until 1999). The price of oil would periodically rise. International trade and investment grew tremendously between the increasingly developed countries, while developing countries increased their foreign debt. In summary, the international economic system became increasingly market-oriented, complex, open to periods of rapid growth and prosperity along with economic instability, recessions, and periodic collapse of different economies throughout the world which the United States and a recovered Europe (the G-8) found increasingly difficult to manage—a trend that has intensified to the present day.

Despite Vietnam and the collapse of the Bretton Woods system, many scholars tend to see continuity in U.S. foreign policy since World War II. Most orthodox scholars tend to emphasize the permanence of containment as the basis of U.S. foreign policy since World War II; many revisionist scholars tend to emphasize the constant role of American economic expansion and management of the international political economy since the war. However, an increasing number of scholars and analysts have begun to conclude that the Vietnam War represented an important break in U.S. foreign policy in the post–World War II period.

At the time, this was probably best represented by **J. William Fulbright**, Chairman of the Senate Foreign Relations Committee and the first prominent critic to receive popular attention. In *The Arrogance of Power* in 1966, Fulbright argued that there were two Americas: one, generous, humane, and judicious; the other, narrowly egotistical and self-righteous. For Fulbright (1966:3), cold war policies and U.S. interventionism abroad indicated that an aggressive and self-righteous America was prevailing in U.S. foreign policy:

> For the most part America has made good use of her blessings, especially in her internal life but also in her foreign relations. Having done so much and succeeded

so well, America is now at that historical point at which a great nation is in danger of losing its perspective on what exactly is within the realm of its power and what is beyond it. Other great nations, reaching this critical juncture, have aspired to do too much, and by overextension of effort have declined and fallen.

The United States, in other words, was beginning to suffer the fate of Rome, Great Britain, and other past imperial powers, in which "power tends to confuse itself with virtue and a great nation is peculiarly susceptible to the idea that its power is a sign of God's favor, conferring upon it a special responsibility for other nations—to make them richer and happier and wise, to remake them, that is, in its own shining image." Thus, U.S. foreign policy, especially as it was being executed in Vietnam, demonstrated an "arrogance of power" by acting as the world's policeman. "In so doing we are not living up to our capacity and promise as a civilized example for the world" (Fulbright 1966:22).

Fulbright was severely criticized by President Johnson, conservatives, and cold warriors. Yet, Fulbright and his liberal internationalist perspective helped to legitimize public dissent and promote a more open dialogue concerning the ends and means of U.S. foreign policy that has carried into the post–Vietnam War and post–cold war years. As we discuss later in this chapter, such controversy and debates about imperial power and the future of U.S. foreign policy resurfaced in the context of the September 11, 2001, terrorist attacks, the war in Iraq, and the economic meltdown of 2008.

The failure in Vietnam and the breakdown of the Bretton Woods system represented international and domestic changes that have resulted in *three new patterns in U.S. foreign policy during the post–Vietnam War era until the late 1980s.* First, with each new administration, there was a modification in the direction of U.S. national security policy. Although a policy of containment continued to have its share of advocates, other policy orientations gained legitimacy and influenced the policymaking process (as illustrated earlier by Fulbright). Second, with the growth of economic problems at home and abroad, foreign economic policy became "high" policy again, becoming a major agenda item facing all presidents. Although most American leaders continued to see the need for a stable and liberal international market economy, they were often unsure over the particular strategy and means to promote economic stability. Third, in contrast to the cold war years, after the Vietnam War it became very difficult for any president or administration to devise a foreign policy that responded successfully to changes in the global environment and obtained substantial domestic support over time. This forced every president to change or modify U.S. foreign policy during his term, usually toward the political center. The result of these three political patterns, which will be discussed throughout the rest of the book, is that the continuity in foreign policy experienced during the cold war years was replaced by much less consistency and much more incoherence since Vietnam.

Although U.S. foreign economic policy became "high" policy with the breakdown of the Bretton Woods system in 1971, foreign economic policy has lacked much coherence over time in an increasingly globalized economy despite the simple rhetoric of "free markets." This is because of the growing difficulty of governments to address complex and intractable economic issues—such as inflation, unemployment, energy needs, deficits, currency fluctuations, "bull" and "bear" markets, environmental concerns, etc.—in both the domestic and international arena. This meant that U.S. foreign economic policy has lacked design and been defensive and reactive to domestic and international economic problems as they have arisen. Part of the problem is that most Americans continue to think of the economy as being "domestic" as opposed to being part of the increasingly globalized economy.

In the national security area, incoherence and inconsistency in U.S. foreign policy also has been visible. The Nixon and Ford administrations represented the first real change from the cold war emphasis on containment of Soviet communism to ensure global security to a "realpolitik" orientation and a policy of "détente" focused on counterbalancing the Soviet Union as a traditional great power in order to promote global stability and order. Although there was much disagreement during the early 1980s as to the nature of the Carter administration's foreign policy, a broad consensus has recently emerged that the administration entered office with a relatively optimistic vision of global change and a liberal internationalist orientation. Disagreement exists, however, concerning to what extent the administration's early foreign policy abandoned the containment strategy. In 1981, U.S. foreign policy under the Reagan administration fully returned to an emphasis on global containment of Soviet communism through the threat and use of force reminiscent of the cold war era of the 1950s and 1960s, while retreating from multilateralism as well, until the latter years when greater cooperation with the Soviet Union emerged with the rise of Mikhail Gorbachev.

Thus, the global era in U.S. foreign policy that began with American involvement in World War II resulted in two globally oriented foreign policy periods separated by the Vietnam War. From World War II until Vietnam, American national security policy was devoted to containing the threat of Soviet communism throughout the globe and was supported by a foreign economic policy based on American leadership of the international political economy. The Vietnam War and the breakdown of the Bretton Woods system represented international and domestic changes that called the ability of the United States to promote a global containment policy and to maintain economic prosperity at home into question. After Vietnam, successive administrations embraced different foreign policy initiatives to address the new context, and foreign economic policy was restored to a significant place on the foreign policy agenda.

The Post–Cold War/Globalization Era

With the collapse of communism in Eastern Europe and the collapse of the Soviet Union, the United States entered a new era in foreign policy—a post–cold war era beginning in the 1990s. The contradictions between the legacy of America's expansive and cold war past, the declining threat of communism and its collapse in the Soviet Union and Eastern Europe, changes in the American and global economy, and the uncertainty of domestic support have intensified. Such an environment predominated for President George H. W. Bush and President Clinton. Presidents George W. Bush and Barack Obama also have had to contend with the terrorist attacks of September 11, 2001, and the Great Recession of 2008. In this respect, *the end of the cold war has provided current and future administrations with new opportunities and constraints in their conduct of foreign policy.*

THE GEORGE H. W. BUSH ADMINISTRATION Straddling the cold war and post–cold war years, the George H. W. Bush administration's foreign policy was shaped by both the strong legacy of the cold war past and the great uncertainty of a post–cold war future. This was perhaps somewhat reminiscent of the Truman administration following World War II, in that the Bush administration was trying to cope with a postwar future of great uncertainty and conflict. Although accused of lacking global vision, George H. W. Bush's foreign policy in fact appeared to be heavily influenced by a pragmatic approach to world politics committed to managing the effects of the dramatic changes in the Soviet Union and elsewhere (Beschloss and Talbott 1994).

Not surprisingly, as David Halberstam (2001:59) described in *War in a Time of Peace,*

the top civilians in the Bush administration were cautious in general, befitting men who had grown up and come to power during a prolonged period of relentless Cold War tensions, tensions made ever more dangerous by the mutual availability of nuclear weapons. . . . The principal military men were cautious, too, but in a different way, befitting men who had experienced the full bitterness of the Vietnam War. Thus for all of the men around Bush, the geopolitical tensions in their lifetimes had been constant, the victories essentially incremental. Keeping things from getting worse was, in itself, a victory. . . . The irony was that the president and his most senior people had come to power in a period that was the exact opposite of what they had trained for.

Facing the dramatic changes caused by the end of the cold war and the collapse of the Soviet Union and communism, no dominant and consistent foreign policy pattern prevailed during the Bush administration. Instead, the Bush administration displayed a "mixture of competence and drift, of tactical mastery set in a larger pattern of strategic indirection" (Deibel 1991:3).

THE CLINTON ADMINISTRATION Overall, despite its liberal internationalist orientation, the Clinton administration, very much like the George H. W. Bush administration, *tended to be "reactive"*—as opposed to "proactive"—abroad, and hence, U.S. foreign policy was somewhat incoherent and inconsistent. Like its predecessor, the Clinton administration faced an increasingly complex international and domestic environment in which the days of the cold war's grand design gave way to a more pragmatic time of muddling through (Danner 1997; Layne 1997; Rosati 1997; Scott 1998).

After entering office in 1993, the Clinton administration was accused of considerable vacillation and hesitancy in the conduct of U.S. foreign policy. President Clinton did manage to initiate several significant foreign policy actions in Haiti, Mexico, Bosnia, and the Middle East. Also, the administration had great difficulty in responding to the continuing Yugoslavian crisis, and getting its NATO allies to work together multilaterally, until war resulted in Kosovo through a massive bombing campaign. For the most part major national security failures were avoided while the administration highlighted domestic policy and international economics. Most prominent in thisregard were passage of the North American Free Trade Agreement (NAFTA) and the Uruguay round of the GATT agreement, which produced the World Trade Organization (WTO).

THE GEORGE W. BUSH ADMINISTRATION AND SEPTEMBER 11

Muddling through continued through the initial months of the new George W. Bush administration. During the 2000 election campaign, much emphasis was on the need to lessen commitments, emphasize vital national interests, and exercise greater humility abroad (see Rice 2000). Once in office, George W. Bush's foreign policy orientation initially seemed reminiscent of his father's approach, perhaps unsurprising since he selected so many foreign policy advisors who had worked with his father.

What did distinguish the administration's foreign policy perspective, according to some observers, was not so much a radical departure from mainstream goals as in the means to achieve them. The administration held a "hegemonist" view of American foreign policy, committed to U.S. power and the willingness to use it. Numerous members of the administration tended to view power, especially military power, as the essential ingredient for American security, while also rejecting traditional emphases on deterrence, containment, multilateralism, and international rules and agreements. It was, in short, a view fundamentally committed to maintaining a unipolar world and acting unilaterally (see Daalder and Lindsay 2003; Ikenberry 2002a).

In reaction to September 11, the new foreign policy orientation of the Bush administration became more pronounced and aggressive, revolving around a global war on terrorism. In the words of National Security Advisor Condoleezza Rice: "I really think that this period is analogous to 1945 to 1947 in that the events so clearly demonstrated that there is a big global threat, and that it's a big global threat to a lot of countries that you would not have normally thought of as being in the coalition. That has started shifting the tectonic plates in international politics" (quoted in Lemann 2002a:44).

New enemies—Osama bin Laden and al-Qaeda, Saddam Hussein and Iraq, and terrorism—replaced the old enemy of communism. The new foreign policy orientation was based on deterrence, containment, and preemptive strikes on terrorism and alleged terrorist threats throughout the world. As Michael Hirsh (2002:18) suggested, after September 11 in the minds of members of the George W. Bush administration, "The United States was [now] faced with an irreconcilable enemy; the sort of black-and-white challenge that had supposedly been transcended in the post–cold war period, when the great clash of ideologies [had] ended, [and] had now reappeared with shocking suddenness." As in the past, the heightened perceptions of threats and enemies led to a series of new, but familiar trade-offs between national security and civil liberties as well (see **The Liberty–Security Dilemma:** War, Peace, and the Pendulum Effect).

THE LIBERTY–SECURITY DILEMMA

War, Peace, and the Pendulum Effect

As a country founded on the principles of liberty and limited government, the United States has regularly grappled with the tension between the requirements of those principles and the demands of national security in an anarchic and dangerous world. One way to understand the consequences of the tension and trade-offs between democracy and national security is to examine the patterns in terms of a pendulum effect. During times of war and danger when perceptions, real and imagined, of threat and fear of enemies increases, U.S. leaders have tended to embrace policies to curtail the civil rights and liberties of Americans, sometimes very dramatically, in the name of national security. As the periods of national emergency and danger pass, and perceptions of threat decline, leaders have generally taken steps to restore and protect liberties and roll back the security measures that were adopted.

Thus, the pendulum swings between these two competing objectives, and has done so throughout U.S. history (see Farber 2008; Stone 2007).

While we could trace this pattern back to the earliest days of the United States (e.g., the passage of the Alien and Sedition Acts in 1798; measures such as the suspension of the writ of habeas corpus and the imposition of martial law during, and after, the American Civil War), let's consider examples of this pendulum effect from the last one hundred years or so to illustrate the actions and reactions that form the pattern for good discussions of the dilemmas between liberty and security over the course of American history).

- During World War I, the U.S. government imposed a broad array of restrictions on socialist, anarchist, and other groups, including German-Americans, in the name of security. This included the Espionage Act of 1917 and the Sedition Act of 1918 (regulating anti-government speech and opinion) and continued with the anti-Bolshevik and anti-socialist Palmer Raids in the 1920s led by J. Edgar Hoover and the early FBI. In the years following World War I, almost all of these restrictions were rolled back by the U.S. Supreme Court and the U.S. Congress.

- World War II led to the infamous presidential decision in Executive Order 9066 to relocate and intern over 100,000 Japanese-Americans in a series of "War Relocation Camps," actions later rescinded in 1945, and the Smith (or Alien Registration) Act of 1940, which required non-U.S. citizens to register with the government and established criminal penalties for advocating—or belonging to a group advocating—the overthrow of the U.S. government.

- During the early cold war, the threat and fear of communism led to numerous congressional investigations (such as by the House Committee on Un-American Activities); loyalty oaths; official lists of supposed subversive organizations; informal "blacklists"; domestic surveillance, investigations, and infiltration of thousands of individuals and groups by the government and local leaders (such as *Operation Cointelpro* under J. Edgar Hoover and the FBI). This came to be known as McCarthyism and produced a powerful backlash with the rise of the civil rights and anti-Vietnam War movements.

- After 9/11, the Bush administration quickly submitted an anti-terrorism bill known as the **USA Patriot Act** (which stands for United and Strengthening America by Providing Appropriate Tools Required to Intercept and Obstruct Terrorism), which became law in October 2001. The USA Patriot Act increased penalties for acts of terrorism and harboring or financing terrorists or terrorist organizations. It expanded the government's ability to conduct electronic surveillance; get subpoenas for e-mail, Internet, and telephone communications; acquire nationwide search warrants; detain immigrants without charges; and penetrate (and sanction) money-laundering banks. It also permitted government officials to share grand jury information to thwart terrorism and relax the conditions under which judges may authorize intelligence wiretaps. Beginning in 2005, when the Iraq War went badly, the act became increasingly controversial, challenged, and modified (but not outright eliminated).

According to Geoffrey Stone (2007), it is almost as if the United States has two constitutions: one for war and one for peace. Or as Richard Hofstadter (1965) has found, times of fear and perceived threats to national security are often accompanied by what he has called "the paranoid style in American politics." This typically occurs because most segments of society tend to rally behind the president and the government in order to fight the enemy abroad (and at home). War and national emergencies, in particular, tend to be times when fear increases and little tolerance exists for individuals and groups that publicly criticize or challenge the government's foreign policy or the status quo within society. Clearly, leaders and citizens of the United States continue to struggle with the dilemmas of liberty and security.

Is the United States currently in a time of war, of peace, or "war in a time of peace"? What should be the appropriate balance between the demands of liberty and security for conducting a war on terrorism?

Bush's global war on terrorism resulted in a major defense buildup, an emphasis on "homeland security," an effort to distinguish between friends and foes, and a heavy reliance on the use of force abroad, especially in Afghanistan and Iraq. The administration's strategy became much more unilateral in orientation, saw little relevance of international organizations like the United Nations, assumed international support is often a function of coercion, that democracy and Western liberalism should and can spread throughout the world, and, most importantly, officially emphasized the threat and use of "overt" preemptive—or preventive—strikes.

Together, such a policy orientation is reflected in what has become known as the **Bush Doctrine** as expressed in George W. Bush's (2002) West Point speech. A much more elaborate and detailed account of the Bush administration's post–September 11 strategy can be found in *The National Security Strategy of the United States of America* published by the White House in September 2002 (U.S., White House 2002), characterized by some as a sweeping redesign of U.S. strategy (Gaddis 2005), and by others as more reflective of continuity with post–World War II policy (Leffler 2004). Whatever the perspective, in many ways, the war on terrorism became the core and the mantra of the George W. Bush administration's foreign policy, to the neglect of numerous other foreign policy issues and approaches, including the international political economy. In the words of one critic, "The Bush Doctrine has been used to justify a new assertiveness abroad unprecedented since the early days of the Cold War—amounting nearly to the declaration of American hegemony—and it has redefined U.S. relationships around the world" (Hirsh 2002:19).

THE BARACK OBAMA ADMINISTRATION AND THE GREAT RECESSION

The Obama administration entered office faced with the need to address the war on terrorism and the legacy of the Iraq War, but also at a time when the American and international political economy were teetering on the brink of collapse, now referred to as the **Global Recession**. The administration's first priority was to prevent the economic situation from further deteriorating and potentially collapsing into a great depression reminiscent of the 1930s. The administration attempted to do so supporting the threatened banks to prevent their collapse and restore the "confidence" and functioning of the credit markets so individuals, institutions, and corporations would have access to loans. In addition, the administration passed a large stimulus package intended to promote confidence among businesses and American consumers (to spend again), since U.S. economic growth is driven by as much as 70 percent consumer spending.

The Obama administration emphasized the need for Keynesian governmental spending and involvement as the primary source for calming the markets, restoring confidence, and increasing the likelihood of an economic recovery—in a very pragmatic and experimental way. The administration also highlighted the need for a multilateral response (through the G-20 countries and international financial institutions) since the economic collapse was global in its scope and the United States could not unilaterally address the problem on its own given the spread of globalization. In fact, what made the global economic crisis so problematic and significant is that it began, not in Third World or emerging market countries, but in the ultimate core of the developed and capitalist market economies—the United States itself (discussed at greater length in Chapter 8).

In addition to urgently needed attention to foreign economic policy, the Obama administration also had to deal with a variety of national security issues inherited from previous administrations. The most pressing was the administration's efforts to withdraw American troops from the Iraq War and turn the war over to the Iraqis while at the same time increasing American troop levels in Afghanistan and operations in Pakistan given the deteriorating and increasingly unstable situations in those countries. In addition, numerous other issues needed to be addressed including North Korea, Iran, and nuclear proliferation, the Arab–Israeli conflict, the future of Russia, oil dependency, immigration, and global warming. Moreover, substantive debates and divisions deepened on questions of the proper nature, uses, and balance among foreign instruments including diplomacy, force, aid, and others.

The Obama administration also was very active in trying to restore confidence in U.S. leadership and promote the likelihood of "multilateral" responses in attempting to react and address such global problems. As President Obama (2009) articulated early on in contradiction to the unilateralism of the Bush administration:

> There are a couple of principles that I've tried to apply across the board: Number one, that the United States remains the most powerful, wealthiest nation on Earth, but we're only one nation, and that the problems that we confront, whether it's drug cartels, climate change, terrorism, you name it, can't be solved just by one country. And I think if you start with that approach, then you are inclined to listen and not just talk. . . . Countries are going to have interests, and changes in foreign policy approaches by my administration aren't suddenly going to make all those interests that may diverge from ours disappear. What it does mean, though, is, at the margins, they are more likely to want to cooperate than not cooperate. It means that where there is resistance to a particular set of policies that we're pursuing, that resistance may turn out just to be based on old preconceptions or ideological dogmas that, when they're cleared away, it turns out that we can actually solve a problem.

Beyond an emphasis on building multilateral responses to international issues, it is unclear how much the Obama administration was driven by an idealistic worldview or by pragmatic efforts to react to the plateful of national security and economic issues it faced. During the 2012 election campaign, President Obama blended these elements of idealism and pragmatism as he defended his foreign policy record against his rival, former Massachusetts governor Mitt Romney. While the 2012 election focused on economic issues, President Obama stressed his administration's practical approach to trade, his aggressive efforts in the war on terrorism -- including the successful raid that killed Osama bin Laden in Pakistan -- and his commitments to a strong defense. At the same time, he also stressed his successful engagement and multilateral cooperation with allies, friends and others to address other problems. This blend of idealism and pragmatism was especially evident in the October 22nd, 2012 foreign policy debate between President Obama and his rival, which the public judged a win for the president, helping him to his electoral victory about two weeks later.

In an August 12, 2010 memorandum written by Obama for his staff in response to the reform movements known as the "Arab spring," the goals of democracy and reform were couched in the language of U.S. interests rather than the sharp moral language that presidents often use in public:

> Increased repression could threaten the political and economic stability of some of our allies, leave us with fewer capable, credible partners who can support our

regional priorities, and further alienate citizens in the region. . . . Moreover, our regional and international credibility will be undermined if we are seen or perceived to be backing repressive regimes and ignoring the rights and aspirations of citizens (Lizza, 2011).

President Obama appeared to seek a delicate balance: to talk like an idealist while often acting like a realist. In the words of one of President Obama's major advisors, "Pursuing our interests and spreading our ideals thus requires stealth and modesty as well as military strength. It's so at odds with the John Wayne expectation for what America is in the world," This balance was on display in the administration's careful reaction to the Arab Spring events and many other matters over his first term. This was apparently effective throughout his successful re-election campaign despite an economy that was slowly recovering -- public approval of Obama's handling of the economy was split. At the same time, President Obama was given higher marks for foreign and national security policy than his rival, an unusual turn of events from previous elections in which Republicans have typically enjoyed the more favorable view on such issues,

Clearly, in a post–cold war world numerous questions emerge: What exactly are America's vital interests in a post–cold war, post–September 11, and post-Great Recession world? To what extent will the American and global economy recover? Will economics continue to play an increasing role in U.S. foreign policy in a world of globalization? To what extent should U.S. foreign policy revolve around the threat of terrorism and what does it mean to conduct a war on terrorism? What role should be played by U.S. force? To what extent will the conflicts in Afghanistan and Pakistan become "Obama's" wars? What other global issues should the United States address into the foreseeable future? Should it emphasize unilateral or multilateral initiatives? To what extent should (or can) the United States be reactive or proactive? None of these questions, nor others, are easy to answer, but they will have to be addressed in one way or another and will impact the Obama administration as well as future ones. Answers to these questions will be heavily impacted by the global environment and American power, to which we now turn.

GLOBALIZATION, AMERICAN POWER, AND THE TWENTY-FIRST CENTURY

The preceding overview emphasized the history of U.S. foreign policy. In addition to historical context, although briefly mentioned and alluded to, the global context and the nature of American power is consequential for foreign policy—the focus of the remainder of the chapter. The **global context**—or setting, environment, or milieu—refers to phenomena beyond or external to the institutions, beliefs, and processes of human interaction in government and society. This context refers to such elements as the country's power (military and economic), resources, level of technology, and the larger global arena of which the United States is a part—all impact the complex politics of U.S. foreign policy in the past, present, and future.

Although frequently obscure in the causal chain of events and therefore difficult to ascertain, *the global environment plays a significant role in the politics of U.S. foreign policy in two principal ways.* First, global structures and patterns set the "underlying" conditions or parameters of likely U.S. foreign policy. For example, the general patterns that prevail throughout the globe affect American power and the United States' international role, thus setting the stage in which the politics of U.S. foreign policy operates in society and government. Second, particular world events and relationships often have an "immediate" impact on domestic politics and the U.S. policymaking process. For example, **international crises** (commonly defined in terms of surprise, a threat to values, and little time to respond) are events that catapult an issue on the political agenda and often play an influential role in the politics of U.S. foreign policy. Therefore, both general patterns and immediate events in America's global context affect one another and are often mutually reinforcing (see Gilpin 1981; Hermann 1969; Lebow 1981; Morse 1973; Waltz 1954).

The underlying and immediate impact of the global context on power and politics occurs in two ways: through the perceptions that people have of the world and by directly affecting the performance and outcome of foreign policy behavior. Such a distinction between the **psychological versus objective environment** is explained by Harold and Margaret Sprout (1965) in *The Ecological Perspective on Human Affair:*

> So far as we can determine, environmental factors (both nonhuman and social) can affect human activities in only two ways: such factors can be perceived, reacted to, and taken into account by the human individual or individuals under consideration. In this way, and in this way only . . . environmental factors can be said to 'influence,' or to 'condition,' or otherwise to 'affect' human values and preferences, moods, and attitudes, choices and decision.

In contrast, environmental factors limit the execution of human undertakings. "Such limitations on performance, accomplishment, outcome, or operational result," the Sprouts assert, "may not—often do not—derive from or depend upon the individual's perception or other psychological behavior."

Although there are numerous ways to organize these larger contextual patterns, it is useful to speak of *three sets of developments, or major stages, in the evolution of the global environment and American power that have been dominant since World War II and which correspond to the history of U.S. globalism:* (1) the rise of a global cold war and American hegemony from the 1940s to 1960s; (2) increasing global complexity and the relative decline of American power from the 1960s to 1980s; and (3) the post–cold war era in world politics and American renewal, from the 1990s into the twenty-first century.

The Global Cold War and American Hegemony

World Wars I and II represented the twentieth-century struggle for European and global hegemony. Entering the twentieth century, France and especially Great Britain were the two global powers that dominated the global status quo. At the same time, Japan and Germany rapidly grew in power and challenged Great Britain, France, and the status quo. The result was war on a global scale. Ironically, rather than creating a new German and Japanese hegemony or restoring the old European hegemony, the two world wars contributed to the demise of Europe as the center of world politics.

With the decline of Europe following World War II, the Soviet Union and the United States filled the political vacuum in world affairs. Actually, the Soviet Union and the United States grew in power throughout the nineteenth and twentieth centuries. As the United States expanded westward and industrialized, a very similar process occurred in the Russian Empire (the predecessor of the Soviet Union). It became a Eurasian power by expanding eastward (and southward) and industrializing (though at a less dynamic pace than the United States) under both the czars and later Bolshevism.

The ascendance of the Soviet Union and the United States in the wake of European collapse resulted in a global context in which an American-Soviet conflict of some type was virtually inevitable for a variety of reasons—setting the stage for what has traditionally been called a global era of **bipolarity**. After the United States entered World War II, the Soviet Union and the United States were cautious partners who found themselves in an alliance of convenience during the war—an alliance that would have great difficulty surviving the postwar peace.

Specific international events and crises reflecting these World War II and postwar developments impacted domestic politics and the government policymaking process in such a way that they spurred the onset of the cold war. Within the United States, for example, disputes over postwar European economic reconstruction; the fate of Germany; the rise of communism in Eastern Europe; the Soviet-American conflict over Iran, Greece, and Turkey; the fall of Chiang Kai-shek and the Nationalist government in China; the North Korean attack on South Korea; and the Soviet explosion of an atomic bomb all contributed to the growing cold war environment both abroad and at home.

With these events, the postwar debate over American foreign policy was soon dominated by a view of the Soviet Union as no longer an ally but an evil enemy attempting to achieve world empire. Americans in both government and society saw a "free world" led by the United States pitted against a "totalitarian world" led by the Soviet Union in a global cold war throughout the 1950s and early 1960s. Hence the rise of the East–West conflict gave rise to presidential preeminence in the making of U.S. foreign policy, allowing the demands of national security to prevail over the demands of democracy.

At the same time, the war effort lifted the American economy out of the Great Depression of the 1930s and catapulted it into unprecedented prosperity. Clearly, the United States was the global power, or *superpower*, of its time. American economic production was the key to Allied success in the war and was responsible for producing almost half the value of the world's goods and services following the conflict. As Godfrey Hodgson (1976:19) has observed:

> In 1945, the United States was bulging with an abundance of every resource that held the key to power in the modern world: with land, food, raw materials, industrial plant, monetary reserves, scientific talent, and trained manpower. It was in the war years that the United States shot ahead of all its rivals economically. In four years, national income, national wealth, and industrial production all doubled or more than doubled. In the same period, . . . every other industrial nation came out of the war poorer and weaker than when it went in.

American multinational corporations and financial investment, which had been expanding since the turn of the century, came to dominate the postwar international marketplace.

The United States emerged from World War II not only as a superpower but as the **hegemonic power** of its time (Ikenberry 1989). In the more common language used by American leaders and the general public, the United States was considered the "world's policeman" and the "world's banker." American power was seen as so immense during the 1950s that the twentieth century was often referred to as the "American century." The consequence of these developments was that American power, as well as the perception of that power, provided the means to intervene throughout the world to contain Soviet communist aggression, defeat threats to the status quo arising from political instability and insurgency, become the bulwark of the Bretton Woods international political economy, and promote what has been called "nation-building" in Third World countries in accordance with the American liberal model of political and economic development.

Global Complexity and American Decline

Between the 1960s and the 1980s, a more pluralistic and interdependent world, combined with the relative decline of American power, made it increasingly difficult for the United States to successfully pursue its cold war policies abroad—as best illustrated by the American failure in the Vietnam War and the ending of the Bretton Woods economic system, based on fixed currency rates and the gold standard. Among the most important global developments have been the economic recovery and rise of Western Europe and Japan, the rise of OPEC, the arrival of new industrializing nations and other actors in the international political economy, the growth of Third World independence and nationalism, and the diffusion of armaments, technology, and communication worldwide.

Newly industrializing countries such as South Korea, Taiwan, Singapore, and Brazil were becoming more competitive in the international economy. With oil as the basic source of energy in industrialized societies, OPEC also became more consequential politically and financially due to its ability to periodically impact oil prices. Third World countries, in general, were becoming increasingly important to industrialized economies as a source of raw materials, as export markets for finished goods, and as borrowers of capital, resulting in large foreign debts. Also, with the rise of détente, the Soviet Union, Eastern Europe, and the People's Republic of China became more intertwined with the global capitalist economy. Furthermore, multinational corporations spread and expanded their influence throughout the globe, gaining greater independence from government control. Finally, the breakdown of the Bretton Woods system increased the political and economic importance of international governmental organizations such as the IMF, World Bank, and GATT on the workings of the international political economy.

As the world became noticeably more pluralistic and interdependent from the 1960s through the 1980s, the United States' economic and military ability to influence the world declined relative to its post–World War II apex. The United States' decline was not in "absolute" or real terms but was "relative" to changes occurring in the global environment. In some respects, the decline of American power was inevitable. The immensity of American power in the late 1940s and early 1950s was clearly extraordinary—and temporary—given the devastation wrought by the war throughout most of the world. As Europe, Japan, and the Soviet Union recovered from the war, American power could only decline in comparison. Many of these changes were a function of the United States' success in promoting a liberal international economic order. This has led to a seeming contradiction in U.S. foreign policy that might be called the **paradox of American power**: The United States continued to be the most powerful country in the world but no longer was as able to exercise the kind of economic, political, and military influence that it enjoyed at its height during the late 1940s and 1950s.

Although the United States remained the preeminent economic power, its economic influence nonetheless declined quite dramatically during the 1960s and 1970s from its post–World War II peak—the time period that provided the foundation for American global interventionism and the rise of presidential power in foreign policy. *A comparison of America's economic role in the world between 1950 and 1976 highlights its relative decline:* (1) the percentage of total world economic production produced within the United States declined from almost 50 percent to 24 percent; (2) the American share of world crude steel production fell from 45 percent to 17 percent; (3) American iron ore production shrank from 42 percent to 10 percent of the world total; (4) crude petroleum production declined from 53 percent to

14 percent; (5) the percentage of international financial reserves decreased from 49 percent to 7 percent; (6) American exports fell from 18 percent to 11 percent of world trade; and (7) even American wheat production as a percentage of global production declined from 17 percent to 14 percent (Krasner 1982:38). Very simply, economic production in Europe and Japan and throughout the world had increased more rapidly than in the United States. In some cases, such as oil, there had actually been an absolute decline in American production.

The relative decline of the American economy was not simply quantitative but qualitative as well. In numerous areas, American companies lost the technological lead to foreign competitors, especially the Japanese. Whereas during the cold war years "Made in the U.S.A." had been considered the mark of excellence, during the 1970s and 1980s American products were no longer held in such high esteem either abroad or at home. Likewise, whereas "Made in Japan" had been an indication of cheap and unreliable goods until as recently as the 1960s, it became the symbol of the highest quality available for manufactured and technological goods.

A similar pattern occurred with respect to U.S. ability to threaten and use force successfully abroad after the Vietnam War. The U.S. government found it increasingly difficult to promote political stability and to exercise overt and covert military force. In Iran, for example, the United States was able to covertly overthrow the Iranian government with relative ease, restoring the shah to power in 1953. Twenty-five years later, however, the United States could not stop the Iranian revolution and the rise of the Ayatollah Khomeini, triggering the Iran hostage crisis in American politics. Even in Central America, the traditional region of American hegemony, the United States faced new obstacles to the exercise of foreign policy influence. Small military or covert U.S. operations had determined the fate of Central American countries throughout most of the twentieth century; by the 1980s, however, the Reagan administration's covert war in Nicaragua involving over ten thousand contras was unable to defeat militarily the Sandinistas. Clearly, quick and easy military victories, such as in Grenada and Panama, were still possible, but they were becoming more costly politically and, with the rise of global complexity, they were becoming the exception to the rule.

The Vietnam War was symptomatic of the increased resistance that the United States found when attempting to exercise political and military force abroad. First, strong multilateral support for American military intervention abroad became less certain. Over fifteen allied countries had supplied combat troops in the Korean War; fewer than five did so in the Vietnam War. Europe not only refused to provide troops but criticized American involvement during the war. Second, beleaguered governments dependent on American support became more difficult to influence. As Lawrence Grinter (1974) demonstrated in "Bargaining Between Saigon and Washington," the governments of South Vietnam and the United States continually worked at cross-purposes with each other. The South Vietnamese leadership aspired to maintain power and attract American assistance during the war, while the American leadership was preoccupied with containing communism and protecting American prestige. The net result was that the South Vietnamese government was not simply a "puppet on a string" but was able to resist and manipulate U.S. policy. A third difficulty that the United States faced was nationalism, a force to be reckoned with. Vietnamese nationalism was the major asset of the Vietnamese communists in defeating the United States and the South Vietnamese. John Mueller (1980) demonstrated in "The Search for the 'Breaking Point' in Vietnam" that the Vietnamese communists were a most formidable enemy able to withstand large casualties: Over the centuries they had resisted and defeated the Chinese, Japanese, French, and finally the Americans. The Soviet Union faced a similar problem in Afghanistan in the 1980s. Finally, the adversary was able to find sources of vital goods and supplies in order to carry outthe war. The Vietnamese communists were able to take advantage of the East–West rivalry and the growing Sino-Soviet split to get Chinese and Soviet support.

The Vietnam War was indicative that the "good old days" of simple power politics—in which great powers could easily dominate lesser powers through the threat of war, the use of force, and covert paramilitary action with minimal political costs—had disappeared. Richard Feinberg (1983:34) wrote in the 1980s:

> Compared to the situation that the colonial powers found in the heyday of imperialism, when a small flotilla of gunboats could manhandle an ancient civilization or conquer disorganized territories, many of today's Third World states wield much more formidable degrees of organized power. . . . While most Third World states may not yet be powerful enough to guarantee their own sovereignty, it has certainly become more problematical for foreign powers arbitrarily to impose their will upon them.

Soviet Collapse, September 11th, and American Renewal

The end of the cold war in 1989 and 1990 made the world an even more complex place, with contradictory implications for American power and U.S. foreign policy. *Thus far, two post–cold war global trends have been most important for the contemporary and future politics of U.S. foreign policy:* (1) the collapse of communism and the rise of globalization and (2) the continuation of global conflicts, crises, and wars.

The most significant long-term development in the global environment has been the collapse of communism, which appears to have reinforced and intensified the changes that have occurred in the politics of U.S. foreign policy since the Vietnam War. The collapse of the Soviet empire was a momentous event in the twentieth century and world history, for it meant the end of the cold war and a world of even greater complexity.

The collapse of communism in the Soviet Union and Eastern Europe has resulted in a single, integrated international political economy of growing interdependence and complexity—commonly referred to as **globalization** (Keohane and Nye 2011). For at least forty years after World War II, the Soviet Union attempted to withdraw and minimize its interaction with the larger, capitalist global economy dominated by the West and the United States—creating its own separate political economy made up of communist/socialist states. The collapse of communism in the Soviet Union and Eastern Europe, along with the economic transition within China since the death of Mao Zedong, has reintegrated these areas of the world within the larger international political economy. This is reinforced by the tremendous rise of international economic transactions and trade with countries such as China as well as the development of the North American Free Trade Agreement (NAFTA) and the creation of the World Trade Organization (WTO). This means that all states and parts of the world, including the United States, are increasingly interdependent economically as the world has become a single international political economic system or globalized world.

The United States, the West, and liberal capitalism appeared to have prevailed as many optimistically proclaimed (see Friedman 1999; Fukuyama 1989). Yet, the international economic crises of the late 1990s and early twenty-first century, such as the collapse of the Mexican peso, of the "Asian tiger" economies, of Argentina and other South American economies, and, most recently, of the 2008 Global Recession, not only highlight the extent to which the United States is heavily interwoven in the fabric of the larger global economic system, but the tendency of market systems to experience both "boom" and "bust." Such a world of global complexity, interdependence, and economic growth and instability is only likely to grow and, thus, become increasingly important for U.S. foreign policy and for Americans into the future.

The end of the cold war neither signified the end of conflict in the world, nor did it mean "peace is at hand." In fact, the cold war's end led to a world of greater complexity, where global issues proliferated and power became more diffused. Although not on the scale of the U.S.-Soviet conflict, the end of the cold war also produced more conflicts and **crisis** with the potential to trigger American intervention in the world.

Since the end of the cold war, the most obvious international conflict, especially for Americans, revolves around terrorism. Although the issues and problems surrounding terrorism have been around for some time throughout the world and in the United States, they became particularly salient for most Americans in the wake of the tragedy and scope of the casualties caused by the direct attacks on important American symbols on American soil—the World Trade Center towers in New York City, which were completely destroyed, and the Pentagon, in Washington, D.C. But unlike the Persian Gulf or Kosovo wars, the war on terrorism will not be an easy war, against an easily identifiable enemy, that can be accomplished quickly and convincingly as Iraq and Afghanistan testify.

In addition to terrorism, other types of conflicts are likely throughout the world, such as:

- disputes arising from traditional rivalries and state boundaries such as in the Middle East and between India and Pakistan,

- changes in the power and influence of state actors, such as in China, Russia, and the European Union,

- nuclear proliferation, such as with Iran and North Korea,

- ethnic groups and loyalties, over and within state boundaries,

- movements and migration of peoples, demographic changes, and growth of refugee populations,

- demands and needs for scarce resources such as water,

- economic competition and growing inequality between rich and poor, around the globe and within regions and states,

- international economic instability and limits to growth, not just for poorer countries but developing and developed countries, especially the core economies of the United States and the European Union,

- profound technological developments occurring with greater speed and uncertainty, especially in information communications technology (ICT), and

- environment and pollution problems including deforestation and global warming and more.

The list is potentially endless and open to the imagination, especially in a world of greater interdependence and complexity in which technology and time seem to be evolving faster and faster as planet earth proceeds into the future.

Clearly, the end of the cold war created increasing global complexity and the rise of globalization, but it also resulted in the proliferation of global conflicts, crises, and wars, and lots of future uncertainty. These contradictions pose both greater opportunities and constraints for the evolution and exercise of American power. However, there is no agreement on how these post–cold war contradictions will play out. In fact, *there are three dominant and competing theoretical perspectives that attempt to explain and understand the fundamental nature of global politics* with potentially profound impact on American power and U.S. foreign policy (see **A Different Perspective:** Competing Global Theories).

Competing Global Theories

In the aftermath of World War II, the study of international relations became a serious discipline, especially within the United States and academia. Since the 1970s, *three different global theoretical approaches (or perspectives or paradigms) have dominated:* (1) classical realism, (2) liberal idealism (or internationalism), and (3) social globalism (see Knutsen 1997).

Classical realism tends to see the world as relatively anarchical and conflictual in which the primary actors are (sovereign and independent) states, the most important issues revolve around national security and the use of force, and the principle motivation is the promotion of national power and wealth and prestige. So-called realists focus on the tremendous uneven distribution of power among states, on great power conflicts (and alliances and empires), the rise and decline of power, the maintenance of stability and order, and the utility of force as a means to settle disputes and international conflict. Conservative realists tend to be more pessimistic about the future possibilities of a world of greater peace, prosperity, and human development. According to Michael Doyle (1997:18) in *Ways of War and Peace*, to realists it is "the nature of humanity, or the character of states, or the structure of international order (or all three together) that allows wars to occur. This possibility of war requires that states follow 'realpolitik': be self-interested, prepare for war, and calculate relative balances of power."

Liberal idealism (or internationalism) tends to see a world of more cooperation and complex interdependence. Although they see states as important actors, they contend that the dominance of states has dimin-

ished with the advent of other influential actors, such as international organizations (governmental like the UN or the IMF, and nongovernmental like private voluntary organizations), multinational corporations, and ethnic groups. Such complexity allows for a much more interdependent (capitalist) international political economy, where a variety of issues may be significant—national security, but also political, economic, social, and cultural issues as well. This suggests that despite a world of considerable conflict, there is also much cooperation and order that regularly does and can occur. Hence, the importance of such forces as international law, international norms and rules, international networks, international markets, finance and commerce, and democratic institutions. Liberal idealists tend to be much more optimistic about the potential for greater cooperation and peace, prosperity, and human development throughout the world. In their view, the state is not a hypothetical single, rational, national actor in a state of war (as it is in the realist ideal), but a coalition or conglomerate of coalitions and interests, representing individuals and groups and transnational actors.

Social globalism tends to see the existence of a global system, but one in which power and wealth is incredibly unevenly distributed throughout the world. The world is often divided into different classes: a small, wealthy class of powerful or "core" states (and actors—basically the "developed" or "First World"); a predominantly poor class of weak or "peripheral" states (and actors—the "developing" or "Third World"); and a small group of industrializing or "semi-periphery" states (and actors—such as India and Brazil). These political and especially economic distinctions between different classes of people also seem to exist within different countries and societies as well. The emphasis is on the international political economy, the dominance of the capitalist system, and the inherent inequalities and dependencies that result for the poor relative to the wealthy that are difficult to change. Social globalists are both extremely pessimistic about the future given the global system of inequality and injustice; at the same time, they remain optimistic or hopeful that major or radical changes can occur to dramatically increase peace, prosperity, and human development for all.

What are the implications of these three competing perspectives for American power and U.S. foreign policy?

IS THE TWENTY-FIRST CENTURY THE AMERICAN CENTURY?

Since the 1980s, there has been considerable disagreement over American decline or revival. And with the collapse of the cold war, the Soviet Union, the September 11 attacks, and the 2008 Global Recession, the United States may have entered an extraordinary period that has generated even more intense controversies about the future of the United States (and the West) in the world. Two major schools of thought prevail.

Declinists tend to emphasize a more pessimistic view of the future of American power in the long run, given the complexity and contradictions of the post–cold war world. In *The Rise and Fall of the Great Powers*, Paul Kennedy (1987) argued that the power of all societies throughout history has been dynamic. Great powers that have risen to global prominence as a result of gains in economic and military power eventually experience decline in world affairs when their economies weaken and they engage in **imperial overstretch**. In other words, decline occurs if the gap widens between a great power's ends and means—between its foreign policy goals and its ability to carry them out. Although Kennedy did not predict collapse or that the United States was absolutely declining or severely declining relative to others, he did warn that, like other great powers before, the United States faced decline unless it could balance its goals and means and protect its technological advantages. He concluded that "What we are witnessing at the moment is the early decades of the ebbing" of America's extraordinary economic power following World War II to its more natural state (Kennedy 1987:5). Consequently, the task facing American political leaders was to ensure that the relative decline occurred slowly and smoothly (Kennedy 1987:533).

Revivalists, on the other hand, argued that the revival of American power in the future was likely. According to Samuel Huntington (1988), claims about American decline were common, widely exaggerated, and ignored the "self-renewing genius" of the American society. (Though, somewhat ironically, with the collapse of the cold war, Huntington [1996] became more pessimistic about America's future given the coming "clash of civilizations.") Likewise, Joseph Nye (1990) acknowledged that the United States experienced relative decline but emphasized that the nation was not as powerful following World War II as declinists often suggest, has not declined as precipitously as the declinists argue, and faces no rival that can replace it as the global power "bound to lead" in world affairs in the future.

Furthermore, the United States continued to enjoy certain advantages, such as the power of ideas, financial flows, and mass communications—what Nye called **soft power** versus **hard power** or military power—that will allow it to exercise global leadership in the future. Finally, Henry Nau (1990) emphasized the increasing convergence toward democracy and freer markets among industrialized countries since World War II (which is somewhat similar to Francis Fukuyama's [1989] argument about "the end of history" due to globalization and triumph of liberalism). From this perspective, a decline in relative American power may actually translate into an overall increase in America's position in the world community if the nation's economy is strengthened.

By the turn of the twenty-first century, with the collapse of the Soviet Union, the triumph of the Gulf War, and the economic recovery and boom of the 1990s, it appeared that the revivalists had prevailed. Yet as Michael Cox (2002:60) summarizes and assesses the debate:

> Of course it is easy to be wise after the event. It is easier still to forget how few analysts failed to predict what happened in the 1990s. Even the revivalists did not get it right. The United States, they argued, possessed structural advantages that meant that it was not in decline. But that was not the same as anticipating the great changes that then occurred. . . . Indeed if we were to take the longer view, and compare America's position in 2000 with that which it held in 1945, a very strong case could be made that it was actually in a far more favorable situation at the end of the century than it was just after the war.

Indeed, some of the nation's most notable commentators and scholars even began to use the term "empire" to refer to the U.S. position in the early twenty-first century. In fact, Michael Cox (2002:63) refers to the 1990s and the United States as a time of "empire strikes back."

By 2013, the debate would come full circle with the war on terrorism, the failure of the Iraq War, the Americanization of the Afghan War, and the near global economic collapse under the Bush and Obama administrations. The dramatic U.S. financial and economic crises, mounting debt, and weakening currency generated significant problems, and one group of important countries—Brazil, Russia, India, and China, also referred to as the BRIC nations—issued vocal appeals for a new world currency to replace the dollar. The American military intervention in Iraq and Afghanistan, controversial tactics in the war on terror, and unilateral rejection of a host of institutions and agreements during the Bush administration combined to heighten anti-American sentiment abroad, damage the very "soft power" Nye called attention to, and alienate allies and friends. Hence, despite the general argument that the United States is the most powerful country in the history of the world, questions about empire, rise, and decline are as popular and controversial as ever (see Cox 2002; Hendrickson 2004; Ikenberry 1996; Judt 2004; Ryan 2008; Zakaria 2008).

Surely, the United States remains the most powerful single actor on the global stage; it is the only complete superpower and its military and economic might are still quite formidable. However, the forces of globalization have unleashed a more complex and uncontrollable world of interdependence, technological change, uneven development, identity and culture clashes, and transnational forces. The old levers of power and influence are harder to identify and still harder to apply, and reliable foreign policy instruments such as military force face new constraints at home and abroad in their application.

The U.S. economy is also petroleum based and increasingly dependent on the importation of oil (and other strategic minerals) from around the world (see **Table 2.2** and **Figure 2.2**). The **petroleum-based economy** of the United States went from being relatively independent during the 1940s and 1950s, to increasingly dependent on foreign oil to the present day (see Halberstam 1986). In the language of Robert Keohane and Joseph Nye (2011), American interdependence has dramatically increased the "vulnerability" and "sensitivity" of American power. Such factors raise new challenges for the present and future administrations, and the American people, to confront.

The Challenge of Hegemony and Legitimacy

The ultimate global challenges that the United States faces might be called the "challenge of hegemony" and the "challenge of legitimacy." Clearly, in the current global environment, according to G. John Ikenberry (2002a:1):

> The preeminence of American power today is unprecedented in modern history. No other great power has enjoyed such formidable advantages in military, economic, technological, cultural, or political capabilities. We live in a one-superpower world, and there is no serious competitor in sight. Other states rival the United States in one area or another, but it is the multi-faceted character of American power that makes it so commanding, far reaching, and provocative.

Such global predominance obviously brings advantages as discussed earlier, but it poses an additional global challenge to such hegemony as well. Among the most significant are the fear and uneasiness it provokes in other countries, even those who are commonly allied with the United States.

Three types of global reactions are often generated in response to the rise of hegemonic states. First, the predominance of American power can prompt others to align

Table 2.2   U.S. Oil Consumption and Net Imports (In Quadrillion British Thermal Units)

Year	Oil Consumed	Oil Imported	Percentage of Oil Imported
1960	19.92	3.97	20.0
1970	29.52	7.47	25.3
1975	32.73	12.95	39.6
1980	34.21	14.66	42.9
1985	30.93	10.61	34.3
1990	33.55	17.12	51.0
1995	34.44	18.88	54.8
2000	38.26	24.53	64.1
2005	40.39	29.25	72.4
2009	35.40	25.16	71.0

SOURCE: U.S. Census Bureau, *Statistical Abstract of the United States.*

Figure 2.2   Top Suppliers of U.S. Crude Oil Imports

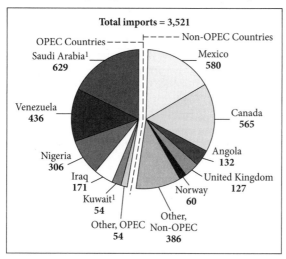

SOURCE: Chart prepared by U.S. Census Bureau.
[1]Imports from the neutral zone between Kuwait and Saudi Arabia are included in Saudi Arabia.

themselves for self-interested reasons with the United States. As Stephen Walt (2005) describes, countries may "bandwagon" (join in), "bond" (build close ties and hope to influence U.S. decisionmaking as a trusted ally), or attempt to "penetrate" American politics (take advantage of the open society and multiple access points to U.S. officials in the executive branch and Congress to persuade decisionmakers to adopt favorable policies) to accommodate and cooperate with the United States. Second, U.S. hegemony is likely to trigger efforts by other countries to reign in U.S. power and resist U.S. domination. According to Walt, their efforts include "balancing" American power and "balking," or ignoring U.S. requests or foot dragging in carrying them out to hinder U.S. efforts. They also include "binding," or attempting to use norms and institutions such as the UN and others to constrain U.S. freedom of action as well as "blackmail," which involves threatening to take action the United States opposes unless the United States offers compensation. Finally, others may attempt "delegitimization," portraying the United States as irresponsible, arrogant, and selfish to encourage resistance to U.S. efforts, actions readily seen in a variety of places in recent years. American decisionmakers will increasingly struggle to grapple with these responses to the global power of the United States.

As Knutsen (1999:67, 272) argues, "if a new world order is to be established under American aegis, then the United States must appear as a just and trustworthy leader." Given the world's complexity and diversity and the United States' tendency to act unilaterally (usually in the name of liberalism, democracy, and human rights), it is likely that the United States will not only remain the most powerful country in the world but may slowly, but inevitably, experience greater challenges to its power and foreign policy in the future (more balancing and delegitimization than bandwagoning?). Such may be the paradoxical nature of American power in the contemporary and future world. Or as Knutsen (1999) states, "Because they confuse their own political mythology with the natural state of affairs, hegemons regularly express a remarkable inability to understand the seething mix of hatred, admiration and ridicule that they inspire abroad. They are not in the habit of examining closely their own myths, rules, laws and values. They simply take them for granted."

According to Richard Betts (2002), "September 11 reminded those Americans with a rosy view that not all the world sees U.S. primacy as benign, that primacy does not guarantee security, and that security may now entail some retreats from the economic globalization that some had identified with American leadership. Primacy has two edges—dominance and provocation." In fact, for Betts (2002:33)

> American global primacy is one of the causes of this war. It animates both the terrorists' purposes and their choice of tactics. To groups like al-Qaeda, the United States is the enemy because American military power dominates their world, supports corrupt governments in their countries, and backs Israelis against Muslims; American [soft] cultural power insults their religion and pollutes their societies; and American economic power makes all these intrusions and desecrations possible. Japan, in contrast, is not high on al-Qaeda's list of targets, because Japan's economic power does not make it a political, military, and cultural behemoth that penetrates their societies.

The vastness and pervasiveness of American power—hard and soft—in other words, have complex and contradictory implications.

Yet, since hegemons are the most powerful and see themselves as the most progressive societies of their age, they are highly susceptible to simplistic images built around an inflated self-concept and fear of others. As Knutsen (1999:215) found, "this fear of the other worked to constrain the liberties which the hegemons, in their fits of self-congratulatory arrogance, flaunted to the world—and which the world after a while interpreted as inconsistency at best or hypocrisy at worst." Senator J. William Fulbright (1966:9) at the height of the Vietnam War described the result in his book *The Arrogance of Power*:

> The tendency of great nations to equate power with virtue and major responsibilities with a universal mission. The dilemmas involved are pre-eminently American dilemmas, not because America has weaknesses that others do not have but because America is powerful as no nation has ever been before, and the discrepancy between her power and the power of others appears to be increasing. One may hope that America, with her vast resources and democratic traditions, will find the wisdom to match her power; but one can hardly be confident because the wisdom required is greater wisdom than any great nation has ever shown before.

So what of the future of the United States and the world? Will the twenty-first century be the "American century"? Although the future of the United States is both promising and full of challenges, it clearly remains uncertain. No one has a crystal ball. But one thing seems relatively clear: We may have entered a time of world history where the future of the United States will probably be unlike that experienced by any other previous great power. Throughout history, great powers in decline have traditionally faced a great power war that accelerated their fall—a most unlikely future scenario for the United States, given the existence and lethality of nuclear weapons and the collapse of the Soviet Union in the cold war. Therefore, the United States is in somewhat of a fortunate situation, allowing the society and government to adapt to and probably muddle through the twenty-first century as an extremely formidable global power facing an increasingly complex and multifaceted global environment in national security and economic affairs. And the controversy about the future of the United States and the world will continue.

Ultimately, it is the dynamic interaction between the government, society, and global/ historical context that will determine the complexity and direction of the future politics of U.S. foreign policy, as is explored at greater length throughout the book. Yet, it is to the government and the policymaking process that we now turn, beginning at the center of the policy process by addressing presidential power and the president's ability to govern U.S. foreign policy.

SUGGESTED SOURCES FOR MORE INFORMATION

Alstyne, Richard W. Van. (1974) *The Rising American Empire*. New York: W.W. Norton. A classic realist revisionist account of the history of U.S. foreign policy.

Cox, Michael. (2002) "September 11th and U.S. Hegemony—Or Will the 21st Century Be American Too?" *International Studies Perspectives* 3:53–70. Excellent overview of the long-running debate about the rise, decline, and revival of American power.

Hendrickson, David C. (2004) "A Dissenter's Guide to Foreign Policy," *World Policy Journal* (Spring): 102–113. Excellent book review essay on competing interpretations of the future of American power.

Judt, Tony. (2004) "Dreams of Empire," *New York Review of Books* (November 4). Excellent book review essay on competing interpretations of the future of American power.

Kennedy, Paul. (1987) *The Rise and Fall of the Great Powers: Economic Change and Military Conflict from 1500 to 2000*. New York: Random House. The classic statement on the rise and decline of American power in world affairs.

Kuttner, Robert. (1991) *The End of Laissez-Faire: National Purpose and the Global Economy After the Cold War*. New York: Knopf. Excellent overview of the international political economy since World War II and the role of the United States within it.

LaFeber, Walter. (1994) *The American Age: U.S. Foreign Policy at Home and Abroad Since 1750*. New York: W.W. Norton. Good overview of the history of U.S. foreign policy.

LaFeber, Walter. (2006) *America, Russia, and the Cold War, 1948–2006*. New York: McGraw-Hill. Informative history of U.S. foreign policy since World War II.

Lizza, Ryan. (2011) "The Consequentialist: How the Arab Spring remade Obama's foreign policy," *The New Yorker* (May 2). Excellent on Obama's initial education as a liberal internationalist, and his evolution as a practitioner to be increasingly pragmatic and realist.

Melanson, Richard A. (1983) *Writing History and Making Policy: The Cold War, Vietnam, and Revisionism.* Lanham, MD: University Press of America. In-depth summary of competing interpretations of the origins of the cold war.

Nobles, Gregory. (1997) *American Frontiers: Cultural Encounters and Continental Conquest*. New York: Hill and Wang. Excellent overview of American continental expansion.

Nye, Joseph S., Jr. (2003) *The Paradox of American Power: Why the World's Only Superpower Can't Go It Alone.* Oxford: Oxford University Press. A synthesis of Nye's works, hard and soft power, and America's future role in the world.

Perkins, Dexter. (1968) *The American Approach to Foreign Policy.* New York: Scribner. A classic orthodox interpretation of the history of U.S. foreign policy.

Ryan, Alan. (2008) "What Happened to the American Empire?" *New York Review of Books* (October 23). Excellent book review essay on competing interpretations of the future of American power.

Stone, Geoffrey (2007). *War and Liberty: An American Dilemma: 1790 to the Present.* New York: W.W. Norton. A good discussions of the dilemmas between liberty and security over the course of American history.

U.S., White House. (2002) September *The National Security Strategy of the United States of America.* September, Washington, D.C. The official national security strategy of the Bush Administration after September 11.

Walker, J. Samuel. (1981) "Historians and Cold War Origins: The New Consensus," in Gerald K. Haines and J. Samuel Walker, eds., *American Foreign Relations: A Historiographical Review.* Westport, CT: Greenwood Press, pp. 207–236. Excellent and succinct overview of competing interpretations of the cold war.

Walt, Stephen. (2005) *Taming American Power: The Global Response to U.S. Primacy.* New York: W.W. Norton. An excellent discussion of the kinds of responses other countries are likely to take to address American hegemony.

KEY CONCEPTS

bipolarity	liberal idealism
cold war	low policy
conservative realism	manifest destiny
containment strategy	nation-building
continental expansion	origins of the cold war
declinists	orthodox interpretation
empire	paradox of American power
global context	postrevisionism
globalization	psychological versus objective
hegemonic power	environment
high policy	revisionism
imperial overstretch	revivalists
imperial republic	social globalism
international crises	sphere of influence
isolationism	

OTHER KEY TERMS

American Revolution
Bretton Woods II
Bretton Woods system
Bush Doctrine
Declaration of Independence
George Washington's Farewell
  Address
Global Recession
height of isolationism
J. William Fulbright

Monroe Doctrine
Northwest Ordinance of 1787
Olney Proclamation
Open Door
petroleum-based economy
Spanish-American War
Treaty of Paris of 1783
Truman Doctrine
USA Patriot Act

GOVERNMENT AND THE POLICYMAKING PROCESS

Part II examines the center of the policymaking process, beginning with the president and moving to the bureaucracy of the executive branch and then to Congress. Chapter 3 discusses the paradox of presidential power, the difficulty of governing in foreign policy, and importance of leadership. Chapter 4 discusses the significance of presidential management of the bureaucracy, focusing on the National Security Council system and process. Chapters 5, 6, and 7 discuss the important bureaucratic roles of the State Department, the military establishment, and the intelligence community in the making of foreign policy. Chapter 8 focuses on the growing role of the foreign economic bureaucracy and the development of the National Economic Council. Chapter 9 provides a synthesis of the overall policymaking process throughout the executive branch by summarizing the major models of decisionmaking theory and discussing important theoretical elements for better understanding policymaking. We then discuss the critical role of the Congress (and the Constitution and the courts) and the nature of legislative–executive relations in Chapter 10.

. . .

PRESIDENT OBAMA RECEIVES A BRIEFING FROM ADVISORS IN THE WHITE HOUSE SITUATION ROOM IN PREPARATION FOR MEETINGS IN ASIA IN MARCH 2012.

PRESIDENTIAL POWER AND LEADERSHIP

Most Americans believe that the president is the most powerful political figure in the United States. In fact, many of us acquire an image of an almost omnipotent president. At a very young age, we are taught that the president is a benevolent father figure who controls the government and represents the American people. As Stanley Hoffmann (1968:289) observed over forty years ago, "The American system of government seems unable to prevent a kind of hand-wringing, starry-eyed, and slightly embarrassing deification of the man in the White House, a doleful celebration of his solitude and his burdens." Naturally, Hoffmann added parenthetically, "when things go badly, there is, of course, a tendency to besmirch the fallen idol."

This chapter examines presidential power and provides an overview of much of the book. It discusses the paradox of presidential power and how this affects the making of foreign policy. More specifically, *we examine the following major questions:* What are the sources and constraints on presidential power? How much power does the president really have in general and in foreign policy? How important is presidential leadership? How have presidents exercised leadership and power since the Great Depression and World War II?

THE PARADOX OF PRESIDENTIAL POWER

When President Lyndon Johnson left office, he offered a warning to his successor, Richard Nixon:

> Before you get to be president you think you can do anything. You think you're the most powerful leader since God. But when you get in that tall chair, as you're gonna find out, Mr. President, you can't count on people. You'll find your hands tied and people cussin' you. The office is kinda like the little country boy found the hoochie-koochie show at the carnival, once he'd paid his dime and got inside the tent: "It ain't exactly as it was advertised." (quoted in Cronin 1979:381)

President's Johnson's characterization nicely captures the tension between the powers and constraints that make up the paradox of presidential power.

The reality is that the president faces a **paradox of presidential power**. The president is the most powerful political actor in the United States. He occupies many constitutional roles and has many capabilities that contribute to his power. However, the president also faces many constraints that limit his power. The successful exercise of presidential power becomes even more problematic when one considers uncertain elements that impact the president, sometimes strengthening his hand and at other times weakening it. Therefore, the president is not nearly as powerful as most Americans believe. While at times he is able to successfully influence—even dominate—the policy process, at other times he has very little impact on that process, regardless of his best efforts to exercise power (see Cronin and Genovese 2009; Neustadt 1960, 1991; Pious 1979).

As President John F. Kennedy understood, the president "is rightly described as a man of extraordinary powers. Yet it is also true that he must wield those powers under extraordinary limitations" (quoted in Sorensen 1963:xii). To better understand this paradox, let's consider the elements of presidential power, limits and constraints on it, and uncertain factors that complicate the ability of the president to lead.

Constitutional Roles and Strengths

The president occupies many different roles, or wears many different hats, that provide him with the capability to exercise considerable power. *The most important roles include the following:*

1. Head of state,

2. Chief diplomat,

3. Commander in chief,

4. Chief executive, and

5. Chief legislator.

These roles have their origins in Article II of the U.S. Constitution and have evolved throughout the history of the United States through constitutional amendments, legislation, judicial rulings, and changes in custom (see Rossiter 1960).

HEAD OF STATE The president is the "head of state" and the government, which means that he also represents the United States of America. Although primarily symbolic, symbolism should not be downplayed for the outcomes of politics are heavily a function of its successful use. To compare Great Britain and the United States, for example, when a foreign head of government arrives in Great Britain, the first official visit, according to the diplomatic protocols of international behavior, is with the queen, for she represents the state. In contrast, the same foreign leader coming to the United States will pay official respects first to the president.

CHIEF DIPLOMAT   The president also is often referred to as the chief diplomat, or chief negotiator representing the United States. This role originates with the president's constitutional duty to nominate the secretary of state and ambassadors to countries abroad, to receive foreign ambassadors, and to negotiate treaties. The president also has the right to offer, or withdraw, official U.S. diplomatic relations with foreign governments. Finally, the president can enter into executive agreements with foreign governments and, with the advice and consent of the Senate, can negotiate treaties that are binding on the United States and have the force of law (more on this in Chapter 10 on Congress).

The president has personally headed American diplomatic delegations and negotiated with foreign leaders, something that has increased in frequency over the last four decades with the rise of "summitry." For example, in 1972 President Nixon led the American delegation to Moscow to complete the first Strategic Arms Limitation Talks (SALT) with the Soviet Union. President Carter spent thirteen days negotiating with President Anwar Sadat of Egypt and Prime Minister Menachem Begin of Israel in 1978 to produce the Camp David Accords. President Reagan had four major summits with Soviet leader Mikhail Gorbachev between 1985 and 1989 (more than any previous president since Franklin Roosevelt). President Clinton led the American delegation that attempted to bring a settlement to the Israeli-Palestinian conflict. President Obama has also traveled extensively throughout the world, meeting with foreign leaders concerning a variety of national security and economic issues. Finally, U.S. presidents participate every year with leaders from the world's major economies (G-8) and developing countries (G-20) in summits to discuss measures to contribute to the stability and growth of the international political economy.

COMMANDER IN CHIEF   According to the Constitution, the president is the commander in chief, which means that he has ultimate authority over the military. By virtue of his position as president, when he gives an order, members of the military and the Department of Defense must comply. This gives the president considerable power because, as commander in chief, he dictates the use of American armed forces abroad.

Since World War II, the president has exercised his powers as commander in chief very broadly. President Harry Truman decided to send American troops to Korea in 1950, while American escalation and the use of armed force in Vietnam throughout the 1950s, 1960s, and 1970s was a result of decisions made by presidents Dwight Eisenhower, John Kennedy, Lyndon Johnson, and Richard Nixon. The decision to secretly support the Contras in their effort to overthrow the Sandinistas in Nicaragua was made by President Ronald Reagan. President George H. W. Bush invaded Panama in 1989 and Iraq in the Persian Gulf War of 1991. President Clinton led a major NATO bombing campaign in the war in Kosovo. President George W. Bush led a global war on terrorism punctuated by two major military operations in Afghanistan and Iraq. President Barack Obama escalated American military involvement in Afghanistan and Pakistan and committed U.S. forces to military action in support of Libyan rebels seeking to overthrow Moammar Ghaddafi. Despite the fact that the Constitution provides Congress the powers to declare wars, raise and support armies, and make rules for their activities, all these examples represent presidential decisions with limited involvement by the U.S. Congress, which authorized the use of force in only a few instances and declared war in none.

CHIEF EXECUTIVE The president is also the chief executive, or head of government, which means he has authority over the executive branch. So, in theory, all the governmental agencies within the executive branch, all the cabinet secretaries, and all the bureaucrats take their direction from the president. One of the major ways the president exercises this administrative power is through appointments. The president selects his personal staff, nominates cabinet secretaries, and appoints most of the high-level officials in each of the departments and agencies that make up the executive branch. The president also establishes the structure and process by which policy is formulated and implemented, which reinforces his roles as commander in chief and chief diplomat as will be discussed in subsequent chapters.

CHIEF LEGISLATOR Although the president is not a member of Congress, he does occupy the role of de facto "chief legislator" because of his ability to both initiate and veto legislation. In the modern relationship between the legislative and executive branches, much of the legislation before Congress originates in the executive branch and is submitted by the president—such as the budget of the U.S. government, as well as programs for defense spending and foreign assistance. Therefore, Congress often responds to the president's agenda, which gives him a political advantage in gaining Congress's acceptance of his programs. The president also has the constitutional right to "veto" legislation. Congress may override a presidential veto with a two-thirds affirmative vote for the legislation in the House of Representatives and in the Senate, but this happens infrequently. For this reason, the president can stop legislation he does not like or, by threatening a veto, force members of Congress to modify legislation to conform to his desires—an important exercise of presidential power in the legislative area.

Limits and Constraints

Clearly, the president occupies a number of important roles that allow him to exercise considerable power. However, as the paradox of presidential power suggests, *the president faces a number of limitations and constraints that make it difficult to get his way, including:*

1. time,
2. information,
3. the bureaucracy,
4. Congress,
5. state and local governments,
6. political parties, and
7. interest groups and social movements.

These limits and constraints on presidential power tend to be strongest when it comes to domestic policy, but they are significant for foreign policy as well.

TIME The president's first major problem is insufficient time to complete all the tasks necessary to govern successfully. The president has one of the most demanding jobs imaginable: He is trying to govern a complex society of over 300 million people and is responsible for representing the United States throughout the globe. The president, however, like any human being, has only so much time to devote to the hundreds of issues and individuals for which he is ultimately responsible. Beyond eating and sleeping and attending to other personal needs, the presidency is a complicated, full-time occupation seven days a week, usually starting early in the morning and lasting late into the night. Much of his day is occupied with staff meetings, entertaining foreign dignitaries, publicly signing new pieces of legislation, or responding to crises and disasters. Although each president has his own style, the job demands a great deal of time and energy, especially if the president wants to govern successfully. For an example of a president's day, see **A Closer Look** on the time constraints presidents face in their daily schedules.

A CLOSER LOOK

Time Constraints and the President's Daily Schedule

The presidency may be the most demanding job in the world. The following schedule records the daily activity of President George H. W. Bush on Tuesday, January 8, 1991, just prior to the beginning of the Persian Gulf War:

7:04 A.M.	The president went to the south grounds of the White House.
7:07	The president went to the Oval Office.
7:12	The president telephoned Senator Malcolm Wallop, Senator John Chafee, and Rep. Mel Levine.
7:21–7:31	The president talked with Senator Wallop.
7:31–7:32	The president talked with Mrs. Virginia Chafee.
7:33–7:56	The president met with John B. Adler.
7:57–8:06	The president talked with Rep. Levine.
8:05–8:24	The president met for an intelligence briefing with William Webster, Director, CIA; [name deleted], briefer, CIA; Brent Scowcroft, Assistant for National Security Affairs; Robert M. Gates, Deputy Assistant for National Security Affairs; John Sununu, Chief of Staff.
8:24–9:10	The president met for a national security briefing

	with Mr. Scowcroft; Mr. Gates; Mr. Sununu.
9:10–9:48	The president met with Mr. Sununu; David F. Demarest, Assistant for Communications.
9:52–10:10	The president went to Room 450 in the Old Executive Office Building to participate in a message taping session for the community of nations united against Iraqi aggression. The message will be broadcast over the U.S. Information Agency WORLDNET satellite network.
10:14	The president returned to the Oval Office.
10:16–11:09	The president participated in a meeting to discuss the proposed National Energy Strategy with the Economic Policy Council in the Cabinet Room.
11:09–11:17	The president met with Richard B. Cheney, Secretary of Defense; Mr. Sununu in the Oval Office.
11:17–12:04	The president met to discuss congressional strategy on the Persian Gulf with administration officials in the Cabinet Room.
12:04–12:10	The president met with Secretary Cheney; Lawrence S. Eagleburger, Deputy Secretary of State; Mr.

	Scowcroft; Mr. Gates; Mr. Sununu, in the Oval Office.
12:10	The president telephoned Rep. Thomas Foley and Rep. Robert Michel.
12:10–12:19	The president talked with Senator Robert Dole.
12:14–12:37	The president met with Mr. Scowcroft.
12:17–12:29	The president met with Mr. Sununu.
12:24–12:26	The president met with Marlin Fitzwater, Assistant and Press Secretary.
12:19–12:21	The president talked with Senator George Mitchell.
12:22–12:26	The president talked with Rep. Foley.
12:30–12:33	The president talked with Rep. Michel.
12:37–12:39	The president met with [names deleted].
12:39–1:26	The presidential party went to the White House Mess for lunch.
1:27–1:33	The president returns to the Oval Office to meet with Mr. Webster; General Colin Powell, Chairman, Joint Chiefs of Staff.
1:33–2:35	The president participated in a meeting with administration officials and Mideast experts.
2:35–2:43	The president met with Secretary Cheney; Mr. Eagleburger.
2:35–2:46	The president met with Mr. Sununu.
2:35–2:54	The president met with Mr. Scowcroft.
2:35–2:49	The president met with Mr. Gates and Richard Haass.
2:54–2:57	The president met with Andrew Card, Asst. and Deputy Chief of Staff
3:00–3:06	The president talked with Charles Black, Jr., Acting Chairman of the RNC.
3:28–3:33	The president met with Robert B. "Bobby" Holt, Chairman of the Republican Eagles.
3:33–3:55	The president and the First Lady met with the leadership of the RNC Eagles in the Roosevelt Room.
3:50–3:55	The president returns to the Oval Office to participate in a photo opportunity with the Republican Eagles.
4:15–4:23	The president met with Mr. Sununu; Edward Derwinski, Secretary of Veterans Affairs.
4:52–5:02	The president met with Mr. Sununu.
5:02–5:43	The president goes to the barber shop for a haircut.
5:11–5:16	The president talked with Secretary of State James Baker in Geneva, Switzerland.
5:43–5:50	The president returned to the Oval Office and meets with Mr. Scowcroft.
5:50–5:55	The president went to Mr. Fitzwater's office to meet with.
5:55	The president returned to the second floor Residence.
6:45–6:47	The president talked with his physician, Dr. Burton J. Lee III.
10:10	The president retired.
10:27–10:29	The president talked with his brother, William H. T. "Bucky" Bush.

How do you think the need to attend to so many different issues in such a crowded schedule affects a president's leadership and decisionmaking?

SOURCE: U.S., White House, George H. W. Bush, *The President's Schedule* (George H. Bush Presidential Library, Texas A&M).

The president's time is limited not only from a daily perspective but in terms of his time in office as well. The president may have as little as four years and certainly no more than eight years (according to the **Twenty-Second Amendment** to the Constitution) to accomplish all that he has set his sights on. Moreover, as we discuss later, presidents tend to have more opportunity early in their terms. Therefore, presidents are forced to be selective as to how they will occupy their time. For those issues on which the president is extremely attentive, he may exercise considerable power. However, for the remaining issues on which he lacks interest or time, the president may find that he is the president in name only.

INFORMATION   Another limitation on presidential power involves information problems. Despite having relevant experience such as being a governor, a member of Congress, or a vice president, much of the president's knowledge is acquired through "on-the-job training" because, unfortunately, there is no existing occupation that can adequately prepare one for becoming president of the United States. This means that presidents must use valuable time and require much staff support for getting information and advice.

The president faces two problems in terms of information: scarcity and overabundance. At times, a president may find that he does not have enough information. This is quite common, especially in the area of foreign policy. Presidents often have great difficulty getting sufficient information about international events, particularly during crises, when time becomes even more limited and important. Yet a president may have no choice but to make decisions. The other problem is that the president often gets too much information in dealing with an issue. The problem here is that, given his pressing schedule, he doesn't have enough time to digest all the available information or he may be provided with contradictory information. Nevertheless, decisions must be made. Having too little or too much information makes it that much more difficult for the president to successfully exercise power.

THE BUREAUCRACY   The third major constraint is the bureaucracy. As chief executive and administrator, the president has great capacity to initiate action. However, the bureaucracy has also become so large and entrenched that it is often unresponsive to the president and his personal staff and policy advisors, with contradictory consequences for presidential power. It can be of great value for the president in his roles as commander in chief, chief diplomat, chief administrator, or chief legislator, yet can also be extremely unresponsive to presidential requests or commands. Hence, as we discuss in Chapter 4 (on national security) and Chapter 8 (on foreign economics), all presidents must grapple with the problem of creating a structure and process to manage and control the far-flung administrative agencies as much as possible. Such efforts are never completely successful, however, because *bureaucratic organizations have a number of advantages* that allow them to remain relatively autonomous and free of presidential control (as we discuss in Chapters 5–7 and 9).

First, a new president enters office with a set of policies and programs administered by the bureaucracy already in place under previous presidents. Each bureaucratic organization, therefore, tends to develop its own goals, subculture, and tasks over time that may be at odds with the policies preferred by the current president. Second, the president is heavily dependent on the bureaucracy for information. The bureaucracy determines not only the quantity of information available to the president but also its quality—its level of comprehensiveness, the interpretation of reality embedded in the language, and the range of viable options for presidential consideration (often protecting and reflecting the agency's position).

Third, members of the bureaucracy have the advantage of time. The president and his personal staff are there for only four, perhaps eight, years, whereas many bureaucrats occupy positions of importance for ten, twenty, or thirty years (and as members of the civil service they have tenure or other rights that make it very difficult for presidents to fire them—even for incompetence). A fourth advantage is that bureaucrats often have close relationships with members of Congress, who ultimately must approve the programs and funding for the executive branch bureaucracy. Therefore, it is not unusual for networks to develop between executive branch employees and members of Congress (and interest groups) around various issues, each dependent on each other. The final advantage is that some bureaucratic organizations enjoy official independence (at least in daily operations) from presidential authority, such as the powerful Federal Reserve Board. These officially autonomous organizations not only can resist the president's exercise of power, but may also have the legal right to ignore presidential requests.

CONGRESS   The president and Congress share power; in fact, there is no constitutional power provided to the president that the Congress does not share in some way. Therefore, while the president initiates and can veto legislation, Congress is often a major constraint on the exercise of presidential power. When the president first enters office, he usually enjoys a brief honeymoon with Congress, during which members are more likely to be responsive to presidential requests in light of the president's recent victory. However, the honeymoon rarely lasts more than a few months, and then it is back to business as usual in which the president quickly finds that Congress is often extremely unresponsive to his requests and can at times be quite obstructionist.

Traditionally, since World War II, members of Congress have been more active on domestic policies and more responsive and less obstructionist in the area of foreign policy. However, Congress became much more independent and assertive in this area as well following the Vietnam War and Watergate. Many members of Congress also have agendas of their own that may be incompatible with the president's agenda. Furthermore, since the Vietnam War, the U.S. government has usually been divided (with a Republican president and a Democrat-run Congress, or vice versa) making it that much more difficult for the president to be effective. In sum, the fact that the legislature is an independent branch with independent power means that Congress and the president will be involved in a constant power struggle (as we discuss in greater depth in Chapter 10).

STATE AND LOCAL GOVERNMENTS   The president may be the commander in chief, the chief of state, and the chief administrator; however, he has little legal authority over state and local governments. State governments in the United States have their own power bases, embodied in the fifty state constitutions. The framers of the Constitution created a federal system of government in which two sets of governments, each with its own sovereignty and authority, were established: a central government, usually referred to as the "federal government" by Americans, and state governments. State and local governments play a particularly important role in economics because they have their own foreign economic policies and compete with each other, impacting the overall foreign economic policies of the United States.

POLITICAL PARTIES   The president is the head of his party, but in the United States this does not translate into great political influence in governing and electoral politics.

Unlike those in most other countries, American political parties, whether Democratic or Republican, are decentralized and weak. For example, presidents cannot force members of their own party to support them in Congress, for congressional members have independent power bases. Nor can the president dictate to the party his heir for the presidential nomination. Therefore, although electoral politics is important the weakness of American parties makes it that much more difficult for the president to exercise power successfully.

INTEREST GROUPS AND SOCIAL MOVEMENTS   A final impediment to the exercise of presidential power is the impact of interest groups and social movements on domestic politics and the governmental process. The United States contains thousands and thousands of groups organized to promote their own goals and interests, regardless of what the president believes or wants. These groups utilize all avenues available to them in making their views known and promoting their interests, including influencing Congress, members of the executive branch bureaucracy, the media, and the American public (and state and local governments).

Presidents who attempt to change aspects of public policy (e.g., think health care or the Israeli-Palestinian question) find resistance not only within the federal bureaucracy and Congress, but throughout society from groups that are quite comfortable with the status quo. At the same time, many social movements and groups demand changes in governmental policy that, if opposed by the president, may result in the creation of political antagonists or enemies. Interest groups and social movements tend to be more visible when it comes to domestic and economic issues, but as discussed in Chapter 12, they have grown in importance in the area of foreign policy as well, thus complicating the lives of presidents even further.

Uncertain Elements

In addition to these constraints and limitations, a number of uncertain elements that a president cannot control affect his ability to govern. Sometimes these elements may work for him, enhancing his power; other times they work against him, acting as another constraint on presidential power. *These **uncertain elements in the makeup of presidential power** include:*

1. the courts,

2. public opinion,

3. the media, and

4. the global and historical context.

THE COURTS   Although the president nominates all federal judges and the Senate tends to approve the nominations, with an occasional controversial exception, this does not guarantee that judges' rulings will support presidential policies (as will be discussed to a greater extent in Chapter 10). The classic example of an appointment run amok, at least from the president's perspective, was President Eisenhower's appointment of Earl Warren as chief justice of the Supreme Court. Eisenhower thought he was appointing a political moderate, but Earl Warren led the Supreme Court in a liberal direction over the course of the next two decades. The uncertainty of predicting the political views of judicial appointees is reinforced by the fact that most judicial rulings are made by federal judges who were appointed by previous presidents. Therefore, while the courts generally tend to play a more passive role in the area of foreign policy, the impact of judicial rulings on presidential power varies.

PUBLIC OPINION The public is an important source of presidential power, as we will find later in this chapter and in Chapter 11. The public elects presidents. Yet, public opinion can also turn against a sitting president, as Johnson, Nixon, Ford, Carter, the elder Bush, the younger Bush, and Obama all discovered. Public opinion tends to be most supportive of the president when he enters office (and during crises), but it tends to decline over time. Therefore, public opinion strengthens a president's power early in office but increasingly constrains presidential power through the president's tenure, as all presidents soon discover. Increasingly unpopular presidents and unpopular policies invite opposition, as well as defection by otherwise supportive individuals and groups.

THE MEDIA The media represent another source of great uncertainty in the exercise of presidential power. In order to better understand media coverage and its impact, discussed in Chapter 13, it is important to remember that different individuals and groups within government and throughout society try to influence the media and the power they have over the communications process to gain control of the government and influence domestic politics. Presidents, in particular, are heavily dependent on the media to help them promote a positive image—both while campaigning and while governing if they want to win and exercise power. Overall, there is a cyclical pattern in the media's impact on presidential power. The media are a crucial source of presidential power early on for gaining the presidential nomination, winning the election, and exercising power in a new administration. However, they are also a source of much of the difficulty that presidents face later in office, regardless of who is in office or his party affiliation, which contributes to the negative impact of the other constraints and uncertainties on presidential power discussed earlier.

GLOBAL AND HISTORICAL CONTEXT The final element that has an inconsistent impact on presidential power is the global and historical context, as already discussed in Chapter 2. First, although presidents make decisions that impact the global environment, they often react to events and developments as they occur abroad. Sometimes international events and crises strengthen the president's exercise of power; sometimes they create problems. For example, President George W. Bush responded to the September 11, 2001, terrorist attacks and the 2008 economic crisis, leaving a legacy of policies and political consequences inherited and "owned" by President Obama.

Not only are presidents unable to control events with which they are faced, but they also have little control over America's global position and power, which reflects a set of underlying, long-term structural trends within the international system. Truman, Eisenhower, Kennedy, and Johnson each had the good fortune to be president during a period in which the United States was clearly the undisputed global superpower in every dimension, and in which a common enemy united American allies. However, subsequent presidents, beginning with Nixon, came to office during a time of relative decline of U.S. power, as reflected in the military challenge of the Soviet Union and the economic challenges posed by Europe, Japan, and the Pacific Rim countries. Post–cold war presidents have been provided with new opportunities for U.S. foreign policy, but also have the disadvantage of exercising power in an increasingly complex and globalized world. They also have to grapple with both the opportunities and the challenges of the remarkable power advantages—some would say hegemonic power—possessed by the United States in an increasingly complex world without a peer rival in the twenty-first century.

THE PATTERNS OF THE PARADOX

The notion of paradox provides us with a general understanding of the nature of presidential power, but when and where is the president most able, and least able, to exercise power? To answer this question, we need a better understanding of the concept of power and how it is exercised. Then we must also be aware of different domains or issue areas in which it is possible to exercise power.

Power, very simply, is the ability to influence the surrounding environment in ways one prefers. *The exercise of power can be accomplished in one of two ways, through:*

1. positive power, and

2. negative power.

The "positive" exercise of power is the ability to initiate, implement, and make something happen. This is what most people think of as the exercise of power. Another way to exercise power may be called "negative" power, which is the ability to negate and to prevent others from doing something against one's wishes. The use of negative power is typically ignored, yet is important in the overall exercise of power (James 1974).

Does a president generally have the upper hand in exercising positive or negative power? On the one hand, to initiate and implement policy, he usually needs the support of others—a tall order to fill given the constraints and uncertainties he faces. He needs to build political coalitions to support his initiatives and, at a minimum, convince others not to oppose his policies. The exercise of negative power, on the other hand, is less demanding. To stifle something, presidents do not have to build or maintain extensive political coalitions in support of policy initiatives as they evolve over time. Preventing an initiative from surfacing on the political agenda or stopping it after it has surfaced is a much simpler task. The president, for example, has the unique ability to block virtually any piece of legislation he chooses through his use of the veto, which is rarely overridden. Although there is no guarantee that the president will succeed in exercising negative power, the odds are much higher than in his efforts to exercise positive power.

In addition to positive and negative power, we also need to discuss the domain, or **issue area**, in which power is exercised. Issues may be classified in a variety of ways, but *a breakdown into three issue areas helps to clarify the paradox of presidential power:*

1. domestic issues,

2. foreign policy issues, and

3. intermestic issues.

For some issues the president is likely to be a powerful political figure, while on other issues he may lack much power (Evangelista 1989; Manning 1977; Potter 1980).

The president tends to have greater strengths and fewer weaknesses in the exercise of power in foreign policy in general and national security policy in particular. Three of the constitutional roles contributing to presidential power really involve only foreign affairs: commander in chief, chief diplomat, and chief of state. While two of these areas are shared with Congress, these roles typically allow the president to exercise more power, both positive and negative, in the foreign policy area, especially during crises. Furthermore, many of the constraints that he faces tend to be weaker in the area of foreign policy. The bureaucracy, Congress, the courts, state and local governments, the public, political parties, the media, and interest groups all play independent roles in the making of U.S. foreign policy, but they tend to be more active and influential concerning domestic policies.

However, with the major technological revolutions of the late twentieth century in information, communication, and transportation, an increasing array of issues straddles this traditional foreign and domestic policy divide. Issues involving economics, trade, immigration, the environment, and others are both international and domestic in orientation—thus, often referred to as **intermestic issues** (Manning 1977). Nowhere is this truer than with what Americans like to call the "domestic economy," which is increasingly foreign economic policy (and has always been) interlinked with the global economy (see Friedman 2000). The economic crisis that began in 2008 reflects these linkages. The so-called American "Great Recession"—involving the banking and financial sector; the rise and collapse of real estate values; exorbitant individual, corporate, and governmental debt; and so on—also affected Europe and the entire global economy.

When it comes to formulating policies to cope with such economic issues, for instance, everyone gets into the act and attempts to exercise influence and outcomes. On such issues, presidents must increasingly grapple with interest groups (especially corporate, financial, and labor), members of Congress, public opinion, and more within the United States, as well as governments, multinational corporations, and international financial institutions throughout the world. Such intermestic issues deeply affect the jobs, the lives, and the communities of peoples at home and abroad, but are very difficult to understand because of their complexity as well as their domestic and international realities. In sum, *economic issues are neither about domestic nor about international politics, but are intermestic*—and, therefore, an issue area of great challenge for presidents (and Americans) that will likely intensify as globalization becomes the norm in the twenty-first century.

Given the discussion thus far, the question of presidential power does not allow for a simple, black-or-white answer. By combining the two ways power can be exercised with the three types of issue areas, we can develop a simple, yet valuable, three-by-two classification scheme for making better sense of the paradox of presidential power (see **Figure 3.1**). The

Figure 3.1 Categorizing Presidential Power

| | The Exercise of Power | |
	Positive	Negative
Foreign Policy	Moderate	High
Issue Area — Intermestic Policy	Moderate	Moderate
Domestic Policy	Low	Moderate

© Cengage Learning

president is most powerful in areas of foreign and national security policy, most constrained in the domestic policy arena, and somewhere in between for intermestic issues. He is most successful in exercising power when he opposes the initiatives of others but requires more skill and luck to promote successfully policies of his own. These are the patterns or trends that make up the paradox of presidential power, making it difficult for a president to govern successfully and, consequently, fulfill the high expectations most Americans have of him.

THE PROBLEM OF PRESIDENTIAL GOVERNANCE

The paradox of presidential power makes it extremely difficult for a president to govern successfully, especially in domestic but also in foreign policy. ***Two patterns seem to affect the president's ability to govern and lead the country:***

1. a president tends to go through a presidential life cycle in which presidents are strongest when they enter office and then their power tends to decline over time, and

2. a crisis of leadership (or governance) now seems to exist in American politics in which no individual or organization, including the presidency, is able to lead the government and country for long.

These patterns have become increasingly visible since the Vietnam War, have continued since the collapse of the Soviet Union and, despite the 9/11 attacks and Great Recession, have important consequences for the foreign policymaking process (see Burns 1984; Cronin and Genovese 2009; Chubb and Peterson 1989; Edwards 2009; Huntington 1981; Lowi 1985; Sundquist 1980).

The Presidential Life Cycle

Most presidents find that their ability to exercise power tends to go through a cyclical process over the course of their term of office: They enter office near the peak of their power, and by the end of their term they are considerably weaker. To explain this **presidential life cycle** we must understand how the paradox of presidential power impacts the president's ability to govern over time.

A president enters office with all of his constitutional roles fully available to him, constraints at their weakest, and with most of the uncertain elements working in his favor. Newly elected presidents usually proclaim an **electoral mandate** for themselves and their policies. During the first few months in office the president enjoys a so-called **honeymoon** period, not only with the Congress but with the media and the public as well. This begins with the president's inauguration, celebrated as a triumph of American democracy in action. People tend to be hopeful and interested in the new president, the first lady, their personal characteristics, and his style of governing, and the president enters a relatively hospitable political environment in which he is provided considerable leeway to initiate new policies. This makes it a most inopportune time for individuals and groups to be too critical of the new leader of the United States.

Within a short period of time—and one that seems to have grown shorter in more recent decades with greater partisanship—the honeymoon with Congress and the media is over. Congress begins to act independently of presidential wishes, especially if the majority party is different from the president's party, a common occurrence since the Vietnam War. Members of the media soon spend more time addressing the issues and critically analyzing presidential policies. Interest groups and social movements descend on the policymaking process. Under such conditions a president quickly finds that he is no longer operating with a clean slate in an optimistic political environment. In fact, the longer the president is in office, the more likely that critical judgments will be made by individuals and groups throughout government and society concerning how well the president is doing and who benefits from his policies. As the political environment becomes more critical and uncontrollable, the president finds that his public approval rating also tends to decline.

Lyndon Johnson, a former majority leader in the U.S. Senate and a shrewd observer of American politics, once gave the following portrayal of the presidential life cycle after his 1964 landslide victory (quoted in Halberstam 1969:424):

> When you win big you can have anything you want for a time. You come home with that big landslide and there isn't a one of them [in Congress] who'll stand in your way. No, they'll be glad to be aboard and to have their photograph taken with you and be part of all that victory. They'll come along and they'll give you almost everything you want for a while and then they'll turn on you. They always do. They'll lay in waiting, waiting for you to make a slip and you will. They'll give you almost everything and then they'll make you pay for it. They'll get tired of all those columnists writing how smart you are and how weak they are and then the pendulum will swing back.

The president's ability to exercise power successfully usually declines significantly as this honeymoon period fades, usually within a few months. During this period, his strengths diminish, his constraints intensify, and the uncertain elements tend to work more often against him than with him. The decline of public support does not occur in a linear pattern, but is a bumpy process, with peaks and valleys. The major exception to this pattern occurs during times of national emergency and crisis, when the constraints on presidential power are temporarily reduced as the public rallies behind the president for leadership and crisis resolution. These spurts of public approval during crises are reinforced by congressional deference to the president, especially in foreign policy, and his tendency to dominate communications and the media. However, once the crisis subsides normal politics resurface and the downward pattern tends to continue. Eventually, the constraints multiply to the point that the president has considerable difficulty exercising power over most issues. By the end of his term, he may be so weak that he is referred to as a **lame-duck** president.

Figure 3.2 demonstrates the overall decline in public approval that every contemporary president has faced through the life cycle of his presidency. With the exception of President Bill Clinton, the trajectory has been downward for every president from the time they entered office to the time they have left office (obviously, the downward trend has been stronger for some presidents than others).

Even with the tremendous political impact of the September 11, 2001, terrorist attacks, President George W. Bush was not able to escape the presidential life cycle. Bush's approval skyrocketed to over 90 percent after the attacks, as the country and Congress rallied around the president and the global war on terror. However, from that high point in late 2001, public approval steadily declined, dropping below 50 percent in early 2005 and down to the mid-30s by the summer of 2006 until the end of his term of office.

Again, Lyndon Johnson had an instinctive feel for the rhythm of the presidency and the president's relationship with Congress (quoted in Smith 1988:333): "You've got to give it all you can, that first year," Johnson told Harry McPherson, a top aide. "Doesn't matter

Figure 3.2   Public Approval of Presidential Performance

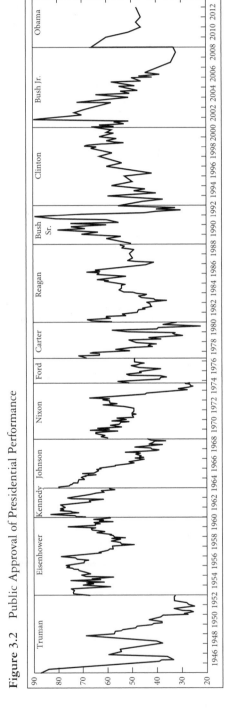

SOURCE: Gallup.

what kind of majority you come in with. You've got just one year when they treat you right and before they start worrying about themselves. The third year, you lose votes. . . . The fourth's all politics. You can't put anything through when half the Congress is thinking how to beat you." In fact, President Bush's approval ratings were so low near the end of his term that they may have reinforced the lack of confidence that existed for the economy in general during the economic crisis of 2008, which also happened to be an election year.

President Obama faced the same pattern. He assumed office with high approval ratings, and tried to take advantage of his honeymoon period in his first year with a flurry of political activity and policy initiatives. And yet, as depicted by **Figure 3.3**, his popularity, once higher than 70 percent, fell to the 50s as early as June 2009, and subsequently into the 40s, where it hovered ever since as Obama advanced an ambitious agenda and confronted a host of controversial issues. By 2012, his declining popularity made him vulnerable in his effort to win reelection.

However, as the economy slowly improved, Obama waged an effective political campaign against former Massachusetts governor Mitt Romney, the Republican nominee. As the campaign unfolded, Obama's favorability and approval ratings once again climbed to the 50 percent mark, and he won re-election with over 50% of the national vote and a decisive electoral vote margin of 332-206. His victory set up a temporary window of opportunity in his second term, which is likely to narrow over his last four years in office.

This cyclical pattern is largely a function of presidential promises and expectations—in the minds of political leaders, the politically involved and active, and especially members of the general public (Brody 1991). During the presidential nomination and general election campaigns, all candidates promise the American people that, if elected, they will improve the quality of voters' lives. They promise to clean up the environment, improve the quality of education, prevent American men and women from dying abroad, and keep America free and strong. Most importantly, candidates promise to restore or maintain economic prosperity, to reduce inflation and unemployment, to improve the economy so that all Americans will have a better chance of attaining the "American Dream."

These promises create expectations among the public that presidents find very difficult if not impossible to fulfill. Why? Because presidents are neither powerful enough nor do they serve long enough. David Halberstam (1969:64), in *The Best and the Brightest*, aptly describes this problem of the modern presidency back in the early 1960s:

Figure 3.3 Public Approval of Barack Obama

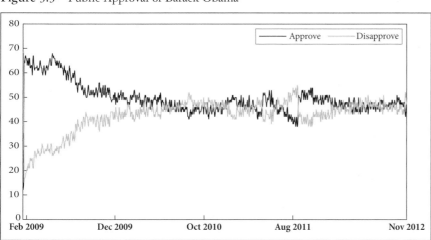

SOURCE: Gallup.

As President, Kennedy was faced with that great gap of any modern politician, but perhaps greatest in contemporary America: the gap between the new unbelievable velocity of modern life which can send information and images hurtling through the air onto the television screen, exciting desires and appetites, changing mores almost overnight, and the slowness of traditional governmental institutions produced by ideas and laws of another era, bound in normal bureaucratic red tape and traditional seniority.

The process of promoting expectations that are likely to remain unfulfilled reinforces the vicious life cycle of presidential power. The paradox of presidential power makes it very difficult for the president to implement his preferred policies. The inability to fulfill the optimism and high expectations created early on means that much of the American public eventually will grow disenchanted with the incumbent president and impatient to see a new individual as president, often from the other party. This sets the stage for a repeat performance of the presidential life cycle for the new president—early optimism eventually replaced by pessimism and frustration.

The Crisis of Leadership

The paradox and life cycle of presidential power have led to a **crisis of leadership (or governance)** in American politics that has heightened since the Vietnam War and the end of the cold war. Presidents are elected to govern and lead the country, but they are unable to do so for political power is dispersed throughout government and society and the president faces major limitations and constraints in the exercise of his power for domestic, intermestic, and foreign policy issues. This means that, even when the problems facing the country are growing in severity, not only are presidents often unable to govern and lead, but their administrations are often seen as failures in the public eye.

The *rise of divided government and partisanship since the 1960s are potentially more problematic for presidential leadership.* Since the Vietnam War and Watergate, divided government, in which the president and Congress are led by people of opposing political parties, has become increasingly the norm. And partisanship has escalated in just about every way imaginable: among party leaders, in congressional voting behavior, and throughout the political arena (see **Table 3.1**). As stated by Todd Purdum (2010), "There's little doubt that the Washington game is more complicated, and lethal, than ever, and it's increasingly difficult to play and win" (see Alter 2010).

Partisanship was extremely evident when every Republican in the House and all but three in the Senate voted against Obama's stimulus package at the very beginning of his presidency, despite the crisis in the U.S. economy. And such partisanship and political polarization have been the case for most major issues since. Even his successful conclusion of a "New START" treaty with Russia to dramatically reduce nuclear arsenals on both sides—a goal that every president since Richard Nixon has sought—faced a fierce partisan debate before it was ratified by the U.S. Senate, and then only after the addition of amendments to placate some Republicans, and only by a 71–26 vote, barely clearing the 67-vote threshold for treaty ratification. No democrats voted against the treaty. Despite his rhetoric about governing in a "post-partisan" environment in Washington, D.C., as a candidate and as president, Obama has faced more, rather than less, division.

In sum, given the popular image of presidential power, presidents receive credit when things are perceived as going well and are blamed when things go badly. Yet, should success or improvement occur, given the lack of presidential power, it is probably not by the

Table 3.1   Party Control of the Presidency and Congress in the Twentieth Century

Congress	Years*	President	Party	Senate D	Senate R	Senate Other	House D	House R	House Other
59th	1905–1907	T. Roosevelt	R	32	58	—	136	250	—
60th	1907–1909	T. Roosevelt	R	31	61	—	164	222	—
61st	1909–1911	Taft	R	32	60	—	172	219	—
62d	1911–1913	Taft	R	44	52	—	228‡	162	1
63d	1913–1915	Wilson	D	51	44	1	290	127	18
64th	1915–1917	Wilson	D	56	40	—	231	193	8
65th	1917–1919	Wilson	D	54	42	—	210	216	9
66th	1919–1921	Wilson	D	47	49‡	—	191	237‡	7
67th	1921–1923	Harding	R	37	59	—	132	300	1
68th	1923–1925	Coolidge	R	42	53	1	207	225	3
69th	1925–1927	Coolidge	R	41	54	1	183	247	5
70th	1927–1929	Coolidge	R	46	48	1	195	237	3
71st	1929–1931	Hoover	R	39	56	1	163	267	1
72d	1931–1933	Hoover	R	47	48	1	216‡	218	1
73d	1933–1935	F. Roosevelt	D	59	36	1	313	117	5
74th	1935–1937	F. Roosevelt	D	69	25	2	322	103	10
75th	1937–1939	F. Roosevelt	D	76	16	4	333	89	13
76th	1939–1941	F. Roosevelt	D	69	23	4	262	169	4
77th	1941–1943	F. Roosevelt	D	66	28	2	267	162	6
78th	1943–1945	F. Roosevelt	D	57	38	1	222	209	4
79th	1945–1947	Truman	D	57	38	1	243	190	2
80th	1947–1949	Truman	D	45	51‡	—	188	246‡	1
81st	1949–1951	Truman	D	54	42	—	263	171	1
82d	1951–1953	Truman	D	49	47	—	234	199	2
83d	1953–1955	Eisenhower	R	47	48	1	213	221	1
84th	1955–1957	Eisenhower	R	48‡	47	1	232‡	203	—
85th	1957–1959	Eisenhower	R	49‡	47	—	234‡	201	—
86th	1959–1961	Eisenhower	R	65‡	35	—	283‡	153	—
87th	1961–1963	Kennedy	D	64	36	—	262	175	—
88th	1963–1965	Kennedy	D	66	34	—	258	176	—
		Johnson	D						
89th	1965–1967	Johnson	D	68	32	—	295	140	—
90th	1967–1969	Johnson	D	64	36	—	248	187	—
91st	1969–1971	Nixon	R	57‡	43	—	243‡	192	—
92d	1971–1973	Nixon	R	54‡	44	2	255‡	180	—
93d	1973–1975	Nixon	R	56‡	42	2	242‡	192	1
		Ford	R						
94th	1975–1977	Ford	R	60‡	38	2	291‡	144	—
95th	1977–1979	Carter	D	61	38	1	292	143	—
96th	1979–1981	Carter	D	58	41	1	277	158	—
97th	1981–1983	Reagan	R	46	53	1	243‡	192	—
98th	1983–1985	Reagan	R	46	54	—	268‡	167	—
99th	1985–1987	Reagan	R	47	53	—	253‡	182	—
100th	1987–1989	Reagan	R	55‡	45	—	258‡	177	—
101st	1989–1991	Bush Sr.	R	55‡	45	—	260‡	175	—
102d	1991–1993	Bush Sr.	R	56‡	44	—	267‡	167	1
103d	1993–1995	Clinton	D	57	43	—	258	176	1
104th	1995–1997	Clinton	D	48	52‡	—	204	230‡	1
105th	1997–1999	Clinton	D	45	55‡	—	206	228‡	1
106th	1999–2001	Clinton	D	45	55‡	—	211	222‡	2
107th	2001–2003	Bush	R	50‡	49	1	212	221	2
108th	2003–2005	Bush	R	48	51	1	204	229	1
109th	2005–2007	Bush	R	44	55	1	202	231	1
110th	2007–2009	Bush	R	49‡	49	2	233‡	202	—
111th	2009–2011	Obama	D	58	40	2	256	178	—
112th	2011–2013	Obama	D	51	47	2	198	241‡	2
113th	2013–2015	Obama	**D**	**53**	**47**	**21**			

D = Democrat, R = Republican

* Represents a two-year period, since Congress officially convenes in January.

‡ Chamber controlled by party other than that of the president.

SOURCE: U.S. House of Representatives; U.S. Senate.

president's own design. Nonetheless, the president—the person perceived to be the leader of the country—will be rewarded in terms of public prestige, greater power, and reelection (for him or his successor). However, if the president is perceived as unsuccessful—a failure—this results not only in a weakened president but one that the public wants replaced, creating the opportunity for challengers such as Republican nominee Mitt Romney in the presidential election of 2012. It also reinforces the imperative that the new president, from whichever party, will distance himself from many of the policies of his predecessor. This contributes to change in the types of public policies pursued by presidents, making it very difficult for the U.S. government to form a coherent long-term program for governing and leading the country into the twenty-first century.

THE IMPORTANCE OF PRESIDENTIAL LEADERSHIP

How do presidents maximize their power and success? How can they overcome or minimize the crisis of governance in American politics? How can they increase their ability to govern foreign policy? The key is **presidential leadership**. Strong leaders, on the one hand, are able to maximize their strengths and capabilities, minimize the constraints they face, and force the uncertain elements to work better and longer in their favor. Strong presidents are more able to exercise power and govern. Weak leaders, on the other hand, have great difficulty exercising power and governing, for they operate in a world dominated by insurmountable obstacles and constraints. Although this is particularly the case in domestic policy, presidential leadership is also important for presidential power and governance in foreign policy (see Burns 1965, 1978; Edward 2009; Skowronek 1997, 2011).

The classic statement on presidential leadership is *Presidential Power: The Politics of Leadership* by Richard Neustadt (1960). Neustadt's basic argument is that the key to presidential power is the **power to persuade**, which is a function of political leadership. Presidents who enter office and expect to "command" are quickly disappointed and frustrated. Barking orders may get results for military leaders, but it does not work within the government. In fact, as Neustadt points out, efforts at exerting presidential power through command are an indication of presidential weakness, for presidents should rely on their legal and formal authority only as a last resort. The command model of governing may be consistent with the way most Americans are raised to think of presidential power, but the key for presidential governance is to persuade others that it is in their best interest to do what the president prefers. *Neustadt identified three crucial elements of political leadership and presidential power:*

1. **professional reputation:** how other political actors inside and outside Washington, D.C., judge the president's ability to get things accomplished,

2. **public prestige:** how other political actors—whether in the bureaucracy, Congress, interest groups, or the media—perceive the level of public support for the president, and

3. **presidential choices:** the choices that only a president can make that impacts his ability to lead and persuade.

This emphasis on professional reputation and prestige underscores the importance of perceptions and images that have always been important in politics, but with the rise of the electronic media, the importance of symbolism and "symbolic politics" has grown. Leadership involves the ability to create the illusion of being powerful. According to Hedrick

Smith (1988:56) in *The Power Game*, "Presidents—past, present, and future—have less power than the country imagines, but the successful ones convey the impression of power and get reputations as strong presidents by playing down their problems and trumpeting their few clear victories."

Much of a president's professional reputation and public prestige is a function of his personality and particular style of operating and presenting himself. As George Reedy (1970:197) stated, the presidency "provides a stage upon which all of his personality traits are magnified and accentuated." Depending upon how his personal characteristics affect his leadership style, it can contribute to or hinder his professional reputation and public prestige. Presidents with a reputation for being very skillful in exercising power and for having to be reckoned with when opposed are most persuasive. Presidents with a positive public image are more powerful because high credibility and popular support throughout the country enable a president to use professional reputation and public prestige to persuade. Presidents who want to exercise power successfully and govern need to be aware of these aspects of leadership long before they decide to run for the office (see Greenstein 2009; Skowronek 2011).

The choices a president makes affect his professional reputation and public prestige. Ultimately, this requires that *the president and his staff need to be skillful in three areas:* (1) managing the executive branch and the decisionmaking process; (2) building coalitions and politically interacting with other players in and out of Washington, D.C.; and (3) symbolically communicating his priorities and preferences to American society and the world. These are political requirements involving important choices for successful presidential leadership and will be discussed throughout the book.

According to Neustadt, "passive" presidents tend to be little more than "clerks" who merely occupy the office. To lead and govern, presidents must be "active"—actively involved in becoming informed, making decisions, and supervising their implementation. They must know on whom they can and cannot rely in the government and beyond. They must be aware of the political implications of what they say and do. In other words, a president's choices are the means by which he exercises leadership and power in the complex politics of U.S. foreign policy.

Richard Pious (1979), in *The American Presidency*, has added important insights into the nature of presidential choice and activism on presidential leadership. He argues that the paradox of presidential power has become so constraining that a president must exercise prerogative government if he wants to govern and lead the country. By **prerogative government**, Pious means that presidents must be very active and arrive at decisions that push the Constitution to its limits in exercising presidential power. Presidents are more likely to exercise presidential power and prerogative government during times of crisis and war. "The president justifies his decisions on constitutional grounds, on powers enumerated, or on those claimed. . . . When his expansive interpretation is challenged, he appeals to the public for support by defining his actions in terms of 'national security' or 'the national interest'" (Pious 1979:47; see also Edwards 2009; Fisher 2007).

Those presidents who have a more expansive view of presidential power tend to be the most successful in governing and go down in history as the best presidents. However, activist presidents who exercise prerogative government also run the political risk of abusing their power, which can damage or destroy them. This is because the Constitution is an ambiguous document, and it is often unclear whether a president is exercising power legitimately or abusing it. However, the final determinant of the legitimate exercise of presidential power is perceptions and politics.

Pious found that, throughout American history, *three political outcomes have occurred when presidents have exercised prerogative government:* frontlash, backlash, and over-shoot and collapse. First, presidents are most successful in exercising prerogative government in the area of foreign affairs during a time of national emergency such as war. During such times, the president is able to legitimately exercise extraordinary powers because of the urgency of the situation. This is what happened under Presidents Abraham Lincoln and Franklin Roosevelt—and perhaps George W. Bush after his first years in office—as they exercised prerogative government in the face of the greatest of all national emergencies, a civil war and a world war. The worst that presidents can expect under such circumstances is what Pious calls "frontlash" after the emergency has subsided. That is, presidents can expect Congress and domestic politics to reassert their significance during times of normalcy, again constraining presidential power.

Second, presidents may experience political "backlash" if they exercise prerogative government, especially over domestic policy, even during a national emergency. In domestic policy, unlike foreign policy, presidents (facing the paradox of power) are not given much leeway or flexibility to respond to crises. Bureaucrats, members of Congress, and other political players are very protective of their positions and roles in the domestic policymaking process. Such was the case with President Harry Truman's seizure of steel mills in 1951 in the name of national security, in response to a strike during the Korean War. The political response was very critical of Truman for his exercise of emergency national security powers involving a labor-management dispute—clearly a domestic issue at the time. Presidents with an expansive view of the Constitution during domestic emergencies will eventually be perceived as abusing power and may expect to suffer severe political setbacks.

Presidents also run the risk of "overshoot and collapse" when exercising prerogative government, resulting in a president's fall from power. This risk is most likely to occur when there is no perception of emergency in society, and is especially acute if domestic affairs are involved. A president exercising prerogative government under these conditions will be widely perceived as abusing his power and oath of office. The domestic political resistance is likely to be so severe that the president may have to fight for his political life. President Nixon suffered from overshoot and collapse as a result of Watergate. President Reagan faced this possibility with the Iran-Contra affair and survived, while President Clinton was able to survive the Monica Lewinsky affair.

President George W. Bush's troubles peaked in his second term and originated, at least in part, in the controversies over the extensive prerogative power sought in the global war on terrorism and aggressive administration actions in making and defending the case for the invasion of Iraq. The consequence: severe backlash. After Democrats gained control over both chambers of Congress in the November 2006 election, the younger Bush's presidency was effectively crippled. His successor, Barack Obama, found himself forced to contend with a legacy of problems from the previous administration and has embraced an aggressive array of policies to confront, especially the economic crisis, as well as the wars in Iraq and Afghanistan and Pakistan. In the 2010 elections Republicans gained control of the House of Representatives, producing a partially divided government (Democrats retained control of the Senate) and further intensified partisanship. Obama's success and assertiveness, especially concerning the (perception of the) state of the American economy, significantly impacted his success in the 2012 campaign, in which he defeated his Republican rival, Mitt Romney.

PRESIDENTIAL POWER IN FOREIGN POLICY

What are the implications for presidential power in foreign policy? Historically, it is important to understand that the president has not consistently dominated the foreign policy process throughout American history. As we discuss in greater depth in Chapter 10, the U.S. Constitution produced a central government with "separate institutions sharing powers," resulting in an "invitation to struggle" between the executive and legislative branches. In fact, executive–legislative relations in foreign policy have been fluid and dynamic and, as described by Arthur Schlesinger, Jr. (1989) in *The Imperial Presidency*, they have been characterized by a kind of "pendulum or cyclical effect." In times of national emergency, particularly war, power tends to flow toward the president and the executive branch. During times of peace, when conflict has subsided, power tends to flow back to Congress. Yet while Congress tends to reassert its constitutional authority and power following war, increases in presidential power during periods of conflict tend to be so extensive that it seldom returns to prewar levels.

The cyclical ebb and flow in executive relations in foreign policy has enabled presidents to steadily accumulate greater power over time, especially on issues of foreign policy and national security affairs. *Since the global Great Depression and World War II, presidential power in foreign policy has gone through four general stages:*

1. during the Great Depression and especially World War II, the modern and the "model" presidency occurred under President Franklin Roosevelt,

2. after World War II and during the cold war, presidential power in the making of foreign policy became supreme,

3. since the Vietnam War, the president's ability to govern and lead foreign policy has declined and become much more complex, and

4. with the end of the cold war, the paradox of presidential power, the presidential life cycle, and the crisis of leadership have further intensified.

The concepts of professional reputation, public prestige, and presidential choices (especially prerogative government) are helpful for understanding the president's ability to lead and govern in general and in foreign affairs in particular. These three elements of presidential leadership help to explain why Franklin Roosevelt was the most successful president in modern times; why presidents Truman, Eisenhower, and Kennedy were able to dominate foreign policy during the cold war; why the situation began to change under President Johnson; and why it has been so difficult for presidents to govern in foreign affairs since the Vietnam War and the end of the cold war.

The Great Depression, World War II, and the Roosevelt Presidency

Regardless of whether one liked the direction in which he led the country, Franklin Delano Roosevelt was one of America's greatest presidents if greatness is measured by ability to govern and lead. He was elected president an unprecedented four times and occupied the office for thirteen years. Why? Because he was a politician with tremendous leadership skills and he became president at a unique time in American history.

Roosevelt enjoyed a strong professional reputation and high public prestige, and he operated during times of domestic and international emergency allowing him to exercise prerogative government (see Burns 1989; Leuchtenburg 2009; Pious 2002). He entered office in 1933, when the United States was experiencing the full force of the Great Depression, the greatest national emergency to confront the United States since the Civil War. As an activist president, he took advantage of the extraordinary situation to move his New Deal legislation through Congress as he presided over the most active first hundred days in the history of legislative–executive relations. Roosevelt was also a consummate politician who personally ran the White House and restored the faith of the American people through his famous "fireside chats" over the radio. Moreover, the Japanese attack on Pearl Harbor in 1941 presented the president and the country with another national emergency, which gave Roosevelt extraordinary powers to wage war as commander in chief. An extremely powerful president and successful political leader, Roosevelt has long been viewed as the **model presidential leader** in modern American politics, and subsequent presidents have found it a great challenge to match his accomplishments.

Presidential Dominance During the Cold War

As a result of World War II and the rise of the cold war, the president became dominant in the making of foreign policy. According to Aaron Wildavsky (1966) and his **two presidencies thesis**, this lead to a powerful presidency in foreign policy and a weak presidency in domestic policy. Examining the legislative–executive relationship during the 1950s and 1960s, Wildavsky found that presidents were much more successful in influencing foreign policy legislation than domestic legislation. According to the two presidencies thesis, the paradox and life cycle of presidential power were operative predominantly in the realm of domestic policy, but the president was able to govern and lead the country when it came to foreign policy (see also Shull 1991).

Before World War II, few governmental institutions were oriented toward foreign affairs and national security—the policymaking elite was extremely small and centered in the State Department. World War II changed this dramatically. Overnight, the U.S. government was redirected to devote itself to fighting a global war: The military expanded enormously and civilian agencies grew to assist the president in fighting the war. The governmental war effort, in turn, put the economy and society on a war footing to provide the necessary personnel, equipment, and services to achieve U.S. victory. After World War II, mutual suspicion and fear between the United States and the Soviet Union escalated, especially with the Korean War, leading to a new global conflict. A brief period of postwar demobilization soon gave way to remobilization and the expansion of efforts to fight a global cold war—another time of national emergency in the minds of most Americans.

This sense of national emergency gave presidents during the 1950s and 1960s extraordinary powers over national security and foreign policy, accounting for the popularity of the two presidencies thesis. The 1950s and 1960s were perceived to be a time when communism directly threatened the security of the United States. During such times of perceived national emergency, the president could exert considerable powers as commander in chief, head of state, chief diplomat, and chief executive. Constraints were relatively weak, and the uncertain elements tended to be supportive of presidential efforts to contain the threat of communism.

The foreign policy bureaucracy, for example, expanded and became an important tool for implementing the president's containment policies. This was also a period in which political party differences were minimal and Congress developed a bipartisan consensus largely supportive of most presidential initiatives in foreign policy. A strong anticommunist consensus also developed among the American citizenry and foreign policy elite, resulting in strong public, media, and interest group support of a policy of containment and presidential actions abroad (while state and local governments and the courts were relatively inactive in foreign policy). This supportive political climate also existed at a time when the United States was the world's preeminent power.

Presidential supremacy developed in foreign policymaking because the superpower conflict was perceived as a permanent time of crisis and national emergency for two decades following World War II. It is not that Truman, Eisenhower, and Kennedy had uniformly great leadership skills stemming from professional reputation and public prestige—the personal situation varied from president to president. Indeed, Truman, for example, had quite low public approval ratings for much of his presidency. The consequential factor was public perception that the cold war represented a contest that the United States and the free world could not afford to lose. It was fought through the strategy of containment, which emphasized the threat and use of force. These cold war beliefs and policies required a strong president who was able to combat the enemy quickly and secretly with public support and little opposition; therefore, the demands of national security took precedence. Presidents were able to exercise prerogative government in foreign policy as the norm for twenty years. Their power was virtually undisputed on questions of war and peace, as demonstrated by the long history of presidential decisions taken by Truman, Eisenhower, Kennedy, and finally Johnson, resulting in the Americanization of the war in Vietnam.

The cold war years of American globalism were thus a time of extraordinary presidential power in foreign affairs—certainly not the norm in the history of U.S. foreign policy. This is not to say that the president faced no opposition or that he controlled all foreign policy issues. Nonetheless, the president was clearly the dominant political figure and exercised a disproportionate amount of influence over U.S. foreign policy within a cold war orientation. Presidents had the ability to formulate and implement policies in accordance with their cold war beliefs (see Hodgson 1976; Piper 1994).

The Decline of Presidential Power Since the Vietnam War

Ironically, the Vietnam War represented not only the height of presidential power, but also the beginning of the end of the extraordinary exercise of prerogative power in foreign affairs. Because of the Vietnam War, presidents were challenged about their conduct in foreign policy for the first time in over twenty years. Once the bipartisan, cold war consensus shattered, what had been accepted as a legitimate exercise of presidential power in the political climate of the cold war years became increasingly considered presidential abuse of power in the political climate of the post–Vietnam War years. The uncertainties and constraints on presidential power, either silent or supportive of the president during the cold war, resurfaced.

The collapse of the anticommunist consensus produced a re-assertive Congress, new and varied interest groups and social movements, a more critical media, and a cynical public. In the past, given the strength of anticommunism and the national security state, the president could lead the country, but only in the direction of fervent anticommunism, containment, and interventionism. Since Vietnam, every president has tried, but failed to generate a new consensus or sustain much support for his policies for any length of time. Moreover, as Destler, Gelb, and Lake (1984:50) argue, "The making of American foreign policy has been growing far more political—or more precisely, far more partisan and ideological." Hence, according to Alexander George (1980b:236), "the necessity for ad hoc day-to-day building of consensus under these circumstances makes it virtually impossible for the President to conduct long-range foreign policy in a coherent, effective manner."

Thus, the era of two presidencies and extraordinary presidential power in foreign policy was over. The high levels of positive and negative power in foreign affairs enjoyed during the cold war diminished after Vietnam, particularly in the area of positive power in foreign policy. Foreign economics and other so-called traditional domestic and "intermestic" issues likewise rose in significance and increasingly became a part of the foreign policy agenda. In fact, studies examining the two presidencies thesis after the Vietnam War tended to restrict—or even reject—the argument (Fleisher, Bond, Krutz, and Hanna 2000; Shull 1991). Even the original author of the idea has acknowledged its limits, concluding that "foreign policy has become much more like domestic policy—a realm marked by serious partisan divisions in which the president cannot count on a free ride" (Oldfield and Wildavsky 1991:188).

Without a state of permanent emergency, the context of the immediate situation and presidential leadership skills involving professional reputation, public prestige, and presidential choices became much more important. Upon examining recent presidents, *strong and durable political leadership does not appear to be a common commodity.* Neither Johnson, Nixon, Ford, nor Carter had strong leadership skills overall. Consequently, these presidents were perceived as failures by the end of their terms of office. Only President Reagan was able to buck the trend, yet even he was politically damaged and considered a lame duck at the close of his term. President Reagan seemed to have maintained high levels of professional reputation and public prestige, which may explain why he has been the most successful of contemporary presidents, even while suffering from the Iran-Contra affair.

THE JOHNSON PRESIDENCY   President Lyndon Johnson was in office for both the height and decline of what became referred to as the **imperial presidency** (Schlesinger 1989; 2005). He was the first victim of the changed political environment facing the president. Known from his days as Senate majority leader for his ability to wheel and deal in Washington's corridors of power, his professional reputation was a result of his overall aggressiveness and strong style of personal interaction. When he assumed the presidency after the 1963 assassination of John Kennedy, his discomfort before the general public became more obvious. He lacked charisma and was unable to display a sense of confidence in public appearances, such as on national television, which hurt his public prestige and contributed to his severely declining popularity after the 1964 electoral landslide as his administration's handling of the Vietnam War was increasingly challenged (see Kearns 1976, 1991).

Operating with cold war beliefs that emphasized the need to contain communist aggression, President Johnson escalated American intervention in Vietnam from 18,000 American troops in 1963 to over 550,000 troops by 1966. While the American role grew and the war continued, President Johnson and other military and administrative leaders told the American people that it was only a matter of time until the Vietnam War would be won—that there was "light at the end of the tunnel." Then in February of 1968, during the Vietnamese holiday Tet, the North Vietnamese army and Vietcong guerrillas launched a major offensive in which most of the country, including cities throughout the south and the U.S. Embassy in Saigon, came under enemy occupation or siege. Although it was repulsed by American and South Vietnamese forces, the **Tet offensive** became a political crisis for the Johnson administration where public optimism about the war and LBJ's credibility with the American people were destroyed.

Although Johnson was in many ways a master of the political smoke-filled room, his weak skills at building public prestige made it impossible for him to overcome the crisis of governance that he experienced over the Vietnam War. The president, the American war effort in Vietnam, and the cold war beliefs on which the containment strategy was founded were increasingly challenged both within the government and throughout the domestic arena by a growing antiwar movement and public disenchantment. Johnson was so deeply affected by his loss of support that, rather than fight the political changes that were taking place around him, he declined to seek the Democratic presidential nomination for the 1968 election and withdrew from public life—the first post–World War II presidential casualty of a failed major U.S. foreign policy initiative.

THE NIXON PRESIDENCY   President Nixon, like Johnson before him, was known for his ruthless exercise of power within Washington. Nixon's professional reputation was neither so strong as Johnson's, nor was his public prestige so weak. President Nixon was able to build a strong staff that centralized and exercised power in the White House. Although not a strong orator, he was better able to communicate to what he called the "silent majority" and, given all his years in public life, he had strong support among more conservative segments of the public (see Wills 1969).

Nixon's downfall came because he did not fully understand (or accept) the extent to which the domestic political environment was changing. As his predecessors had, Nixon tried to govern foreign policy with a free hand, while more and more Americans doubted the validity of communism as the major threat to the United States and questioned the basis of twenty years of containment policies and of presidential prerogative government in foreign affairs. From Nixon's perspective, the traditional authority of presidential power in national security affairs was being challenged. His reaction was to set in motion activities to fight the domestic political opposition, leading to Watergate and the abuse of presidential power.

The key to understanding the fate of President Nixon was his policy toward the war in Vietnam. He had told the American public in 1968 that he had a "secret plan" to end the Vietnam War, which would restore peace while maintaining American honor. The secret plan consisted of a strategy involving simultaneous de-escalation, escalation, and negotiations. De-escalation meant that U.S. troops were slowly phased out through a process of "Vietnamization." Escalation entailed stepped-up American bombing of Indochina as well as invading guerrilla sanctuaries in neighboring Cambodia and Laos. De-escalation and escalation, reinforced by détente initiatives with the Soviet Union and the People's Republic of China, were intended to elicit a negotiated agreement with the North Vietnamese, producing "peace with honor" and buying South Vietnam a "decent interval" for survival.

However, with the escalation the antiwar movement reached its height, calling for the immediate withdrawal of all U.S. forces from Indochina and challenged American interventionism abroad. Nixon, a scrappy fighter from his earliest political days, responded by attacking the domestic opposition as if it were the enemy. This led to a number of illegal and unconstitutional activities by the Nixon White House and came to be known as **Watergate** (see **The Liberty–Security Dilemma** box).

Revelations about Nixon's abuse of presidential power led to his downfall and the diminution of presidential power. First, a Senate committee held hearings, followed by House Judiciary Committee hearings, which voted three counts of impeachment. This led President Nixon to resign in 1974, fearing a near-certain House of Representatives vote in favor

What Watergate Was All About

As opposition to his Vietnamization policy grew, especially with military escalation, President Nixon responded by turning to members of his White House staff to conduct a series of illegal and unconstitutional activities, illustrating the tension that can develop between the demands of national security and democracy. First, Nixon ordered wiretaps of members of the National Security Council staff and a number of journalists in an effort to determine who was leaking information to the media (about the secret U.S. bombing of Cambodia)—hence, referred to as the "plumbers." Second, these efforts soon grew into broader attempts to discredit, disrupt, and derail the antiwar movement and critics of the Nixon administration, such as the surveillance of activist groups and sabotage of demonstrations, use of the Federal Communications Commission to coerce the news media into providing less negative coverage of the administration, threatening individuals with tax audits by the Internal Revenue Service, and burglarizing Daniel Ellsberg's psychiatrist's office in an effort to find scandalous information that would discredit Ellsberg, who had been responsible for leaking the explosive *Pentagon Papers* to the media (which had exposed the government's Vietnam policy process in the 1960s).

Eventually, given the growing antiwar opposition throughout the country, President Nixon's reelection fears resulted in White House involvement in a number of dirty tricks and illegal activities designed to ensure the president's reelection in 1972. Taking no chances, the Nixon White House attempted to sabotage the campaigns of the political opposition, including Edward Kennedy and Edmund Muskie. It was this type of activity that led to the burglary of the Democratic Party headquarters in the Watergate Hotel in Washington, D.C., which gave the ensuing scandal its name and publicly exposed the wide-ranging illegalities and subsequent cover-up by President Nixon. From wiretapping, to an "enemies project," to efforts to ensure the reelection of the president, and finally to the cover-up, the legacy of these illegal and unconstitutional activities was a destroyed president and a successful challenge to Nixon's claims of prerogative government in the name of national security to the demands of democracy (see Bernstein and Woodward 1974; Dean 1977; Lukas 1973).

What are the implications of the Watergate scandal for the tension between liberty and security?

of impeachment and conviction in the Senate. Therefore, soon after his triumphant reelection in 1972, Nixon was forced to leave office in disgrace—only the second president in American history to face impeachment for "high crimes and misdemeanors," and the second presidential casualty of U.S. foreign policy in Vietnam.

The overshoot and collapse of the Nixon presidency thus came about in part because of difficulties of his own making because he had failed to understand the limitations and constraints on the exercise of presidential power generated by events such as the Vietnam War. This new political environment had new negative consequences for presidential exercise of prerogative government, which Nixon failed to recognize or adapt. At the same time, the administration's failure also came about because of the fragility of Nixon's public prestige. He created many political enemies during his career and was not particularly admired or well liked by either his political peers or the general public. He had acquired a reputation as a mean-spirited politician (symbolized by the popular nickname "Tricky Dick"). The weak foundation of Nixon's public prestige, therefore, made him politically vulnerable during Watergate.

THE FORD PRESIDENCY Gerald Ford was a relatively passive president who had low levels of professional reputation and public prestige. Ford was a likable person but never would have become president on his own. Nixon had picked him as vice president to replace Spiro T. Agnew, who had been forced to resign on charges of corruption. Not only was Ford catapulted overnight into the presidency after having been minority leader in the House of Representatives, but he also possessed no election mandate. These circumstances were reinforced by his passivity in managing the government and the general public perception that he was not a particularly "presidential" individual.

President Ford was unable to overcome the stigma of Watergate and his pardon of President Nixon. He continued to pursue many of the policies emphasized during the Nixon administration, as reflected in his retaining Henry Kissinger as secretary of state, but now they were under attack. Liberal opponents who feared another Vietnam stopped American covert intervention in Angola. Conservative anticommunists within his own party attacked Détente with the Soviet Union and efforts to normalize relations with the People's Republic of China for being too "soft." In fact, Ford barely survived a challenge by Ronald Reagan for the Republican presidential nomination. The situation got so bad that Ford and Kissinger no longer used the word *détente* when discussing U.S. foreign policy. Given his low levels of professional reputation and public prestige, it was not surprising that Ford was voted out of office in 1976 after having been president only three years—another failed president.

THE CARTER PRESIDENCY Jimmy Carter attempted to put the tragic episodes of Vietnam and Watergate behind the country by instilling in the office a new spirit of honesty and idealism, represented by his commitment to human rights and peace. Carter was the first person to gain the presidency by running against Washington, pledging that he would clean up governmental corruption and discard the politics-as-usual approach. As a true "outsider" to national politics, his political experience had been as governor of Georgia, he entered office resistant to the politics of Washington and with few political friends, but a public presence that initially instilled hope and high public expectations about the future, especially among the more liberal segments of the population.

Though extremely intelligent, President Carter was naive about the importance of presidential leadership and the difficulties of exercising political power within Washington, D.C. He entered office as an activist president with relatively high public prestige and very low professional reputation. Early on, he antagonized members of Congress and the bureaucracy, thus destroying his honeymoon and his professional reputation. Despite the popularity of his human rights campaign and his ability to bring peace to Egypt and Israel with the Camp David accords, by the end of his administration the economy went into a tailspin with double-digit inflation and unemployment.

The public's perception of his mishandling of U.S. foreign policy abroad haunted him as it had his predecessors, especially the **Iran hostage crisis**. After years of U.S. support since the 1950s, the Shah of Iran fell from power in 1979. Ayatollah Khomeini, a prominent religious figure, became Iran's new leader, and in the political turmoil fifty-two American diplomatic personnel were taken hostage in Teheran. For 444 days, the hostage crisis was the lead story in American politics. This initially resulted in a rise in public support for the president during a crisis, but Carter's inability to free the American hostages destroyed the earlier optimism that had surrounded his presidency. Americans became frustrated, which intensified when the Soviet Union invaded neighboring Afghanistan in 1979 to prop up their allied regime in Kabul. President Carter was never able to recover politically from the economy and the events in Iran and Afghanistan—he became another victim of the crisis of leadership, written off by most of the public as a failure (see Glad 1980; Jordan 1982; Rosati 1987). Only after he left office did popular approval and admiration for Jimmy Carter as an "ex-president" grow (see Chambers 1998; Rozell 1993).

THE REAGAN PRESIDENCY   Ronald Reagan was the only president since the Vietnam War and before the collapse of the cold war who was able to overcome the paradox and life cycle of presidential power. But even Reagan experienced a major crisis of governance during his administration—the Iran-Contra affair—where at the height of the crisis in 1987 it was unclear whether President Reagan would survive politically (Cannon 1991; Wills 1988).

As the only contemporary president who has enjoyed high levels of both public prestige and professional reputation, Ronald Reagan was able to overcome the constraints and uncertainties that a president faces throughout his term of office. Once written off as a conservative ideologue and two-bit actor, he soon proved the political pundits wrong.

Reagan was, in fact, a complex man of many contradictions. While he rarely immersed himself in the issues, he entered office with a very active agenda. Although he was relatively uninvolved in the daily operations of presidential governance, he recruited a strong presidential staff that was capable of pursuing his policies. This played to his greatest strength: his ability to communicate to the general public. Reagan was also well liked by the American people, especially after his 1981 assassination attempt. Eventually regarded as the "great communicator," he had the ability to speak to them and gain their support by using language and symbols that most Americans understood and to which they responded. It was his rise in public prestige, reinforced by his growing professional reputation, which was the key to his ability to govern, lead, and survive.

President Reagan assumed office prepared to initiate a new conservative agenda: to strengthen American defense forces and resolve overseas while unleashing the market to restore economic prosperity at home and abroad. He pledged to renew and strengthen America's efforts to combat communism and terrorism abroad. The Reagan administration's high priority was to defeat and contain the communist threat posed by the Soviet Union, especially in Central America. In that region, the goal of U.S. foreign policy was to defeat the Marxist-Leninist–led guerrillas in El Salvador and to overthrow the Sandinista revolutionary regime in Nicaragua through the threat and use of force. The U.S. government provided financial and military support to friendly regimes in the region, such as El Salvador, Guatemala, and Honduras, to help them in their fight. Covertly, the Central Intelligence Agency (CIA) became responsible for creating, arming, and supporting a counterrevolutionary group to overthrow the Sandinistas known as the "Contras."

To finance his Central American policy, President Reagan requested large amounts of assistance from Congress. Despite Reagan's efforts to raise public consciousness about the gravity of the situation, the threat of communism in Central America never became a high-priority issue among the majority of the public, and there was much public criticism of his policies. Members of Congress initially granted the Reagan administration only a portion of the assistance it wanted during the first few years, but the issue became so politicized that Congress prohibited the U.S. government from providing any support or assistance to the Contras at all during 1985 and 1986.

This set the stage for the **Iran-Contra affair**. Regardless of the congressional ban, Reagan decided that the threat of communism and the future of Nicaragua required that the administration continue covert support to the Contras (these operations are discussed in greater depth in Chapter 7 on the intelligence community). President Reagan also decided that he was willing to sell arms to Iran covertly in exchange for American hostages. It was not long before White House operations in support of the Contras leaked to the press.

The public revelation that really came to haunt the Reagan presidency, however, involved the story that the United States was trading arms for hostages with Iran. After being told by Reagan that he would never negotiate secretly with terrorists and that they only understood force, most Americans could not believe that the president had agreed to negotiate with the so-called leading terrorist of them all, the Ayatollah Khomeini. President Reagan's denials only made the political situation worse for him and his administration. Then the public learned that some of the money the administration had received from the Iranian arms deal had been illegally diverted from the U.S. treasury to the Contras.

As with Watergate, a congressional investigation proceeded to determine the level of presidential abuse of power, and members of the Reagan administration were indicted. For almost a year President Reagan and his administration were badly shaken and on the defensive about Iran-Contra, which included joint Congressional hearings of the administration's activities. Ultimately, President Reagan was able to survive the crisis and complete his term, though he was considerably diminished in power and public prestige. (See **A Different Perspective** on the stress presidents face in office and the toll it takes on them.)

A DIFFERENT PERSPECTIVE

The Stress and Toll of the Office

Although Americans tend to view presidents as almost all-powerful policymakers, the view from inside the Oval Office is quite different. Modern presidents have experienced considerable problems in governing and leading the country. Presidents Johnson, Nixon, Carter, Reagan, Clinton, and the younger Bush all experienced a crisis of governance in foreign policy that gave rise to a major political crisis. In fact, the crises became so severe that each president became overwhelmed by them. Each found little time and energy to respond to other issues and presidential responsibilities, which were either put on hold or carried out by subordinates with little presidential supervision. Clearly, the stress and toll of the office is immense, causing many presidents to noticeably age during their presidencies.

President Johnson was constantly preoccupied by the Vietnam quagmire during the last three years of his administration, to the point that it was difficult for his advisors and staff to get his attention on other matters. As President Nixon's cover-up of Watergate unraveled, he devoted himself to "damage control." As Congress came closer to impeaching him, his moods would swing from tenacious defense of his office to incredible despair, hopelessness, and obsession with little else but the future of his presidency (to the point that Henry Kissinger, who now enjoyed the roles of both national security advisors and secretary of state, was virtually in charge of U.S. foreign policy). Jimmy Carter became preoccupied with the release of the hostages. For one year the Monica Lewinsky affair dominated Clinton's presidency and all of American politics. And the Iraq War overwhelmed much of the agenda within the George W. Bush White House.

In some ways, Ronald Reagan may have been affected the most by his political crisis. Reagan was completely "shocked" by the political damage that the Iran-Contra revelations produced. Here was an individual who had beat the odds all his life—first as an actor in Hollywood, then in the California governorship, and finally with the U.S. presidency. Even though he was heavily criticized throughout his tenure, President Reagan was extremely popular with the American people, was very successful in exercising power, and won a landslide reelection in 1984.

Then, suddenly the world turned upside down. Such is the contemporary nature of presidential politics. When Americans learned that President Reagan had sold arms to and negotiated with the Khomeini regime, they couldn't believe it. When Reagan denied any involvement, his credibility was questioned for the first time, and the so-called "Teflon" presidency collapsed. And when it was learned that some of the money received in the arms-for-hostages deals had gone to the Contras, in direct opposition to a congressional ban on all Contra aid, congressional investigations were triggered to examine Iran-Contra and determine whether the president had abused the powers of his office.

President Reagan, who had appeared at the height of his power, was now on the defensive, trying to minimize the political damage. Reagan, never one to be too heavily involved in the day-to-day details of governing, was so badly shaken that for a time he became virtually paralyzed as president. It was reported that the situation became so bad at one point that his advisors began to discuss seriously whether they should invoke the **Twenty-Fifth Amendment**, which allows the vice president to temporarily act as president if the sitting president becomes physically or emotionally disabled. Although badly shaken and damaged politically, Reagan ultimately survived and recovered, although much weaker and older to complete his term of office (see Mayer and McManus 1988).

What specific effects do you think the stresses of high office and the consequences of controversy have on presidential leadership and power in foreign policy?

Iran-Contra demonstrates that Reagan also was a president willing to exercise prerogative government in support of foreign policy goals that he deemed vital. Like Nixon before him, he acted as if the political environment had not changed since the 1950s. He felt that the president, as commander in chief, possessed the same right as presidents before him during the earlier cold war—to conduct U.S. foreign policy as he saw fit. As long as the operations involving Nicaragua and Iran remained covert or were kept off the public agenda, Reagan was a formidable president. However, once the stories broke, Reagan experienced a crisis of governance that damaged both his professional reputation and public prestige. Unlike Nixon, Reagan's presidential abuse of power was not considered as severe, limited as it was to the conduct of foreign policy, and his high level of public prestige allowed him to weather the political storm and leave office with a general reputation as a successful president.

POST–COLD WAR OPPORTUNITIES AND RISKS

The end of the cold war created new opportunities for U.S. foreign policy, but it also exacerbated the difficulties that a president faces in exercising power in general and in the area of foreign policy. It is very difficult for post–cold war presidents to govern foreign policy, lead the country, and manage the executive branch to produce a consistent and coherent foreign policy in both national security and economic affairs. In short, lack of consensus on foreign policy, more diffuse international security risks, and an interdependent world economy seem to have combined to increase the constraints and challenges facing presidents. The cold war and the existence of a permanent crisis state was an anomaly in the history of U.S. foreign policy after all. Certainly, this sense of permanent crisis declined with the tragedy of Vietnam and disappeared with the collapse of the Soviet Union and the cold war.

Crises still occur and allow presidents to be extremely powerful, but this tends to be only temporary and for limited foreign-policy scope. This is certainly what President George H. W. Bush experienced with the Persian Gulf War—all-time highest public approval ratings in 1991 only to be defeated for reelection in 1992. Similarly, the terrorist attacks of September 11 created a new period of crisis and national emergency, which made President George W. Bush supreme in the making of foreign policy like former cold war presidents. However, as time passed from the crisis and Bush's policies began to suffer from various setbacks, the initially overwhelming political support he experienced began to decline. In particular, the increasingly costly war in Iraq produced serious fissures in congressional and public support for the president—even within his own party.

The collapse of the cold war has produced an interesting paradox for presidential leadership relative to the future of U.S. foreign policy: It gives the president great opportunities but also creates great risks. Unlike those of the cold war era, contemporary presidents are no longer driven to pursue only an anticommunist containment policy. They now have more flexibility to pursue a wider range of foreign policy options abroad. At the same time, strong and judicious presidential leadership has become increasingly important for it is unclear how far a president may go in pursuing any policy before losing public and governmental support (Hastedt and Eksterowicz 1993; Mann 1990a; Rosati 1992, 1997; Scott 1998; Skowronek 2011).

Clearly, presidential reputation, public prestige, and presidential choices, including the resort to prerogative government, are necessary for presidents to successfully govern in the post–cold war era. Yet, regardless of what the president has promised in either domestic or foreign policy, he usually is unable to fulfill expectations for long. The complexity of the domestic environment, reinforced by the complexity of the global system, with increasing economic interdependence and globalization, simply no longer allows much latitude for presidential success. This has been reinforced by the complex and multifaceted nature of contemporary foreign policy as the differences between foreign and domestic policy are less clear and the issue agenda less obviously dominated by security concerns. The net result of this crisis of leadership has been that with each new administration, as well as over the course of the same administration, U.S. foreign policy has tended to become increasingly "reactive"—as opposed to "proactive"—as U.S. behavior during the administrations of the elder Bush, Clinton, the younger Bush, and Obama indicate. This is likely to continue, making it very difficult for the United States to exercise the kind of sustained global leadership that so many seem to hope for or fear.

The George H. W. Bush Presidency

George H. W. Bush became president just before the collapse of the Soviet Union and communism in Eastern Europe and was widely considered to be a strong president in the realm of foreign policy. Nevertheless, he was unable to take advantage of the favorable post–cold war environment and a tremendously successful and popular war in the Persian Gulf, and lost his bid for reelection in 1992.

Bush entered office pledging to use his considerable governmental experience to continue most of the policies of his predecessor, but with a "kinder and gentler" style. Bush's leadership style was quite different from Reagan's: more informal and low-keyed, more active and hands-on, less ideological, and more politically sensitive. The most common criticisms of Bush were that he attempted to govern without a vision or an agenda, that his presidency was too reactive and cautious, and that he was too sensitive to public relations and politics. Yet early on, Bush's leadership style paid off. His public approval ratings into his third year were over 70 percent, then an all-time high for post–World War II presidents.

However, as we have learned, to begin office strong is not unusual. Although his public approval was high, Bush, unlike Reagan and many of his predecessors, lacked truly strong political support. Also, he was not a particularly good public speaker and, moreover, did not develop an active domestic agenda and faced an economic recession. His pragmatic, real-politick approach to foreign policy, while successful, did not inspire confidence or passion and often appeared reactive to events and initiatives taken by others. Thus, despite his great victory in the Persian Gulf War and public approval ratings approaching 90 percent, he was voted out of office after just one term, largely due to perceptions that he did little to address the nation's domestic ills.

The Clinton Presidency

President Bill Clinton experienced considerable difficulty in governing throughout his tenure both at home and abroad. Yet Clinton managed to escape the presidential life cycle, won reelection against a weak Republican candidate, and completed his second term of office with more popularity—despite the Monica Lewinsky affair—than he enjoyed when he started his first term. In fact, he is the first Democratic president to be reelected since FDR, over fifty years ago—and the only president since World War II to leave office with higher public approval than when he entered (review Figure 3.2).

Bill Clinton appears to be a very complex man who seemed to have contradictory leadership styles. On one hand, he had a strong interest and concern for both policy and politics. His verbal facility and intelligence is formidable, and he brought energy and optimism to the White House. In the words of Jack Watson (1993:431), a former White House chief of staff, he was "exuberant, informal, interactive, nonhierarchical, and indefatigable." On the other hand, Clinton often got himself into trouble by lacking self-discipline and not focusing on a set of specific goals. He was amiable to the point of being ingratiating with friends as well as foes. He was very articulate, but his ability to communicate in public was counteracted by his tendency to become too long-winded and mired in detailed lists (see Greenstein 1994).

Clinton suffered early political defeats, such as with appointments and, in particular, over his effort to legitimize "gays in the military"—which hurt his public prestige and professional reputation. Commonly perceived as trying to do too much too quickly, during his first two years he failed even to get major parts of his legislative program (such as his first budget and his major initiative to reform health care) through a Congress controlled by his own party. And then, in 1994, the Democratic Party suffered a huge electoral defeat, with the Republican Party gaining control of both the Senate and the House of Representatives—for the first time since 1954—producing divided government once again. But he was able to rebound politically when he won a major showdown with the Republican-led Congress in late 1995 and early 1996 over the budget—which included two government shutdowns.

President Clinton was also accused of considerable vacillation and hesitancy in the conduct of U.S. foreign policy, especially in his first term. Highly publicized failures in Somalia and what appeared to be a two-year equivocation on the crisis in the former Yugoslavia were among the early setbacks stemming in part from efforts to promote a more multilateral foreign policy. As his first term wound on, however, President Clinton did manage to initiate several significant foreign policy actions such as the military interventions in Haiti and Kosovo, as well as the bailouts of the Mexican peso and Asian financial crisis, in which he exercised a certain amount of prerogative government.

In each case the administration was faced with considerable public and congressional opposition to each initiative and proceeded nonetheless. In each case there were many in Congress who argued that the president did not have the authority to act alone, and yet he did so. Furthermore, each of these instances of prerogative government occurred in the absence of any semblance of national emergency in the post–cold war environment. And yet in none of the cases did the Clinton administration suffer from "backlash" or "overshoot and collapse." Thus, major foreign policy failures were avoided while the administration chose to emphasize domestic policy and international economics. Most prominent in this regard were passage of the North American Free Trade Agreement (NAFTA); the Uruguay round of the GATT, producing the World Trade Organization; the expansion of NATO; and normalized trade relations with China.

Clinton very easily could have been another failed president, a victim of a year-long crisis of governance over the **Monica Lewinsky affair**—involving the president's sexual relations with a former White House intern. Against the wishes of a majority of the American public (who opposed Clinton's personal behavior but deemed it to be more of a private matter), a Republican special prosecutor and Congress conducted numerous and intensive investigations of the Clintons, eventually voting articles of impeachment for presidential abuse of power. The articles of impeachment were voted down in the Senate on a highly politicized and partisan vote (all Democrats voting against impeachment, almost all Republicans voting in favor). Clinton not only survived politically but was able to maintain an active agenda until the end of his term.

In fact, he left office with greater public approval than when he entered. Bill Clinton's political success may have been in part due to most Americans' lowered expectations, at least relative to him and his presidency. Also, he was the beneficiary of an economy that not only avoided going into recession but actually grew strongly throughout his presidency. Somewhat like Ronald Reagan's Teflon presidency, but for very different reasons, nothing seemed to politically damage Clinton too much or for too long (see Harris 2005; Maranis 1995; Renshon 2000).

The George W. Bush Presidency

George W. Bush had a very inauspicious beginning as president. He was elected in 2000 with a smaller popular vote than Al Gore, the Democratic candidate. The electoral votes and Electoral College were under challenge, especially in Florida, where Bush's brother was governor. And ultimately his election as the forty-third president of the United States was decided by a 5–4 U.S. Supreme Court decision. So President Bush began his term of office with a rather low sense of national legitimacy. Moreover, as former Bush speechwriter David Frum (quoted in Lindsay 2003:537) observed, "On September 10, 2001, George Bush was not on his way to a very successful presidency."

Although Bush was previously governor of Texas and ran for president as a "compassionate conservative," he was not widely respected or admired for his political focus, background, or knowledge—especially in the area of foreign policy. The conventional wisdom was that he picked a seasoned foreign policy team that would make up for what he lacked in knowledge about U.S. foreign policy and world politics. President Bush initially offered no grand vision and his first few months in office were rather uneventful. Most of the president's focus seemed to be on domestic politics—in particular, successfully passing a large tax cut.

And then came September 11, 2001. In addition to the thousands of dead and wounded, prominent American symbols on United States soil were attacked, and most Americans were in a state of shock and disbelief. Quickly reacting to the disaster and ensuing crisis, President Bush seemed to become a new man and a new president over the course of the next few weeks. The immediate response was that the country (and much of the world) rallied around the flag and the president. For the next few months, public approval of presidential behavior surged to around 90 percent. Overnight, George W. Bush became the "war president" focused on the global war on terrorism (see Conley 2004; Renshon 2004).

According to the Bush administration, the United States had entered a new era of national emergency and permanent crisis, similar to what President Truman faced following World War II, in which the United States would have to respond with all its energy and might to eradicate the new global threat. The Bush administration proclaimed a new vision of a **"unitary executive theory"** in which the presidency was once again supreme in foreign policy with virtually unlimited ability to exercise prerogative government, and could ignore or override laws of Congress that interfere with his duties as commander in chief. In fact, as one reporter noted, "on a wide variety of fronts, the administration . . . moved to seize power that it has shared with other branches of government" (Goldsmith 2007; Milbank 2001:A1; see also Daalder and Lindsay 2003; Fisher 2007; Yoo 1996, 2005).

Bush immediately set about refocusing his administration to engage in a global war on terrorism, beginning with Afghanistan to overthrow the Taliban and turning to Iraq to depose Saddam Hussein. No issue seemed to be more central to the administration than Iraq. Galvanized by the desire to be aggressive in its global war on terror, the administration had barely completed its successful invasion in Afghanistan before it began to lay the groundwork for an invasion of Iraq. In spite of international resistance and some internal disagreement, once Bush decided to use force to remove Hussein from power, administration officials and the president himself forcefully advanced the case that Iraq's possession of weapons of mass destruction and ties to al-Qaeda required assertive military action (see Woodward 2004). After securing congressional support and despite resistance from much of the international community, especially France, Russia, and China on the UN Security Council, the administration, in concert with a "coalition of the willing" composed chiefly of Great Britain and a few other countries, invaded Iraq in 2003. By May, U.S. military forces had captured Baghdad and forced the Hussein regime out, and President Bush officially declared "mission accomplished" on May 2, 2003.

The public and Congress initially rallied around the military action (note the spike in public approval at the time of the invasion, as shown in Figure 3.2). However, with the initial military campaign over, the more difficult task of rebuilding the Iraqi government and nation-building ensued. Resistance to the American occupation soon grew and violence seemed to increase daily. Moreover, the weapons of mass destruction that Iraq was alleged to possess were never found, and the American-led search units soon officially concluded that they had never been there. Nor were any ties to al-Qaeda discovered, although al-Qaeda soon became active in the insurgency against the U.S. forces and the Iraqi regime that the U.S. sought to empower. Indeed, far from justifying the president's decision, postwar events cast doubt on the administration's prewar claims and justifications (see Cirincione, Mathews, Perkovitch, and Orton 2004; Powers 2003).

With the costs of the war thus spiraling upward, Bush began to face increased unrest and challenges, and his public approval began to steadily decline. While he secured a victory in the bitterly contested 2004 presidential election over Democratic nominee John Kerry, Bush's popularity continued to decline soon after. Distance from the 9/11 attacks, coupled with increasing costs in Iraq, persistent questions about the success of his global war on terrorism, and lingering concerns about the administration's use (or misuse) of intelligence (and other national security powers) combined with natural disasters such as Hurricane Katrina and a collapsing economy continued to erode Bush's support and exacerbate his lame duck status to the point that he was essentially ineffective by the end of his term in office. In fact, his presidency was effectively crippled in November 2006, when the Democrats seized control of both houses of Congress in a stunning political backlash against Bush.

Hence, what initially appeared to be a time of permanent national emergency and a renewed supremacy in presidential power unraveled into a more complicated and now-familiar post–cold war scenario. The changing sense of threat, coupled with declining policy success, led to increased criticism even within the Republican-led Congress. Bush's inability to prevail on a variety of policy initiatives in his second term, the increasing opposition to his signature policies on the global war on terror, and concerns over his relative neglect of other domestic and foreign policy issues—especially the economic crisis that began in 2008—provide ample evidence that *a weakened post-Vietnam and post–cold war presidency is still quite applicable, even in a political environment in which the president was able to exercise considerable prerogative government for awhile.*

The Obama Presidency

The presidency of Barack Obama is of great significance for many reasons. This was the first time the country nominated and elected a "black" (or African-American or biracial) man as president of the United States in its history, just forty-five years after Martin Luther King, Jr.'s "I Have a Dream" speech. Second, Obama entered office inheriting an (American and global) economy on the verge of a collapse often compared to the Great Depression. Third, numerous national security issues had to be faced, including potential nuclear proliferation in North Korea and Iran, the withdrawal of American troops and "Iraqification" of the war in Iraq, and an escalation in the war on terrorism in both Afghanistan and Pakistan. Finally, the presidential campaign of 2008 raised difficult new issues, including reforming health care, the need for alternative energy policies, and global warming.

President Obama entered office determined to break with the policies of his predecessor and chart a new course. In a flurry of activity, the Obama Administration attempted to take advantage of the honeymoon period to advance an ambitious agenda somewhat reminiscent of the FDR administration and its "first 100 days." Although the problems Obama faced as he began his efforts were not as dramatic as those of the economic depression and global war of the 1930s and 1940s, few presidents since World War II have faced such a daunting array of challenges. In addition to contending with the legacy of the Iraq invasion, Obama faced challenges stemming from the deteriorating situation in Afghanistan and Pakistan (where the Taliban and al-Qaeda had reemerged as viable opponents), a severe global economic crisis, urgent environmental and energy policy issues, and regional security and nonproliferation challenges in North Korea and Iran, among other problems. Obama also faced a political environment in Washington, D.C., more divided along partisan lines than ever before in recent memory. Therefore, although the times and the initial honeymoon usually helps to strengthen presidential power, the successful exercise of prerogative government cannot be safely assumed and presidential leadership remained as crucial as ever.

From the start, Barack Obama developed and led an activist presidency and administration. His initial focus was on the deteriorating economy, followed closely by the wars in Iraq and Afghanistan. He took numerous international trips, visiting many countries and many political leaders in efforts to address international issues in a more multilateral way. In addition to winning the Nobel Peace prize in his first year (a very controversial decision), in subsequent years he successfully concluded a new nuclear arms treaty with Russia, deployed force against Libya, and authorized the successful raid into Pakistan that killed Osama bin Laden. He also took the initiative for major health care reform, and promoted greater fossil fuel efficiency, alternative energy sources, and increased environmental regulation. This was an expansive presidential agenda—in part reactive, in part proactive.

President Obama's leadership style initially seemed to resonate with much of the American people (and much of the world). From the start, he appeared active, calm and patient, bright and articulate, thoughtful, politically astute, tireless, friendly, having a sense of self-deprecation and humility, and a powerful communicator—a potentially impressive package of personal characteristics that helped to maximize his presidential leadership and power of persuasion. In the language of James MacGregor Burns (1978), Obama displayed "transformational" leadership (more strategic and long-term oriented that may profoundly affect future policies and the future of the country), as opposed to the "transactional" leadership (more short-term and politically motivated–oriented) that one commonly tends to see.

President Obama also took advantage of his initial honeymoon period and initial strengths in the presidential life cycle. At least initially, he maintained significant public approval, although his support fell from highs in the 60–70 percent range to the mid-40s by 2010, where it remained (review Figure 3.3). In addition to high levels of public prestige, he also tried to capitalize on his generally positive professional reputation by moving boldly and quickly on many fronts, dominating the policy agenda, refocusing U.S. foreign policy by breaking with past actions, and getting important legislation through Congress. His critics voiced strong verbal opposition and Republicans voted in virtual unison against major legislation, but were not initially successful in preventing its passage (until later on). And Obama exerted much prerogative government, both in national security affairs and, maybe more importantly, in addressing the economic meltdown (especially at home but also abroad).

With respect to the American and global economy, he promoted and adapted a strong set of policies in an effort to prevent further economic collapse and hopefully stimulate economic recovery. His administration helped to restore confidence in the credit and financial markets as well as the economy in general. Governmental spending, governmental debt, and governmental involvement in the economy reached levels not seen since the 1930s or the 1960s, given the severity of the economic meltdown. And yet the administration's policies received considerable public support initially, but also severe political criticism, especially from conservatives and the Republican Party. Given the controversial nature of the policy problems to which he devoted his attention, such criticism was inevitable.

In national security affairs, the Obama administration initiated and carried out a plan to withdraw American troops from Iraq by 2010 while trying to maintain the country's stability. At the same time, President Obama also made early decisions to intensify the American "footprint" in Afghanistan and Pakistan, dispatching an additional 21,000 troops in early 2009 and a subsequent surge of 40,000 troops in the fall of the same year in an effort to prevent further destabilization, with a promise to begin the withdrawal of American troops in 2012.

For the most part, these policies received initial political support, but they also were increasingly overshadowed by the focus on the economy and health care. Despite preventing economic collapse and attempting to stimulate a recovery, by the middle of 2009, public approval of the Obama administration began to decline, especially over the state of the economy. The political focus was no longer on saving the economy, but recovering from the Great Recession.

President Obama's public prestige and professional reputation also began to suffer. The so-called grassroots movement known as the "Tea Party" rose to challenge his policy agenda, and even his legitimacy in office. The Republican Party consistently fought the initiatives and legislation of the Democrats and President Obama and, in the election of 2010, gained control of the House narrowed the Democrat majority in the Senate. Not only were the partisan politics and Washington, D.C., political subculture not reformed or fixed (as promised during the campaign), partisanship got worse and presidential-legislative relations seemed to continually consist of political battles and stalemates. President Obama and his administration also began to be criticized by liberals and Democrats for being too "centrist" and too willing to "compromise." Instead of transformational leadership, President Obama increasingly looked like a transactional leader (see Alter 2010; Bai 2010; Judis 2010; Lizza 2012; Purdum 2010; Wolfe 2010).

In Bob Woodward's terms, the president intellectualized and then charted a way forward despite domestic and international complexities, illustrating the dichotomy of the visionary and functionally pragmatic man who wanted results (Woodward 2010, 38). Jonathan Alter saw the president as an active pragmatist who believed he could change or operate above the "inside the beltway subculture" with no coherent government philosophy and reactive by nature (Alter 2010). Richard Wolffe called it finding a balance between the "renegade rule breaker" and the "conventional rule follower," where the "hope filled rhetoric" of the administration co-existed with the "coldly pragmatic set of compromises" it had made (Wolffe 2010: 28, 39). Ryan Lizza noted that his advisors referred to Obama as a "consequentialist" (Lizza 2011; see also Garrison, Rosati and Scott, 2012).

President Obama clearly lost control of the political agenda. Despite the oratorical skills he had demonstrated during the 2008 campaign, he seemed unwilling and/or unable to communicate his purpose and means. In the words of Jonathan Alter in *The Promise* (2010:xv):

> The great irony was that a candidate who came to office in part because of his silver tongue was unable . . . to explain convincingly why the country should follow him . . . The president had trouble mastering the persuasive powers of the office. He failed to give voice to public anger or to convince the middle class that he was focused enough on their number one concern: jobs. He failed to persuade his fellow Democrats to use their fleeting sixty-vote supermajority in the Senate to enact more of his program.

In effect, President Obama and his administration faced the paradox of presidential power, fell prey to the paradox of presidential power, to the presidential life cycle, and to the crisis of leadership just like his predecessors that seems to eventually prevail since the Vietnam War and the end of the cold war. These factors impacted the 2012 election . . . And yet, despite these forces, the gradual improvement of the US economy, coupled with foreign policy successes and an effective campaign led Obama to a successful bid for re-election and a second term in the White House. As his second term began, President Obama faced these similar forces yet again, with a window of opportunity for leadership after re-election closing with the passing of time. However, President Obama marked the third straight two-term presidency, something that had not occurred since the early 19th century.

SUMMARY AND CHALLENGES OF THE POST–COLD WAR WORLD

This chapter *provides an overview of the politics of U.S. foreign policy.* We found that, while most Americans have high expectations of presidential power, in reality, there is a paradox of presidential power. Although presidents possess significant constitutional roles and strengths, they also face important constraints and uncertainties. Presidents usually go through a presidential life cycle in which they leave office much weaker than they were when they entered and often experience a crisis of leadership (or governance), making it difficult for any president to govern successfully and lead the country in a direction consistent with his beliefs. Although these patterns of presidential power are strongest in the area of domestic policy, they have also impacted foreign policy in the years since the Vietnam War and the end of the cold war. Therefore, the two presidencies thesis of the cold war years appears to no longer operate in a political environment where presidential leadership is more important than ever.

The discussion of presidential power and governance provides an initial *overview of the three foreign policymaking themes*—the president's ability to govern, continuity and change, and the tension between democracy and national security—addressed throughout this book. First, presidents have had a much more difficult time governing and leading the nation since the end of the Vietnam War and the cold war, even in the area of foreign policy, making presidential leadership skills much more important. Second, the foreign policy process has become more complex because of the changes that have occurred in the wake of the Vietnam War and the end of the cold war where Presidents now face more constraints and opposition throughout government, society, and the global environment in the conduct of foreign policy. Third, whenever presidents have exerted prerogative government and pressed assertive foreign policies since the Vietnam War, tensions between democracy and national security have increased, peaking initially during Watergate, and destroying President Nixon. Tension rose again during the Iran-Contra affair, but President Reagan and his presidency survived.

In sum, presidents must realize that they can no longer exercise power and prerogative government in the name of national security (or foreign policy crises), as commonly occurred during the cold war, without risking considerable political backlash and possible overshoot and collapse. Not even Ronald Reagan, with his tremendous symbolic skills and prestige with the American people, was able to rise above the paradox of presidential power. And if Reagan was unable to avoid a crisis of governance and the presidential life cycle, what is the omen for presidents with lesser leadership skills?

This means that the fragmented and pluralist political environment that has prevailed since the Vietnam War will likely continue in the post–cold war era into the twenty-first century, posing greater foreign policy opportunities and political risks for presidents and American leadership abroad. Much will depend on the perceptions Americans have of threat in the world, a president's policies, leadership skills, and of their relative success at home and abroad.

For a short time after 9/11, it appeared that President George W. Bush's war on terrorism would resonate throughout the international community, the domestic political environment, and the American people, producing a new permanent crisis and sense of national emergency, only to produce another failed presidency. President Obama faced the same constraints of other post–Vietnam and post–cold war presidents with the grave challenges he faces in the national security and economic arenas and a savagely partisan atmosphere of Washington, D.C. His initial success turned in part on his reputation, prestige and choices, and these factors will affect the next president as well. We now turn to one of the most significant sources that a president has to exercise leadership and power—his efforts to manage the executive branch and the foreign policy bureaucracy.

SUGGESTED SOURCES FOR MORE INFORMATION

Alter, Jonathan. (2010) *The Promise: President Obama, Year 1*. New York: Simon and Schuster. Excellent overview and analysis of Obama Administration's policymaking process during the economic crisis, Iraq and Afghanistan, and health care, including Obama's personality and leadership skills.

Burns, James MacGregor. (1978) *Leadership.* New York: Harper Torchbooks. Classic on political leadership in general.

Cronin, Thomas E. and Michael A Genovese. (2009) *The Paradoxes of the American Presidency*. New York: Oxford University Press. Good overview.

Destler, I. M., Leslie H. Gelb, and Anthony Lake. (1984) *Our Own Worst Enemy: The Unmaking of American Foreign Policy*. New York: Simon and Schuster. Impressively captures the changes since the Vietnam War.

Goldsmith, Jack L. (2007) *The Terror Presidency: Law and Judgement Inside the Bush Administration*. New York: W.W. Norton. Excellent overview on the rise of the unitary executive theory by an initial supporter and member of the Bush Administration.

Greenstein, Fred I. (2009) *The Presidential Difference: Leadership Style from FDR to Barack Obama*. New York: Free Press. Good overview.

Hook, Steven and James M. Scott. (2012) *U.S. Foreign Policy Today: American Renewal?* Washington: CQ Press. An examination of the foreign policy processes and policies of the early Obama administration by contributing authors.

Judis, John. (2010) "The Unnecessary Fall," *The New Republic* (September 2). On President Obama's inability and unwillingness to be more "populist"—critical to political success—once he became president.

Lizza, Ryan. (2012) "The Obama Memos: The Making of a Post-Post-Partisan Presidency," *The New Yorker* (January 30), pp. 36–49. Excellent analyses and description of Obama's initial beliefs in creating a post-partisan presidency and the reality of how he operated in a partisan-dominated Washington political environment.

Neustadt, Richard E. (1960) *Presidential Power: The Politics of Leadership*. New York: John Wiley & Sons. The classic statement on presidential power and presidential leadership.

Pious, Richard M. (1996) *The American Presidency.* New York: Basic Books. Excellent work on prerogative government.

Schlesinger, Jr., Arthur M. (1989) *The Imperial Presidency.* New York: Houghton Mifflin. Provides an excellent history of the evolution of executive–legislative relations in foreign affairs by describing the growth of presidential power leading up to Watergate.

Scott, James M. (1998) *After the End: Making U.S. Foreign Policy in the Post-Cold War World.* Durham, N.C.: Duke University Press. Excellent overview, including focus on key actors and issues.

Shull, Steven A., ed. (1991) *The Two Presidencies: A Quarter Century Assessment.* Chicago: Nelson-Hall. For a general assessment.

Smith, Hedrick. (1988, 1996) *The Power Game: How Washington Works.* New York: Ballantine. Provides an excellent discussion and feel for the realities of presidential power and American politics during the Reagan years.

KEY CONCEPTS

crisis of leadership (or governance)	power to persuade
electoral mandate	prerogative government
honeymoon	presidential choices
imperial presidency	presidential leadership
intermestic issues	presidential life cycle
issue area	professional reputation
lame duck	public prestige
model presidential leader	two presidencies thesis
paradox of presidential power	unitary executive theory
power	

OTHER KEY TERMS

Iran hostage crisis	Tet offensive
Iran-Contra affair	Twenty-Fifth Amendment
Monica Lewinsky affair	Twenty-Second Amendment
Teflon presidency	Watergate

PRESIDENT BARACK OBAMA AND HIS NATIONAL SECURITY ADVISOR THOMAS DONILON
IN INFORMAL CONSULTATION ON THE WAY TO A MEETING IN THE WEST WING.

THE BUREAUCRACY, PRESIDENTIAL MANAGEMENT, AND THE NATIONAL SECURITY COUNCIL

The president's beliefs about the nature of the world and America's role within it are a very important guide to the type of foreign policy that will be pursued under his administration. Setting the general direction and tone of an administration, however, does not guarantee that a president's vision and priorities will prevail. In fact, much of the government's foreign policy is made and carried out by the bureaucracy. This creates *a significant paradox: The president's ability to govern is heavily dependent on the foreign policy bureaucracy, yet the bureaucracy is so large and complex that it is very difficult to control.* Presidential governance, therefore, requires that presidents be not only strong political leaders, but strong managers as well. In this chapter, *we address the following major questions:* Why is presidential management so important? How do presidents manage the large and complex bureaucracy? What role does the National Security Council (NSC) system play in managing and governing foreign policy? As we will see, a president's success in managing the bureaucracy is very much a function of his choices concerning his personal agenda and level of involvement, the personnel who staff his administration, and how he organizes the foreign policymaking process, in particular the operations of the White House and NSC.

A HUGE AND COMPLEX FOREIGN POLICY BUREAUCRACY

The president is the chief administrator of a sprawling bureaucracy, much of which is beyond presidential control. Hence, as we discussed in Chapter 3, the bureaucracy is both a source of and a constraint on presidential power. If the president is to exercise much power in his efforts to govern, whether in foreign or domestic policy, he must attempt to manage and control the federal bureaucracy, which is no easy task. ***Three key aspects of the bureaucracy complicate the president's task of its management and administration:*** (1) size, (2) complexity, and (3) historical development.

Bureaucratic Size

The president presides over five million personnel, located in fifteen major departments and hundreds of other organizations and agencies, who now spend over $3 trillion a year on thousands of programs and policies throughout the United States and the world. The executive branch is so large that the president cannot manage it alone. Within this sprawling array of organizations, the **foreign policy bureaucracy** is made up of those agencies that have foreign policy roles. The main elements of the foreign policy bureaucracy include the Department of Defense (DOD), which is the largest of all executive branch organizations. It employs over three million civilian and military personnel (including reserves) throughout the world and now spends over $700 billion a year. Along with the DOD, the foreign policy bureaucracy includes Department of State, with its professional diplomatic corps, and the Central Intelligence Agency (CIA) and other specialized parts of the intelligence community, who engage in intelligence-gathering and analysis devoted to foreign affairs. Other agencies have important foreign policy roles as well, including the Department of the Treasury and the Department of Homeland Security (DHS) created in 2002. These are just the most obvious agencies: ***virtually every department and agency in the executive branch contains an international component.***

As **Table 4.1** reveals, there are many agencies that are involved in foreign policy. For example, the Department of Transportation is responsible for the government's policy on international aviation and maritime issues through the Office of the Assistant Secretary for Aviation and International Affairs, the Federal Aviation Administration, and the Maritime Administration. The Department of Justice contains the Federal Bureau of Investigation (FBI), which plays an important role in counterterrorism, and the Drug Enforcement Agency, the lead agency in fighting the drug war. As noted in Table 4.1, there are also a number of independent agencies and governmental corporations with a role in global affairs, including the Environmental Protection Agency, the Federal Maritime Commission (which regulates waterborne domestic and foreign commerce), and the National Endowment for Democracy, a quasi-governmental foundation that distributes democracy assistance grants. All together, we're talking about a huge foreign policy bureaucracy.

Bureaucratic Complexity

The bureaucracy is also incredibly complex. Whatever their specific size, each agency and department has its subculture, and sometimes more than one, as well as its own set of goals and missions. Many times the tasks of different organizations overlap. For instance, the intelligence community, discussed in Chapter 7, is made up of many executive branch organizations that contribute information and analyses to high-level policymakers. These agencies overlap and often compete with

Table 4.1   The Foreign Policy Bureaucracy

	Internationally Oriented Agencies	Domestically Oriented Agencies
Executive Office of the President	National Security Council	White House Office
	National Economic Council	Office of Management and Budget
	White House Office of Global Communications	Office of Science and Technology Policy
	Office of the Director of National Intelligence	Office of National Drug Control Policy
	Office of the U.S. Trade Representative	Office of National AIDS Policy
Presidential Departments and Agencies	Department of State	Department of Agriculture
	Department of Defense	Department of Commerce
	Department of Treasury	Department of Labor
	Department of Energy	Department of Justice
	Department of Homeland Security	Department of Veterans Affairs
	Central Intelligence Agency	Department of Transportation
	U.S. Agency for International Development	Department of Health and Human Services
	Peace Corps	
Independent Agencies	International Trade Commission	Federal Reserve Board
	Export-Import Bank Overseas Protection Investment Corporation	National Aeronautics and Space Administration
	Trade and Development Agency	Environmental Protection Agency
	International Broadcasting Bureau	Federal Maritime Commission
	National Endowment for Democracy	
	African Development Foundation	
	Inter-American Foundation	
	Panama Canal Commission	
	U.S. Institute for Peace	

SOURCE: *United States Government Manual.*

each other and sometimes have problems coordinating. These various organizations also have different levels of autonomy from presidential authority. The president has legal authority within the executive branch over those organizations located in the Executive Office of the Presidency, classified as cabinet departments, or presidential agencies. However, most of the organizations classified as independent agencies in Table 4.1 are independent of presidential authority.

The forces of globalization and interdependence have added to the complexity of the foreign policy bureaucracy over the last several decades by fostering the fading distinction between foreign and domestic policy bureaucracies. Once, traditional national security bureaucracies were easy to identify, such as the State Department, the military, and, after World War II, the intelligence community. However, with the growth of interdependence and the boundary-reducing forces of globalization, these distinctions have lost much of their meaning. U.S. foreign policy now involves intermestic policies in such areas as economics, immigration, the environment, transportation and communications, technology, and narcotics, and a host of bureaucratic agencies that have responsibilities in these areas. Now, in part because of the **internationalization of domestic bureaucracies** and the development of global networks of bureaucratic (personnel) interaction, especially in the "principal areas of food, energy, finance, communication, environment, economic growth, and the spread of technology" (Hopkins 1978:31), most of the departments and ministries of modern governments associated with predominantly domestic areas have some kind of international bureau. In fact, the rise in the importance of the foreign economic bureaucracy, which we discuss in Chapter 8, is one of the main consequences of this shift.

Historical Development of the Bureaucracy

Two hundred years ago the U.S. government was tiny compared to what it is today; it was composed of the president, the vice president, a small personal staff, and four small departments: State, Treasury, War, and Justice. Prior to World War II, foreign policy was conducted by "the president and secretary of state; a handful of administration appointees in the Department of State and major embassies; the senior diplomats of a tiny but adequate Foreign Service; a few military and naval officers serving in important commands or as attaches; and a constellation of influential lawyers and bankers, involved in the Council on Foreign Relations and largely residing on the East Coast" (Maechling 1976:6).

Since the nineteenth century, most bureaucratic growth has taken place in four successive waves:

1. in domestic and economic agencies as a result of the New Deal legislation of the 1930s under president Franklin Roosevelt,

2. in national security and foreign affairs during World War II and the cold war under presidents Franklin Roosevelt, Harry Truman, and Dwight Eisenhower (Zegart 1999),

3. as a consequence of President Lyndon Johnson's Great Society programs of the 1960s,

4. in the post-September 11, 2001, context with President George W. Bush's global war on terrorism and President Obama's response to the global economic recession.

In each of these waves, the expansion of the bureaucracy came from government's responses to the urgency of events and the times. New bureaucratic agencies with new organizational goals and missions were created to respond to new problems, often perceived as so dire and widespread that only the federal government could address them. However, such growth has generated the bureaucratic complexity that makes it so difficult for presidents to act as chief executives.

The national security bureaucracy's tremendous expansion took place over two decades in response to two major conflicts, World War II and the cold war. The key law that was the basis for the permanent expansion of the foreign policy bureaucracy was the **National Security Act of 1947**. It was one of the most important acts ever passed by Congress and signed by the president, because it laid the foundation for the modern foreign policy bureaucracy. This restructuring was intended to produce a more efficient national security process that would be more valuable to the president in his conduct of foreign policy. *The act restructured the national security process in three major areas:*

1. the military, by creating the National Military Establishment (forerunner to the DOD), consisting of the secretary of defense, the Joint Chiefs of Staff (JCS), and the Departments of Army, Navy, and Air Force,

2. intelligence, by creating the CIA and the director of central intelligence, and

3. national security advice to the president, by creating the NSC.

The most recent expansion of the national security bureaucracy came in response to the September 11, 2001, terrorist attacks. In addition to providing large budgetary increases for the military and the intelligence community, President George W. Bush first created the Office of Homeland Security (OHS) by executive order to coordinate the government's counterterrorist efforts. In 2002, Congress, over the initial objections of President Bush and his advisors, turned the office into a full-fledged Department of Homeland Security in order to reorganize numerous executive branch agencies involved in counterterrorism and give it greater stature to help coordinate and lead the counterterrorism effort. Additionally, following the recommendation of a commission that studied the September 11 attacks, the Bush administration also lobbied successfully for a new Office of the Director for National Intelligence (ODNI), created by the Intelligence Reform and Prevention of Terrorism Act of 2004 (P.L. 108-458), which removed the coordinating role from the director of the CIA and provided the new Director of National Intelligence with some expanded powers to coordinate the decentralized intelligence community. (Chapter 7 discusses both the DHS and ODNI in greater detail.) In spite of both changes, much of the intelligence community, especially the FBI and the CIA, remained largely untouched, and many relevant agencies remained outside the direct control of either of the new organizations. The foreign economic bureaucracy has also been expanding under the Obama Administration in response to the global economic recession (discussed in Chapter 8).

PRESIDENTIAL MANAGEMENT

The size and complexity of the foreign policy bureaucracy causes decentralization and coordination problems in the government's policymaking process, which make presidential management of the foreign policy bureaucracy and foreign policy process crucial. But, how can a president manage the bureaucracy and make it work for him? *Three sets of presidential choices are vital:* (1) the president's foreign policy orientation, agenda, and level of involvement; (2) the appointment of executive branch personnel; and (3) the organization of the foreign policymaking process (Edwards and Wayne 2005). These decisions are critical if a president wants to enter office ready to exercise power and govern, poised to take advantage of the honeymoon period and early optimism that surrounds the start of a new administration (Burke 2001, 2009c). These choices are so important that the candidate who has been newly elected in November will have made many of these decisions during the three-month **presidential transition period**, as we saw most recently with a very active Obama transition team.

The President's Orientation, Agenda, and Level of Involvement

The president's beliefs and worldview set the general direction and foreign policy orientation for the administration. Presidents try to set goals and promote policies that reflect their foreign policy orientation and agenda. This is critical because the role of the bureaucracy is too important to be left to chance; a president must be attentive to and actively involved in the bureaucracy's operations to ensure that U.S. foreign policy during his administration accords with his preferences. As Brent Scowcroft, who served as national security advisor to both President Ford and the first President Bush, suggested, "the NSC system was really developed to serve an activist president in foreign policy" (National Security Council Project 1999a:35). The more a president is attentive to and involved in what goes on throughout the executive branch, the more likely he will influence and manage the bureaucracy in accordance with a foreign policy orientation and agenda of his choosing.

Because the bureaucracy is so large and complex, a president must be selective as to the issues most important to him and the agenda he decides to promote, given the time and information constraints he faces. He must understand that the bureaucracy will be most responsive to those issues and agenda items that he most prizes and is most active in promoting. General "policy reviews," especially at the beginning of a new administration; involvement in the policymaking process; and "presidential speeches" offer unique opportunities for the president to gain control over the bureaucracy and foreign policy (Goldgeier 2000). Ultimately, the president must rely on others to assist him in governing, in exercising presidential leadership, and in managing the bureaucracy. Hence, presidential staff and advisors, and the policymaking process, are absolutely critical in affecting the bureaucracy's response to the president's orientation and agenda.

Appointment of Staff and Advisors

The president is not alone and is dependent on others in efforts to govern and to manage the bureaucracy. The president (as an individual) operates within the institution or office of the presidency, which is composed of the president and other individuals and organizations working for the president. Therefore, presidential choices about who to appoint for his staff and advisors are quite critical.

In deciding who will serve in his administration, the president must make *three general sets of presidential appointments:*

1. personal presidential staff,

2. major policy advisors, and

3. high-level officials responsible for other cabinet departments and executive agencies.

These individuals affect the president's ability to manage the bureaucracy and exercise presidential leadership and power. Consequently, with each new president there is considerable change in top-level personnel, which not only empowers the president to populate the bureaucracy with people of his own choosing, but also threatens policy continuity and consistency. Even leaving aside mid- and lower-level appointees, consider, for example, that while the United States has had eight presidents since John Kennedy's assassination, they have appointed thirteen Secretaries of State, thirteen Secretaries of Defense, seventeen Directors of the Central Intelligence (and four Directors of National Intelligence), and seventeen national security advisors (President Reagan alone appointed six in his eight years!).

Building on the recommendations of the 1936 Brownlow Commission, Franklin Roosevelt was the first modern president to expand his personal staff by creating the **Executive Office of the Presidency (EOP)** to cope with a rapidly growing bureaucracy. Today, the EOP contains the people and organizations that a president tends to rely on most in managing the bureaucracy and governing, including the White House Office (WHO), Office of Management and Budget (OMB), NSC, and National Economic Council (NEC) (see **Figure 4.1**). All told, about two thousand people work in the EOP, and its budget has grown from about $12 million in 1962 to about $3.5 billion today.

The president relies most directly on his personal staff, who occupy positions in the **White House Office (WHO)** and therefore play a unique role within the EOP. These are the people who act as the eyes and ears of the president and who are preoccupied with protecting and promoting his professional reputation, public prestige, and presidential choices. They are responsible for the president's daily activities and help him prepare for public appearances. Given their proximity and importance to the presidency, they have also become significantly more involved in the making of U.S. foreign policy (Cohen, Dolan and Rosati 2002; Walcott, Warshaw and Wayne 2001).

The **chief of staff** is the most significant of the president's personal staff and interacts with the president more frequently than anyone else. The chief of staff is responsible for the president's daily schedule and oversees the rest of the White House staff. This is a very influential position because the chief of staff usually acts as the intermediary between the

Figure 4.1   The Executive Branch

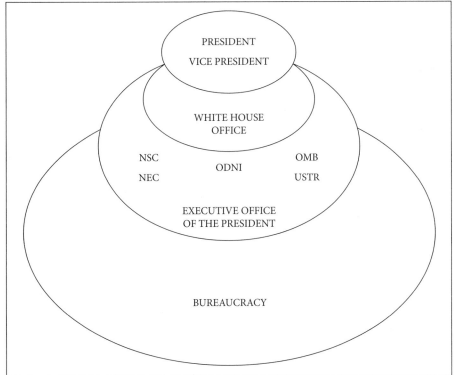

© Cengage Learning

president and all staff and advisors who interact with him. Since the 1970s, the chief of staff has frequently played a more important role in foreign policy as well, often using the **gatekeeping** role to great advantage.

For example, Leon Panetta, President Clinton's second chief of staff, and each of his successors were made formal members of the NSC Principals Committee (see our discussion later in this chapter); Panetta also instituted a structure that required all paperwork to route through his office (including foreign policy paperwork), and carefully controlled access to the president. He also joined President Clinton in all foreign policy and intelligence briefings. Similarly, George W. Bush's first chief of staff—Andrew Card—was a formal member of the NSC and a valued informal advisor, and his successor, Joshua Bolten, played a comparable role. In the Obama administration, the White House staff was heavily involved in foreign policy discussions and communication and President Obama had three different chiefs of staff in his first term—Rahm Emmanuel, William Daley, and Jacob Lew, each of whom was similarly engaged. Finally, another position that has become increasingly central to foreign policy for the most recent presidents (with both positive and negative consequences) is that of the **office of the vice president** (see **A Closer Look** on the vice presidency).

Transforming the Vice Presidency, From Gore to Cheney to Biden

Throughout much of American history, the person in the role of vice president has been a relatively insignificant player in the policymaking process, usually chosen to "balance" the ticket for the presidential election and relegated to symbolic and unimportant activities (such as to preside over the Senate as stipulated in the Constitution). The vice presidency, however, has been an important stepping stone for eventually gaining the party's nomination to run for president (after the president's term of office has ended). Thomas Marshall, vice president under Woodrow Wilson, described the job by saying, "The only business of the vice president is to ring the White House bell every morning and ask what is the state of health of the president."

This began to change in the late 1970s under President Jimmy Carter, who turned increasingly to Vice President Walter Mondale for counsel and political support, and continued through Presidents Ronald Reagan and George H. W. Bush and their vice presidents. However, under the last three presidents, the office of the vice president has become a much enhanced position of power and respect.

Albert Gore, Jr., was the son of a U.S. senator from Tennessee. After serving in the army during the Vietnam War as a journalist, he was eventually elected to the U.S. House and then the Senate from the state of Tennessee. Gore was selected as Bill Clinton's running mate in 1992 and, after their election victory, Gore became an active participant and trusted advisor in the Clinton White House, including in the area of national security affairs—an area that Gore has dealt with for many years and in which Clinton was much more of a novice. Perhaps Gore's most defining issue was his commitment to the environment and to "reinvent government" by lessening red tape and making governmental bodies more efficient. However, Gore was also an active participant in most foreign policy debates. Gore was one of the first vice presidents to effectively promote high-profile national issues.

Under President George W. Bush, **Dick Cheney** became the most powerful vice president ever, especially in foreign policy. Cheney entered office with broad experience, tremendous contacts, and a strong personality under a president with little experience and knowledge about foreign affairs. Cheney, who served in the Nixon, Ford, and elder Bush administrations, successfully ran for office as a congressman from Wyoming in 1978, leaving the institution in March 1989 to become President George H. W. Bush's secretary of defense. Cheney moved into private business after Bill Clinton defeated Bush, becoming chief executive of Halliburton—the largest oildrilling, engineering, and construction services firm in the world. In George W. Bush's administration, it was clear that Cheney was to play a more influential role than any previous vice president. Not only was he a presidential confidant, but Cheney also moved aggressively to strengthen his role in the formal policy process as well. He expanded the office of the vice president, hiring a dozen staff members to create what some consider a mini-NSC staff of his own. He then ensured that his staff had representation in the interagency working groups, took the unusual step of getting himself placed on to the NSC Principals Committee, and even lobbied to be the chair of that committee, which would have put the national security advisor under his direction. Although unsuccessful, he remained an assertive participant in the committee, and used his staff to work outside the official interagency process to gain even more influence. Indeed, reflecting on his influence within the administration, one sympathetic observer told Bob Woodward that Cheney's advice was "the most important, the Cadillac" of all the participants in foreign policymaking. Others forcefully argue that Cheney bore heavy responsibility for the failures of the NSC system during the younger Bush's administration.

Joseph Biden assumed the office of vice president on the heels of important precedents expanding its role. A long-serving senator from Delaware, Biden was born in Pennsylvania, and was first elected to the U.S. Senate in 1972. With a long record of public service and experience on foreign policy issues in the Senate, Biden played an important role in the Obama administration. Yet, Biden was also a forceful critic of his predecessor, who he once called the "most dangerous vice president we've had probably in American history." As vice president, Biden was "'a total utility player,' as Mrs. Clinton described Mr. Biden, or 'the guy who does a bunch of things that don't show up on the stat sheet,' as Mr. Obama once put it" (Leibovich 2012). Among other things, these roles included designated contrarian in policy discussions, including the Afghanistan War, and advice on dealing with Congress (see also Daalder and Lindsay 2003; Fineman 2003; Light 1984; Woodward 2004).

What are the main consequences of this changing vice presidential role for presidential power and management of the foreign policy process?

The president must also decide who will occupy major policy positions in the U.S. government and act as his policy advisors. Of the many appointments a president makes, *six key foreign policy appointments stand out:*

1. the national security advisor (sometimes called the NSC advisor),

2. secretary of state,

3. secretary of defense,

4. director of central intelligence and, since 2005, the director of national intelligence,

5. special assistant to the president for economic affairs (called the national economic advisor or NEC advisor), and

6. secretary of the treasury.

These officials are responsible for the most important foreign policy organizations within the executive branch. They are the people with whom the president interacts most on a daily basis in making foreign policy, with the national economic advisor and secretary of the treasury most instrumental for foreign economic policy and the other officials more consequential in the national security area.

The president also appoints hundreds of other high-level officials to fill positions throughout the executive branch. For most agencies, he appoints the head or director and the positions at the next three or four hierarchical levels within the agency, usually collaborating with agency heads to select nominees. In the State Department, the president has the authority to make appointments at the five highest hierarchical levels: the secretary of state, deputy secretary of state, undersecretaries of state, assistant secretaries of state, and deputy assistant secretaries of state. These appointments do not guarantee presidential control, as we will see in greater depth in the next few chapters, because the bureaucracy has a life of its own and often "captures" appointees to reflect bureaucratic interests. Yet these appointments are one of the key means available for a president to manage the bureaucracy (Patterson and Pfiffner 2001).

Certain selection criteria tend to influence presidential appointments. Presidents try to appoint people who are knowledgeable and who share their ideological outlook and worldview. They also usually select people with whom they are comfortable and whom they believe to be loyal. Most members of the White House staff, for example, usually consist of people with whom the president has grown familiar and comfortable, often recruited from his campaign team. Quite commonly the chief of staff, and maybe one or two others on the White House staff, are the president's close personal friends and, consequently, may also act as trusted policy advisors as well. The people during the campaign who acted as his advisors (for both domestic and foreign policy), briefed him, and wrote his foreign policy speeches often are appointed to key positions and become major policy advisors. For other high-level officials, the president must rely on his personal staff for information and recommendations, where most come from the following professions: (1) law, (2) business, (3), politics and government, and (4) academia and research institutes (see **Table 4.2** for President Obama's major staff and foreign policy advisors during his first term).

Time also affects these decisions and presidential management, for many are made by the president-elect during the brief transition period. And there is no guarantee that people will accept when asked—President Clinton repeatedly struggled to find a director of central intelligence, for example, and President George W. Bush did not secure his first choice for the new director of national intelligence position either, settling on John Negroponte only after others had declined. From a presidential perspective, it is important that appointments be done expeditiously, or bureaucratic agencies are left in the hands of individuals appointed by the previous president. Such developments affect the president's success in moving forward on his agenda.

Another important issue is Senate approval. Appointments to staff agencies within the EOP, such as the WHO and the NSC, do not require Senate approval. From a constitutional

Table 4.2 President Obama's Major Staff and Foreign Policy Advisors

Position	Name	Background
Vice President	Joseph Biden	Politics and Government
Chief of Staff	Rahm Emmanuel	Politics and Government
	William Daley	Law, Business and Government
	Jacob Lew	Law and Government
Senior Advisor and Assistant to the President	David Axelrod	Campaign team and Communications
	Pete Rouse	Politics and Government
	Valerie Jarrett	Friend and Campaign team
White House Counselor	Gregory Craig	Law and Campaign team
	Robert Bauer	Law
	Kathryn Ruemmler	Law
Communications director	Ellen Moran	Labor and Politics
	Anita Dunn	Politics and Campaign team
	Dan Pfeiffer	Campaign team
Press Secretary	Robert Gibbs	Campaign team and Politics
	Jay Carney	Media and Journalism
National Security Advisor	James Jones	Military and Government
	Thomas Donilon	Government and Law
National Economic Advisor	Lawrence Summers	Government and Academia
	Gene Sperling	Economics and Government
Secretary of State	Hillary Clinton	Law, Politics, and Government
Secretary of Defense	Robert Gates	Government
	Leon Panetta	Politics and Government
Chairman of JCS	Michael Mullen	Military
	Martin Dempsey	Military
CIA Director	Leon Panetta	Politics and Government
	David Petraeus	Military
Director of National Intelligence	Dennis Blair	Military and Government
	James Clapper	Military and Government
Secretary of the Treasury	Timothy Geithner	Business and Government

perspective, these personnel and agencies are considered the president's personal staff. Most other high-level appointments in the executive branch require the **advice and consent** of the Senate. A president tries to nominate people who will gain Senate approval as soon as possible, thereby getting his people in position to help him manage the bureaucracy. As we discuss in Chapter 10, approval is the norm, but most presidents have experienced difficulty with a few appointments.

The major staff and advisors to the president who work in the White House tend to get, and often fight for, the largest, nicest, most prominent, and closest offices to the president (usually an indication of prestige and power). **Figure 4.2** shows the location of White House staff and offices in the West Wing during the Obama presidency. Notice the location of the offices of the most prominent personal staff and foreign policy advisors to the president listed in Table 4.2 (despite staff turnover). Naturally, cabinet secretaries and the chair of the JCS have the most prominent offices within their main departmental buildings separate from the White House.

Figure 4.2   White House Staff and Offices in the West Wing, 2009

Inside the West Wing

Location, location, location. The Obama transition has settled on virtually all the staff members who will occupy the most coveted offices in Washington, the ones in the West Wing of the White House. Some, like press secretary Robert Gibbs's office, are spacious. Others are cubbyholes. But they are all in the same building as the president's Oval Office. Here are the offices senior White House aides are moving into today:

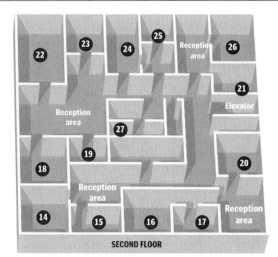

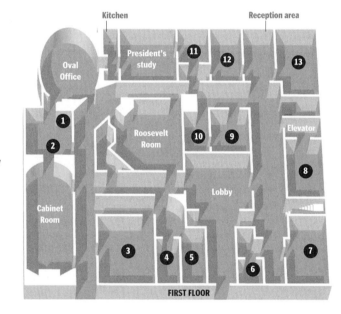

FIRST FLOOR:

1. Katie Johnson, personal secretary to the president
2. Reggie Love, personal aide to the president
3. Robert Gibbs, press secretary
4. Ellen Moran, communications director
5. Dan Pfeiffer, deputy communications director
6. Thomas E. Donilon, deputy national security adviser
7. Gen. James L. Jones, national security adviser
8. Joseph R. Biden Jr., vice president
9. Mona Sutphen, deputy chief of staff
10. Jim Messina, deputy chief of staff
11. David Axelrod, senior adviser
12. Pete Rouse, senior adviser
13. Rahm Emanuel, chief of staff *(his aides seated nearby will be Sean Sweeney, Sarah Feinberg and Amanda Anderson)*

SECOND FLOOR:

14. Melody Barnes, director of the Domestic Policy Council
15. Heather Higginbottom, deputy director of the Domestic Policy Council
16. Phil Schiliro, director of legislative affairs
17. Lisa Konwinski, deputy director of legislative affairs
18. Lawrence H. Summers, director of the National Economic Council
19. Office to be assigned
20. Patrick Gaspard, director of the Office of Political Affairs
21. Office to be assigned
22. Tina Tchen, director of public liaison
23. Cecilia Muñoz, director of intergovernmental affairs
24. Valerie Jarrett, senior adviser
25. Cassandra Butts, deputy counsel to the president
26. Gregory Craig, counsel to the president
27. Chris Lu, Cabinet secretary

NOTE: Floor plan is schematic based on Washington Post staff tour of the White House.

GROUND FLOOR (not shown):
Alyssa Mastromonaco, director of scheduling and advance
Lisa Brown, staff secretary
Jon Favreau, director of speechwriting
Thomas A. Daschle, director of White House Office of Health Reform
Lt. Gen. Douglas E. Lute, deputy national security adviser for Iraq and Afghanistan

John O. Brennan, deputy national security adviser for homeland security
Denis McDonough, foreign policy adviser
Mark Lippert, chief of staff for National Security Council
Pete Souza, chief White House photographer
White House Photo Office

THE WASHINGTON POST

SOURCE: Washington Post.

Organizing the Policymaking Process

The president must decide not only who will staff his administration, but how they will interact so that he is kept informed and able to make decisions and implement them according to his wishes. The president cannot assume when he takes office that the policymaking system in place will automatically do these things for him, allowing him to manage the bureaucracy. On the contrary, if a president wants to manage the bureaucracy, as opposed to responding to bureaucratic momentum, he must initiate a policy process that responds to his demands and fits his personal style.

Important questions about how to organize the policymaking process that a president must address include whether the process should be:

1. White House centered, State Department centered, or mixed/ad hoc?

2. centralized or decentralized?

3. open or closed to staff and advisors?

The president must decide whether to rely on a lead agency to be responsible for coordinating the foreign policy process; whether to have only a few individuals who are allowed to act in the president's name responsible for the overall conduct of foreign policy or to have power more decentralized throughout the foreign policy bureaucracy; and what level of access to grant different policymaking officials in the process, especially at the presidential level.

Decisions about these issues determine how the foreign policymaking process will operate. If the president, or his personal staff, is reluctant to be involved in influencing the policymaking process, policies will soon develop by fait accompli without presidential input, thereby weakening the president's ability to manage the foreign policy bureaucracy. As Richard Neustadt (1960) would say, unless the president is willing and able to make hard choices, he is more likely to act as a "clerk" than a leader. These are crucial decisions, for how the policy process operates determines the extent to which information and policy alternatives flow to the president, whether the bureaucracy is responsive to his agenda, and whether policies are implemented in accordance with his decisions.

It is not unusual for presidents to enter office claiming that they will rely on **cabinet government** as their principal means of managing the bureaucracy. This means that the president plans to rely heavily on his cabinet secretaries and departments for information and advice. Such a policymaking process tends to be highly decentralized and open, often allowing the State Department to act as the lead agency responsible for coordinating the conduct of U.S. foreign policy. In this scenario, the secretary of state is typically the principal spokesperson for U.S. foreign policy, acting as the major advisor to the president, and the State Department is responsible for coordinating the policy process within the rest of the foreign policy bureaucracy (Destler 1972).

Cabinet government and a **State Department–centered system** constitute the popular perception of presidential power and executive branch operation. Unfortunately, a president who attempts to operate this way quickly discovers that the bureaucracy, including the cabinet departments and many of the cabinet secretaries whom he appointed himself, are not very responsive to him. Presidents quickly learn that this is not the way to manage effectively the foreign policy bureaucracy and maximize presidential power. Instead, *three general patterns have prevailed in the foreign policy process* for most presidents since World War II:

1. presidents tend to rely on a White House–centered system,

2. the policymaking process tends to become more centralized with time, and

3. the level of participation in the process tends to narrow and close over time.

Presidents quickly turn to those they trust most, who tend to be the White House staff and agencies within the EOP, and the number of such advisors tends to shrink. This occurs because of time constraints on the president and increasing familiarity among the president and his advisors. As the president begins to interact with his advisors, he learns more about their policy views, personalities, and operating styles and makes judgments about the value of their advice, trust, and friendship. With time the president tends to become more selective as to whom he interacts with and relies on for advice. This often tends to "close" the policymaking process and narrow the range of information and opinions that come before the president, because the presidency is such an "awesome office . . . where no one really stands up to the president, where there is no equality, where no one tells the president he is wrong." In other words, inevitably the office "tends by its nature to inhibit dissent and opposition" (Halberstam 1969:456).

In managing the foreign policymaking process, presidents have increasingly relied on a **White House–centered system**, revolving around the national security advisor and the NSC staff. Unlike much of the established and entrenched bureaucracy, including the Department of State and the DOD, members of the WHO and the NSC are most responsive to the president. They lack an independent base of power, working only for him and under his complete authority.

To sum up, the key to presidential management of the foreign policy bureaucracy involves the choices the president makes concerning his foreign policy orientation and personal agenda, his level of involvement, his executive-level appointments, and the dynamics of the policymaking process. These presidential choices determine the extent to which the president will manage the bureaucracy and make it responsive to him. However, what works for one president may not work for others. *These presidential choices are very much a function of a president's personal characteristics*—his beliefs, personality, and operating style (George 1980b).

Therefore, it is not surprising that presidential management of foreign policy tends to revolve around a White House–centered system that becomes more centralized and closed over time, for it is most responsive to presidents and their personal characteristics. To better understand presidential management of the foreign policy bureaucracy and the operations of a White House–centered system, especially in the area of national security, we must examine the NSC in some detail and the process by which it operates.

THE NATIONAL SECURITY COUNCIL SYSTEM

Since its creation in the 1947 National Security Act, the **National Security Council (NSC)** has evolved into an **NSC system** that bears little resemblance to the original council. Although it was once an important advisory and decisionmaking body, *the NSC has subsequently declined and been superseded by a NSC system made up of three main components:*

1. the special to the president for national security affairs (better known as the national security advisor or NSC advisor),

2. the NSC staff, and

3. the **NSC interagency process** by which national policy is formulated, implemented, and evaluated.

The NSC, within the EOP, is the key agency or organization on which presidents have relied since World War II. Its chief director—the national security advisor—is often regarded as the single most important appointment the president makes because that person usually becomes the most important policy advisor to the president and is responsible for coordinating the foreign policymaking process within the larger executive branch. The NSC staff serves the national security advisor and, therefore, works directly for the president as his personal foreign policy staff. Typically, the national security advisor and the NSC staff are at the heart of the NSC interagency process. To understand how the president manages American foreign policy, we discuss the origins, evolution, and operations of the NSC system, first by considering the NSC and national security advisor, and then turning to the NSC staff and NSC interagency structures in more detail later in the chapter.

Origins

As discussed previously, the NSC came into existence in 1947 with the passage of the National Security Act, which restructured the policy process in the areas of defense, intelligence, and national security advice to the president. *The NSC was created to serve three principal functions:*

1. advise the president,

2. act as a vehicle for long-range planning, and

3. promote the coordination and integration of the national security process.

To do so, the structure of the NSC originally consisted of (1) a formal decisionmaking council composed of high-level foreign policy officials and (2) a small support staff headed by an executive secretary.

Although the list was soon revised, the "original statutory members" of the NSC included the president, secretary of state, secretary of defense, secretary of the Army, secretary of the Navy, secretary of the Air Force, and the chairman of the National Security Resources Board (responsible for emergency planning and civil defense), but the president could also invite others to attend the meetings. A small staff, headed by a civilian executive secretary, provided support for the formal council advisory meetings, helped coordinate the policy process, and conducted long-range planning.

The purpose of the National Security Act was to rationalize the national security process and force the president to be more responsive to formal lines of authority in the foreign policy bureaucracy, especially within the military. The act's formulation and passage was a response to what many people, in both Congress and the executive branch, thought was a chaotic national security policymaking process during World War II. In addition, many people were unhappy with President Roosevelt's management style. Roosevelt avoided formal channels of communication and instead relied on an informal, ad hoc managerial style. He oversaw the bureaucracy and made policy by relying on a variety of individuals of different ranks located throughout the bureaucracy. This managerial style served Roosevelt well as president, but displeased many high-level officials, especially within the military, whom Roosevelt bypassed in the formal chain of command. These concerns increased with the rise to the presidency of Harry Truman, who lacked experience in foreign policy.

Hence, the desire to provide the U.S. government with a policymaking apparatus that would promote greater efficiency and preparedness in the national security process accounts for the NSC's advice, long-term planning, and coordination functions. At the same time, to force the president to comply with a more formal process and adhere to the chain of command, the membership of NSC was set by law and composed largely of members of the newly created National Military Establishment (forerunner to the DOD). Modeled after the British war cabinet, it was a means of imposing a cabinet government on the president when national security decisions were involved. The only legal flexibility that the original act gave the president was the ability to invite officials to NSC meetings in addition to the statutory members.

Changing Patterns in the NSC

Presidents have found the NSC, as originally designed, to be both a potentially useful tool and a source of frustration in managing foreign policy. It should not be surprising to learn that presidents have used those aspects of the NSC they have found useful while ignoring or circumventing those aspects they have found constraining. *Two major changes to the original NSC under postwar presidents are evident:*

1. Providing policy advice and coordinating the policy process for the president have become NSC's two major functions, while long-term planning has become less important.

2. The NSC staff (and the national security advisor, which was not created until 1957) has become more significant over time, while the NSC as a decisionmaking body has declined in importance.

Advising the president and coordinating the foreign policy machinery remain NSC's two major functions. However, the third function, **long-term planning**, has almost never been implemented. The one exception involved the Truman administration and the development of **NSC-68**. NSC memorandum 68 was a staff document approved by the president in 1950. It represented a concerted effort by members of the NSC staff to predict U.S.–Soviet relations into the 1950s and recommend U.S. foreign policy alternatives for presidential consideration. NSC-68 provided the official justification of the policy of global containment of Soviet communism and, through the institutionalization of this policy due to the Korean War, influenced the foreign policies of subsequent administrations during the cold war.

The National Security Act also legally defined who the president must accept as his major foreign advisors. Clearly, this is not acceptable to most presidents. If a president wants to exercise power, as opposed to being a clerk, he must be allowed to determine on whom he will rely for foreign policy advice. Changes in the law have been made over the years reflecting this concern: the NSC now formally includes the president, vice president, secretary of state, and secretary of defense as statutory members, with the chairman of the Joint Chiefs of Staff and the Director of National Intelligence as advisory members. However, as has always been the case, the president can invite other individuals to participate as he sees fit. Very simply, presidents will interact with those policymakers they trust the most and will avoid officials with whom they have policy disagreements or personality conflicts. Each president has used the NSC as it has suited him.

This has ultimately resulted in *the decline of the NSC itself as a formal decisionmaking body,* and the rise of the NSC system as the foreign policy process has gradually become White House–centered. Hence, the president has increasingly relied on the national security advisor and the NSC staff to manage the process and provide him with an independent source of information and advice (see **Table 4.3** for a list of national security advisors and their backgrounds). *Accordingly, the role of the national security advisor has evolved considerably.* Henry Kissinger, who served as Richard Nixon's national security advisor, probably elevated the role more than anyone. However, the centrality of the position had been growing over the previous decade, from little more than an executive secretary under Truman and Eisenhower to increasingly central advisors and process managers. Kissinger thrust the position into prominence during the Nixon administration and, by the time George H. W. Bush appointed Brent Scowcroft as his national security advisor, a kind of consensus had emerged on the importance of the position as both central process manager (and honest broker) and policy advisor. Scowcroft's successors in subsequent administrations largely modeled their behavior after him (National Security Council Project 1999a; Burke 2009b).

There is obviously variation in the behavior of national security advisors over time, which is largely attributable to presidential preferences. However, with the first six years of the Reagan administration as the exception, there has been a general trend toward relying on the national security advisor to exercise institutional control over the foreign policy

Table 4.3   National Security Advisors

Name	Year	President	Background
Sidney W. Souers	1947	Truman	Business and Navy
James S. Lay, Jr.	1950	Truman	Business and Army
Robert Cutler	1953	Eisenhower	Law and Army
Dillon Anderson	1955	Eisenhower	Law and Army
William Jackson	1956	Eisenhower	Law, Business, and Army
Robert Cutler	1957	Eisenhower	Law and Army
Gordon Gray	1958	Eisenhower	Law and Army
McGeorge Bundy	1961	Johnson	Law, Army, and Journalism
Walt W. Rostow	1966	Johnson	Academia
Henry A. Kissinger	1969	Nixon	Academia and Government
Brent Scowcroft	1975	Ford	Academia and Air Force
Zbigniew Brzezinski	1977	Carter	Academia
Richard V. Allen	1981	Reagan	Academia and Government
William P. Clark	1982	Reagan	Law
Robert C. McFarlane	1983	Reagan	Army and Government
John M. Poindexter	1985	Reagan	Navy
Frank C. Carlucci	1987	Reagan	Business and Government
Colin L. Powell	1987	Reagan	Army
Brent Scowcroft	1989	George H. W. Bush	Air Force and Academia
Anthony Lake	1993	Clinton	Academia and Government
Samuel "Sandy" Berger	1997	Clinton	Law and Government
Condoleezza Rice	2001	George W. Bush	Academia and Government
Steven Hadley	2005	George W. Bush	Law and Government
James Jones	2009	Obama	Military, Government
Thomas Donilon	2010	Obama	Government and Law

bureaucracy and process. In this trend, the role of the advisor as a central player is generally accepted. For example, an extensive 1999 discussion with eight previous national security advisors (Allen, Berger, Carlucci, Lake, MacFarlane, Powell, Poindexter, Rostow, and Scowcroft) revealed substantial consensus on the mix of **honest broker**, process manager, and personal advisor while emphasizing the need for the national security advisor to be the central manager of the policy process. As Powell summarized:

> It is the role of the national security advisor to get it all out—all the agendas, all the facts, all the opinions, all of the gray and white and black areas written down—and use a highly qualified staff, the National Security Council staff, to put all of these agreements and disagreements into a form that can be sent back to . . . however many people are debating the issue, and say: "this is the issue as we understand it. These are the points of agreement and disagreement. We agree and disagree. So, let's have a meeting. Let's fight it out." And at some point it's up to the national security advisor to take all of those points, do an integral calculus of the whole thing . . . and to say to the president: "Mr. President, we have heard all these points of view and . . . this is what I think and this is my recommendation to you." You make that recommendation, with both the secretaries of state and defense and all the other cabinet officers and agencies involved knowing what you're going to recommend. And then the president decides. (National Security Council Project 2000:51)

This is ideally how the national security advisor and the NSC system should work, but much depends on a president's management style.

PRESIDENTIAL MANAGEMENT STYLES AND THE ROLE OF THE NSC SYSTEM

Presidential management styles have differed with each president and have evolved over time. It should therefore be no surprise that the NSC system has also evolved and varied as well. As Colin Powell observed, "the duty of the National Security Council staff and the [national security advisor] is to mold themselves to the personality of the president . . . the NSC has to mold itself to the will and desire and feelings of the president" (National Security Council Project 2000:52). Overall, *the policymaking process and the NSC system at the presidential level have tended to operate at two overlapping levels:*

1. an informal process (face-to face meetings or private phone calls) among the president's closest advisors, and

2. a formal NSC interagency process through use of the national security advisor and the NSC staff.

To better understand how contemporary presidents have managed the executive branch, a more detailed look at the actual operation of the general foreign policymaking process and the NSC system is needed. According to I. M. Destler, Leslie H. Gelb, and Anthony Lake (1984), *there have been three major stages in the evolution of the NSC system* and the foreign policy process at the presidential level: (1) presidents Truman and Eisenhower used the NSC Council as an advisory body with a staff to support their reliance on cabinet secretaries and their departments; (2) under presidents Kennedy and Johnson, the NSC Council was eclipsed, and the traditional role of the cabinet, especially the State Department, was challenged by the rise of the national security advisor and staff; and (3) beginning with President Nixon, the national security advisor and staff became ascendant in the policymaking process.

The Early NSC as Advisory Body, 1947–1960

During the 1950s, the NSC was used as an advisory body to assist the president in making foreign policy. Even though NSC provided information and advice to the president, *the secretary of state remained the chief foreign policy spokesperson and advisor to the president,* and the State Department often acted as the lead organization in formulating and implementing foreign policy. Both presidents Truman and Eisenhower relied on strong cabinet officers, such as the secretary of state, for information and advice. Truman relied on the secretary of state, Dean Acheson, and the secretary of defense, General George C. Marshall, for counsel and to carry out presidential policy. Along with his White House presidential counselor, Clark Clifford, an informal advisory process developed between President Truman and these officials. Truman was also hesitant to compromise his independence by relying on NSC, initially refusing to attend its meetings, but following the North Korean attack on South Korea in 1950, it became a regular forum for discussion. The NSC staff was kept very small, consisting of roughly twenty people under an executive director who organized and provided support for the council meetings.

President Eisenhower relied heavily on the formal NSC as an advisory body. In eight years, the NSC held three hundred and forty-six meetings, roughly one each week, as compared to hundred and twenty-eight meetings in over five years under President Truman. Most of the meetings lasted two and a half hours, with President Eisenhower usually presiding (Destler, Gelb, and Lake 1984:172). And the position of **special assistant to the president for national security affairs** (national security advisor) was created to supervise the staff. Two interagency committees, both managed by the national security advisor, were created to assist in the preparation of the formal meetings and to oversee policy implementation. The NSC staff tripled in size and became the major vehicle for coordinating the information and advice provided to the president by the national security departments and agencies. **John Foster Dulles**, the secretary of state, was the major foreign policy spokesperson throughout the administration and acted as a major advisor to the president. Furthermore, Eisenhower also relied on more informal channels of interaction, especially when it came to fast-moving developments and crises.

The Rise of the NSC Advisor and Staff, 1961–1968

Beginning with the Kennedy administration, the NSC declined as a formal advisory body, while the national security advisor and staff grew as independent sources of information and advice for the president. By the early 1960s, the modern NSC process was in place and *three contemporary characteristics have become commonplace for presidential management:*

1. The formal NSC as advisory body was replaced by interagency groups whose membership was determined by the president.

2. The NSC staff became the personal staff to the president for foreign policy.

3. The national security advisor became the key official responsible for managing the interagency groups and coordinating the policy process, as well as for providing information and advice to the president.

Presidential management of the foreign policymaking process, in other words, came to rely increasingly on a White House–centered system that emphasized the use of the national security advisor, staff, and interagency groups—referred to as the NSC system (Rockman 1981).

John Kennedy entered office with a personal management style that tended to be very informal. He quickly scrapped Eisenhower's formal foreign policy apparatus, but his failure to develop an alternative decisionmaking structure resulted in ad hoc structures, processes, and interaction among his foreign policy advisors. This approach lasted only a few months—until the **Bay of Pigs** fiasco. The covert effort to train a Cuban military force and overthrow Castro by invading Cuba, which began under President Eisenhower, failed miserably in large measure because of the decentralized and chaotic nature of the decisionmaking process. To address the problem, the decisionmaking process became more centralized in the White House through the national security advisor, McGeorge Bundy, who managed the working groups and ensured that information and advice reached the president. In this climate, Bundy and his successors increasingly came to act as a personal advisor to the president as well as a manager. This advisory role was reinforced by the substantial growth in foreign policy expertise and specialization in the NSC staff, providing the president with an independent source of information and advice (Daalder and Destler 2009). Such White House activism was reinforced by President Kennedy's low regard for the competence of the State Department and his growing frustration with Dean Rusk as secretary of state. A "situation room" for crisis management was also set up in the White House basement, enabling the president to receive and transmit international communications as well as hold meetings and manage interagency coordination.

President Lyndon Johnson, initially decided to work with Kennedy's appointees to maintain continuity and promote legitimacy for his presidency. However, with time, President Johnson came to rely on his own group of loyal, supportive advisors and replaced many of Kennedy's appointees, such as McGeorge Bundy with Walt Rostow was national security advisor in March 1966. Johnson preferred to delegate authority to people such as Robert McNamara at the Defense Department and Dean Rusk at the State Department. When he wanted additional advice, he did not turn to his staff, as Kennedy had, but rather to those senior political figures he knew well, such as former advisors Dean Acheson and Clark Clifford. When he did get highly involved, he tended to dominate the policy process. Although interagency groups did operate through the NSC, key presidential decisions were made in informal sessions with his closest advisors (Rothkopf 2005b; Daalder and Destler2009). Many of his most important decisions involving Vietnam, for instance, were made during his **Tuesday Lunch group**, composed of senior advisors Clifford, McNamara, Rostow, and Rusk.

The NSC Advisor and Staff Ascendant, 1969–1988

Beginning with President Nixon, the national security advisor and staff became ascendant over the cabinet officers and departments for information, advice, and management of the foreign policy process for the president. The advisor also began to act as a spokesperson for the president and became active in the actual operations and conduct of U.S. foreign policy. To assist the national security advisor, the staff grew in size and influence as well.

Richard Nixon came to the presidency with a strong interest in foreign affairs and a great distrust of the bureaucracy, which he felt tended to limit information and options available to the president. President Nixon's management strategy was to use the White House to control or circumvent the bureaucracy, establishing a very centralized decisionmaking structure that relied on the national security advisor, Henry Kissinger, and his staff (Hersh 1983; Morris 1977). The Nixon-Kissinger NSC system created numerous interagency committees, chaired by Kissinger, or his deputy, designed to provide information and options to the president. President Nixon, always the loner, rarely attended NSC meetings, preferring to consider the products of the committees by himself and personally consult with his closest advisors, especially Henry Kissinger (Daalder and Destler 2009).

Nixon and Kissinger activated the bureaucracy by issuing national security study memoranda (NSSM), which laid out the issue to be addressed, the agencies involved, and presented deadlines for agency submission of policy recommendations. Subsequent interagency meetings chaired by Kissinger considered options and made recommendations for the president. Once the president decided on a particular course of action, often in consultation with Kissinger, a national security decision memorandum (NSDM) would be issued by Kissinger and his staff to instruct the bureaucracy on the policy's implementation. Soon, Kissinger became the president's manager, major advisor, spokesman, and, in some cases, implementer of foreign policy. Kissinger's power was symbolized by his movement from the basement of the White House to a prestigious office on the main floor of the West Wing, down the hall from the Oval Office. The policy process became so centralized in Kissinger's hands, usually with Nixon's blessing, that the ability of many traditional foreign policy agencies and high-level officials to influence the process dwindled. Kissinger and his staff, nevertheless, did develop important contacts and networks with trusted lower-level officials throughout the bureaucracy. Given Kissinger's crucial role, the size of the NSC staff increased to over 100 staffers during this period.

As national security advisor, Henry Kissinger, reached a pinnacle of power under President Nixon that no single presidential advisor experienced before or since. When William Rogers eventually resigned in 1973, Nixon appointed Kissinger as secretary of state as well, and one man held the two most important foreign policy positions in the U.S. government. Such a centralized policy process was clearly responsive to Nixon and Kissinger, but few policy alternatives tended to be considered, and there was considerable internal dissent—even outright rebellion—throughout the executive branch at their heavy-handed approach.

This White House–centered system under Henry Kissinger continued to operate after Nixon's resignation because of President Ford's management style, though with some modifications. In 1975, Lieutenant General Brent Scowcroft, Kissinger's deputy national security assistant since 1973, became the national security advisor and managed the day-to-day NSC process. Scowcroft emphasized his role as process manager (and honest broker) more than Kissinger did, and opened the policy process to other officials such as Donald Rumsfeld as secretary of defense. Nonetheless, Gerald Ford, who had minimal exposure to foreign affairs, developed a close working relationship with Henry Kissinger and remained dependent on his secretary of state throughout his term of office.

In many respects, the Carter and Reagan administrations that followed Nixon and Ford represented reactions to the highly centralized Nixon-Kissinger system. President Carter adopted a similar foreign policymaking apparatus, but sought to reduce its centralization enough to remain relatively open to input by cabinet officials and departments (Moens 1990; Rosati 1987). Eschewing the NSC of his recent predecessors, Carter relied on two formal interagency groups within the NSC system, which became primarily responsible for the working operations of the foreign policy process. The Policy Review Committee (PRC) was established to develop policy at the secretarial level on issues for which one department had been designated as the lead agency by the president. The Special Coordinating Committee (SCC) was established to deal with crosscutting issues, such as arms control and crisis management, and was chaired by National Security Advisor Zbigniew Brzezinski. At the lowest level of the NSC system were two working groups at the assistant secretary level that did much of the legwork for the PRC and SCC and were also responsible for issues of lesser significance.

President Carter relied principally on **Zbigniew Brzezinski** and **Cyrus Vance**. Brzezinski, as national security advisor and head of the NSC staff, was primarily responsible for coordinating the interagency operations of the NSC system, while Secretary of State Vance was the chief negotiator and major spokesperson for the president. However, this arrangement soon began to suffer. Not only did Brzezinski and Vance increasingly differ over proper policy, but their personal styles exacerbated the situation. The growing conflict over policy and personal style resulted in considerable bureaucratic infighting, especially between the staffs of Brzezinski and Vance (Rosati 1987). With the taking of American hostages in Iran and the Soviet intervention in Afghanistan in late 1979, President Carter supported Brzezinski over Vance, reinstating containment as the cornerstone of U.S. foreign policy. President Carter also decided to attempt a military rescue of the hostages, a decision arrived at while Vance, the lone dissenter, was vacationing in Florida. Increasingly isolated within the administration, Vance soon resigned, convinced that he no longer enjoyed the president's support. He was replaced by Edmund Muskie, but Zbigniew Brzezinski and his NSC staff had clearly become ascendant within the foreign policy process by the end of Carter's term of office.

President Reagan entered office committed to reversing the Nixon-Kissinger and Carter trend toward a strong national security advisor and NSC staff. Reagan preferred to rely on his foreign policy officials and their agencies for information and advice, set the broad principles and directions of policy, and delegate to his advisors. Unlike his recent predecessors, Reagan's national security advisor and staff were supposed to act as little more than custodians responsible for coordinating the process, reminiscent of their role during the early NSC days (Daalder and Destler 2009). President Reagan preferred to delegate authority, tended to remain uninvolved in daily operations, and lacked considerable experience and knowledge of foreign affairs. The national security advisor's job was to supervise the staff and provide support for the formal NSC process described above. Unlike Kissinger, who chaired all the interagency committees, or Brzezinski, who chaired some, the national security advisor in the Reagan administration initially chaired no committees.

President Reagan, unlike his predecessors, initially also had the national security advisor (and other foreign policy advisors) report to him through the White House staff rather than directly. This placed the "troika" of James Baker as chief of staff, Michael Deaver as deputy chief of staff, and Edwin Meese as political counselor during his first term — with Baker replaced by Donald Regan and then Howard Baker during Reagan's second term — in important gatekeeping roles vis-à-vis the national security advisor. As a further indication of the decline in the national security advisor's stature and influence within the Reagan administration, his office was moved away from the president into the White House basement.

From the beginning, however, the foreign policymaking process failed to function smoothly. For one, the secretary of state, Alexander Haig, thought that he was going to be the "vicar" of the Reagan administration's foreign policy, responsible for developing a State Department–centered system for the president. Haig could not understand that, even though Reagan had deemphasized the role of the national security advisor and staff, he preferred a White House–centered system that relied on his personal staff. The result was constant political infighting between Haig and the White House staff until President Reagan finally accepted his resignation in 1982. Second, key personnel changed frequently. President Reagan had six national security advisors, each one lasting little more than a year. Richard Allen was replaced by William Clark, then by Robert McFarlane, John Poindexter, Frank Carlucci, and finally Colin Powell. These constant changes of crucial personnel reduced the national security advisor's clout within the executive branch even further than originally intended by President Reagan.

There was so little management of the policy process by the middle years of the Reagan administration that informal coalitions between officials and groups developed over different issues. For example, despite a consensus within the administration in support of the Contras and their effort to overthrow the Sandinistas in Nicaragua, even after American assistance was banned by Congress, there was considerable disagreement among Reagan's advisors over exchanging arms for hostages with Iran. Secretary of State George Shultz and Secretary of Defense Caspar Weinberger fought the initiative. President Reagan, however, was committed to the Iran venture, and, consequently, the circle of participants within the policy process narrowed: the White House, NSC, and CIA remained involved, while the secretary of state and the secretary of defense were eliminated or circumvented. The actual implementation of both these initiatives was taken by the NSC staff. Thus, the **operational NSC staff**, begun under Kissinger, reached its height under the Reagan administration and helped produce the Iran-Contra affair.

For a number of reasons, management of the bureaucracy improved in the latter years of the administration. First, Frank Carlucci and then Colin Powell were brought in as national security advisor, restoring the stature of the position and the NSC staff and increasing their influence over the policy process. Two of the dominant personalities and foreign policy officials within the Reagan administration also departed—Secretary of Defense Weinberger returned to private life and Director of Central Intelligence Casey died in office—leaving George Shultz in a strengthened position. Finally, former Senator Howard Baker replaced the ineffective Donald Regan as chief of staff, helping to make the policy process work more efficiently for the president. When Reagan left office, his NSC system was in considerably better shape than any other time in his two terms.

The Contemporary NSC Model, from 1989–Present

GEORGE H. W. BUSH'S NSC SYSTEM When George H. W. Bush took office in 1989, he and his National Security Advisor Brent Scowcroft established an NSC system and process that reflected the emerging consensus on the role of the national security advisor (see **A Different Perspective** on the role of the national security advisor and staff), and the negative lessons of both the Nixon-Kissinger system and those Bush learned as Reagan's vice president. Hence, Bush established a White House–centered system revolving around an NSC process in which cabinet officials and departments played a prominent role. President Bush was comfortable with such a White House–centered policymaking process because of the foreign policy expertise and policymaking experience he acquired during the Nixon, Ford, and Reagan years, especially as director of central intelligence, U.S. ambassador to the United Nations, and vice president (Mulcahy 1991). Highly regarded by virtually all those who observed or participated, the NSC system the elder Bush and Scowcroft constructed become the model on which all subsequent administrations have depended (Burke 2009b).

George H. W. Bush established a three-tiered formal interagency policy process dependent on the NSC staff and the coordination of national security advisor. At the top, Scowcroft and his deputy national security advisor served as chairs of the two key NSC committees coordinating the Bush administration's foreign policy machinery—the NSC **Principals Committee** (PC, a secretary-level group) and the NSC **Deputies Committee** (DC, a deputy secretary-level group). Below these committees, the Bush White House established a series of NSC interagency working groups (WGs). In the Bush administration's system, these interagency WGs, or "policy coordinating committees," as the Bush administration labeled them, did most of the work to formulate policy options for higher-level consideration and also to supervise and coordinate the implementation of policy choices. Organized into various regional

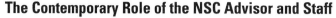

The Contemporary Role of the NSC Advisor and Staff

Despite all the public attention focused on the national security advisor as a consequence of assertive individuals in that position (Kissinger, Brzezinski) and controversies over their behavior (McFarlane, Poindexter), the view from the inside has evolved. As two long-time practitioners/analysts of the policy process summarize:

A consensus has emerged on the importance of the position as predominantly central process manager and honest broker—as a means to promote and protect the president . . . [T]here are some tasks that the NSC advisor and staff are uniquely placed to undertake, and it is their responsibility to make sure that they do so. These include:

- Staffing the president's daily foreign policy activity: his communications with foreign leaders and the

preparation and conduct of his trips overseas;

- Managing the process of making decisions on major foreign and national security issues
- Driving the policymaking process to make real choices, in a timely manner;
- Overseeing the full implementation of the decisions the president has made.

All of these tasks are important—and none can be left to others (Daalder and Destler 2009:318–319).

Given this insider view, consider our description of the evolution of the national security advisor and NSC system.

What do you think are the essential characteristics necessary for the person holding the national security advisor position?

(e.g., Europe, Soviet Union, Latin America) and functional units (e.g., arms control, defense, intelligence). These working groups were chaired by assistant secretaries of state for the regional units, and assistant secretaries (or their equivalents) from Defense, Treasury, the CIA, and elsewhere for functional units. However, an NSC staff member served as executive secretary for each working group so as to increase White House control and policy coordination (see **Figure 4.3** for an overview of the elder Bush's structure and process).

The PC–DC process helped to further centralize policy control by the White House, national security advisor, and NSC staff. The DC, through the deputy national security advisor and the NSC staff, reviewed all work from the coordinating committees and made recommendations to the PC, under the leadership of the national security advisor. Effectively, the PC served as a White House-led center for considering all national security questions. President Bush attended most of the PC meetings himself (National Security Council Project 1999b). Bush supplemented this formal structure and process with an informal advisory process that usually included National Security Advisor Brent Scowcroft, the White House chief of staff (initially John Sununu, then Samuel Skinner), Secretary of State James Baker, Secretary of Defense Richard Cheney, and Chairman of the Joint Chiefs of Staff Colin Powell. Emphasis was on loyalty and quiet teamwork, "in marked contrast to the public feuds over policy and bureaucratic turf in previous administrations—the Shultz-Weinberger, Vance-Brzezinski, or Rogers-Kissinger battles" (Deibel 1991:5).

Figure 4.3   George H. W. Bush's Foreign Policy System

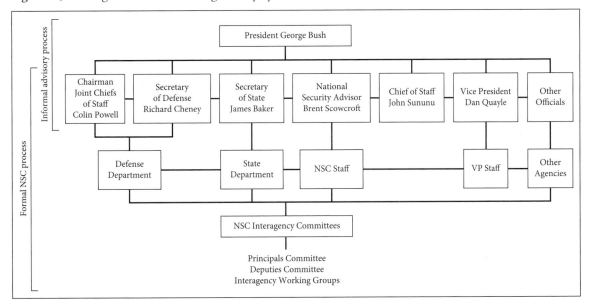

BILL CLINTON'S NSC SYSTEM President Bill Clinton recognized the merits of his predecessor's approach and adopted it for his own administration. The basic structure remained three-tiered, although Clinton broadened the circle of PC members to include the secretary of the treasury, the U.S. ambassador to the United Nations, the special assistant to the president for economic policy, and the White House chief of staff, in part reflecting the importance of economic issues and the changing political context of the post–cold war world. The national security advisor and his deputy chaired the PC and DC, while assistant secretaries generally chaired the working groups which prepared policy studies and facilitated implementation of decisions. Clinton also determined to improve the coordination and centralization of economic policy, both foreign and domestic, and therefore created the "National Economic Council," modeled on the NSC. We discuss the role of the foreign economic policymaking process, in general, and the NEC and the national economic advisor under Bill Clinton and his successors in greater detail in Chapter 8.

However, in practice Clinton's personal style and relative inexperience with foreign policy created challenges for this system that his more disciplined and experienced predecessor had not faced. In his first term, Clinton showed a strong preference for informal meetings with his closest advisors, especially Secretary of State Warren Christopher, National Security Advisor Anthony Lake, and Defense Secretary Les Aspin and, later, Aspin's successor, William Perry. In fact, early on in the administration, Clinton's apparent unwillingness to establish more frequent formal meetings on foreign policy created concern among advisors like Secretary of State Christopher. Much of the president's time, especially early on, was spent cramming to get up to speed on foreign policy. Clinton's preference was to set broad guidelines and pay spasmodic attention to different issues as they arose. As Secretary of State Warren Christopher delicately put it, President Clinton laid down "the broad guidelines of foreign policy, expecting his State Department and national security advisors to implement them as a team, working together, and holding them accountable if they don't carry it out in a fairly straightforward way" (quoted in Friedman and Sciolino 1993:A3).

The functioning of Clinton's system evolved considerably over his two terms. The first national security advisor—**Anthony Lake**—tried to emphasize his role as coordinator of the policy process and prevent the bitter infighting that often occurred between the occupants of his position and secretaries of state in past administrations. However, Lake and his deputy, Sandy Berger, were criticized for putting too much emphasis on presenting consensus positions to the president, and for not being proactive enough in the important tasks of managing the NSC staff and interagency process and bringing the president's attention to focus on national security. Many of these problems were most visible in the Clinton administration's policy toward the former Yugoslavia (Rothkopf 2005b; Daalder and Destler 2009). Policymaking improved in 1995, when Leon Panetta took over as chief of staff from Clinton's friend Thomas "Mack" McClarty and imposed more structure and a more orderly process on the White House.

In the second term, things improved even more when Sandy Berger (who had a much closer relationship with President Clinton than Lake and was a more aggressive manager of the process) became national security advisor; Madeleine Albright, former ambassador to the United Nations, became secretary of state; and William Cohen (a former senator from Maine and the only major Clinton appointee from the Republican party) became secretary of defense. Clinton's increasing comfort with and interest in foreign policy led him to pay more attention to national security issues, and many of the early problems largely disappeared (National Security Council Project 2000; Daalder and Destler 2009).

GEORGE W. BUSH'S NSC SYSTEM   George W. Bush continued to use the formal three-tiered NSC interagency process established by his father, while supplementing it with a heavy reliance upon informal meetings among his principal foreign policy advisors, especially after the attacks of September 11. Throughout his administration, these advisors included Condoleezza Rice, first as national security advisor and then as secretary of state; Colin Powell as secretary of state; Donald Rumsfeld as secretary of defense; General Richard Myers as chairman of the Joint Chiefs of Staff (CJCS), and Dick Cheney as vice president. Until his resignation, CIA director George Tenet was also a member of this inner circle, while White House staff including Andrew Card (chief of staff), Karl Rove (senior advisor), and Karen Hughes (White House counselor and director of communications) were also key members of the informal advisory system.

While the younger Bush's foreign policy structure resembled that of his father, the results were very different, demonstrating that getting the structure "right" is only part of the battle for effective foreign policy. This was due to a combination of several factors. First, while the younger Bush drew wide praise for assembling a strong team of advisors such as Powell, Rumsfeld, and Cheney, *among these heavyweights there were significant policy differences,* especially between Rumsfeld and Cheney on the one hand, and Colin Powell on the other. Cheney and Rumsfeld, an experienced secretary of defense known for his skills as a bureaucratic infighter, favored a strong assertive nationalism—or hegemonist approach in one formulation—to the U.S. role abroad (Daalder and Lindsay 2003). Powell reflected a more selective and pragmatic realist orientation. These differences surfaced on a variety of issues both before and after the September 11 attacks, including how to deal with North Korea, Iran, the war on terrorism, and Iraq, to name a few. Nor were these rifts contained to the top level advisors. In fact, they extended to the mid- and lower levels as well, with tensions between State and Defense appointees, Defense appointees and the uniformed military, and Defense and the CIA. One critical aspect of these disputes pitted the administration's neoconservatives, or "neocons," against other more traditional conservative nationalists and internationalists. For example, Deputy Secretary of Defense Wolfowitz, a neocon, and

Deputy Secretary of State Richard Armitage, a more pragmatic conservative, clashed regularly on a wide variety of issues. As one observation noted, "the Bush administration had trouble singing from the same foreign policy hymnal" (Walcott and Hult 2003). Powell's isolation, in particular, probably contributed to his decision to resign his post at the end of Bush's first term (Duffy and Shannon 2005:36).

Second, disagreements among his advisors were exacerbated by the performance of **Condoleezza Rice** as national security advisor, who proved considerably less effective than her mentor, Brent Scowcroft. Many observers of the foreign policy process "consider her one of the weakest national security advisors in recent history in terms of managing interagency conflicts" (Kessler and Ricks 2004:7). She was relatively unsuccessful in her role as central manager of the NSC system and the NSC interagency process, emphasizing her close personal relationship with the president over her role as honest broker (Baker 2008; Burke 2005; Daalder and Destler 2009; Packer 2005). From the start, Rice failed to drive the foreign policy process effectively. For example, Richard Clarke, an NSC staff member in charge of counterterrorism for Clinton and Bush until 2003, pressed her to hold early, high-level NSC interagency meetings on the threat posed by al-Qaeda, but Rice failed to respond to his requests and a series of increasingly urgent warnings throughout the summer of 2001, waiting until September 4, 2001, to hold the first PC meeting (Clarke 2004). Similarly, critics argue that disputes over issues such as North Korea and Iran were never resolved through the NSC interagency process (Kessler and Ricks 2004), and Colin Powell asserts that the formal NSC never consistently met formally to consider, debate, and decide the variety of information and alternatives that resulted in the 2003 military invasion of Iraq (Powell 2012).

Third, even a more experienced and aggressive national security advisor would have struggled to contend with the administration's foreign policy heavyweights. But Rice and her successor Stephen Hadley faced the problem of the unprecedented role of Vice President Dick Cheney in the foreign policy process. As we discussed in **A Closer Look**, Cheney first assembled a mini-NSC staff in his own office, then pressed hard—and ultimately unsuccessfully—to chair the PC, and then ensconced himself on that committee and salted the other interagency groups with members of his staff. Moreover, he worked closely with ally Don Rumsfeld to press their more assertive positions (as well as to undermine Powell), ignoring Rice's attempts at control. Both Cheney and Rumsfeld conducted significant portions of their foreign policy discussions and advising outside the structures of the NSC system, making it even more difficult for Rice (Elliott and Calabresi 2004; see **The Liberty-Security Dilemma** on Cheney and fighting the war on terrorism).

Finally, the NSC process and role of the national security advisor as coordinator were downplayed and kept at very low profile by the president and his management style. Initially, Bush adopted a less engaged and less collegial "**CEO style.**" After September 11, the Bush system became more informal and ad hoc in nature (Milbank and Graham 2001; Thomas 2002a). President Bush, however, became so engaged and forceful once he had made up his mind to take the nation on a war on terrorism, that the policymaking process at the presidential level became increasingly closed and the range of views expressed was very narrow, such as over the invasion of Iraq (see Badie 2010; Woodward 2002, 2004, 2006). The net result in the words of some is that, "It's not that he is a socially awkward loner or a paranoid. He can charm and joke like the frat president he was. Still, beneath a hail-fellow manner, Bush has a defensive edge, a don't-tread-on-me prickliness . . . In the Bush White House, disagreement is often equated with disloyalty" (Thomas and Wolffe 2005:33,34). This weakened Secretary of State Powell and strengthened the influence of Vice President Cheney and Secretary of Defense Rumsfeld within these informal group sessions and it gave them greater leeway to circumvent the NSC system altogether.

Dealing with Terrorists, Circumventing the Process . . . and the Law?

Barton Gellman (2008:162–168) provides this revealing account of Vice President Dick Cheney's willingness to circumvent the NSC system and process, raising important questions about the tension between national security needs and the rule of law:

Just past the Oval Office, in the private dining room overlooking the South Lawn, Cheney joined Bush for lunch on November 13, 2001. . . . Cheney brought a four-page text. David Addington, his lawyer, had drafted it in strict secrecy.

The United States was at war in Afghanistan, Osama bin Laden's base of operations. It was the first substantial response to September 11. Now U.S. troops faced a question: What should they do with a captured fighter from al Qaeda or the Taliban?

Questions like that nearly always get scrubbed in an "interagency review." Secretary of State Colin Powell appointed Pierre Prosper, ambassador-at-large for war crimes to lead a working group. . . . Prosper convened representatives from Justice, Defense and the Joint Chiefs of Staff. Condi Rice and Alberto Gonzales sent lawyers. . . . Cheney's staff did not show up. Addington knew what his client wanted, and the "interagency was just constipated," said Jim Haynes, his ally at the Pentagon.

Addington typed out an order that stripped foreign terrorist suspects of access to any court—civilian or military, domestic or foreign. They could be confined indefinitely, without charge. They would be tried, if at all, in closed "military commissions," modeled on the ones Franklin

Roosevelt set up for Nazi saboteurs in World War II. . . . By relying on Roosevelt's model and on the 1942 Supreme Court case upholding it, Addington discarded six decades of intervening laws and treaties. Since then, the United States had led the world in creating . . . international institutions and international law, some of it enacted into U.S. statutes. . . .

It was difficult to tell what the president knew, if anything, about the military order now heading toward his lunch table. Certainly he approved the idea that this was going to be a new kind of war, without a lot of lawyerly coddling for terrorists. When details became important, someone was supposed to tell him. Was he aware of [the Attorney General's] objections? Had anyone offered a heads-up on the legal risks, or the likely reaction of allies? Did Bush intend to keep his national security advisor and secretary of state out of the loop?

. . . Three days later, Cheney brought the order to lunch with the president. No one told Colin Powell or Condi Rice. No one told their lawyers, William H. Taft IV and John Bellinger. No one told Pierre Prosper, who was waiting for a reply to the option paper he sent the White House. Jim Haynes, the Pentagon lawyer, said the order "was very closely held because it was coming right from the top."

Cheney emerged from lunch with a thumbs up from the president. . . . The vice president chanced no last-minute protest. He sent the order on a swift path to execution, leaving no trace of his touch. In less than an hour the document traversed a West Wing circuit that gave its words the power of command. . . . Bush was standing, ready to depart, when [deputy staff secretary Stuart] Bowen arrived in the Oval Office. Addington's words were now bound in a blue portfolio, embossed with the presidential seal. . . . Bush pulled out a Sharpie from his breast pocket and signed. . . .

Bush was airborne for Crawford when CNN broke into its broadcast with the news. Condi Rice, furious, sent [senior national security lawyer] John Bellinger to complain.

Colin Powell had the television going in his office. He picked up the phone to Pierre Prosper.

"What the hell just happened?" he asked.

How was the vice president able to accomplish this and what are the implications for the rule of law and presidential management of the foreign policy process?

Bush's second term saw some of these problems reduced. Ironically, with the resignation of Colin Powell and Rice's move to the State Department, the NSC system in the second term appeared in some ways to be in better shape than in the first term. For one, Rice retained her close personal relationship with President Bush, an advantage Colin Powell never had in attempting to press his policy positions. Also, with her former deputy national security advisor Stephen Hadley becoming national security advisor, Rice had an ally in the policymaking process, enabling her to balance more effectively the views of other participants (Allen 2004; Ratnesar 2005). Further, because Hadley lacked Rice's close relationship with the president, he focused more on the process manager side of the national security advisor role (Daalder and Destler 2009). Finally, persistent criticism of Dick Cheney for his role in the prewar intelligence fiasco and in the leaking of a CIA operative's name, among other things, coupled with Bush's greater confidence in his own foreign policy judgments, combined to reduce the overpowering impact of the vice president on the administration's foreign policy (Woodward 2008).

BARACK OBAMA'S NSC SYSTEM   President Obama quickly established a formal NSC system that reflected the Bush-Scowcroft model. The same three tiers remained, with the same basic responsibilities: a PC at the top, a DC in the middle, and a series of "Interagency Policy Committees" at the bottom (Presidential Policy Directive 1, February 13, 2009). President Obama added the secretaries of energy, treasury, and homeland security, the attorney general, the White House chief of staff, the UN ambassador to the PC, as well as the director of national intelligence, CJCS and the director of the Office of Management and Budget as advisory members. The counsel to the president, the vice president's personal national security advisor, and the deputies to the national security advisor and the secretary of state were invited to attend any meeting, while other individuals were included according to the issue at hand.

In a signal of his determination to establish a strongly centralized White House-dominated structure and process, President Obama designated his first national security advisor (former Marine General Jim Jones), deputy national security advisor (Thomas Donilon, a former State department appointee), and NSC Staff members as chairs of all the relevant committees from the PC to the policy committees. This move was also viewed as part of an effort by President Obama and his national security advisor to correct the problems of his predecessor. According to one account, "Jones, a retired Marine general, made it clear that he will run the process and be the primary conduit of national security advice to Obama, eliminating the 'back channels' that at times in the Bush administration allowed Cabinet secretaries and the vice president's office to unilaterally influence and make policy out of view of the others" (DeYoung 2009:A1). As one official stated, "We have reenergized the interagency process and are aggressively putting together new policy on a range of issues. The NSC should be at the center of that process: coordinating, making sure everyone with equities is engaged and is heard. It is working as it should" (Rozen 2009).

Second, President Obama continued the trend of the past two decades of integrating a wider array of agencies and issues into the NSC system. Spurred by a complex issue agenda that included traditional national security issues, such as the ongoing wars in Afghanistan and Iraq, the global economic crisis, and a host of additional issues ranging from counterterrorism to the global environment, Obama's NSC system included "new NSC directorates [to deal with] such department-spanning 21st-century issues as cybersecurity, energy, climate change, nation-building and infrastructure" and, perhaps most broadly, global engagement (DeYoung 2009:A1).

Finally, President Obama's White House staff played a more important role in the NSC process, including the chief of staff Rahm Emmanual, William Daley, and then Jacob Lew; counselor to the president David Axelrod; and other personal aides (Hoagland 2009). Stemming from the continued need for presidents to maintain White House leadership of an increasingly sprawling foreign policy bureaucracy, this trend also suggests the extent to which political calculations and "message cohesion and control" increasingly influence policymaking.

Despite these adjustments, the NSC system under Obama reflected more continuity than change (Burke 2009a). And, not surprisingly, some of the problems that emerged were similar to those of the past as well. For one, Obama's first national security advisor—James Jones—was relatively ineffective. Not only was he a relatively passive manager of the process, his style did not mesh well with the president's "informal, substantively intense" approach (Destler 2009), and he approached his role with considerably less energy than most of his predecessors (Lee 2010).

Because of these and other concerns, President Obama replaced Jones with Thomas Donilon in October 2010. In contrast to Jones, Donilon was more seasoned in the ways of the bureaucracy, and more energetic and focused on the management of the process and the provision of advice to the president. He also enjoyed a close personal relationship with the president, who trusted him (Destler 2010). Donilon's approach as process manager had a positive effect. According to one observer:

> The NSC became more organized and disciplined, with effective paper trails being created, and a network of effective oral communications between members being instituted. . . . [D]uring the Libyan crisis of 2011, Donilon did what he was expected to do by Obama. He set up decision-making and policy-making processes for the president to make his choices and in ways that would allow his orders to be properly implemented (Jackson 2012).

President Obama's style also affected the way the system functioned. On the one hand, the president approached the process with discipline and engagement. As some observers noted, Obama, relied on and valued the NSC machinery, insisted on a regular process to in an effort to try to avoid back-channel end-runs, and actively participated in the discussions and decisions (Isaacson 2011; Jackson 2012). However, the president also tended to put himself at the center of the discussions and deliberations, often trying to play the role of his own honest broker. Given his limited experience and knowledge this sometimes backfired.

In particular, during the 2009 debate about whether to employ a military "surge" in Afghanistan, for example, President Obama was proactive, but had difficulty in getting the military and Secretary of Defense Gates to cooperate and avoid end-runs. He even tried to prepare his own memos outlining his thinking and seeking a greater range of options—the job of the national security advisor — reflecting his frustration with James Jones! According to one report, the President instructed, "Get me some other people's opinions on this . . . I want more than what's in this room" (Rudalevige 2009).

There are benefits from such engagement, but there are also costs, as the president can easily lose control of the process by becoming his own national security advisor and/or come to dominate the process and stifle discussion and debate if his preferences are too obvious (Alter 2010; Garrison, Rosati and Scott 2012; Jackson 2012; Woodward 2010). After 2010, although Obama remained an active and assertive participant, with the change from Jones to Donilon, the tendency for the president to act as his own national security advisor was reduced, largely because Donilon managed the process better than Jones, served as a better honest-broker, and enjoyed the president's trust.

After his re-election in 2012, President Obama faced the task of replacing key personnel in his NSC system. In particular, his Secretary of State, Hillary Clinton, prepared to step down in 2013. Others, including Defense secretary Leon Panetta and Treasury secretary Timothy Geithner were also expected to move on from cabinet positions. Hence, President Obama faced another challenge in assembling a new national security team while ensuring continuity and capitalizing on the hard-won lessons of his first term.

THE NSC AND PRESIDENTIAL MANAGEMENT TYPES IN PERSPECTIVE

All post–World War II presidents have had mixed success in managing the foreign policy bureaucracy. Presidential management depends on the important choices a president makes about his foreign policy orientation, his political agenda and level of involvement therein, his presidential appointments, and the organization of the decisionmaking process. As the bureaucracy has grown in size and complexity, the NSC has come to be the major institution involved in managing the foreign policy bureaucracy, though not as originally intended. The president has come to rely increasingly on a White House–centered foreign policy process managed by the national security advisor and staff.

From the perspective of the years since World War II, there has been both continuity and change in the overall making of U.S. foreign policy. There has been considerable continuity in the national security process and reliance on the NSC. Several major changes are worth noting, however. One such change has been in the issues that presidents must manage. For example, foreign economic policymaking no longer takes a backseat to national security policymaking, as it did during the cold war. Therefore, under President Clinton the White House-based NEC was created and has been relied upon since to coordinate much of the process, which continued under President Bush and especially President Obama given the global recession. The current context suggests that the NSC system is adapting to strengthen the White House's ability to manage new issues as well. A second change has been the rise of the White House staff as participants in the NSC system and process. Presidents want their most trusted staff and advisors to assist them, so it is no surprise that, as the players and agencies involved in the process expand, presidents turn to White House staff to help them manage the increasingly complicated process.

Ultimately, the NSC system exists for presidential management. It is meant to provide structure and process for the president to receive the best information, make the best decisions, and ensure that those decisions are carried out. Because, as we have seen, presidential styles vary, it is meant to support a president's strengths and minimize his weaknesses, while helping the president to meet the challenges of foreign policymaking in an increasingly complex world. As the U.S. role in the world has grown, so too has the "footprint" of the foreign policy bureaucracy, which has helped speed the development of a White House–centered system. As the Brownloe Commission concluded in the 1930s, "the President needs help." Since World War II, presidents have increasingly turned to the national security advisor and staff and the NSC system to provide that help. None of the presidents of the past twenty years has experimented with a cabinet-based system. In addition to the forces and factors we have discussed in this chapter, this is also the case because of the nature of the foreign policy bureaucracy, to which the next several chapters turn.

SUGGESTED SOURCES FOR MORE INFORMATION

Alter, Jonathan. (2010) *The Promise: President Obama, Year 1*. New York: Simon and Schuster. Excellent overview and analysis of Obama Administration's policymaking process, Iraq and Afghanistan.

Badie, Dina. (2010) Groupthink, Iraq, and the War on Terror: Explaining US Policy Shift toward Iraq. *Foreign Policy Analysis* 6:4 (October): 277–296. Very good overview of the closed and narrow policymaking process under George W. Bush that led to the invasion of Iraq.

Baker, Russell. (2008) Condi and the Boys. *The New York Review of Books* (April 3). Excellent overview on Condoleezza Rice, her personality, and inability to manage the NSC system.

Brookings Institution. (1998–2001) *NSC Oral History Roundtables,* http://www.brookings.edu/projects/archive/nsc/oralhistories.aspx. Provides roundtable transcripts and reports on the Nixon, Bush, and Clinton administrations, the role of the national security advisor, and a variety of related issues.

Burke John P. (2009b). Honest Broker?: The National Security Advisor and Presidential Decision Making. College Station, TX: Texas A&M University Press. Good overview of the rise of the national security advisor and honest broker role, and to what extent it has been implemented under different presidents.

Daalder, Ivo H., and I. M. Destler. (2009) *In the Shadow of the Oval Office: Profiles of the National Security Advisors and the Presidents They Served—From JFK to George W. Bush*. New York: Simon and Schuster. An insightful analysis of the advisory roles and structures in action.

Daalder, Ivo H., and James M. Lindsay. (2003) *America Unbound: The Bush Revolution in Foreign Policy.* Washington, DC: Brookings Institution Press, 2003. An excellent overview of the policymaking process within the younger Bush's administration

Destler, I. M., Leslie H. Gelb, and Anthony Lake. (1984). *Our Own Worst Enemy: The Unmaking of American Foreign Policy.* New York: Simon and Schuster. An excellent overview of the evolution of the policy process and the NSC.

George, Alexander L. (1980b) *Presidential Decisionmaking: The Effective Use of Information and Advice.* Boulder, CO: Westview Press. A good overview of presidential management styles and models.

Halberstam, David. (2001). *War in a Time of Peace: Bush, Clinton, and the Generals.* New York: Scribner. A good discussion of foreign policy dynamics, divisions, and personalities during the Bush and Clinton administrations.

Rothkopf, David. (2005b) *Running the World: the Inside Story of the National Security Council and the Architects of American Power.* New York: Public Affairs. An insider account of the evolution and dynamics of the NSC system.

Woodward, Bob. (2002). *Bush at War.* New York: Simon and Schuster.

____. (2004) *Plan of Attack.* New York: Simon and Schuster.

____. (2006) *State of Denial.* New York: Simon and Shuster.

____. (2008) *The War Within.* New York: Simon and Schuster.

____. (2010) *Obama's Wars.* NewYork: Simon and Schuster. Woodward's four books are detailed accounts of the decisions and processes of George W. Bush's administration. His fifth book provides an account inside the Obama Administration.

Zegart, Amy B. (1999) *Flawed by Design: The Evolution of the CIA, JCS, and NSC* (Stanford, CA: Stanford University Press). An excellent exploration of the creation of key elements of the national security bureaucracy.

KEY CONCEPTS

cabinet government	long-term planning
CEO style	NSC system
Executive Office of the Presidency (EOP)	presidency
foreign policy bureaucracy	presidential transition period
gatekeeping	State Department–centered system
honest broker	White House–centered system
internationalization of domestic bureaucracies	

OTHER KEY TERMS

Al Gore	NSC staff
Bay of Pigs	NSC-68
chief of staff	office of the vice president
Dick Cheney	operational NSC staff
deputies committee	presidential appointments
John Foster Dulles	principals committee
Joseph Biden	special assistant to the president for national security affairs
National Security Act of 1947	
national security advisor	Tuesday Lunch group
National Security Council (NSC)	White House Office (WHO)
NSC interagency process	

U.S. SECRETARY OF STATE HILLARY CLINTON (WITH U.S. TREASURY SECRETARY TIMOTHY GEITHNER ON HER RIGHT) ON A DIPLOMATIC MISSION TO CHINA IN 2012.

UNDERSTANDING BUREAUCRACY: THE STATE DEPARTMENT AT HOME AND ABROAD

The foreign policy bureaucracy is large and complex, and poses many management challenges for the country's elected leaders, especially the president. Among the main components of the foreign policy bureaucracy, the Department of State is one of the most important executive branch organizations. One of four original cabinet departments created as part of the new government of the United States in 1789, throughout most of American history the State Department was the lead organization responsible for the conduct of U.S. foreign policy. However, with the rise of the cold war, the containment strategy, and the president's effort to manage foreign policy, the State Department's influence declined. Nevertheless, while the policymaking process is no longer State Department–centered, the department remains an important bureaucratic institution involved in foreign policy. In this chapter, *we briefly discuss the context of bureaucracy in general to build a foundation for this and the following three chapters. Then, we consider the diminishing role of the State Department; its organization and operation; and the role/influence of the secretary and the department in the contemporary environment.*

A CONCEPTUAL APPROACH FOR UNDERSTANDING BUREAUCRACY

Understanding the foreign policy **bureaucracy** is essential for comprehending the foreign policymaking process and the roles that institutions like the Department of State, Department of Defense (DOD), and intelligence community play in it. After all, it is the bureaucracy that is responsible for most governmental behavior, and it is central to both the formulation and implementation of governmental policies.

A bureaucracy, whether public or private, consists of an organization with the following characteristics: (1) hierarchy (of authority and status), (2) specialization, and (3) routinization. Bureaucratic organizations usually are hierarchically structured with divisions of authority and labor specified throughout. Hierarchy involves a top-down division of authority in which every official occupies a particular role. People in positions near the top of the organization not only enjoy more authority, they also require more general knowledge and skills since they deal with large questions and the "bigger picture." As one moves down the bureaucratic hierarchy, positions become increasingly specialized and routinized with individuals having less and less authority to act independently of superiors and increasingly likely to repeatedly perform the same tasks that involve a tiny facet of the organization's operation.

Understanding any bureaucratic organization requires examining at least **four key factors**: (1) the historical context, (2) the functions (or mission or tasks), (3) the structure (or organization), and (4) the subculture (see **Figure 5.1** for a visual summary). We focus on these core elements of the State Department in this chapter to better understand its role and evolution in the making of U.S. foreign policy. Our examination also enhances our understanding of how bureaucracies operate in general and their implications for presidential governance of U.S. foreign policy (see Halperin 1974; Heclo 1977; Wilson 1989).

THE CONTEXT OF THE DECLINE OF STATE'S HISTORIC ROLE

The historical context is important for understanding the role of a bureaucracy. For more than 150 years, *until World War II, the State Department was the major organization responsible for foreign affairs.* U.S. foreign policy was made within the State Department,

Figure 5.1   Explaining Bureaucratic Organizations

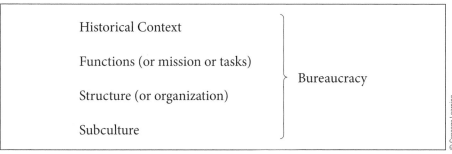

managed by its members, and carried out by ambassadors and other department members abroad. Other organizations within the government, such as the Treasury Department and especially the military, were involved in the conduct of U.S. foreign policy, but the State Department was the dominant agency. During the twentieth century, however, power began to flow to other agencies in the governmental bureaucracy and to the White House. Thus, the State Department has experienced a real decline in its overall influence in the conduct of U.S. foreign policy.

Five global and historical patterns account for the decline of the State Department's central importance in the making of U.S. foreign policy: (1) the growing importance of international affairs for the United States; (2) the growing power of the United States in the world; (3) the global communications revolution; (4) the rise in the use of force as an instrument in U.S. foreign policy; and (5) the increasing importance of international economics. These broad patterns of change throughout the world and within the United States set the stage for the rise of the presidency and other foreign policy agencies at the expense of the State Department.

Increasing Importance of International Affairs

During the twentieth century, international affairs became increasingly important for the United States. Surrounded by two oceans and relatively weak neighbors, the U.S. government was able to concentrate on internal development and expansion across the North American continent with minimal opposition from the time of its inception to the early 20th century. However, with World War I, the global depression of the 1930s, the global war of the 1940s, the cold war after World War II, the increasing interdependence of the international political economy, and the rise of transnational threats such as terrorism, disease, global environmental issues, events far beyond American borders became increasingly important. The U.S. government, including the president, can no longer afford to concentrate on domestic affairs and be unresponsive to the international scene. With the creation and expansion of the National Security Council (NSC), DOD, intelligence community, Department of the Treasury, and other foreign affairs agencies, the foreign policy bureaucracy has grown in size and complexity. Consequently, the State Department is no longer the only organization within the executive branch with major responsibilities for the conduct of foreign affairs.

Rise of American Power

By World War II, the United States was the most powerful country in the history of the world. Therefore, not only was the United States increasingly impacted by the international system, but U.S. foreign policy increasingly affected the workings of that system. America's growing global role during World War II and the cold war increased presidential power in the making of foreign policy. The global power and role of the United States was so large that the conduct of foreign policy could no longer be left to the State Department. Instead, presidents attempted to lead foreign policy directly and to manage the growing foreign policy bureaucracy through a White House–centered system using the national security advisor and NSC staff.

The Global Communications Revolution

The third major reason for the decline in the influence of the State Department was the communications revolution. Before the existence of the airplane and telephone, it took months for American officials in different parts of the world to travel or communicate with each other via diplomatic pouch. The president was dependent on the State Department and its members located abroad to officially represent the U.S. government. American ambassadors and other

State Department employees consequently had wide latitude in influencing negotiating positions or other important aspects of U.S. foreign policy. Changes in technology and the development of instant communications have allowed the president to become less dependent on the State Department in the day-to-day management of foreign policy (see Dizard 2001).

Increasing Reliance on Force

A fourth reason for the State Department's fall from its leading position in the policymaking process has been the reliance on force as a major instrument in U.S. foreign policy. With the rise of the cold war, U.S. foreign policy focused on the need to contain the threat of Soviet communism throughout the globe. The basis of the containment strategy—the effort to confine the Soviet empire to Eastern Europe and China—was to deter or reverse a Soviet challenge to the international status quo through the threat and use of force. The containment policy resulted in the expansion of America's military capabilities through the development of nuclear weapons, a large standing conventional military force, counterinsurgency forces, and covert operations. This meant not only the growth of the military and the Central Intelligence Agency (CIA), but the president's increasing use of these organizations as the means of conducting U.S. foreign policy. Similarly, in the twenty-first century, the centrality of the global war on terror also contributed to State's waning influence in much the same way. After 9/11, for example, it was the military and intelligence agencies that received most of the budget increases and new policy authority. Hence, diplomacy, the strength of the State Department, was superseded by the threat and use of force in the post–World War II period, and these newly formed bureaucratic organizations also became serious rivals in the policy process.

Increasing Importance of International Economics

Finally, as the forces of economic globalization have accelerated, especially over the past several decades, the State Department has faced challenges from the foreign economic bureaucracy as those agencies have played a more central role in policy deliberation and implementation. This has resulted in more salient foreign policy roles for treasury secretaries and other economic policy advisors and agencies, especially in the past two decades. Moreover, new structures for White House coordination in this issue area such as the National Economic Council, which was first established in the Clinton administration, have also forced State to contend with a more diverse range of rivals.

STATE'S FUNCTIONS OVER TIME

Each bureaucracy develops its own set of functions or missions or tasks over time. Although the State Department continues to be an important part of the foreign policy bureaucracy, its relative influence has declined in the foreign policy process. Nevertheless, it remains oriented to fulfilling the *five major purposes or missions for which it was originally created* (see Campbell 1971; Rubin 1985):

1. to represent the government overseas,

2. to present the views of foreigners to the U.S. government,

3. to engage in diplomacy and negotiations,

4. to analyze and report on events abroad, and

5. to provide policy advice.

One of the most important purposes of the State Department is to represent the U.S. government overseas, usually to foreign governments. The members of the State Department who are part of the foreign service (known as **foreign service officers**, or FSOs) serve abroad in embassies in the capital cities of foreign countries, in consulates in major cities of foreign countries, in other missions abroad, and in international governmental organizations such as the United Nations. In this role, the U.S. ambassador and the FSO act in the name of the U.S. government and communicate the official foreign policy of the United States to people abroad. Given the primitive nature of transportation and communications fifty years ago, this was a crucial role because the FSO was the principal channel through which governments communicated. Today, with more and more organizations of the U.S. government employing official representatives overseas, this unique role of the FSO has declined in importance. Also, with the technological revolution in transportation and instant communications, the U.S. president and foreign leaders no longer are dependent on FSOs to communicate official governmental policy.

The second major State Department purpose is to represent the views of foreigners, usually foreign governments, to the U.S. government. An important job of the foreign service is to interact with foreign government officials in the United States and abroad, learn their official positions on international issues, and communicate their views to other parts of the U.S. government. The fact that the State Department represents the views of a certain constituency is not unique within the bureaucracy. For example, for the Department of Labor often represents the views of unions, the Department of Commerce represents business, the Department of Agriculture represents farmers, and so on. However, the fact that the State Department represents the views of foreign governments, as opposed to organized domestic interests, is unique within the bureaucracy. It also contributes heavily to charges of **clientelism** among State Department officers, who are regularly accused of weighing the interests and concerns of their assigned countries more heavily than those of the United States. Also, with the rise of other bureaucratic agencies and the mass media, contemporary presidents are no longer as dependent on the State Department for learning the foreign policies of other governments.

The third major purpose of the State Department is to conduct diplomacy and negotiations abroad. In the past, if the president wanted to conclude a treaty or come to some common understanding with an adversary or friend, he had to rely on ambassadors and FSOs to negotiate in the name of the U.S. government. Communications were so slow that the president had little choice but to entrust considerable authority to his ambassadors and subordinates abroad. This is no longer the case. The speed of communications now gives presidents the ability to control negotiations on those issues they deem most important. In addition to engaging in substantially more diplomacy themselves, such as through summitry, presidents have also increasingly turned to special envoys and others outside the State Department for their diplomatic initiatives. For example, President Richard Nixon believed that opening relations with the People's Republic of China and concluding the first SALT treaty with the Soviet Union were too important to entrust to the bureaucracy, so he relied instead on the personal diplomacy of national security advisor Henry Kissinger. Nor is it unusual for the president, or his closest advisors, to pick up the phone and communicate directly with international leaders, or for the president to appoint a special envoy to represent the U.S. government in his name for a particular foreign policy issue. Examples include Reagan's appointment of former diplomat Philip Habib to lead U.S. efforts on Lebanon in the early 1980s, and Obama's appointments of former senator George Mitchell as special envoy for the Middle East, diplomat and former U.S. ambassador to the UN Richard Holbrooke as special envoy to Afghanistan and Pakistan, foreign policy specialist Frank

Wisner as special envoy to Cairo during the 2011 "Arab Spring" uprising there, and former president Bill Clinton as special envoy to Haiti in 2009.

The State Department's fourth major purpose is to analyze and report on foreign events. Most FSOs located abroad spend the bulk of their time analyzing events and transmitting these analyses through cables back to the State Department in Washington, D.C. Most of the FSOs in Washington spend much of their time reading the cables, using them as the principal source of information for communicating with their superiors—ultimately the secretary of state—and fulfilling their foreign policy functions. Decisions and directions for implementing and representing U.S. foreign policy abroad are subsequently communicated via cable to the embassies, consulates, and missions in the field. In some ways, the **cable traffic** remains the heart and soul of the contemporary State Department—consisting of over 2.5 million cables and 25 million e-mail messages a year (Zimmerman 1997). Yet, whereas past presidents may have relied to a considerable extent on reports and analyses of foreign events provided by the State Department, they now also tend to rely on their own staff through the national security advisor, have a large bureaucracy at their disposal (including the intelligence community), and consult the mass media to keep informed about world politics.

State's final major function is to provide policy advice to the president. No department function has suffered more than this one. The foreign policy process tended to be State Department–centered before World War II but has become increasingly White House–centered since the 1940s. Whatever information and advice does seep up to the White House from the State Department must work its way through the formal NSC process used by the president for managing U.S. foreign policy. In more recent years, new White House–based structures for homeland security and economics have further diffused State's role and access. The president also tends to rely on a small informal circle of major advisors, only one of whom may be the secretary of state. Thus, the overall policy influence of State may depend heavily on the working relationship between the president and the secretary of state.

BUREAUCRATIC ORGANIZATION AND STRUCTURE

The State Department began in 1789 with a staff of six, a budget of $7,961, and two diplomatic missions. By 2012, the State Department had a budget of about $50 billion (which includes US Agency for International Development funds and other international programming) and operated more than 250 diplomatic missions, in almost every country and in many international organizations. However, while the State Department is a very complex organization with a broad mandate, in comparison to most contemporary bureaucracies within the U.S. government, *the State Department is actually relatively small.* In fact, because of its geographic scope and the foreign service subculture (which we discuss later in this chapter), in spite of its relatively small size the State Department has come to operate as if it were a very large bureaucratic organization both at home and abroad. Of its approximately 60,000 employees, there are about 13,500 foreign service professionals: 6,500 FSOs and 5,000 Foreign Service Specialists in the State Department, another 1,200 in the foreign service of the United States Agency for International Development (USAID), with the balance in other agencies. Other employees are basically support personnel: doctors, security officers, secretaries, drivers, other workers, and foreign nationals, all of whom assist the FSOs, who have primary responsibility for fulfilling the State Department's major functions. Roughly two-thirds of all department employees are located in its home office in **Foggy Bottom** neighborhood of Washington, D.C., and the remaining third are located abroad. For FSOs within the department, the reverse is true; roughly one-third of all FSOs are located in Washington, D.C., while the other two-thirds are located at missions abroad.

At Home

The State Department shares the common elements found in any government or private sector bureaucracy: hierarchy, specialization, and routinization. **Figure 5.2** and **Figure 5.3** show that there are *five major hierarchical levels within the State Department:* the secretary of state, deputy secretary of state, undersecretaries of state, assistant secretaries of state, and deputy assistant secretaries of state. The top three levels of officials are referred to as the "seventh floor principals" because their offices are on the top, or seventh, floor of the State Department

Figure 5.2 Overview of State Department Organization in 2012

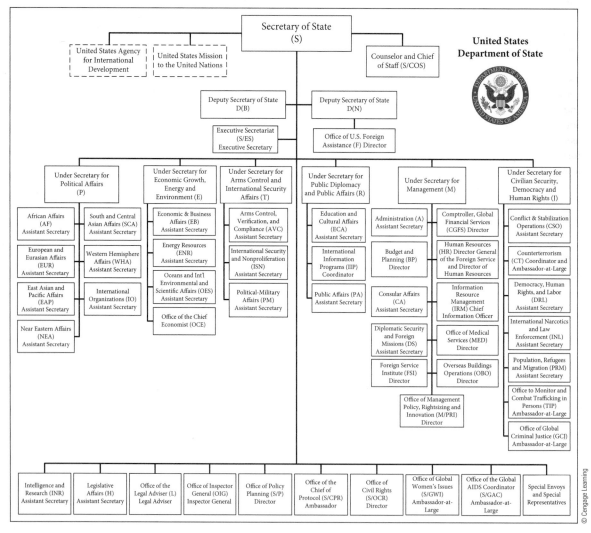

© Cengage Learning

building in Washington, D.C. The **secretary of state** is the chief officer responsible for governing and managing the State Department for the president. There are now two **deputy secretaries** of state — one is the principal advisor to the secretary, and one serves as the chief operating officer of the agency. The department underwent reorganization in 1999 and again in 2010, so that now the secretaries and deputy secretary have the support of six (up from four) **undersecretaries, each** responsible for supervising one of the following broad areas: political affairs; economic growth, energy and environment; arms control and international security affairs; civilian security, democracy and human rights; public diplomacy and public affairs; and management (including budget and personnel). A counselor and other units that report directly to the secretary, such as the Policy Planning Staff and the Bureau of Intelligence and Research, play significant roles at times as well. These offices were created during the cold war to assist the secretary in providing a broader long-term perspective. However, they have been used in various ways by the secretary, often as personal staff, depending largely on the personalities involved.

As the highest-ranking officials in the State Department, the seventh-floor principals tend to be generalists and are responsible for the department's overall conduct. Most of the specialized work of the department, however, occurs at the **bureau** level. Like most foreign policy bureaucracies, the State Department is organized into both geographic and issue-oriented bureaus. There are six geographic bureaus, often referred to as the "baronies" because of their centrality to the State Department's functions: African Affairs, East Asian and Pacific Affairs, European and Eurasian Affairs (including Russia), Near Eastern Affairs, South and Central Asian Affairs, and Western Hemisphere Affairs. The bureaus are run by **assistant secretaries,** with **deputy assistant secretaries** (or directors and deputy directors)—referred to as "bureau principals"— under them as the fourth and fifth hierarchical levels in the State Department (see Figure 5.3).

Within a geographic bureau, the assistant secretary has one or more deputies, and the bureau's area focus is subdivided into regions, and then countries. For example, as Figure 5.3 shows, the African Affairs Bureau is divided into west, central and east, and southern African affairs, each of which then includes country subdivisions. Each country, in turn, is managed

Figure 5.3   Organization of African Affairs Bureau

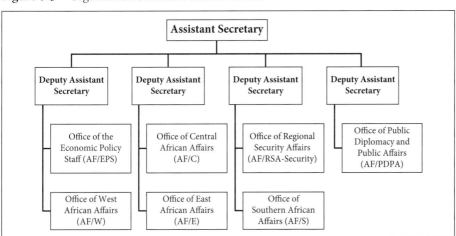

by a **country director**—or desk officer—who reports to one of the deputy assistant secretaries responsible for that part of the region, who in turn reports to the assistant secretary. Thus, the assistant secretary and the deputy assistant secretaries develop expertise and have responsibilities at the regional level. The assistant secretary for African Affairs, for example, is likely to be a principal advisor to the undersecretary of state for political affairs and possibly the secretary of state (and his or her deputy) on African issues. The country director for South Africa within the bureau is the specialist, the expert, on the current situation in that particular country and the key link in all of the information and decisions communicated—through the cable traffic—between his superiors at home and those in the field.

Abroad

In the State Department abroad, more than 250 diplomatic missions are operated internationally. About 180 of these are embassy missions (usually called **embassies**) in countries with which the United States maintains official diplomatic relations. The remaining hundred or so missions are **consular posts** that provide various services for Americans and issue visas to foreigners for travel to the United States, support the main embassy in larger metropolitan areas, and maintain other permanent missions, such as to international organizations like the United Nations or Organization of American States. In a few special cases, the United States does not have full diplomatic relations with a country (such as Cuba). In such cases, the United States is usually represented by a U.S. Liaison Office or U.S. Interests Section. The size and complexity of embassies vary enormously, though they are all organized in a similar bureaucratic fashion. For a long time, the largest embassy was in London with a staff approaching 300; today the embassy in Iraq is the largest as a result of the war—with dozens of buildings and thousands of staff. Smaller embassies such as many in Africa often have staffs of only a few people.

Figure 5.4 gives an idea of how an overseas mission, such as an embassy, is organized. The common bureaucratic elements of hierarchy, specialization, and routinization are evident here as well. The **ambassador** is the chief of mission, the highest representative of the United States stationed abroad, with responsibility over those individuals employed by the embassy. He has the assistance of a deputy chief of mission and a country team, composed of FSOs from the State Department and other governmental agencies with more specific areas of responsibility (Dorman 2005; Miller 1992; U.S. Congress, General Accounting Office 1993).

An interesting aspect of Figure 5.4 is the *overseas presence of personnel from agencies other than the State Department.* Until World War II, most officials stationed abroad as representatives of the U.S. government were from the State Department. This is no longer the case. The U.S. government now has over 30,000 employees abroad (not counting American troops in military bases or CIA personnel). Of these, State Department personnel comprise roughly 30 percent of the total, a sizable segment but not as dominant as in the past. In addition to the State Department, many government personnel abroad work for the Agency for International Development (about 20 percent), DOD (about 25 percent, excluding troops), and the Peace Corps (about 20 percent). The presence of some of these agencies is so large that they may have their own facilities separate from the main embassy, although the ambassador remains the senior U.S. governmental official within the country. One agency that is not depicted in Figure 5.4 is the CIA. It does have a major presence abroad but is officially kept secret. The **CIA station chief**, for instance, is likely to have an official position attached to the embassy in order to provide "cover" and diplomatic immunity. Other intelligence personnel and operatives will either be attached to the embassy or occupy private roles within the country (such as working for a multinational corporation).

Figure 5.4   An Embassy Organizational Chart

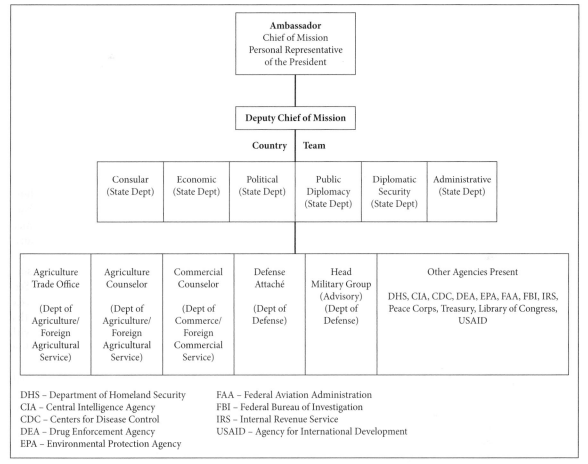

SOURCE: Shawn Dorman, ed., *Inside a U.S. Embassy: How the Foreign Service Works for America* (Washington, D.C.: American Foreign Service Association, 2005).

As discussed in Chapter 4, almost every department and agency within the executive branch is internationally involved in some way and has representatives overseas. Examining the government's official presence abroad reinforces the conclusions drawn earlier concerning changes in the foreign policy bureaucracy over time; while the State Department's influence has declined, the influence of other agencies, such as the Defense Department and the CIA, has increased tremendously.

Overall Bureaucratic Patterns

Three patterns concerning bureaucratic structure within the State Department must be kept in mind:

1. it is a hierarchical organization,

2. the policy process is complex and issue dependent, and

3. the presidential appointment process has produced controversy.

These patterns are not unique to the State Department but apply to other organizations within the foreign policy bureaucracy, as well.

First, the State Department is hierarchically organized and structured. Not only is there a top-to-bottom hierarchy of authority and labor, but a **pecking order** also exists within each level. For example, at the undersecretary level, management is considered the least significant and prestigious of the six positions, while Political Affairs is considered the most significant and prestigious by members of the foreign service. A similar pecking order exists at the bureau level and abroad. The geographic bureaus—the baronies—are considered more important and prestigious than those that involve crosscutting issues, with the European Bureau traditionally the most prestigious and the African Bureau the least prestigious (rarely an important area in U.S. foreign policy). The issue-oriented bureaus that are involved in political matters, such as the bureaus for Political-Military affairs and International Security and Nonproliferation, are also considered more important than those concerned with global affairs, such as Oceans and International Environment and Scientific Affairs and Democracy, Human Rights and Labor.

Abroad, large embassies in industrialized countries, such as the London embassy, are more desirable and prestigious assignments than small embassies in Third World countries, such as Brazzaville, Congo. Likewise, within the foreign service, five "career cones" are similarly structured, with a hierarchy placing the political cone ahead of the economic, consular, management, and, since 1999, public diplomacy cones. These patterns of hierarchy and prestige tend to hold generally, but the rise of "hot" issues will temporarily enhance one bureau or position over another, as when the Vietnam War increased the importance of the East Asian and Pacific Bureau and the Southeast Asia embassies during the 1960s; the conflicts in El Salvador and Nicaragua increased the importance of the Western Hemisphere Bureau and the regional embassies during the 1980s; and since 2001, the war on terrorism and conflicts in the Middle East and between Pakistan and India have made the Near Eastern and South and Central Asian Bureaus more prominent.

Second, the nature of the policy process within the State Department is heavily dependent on the importance of the foreign policy issue involved. To understand this process, it is helpful to see the department as a complex bureaucracy addressing numerous issues that determine who will be involved and at what level. The secretary of state, like the president, is most influential for those issues in which he or she is most interested and involved. Yet most issues are routine (involving visas, a report, or a local incident abroad) and can be handled by a few people in the appropriate bureau at home and in the field abroad. In these cases, a bureaucratic process exists in which information and decisions routinely flow up and down within the department at home as well as through regularized channels between Washington, D.C., and the field offices.

Those issues perceived to be more significant for U.S. foreign policy involve a much larger process, including higher-level officials within and beyond the State Department. This can be illustrated by the U.S. government's repeated efforts to further a comprehensive settlement of the Arab-Israeli conflict. The issue falls within the immediate jurisdiction of the Bureau for Near Eastern Affairs and involves the most relevant assistant secretary and country directors (for Israel, Jordan, Egypt, Syria, and Lebanon) and relevant embassies in the field. But the importance of the issue often increases the scope of the participants. The Near Eastern Affairs Bureau principals and many of the seventh-floor principals, possibly including the secretary of state, are likely to be involved and kept abreast of matters. Currently, the Middle East has important implications for other country directors within the bureau and for other bureaus—such as European Affairs (given their dependency on

Arab oil); Political-Military Affairs (since it is the site of a major military conflict); Democracy, Human Rights, and Labor; and Population, Refugees, and Migration (given the Palestinian refugee status and violence in the West Bank and Gaza Strip); Legal Affairs (for questions involving international law); Legislative Affairs (given the interest of certain members and committees of Congress); and Public Affairs (given the interest of the media and the public).

Nor is the issue restricted to the State Department. As early events in the Obama administration nicely illustrate, presidential envoys (e.g., former senator George Mitchell, diplomat Frank Wisner), White House officials such as the national security advisor, and officials from other foreign policy agencies such as the DOD are likely to be involved. Indeed, the White House is likely to desire policy control, and presidents themselves may prioritize the issue and place themselves at the forefront when important issues occur such as the 2011–2012 "Arab Spring" uprisings across the region. When this happens, high-profile diplomatic efforts and even trips to the region such as those of President Obama in June 2009 may ensue. Therefore, the more an issue is perceived as significant, the more likely a variety of bureaus will be involved, the higher up the issue will go within the department, and the more likely other elements of the foreign policy bureaucracy and the White House will also be involved, resulting in a larger, more complex policy process.

The third important point concerns the controversy over the appointment process and personnel. The president technically appoints all ambassadors and major officials within the State Department down to the deputy assistant secretary. Since the president is not likely to have much foreign policy expertise, he typically relies on his personal staff and the secretary of state for selecting appropriate people. Remaining policy positions, such as country directors at home or members of the embassies abroad, are staffed by FSOs who are placed through an established personnel system administered by the director general of the foreign service under the undersecretary for management. As with the civil and military services, the president has very little, if any, influence over personnel decisions within the foreign service.

Controversy has always surrounded presidential appointments. Members of the foreign service tend to believe that appointments to ambassadorships and high-level positions below the secretary of state should go to FSOs, for they have the greatest expertise and understand the workings of the State Department. Some presidents have appointed more FSOs to important policy positions than others, but non-FSOs have been increasingly appointed at the assistant secretary and deputy assistant secretary levels as well as to ambassadorships. FSOs have been getting fewer significant appointments at home and often become ambassadors to smaller, less important countries. Outside appointees tend to be from business, academia and research institutes, or government, and they may be knowledgeable about foreign affairs but not about the foreign service or the operations of the department.

Particularly irksome to the foreign service are presidential **political appointments**. This refers to those individuals, such as ambassadors, who are basically unqualified for the job—they are friends or, more often, major contributors to the president's campaign who possess little foreign policy interest or knowledge. In these cases, the prestige of being appointed ambassador, a title that reverts to the individual for life, is thought to be a personal thank-you for friendship and political support, not a request for commitment and hard work. Although political appointees can sometimes cause controversy and diplomatic faux pas abroad, they can breathe fresh air into U.S. embassy and form a strong team with a capable FSO as the deputy chief of mission. Such appointees can also make constructive use of their personal connections with the president.

Continuing a tradition that extended back to President Andrew Jackson in the early nineteenth century, under President George H. W. Bush, roughly one-third of the ambassadors were non-foreign-service-career appointees, and more than 50 percent of those ambassadorships were considered political appointments. Presidents Bill Clinton, George W. Bush, and Barack Obama continued this practice—with the regular blessing of the U.S. Senate, which usually approves presidential appointments with little or no dissent (see Lacey and Bonner 2001; Sciolino 1989; U.S. Congress, Senate, Committee on Foreign Relations 1981).

A few recent examples illustrate the more controversial ambassadorial appointments by a president: in 1989, Peter Secchia, a multimillionaire lumber tycoon who was crucial in the elder Bush's victory in the Michigan Republican party caucus over presidential challenger Pat Robertson, was appointed ambassador to Italy. Ambassador Secchia created constant controversy in Italy by his tendency to use profanity and make sexist remarks in public. In 2009, President Obama named attorney John Roos as ambassador to Japan despite the fact that he had almost no experience in the region, no diplomatic background, and few political credentials other than having raised more than half a million dollars for Obama's political campaign. Major fundraisers were also appointed as ambassadors to the United Kingdom (a former vice president of Citibank) and France (the former president of the Jim Henson Company—of the "Muppets" fame).

In sum, *the bureaucratic patterns found in the State Department are common to bureaucracies in general,* including other foreign policy agencies within the executive branch. Bureaucracies like the State Department are complex institutions of hierarchy, specialization, and routinization in which the policymaking process is affected by the nature of the issue. This often produces political tension between bureaucratic **insiders versus outsiders**: career members of the permanent bureaucracy versus presidential appointees, who are often referred to as "in-outers" since they tend to go back and forth between the government and private sectors and from one government position to another. Insiders, such as the foreign service in the State Department, tend to be part of a particular subculture and loyal to the institution where they have worked for years. In-outers tend to have little understanding or allegiance to the particular bureaucracy for which they work. How this tension between insiders and in-outers plays itself out has important ramifications for the policymaking process in general, including the particular role of the State Department and the foreign service (Halperin 1974; Heclo 1988; Rockman 1981).

USAID: AFFILIATED YET AUTONOMOUS

Ever since the **Foreign Affairs Reform and Restructuring Act** of 1998, the U.S. Agency for International Development has been housed within the Department of State, and its director reports to the secretary of state. However, USAID remains largely autonomous and was, from its 1961 inception until 1998, separate from the department. Indeed, it still maintains separate offices, with State in the complex at Foggy Bottom, and USAID in the Ronald Reagan Building. However, in recent years, greater effort to coordinate the goals and purposes of the two organizations has occurred. For example, since 2003, State and USAID have collaborated to produce a single, integrated strategic plan to better coordinate foreign policy and development programs.

The **Agency for International Development (USAID)**, its traditional name, was established in 1961 by President John F. Kennedy (along with the Peace Corps) to help Third World countries develop and to counter the expansion of Soviet influence around the world. Since then, USAID has provided loans, grants, and technical assistance to developing countries to spur economic and political development, with priority targets shifting with the context of the times (see Kirschten 1993; *U.S. Foreign Aid* 2004). Since 1961, USAID has been responsible for most U.S. economic assistance programs, administering a total of about $350 billion in such aid during that period. The agency administers its bilateral assistance programs through a central headquarters and overseas offices, with a workforce composed of direct hires and personal services contractors (both U.S. and foreign national personnel). As discussed earlier, USAID often has a larger overseas presence than the foreign service in a developing country (see **A Closer Look** for an overview of U.S. foreign assistance).

A CLOSER LOOK

U.S. Foreign Assistance and Nation-Building

Foreign assistance involves a variety of aid programs and government agencies. Security-related assistance—that is, programs that are targeted to stabilize foreign governments and strengthen police and military forces—is provided covertly by the CIA and, principally, by the DOD. Economic developmental assistance—programs to promote human welfare, economic development, and political stability in other societies—is provided by the Department of Agriculture (Food for Peace Program); the Department of the Treasury (through multilateral assistance to international governmental organizations, such as the World Bank, African Development Bank, Asian Development Bank, Inter-American Development Bank, and other United Nations agencies); the **Peace Corps** (created by President John Kennedy to help people in developing countries—there are over 6,000 volunteers today in more than seventy countries—meet basic needs for health, food, shelter, and education); and, most importantly, USAID.

Following World War II, the U.S. government began to engage in the practice of **foreign assistance**. Most of this assistance in the postwar years went to Western Europe in the form of the **Marshall Plan** to help those countries reconstruct their economies

and stabilize their political systems. As Western Europe recovered from the war and the cold war began, more and more of American foreign assistance was directed to other areas of the world as part of the United States' larger strategy to contain the Soviet Union and communism. Since the 1990s, U.S. foreign assistance has fluctuated between $15 and $30 billion a year, with security-related and developmental aid to other countries around two-thirds and one-third of the total, respectively. The largest recipients over the past two decades have been Egypt (about $1.5 billion) and Israel (between $2 and $3 billion), which together have received the two largest shares of American assistance since the signing of the Camp David Accords in 1979 brought peace between the two countries. Since the September 11 attacks, assistance has increased to countries in the Middle East and South Asia—Pakistan, for example, has been given over $1 billion a year to support the U.S. war on terrorism.

In the cold war era, foreign aid was partly justified as a way to counter Soviet influence. Since the end of the cold war, other priorities, including sustainable development, transnational and humanitarian issues, and democracy and "transformational aid" for **nation-building**, have been central. Recent interventions in Panama, Somalia, Haiti, Afghanistan, and Iraq illustrate nation-building and other purposes and suggest that the American effort to

Continued

build stable and modernizing nations, even in a post–cold war environment, continues to be problematic at best.

However, in today's political environment foreign aid is a particularly difficult sell. Questions continue to be raised about the effectiveness and purpose of foreign assistance. Members of Congress, who heavily influence foreign assistance legislation and budgets, do not believe that foreign aid is a salient issue with voters; and public opinion on foreign aid often gives policymakers contradictory signals: Americans believe in helping those in need but are much more concerned with the needs of American society at home than of societies abroad. In fact, most Americans actually tend to greatly overestimate the amount the United States spends on foreign assis-

tance. They would be surprised to know that the foreign assistance budget is less than one-fourth of 1 percent of the total federal budget and that it has not grown in constant dollars in over a decade (thus actually declining quite a bit in real dollars). And in addition to providing assistance for strategic motives, many of the foreign assistance laws require donor countries to purchase American products. Yet Americans typically see foreign assistance as "charity," which makes such programs vulnerable to domestic politics (see Packenham 1973; Ruttan 1996; U.S. Foreign Aid 2004).

What challenges do these characteristics of U.S. foreign assistance pose to presidential leadership and policies?

Beginning with the rise of East-West détente in the 1970s, but especially with the collapse of the Soviet Union, USAID's policies have been redirected increasingly away from security concerns. Currently, its seven core strategic goals (2007–2012), developed jointly with the Department of State, emphasize "transformational diplomacy" and include: (1) achieving peace and security); (2) governing justly and democratically; (3) investing in people; (4) promoting economic growth and prosperity; (5) providing humanitarian assistance; (6) promoting international understanding; (7) strengthening consular and management capabilities (U.S. Department of State and U.S. Agency for International Development 2007). To tackle these broad challenges, USAID's budget is approximately $10 billion, and it implements programs of technical assistance and financial support for various in-country projects in about ninety countries through its field missions that can range from three to four people to more than thirty at "mega-missions" in Iraq and Afghanistan. USAID also works very closely with a variety of IOs (international organizations) and PVOs (private voluntary organizations) that are actively engaged in development abroad.

USAID's small piece of the budget pie has been shrinking. In recent years, it responded by embarking on ambitious reform plans and cutting over 1,800 staff and dozens of organizational units. The agency has attempted to shed programs that are not clearly related to development and has reevaluated the countries and programs receiving aid. In addition to organizational reform, USAID has attempted to reform a scandal-ridden procurement process (for purchasing technical and material support) and to respond to criticisms that its policies were helping American businesses locate overseas at the expense of American jobs. USAID has also been increasingly subcontracting out development projects to PVOs and private companies, including in Afghanistan and Iraq, which has created a whole new set of problems in terms of designing and completing projects to help local people (Stephens and Ottaway 2005). These may have saved the agency from further budget cuts and threats to USAID's organizational existence, especially from critics in Congress such as the late

Republican Senator Jesse Helms of North Carolina and others. Hence, USAID is likely to continue to play an important role in foreign assistance, nation-building, and U.S. foreign policy around the world.

PUBLIC DIPLOMACY: A DIFFICULT AFFILIATION

For most of the past sixty years, the U.S. government has been involved in disseminating information about the United States and in promoting U.S. cultural activities abroad. Until 1999, the responsibility for these activities rested in the **United States Information Agency (USIA)**, a small yet significant agency administering a worldwide network of international broadcasting, film, and videotape/DVD programs; magazines and other print media; and a variety of informational, educational, and cultural activities, including the maintenance of libraries and book programs, lectures and cultural presentations, and English instruction. USIA also administered a number of **international exchange programs**, such as the Fulbright program, involving over 20,000 students, scholars, and practitioners from America and abroad. (This is actually one large part of over seventy international exchange and training programs administered in more then fifteen federal departments and agencies involving over 60,000 people.) The purpose behind USIA's activities was to promote cross-cultural knowledge and understanding to foster a more supportive environment for U.S. foreign policy (Hansen 1984; U.S. Congress, General Accounting Office 1993; U.S. Information Agency 1990).

As a consequence of the Foreign Affairs Reform and Restructuring Act, *in 1998 the USIA was abolished and its programs dispersed.* The broadcast elements were housed under the Broadcasting Board of Governors (BBG) in the International Broadcast Bureau (IBB), which continued to administer such entities as the well-known **Voice of America (VOA)**, the major broadcasting arm and official voice of the U.S. government. Begun during World War II as part of the war effort, VOA broadcasts a mixture of general news, public affairs programs, music, and entertainment throughout the world in over forty languages on radio, satellite television, and the Internet to an estimated audience of over 100 million people. It is currently staffed by approximately 1,100 individuals, most of whom work in the United States. In addition to the VOA, the IBB administers a range of additional operations, including Radio Free Europe/Radio Liberty; Radio Free Asia; Radio/Television Marti, created by the Reagan administration to propagandize the virtues of the American way of life to the people of Cuba; and Alhurra Television and Radio Sawa, created under President George W. Bush to broadcast in the Middle East after the September 11, 2001, events.

Such programs have always been controversial. Some believe the operations should serve purely as a propaganda outlet in which the United States is portrayed in a positive light while American adversaries are portrayed negatively; others believe that they should operate more subtly, reflecting some of the norms of the journalism profession and the American national media. Hence, it is not surprising that programming has fluctuated under different administrations. Of course, the collapse of the communist regimes in the Soviet Union and Eastern Europe deeply affected all the broadcast programs, but especially Radio Liberty and Radio Free Europe, raising questions concerning their future and ultimate purpose and forcing serious downsizing until the post–9/11 environment prompted modest increases. More recently George W. Bush's administration attempted to use the VOA and new outlets like Radio Sawa and Alhurra Television to improve the U.S. image around the world, especially in the Middle East, as part of a broader campaign to reduce anti-Americanism in the region (LaFranchi 2001; Ungar 2005).

The remainder of the old USIA mission—public diplomacy and cultural exchanges—were integrated into the Department of State. First, a new undersecretary of public diplomacy and public affairs was established, with bureaus for educational and cultural affairs (now housing the Fulbright and cultural exchange programs), international information programs (now managing the production of media and information packages), and traditional public affairs. Additionally, public diplomacy officers were assigned to each regional and functional bureau of the department; in 2005, these officers were upgraded to deputy assistant rank to improve their performance and influence. Also, the younger Bush's White House sought to elevate public diplomacy as well, introducing the short-lived Office of Global Communications in 2002 and the Strategic Communications Public Diplomacy Coordinating Committee (in the EOP) a year later to better coordinate public diplomacy activities. These steps were designed to overcome the fundamental tension that exists within the department between the policy-oriented foreign service, and the program-oriented public diplomacy people, which has resulted in the marginalization of the public diplomacy personnel who fit rather uneasily in the dominant subculture of the department.

With the post–9/11 environment providing the motivation, the younger Bush's administration also sought to harness public diplomacy to the broader campaign against terrorism and anti-American sentiments. In 2005, the effort received a boost when the new secretary of state, Condoleezza Rice, persuaded long-time Bush confidante Karen Hughes to take up the role of undersecretary for public diplomacy and public affairs. Hughes brought her high-profile efforts to bear on improving the public diplomacy operations, and relied on her close relationships with Rice and the White House to strengthen the operations. Her efforts included a rapid response office to counter critical international news reports about the United States in the Middle East, and a program to increase pro-American speakers on the influential Al-Jazeera television network (Hand 2005). President Barack Obama has had three undersecretaries of public diplomacy (including the former president and CEU of Discovery Communications), each of whom has had a record of experience in government and in broadcast, print and online journalism.

THE FOREIGN SERVICE SUBCULTURE

To fully understand the behavior of a bureaucracy like the State Department, it is vital that we examine a fourth basic characteristic: its **organizational subculture**. Every organization or bureaucracy eventually develops a subculture, or a number of subcultures. Subculture refers to the common set of goals and norms acquired by individuals within a group or organization, such as the State Department's foreign service. These beliefs and norms result in certain incentives and disincentives that influence the behavior of individuals within the organization. The subculture, according to James Q. Wilson (1989:91) in *Bureaucracy*, produces "a persistent, patterned way of thinking about the central tasks of and human relationships within an organization. Culture is to an organization what personality is to an individual. Like human culture generally, it is passed on from one generation to the next. It changes slowly, if at all" (see also Scott 1969; Whyte 1956).

New members quickly discover they are expected to learn and absorb the rules and norms that pervade the organization. These rules and norms are formally or officially communicated and enforced (e.g., by disseminating departmental guidelines on appropriate "professional" behavior or by affecting career advancement through the personnel evaluation and promotion system) and informally enforced (e.g., through peer interaction). People quickly learn to play by the rules of the game if they want to be accepted by their peers and be professionally successful within the organization. This produces conformity in the behavior of most individuals, thereby reinforcing and promoting the organizational subculture. The subculture of the foreign service is particularly strong because of its small size—only 6,500 FSOs—relative to other bureaucratic organizations. Together, the structure and subculture of the State Department bureaucracy determine how well the department fulfills its primary functions and influences the overall policymaking process (see Schake 2012; Kopp and Gillespie 2008).

Identifying and describing a subculture is no simple feat. Discussing the major beliefs and norms that prevail in a group or organization necessarily results in broad generalizations that oversimplify the organization's complexity and are unlikely to apply to any one individual. Despite these complications, much work has been done on the subculture of the foreign service, and a strong consensus exists on its major attributes (see also Clarke 1987; Crosby 1991; Rockman 1981; Rubin 1985; U.S., Department of State 1992). It is commonly argued that *five key characteristics comprise the subculture of the FSO:*

1. a tendency to be elitist or exclusivist,

2. a preference for overseas experience and to identify with foreign viewpoints,

3. an emphasis on the policy instruments of diplomacy and negotiation,

4. a tendency to be generalists, and

5. a tendency to be loyal and cautious.

The foreign service is commonly considered an elitist or exclusivist group. This elitism takes two forms. First, the foreign service is elitist in the sense that it is difficult to become an FSO and FSOs consider themselves to be the crème de la crème of the government in foreign policy expertise. There is much truth to this, for the demand to join the foreign service is extraordinarily high and the job openings are few. The Foreign Service Exam is also extremely demanding. Few applicants do well, and those who score high have no guarantee that a position will be found for them.

The foreign service is also considered elitist in another sense: Throughout most of its history, membership in the foreign service consisted of men who were White Anglo-Saxon Protestants (WASPs) from wealthy, urbane families who often attended Ivy League schools. In other words, the foreign service consisted of a very exclusive **old boy network**. Entrance into the foreign service was based on anything but merit. Instead, the key was an individual's "pedigree"—family, background, education—and his connections. This exclusiveness resulted in an air of superiority among FSOs relative to other government employees, especially as other foreign policy bureaucracies expanded during World War II and the cold war (Weil 1978).

Much has changed within the State Department, especially over the last thirty years. The old boy system has opened up to new entrants. Connections and pedigrees have been replaced by a more demanding merit system based upon the Foreign Service Exam. Women, minorities, and individuals who are not from the Northeast, not Protestant, and not upper or upper-middle class, have become part of the foreign service. Nonetheless, the process of change has been a slow one, and the foreign service continues to be dominated by white men from affluent segments of society. (See **A Different Perspective** on gender and race discrimination in hiring and personnel systems.)

A second characteristic of the foreign service subculture is that FSOs usually prefer to be stationed abroad and tend to identify with foreign viewpoints. For an FSO, to be abroad rather than in Washington, D.C., is to be where the action and excitement is—in the field.

It is also a way to see and experience the world, often a key motivating factor among foreign service applicants (e.g., Kopp and Gillespie 2008). This is reinforced by an FSO's privileged lifestyle abroad and constant interaction with foreign elites. The preference is not only for overseas experience but also for choice assignments such as London, Paris, and Rome. This orientation toward overseas experience and identifying with foreign countries is reinforced by the foreign service personnel system, in which career advancement is based on service abroad. To be posted in Washington, D.C., too often or too long may hurt career opportunities. In fact, the typical career goal of an FSO is to become an ambassador, not secretary of state or another major policymaking official close to the president.

This emphasis on overseas experience and identifying with foreign viewpoints often is detrimental to the ability of FSOs to operate successfully in the foreign policy maze at home. Because FSOs are more interested and knowledgeable about what is happening abroad than at home, they may not be motivated or equipped to influence the policymaking process outside the State Department. Often they are accused of allowing the interests of the countries in which they serve to trump U.S. interests, to the frustration of the White House and senior appointees. Recently, for example, objections by Arab leaders led officers in State's Middle East bureau to water down ambitious proposals for a U.S. democracy promotion plan in the region, while a number of FSOs serving as ambassadors in the region refused to use White House–approved talking points explaining and defending the U.S. position on Iraq for fear of offending their hosts (Kaplan 2004). Such behavior frequently results in accusations that members of the foreign service so identify with foreign viewpoints that they have "gone native," and other officials in the policymaking process may therefore not take an FSO's policy positions seriously. These subcultural traits make it difficult for the State Department as an organization to influence strongly the foreign policymaking process (Kaplan 1994).

A DIFFERENT PERSPECTIVE

Gender and Race Discrimination in Hiring and Personnel Systems

Being a woman in the world of U.S. diplomacy has historically involved vastly different experiences and perspectives than those of their male counterparts, and considerable controversy has existed over the composition of the foreign service. Even though personnel selection and promotion is currently based on a merit system, most FSOs are white men from more privileged backgrounds. More women and minorities have gained entry to the foreign service in the last few decades, but they remain underrepresented in comparison to their numbers in society. This pattern becomes even more noticeable as one moves up the career ladder

to more senior positions in the foreign service. In fact, prior to 1980, no woman had ever been put in charge of any of the major regional bureaus.

In a 1989 class action suit, a U.S. Court of Appeals found the State Department guilty of **sex discrimination** against women in its hiring and promotion practices and ordered that such promotion practices be remedied and the Foreign Service Exam revised. Subsequently, in the elder Bush administration, women were named to 23.2 percent of the appointments at the top six levels of the department. Under Clinton, that figure rose to 28.2 percent. Yet some people remain frustrated with the gradual nature of the changing composition and emphasize the need to make the foreign service more democratic and more representative, arguing that diversity can be a source of strength to the department's international efforts in a world of great heterogeneity.

Although slow to change, the State Department's personnel system is becoming more merit oriented. Yet because the Foreign Service Exam is so demanding, those from more privileged backgrounds are likely to perform better. Also, because of the foreign service's small size, job openings are few and the rate of turnover is slow. New personnel problems are also arising. Whereas once the spouse (and children) accompanied the FSO from post to post and played the important role of host, the rise of professional careers for both the husband and the wife has generated much frustration with the rotation tradition of "worldwide availability." As always, controversies over personnel are likely to plague the State Department, and other governmental organizations, into the future (see Olmstead, Baer, Joyce and Prince 1984; Scott and Rexford 1997; U.S. GAO, State Department 1989).

In a society where women are highly underrepresented throughout government, particularly at the higher levels, even the image of breaking into top positions offers encouragement to the ranks of women and minorities hoping to garner employment in foreign policy. In the Department of State, three of the last four secretaries of state have been women, signaling a major shift from a history of male dominance in that position: Madeleine Albright (Clinton), Condoleezza Rice (George W. Bush), and Hillary Rodham Clinton (Obama). Fittingly, one journalist wrote of **Madeline Albright's** 1997 appointment as secretary of state: "The image of a woman leading American diplomacy makes a statement that no slogan can" (Cooper and Liu 1997). Similarly, Condoleezza Rice has noted that "If somebody . . . in 1954 . . . had said the secretary of state will be a black woman—and by the way, that will be after the last secretary of state was a black man and the secretary of state before that was a woman—people would have said 'No, really—are you kidding?' " (Ratnesar et al. 2005). With Hillary Clinton's 2009 appointment as secretary of state following those of Albright and Rice, the glass ceiling in the oldest of all U.S. foreign policy agencies appears to have been shattered (see Cooper and Liu 1997; Duffy and Shannon 2005; Gibbs 1997; Isaacson 1999; Keating 2009; Ratnesar et al. 2005).

What do you think is the impact of greater numbers, roles, and authority for women in the diplomatic corps for U.S. foreign policy and policymaking?

The third major characteristic of the foreign service is its emphasis on diplomacy as the principal tool of U.S. foreign policy. FSOs see themselves as diplomats—a long-honored profession in the history of world politics. And the ability to engage in diplomacy and conduct negotiations is an art—mastery of which is not learned in a book but through field experience overseas (or in earlier times, it was part of an elitist subculture into which one was born). The problem with the foreign service's focus on diplomacy is that, with the rise of the cold war, that approach was superseded by increased reliance on the military, economic, and cultural instruments of foreign policy: force, covert operations, assistance, trade, economic sanctions, cultural programs, and international broadcasting. Even after the end of the cold war, as the instruments to support America's global policy have multiplied, the foreign service's emphasis on the role of diplomacy has contributed to the decline of the State Department.

The fourth characteristic of FSOs is their tendency to be generalists. Although the foreign service prides itself on its foreign policy expertise, most FSOs are not specialists. This is a function of the **foreign service personnel system**. Not only is there an emphasis on overseas service, as discussed, but a rotation system operates based usually on three-year tours. This means that every three years an FSO is stationed in a new post abroad (though every third or fourth tour may be at home), often in a new region of the world. It is not unusual, for example, to find a new FSO with a degree in East Asian studies posted first in Haiti, then maybe in Somalia, then in Washington, D.C., in the Western Hemisphere bureau, abroad again in Cameroon, and so on, maybe never getting the opportunity to use his or her original East Asian training. The little specialized training that does take place occurs within the State Department (no bureaucratic incentives exist to obtain graduate degrees) and in the Foreign Service Institute. The emphasis, rather, is to produce well-rounded experts with wide-ranging experience and intuitive understanding, able to fulfill any foreign policy position. Those individuals who prefer to stay within a region and specialize do so at the risk of career advancement. The major exception to this pattern is when an FSO begins to gain considerable seniority; at that point an area of specialization may be carved out (Ayres 1983a; Bacchus 1983).

This emphasis on the creation of well-rounded, generalist diplomats runs counter to the expansion of bureaucracy, which emphasizes the development of specialists. On the one hand, the development of personnel with general knowledge and a broader perspective allows for the integration of context and history in policy analysis, something that has eroded with the growth of specialization on top of specialization. On the other hand, FSOs are often at a disadvantage with their counterparts from other bureaucracies because they may lack detailed knowledge vital to an issue making its way through the policy process. When coupled with the other characteristics, it also helps to explain why governmental politics tends to be an FSO's weakest suit. Their elitism, parochialism, emphasis on diplomacy, and generalist training frequently hamstring their participation in interagency processes, as does their frequently aggressive resistance to ideas and information that originate outside their particular spheres. The rotation system also provides little incentive for learning the local language and culture, since each posting tends to be a temporary stop.

The fifth characteristic common to FSOs is their tendency to be loyal and cautious. FSOs are loyal to the foreign service and identify closely with the State Department as an institution. Such loyalty is easy to understand, for most FSOs spend their adult careers within the foreign service and the State Department. Given the limited number of FSOs, an FSO ends up working and interacting with familiar colleagues over fifteen or twenty years. Informal networks of relationships that build up with time are reinforced by the formal personnel process in which one's immediate superiors regularly evaluate one's performance. In addition, FSOs are also known for being cautious. They are hesitant about bucking the dominant beliefs and norms of the foreign service, and they also often provide "low-risk" advice and are reluctant to take individual policy initiatives. For example, before a request or decision is cabled abroad, for instance, the desk officer with primary jurisdiction must make sure it has been cleared (approved) by all other officials interested in the issue. If an issue triggers the participation of officials from seven or eight bureaus, no matter how distant their involvement, all the participants are kept apprised of the process and sign off on any decisions, no matter how minor. The result tends to be a cautious, cumbersome process built around compromise and consensus.

Such caution and loyalty can be found in the history of the State Department from its beginning, and the evaluation and promotion procedures of the department are partly to blame as well. However, the traits intensified after World War II and the coming of the cold war, which ushered in the rise of anticommunism and McCarthyism in the country and the government, especially in Congress. And the State Department, especially those focusing on Asia, was badly damaged (see **The Liberty–Security Dilemma**).

THE LIBERTY–SECURITY DILEMMA

Traitors and Purges in the State Department

McCarthyism resulted in political charges of un-Americanism and communism against individuals and institutions, especially the State Department for "losing the cold war and selling out America to communism." **Alger Hiss**, a high-level State Department official, was accused in 1948 of being a traitor for his activities during World War II and was convicted of perjury (resulting in the rise of Congressman Richard Nixon, who led the political attack against Hiss). With the "fall" of China in 1949, senior officials of the Far Eastern bureau, who predicted that the Chinese Nationalists, given their corruption and brutal authoritarian behavior, would lose the civil war to the Chinese Communists, became scapegoats and were forced out of the department and their careers destroyed.

By the early 1950s, McCarthyism became so powerful and reckless that high-level officials within the Harry Truman administration were attacked for being "appeasers" and "fellow travelers" of communism. The secretary of state and the department were, for example, referred to as the "Dean Acheson College for Cowardly Containment of Communism" by Congressman Richard Nixon. With the attacks continuing under Truman and after the election of Dwight Eisenhower as a Republican president, loyalty oaths and loyalty programs were instituted throughout the government, and the practice developed of expanding the

scope of classified information, making it unavailable to the public in the name of national security.

In this political climate, many officials were purged from the State Department for not having sufficiently "hard-line" anticommunist views. Journalist David Halberstam described the situation among the East Asian specialists: "The best had been destroyed and the new experts were different, lesser men who had learned their lessons, and who were first and foremost good anti-communists" (Halberstam 1969:390). Survivors of the political attacks and purges within the State Department—such as Dean Rusk, who was in the Far Eastern bureau at the time and later became secretary of state under Presidents Kennedy and Johnson—drew the obvious lesson that to take the initiative and stand out from the pack in foreign policy was a major risk to one's career. Thus, cautiousness and secrecy increased within the foreign service, and an extensive clearance procedure was instituted within the State Department to ensure that an individual was not alone in approving decisions that might become politically controversial (see Halberstam 1969; Kahn 1972; Newman 1992).

How did the virulent anticommunism of the early Cold War and the internal security concerns it spawned affect the Department of State and its role/influence in foreign policy, then and now?

This portrait of the foreign service subculture is not particularly complimentary. Many FSOs are likely to disagree with what they might consider to be a caricature of the foreign service. However, this is the consensus position within the foreign policy literature, and this perspective also tends to be shared by other members of the foreign policy bureaucracy, including the White House, as we discuss in the next section.

CONSEQUENCES FOR PRESIDENTIAL RELIANCE ON STATE

Presidents and their closest advisors have generally had a negative perception of the State Department's performance in the last few decades. John Kennedy, for example, referred to the State Department as a "bowl of jelly." Lyndon Johnson considered members of the foreign service to be "sissies, snobs, and lightweights who sacrificed too little and thought themselves better than their country." Richard Nixon declared in the 1968 campaign that "I want a secretary of state who will join me in cleaning house in the State Department" (Halberstam 1969:299); and Condoleezza Rice's appointment as secretary of state in the younger Bush's second term prompted a former advisor to note, "you can't be true to the president's foreign policy and be 'nice' to the Foreign Service" (Kaplan 2004). These negative images of and experiences in working with the State Department have contributed to presidents' increasing reliance on a White House–centered policymaking process.

Although Barack Obama relied more heavily on diplomacy in his first term, and Hillary Clinton worked strenuously to elevate the role of the State Department and its FSOs in the policy process, the department remains just one voice among many in the widening foreign policy bureaucracy. Consequently, the department has not escaped or overcome the persistent problems it has faced as its influence and role eroded after World War II. From a presidential perspective, six complaints are often voiced about the State Department's performance:

1. inefficient and slow,

2. poor staff work,

3. unresponsive,

4. resistant to change,

5. incapable of putting its house in order, and

6. unable to lead.

It is often argued that the State Department is inefficient and slow. As discussed earlier, the State Department operates as a very large, cumbersome bureaucracy with an extended clearance procedure that involves numerous officials and bureaus for any issue. The president and other major foreign policy officials have often found that the State Department moves too slowly, especially if there is a pressing issue at hand. When the State Department does respond, another complaint is that the staff work is often poor. National Security Advisor Kissinger, after issuing a National Security Study Memorandum directing the bureaucracy to provide information, analyses, and policy alternatives, was often frustrated with the work produced by the State Department and frequently forced the department to prepare new studies.

A third complaint is that the State Department is unresponsive to the president. Presidents and their advisors frequently argue that State personnel refuse to follow orders. The department is perceived as being unresponsive since FSOs are permanent members of the bureaucracy who will outlive the short political life of any president. Furthermore, given the foreign service's particular subculture, FSOs often seem to act as if they know what is best for U.S. foreign policy. A closely related complaint often heard is that the State Department resists change (e.g., Schake 2012). Bureaucratic resistance to change is not unique to the State Department; all bureaucracies develop patterns and policies over time, making them resistant to changes the president may want to initiate.

The fifth common complaint is that the State Department is incapable of putting its own house in order. In other words, the State Department has not been successful in reforming its structure and subculture so that it operates more efficiently, produces higher quality staff work, and is more responsive to presidential orders and initiatives (e.g., Schake 2012). Endless studies of the operations of the State Department have been conducted, and a number of efforts at reorganization have occurred since World War II. Under Hillary Clinton, for example, another round of shuffling occurred at State. Among other things, energy and the environment were moved from global affairs and into economic and business affairs (newly named "economic growth, energy and the environment"). Global affairs, in turn, was reorganized to include a greater focus on human rights and human security.

In general, the net result has been superficial change in the formal organizational chart, while the foreign service subculture and day-to-day bureaucratic operations of the State Department remain intact. The difficulty in changing a bureaucratic organization, from without or within, is not limited to the State Department. The subculture of any organization tends to produce bureaucrats—FSOs in the case of the State Department— who believe that they are performing their jobs properly, helping to fulfill the functions of the organization, and making a contribution to the public policy of the U.S. government.

Considering these complaints, it is not surprising that presidents have found the State Department unable to lead U.S. foreign policy—the final complaint commonly heard. No matter how much a president may want to rely on the State Department for the conduct of U.S. foreign policy, he soon finds that State is unable to lead, for it has resisted change in the internal workings of the department and the foreign service. This is why the roles of the national security advisor and staff have grown tremendously over time to the detriment of the State Department. Indeed, reflecting on foreign policymaking, a group of NSC staffers from George H. W. Bush's administration observed that interagency groups chaired by State were more often ineffective than those chaired by NSC staff (National Security Council Project 1999). In the Obama administration, NSC officials not only chair the principals and deputies committees, but all the interagency policy committees as well, including the regional committees, which were usually chaired by State Department officials (Presidential Policy Directive 1, February 13, 2009).

Such perceptions quite naturally have serious policymaking consequences. One recent example will suffice to highlight not only the bureaucratic divisions that often stymie American foreign policy, but also the deterioration of State's influence resulting from the combination of its behavior and perceptions of it by others. Not long after the Bush administration was wrapping up its military campaign in Afghanistan, top foreign policy officials began to target Iraq for subsequent military operations to remove Saddam Hussein from power. Consequently, in the Department of State, Thomas Warrick, a careerist working in the Middle East bureau, headed a **Future of Iraq Project** designed to consider the issues and challenges of a post–Hussein Iraq (Fallows 2004; Rieff 2003). Wide-ranging, drawing on experts at State, USAID, and other agencies, representatives of NGOs (nongovernmental organizations), as well as many Iraqi exiles representing a broad range of views, the project consisted of numerous working groups on just about every aspect of the issue. Both the CIA and the Defense Department were also involved. Eventually, under Warrick's direction, the many working groups of the project produced thirteen volumes—thousands of pages—of material that explored "almost everything, good and bad, that has happened in Iraq since the fall of Saddam Hussein," but well before the U.S. military operation ever began (Fallows 2004:52).

However, Secretary of Defense Donald Rumsfeld and his subordinates completely ignored the need for postwar planning, even when the Defense Department was charged with the responsibility. Finally, in late January 2003, DOD formed the Office of Reconstruction and Humanitarian Assistance just two months before the war would begin. General Jay Garner, tapped to lead the effort, immediately asked for Thomas Warrick to be named to his team. He was turned down by the Office of the Secretary of Defense. When he requested information from the Future of Iraq Project, again, according to Garner, his superiors refused, telling him to ignore the work. Why? "The Pentagon didn't want to touch anything connected to the Department of State" (Rieff 2003:32). State was apparently simply frozen out of the policymaking loop, in large measure because its conclusions did not match those of the civilian leadership in the DOD. Consequently, as one observer glibly characterized it, "Donald Rumsfeld's Defense Department ended up administering postwar Iraq but being surprised by the electricity problems, while Colin Powell's State Department was marginalized but fully aware of it" (Drezner 2003:2). Of course, the consequences were far more serious, as the rushed planning led by Garner and the military precipitated a myriad of postwar failures and contributed to increased instability, a rising insurgency, and a continuing Iraq War (see Chapter 9 for more on the decisionmaking dynamics on Iraq's postwar reconstruction efforts).

The Secretary of State

Despite the decline of the State Department as an institution, individual State Department officials have played influential roles in the making of U.S. foreign policy for the president and within the policymaking process. *The distinction between the State Department as an institution and individuals within the State Department is very important to understand.* Secretaries of state often act as major spokespersons for the administration in foreign policy and major advisors to the president, as was discussed in Chapter 4, about presidential management of the foreign policy process. And lower-level State Department officials may also play important roles, depending on the people involved and the issue.

Table 5.1 details the secretaries of state since the Roosevelt years. Many of the people who have served as secretary of state have been consequential in the making of U.S. foreign policy. Henry Kissinger, Cyrus Vance, George Shultz, James Baker, Warren Christopher, Madeleine Albright, Condoleezza Rice, and Hillary Clinton are all examples of strong and powerful secretaries of state in U.S. foreign policy who have had good relationships with the president since the ascendancy of a White House–centered system.

Strong and powerful secretaries of state, in turn, rely heavily on many officials within the State Department (some of which are in-outers) for the information and advice in

Table 5.1   Secretaries of State

Name	Year	President	Background
Edward R. Stettinius	1944	Truman	Business and Government
James F. Byrnes	1945	Truman	Law, Congress, and Supreme Court
George C. Marshall	1947	Truman	Army
Dean Acheson	1949	Truman	Law and Government
John Foster Dulles	1953	Eisenhower	Law and Government
Christian A. Herter	1959	Eisenhower	Congress and Government
Dean Rusk	1961	Kennedy	Foundation and Government
William P. Rogers	1969	Nixon	Law and Government
Henry Kissinger	1973	Nixon	Academia and Government
Cyrus R. Vance	1977	Carter	Law and Government
Edmund S. Muskie	1980	Carter	Law, Congress, and Government
Alexander M. Haig	1981	Reagan	Army and Government
George P. Shultz	1982	Reagan	Academia, business, and Government
James A. Baker, III	1989	George H. W. Bush	Law and Government
Lawrence S. Eagleburger	1992	George H. W. Bush	Government
Warren M. Christopher	1993	Clinton	Law and Government
Madeleine K. Albright	1997	Clinton	Academia and Government
Colin Powell	2001	George W. Bush	Army and Government
Condoleezza Rice	2005	George W. Bush	Academia and Government
Hillary Clinton	2009	Obama	Government and Law

© Cengage Learning

formulating their policy positions. They may also opt to work with and empower the careerists within the department. Hence, the decline of the State Department as an institution in the formal policymaking process has not foreclosed key State Department officials from exercising influence in the foreign policymaking process. However, since World War II, and especially since the Kennedy administration and the rise of White House–centered policymaking, secretaries of state have faced a fundamental choice. On the one hand, they can stress their role as advisor and spokesperson for the president, and thus preserve policy influence; on the other, they can emphasize their role as manager of the department, advocating for and relying on the resources, recommendations, and personnel of the department. Over the past five decades or so, this **inside-outside dilemma** has challenged all who have held the position.

The most recent occupants of the position nicely illustrate the dilemma. When George W. Bush nominated Colin Powell to serve as secretary of state, the outpouring of praise was instant. Almost from the start, Powell sought to empower the department and its personnel, and to rally morale among its careerists (McGeary 2001:24–32). He also emphasized career personnel in mid-level and ambassadorial appointments and other responsibilities. Moreover, he sought to inject State Department analyses into policy discussions. The consequence was that "State Department officials . . . love Powell" (Kessler and Ricks 2004:A7). Indeed, career State Department employees recently told the authors that the mere mention of Powell in an audience of FSOs prompts an outpouring of praise. However, in contrast to these positive views within the agency, Powell was cynically regarded as "Foreign Service officer-in-chief" outside the department (Kaplan 2004). Consequently, Powell soon found himself on the losing end of the contest for policy influence (see Kitfield 2001; also Daalder and Lindsay 2003; Woodward 2004, 2007). Even as early as September 2001, Powell was being characterized in the press as the "odd man out" (McGeary 2001). After the presidential election of 2004, Powell quietly resigned and was replaced by Condoleezza Rice as Secretary of State.

Powell's successor, **Condoleezza Rice**, followed Madeleine Albright as the second woman to hold the post of secretary of state. Rice moved to State from her role as national security advisor, a position she gained largely by virtue of her role as a key foreign policy advisor to George W. Bush during the 2000 campaign. In stark contrast to Powell, however, Rice leaned heavily on her extraordinarily close relationship with the president. Their relationship, clearly closer than any similar relationship since George H. W. Bush and his secretary of state James Baker, was so extensive that one observer characterized her as the president's "alter ego" (Kaplan 2004). To be sure, Rice made efforts to signal the State Department's employees that she would be their secretary of state, offering pep talks, advocating for and defending their roles in key issues, such as negotiations with North Korea, where she successfully lobbied the White House to allow assistant secretary of state Christopher Hill to talk with the North Koreans face-to-face, and other gestures (see Diehl 2005; Duffy and Shannon 2005; Ratnesar et al. 2005). However, her overall orientation, and the most significant element of her influence, remained her connection to the White House.

Barack Obama's choice for secretary of state was **Hillary Rodham Clinton**. President Obama thus turned his main rival for the presidential nomination in 2009 from an independent senator into part of his team. As secretary of state, Clinton took up a central role in policy formulation by walking a fine line between the two ends of the inside-outside dilemma. Given substantial autonomy by President Obama in her role as secretary of state, Clinton drew on her substantial political capital and skills to emerge as the president's leading foreign policy voice, aided in part by the ineffectiveness of Obama's first national security advisor, Jim Jones, and later by her good relationship with Jones's replacement, Tom Donilon. According to one account, she managed this by deftly combining a mix of outsiders and career diplomats throughout the upper and middle levels of the department and effectively engaging in the advisory process (Keating 2009).

From the start, Clinton sought—and was given—almost total authority over hiring at State, which enabled her to build her team at the agency. While Obama's first national security advisor, Jim Jones, stressed process, Clinton aggressively championed a shift away from the confrontational, military-dominated policies of the previous administration toward great cooperation, engagement, and diplomacy (Rothkopf 2009). She assiduously advanced the president's agenda and kept close to him as she assumed the leading role on foreign policy. One key policy deputy—James Steinberg (who served as deputy national security advisor in the Clinton administration, and as a foreign policy advisor to the Obama campaign)—worked closely with Donilon, who was first deputy national security advisor and then national security advisor (Donilon also served in the Clinton administration's State Department) to improve State–White House collaboration (Rothkopf 2009). Also her first deputy secretary of state, Jacob Lew, was well respected by the White House as well (he became the director of the Office of Management and Budget in 2010, and the White House Chief of Staff in 2012!).

Within the agency, Clinton "made a vigorous effort to widen her circle, wooing and pulling into her orbit the agency's Foreign Service and civil service officials, many of whom said in interviews that she . . . brought a new energy to the building" (Romano 2010). According to a number of State Department employees at various levels, Clinton had success "heading off the historical tensions between career employees and quadrennial political newcomers by relying on the counsel of senior Foreign Service operatives and reaching out in general" (Romano 2010). As one colorful account notes:

> She has walked the halls and popped into offices unexpectedly, created an electronic "sounding board," and held seven internal town hall meetings to listen to gripes about everything from policy to cafeteria food to bullying in the workplace. She installed six new showers that joggers requested, is taking steps to remedy overseas pay inequities and instituted a policy that allows partners of gay diplomats to receive benefits. She became a heroine to the Foreign Service when she went to bat to get funding for 3,000 new Foreign Service positions for State operations and the U.S. Agency for International Development—the first boost of this magnitude in two decades. (Romano 2010)

Hillary Clinton is not the first secretary of state to try to thread the needle on the insider-outsider dilemma. However, by the end of 2012, she had managed to walk that line at least as effectively as anyone before her, and better than most. In 2012, Robert Gates—her counterpart as secretary of defense for the first two years of the Obama administration—wrote of her in an essay naming her as one of *Time Magazine*'s Top 100 influential people in the world. According to Gates (2012)—no stranger to the challenges of presidential advising and bureaucratic management—Clinton excelled:

> In a world that is ever more complex, turbulent and dangerous, Secretary Clinton . . . has made a singular contribution to strengthening this country's relationships with allies, partners and friends; rallying other countries to join us in dealing with challenges to the global order, from Libya and Iran to the South China Sea; and reaching out to people in scores of countries to demonstrate that America cares about them.
>
> She has developed, for the first time, long-range, comprehensive strategies for diplomacy and development that will strengthen the critical civilian contribution to America's national security abroad. We worked closely together to integrate and coordinate the efforts of the departments of State and Defense.
>
> Equally important, Secretary Clinton has been thoughtful and tough-minded about where and how the U.S. should engage its prestige, its resources and its men and women in the field, both civilian and military. She is an idealistic realist and a superb Secretary of State and has well served the President and our country.

In 2012, Hillary Clinton announced her plans to step down as secretary of state after President Obama's first term. She promised to stay in the position until a smooth transition could be organized with a new successor after Obama's election victory in November.

THE FUTURE?

With the end of the cold war, the State Department appeared poised to play a more prominent role in the making of U.S. foreign policy. However, negative perceptions of the department's competency shared by political leaders, along with persistent conflicts, such as the Persian Gulf, Kosovo, Afghanistan, and Iraq wars and the global war on terrorism, and the increasingly significant global economic challenges suggest that the department's status is not likely to change dramatically.

This is the conclusion of a task force commissioned by the Department of State to examine its own role and needs into the future given the collapse of the cold war. Entitled *State 2000: A New Model for Managing Foreign Affairs*, the study (U.S. Department of State, 1992:79–80) also acknowledged that it will be "a difficult adaptation for an institution bound in tradition" and "there are, of course, limits to what the leadership of the Department can do about the culture of the institution." Unfortunately, most observers would say that too little has changed in the two decades since the publication of report.

Therefore, it should no longer be surprising that, although the State Department remains a key agency in the foreign policy bureaucracy and individual officials within the department will continue to play significant roles, the president has turned to other agencies within the government for information, advice, and management of the national security process, such as the DOD and the intelligence community in addition to the NSC. Yet, as we will see in Chapters 6 and 7, the president has had problems in managing these bureaucratic organizations as well.

SUGGESTED SOURCES FOR MORE INFORMATION

Clarke, Duncan. (1987) "Why State Can't Lead," *Foreign Policy* (Spring):128–142. Insightful and still relevant discussion of the foreign service subculture and its impact on the State Department's role in the policy process.

Dorman, Shawn, ed. (2005) *Inside a U.S. Embassy: How the Foreign Service Works for America.* Washington, D.C.: American Foreign Service Association. A look at the inside workings of an embassy.

Kopp, Harry and Charles Gillespie. (2008) *Career Diplomacy: Life and Work in the Foreign Service.* Washington, D.C.: Georgetown University Press. A discussion of the nature and role of foreign service officers, including day-to-day life.

Lake, Anthony. (1989) *Somoza Falling* (Boston: Houghton Mifflin, 1989). Informative analysis of State Department policymaking in the Carter administration's policy toward Nicaragua.

Rubin, Barry. (1995) *Secrets of State: The State Department and the Struggle over U.S. Foreign Policy.* New York: Oxford University Press. A good history and overview.

Schake, Kori N. (2012) *State of Disrepair: Fixing the Culture and Practices of the State Department.* Stanford, CA: Hoover Institution Press. A discussion of the foreign service officers subculture.

Talbott, Strobe. (1997) "Globalization and Diplomacy: A Practitioner's Perspective," *Foreign Policy* (Fall 1997):69–83.

U.S. Department of State. (1992) *State 2000: A New Model for Managing Foreign Affairs* (December). Report on the opportunities and challenges facing State after the cold war's end.

KEY CONCEPTS

bureaucracy
bureaus
cable traffic
clientelism
foreign assistance
foreign service personnel system
inside-outside dilemma
insiders versus outsiders

nation-building
old boy network
organizational subculture
pecking order
political appointments
secretary of state
sex discrimination

OTHER KEY TERMS

Agency for International
    Development (USAID)
ambassador
Alger Hiss
assistant secretary
CIA station chief
Condoleezza Rice
consular posts
country director
deputy assistant secretary
deputy secretary of state
embassies
Foggy Bottom

Foreign Affairs Reform and
    Restructuring Act (1998)
foreign service officer (FSO)
Future of Iraq Project
Hillary Rodham Clinton
international exchange programs
Madeleine Albright
Marshall Plan
Peace Corps
undersecretary
United States Information
    Agency (USIA)
Voice of America (VOA)

CHAPTER 6

ROMEO GACAD/AFP/Getty Images

U.S. Soldiers on Patrol in a Village in Afghanistan, 2012.

THE MILITARY ESTABLISHMENT

As an institution, the U.S. military experienced tremendous growth in the twentieth century. Throughout most of its history, the United States had a modest-sized military that was distant from much of American society. But with World War II and the rise of the cold war, the military grew to be the largest bureaucratic institution in the United States and a major force in U.S. foreign policy. Since the end of the cold war, despite some downsizing, the military continued to be important as a tool of U.S. foreign policy.

This chapter examines the basic functions (or missions), historical evolution, organizational structure, and subcultures of the military establishment. We discuss the use of force in the conduct of U.S. foreign policy and the military's effects on the policymaking process. The chapter begins with a brief overview of the military's general functions and its history, followed by an examination of three phases: the post–World War II modern military, the military after the Goldwater-Nichols Act of 1986, and the military since 9/11, including the Iraq and Afghan wars.

FUNCTIONS OF THE MILITARY

Although the military has developed into a large, permanent, professional force during peacetime and has grown enormously in size and scope, the *basic functions or purposes of the military have remained basically the same* from the beginning. The general purpose of the military is to "defend and protect" the government and the state. A second important function of the U.S. military is to conduct military operations at the direction of the political and civilian leadership, as stipulated in the U.S. Constitution. Finally, the third function is to fight and destroy in support of the country (and for the individual soldier, be willing to give up one's life). This is such a unique function, in comparison to any other organization within the government or society, that it requires unique training to "re-socialize" individuals to accept and engage.

The use of military force, or hard power, by a permanent, large bureaucracy became the foundation for the U.S. policy of containment during the cold war, which tended to revolve around a "threat-oriented" foreign policy. From 1946 to 1994, American policymakers used the armed forces as a "political" instrument to influence the actions of other countries almost 400 times (Blechman and Kaplan 1978; Fordham 1998), and the threat and use of military force continues to the present day.

THE HISTORICAL U.S. MILITARY

From independence until World War II, *three general characteristics prevailed in the U.S. military.* First, the United States generally maintained only a small career military (see Millet and Maslowski 1985; Perret 1990). During times of conflict—such as the War of 1812, the Mexican-American War, the Civil War, and World War I—the U.S. government recruited a "citizen militia" to form a large military to fight the war that was then quickly demobilized when hostilities ceased. Much of this can be explained by the advantages of the geographic location of the United States between two oceans and the relative weakness of its two neighbors. This policy was reinforced by a popular distrust of the large, professional military establishments that existed in the Old (European) World.

The military was also highly fragmented and decentralized during this period. Instead of a unified military with different services responsible for different missions, the U.S. government maintained two separate military departments: a **Department of the Navy** (including the Marines) and a **War Department** (consisting of the army and later an army air corps—from which today's separate air force emerged). Overall direction and coordination were the responsibility not of the military, but of the civilian commander in chief, the president of the United States.

A third important characteristic of the pre–World War II military was that it was an important source of political recruitment. Many of America's major political leaders were once generals in the U.S. Army. For example, Presidents George Washington, Andrew Jackson, Ulysses S. Grant, and Dwight Eisenhower, to name a few, were prominent generals in the army. Since the Vietnam War military experience lost much of its value in the recruitment of candidates and in political campaigning, but it can occasionally become a controversial campaign issue: as in 1992 over the question of Bill Clinton's avoidance of the draft, in 2004 on President George W. Bush's national guard status and John Kerry's Vietnam experience, and in 2008 when it was made an issue by Republican candidate John McCain in his election contest with eventual victor Barack Obama.

THE TRANSFORMATION OF THE POST–WORLD WAR II MODERN MILITARY ESTABLISHMENT

America's entry into World War II and its efforts to contain the threat of Soviet communism during the subsequent cold war resulted in *three major changes that transformed the old military into a modern military establishment:*

1. greater centralization and specialization,

2. emergence of a large, permanent professional military, and

3. tremendous expansion in bureaucratic size and scope.

Efforts at Greater Unification and Specialization

The experience of World War II created concern for the need to create unity of effort within the military, as symbolized by the passage of the National Security Act of 1947. American leaders were concerned not only over the policymaking process at the presidential level during World War II, prompting the creation of the National Security Council, but also about the fragmentation, lack of coordination, and in-fighting among the different armed services supporting the war effort. Nowhere was this more noticeable than in the Pacific theater, where jurisdiction was divided between the Army and the Navy. General Douglas MacArthur was in charge of American forces in the Southeastern Asian theater (with General Joseph W. Stilwell in charge of the China-Burma-India theater), while Admiral Chester Nimitz was responsible for military operations throughout the northern and central Pacific. This division of authority resulted in competing, and not always complementary, military strategies being implemented by the United States in the Pacific.

Following the war a major debate ensued in which the Army favored a highly integrated military system, but the Navy strongly opposed this. The National Security Act of 1947 reflected a compromise: The old War and Navy departments were replaced by a single Department of Defense (after the creation initially of the National Military Establishment), composed of a loose confederation of three military departments: the Army, Navy (including the Marines), and Air Force. Coordination of service activities was to be accomplished by the Joint Chiefs of Staff, and the Office of the Secretary of Defense was created to make the military more responsive to the president as the commander in chief (Zegart 1999).

Large, Permanent Military

The second major change was the development of a large, permanent military, replacing the small career force that temporarily grew in size during wartime. Although the U.S. military did begin to demobilize after World War II, the rise of the cold war resulted in reinstitution of the draft in 1947 in order to maintain a large military force that received extensive training even in peacetime (i.e., when a major "hot war" did not exist).

This revolutionary transformation in the U.S. military did not come easily and was bitterly fought over in Congress during the late 1940s, until the Korean War resulted in U.S. military intervention (Halberstam 2007). This change occurred because, for the first time since 1812, most Americans feared for the security of their country and believed that the threat of communism required the development of a large, permanent, professional military to keep the peace.

Expansion in Size and Scope

Following World War II and the Korean War, the **Department of Defense (DOD)** *became the largest bureaucracy in the U.S. government and American society.* By 1989—the year the Berlin Wall came down—the DOD spent almost $300 billion per year and employed well over 4 million people: about 2 million full-time soldiers, 1.5 million troops in the reserves and National Guard, and 1 million civilians (plus contractors). Military spending represented roughly 30 percent of total expenditures by the U.S. government (as high as 50 percent during the 1950s); DOD also employed roughly 60 percent of all full-time U.S. government employees (not including members of the reserves and the National Guard) and one-third of all federal civil servants. DOD personnel were located on over 1,000 military bases and other properties in every state of the Union. Some 500,000 troops were permanently stationed throughout the world in over 3,000 installations, including over 330 major military bases in over twenty countries and twenty-five U.S. overseas territories (such as the Panama Canal Zone), predominantly in Europe, Asia, and the Pacific. With military personnel in over 130 countries, the United States provided military training, in one form or another, to 75 percent of the world's armed forces (U.S. Senate 1989). Since the collapse of the Soviet Union and the cold war, the DOD has experienced some downsizing (or in military jargon, there has been a "drawdown"), but it increased again following the events of September 11, 2001, along with its budget.

In many ways, the military now exists as a *society within American society.* It has its own system of laws, courts, and military police (MP), and most military bases are relatively large, urban complexes that maintain barracks and residential facilities for families. They also have medical (e.g., hospitals) and educational facilities (from kindergarten to adult extension college classes), commissaries (military supermarkets and department stores), and recreational facilities (bowling alleys, movie theaters, and country clubs). The military has made an effort to provide its personnel with every amenity of modern life, at least in terms of material comfort, at home as well as abroad, including in war zones such as Iraq and Afghanistan.

In addition to the Army, Navy, and Air Force academies, the military operates its own system of graduate colleges and universities for preparing its middle officers for senior staff and command positions, including the Army War College, Naval War College, Air University, Armed Forces Staff College, Defense Systems Management School, and the National Defense University, which consists of the National War College and Industrial College of the Armed Forces. The military services, individually and jointly, also maintain a number of colleges and research institutes in the health sciences as well as Reserve Officer Training Corps (ROTC) programs located in most public colleges and universities in the country. DOD also owns more than seventy industrial plants and facilities, many dating back to World War II.

Furthermore, *the military is considerably more than just the Department of Defense.* For example, the Department of Homeland Security includes the Coast Guard (with over 35,000 personnel), which has important military functions. The Department of Veterans Affairs (VA) was created to assist wounded war veterans and maintains an extensive system of VA hospitals throughout the country. The space program within the National Aeronautics and Space Administration (NASA), originally a civilian-run organization to promote a nonmilitary space mission, supports more military than civilian missions today. The Department of Energy oversees about twenty government-owned plants, privately operated by industry and universities (such as the Savannah River Plant in South Carolina) responsible for the design, manufacturing, testing, and retirement of nuclear weapons going back to the "Manhattan Project." When the Soviet Union detonated an atomic device in 1949, this event not only intensified the cold war and growing fears of communism, it also resulted in maximum production and maximum secrecy in the U.S. government as it developed the hydrogen bomb and expanded America's nuclear weapons stockpile at the likely detriment to the health of thousands of Americans (see **The Liberty–Security Dilemma**). From its height of over 140,000 workers in the 1980s, the nuclear weapons production process has shrunk, but the Department of Energy remains responsible for storage of vast hazardous substances and environmental cleanup (Cochran, Arkin, Norris and Hoenig 1987; U.S. Congress 1994).

THE LIBERTY–SECURITY DILEMMA

Nuclear Testing, Downwinders, and Human Safety

As part of the research and development of nuclear weapons, an **atomic testing program** was conducted by the Atomic Energy Commission (AEC, forerunner to the Department of Energy) from 1951 to 1958 at the Nevada Test Site, northwest of Las Vegas, where almost one hundred nuclear devices were tested above ground. Over 100,000 people who lived downwind from the Nevada Test Site felt the nuclear blasts and were exposed to the resulting radioactive fallout. These people were predominantly Mormons, very patriotic believers in God and country, who lived in small towns in Nevada and Utah.

When some of the so-called "downwinders" began to express concern about the fallout, the U.S. government—with the support of local political, business, and religious leaders—initiated a campaign to educate the public. Local citizens were told by the U.S. government that there was no need to worry because radioactive fallout is harmless (no more dangerous than medical X-rays) and that the atomic tests were a crucial component of efforts to safeguard the security of the United States. This public relations effort included this message from the Nevada Test Site manager in a 1955 AEC pamphlet given to schoolchildren and their parents:

> You are in a very real sense active participants in the Nation's atomic test program. You have been close observers of tests which have contributed greatly to building the defenses of our country and of the free world. . . . Some of you have been inconvenienced by our test operations. At times, some of you have been exposed to potential risk from flash, blast, or fallout. You have accepted the inconvenience or the risk without fuss, without alarm and without panic. Your cooperation has helped achieve an unusual record of safety. . . . I want you to know that each shot is justified by national or international security need and that none will be fired unless there is adequate assurance of public safety. We are grateful for your continued cooperation and your understanding. (quoted in Ball 1986:73)

By the late 1950s, many local citizens became increasingly skeptical of the U.S. government's bland assurances of their safety. Medical research indicated that radioactive fallout was extremely harmful and in the 1960s there was an alarming increase in the number of leukemia patients detected in the small communities that were downwind from the Nevada Test Site, particularly among the young (the most vulnerable). Feelings of great bitterness resulted. As expressed by one local citizen, "We trusted the government when they told us that it was safe and so we didn't take precautions that we might have otherwise done had they told us the methods to protect ourselves" (quoted in Ball 1986:92).

In the late 1970s, after the Vietnam War, the AEC was forced to release classified information, demonstrating that members of the AEC and the U.S. government had shown little interest in questions of safety during the nuclear testing program, "knowingly" lied about the harmlessness of radioactive fallout, and kept medical studies classified indicating the dangerous effects of low-level radiation in order to avoid adverse publicity. Nevertheless, federal courts typically ruled in favor of the U.S. government, while the U.S. Congress failed to pass legislation compensating the downwinders.

Such governmental practices were not confined to the Nevada Test Site case. Islanders were exposed to radioactive fallout from nuclear tests in the Pacific; military troops were exposed to radioactive fallout while engaged in war exercises following nuclear tests in the Pacific and the Nevada Test Site; civilians were exposed to dangerous bacteria as a result of the Army's germ warfare tests over populated areas; civilians were injected with radioactive substances in experiments to determine the effects

of radiation; miners and nearby residents were exposed to radioactive material from uranium mines; Vietnam veterans (and countless local Vietnamese) were exposed to dioxin in the chemical defoliant Agent Orange; and military personnel and civilians are exposed to military toxic wastes while they work and live near toxic waste dumps on military bases (see Cole 1988; D'Antonio 1993; Gallagher 1993; Honicker 1989; Saffer and Kelly 1982; Welsome 1999).

Overall, millions of Americans, military and civilian, have been exposed to radioactive and toxic substances used by the U.S. government and the military in the name of national security. Since Vietnam more information about threats to public health has come to light, but in each situation the government response tends to be the same: The substances and facilities are claimed to be safe for humans, the release of relevant information is resisted, and any political or legal challenge that arises is fought. There have been some court settlements, and the U.S. government, usually through the VA, has been forced to be somewhat more responsive.

To what extent do national security practices prevail over the safety and rights of American citizens today?

THE NATURE OF THE MODERN MILITARY ESTABLISHMENT

As a consequence of these three major changes, *a modern military establishment has developed.* To understand its nature, let's examine three aspects in some depth:

1. the organizational structure and process,

2. the military subculture, and

3. the American way of war.

In the modern military, a number of important changes (as well as continuities) occurred since the 1980s, beginning with the Goldwater-Nichols Act of 1986, but they will be discussed later in the chapter.

DOD's Organizational Ideal Versus Political Reality

The DOD expanded into an enormous national and global bureaucracy during the cold war characterized by hierarchy, specialization, and routinization (or standard operating procedures) common to all bureaucracies, as discussed in Chapter 5. To better understand the dynamics of the defense process, we have to compare the formal organizational model to political reality.

According to the formal organization chart and the ideal bureaucratic model, the DOD operates very rationally within a pyramid-like structure composed of three levels. The individual services implement and carry out the plans and policies of their superiors— the Joint Chiefs of Staff, who consist of the senior military officers, and the Office of the Secretary of Defense, which represents the president and the civilian control dictated by the Constitution. Unfortunately, the political reality of the policymaking process within the Defense Department is far removed from the ideal and among the most complex of any governmental bureaucracy (see **Figure 6.1**).

The military became so enormous and remained so decentralized during the cold war that each of the military services possessed their own missions, standard operating procedures, and subcultures over which the president has been able to exercise only limited control, producing a particular American way of war that was not always that effective during times of conflict. This is better understood by considering the role of the services, the Joint Chiefs of Staff, and the Office of Secretary of Defense (see Coates and Kilian 1985; Luttwak 1985; Perry 1989).

The **services** were created to implement U.S. defense policy where the Army, Navy, Marines, and Air Force each have specialized responsibilities in preparing for and engaging in war. The Army was primarily responsible for land warfare. The Navy maintained over 500 ships, including twelve aircraft carriers with hundreds of aircraft, for sea and coastal warfare. The Marine Corps was an assault force, maintaining its own air and landing craft. The Air Force operated over 2,000 aircraft in support of its air warfare mission. Day-to-day military operations were based on clearly defined divisions of labor (between and within services) and rank (from general down to army private) during the cold war.

The **Joint Chiefs of Staff (JCS)** was created after World War II to coordinate military strategy among the services and represented the entire military in advising the secretary of defense and the president. The JCS originally consisted of the four highest military officers: the chair, chief of staff of the Army, chief of naval operations, and chief of staff of the Air Force (the commandant of the Marine Corps was added in 1958). The chair of the JCS was appointed by the president for up to four years, while the other positions were a function of the personnel systems within the individual services. A joint staff, no larger than a few hundred military officers on loan from the individual services for a limited term, existed to support the JCS's work and mission.

The JCS was a weak body for its first four decades, unable to enforce a coherent military policy and coordinate the individual services. The chairman of the JCS, the only presidential appointment representing the entire military, had only one vote and no power to force the other members to support him (until the Goldwater-Nichols Act). Each of the other four members represented the interests of their individual services. Decisions over issues tended to produce competing interests that were resolved through compromise and consensus within the JCS, and each service tended to get most but not all of its demands met. In this way, the JCS was able to symbolically present a unified military position that the civilians in the Office of the Secretary of Defense and the president found difficult to combat.

Figure 6.1 The Department of Defense Organizational Dynamics

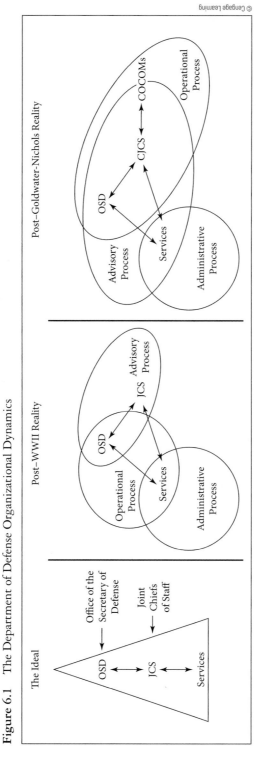

NOTE: COCOMs, Combatant Commander; CJCS, chair of the Joint Chief of Staff; JCS, Joint Chiefs of Staff; OSD, office of the Secretary of Defense.

The **Office of the Secretary of Defense (OSD)** was created to provide better civilian control of the military and to advise the president. OSD is the predominantly civilian side of the DOD. The major hierarchy of administrative officers are the secretary of defense, a deputy secretary, undersecretaries, assistant secretaries, and deputy assistant secretaries, all nominated by the president and confirmed by the U.S. Senate. Most of the routine day-to-day activity within OSD takes place in organizational units or bureaus that specialize in certain defense subjects and issues. The Defense Department's structure allowed for the military, through the OSD, to serve the president in his constitutional role as commander in chief.

In practice, the OSD had little legal authority (until Goldwater-Nichols) to influence the operations of the JCS or the individual services. To illustrate the fragmentation within the DOD and the independent autonomy of the individual services, official U.S. governmental publications such as the *United States Government Manual* and the *Congressional Directory* list the Army, Navy, and Air Force as separate "departments" within the executive branch (the Marine Corps is an autonomous part of the Navy), even though they are officially a part of the DOD, indicative of their autonomous power.

The key to understanding the decentralized process of the DOD in the post–World War II era is to examine who controlled the **budget and personnel systems**, for they determine how any organization actually operates. Decisions about the military budget (how to spend the money available) and military personnel (tours of duty and promotions) have been made within each of the services. Furthermore, the budgetary and personnel practices within each service became institutionalized and standardized, making them very resistant to change. As General David C. Jones (1982:79), former chairman of the JCS, has stated, "He who controls dollars, promotions, and assignments controls the organization—and the services so control, especially with regard to personnel actions."

Decisions over which weapons to build, where to deploy them, and how to use them in combat were typically made within an individual service, validated by the JCS, and usually approved by OSD—all within the constraints of the overall military budget. The president and the secretary of defense might exercise influence on those issues in which they were most interested and attentive, otherwise they had limited impact on the actual operations of the services—the heart and soul of the military.

With the dramatic expansion, enormous bureaucratic size at home and abroad, and relative decentralization of the military establishment brought about by the rise of the cold war, *numerous organizational and political trends that were often problematic developed, including* information problems, duplication and overlapping of activities, and difficulty of military coordination.

These are three major problems common to all complex bureaucracies, but they are especially important in the DOD, given its role and functions in national defense. Overall, the U.S. military "war machine" has been big and powerful since World War II, yet a close examination demonstrates that it was not nearly as effective a fighting force or as finely tuned an organization during war or peace as many Americans commonly believed.

PROBLEMS OF INFORMATION   Beyond the difficulty of communicating within such an enormous bureaucracy, other information problems plagued the military. The first was a heavy reliance on obtaining measurable indicators of military capabilities and operations, while deemphasizing the more intangible or human dimensions of warfare. Second was a tendency to inflate or deflate the information in accordance with service "political" interests.

Not surprisingly, one of the major lessons of the Vietnam War that continues to have a major impact is that, during wartime, information needs to be closely controlled by the military and the DOD.

In Vietnam, for example, under General William Westmoreland and Secretary of Defense Robert McNamara, **body counts** became the ultimate "objective" indicator of how well or poorly the United States was performing in the war. Thus, if enemy body counts went up, this was used as an indication to the DOD and the country that the United States was winning. Not surprisingly, after a firefight soldiers on the ground made estimates of body counts from a distance (as opposed to risking ambush) and learned to error on the side of higher body counts to please their superiors and advance their careers, resulting in the over-reporting of enemy-killed-in-action figures. At the same time, there were also incentives to deflate the number of North Vietnamese Army (NVA) troops coming down the Ho Chi Minh Trail into South Vietnam.

Political battles were also fought over the "order of battle"—that is, the size of enemy forces in South Vietnam—with CIA estimates much higher than MACV's (Military Assistance Command in Vietnam), especially throughout 1967. The military won the political fight in Washington, but historical hindsight supports the CIA position. Ironically, the military leadership, including General Westmoreland and the JCS, the civilian leadership, including President Johnson, were aware of the accuracy of the larger enemy numbers. They simply found the lower estimates more politically appealing for boosting public optimism and combating the antiwar demonstrations that were increasing on the home front, giving a false impression to the American people of "light at the end of the tunnel" that was overwhelmed by the Tet Offensive (Berman 1989).

DUPLICATION AND OVERLAP OF ACTIVITIES Given the size and autonomy of and competition between the services, considerable duplication and overlap of activities have resulted. Although most Americans believe that there is but one Air Force, the U.S. military actually has four major air forces: the Air Force itself; the Army Air Force (consisting primarily of helicopters to support the Army's land mission), which maintains more aircraft than the Air Force; the naval air arm, involving a large carrier air force to defend the Navy fleet and undertake air strikes; and the Marine Air Force to support its own mission. Why has each service had its own air force and flown its own missions? The absence of dependable support from the other services—such as air support from the Air Force for Army troops—forced each service to fend for itself, promoting duplication. Some duplication may be helpful to ensure the success of a mission, but the military services have been so decentralized and autonomous that excessive duplication became the norm.

Using Vietnam as an example again, while the services ran their own air wars in the south, President Johnson and his foreign policy advisors controlled the air war over North Vietnam. Furthermore, the CIA maintained its own air force in support of its covert missions. In fact, the best way to understand the Americanization of the war in Vietnam is not as a unified military effort under a single commander, but as a number of different wars fought by different components of the U.S. government.

COORDINATION PROBLEMS During the cold war, lack of coordination among the services made it difficult to develop a truly unified and mutually reinforcing military orientation that cohered overall. Each service tended to pursue its own mission and tactical orientation largely independent of the others, resulting in a patchwork military strategy, which together may or may not have promoted the overriding goals of U.S. foreign policy.

Why? The tremendous size, decentralization, specialization, and strength of the service subcultures allowed minimal military as well as civilian control, which often led to considerable **interservice rivalry**. Even though the military enjoyed substantial political and financial support from the president, Congress, and the public at large, the Army, Navy, Marines, and Air Force intensely competed with each other for resources, control, and preeminence—the ultimate indicators of success and the main tools for building a modern force (see Halperin and Halperin 1984). The same lack of real coordination often existed in military operations. Once American forces were engaged in combat abroad, every service expected to get a piece of the action. In the Vietnam War, not only were the Army, Navy, Marines, and Air Force all involved, but the U.S. Coast Guard patrolled the inland waterways along the Mekong Delta.

In addition to the strong interservice rivalry (between services), much **intraservice rivalry** (within a service) existed as well. Each service is organized into different branches and commands (such as infantry, armor, and artillery within the Army) that develop particular subcultures, with which personnel tend to identify strongly and compete for resources. This intraservice rivalry impeded the Army's ability to conduct war successfully in Vietnam. Under President Kennedy most of the 18,000 troops sent were **Army Special Forces** (or **Green Berets**). Although originally organized in the late 1950s to conduct behind-the-lines training of partisan forces against the United States' cold war enemies, during the early 1960s Green Berets became specially trained to perform counterinsurgency (and antiguerilla) operations—which required certain political, economic, and cultural skills (such as language training), in addition to military skills, to help the population defend itself. However, by the mid-1960s more and more conventionally trained soldiers were sent to Vietnam, pushing counterinsurgency into the background. This was reinforced by the dominant Army view that Green Berets, though held in high regard for their prowess, were not trained to do things the conventional army way. Hence, as the war became Americanized, the conventional Army came to rely on the helicopter and the air cavalry—the latest technologies for concentrating firepower by quickly moving personnel and equipment in support of "search and destroy" operations (Betts 1977).

The Modern Military Subculture

Examining the department's organizational subcultures helps to understand the workings of the military and civil-military relations within the DOD. With both civilian and military personnel, different services, and differences between officers and enlisted personnel, the DOD bureaucracy is not only enormous, but also diverse, composed of many different elements. Consequently, the department does not have a single subculture. However, a number of general characteristics have pervaded the military over the cold war years (see Allard 1990; Betts 1977; Fallows 1981; Hadley 1986; Luttwak 1985; Yarmolinsky 1971). *Most members of the military, especially career officers, have tended to share five characteristics:*

1. a managerial style,

2. pursuit of procurement and high technology,

3. preoccupation with careerism,

4. belief in the separation of politics and military combat, and

5. promotion of the principle of concentration in warfare strategy.

First, it is commonly argued that the military no longer produces warriors, but rather a "managerial class" of military leaders. The primary purpose of the military is to prepare and engage in war and, historically, carrying out this function required the development of a warrior class in society. In the United States, the military has been the institution where this warrior tradition was fostered. However, the manager has become ascendant over the warrior since modern bureaucratic warfare demands the ability of officers to become "managers of violence." Or maybe to be more accurate, officers are now expected to be both warriors and administrators. Given the enormous expansion of the military bureaucracy in size, scope, and complexity, this is a natural development and was reinforced by the civilian leadership, especially under Secretary of Defense Robert McNamara.

Robert McNamara entered office committed to seizing control of the DOD and making it more efficient and responsive to the president. McNamara's background was in the corporate world, and he had gained a reputation as an excellent manager while chief executive officer of the Ford Corporation. During the Kennedy and Johnson administrations, McNamara appointed numerous "whiz kids" to positions in the OSD in his effort to restructure the department as well as streamline and improve the flow of information and the budgetary process. Although the basic military missions of the services continued, McNamara was successful in spreading his managerial approach throughout the military during the Vietnam War.

The most successful military officers in the military became those with administrative skills. Symptomatic of this change were the postgraduate degrees and curricula pursued by senior officers. Where history and military strategy were once the norm, the emphasis became business administration, public administration, and engineering. Even at U.S. military colleges, knowledge of military history, international conflict, and military strategy no longer became dominant (except at the "war colleges" for senior officers). The emphasis has not been on the art of war but on learning how to administer a large bureaucracy. This has been accompanied by the rise of "bureaucratese" within the military—the development of a technical language among a select group of professionals and bureaucrats (including academics). Acronyms and jargon, such as MAD (mutual-assured destruction), KIA (killed in action), and "collateral damage" (civilian injuries and fatalities and property damage), have proliferated, distancing the military and civilian managers from the brutality of war (see Creveld 1989; U.S. Congress, General Accounting Office 1991).

The rise of "managerialism" has been reinforced by a second characteristic of the military subculture, the quest for more procurement and high technology. A strong norm developed that a modern military requires expensive "hardware" (weaponry and support facilities). Not unique to the military, much of American society has an abiding faith in the promise of technology. The goal is not only to deter and win wars, but to gain the symbolic value and prestige conferred by state-of-the-art weapons.

This "materialist" bias for more weapons, particularly those that are state-of-the-art, reinforced a decline in the importance of the soldier-warrior, required more expert personnel to maintain and administer the hardware, and deemphasized the importance of intangibles—such as leadership and will—during time of conflict. It also led the upper echelons of the military to take a much more active political role in civil–military relations: influencing the president, lobbying Congress, using the media, and campaigning to build public support for more procurement and high technology. Thus, the military, along with its supporters, became a potent political force in the politics of national defense, reducing military accountability to civilian leadership and exacerbating the difficulties the president faced as commander in chief.

A third characteristic of the military subculture is the rise of **careerism**. A personnel system developed within each of the services that promotes individual conformity to the dominant norms and status quo and places a premium on individual preoccupation with career advancement. There has been an "up or out" expectation according to which either an officer is regularly promoted within the service, requiring very high evaluations from his or her superiors, or his career will suffer. Furthermore, officers have been expected to "punch their tickets"—that is, serve in a variety of specified positions and roles throughout their service. This normally includes a combat record, which is usually crucial to high career advancement. As many observers have pointed out, the military career ladder has become little different from the governmental or corporate career ladder, typical of any large bureaucracy. In each of the services, the end product became an "organization man or woman" who learned organizational norms and was able to contribute to the performance of the individual services' missions.

The fourth characteristic of the military's subculture is a belief in the separation of politics and military combat. The military perspective has been that the civilian leadership, symbolized by the president and the Congress, decide when and where to go to war; but once the decision has been made, it is time for the politicians and civilians to stand aside and let the military do what it does best: fight wars. Most presidents and civilian leaders see the nature of civil-military relations quite differently—that the president is the commander in chief before, during, and after a war, as stipulated in the U.S. Constitution (see Huntington 1957).

Given such differing interpretations, the military and civilian leadership often have found themselves in political battles during times of peace and war. For example, during the Korean War President Harry Truman relieved **General Douglas MacArthur** from his command of the United Nations forces for insubordination, triggering a national controversy over the conduct of the war and the containment policy (see Halberstam 2007). The American failure in the Vietnam War fueled a similar debate, for many attributed the loss of the war to civilian interference with the military's ability to perform its mission, while others blamed the military's inability to succeed within the appropriately described limitations set by the civilian leadership.

The final characteristic that is part of the socialization or conditioning of military personnel is the belief in the principle of concentration of forces and firepower (or attrition warfare) as the most effective strategy to deter, weaken, exhaust, and ultimately defeat the enemy. This is what the conventional U.S. military has been fundamentally organized, equipped, and trained to do. Given the different responsibilities and missions of each service, this emphasis has resulted in the historical development of three different warfare strategies. The army emphasized control of land through the destruction of the enemy's army and occupation of its territory (for the Marines preferably through amphibious landings); the Navy has emphasized a maritime strategy of control of the sea by decisive defeat of the enemy's fleet; and the Air Force asserts the primacy of airpower over every other form of combat for defeating the enemy (see Davis 1967; Wylie 1966). Together, this has produced an American way of war.

The American Way of War

The basic functions of the modern military establishment, its organizational reality and complexity, and its dominant military subculture have *produced an American way of war and a tremendous military paradox:* The U.S. military has become a very powerful force over time, yet it has been relatively limited in what it has been able to perform well. The military primarily has been organized and trained to fight nuclear and conventional wars—the American way of war. Only limited military forces have been devoted to unconventional or "low-intensity" warfare. In many ways, however, the military's performance in warfare since World War II and the quality of its performance prior to Goldwater-Nichols has been unimpressive, except for those few occasions involving more classic conventional warfare.

WARFARE BEFORE AND AFTER WORLD WAR II Throughout its history, the U.S. military has been organized and trained for classic conventional warfare. The great military strategies and wars that have influenced the U.S. military historically have been European— the British military being the main model for emulation. World Wars I and II, the greatest conventional military clashes in world history, demonstrated the need to organize and train for massive, general conventional war and called for a strategy of concentration of forces and attrition to defeat the enemy.

This was reinforced by the **Korean War**, the first major military conflict of the cold war. The Korean War of 1950 was a "limited" war where the U.S. military was successful in stopping the North Korean invasion of South Korea after the peninsula was divided following World War II, but General MacArthur was unsuccessful in his determination to reunify the entire peninsula, only to trigger Chinese military intervention that produced prolonged military stalemate until the cease fire in 1953 (and led to MacArthur's firing by President Truman; see Halberstam 2007).

Although nuclear weapons were not used in the Korean War, initially they were part of the general arsenal in support of the conventional strategy of attrition. The increasing destructiveness of nuclear weapons and advances in missile technology during the 1950s resulted in the military also being organized and trained for a new, nuclear form of war. *Therefore, following World War II, the U.S. military was prepared to fight principally two types of wars:* a conventional war and a nuclear war.

For forty years, the U.S. military plans focused on conventional and nuclear war with the Soviet Union. This preparation was the foundation of containment and the **deterrence strategy**, to stop Soviet expansionism through the threat and use of military force. Such a strategy presupposed a conventional war most likely occurring in central Europe and then on the Korean Peninsula in Asia. It also was based on the likelihood of a nuclear battle predominantly fought on the territories of the United States and the Soviet Union. Refinements were made to these general strategies, such as a concern with limited nuclear war and limited conventional war directed predominantly at the Soviet Union and its surrogates (see Brodie 1973).

Historically, reliance on a conventionally trained military did not pose a problem for dealing with uprisings or guerrilla war. Such conflicts were not widespread and were often subdued by sending American marines to restore stability in places like Nicaragua, as was often done during the early part of the twentieth century (with the possible exception of the Philippine insurrection of 1899–1902). However, in the years following World War II, there has been an explosion of nationalism, an increase in new state and nonstate actors, and a proliferation of weaponry throughout the globe with major implications for contemporary warfare. First, Third World states have become better able to resist militarily the projection of great-power military force abroad. And second, most of the actual low-intensity conflicts throughout the world, such as civil wars, guerrilla wars, and terrorism, began to involve the great powers directly. This meant that use of conventional force became less appropriate with time and has had greater difficulty succeeding. This situation is not unique to the United States but confronts all conventionally oriented military forces (as illustrated by the Soviet experience in Afghanistan in the 1980s and 1990s and American support for the Afghan resistance fighters, the mujahadeen).

THE VIETNAM WAR   The United States first faced this new environment in Vietnam. Most American leaders, and the public, operated under the assumption that the projection of U.S. military force into Vietnam would quickly contain the enemy and stabilize the situation. Yet the United States and the U.S. military were poorly prepared for a war where there were no front lines, where distinguishing between friend and foe was nearly impossible, where a peasant by day could be a Viet Cong guerrilla by night, and where the enemy's will to resist was greater than the American will to win. Thus, a conventionally trained military of over 550,000 troops by 1966 was thrown into a most unconventional war. And the military and the United States suffered their first major defeat in war.

The **military lessons of Vietnam** have been hotly debated. *On Strategy* by Harry Summers (1982), a retired colonel in the U.S. Army, was the first major analysis of American's military experience in Vietnam to be well received within the military. Summers argued that the U.S. military mistakenly tried to adapt its strategy and tactics to fight a counterinsurgency war, when in fact the enemy by the mid-1960s was engaged predominantly in conventional combat. He argued that the United States should have allowed the Army of the Republic of Vietnam (ARVN) to pursue counterinsurgency in South Vietnam while the U.S. military formed a conventional front along the demilitarized zone between North and South Vietnam (the DMZ) and, by invading Laos, extend it across Laos to the Thai border to prevent North Vietnamese infiltration into South Vietnam (see **Map 6.1**).

According to critics, besides overlooking the difficulty of training the South Vietnamese Army in counterinsurgency warfare (for which the U.S. military was ill equipped) and the support provided by China and the Soviet Union, Summers misconstrued the nature of the Vietnam War. As Major Andrew Krepinevich (1986) argued in *The Army and Vietnam*, the enemy relied on an unconventional strategy until the latter years of the war. Despite tactical modifications, the U.S. military was ill-equipped and ill-trained for the war throughout both the "advisory" and intervention periods that lasted from 1954 to 1973. One quote by an Army general is particularly telling:

> General Williams agreed that "if you really want to be cost-effective, you have to fight the war the way the VC [Vietcong] fought it. You have to fight it down in the muck and in the mud and at night, and on a day-to-day basis." Yet, the general told the correspondent, "that's not the American way, and you are not going to get the American soldier to fight that way" (Krepinevich 1986:171; see also Shafer 1988).

In *The Limits of Air Power*, Mark Clodfelter (1989), an Air Force major, concluded that although the United States dropped more bombs in Indochina than all the allies dropped during World War II, the conventional use of air power failed to deter the enemy.

President Johnson made certain operations off-limits, such as attacking Cambodia, Laos, or North Vietnam, for fear of triggering the military intervention of the People's Republic of China (as occurred during the Korean War when American troops pushed up

Map 6.1   Vietnam War Map

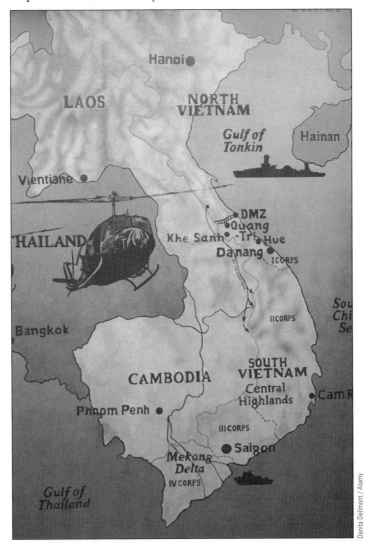

SOURCE: http://www.historyplace.com/unitedstates/
vietnam/vietnam-map.htm

the Korean Peninsula approaching the Chinese border). Although certain political restrictions have always been imposed by civilian leaders during war, actual military operations were conducted by the unified commands and the services. Thus, the basic tactical strategy of "search and destroy" (using mobility to transport and conentrate firepower to destroy the enemy) was selected by General William Westmoreland, the commander in chief of American forces in Vietnam (see Kinnard 1977).

AFTER VIETNAM TO THE 1980s The failure of the U.S. effort in Vietnam reinforced the bureaucratic structure and subculture of the military against unconventional warfare and in continuing support of the principle of concentration—to overwhelm the enemy with a quick delivery of massive firepower—along with a new interest in force mobility. Yet, military performance since Vietnam throughout the 1970s and 1980s has been often found lacking. As military strategist Edward Luttwak (1985:17) concluded in *The Pentagon and the Art of War*:

> Irrefutable facts overwhelm the patriotic impulse to overlook our failures in war— from Vietnam in its most varied and prolonged entirety; to the clumsy Mayaguez raid of 1975, in which forty-one died to save forty; to the Iran rescue attempt in 1980, which ended in bitter humiliation, with eight dead and none rescued; to the avoidable tragedy of Beirut, which took the lives of 241 Marines and other servicemen in October 1983; to the Grenada operation of the same month . . . ; to the Lebanon bombing raid of December 4, 1983, in which the Navy lost two costly aircraft.

Knowledge of the U.S. military's actual performance, however, largely has remained hidden from the American public, especially as a result of the Pentagon's effort to strengthen public support by controlling the information communicated through the media when American troops are engaged abroad. This was a major lesson the military learned from the Vietnam War—that the press contributed to the military's failure and needed to be controlled. A policy of media censorship by the government, in fact, has prevailed in war since the Grenada invasion, when President Reagan proclaimed it a great triumph. On the contrary, U.S. military incompetence after the Vietnam War reached its peak during the **Grenada invasion**, as described in **A Closer Look**, prompting military reforms such as the Goldwater-Nichols Act.

THE POST–GOLDWATER-NICHOLS MILITARY

The problems of military organization, military subculture, and military performance of the American way of war spurred debate on reform of the military and JCS, led by then JCS chairman General David Jones (1982). The debate and calls for reform were taken up by Congress and eventually resulted in the Goldwater-Nichols Act of 1986 (Roman and Tarr 1998).

The **Goldwater-Nichols Act** addressed three general issues within the military establishment:

1. strengthened the chair of the JCS (CJCS) as head of the military and advisor to the president,

2. clarified the military operational chain of command, and

3. made joint service of great significance.

Ultimately, the Goldwater-Nichols act had a major impact on the military and its role in U.S. foreign policy to the present day (Kitfield 1995; Locker 2002).

First, the act redefined the role of the CJCS, making him the sole advisor to the president and requiring him to inform the president only of dissenting service chief opinion. This removed the old corporate system of advisory consensus. The act also increased the power of the CJCS by providing him with a vice chair and a joint staff responsive to him, further solidifying his role as preeminent advisor to the president on military affairs. Second, the act clarified the operational chain of command of the regional commanders in chiefs and made them directly responsible to the secretary of defense and the president, removing service competition and duplication of effort in a theater of operation. Last, the act made joint service or "Joint Time" mandatory for all officers who wished to be promoted to general, thus removing any stigma associated with service on the Joint Staff. Officers now seek out Joint Staff service, with only the "best and the brightest" receiving such assignments, which mark them for continued service and potential to rise to the very top of the military hierarchy.

The Grenada Victory as Military Fiasco

What should have been a quick military advance and mopping-up exercise became an incredibly slow, cumbersome, and inefficient military operation. Consider the mission: to defeat a token force of 679 Cubans, most of whom were construction workers, and a few Grenadians on an island that was only 133 square miles (twice the size of the District of Columbia). Yet *Operation Urgent Fury* required three days and over 7,000 Marines, Army rangers, paratroopers, and independent commando teams from all the services to subdue the enemy and occupy the island—all for the official purpose of rescuing predominantly American medical students who were never in danger.

The problems were endless. First, intelligence was poor. The intelligence community did not know the number of enemy troops or how well they were equipped. When the military operations bogged down after the first day, estimates escalated to as high as several thousand Cuban troops. In fact, the military did not have maps of the island, requiring many of the invading troops to rely on tourist maps from Michelin during the three-day operation. And the invading troops were never briefed about a second medical school campus with American students.

Second, the command structure was inappropriate for the task. Although a land

operation, the military strategy was planned and commanded by naval officers for the simple reason that Grenada was geographically located within the boundaries of the Navy-dominated Atlantic Command headquartered in Norfolk, Virginia. Thus, the operational commander was a vice admiral on the aircraft carrier *Independence*, while there was never any agreement concerning the existence of a single commander for the ground forces and every service naturally had to play a role in the invasion.

Third, the military operations were slow and inefficient. The rangers (the Army's elite conventional troops) invaded from the north, while the Marines invaded from the south. Yet, advances were repeatedly stalled by sporadic enemy fire and inflated reports of enemy strength where rangers and Marines had to be reinforced by paratroopers from the Army's 82nd Airborne Division on the second and third days. A team of the Navy's elite troops, the SEALs, not only failed to rescue the governor-general of Grenada but became trapped with the governor and his family in the governor's residence. A secret Delta Force of elite army commandos failed in its mission to rescue political prisoners. Both the SEALs and the Delta Force eventually were rescued by the Marines.

Fourth, units from the various services had difficulty communicating with one

(Continued)

another. In one case, it was reported that a ranger unit was unable to call in an air strike to the Navy command. To overcome this obstacle an ingenious soldier slipped into a nearby phone booth and used his AT&T long-distance card to reach Fort Bragg, North Carolina, which relayed the request through the Pentagon to the *Independence* for the air strike.

In the end, U.S. forces suffered eighteen killed and 116 wounded (as opposed to twenty-five Cubans killed), many due to accidents and friendly fire. The operation was so slow in rescuing the 224 American medical students (which was the official justification for the invasion following a successful military coup) that many of them may have been placed at greater risk by the operation itself since they were completely at the mercy of the Cubans and Grenadians. However sloppy the operation, the Reagan administration's response was to issue over 1,600 medals for meritorious service and heroism, even though only 7,000 American troops set foot on the island and a much smaller number were actually involved in combat (see Adkin 1989; Ayres 1983b; Taylor 1983).

How do the reforms of Goldwater-Nichols make a military fiasco like Grenada less likely?

The powerful results of the changes in the CJCS's role were not initially apparent. Admiral William Crowe implemented the changes, focusing on gradually and quietly consolidating the power of the CJCS. It is said that Crowe planted the vineyard of the CJCS and **General Colin Powell** reaped the harvest of grapes (Roman and Tarr 1998). The appointment of Powell in 1989 increased the power of the JCS chair because of his considerable political skills in operating within the military and as a presidential advisor. This has made the presidential appointment of the CJCS even more important and "politicized." In fact, a trend has begun to develop wherein the appointment of a chair to the JCS increasingly represents the presidential desires of the time (rather than seniority and JCS successor norms).

At the operational level, the services used to dominate military operations through the so-called unified commands. Unified commands contain forces from two or more services (the Navy and Marine Corps are considered within the same department) and are regional or functional in orientation. However, the new unified **Combatant Commander (COCOM;** formerly called commander in chiefs, CINCs) is no longer responsible to the head of his service (such as the Army chief of staff or the chief of naval operations). Goldwater-Nichols changed the operational chain of command so that the COCOM reports directly to the secretary of defense and the president, usually through the chair of the JCS. This has not only increased the power of the civilians and the CJCS but has made each COCOM extremely powerful.

During a time of mobilization or war, the relevant COCOM now has the authority and power to call up and deploy forces from the different services. Journalist Dana Priest (2002, 2003) has described the COCOMs as the "modern-day equivalent of the Roman Empire's proconsuls," exerting more influence than most civilian diplomats and extremely "well-funded, semiautonomous centers of U.S. foreign policy." In conducting military operations, the world is divided up into six major regions and four major functional areas, each led by a COCOM (see **Table 6.1** for an overview of the unified commands and how the military geographically divides the world).

Table 6.1 The Military's Unified Command Structure

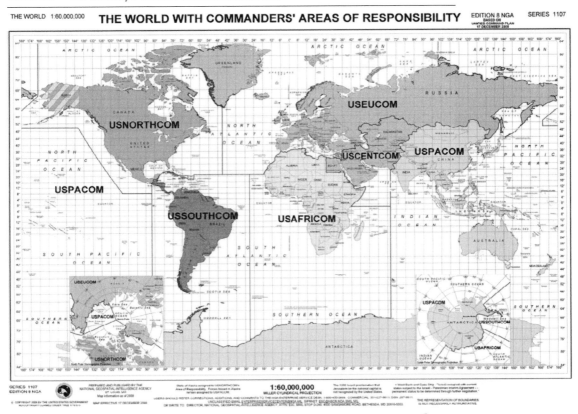

THE WORLD 1:60,000,000 **THE WORLD WITH COMMANDERS' AREAS OF RESPONSIBILITY** EDITION 8 NGA SERIES 1107

Commands	Area of Responsibility	Traditional Combat Commander
Regional		
Africa Command (AFRICOM)	African continent with the exception of Egypt	Army general
European Command (EUCOM)	Europe and Israel	Army or Air Force general
Pacific Command (PACOM)	The Pacific, Asia, and the Indian Ocean	Navy admiral
Central Command (CENTCOM)	Mideast and Egypt	Army or Marine general
Southern Command (SOUTHCOM)	Central and South America	Army general
Northern Command (NORTHCOM)	North America, the Caribbean, and coastal waters	Marine general or Navy admiral
Functional		
Strategic Command (STRATCOM)	Nuclear Forces, Space Operations, and Satellites	Air Force general
Transportation Command (TRANSCOM)	Movement of forces and material	Air Force general
Special Operations Command (SOCOM)	Special-purpose forces of all services	Army general
Joint Forces Command (JFCOM)	Force provider to the CINCs to fulfill future Joint Vision 2020	Army general

SOURCE: U.S. Department of Defense.

Although the rivalry between and within the services continues since the Goldwater-Nichols Act, there has developed a new military emphasis on "**jointness.**" This is especially the case at the operational level, with stronger unified commands and a stronger chair of the JCS providing military advice. The military subculture also is incorporating more of a joint orientation, especially at the more senior levels. All senior officers are now expected to complete at least two years of "Joint Duty," those who get the opportunity attend a war college of another service, and the joint staff of the JCS is now considered a significant duty and an important stepping-stone to career advancement.

Three questions about the impact of Goldwater-Nichols on the military warrant our attention:

1. whether the organizational reality, although still incredibly complex, has become more efficient and effective,

2. whether the value of military advice, despite problems with the military subculture and civil-military relations, may have increased in importance, and

3. whether and to what extent the U.S. military is better able to operate in low-intensity conflicts, given the American way of war.

A More Efficient But Incredibly Complex Organizational Process?

The DOD has become such an enormous, complex, and confusing enterprise that probably no one really understands how the entire process operates. Nevertheless, it is possible to identify general patterns of behavior within DOD. Rather than a simple top-down, centralized civilian-controlled process, *the workings of the DOD can be better understood if seen as three independent but overlapping systems or processes:* administration (involving the military's basic infrastructure), operations and military conduct on the ground (the meat of the military), and advice about the use of force (which will be discussed in the next subsection). This simplifies the complex policy process within the department yet provides a means for making sense of the basic operating patterns and understanding the implications for presidential governance of foreign policy (see Figure 6.1 again).

The least exciting but very important process within the DOD is the "administrative process." This involves day-to-day management of the military and remains pretty much controlled by the individual services. Personnel decisions about recruiting, training, tours (including joint tours of duty), and promotion are individual service affairs, as are the daily routines and activities concerning health, schooling, provisions, recreation, security, and so on. Requests for weaponry are also heavily influenced within each of the services, ultimately through the chief of staff and the JCS.

The "operational" process includes the military strategy and tactics employed by the armed forces and involves both the individual services, the OSD, and since the Goldwater-Nichols Act, the CJCS and the relevant combat commander. The secretary of defense and OSD clearly have their greatest independent impact, when they have any impact at all, at the "strategic level." A president through OSD may be able to affect war preparations, national military strategy, and overall force structure (and the development of large weapons systems), depending on the level of interest and attention displayed by the president, the secretary of defense, the secretary's immediate subordinates (as well as their working relationship with the JCS, especially the chair), and, naturally, Congress.

At the tactical level, the president usually has little control over the existing command structure and set of bureaucratic standard operating procedures for operations and military conduct on the ground. Since Goldwater-Nichols, usually the regional combat commander is the main military official responsible for employing the forces of the different services and has considerable leeway in doing so through use of his subordinate officers. A president, through the secretary of defense and OSD and the advice of the chair of the JCS, may be able to fine-tune specific military tactics, but more than this is usually beyond his competence and control.

The Value of Military Advice?

What about the value of military advice to go to war? Many Americans do not realize that since the Korean War the civilian leadership, including the secretary of defense and the president, have often been skeptical of military advice. The president is the commander in chief and determines when and where to use armed force abroad. Most presidents rely on their most trusted foreign policy advisors, including the national security advisor and secretary of defense, when it comes to such important decisions. Since Goldwater-Nichols and the increased prominence of the CJCS and the relevant COCOM, the credibility of military advice appears to have improved under presidents Reagan, the elder Bush, and Clinton. As we discuss later in this chapter, military-civil advisory relations became more problematic and tense during the younger Bush and Obama administrations.

The conventional stereotype (especially in movies) portrays the military as always recommending the use of force to deal with international crises. In fact, studies of military advice during crises suggest that the military tends to be reluctant to initiate the use of force. In *Soldiers, Statesmen, and Cold War Crises*, Richard Betts (1977) found the Army to be the most cautious in recommending force (since it takes the brunt of the casualties), while the Air Force tends to be most optimistic about force, especially the use of air power. He also found that the military has its greatest impact on civilian leadership when military advice "opposes" the use of force (since this is the unexpected position), while it is least credible when it recommends force. The military may be eager to expand its capabilities through more sophisticated weaponry and more personnel, but it tends to be reluctant to put them at risk. However, once a decision to use force has been made, the military aggressively argues that civilians should stand aside and allow the military to do whatever is necessary to succeed, which may require escalation.

Through most of the cold war years, in fact, civilians tended to be much more "hardline" and quicker to recommend force to impress military leaders, as occurred during and since the Vietnam War (see Halberstam 1969). During the Reagan administration, Secretary of State Alexander Haig and then George Shultz were the major advocates of military force, while Secretary of Defense Caspar Weinberger, representing the military, was reluctant to use force unless it had the full support of the American public. Likewise, President George H. W. Bush and National Security Advisor Brent Scowcroft were the most vehement in support of a major military response to the Iraqi invasion of Kuwait and the need to take Saddam Hussein to the brink of war to compel his withdrawal, while Secretary of State James Baker and CJCS Colin Powell were much more cautious, preferring economic sanctions over force. A similar situation arose between military and civilian leaders (such as Secretary of State Madeline Albright) over Bosnia and Kosovo during the Clinton administration (see Halberstam 2001; Woodward 1991). Clearly, one of the major lessons learned by the military from the Vietnam War, especially within the Army, was to avoid the use of troops unless overwhelming force will be used and there is strong and visible public backing.

Military failures in Vietnam, Beirut, and Grenada led to what is commonly referred to as the **Weinberger-Powell Doctrine**, which became the popular military paradigm until September 11, 2001. The keys to this doctrine were spelled out first by Secretary of Defense Caspar Weinberger in Washington, D.C., on November 28, 1984, at an address to the Washington Press Club in which he *defined six criteria for the use of force:* (1) The United States should not commit forces to combat overseas unless the particular engagement or occasion is deemed vital to its national interests or its allies' interests, and the conflict should be declared before the United States takes action; (2) once ground troops are committed, they should be supported wholeheartedly; (3) if the United States decides to commit forces overseas, it should have clearly defined political and military objectives; (4) the relationship between U.S. objectives and the forces committed must be continually reassessed and adjusted if necessary; (5) before the United States commits forces to combat abroad, support must be assured by the American people and Congress; and (6) the commitment of U.S. forces should be a last resort. These criteria were aimed at defining the role of the U.S. military in the future to ensure another Vietnam did not occur.

Some took these criteria as a checklist for deciding whether to commit forces to combat. In 1992, then-CJCS Colin Powell, wrote an article in *Foreign Affairs* titled "U.S. Forces and the Challenges Ahead" in which he redefined the checklist approach to committing U.S. troops, citing the success of U.S. forces in Panama and the Gulf War, which were tailored in both cases to meet the threats presented. He highlighted that Weinberger's six points be used only as a guide to the commitment of troops. Overall, he espoused the use of decisive force to overcome a threat, clearly defined rules of engagement (ROE), and an exit strategy to avoid mission creep (i.e., the adding of extra tasks and goals), and excessive casualties. In short, the military should not be placed in a situation where it cannot utilize overwhelming force, win, and come home swiftly with strong public support (see also Halberstam 2001).

Overall, the president is faced with certain limitations in his choices regarding the use of force. First, given the American way of war, the president has limited viable military options from which to choose: principally some type of nuclear strike or conventional strike in a world where nuclear war has been avoided and major conventional battles appear to be relatively infrequent. As Eliot Cohen (1984:165) concluded, "The most substantial constraints on America's ability to conduct small wars result from the resistance of the American defense establishment to the very notion of engaging in such conflicts, and from the unsuitability of that establishment for fighting such wars."

In addition, presidents have to be much more cautious than they were during the cold war because of the breakdown of consensus and the fact that Americans have high expectations for quick success. It is important to remember that the country was significantly divided when President George H. W. Bush took it to war in the Persian Gulf on January 17, 1991, and President Clinton exercised prerogative government as commander in chief to launch a war in Kosovo that was a low priority in the minds of most Americans. Although quickly forgotten in victory, at the time these were difficult and politically risky decisions made by presidents concerning the use of force, and there were no guarantees of military success with minimal American casualties. Both wars highly exceeded expectations (among the leadership of the military as well as civilian military strategists) despite their conventional nature, and both were quick success stories with very few American casualties.

In sum, decisions to use American armed forces are dominated by the civilian leadership, while decisions concerning administration and basic military operations of the armed forces tend to be made within the military. In other words, presidents can begin and end wars, but the military fights them. This is the kind of division of labor that is preferred by most within the military but that often frustrates presidents who want to control and govern U.S. foreign policy.

The American Way of War, Low-Intensity Conflict, and Unconventional Warfare?

Goldwater-Nichols has had a major impact on the military's conduct, helping to alleviate (but not eliminate) coordination, information, and duplication problems that have made the military more successful during the use of force and troops. The U.S. military has experienced important military successes in Panama, the Gulf War, and Kosovo, certain problems notwithstanding.

The December 1989 invasion of Panama was successful in overthrowing General Manuel Noriega—perhaps an exceptional case given its location and unique history. Much of this was due to the fact that, as the *New York Times* reported, "the main part of the Panama attack was a virtual replay of a World War II battle, with paratroops dropping from the sky and tanks blasting through a city to overwhelm the opposition" (Trainor 1989:1). The victory came at the cost of twenty-five American soldiers killed and hundreds wounded (many due to friendly fire); thousands of Panamanian civilian casualties (and displaced persons) through indiscriminate bombing and shelling; the maintenance of a large U.S. military occupation force; the provision of millions of dollars in reconstruction aid to the new government, which quickly resorted to old, corrupt ways; and widespread global condemnation for American gunboat diplomacy, especially given its twelve previous invasions of Panama.

The **Persian Gulf War** was a tremendous military success that also used a major military innovation. The Army adopted the "air-land battle doctrine," which emphasized mobility and flexibility in the concentration and application of firepower on the ground with the support of the other services in the air to attack the enemy where they might be most vulnerable. This stunning success in light of past performances raises the question: Why did the U.S. military perform so successfully in the Persian Gulf War? Principally because this was the kind of conventional war (or battle) that the U.S. military is best trained and equipped to fight. According to military strategist Eliot Cohen (1991:22), "the United States fought in a theater ideally suited to our military strengths, an empty desert. . . . We had half a year to mass and train troops, and to prepare elaborate plans to attack. . . . We also had the luxury of one of the best port, road, and air base networks in the world, including military facilities built by our engineers, and the support of a wealthy and cooperative host nation [that is, Saudi Arabia]." Also, with Iraq facing global economic sanctions, the United States "could bring to bear the weight of our cold war–rich armed forces without fear of Soviet opposition in the theater or aggression elsewhere." The Persian Gulf War, in other words, represented a classic conventional confrontation. President Bush decided to halt the war short of a full-scale invasion and occupation of Iraq.

The successful Kosovo War under President Clinton had many similarities. Although the physical environment of the former Yugoslavia was not nearly as ideal as the desert, Serbia was a weaker (and more overextended) conventional military adversary than Iraq. Regardless, the American-led NATO attack and massive bombing of Kosovo and Serbia, reinforced by the threat of a ground invasion, were very successful in persuading Serbia's leadership to capitulate and withdraw its forces within weeks. What makes this victory particularly unique was that it was accomplished purely through an air war without the use of any ground troops—a military first. This raises questions that go back decades, and which have been mulled over for years by military strategists, about the superiority of air power and whether advances in technology are sufficient to win wars.

In responding to the challenges of the 1990s and the new century, the military also has placed a somewhat greater emphasis on money, resources, personnel, and training for "unconventional war," low-intensity conflict (or small wars). Such operations focus on less conventional military/civilian operations that developed in the 1990s, such as humanitarian, peacekeeping, peace enforcement missions, and nation-building, which have increased since the end of the cold war (at home, this might include disaster relief activities such as after Hurricane Katrina in 2005).

Although there has been little official specification within the U.S. military's overall strategic doctrine, its training and education, and its specific manuals on operational conduct (until the Iraq War), the American soldier and commander are often able to improvise. At the same time, it's one thing to be involved in relatively small or specific missions of this kind, including postwar reconstruction in Kosovo (along with a large multilateral presence of NATO countries and international organizations). It is another thing to be ill-prepared for major stability and reconstruction operations after a major war in such a large theater as Iraq, especially with few allies and little international support.

THE MILITARY SINCE 9/11 AND THE IRAQ AND AFGHAN WARS

Since September 11, 2001, the U.S. military has been involved in two major military wars in Afghanistan and Iraq. Like the Vietnam War, the Iraq and Afghan Wars have raised numerous issues for the military and DOD, including:

1. the nature and effectiveness of the civilian leadership of Secretary of Defense Donald Rumsfeld and President George W. Bush given the failure of postwar reconstruction in Iraq,

2. military strategy and its role in decisionmaking under President Obama given the expansion of the Afghan War, and

3. the future of the military and hard power.

Rummy, Military Transformation, and the Success and Unraveling of the Iraq War

According to most observers and analysts, under President George W. Bush, **Donald Rumsfeld** became the most powerful (and controversial) secretary of defense since Robert McNamara, and probably since the creation of the National Security Act of 1947 and the creation of the modern DOD. Defense Secretary Rumsfeld attempted to make major and controversial changes in promoting a smaller, more mobile, and more technologically advanced conventional military force structure, strategy, and tactics, which triggered considerable military resentment. After 9/11, the civilian leadership, especially President Bush and Secretary of Defense Rumsfeld (and Vice President Cheney), was the most vocal for a quick military response and unhappy with the initial war plans for Afghanistan and Iraq provided by the military. Their persistence and decisions contributed to the initial success of the Afghanistan and Iraq Wars, as well as their unraveling, with important military implications.

Rumsfeld became powerful for a variety of different reasons. First, Rumsfeld had over three decades of experience as a prominent Washington insider, occupying important positions of power within Republican administrations going back to President Nixon. Second, Rumsfeld had a very strong and domineering personality, along with being a tough "hands-on" manager and a fierce bureaucratic infighter. Third, Rumsfeld was loyal to President Bush and had strong support of the president until 2006. Fourth, Rumsfeld had very strong and forceful officials within the OSD, most notably Deputy Secretary of Defense Paul Wolfowitz and Undersecretary of Defense Douglas Feith. Fifth, Rumsfeld also had very strong relationships with other prominent members of the administration, most notably Vice President Richard Cheney (who was selected by Rumsfeld as his Deputy Chief of Staff under President Ford over thirty years ago). Sixth, Rumsfeld became secretary of defense at a time when the chair of the JCS was not as strong or visible as it was under CJCS Crowe and Powell. Finally, Condoleezza Rice, Bush's first-term national security advisor, was not a strong manager of the national security process, allowing power vacuums to occur. This reinforced President Bush's tendency to delegate important responsibilities to key individuals and organizations outside the White House, often to the advantage of Rumsfeld and DOD (see Mann 2004; Packer 2005; Woodward 2002, 2004).

Although a cold warrior and believer in the use of power, Donald Rumsfeld began his tenure as secretary of defense with one major goal in mind: the need to transform the U.S. military into a leaner, swifter, high-tech, more effective fighting force. The ideas behind the need for **military transformation** had been around for years, both within the military and especially among civilians. Despite considerable military resistance, Rumsfeld was convinced that there should be much greater emphasis on newer military technologies, smaller numbers of "boots (troops) on the ground," precision bombing and the use of special forces, and "command and control" in linking combat operations together as a unified whole. This would allow for smaller and faster military strikes, throwing the enemy off balance, and ultimately resulting in greater military success—with fewer American casualties (see Boot 2003; Kaplan 2005).

The terrorist attacks of September 11, 2001 changed Secretary of Defense Rumsfeld's strategy. Rather than focusing on trying to alter and transform the organizational structures and subcultures within the military in accordance with this vision (in the face of tremendous institutional resistance), Rumsfeld and his DOD team had to conduct a global war on terrorism. This meant that Rumsfeld's focus would be to attempt to transform actual combat operations, which historically had been dominated either by the different military services or, after Goldwater-Nichols, by the combat commander(s) and the chair of the JCS. And in some ways Rumsfeld was successful given the swift military victories in Afghanistan and Iraq. However, the initial military success of the wars in Afghanistan and, especially, Iraq was not followed by relative peace, stability, and reconstruction in either of the countries—becoming the major challenges of President Bush and his war presidency (see Biddle 2003; Boot 2005).

In sum, the Bush administration, the White House, the president's national security team, and, in particular, the OSD led by Donald Rumsfeld have been relatively successful in the "short term" in imposing civilian control over the military. However, *such strong civilian control may have hampered the outcome of the Iraq and Afghan Wars in the long run in a variety of ways.*

First, Rumsfeld, with the support of the president, opposed the initial Iraqi war plan by CENTCOM, calling for roughly 400,000 troops (for the war and especially for postwar reconstruction) and consistently streamlined and trimmed the invasion plan to around 160,000 troops (predominantly U.S. and a few thousand British as part of the "coalition of the willing"), with a heavy reliance on speed and special forces consistent with his vision of military transformation. Second, the president and the national security advisor delegated the "postreconstruction" Phase IV stage of the war outside the supervision of the White House and the NSC, giving OSD and Secretary of Defense Rumsfeld the authority and responsibility. Amazingly, Rumsfeld, Deputy Secretary Wolfowitz, and Undersecretary Douglas Feith (who was put in charge of DOD postwar reconstruction) had incredibly optimistic assumptions about how the Americans would be treated as liberators; that stability, security, and the day-to-day infrastructure (such as electricity) would be easily restored; and that an Iraqi national government could quickly be formed and gain political control (comprised predominantly of exiled elites led by Ahmed Chalabi and the Iraqi National Congress—who were flown into Iraq by the military shortly after the invasion but received a poor reception among Iraqis). In other words, beyond assuming that there was no real need for postwar reconstruction planning, the final invasion plan also assumed that almost all American troops could return home within three months after the end of the actual (Phase III) war. In fact, much of the bureaucracy had extensive reconstruction plans prepared based on much more pessimistic assumptions about postwar security and stability that were all ignored by Rumsfeld and his OSD team, with the support of the White House (Fallows 2004; further discussed in Chapter 9 on the overall policymaking process).

Third, there was much confusion between the civilians (especially at OSD) in Washington, D.C., the military on the ground within CENTCOM, and the civilians on the ground in the Civil Provisional Authority (CPA)—the initial governing body responsible for reconstruction and the transfer of power to a new Iraqi government (in which CPA would then revert to the American embassy in Iraq). Under the leadership of Paul Bremer, a foreign service officer in the Department of State, CPA made numerous decisions that inadvertently contributed to the rise of the insurgency (such as the decision to disband the Iraqi army completely as opposed to only its leadership). This was reinforced by the relative isolation of the CPA within the so-called Green Zone (a relatively secure area in Baghdad that was formerly the seat of the Hussein regime) in which the soldiers who fought throughout Iraq often referred to CPA as "Can't Provide Anything" (Hammer 2004; Packer 2005) (see **Map 6.2** showing Iraq).

Finally, with the insurgency steadily increasing in attacks and the general situation in Iraq steadily deteriorating, by 2004 the military found itself increasingly fighting a guerilla war. The military attempted to fight and adapt as best it could to its changing political-military environment, but the troops had little knowledge of the culture, the language, and almost no intelligence about the insurgency. This led to a number of controversial decisions in Washington, D.C. and in Iraq, where large numbers of Iraqis were detained, imprisoned, and, to the world's disbelief, tortured by American military troops and intelligence personnel in order to gain desperately needed intelligence (best illustrated by the photographs and stories of Abuh Ghraib prison, Saddam's Hussein's favorite prison and torture chamber). Such decisions on enemy combatants, prisoners, interrogation techniques, and ultimately torture were made and approved at the highest level within the Bush administration, especially within the Office of Secretary of Defense and by Secretary of Defense Rumsfeld (Hersh 2004; more about this in Chapter 7, on intelligence).

In sum, President George H. W. Bush tried to heal the powerful legacy and wounds of the Vietnam War in the 1991 Persian Gulf War involving Iraq. In contrast, many of the decisions by the administration of President George W. Bush and by Secretary of Defense Rumsfeld, with the support of almost all major foreign policy advisors, resulted

Map 6.2   Iraq

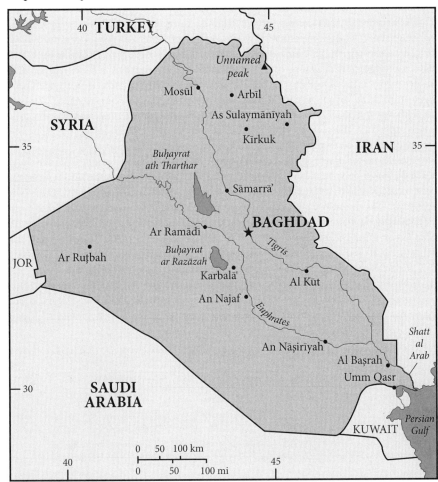

in an unanticipated second war with Iraq as part of the war on terrorism that led to a major political backlash (against the president's public prestige in general) and a semi-military revolt against Rumsfeld's civilian leadership. They also led to a de-emphasis on the war in Afghanistan, which began to unravel in the second Bush term. Despite President George W. Bush's decision and the relative success of the so-called "surge" beginning in 2007, the American public and political system turned against the Iraq War (see Ricks 2009).

Obama's Wars and U.S. Military Withdrawal

The Obama administration retained Robert Gates (after Rumsfeld resigned in 2006) as secretary of defense for its first two years in an effort to reinvigorate and promote reform within the military at home and abroad. Yet, the administration inherited a hornet's nest. With respect to Iraq, in accordance with his campaign pledge, the strategy was to increasingly turn over the war to the Iraqis with the number of American troops steadily declining with the hope that sufficient stability could be maintained throughout Iraq—a type of "Iraqification" similar to "Vietnamization" over a generation ago. President Obama officially declared that U.S. combat troops were completely withdrawn in 2011 (despite leaving thousands of so-called military advisors to the present day).

The "long war" in Afghanistan also deteriorated since the successful invasion with the resurgence of the Taliban compounded by the decline of American public support. Nevertheless, consistent with his campaign statements, early in his administration President Obama made important decisions to escalate the American presence in both Afghanistan and an increasingly unstable Pakistan in the continuing war on terrorism. With the growing "Americanization" of the war in Afghanistan (more U.S. troops alongside NATO forces, and increased numbers of civilian embassy personnel and contractors, making the total "footprint" approach the scale of U.S. involvement in the Iraq War), it became "Obama's War" (see **Figure 6.2** on Boots on the Ground in Afghanistan and Iraq).

Despite the media coverage and public perception of a cordial and collegial inner circle, tensions and conflict grew between the Pentagon (Secretary Gates; General David Petraeus, the Combat Commander for CENTCOM; and CJCS Admiral Mike Mullen) and the White House staff, especially over the escalation decisions for the AfPak (Afghanistan-Pakistan) War. An important geo-strategic interest in the aftermath of the September 11, 2001 terrorist attacks, Afghanistan has long been a "graveyard" for great powers throughout its long history. Its outcome is significant for the region, the present and future administrations, and the military (see **Map 6.3** on Afghanistan, its provinces and major cities, its terrain, and neighboring countries).

In March 2009, President Obama approved a Pentagon request for an additional 30,000 troops that President Bush deferred to his successor. At the time, Obama relied heavily on the judgment of Mullins and especially Gates (supported by Secretary Clinton),

Figure 6.2   Boots on the Ground in Afghanistan and Iraq

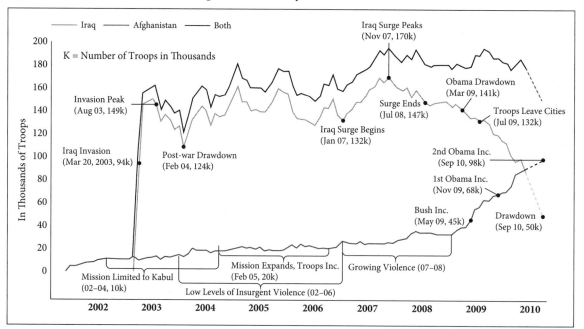

SOURCE: U.S. Congressional Research Service, *The Cost of Iraq, Afghanistan, and Other Global War on Terror Operations Since 9/11* (www.crs.gov: March 29, 2011), p. 12.

Map 6.3 Map of Afghanistan with its Neighboring Countries

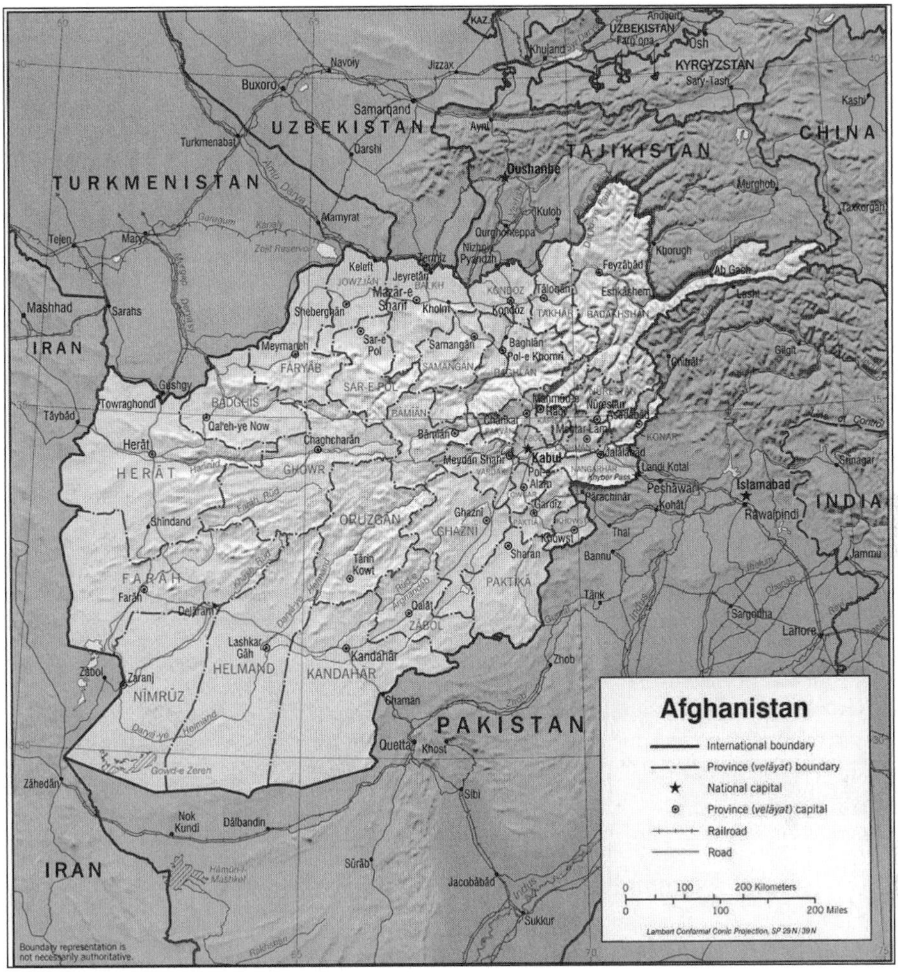

SOURCE: University of Texas Libraries.

in part because of his lack of knowledge about national security and because he was preoccupied with the state of the economy.

Five months later Gates, Mullen, and Petraeus came back with a request for an additional 40,000 troops and the implementation of a full spectrum "counterinsurgency" strategy with the **McChrystal Report** (the U.S. Commander in Afghanistan). President Obama and his White House staff felt "blindsided" and "boxed in" by the Pentagon's second large, request before the previous decision was implemented and reviewed.

Limited by the McChrystal Report, President Obama's involvement and deliberative style did not produce the variety of information and policy options that he coveted among members of his national security inner circle. The president, who often acted as his own national security advisor most of the time because of his growing frustration with National Security Advisor James Jones (see Chapter 4), may have been too proactive given his inexperience. He allowed the Pentagon to be unresponsive and to circumvent the civilian-led process, which may have contributed to final group unanimity very similar to General McCrystal's recommendations despite policy differences.

Obama's deliberative process reflected significant policy disagreements. Vice President Joe Biden and the White House staff were the major proponents of limited escalation and a counter-terrorism strategy focusing on Al Qaeda, while the Pentagon argued for 40,000 more troops and a strategy of counterinsurgency. According to some, The behavior and action of the major civilian and military players within DOD, especially Gates, Petraeus, and Mullin, approached insubordination against a president who was unable to manage his own White House staff, let alone the entire NSC process (see Alter 2010; Crowley 2009; Hastings, 2010; Kaplan 2010; Kornblut, Wilson and DeYoung 2009; Woodward 2010).

The four-month decision process produced a compromise decision (that the Pentagon could happily live with) announced at West Point in December 2009: a "surge" of 40,000 troops and a hybrid "counterinsurgency" strategy (based on "clear, hold and transfer") — along with a more "covert counter-terrorism" plan to go after the Taliban and al-Qaeda that was not made public by the president. The compromise behind the surge was to bolster the Afghan government and the training of the Afghan military/police, rather than to defeat the Taliban (see **A Different Perspective** on counterinsurgency).

After three more years of fighting and after a two-day summit in Chicago attended by leaders of over 50 countries, including 28 NATO countries and the presidents of Afghanistan and Pakistan (but not the Taliban or other so-called enemy forces), a final communiqué was agreed to on May 21, 2012, in which the U.S.-NATO alliance would hand over command of all combat missions to Afghan forces by the middle of 2013; withdraw most of the over 130,000 foreign troops by the end of 2014; and continue to advise, train, and assist Afghan forces beyond 2014. As in Iraq, a surge followed by eventual withdrawal of foreign

---

Role of Asymmetrical Warfare and Counterinsurgency (COIN)

A **counterinsurgency (or COIN)** strategy has been very controversial within the military, especially within the Army and the Marines. The unconventional warfare in Iraq, Afghanistan, and Pakistan would seem to be the kind of war for which much of the conventionally trained U.S. military is still unprepared to fight—and yet the kind of warfare that it may have to wage for the immediate future. In fact, despite its reluctance, the U.S. military has always fought "small wars," that is, unconventional forms of warfare that have, in recent history, gone by such names as "counterinsurgencies," "low-intensity conflicts," "stability and reconstruction operations" (SRO), and **asymmetrical warfare**.

As the military effort in Iraq deteriorated, a network of individuals within the Army (sometimes labeled "COINdinistas") gained in credibility and produced the first *Counterinsurgency Field Manual* in 2006 since the Vietnam War. And they began to implement it, first in Iraq in 2007 with the surge and then in Afghanistan by the summer of 2009, with General Petraeus playing a critical role in each stage. Counterinsurgency emphasizes not the killing of the enemy, but the protection of the population and promotion of a stable, legitimate government. A table is provided within the manual that summarizes the Dos and Don'ts of the doctrine for both officers and troops (see **Table 6.2**).

The effectiveness of such operations should not be underestimated given the military's long history, their increased involvement (however improvised) in such missions overseas in the last two decades, and the increased training in response to mission-specific scenarios—all of which better prepares military operational execution abroad. Such unconventional operations are being integrated within U.S. national military strategy and doctrine, as well as military education and training. However, much will depend on the outcome of the Iraq and Afghan wars (see Cordesman 2012; Davidson 2010; Hastings 2011; Kilcullen 2009; U.S., Department of the Army 2006).

To what extent should the U.S. military be oriented to fight three types of wars—nuclear, conventional, and asymmetrical?

Table 6.2   Successful and Unsuccessful Counterinsurgency Operational Practices

Successful Practices	*Unsuccessful Practices*
• Emphasize intelligence.	• Overemphasize killing and capturing the enemy rather than securing and engaging the populace.
• Focus on the population, its needs, and its security.	• Conduct large-scale operations as the norm.
• Establish and expand secure areas.	• Concentrate military forces in large bases for protection.
• Isolate insurgents from the populace (population control).	• Focus special forces primarily on raiding.
• Conduct effective, prevasive, and continuous information operations.	• Place low priority on assigning quality advisors to host-nation forces.
• Provide amnesty and rehabilitation for those willing to support the new government.	• Build and train host-nation security forces in the U.S. military's image.
• Place host-nation police in the lead with military support as soon as the security situation permits.	• Ignore peacetime government processes, including legal procedures.
• Expand and diversity the host-nation police force.	• Allow open borders, airspace, and coastlines.
• Train military forces to conduct counterinsurgency operations.	
• Embed quality advisors and special forces with host-nation forces.	
• Deny sanctuary to insurgents.	
• Encourage strong political and military cooperation and information sharing.	
• Secure host-nation borders.	
• Protect key infrastructure.	

SOURCE: U.S., Department of the Army, *Counterinsurgency* Field Manual 3-24 (December 2006), page 1–29.

combat troops would hopefully lead to a more stable and legitimate Afghanistan—a type of "Afghanistanization."

The Future of the Military and Hard Power

Despite the end of the cold war and because of the 9/11 attacks, the military has become more active in a variety of missions and has seen its budget increase substantially. As Dana Priest (2003:11) argues in *The Mission*, "U.S. leaders have been turning more and more to the military to solve problems that are often, at their root, political and economic. This has become the U.S. military's mission and it has been going on for more than a decade without much public discussion or debate." The Iraq and Afghan wars have put the future role of the military on the public agenda that Obama and future administrations must deal with, including: (1) recruitment and the rise of a diverse, all-volunteer military; (2) leadership and morale; and (3) how much is enough?

RECRUITMENT AND A DIVERSE, ALL-VOLUNTEER MILITARY The peacetime draft was abolished in 1973 in reaction to the Vietnam War, and polls indicate that most Americans (especially young Americans) remain strongly opposed to a draft. However, the all-volunteer force presents new problems for the U.S. military and its foreign policy. The armed services, particularly the Army, has had difficulty recruiting sufficient numbers of skilled individuals, especially if it is highly likely that one will go to war. This tends to be less of a problem when unemployment increases because the services become a more attractive option for the unemployed (see Korb 2004). Both presidents Clinton and Obama have raised the possibility of having all Americans provide some type of "national service" to their country in either a military or civilian capacity (but this idea has not gained much political support).

This raises another concern about the overall "diversity" and "representativeness" of the military in a democratic society. The last few decades have witnessed a considerable change in the demographic makeup of the U.S. military: "Once peopled mostly by young, unmarried, white males, today's armed forces are composed of unprecedented proportions of minorities, women, married couples, and single parents and are dependent more than ever before on part-time reservists" (Binkin 1991:7; see also Butler 1996; Shilts 1993; Vistica 1996). Such changes parallel changes within American society, but special problems may exist, given the military subculture and the unique function of the military to engage in war, given issues of class, race, gender, sexual harassment, gays in the military, and so on. This also raises the question about the fairness of a situation in which the least advantaged bear the burden of defending all Americans, as well as important public policy decisions about defense spending and military force that are increasingly made and influenced by civilian leaders and a public with little experience and knowledge of the military. This is a position tackled head-on in a provocative book by Andrew Bacevich (2005) entitled *The New Militarism: How Americans Are Seduced by War*.

LEADERSHIP AND MORALE As the military has become increasingly bureaucratic and managerial, strong leadership, especially on the battlefield, and the morale of the combat soldier have suffered. This was particularly an issue with the Vietnam War: there were no homecoming parades, and Vietnam veterans had to deal on their own with the war and personal problems they might have developed (see MacPherson 1984; Severo and Milford 1989). The completion of the **Vietnam War Memorial** in Washington, D.C. helped to heal many of these wounds of war.

Unfortunately, the Iraq and Afghanistan wars have once again raised issues about military leadership and soldier morale, especially in the Army and the Marines since they are doing the brunt of the fighting, and many soldiers have had their "tours of duty" in Iraq extended time and time again (whether in the active military, reserve, or National Guard). Although physical casualties have declined in Iraq, **posttraumatic stress disorder (PTSD)** and other psychological casualties have increased tremendously compared to Vietnam — it may be as high as one out of every three who served in the Iraq and Afghan Wars (Friedman 2004). Therefore, the conduct of the military and the lack of operational success in the Iraq and Afghanistan wars have opened old wounds and renewed questions about morale, leadership, and all the issues raised here, especially, how much is enough?

HOW MUCH IS ENOUGH AND FOR WHAT? What type of military establishment should the United States have for the twenty-first century: *How much is enough and for what purposes?* The U.S. DOD budget now exceeds $700 billion (and this excludes military spending for such departments as Energy, the Coast Guard, NASA, and the Veterans Administration) and has been increasing at a time when no major adversary such as the Soviet Union exists. To place this in comparative context, the U.S. government accounts for about half of the world's military expenditures (see **Figure 6.3** for comparative defense statistics). Members of NATO, including the United States, account for almost 80 percent of the world's military expenditures, while China spends about 10 percent. And then there are traditional U.S. allies that are not part of NATO—such as Japan, Taiwan, South Korea, and Australia. Throwing money to the military to address the complexity of the post–cold war environment and the war on terrorism appears to be a major part of U.S. foreign policy. But how much is enough?

Then there is the question of *how much is enough in terms of military personnel* in a post–cold war and post–September 11 environment? Many argue that the military does not have sufficient manpower to perform all these missions and that constant activation has hurt military readiness. There are currently around 1.4 million active full-time soldiers. What is less well known is that since the Persian Gulf War the reserves and the National Guard have constantly been activated and engaged in a variety of military missions abroad. Unlike the Vietnam War, joining the reserves and National Guard is no longer a way to avoid the active military; they are an integral part of the overall military that is on constant call and is regularly activated as is commonly the case in Afghanistan and Iraq (and at a lower cost, since reserve and Guard members are employed only part-time until activated). Currently, there are also almost 400,000 personnel in the reserves and almost 500,000 in the National Guard. Together, the active military, the reserves, and the National Guard comprise the **Total Force Structure** of over 2.2 million (see **Table 6.3**). And this does not include the increasing use of "contractors" and so-called "corporate warriors" worldwide, such as the more than 50,000 operating in both in Iraq (at its peak in 2006) and Afghanistan (as of 2013) (see Singer 2003, 2005).

And *how much of a permanent military presence should the U.S. have abroad?* The number of military bases in the United States and abroad has also been reduced somewhat, but almost 300,000 active-duty personnel remain stationed abroad. **Figure 6.4** provides an idea of where most of the active-duty military are permanently stationed abroad. Altogether, the United States maintains over 200 military bases in over thirty-five different countries and territories (see **Table 6.4**). Furthermore, about 50,000 active-duty military are regularly stationed "afloat" (such as on aircraft carriers). And

Figure 6.3   Comparative Defense Statistics

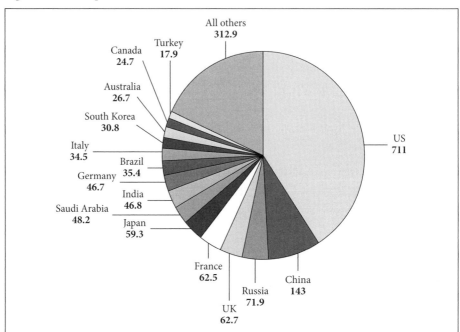

SOURCE: Created from data contained in International Institute of Strategic Studies, 2012.

Table 6.3   U.S. Total Military Force Structure (in thousands)

	Total Personnel	Army	Navy	Marine Corps	Air Force
Active	1,373	525	329	189	330
Reserves	381	205	68	40	68
Guard	458	351	0	0	107
Total	2,212	1,081	397	229	505

SOURCE: CRS Report No. RL34590: *FY2010 National Defense Authorization Act: Selected Military Personnel Policy Issues. FY2010 National Defense Authorization Act, Title IV, Military Personnel Authorizations, Subtitle A-Active Forces.*

thousands of active-duty military, reserve, and National Guard units are temporarily stationed abroad on a rotational basis, which gives the U.S. military a considerable "footprint" throughout the world.

How much is enough depends considerably upon *the national military strategy agreed to by civilians and the military.* The assumption that drove the official pre-9/11 national military strategy was to be prepared for engaging simultaneously in "two major regional conflicts" (such as in the Persian Gulf and the Korean Peninsula) contemplated in the *2001 Quadrennial Defense Review* (QDR, conducted every four years), justifying the force requirements for each of the services as well as for maintaining the U.S. government's global military primacy, and preventing the rise of any new, major adversaries.

Figure 6.4 U.S. Military Personnel on Active Duty Abroad

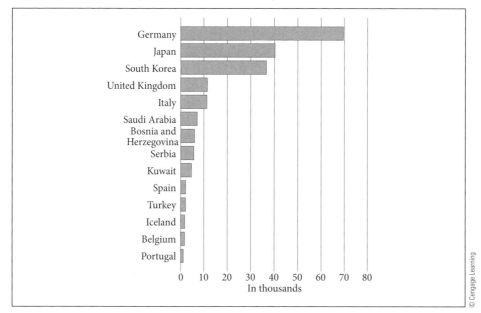

The QDR and the overall national military strategy have since been dramatically amended in light of 9/11, and the Iraq and Afghan wars. *The National Defense Strategy of 2008* (U.S. DOD 2009:1) states, "The United States, our allies, and our partners face a spectrum of challenges, including violent transnational extremist networks, hostile states armed with weapons of mass destruction, rising regional powers, emerging space and cyber threats, natural and pandemic disasters, and a growing competition for resources," quite an expansive and enormous undertaking that now incorporates asymmetrical along with conventional and nuclear war. And the *2010* QDR states, "This is a truly wartime QDR. . . . it places the current conflicts at the top of our budgeting, policy and program priorities. . . . We must recognize that first and foremost the United States is a nation at war," in Afghanistan and Iraq (U.S., DOD 2010: i, iii; see also U.S., CJCS 2011). Is it appropriate? Does it respond to the major global issues and threats of the twenty-first century? What does this mean for the future of the military and its use both at home and abroad?

Clearly, there are no simple solutions concerning appropriate military force structure, military strategy, and the use of the military in a post–cold war environment of great complexity. Some argue that the U.S. government and military should continue to rely on its principal nuclear and conventional missions, and not risk getting bogged down in new Vietnams, such as Iraq and Afghanistan. Others argue that if U.S. foreign policy is to continue to rely on the threat and use of force as well as engage on a war on terrorism, the military must be reformed to improve its conventional performance and gain a real capability in asymmetrical warfare. In the final analysis, the extent to which change and reform in the future military will occur depends on the politics and outcome of the military establishment and U.S. foreign policy, especially the military's conduct of war abroad.

Table 6.4   Military Bases and Installations Outside the United States

AMERICAN SAMOA (1) Army Reserves (1)	**GERMANY (54)** Air Force (8) Army (42) Joint Service Installation (2)	Navy (7) United Nations (1)	Army National Guard (2) Naval Reserve (1) Navy (2)
ANTIGUA (1) Air Force (1)		**JOHNSON ATOLL (1)** Army (1)	**SAINT HELENA (1)** Air Force (1)
AUSTRALIA (2) Air Force (2)	**GREECE (2)** Air Force (1) Navy (1)	**KOREA, REPUBLIC OF (37)** Air Force (4) Army (32) Navy (1)	**SAUDI ARABIA (2)** Air Force (2)
BAHAMAS (1) Navy (1)	**GREENLAND (1)** Air Force (1)		**SINGAPORE (1)** Navy (1)
BAHRAIN (1) Navy (1)	**GUAM (6)** Air Force (1) Army National Guard (1) Navy (4)	**KYRGYZSTAN (1)** Air Force (1)	**SPAIN (2)** Air Force (1) Navy (1)
BELGIUM (5) Air Force (1) Army (4)		**LUXEMBOURG (1)** Army (1)	**THAILAND (1)** Air Force (1)
CANADA (1) Air Force (1)	**HONDURAS (3)** Air Force (1) Army (1) Joint Service Installation (1)	**MARSHALL ISLANDS (1)** Army (1)	**TURKEY (4)** Air Force (3) NATO (1)
CUBA (1) Navy (1)		**NETHERLANDS (7)** Air Force (1) Army (6)	**UNITED ARAB EMIRATES (1)** Air Force (1)
DENMARK (1) Air Force (1)	**ICELAND (1)** Navy (1)	**NORWAY (1)** Air Force (1)	**UNITED KINGDOM (16)** Air Force (10) Army (2) DOD (1) Navy (3)
DIEGO GARCIA (1) Navy (1)	**ITALY (11)** Air Force (3) Army (3) Navy (4)	**OMAN (1)** Air Force (1)	
DJIBOUTI (1) Navy (1)		**PANAMA (6)** Air Force (1) Army (4) Navy (1)	**VIRGIN ISLANDS (1)** Army National Guard (1)
EGYPT (1) Multinational Base (1)	**JAPAN (28)** Air Force (3) Army (4) DOD (1) Joint Service Installation (2) Marine Corps (9)	**PORTUGAL (1)** Joint Service Installation (1)	**WAKE ISLAND (1)** Army (1)
EQUADOR (1) Air Force (1)			
FRANCE (1) Air Force (1)		**PUERTO RICO (6)** Army (1)	

Total = 218 in 42 Countries and Territories

SOURCE: U.S. Department of Defense, Office of the Deputy Under Secretary of Defense, *Base Structure Report Fiscal Year 2010.*

SUGGESTED SOURCES FOR MORE INFORMATION

Bacevich, Andrew, ed. (2007) "The *Long War: A New History of US National Security Policy Since World War II*," New York: Columbia University Press. An excellent collection of chapters on significant and diverse topics by prominent miitary analysts.

Betts, Richard K. (1977) *Soldiers,Statesmen, and Cold War Crises.* Cambridge, MA: Harvard University Press. A classic account of civil–military relations and military advice on the use of force.

Boot Max. (2005) "The Struggle to Transform the Military." *Foreign Affairs* (March–April): 103–118. On Secretary of Defense Donald Rumsfeld, military transformation, and the Iraq War.

Cordesman, Anthony H. (2012) "Afghanistan: The Death of a Strategy," CSIS: Center for Strategic & International Studies, February 27. Excellent critique of the war and COIN fought in Afghanistan.

Davidson, Janine Ann. (2010) *Lifting the Fog of Peace: How Americans Learned to Fight Modern War.* Michigan: University of Michigan Press. Superb overview of the United State's historical role in small wars, with an emphasis of the recent evolution of counterinsurgency within the military.

Fallows, James. (2006) *Blind into Baghdad.* New York: Random House. Excellent overview of the postwar reconstruction planning controversy.

Finkel, David. (2009) *The Good Soldiers.* New York: Farrar, Straus and Giroux. Superb book on the the reality of war on the ground as seen by the soldiers during the surge in Iraq.

Halberstam, David. (1969) *The Best and the Brightest.* New York: Random House. Excellent portrayal of the policymaking process that led to Americanization, hubris and ultimately defeat of the war in Vietnam.

Halberstam, David. (2001) *War in a Time of Peace: Bush, Clinton, and the Generals.* New York: Scribner. Very good on civil–military relations, the Powell Doctrine, the utility of force, and the critical role of individuals and institutions during the George H. W. Bush and Bill Clinton administrations.

Hastings, Michael. (2010) "The Runaway General," *Rolling Stone* (June 25). The article that broke the story on the McCrystal Report and the internal battles within the Obama Administration.

Krepinevich, Andrew. (2009) *7 Deadly Scenarios: A Military Futurist Explores War in the 21st Century.* New York: Bantam Books. An interesting look into current and future defense planning and military/political strategy.

Packer, George. (2005) *The Assassin's Gate: America in Iraq.* New York: Farrar, Straus and Giroux. Masterful overview of the Iraq War from Washington, D.C., to Baghdad.

Priest, Dana. (2003) *The Mission: Waging War and Keeping Peace with America's Military.* New York: W.W. Norton. On the military significance of the Goldwater-Nichols Act.

Ricks, Thomas E. (2006) *Fiasco: The American Military Adventure in Iraq.* New York: Penguin. Very good on the first few years of the Iraq War.

Ricks, Thomas E. (2009) *The Gamble: General David Patraeus and the American Military Adventure in Iraq, 2006–2008.* New York: Penguin. Very good on the military surge in Iraq.

KEY CONCEPTS

asymmetrical warfare	intraservice rivalry
atomic testing program	jointness
budget and personnel systems	military establishment
careerism	military transformation
Counterinsurgency (and COIN)	posttraumatic stress disorder (PTSD)
deterrence strategy	Total Force Structure
interservice rivalry	Weinberger-Powell Doctrine

OTHER KEY TERMS

Army Special Forces (Green Berets)
body counts
Combatant Commander (COCOM)
Department of Defense (DOD)
Department of the Navy
Donald Rumsfeld
General Colin Powell
General Douglas MacArthur
Goldwater-Nichols Act
Grenada invasion
Iraq War

Joint Chiefs of Staff (JCS)
Korean War
McChrystal Report
McNamara, Robert
military lessons of Vietnam
Office of the Secretary of Defense
   (OSD)
Persian Gulf War
services
Vietnam War Memorial
War Department

THE MAIN ENTRY HALL OF THE CIA BUILDING IN LANGLEY, VIRGINIA, LOCATED ON THE POTOMAC RIVER ABOUT NINE MILES NORTHWEST OF THE WHITE HOUSE.

THE INTELLIGENCE COMMUNITY

After World War II, the United States developed an extensive intelligence community within the executive branch, which has had important effects on the process and content of U.S. foreign policy. With components scattered across many bureaucratic agencies, the intelligence community has presented unique challenges for management and coordination in the foreign policy process. *This chapter addresses the following questions:* What are the intelligence community's major purposes and primary activities? How is the intelligence community organized? What are some of the major issues and tensions affecting the quality of intelligence? What role has the Central Intelligence Agency (CIA) and covert operations played in U.S. foreign policy since World War II? All of these questions and issues are of particular importance in the post-9/11 environment, as are the significant tensions that exist between the demands of national security and democracy.

PURPOSE AND ACTIVITIES OF INTELLIGENCE

In the early twentieth century, **intelligence** simply referred to information or news. Since the 1950s, however, *intelligence has come to include three broad sets of activities* managed by organizations within the U.S. government:

1. data collection and analysis,

2. counterintelligence, and

3. political and paramilitary intervention.

There also is a fourth unique function of managing and coordinating intelligence activities and the intelligence community that will be discussed below.

The primary purpose of the intelligence community is to collect and analyze information for military and civilian policymakers in the executive branch. This activity is referred to as the **intelligence cycle** or process. Most intelligence organizations are engaged in collecting and analyzing information for policymakers (see Johnson and Wirtz 2004; Lowenthal 2011).

The intelligence cycle is comprised of five activities that generate a continuous process of interaction between intelligence collectors, producers, and consumers: (1) planning and direction, (2) collection, (3) processing, (4) production and analysis, and (5) dissemination (see **Figure 7.1**). The United States currently possesses many methods of gathering (or collecting) intelligence. They are, however, a finite resource. The intelligence community requires direction (or stated requirements) in order to accurately meet consumer (policymaker) needs.

The intelligence process begins with planning, direction, and "tasking", which usually responds to the climate of the times (e.g., strategic intelligence about the Soviet Union during the cold war or, in recent times, about terrorism). In 2005, for example, the country's first *National Intelligence Strategy* emphasized the need to focus on terrorism, the proliferation of weapons of mass destruction (WMDs), democratization, the ability to penetrate difficult organizations and closed societies, and other objectives as the central priorities. After taking office in 2009, the Obama administration shifted focus to some new or revised tasks, including combating violent extremism, providing strategic intelligence and warning, integrating counterintelligence capabilities, and enhancing cybersecurity, the latter two of which received heightened attention and their own offices and coordinators.

Once requirements are received, collection techniques are allocated to gather the data. The United States has developed a very large array of methods for collecting intelligence, ranging from the simple to the extremely complex. *Four of the most common methods of collection are:* (1) information from electronic signals (SIGINT); (2) from photography (PHOTINT or IMINT); (3) from human sources (HUMINT); and (4) from "open sources" publicly available (such as radio, television, newspapers, and the Internet).

Once collected, the raw information is processed. Because raw information from the collection stage is almost never useful, processing is required to render complex data into an intelligence picture. During the analysis and production stage, pieces of information from various sources are pulled together to paint this intelligence picture. A complete intelligence

Figure 7.1   The Intelligence Community

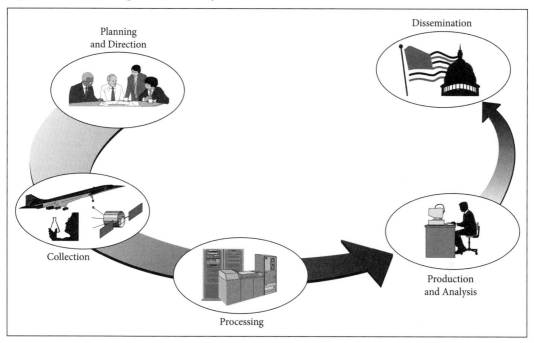

SOURCE: Adapted from Office of Public Affairs, Central Intelligence Agency, *Fact Book on Intelligence* (2005).

picture is ideally constructed from several different sources and methods (e.g., information gathered through human sources is confirmed or denied by electronic and photography methods). The people who do this are called **all-source analysts**. All-source analysts carefully weigh the raw data to evaluate its credibility and reliability, and they synthesize information from the various collection means and methods to which they have access within the intelligence community. The intelligence community thus makes a clear distinction between raw information and intelligence, referring to the products that have been through this cycle and disseminated to policymakers as **finished intelligence**. Among the most important finished intelligence products are National Intelligence Estimates (NIEs) and Intelligence Community Briefs (ICB). An NIE is a relatively regular, updated document that provides a synthesis of the most authoritative judgments of the intelligence community on subjects of concern to U.S. policymakers, while an ICB is a shorter, special document on urgent issues of particular concern at a given time.

A second important function is **counterintelligence (CI)**. Those assigned to this area are responsible for the protection of secrets from the prying eyes and ears of foreign intelligence agencies, both at home and abroad. For forty years, American CI focused on protecting the national security bureaucracy from penetration by its major adversary, the Soviet Union, and its allies. The duties of the men and women of CI range widely and include the prevention and investigation of espionage, subversion, and sabotage against American targets. The functions performed by CI are of the highest priority, for they are intended to protect American secrets from those who would use such information to harm the United States.

In addition to these two traditional intelligence functions, American intelligence agencies are also tasked with covert political and paramilitary operations in support of U.S.

foreign policy. These involve governmental acts, such as propaganda campaigns, psychological warfare, secret financial assistance, destabilization campaigns, partisan resistance movements, assassinations, and coups d'état. The CIA, the organization most (but not exclusively) involved in this area, has developed a certain notoriety for its covert operations over the years, as we discuss later in the chapter.

THE MAJOR INTELLIGENCE ORGANIZATIONS

Although the public generally thinks of the CIA when intelligence activities are mentioned, the intelligence community is much larger and has been expanding since the 1940s. Its sprawling size and challenges have prompted regular calls to reform or restructure its organization to improve its coordination and activities. While these calls produced few results until 2001, the intelligence failures surrounding the 9/11 attacks and Iraq finally led to some structural and procedural changes, although their impact has been relatively limited to date.

As **Figure 7.2** shows, the **intelligence community (IC)** includes parts of 17 federal organizations. The major components are: (1) the National Security Agency (NSA); (2) intelligence units within each of the military services; (3) the National Reconnaissance Office (NRO) and the National Geo-spatial Intelligence Agency; (4) the Defense Intelligence Agency; (5) the State Department's Intelligence and Research Bureau; (6) the Federal Bureau of Investigation; (7) other agencies in the executive branch, such as the Departments of Energy, Treasury, and the Drug Enforcement Administration, that are engaged in intelligence activities; (8) the CIA; and (9) the most recent addition, the Office of the Director of National Intelligence (ODNI), which has the daunting task of coordinating this community (see pp. 213–216 on the recently created Department of Homeland Security (DHS).

Figure 7.2   The Intelligence Community: An Organizational Overview

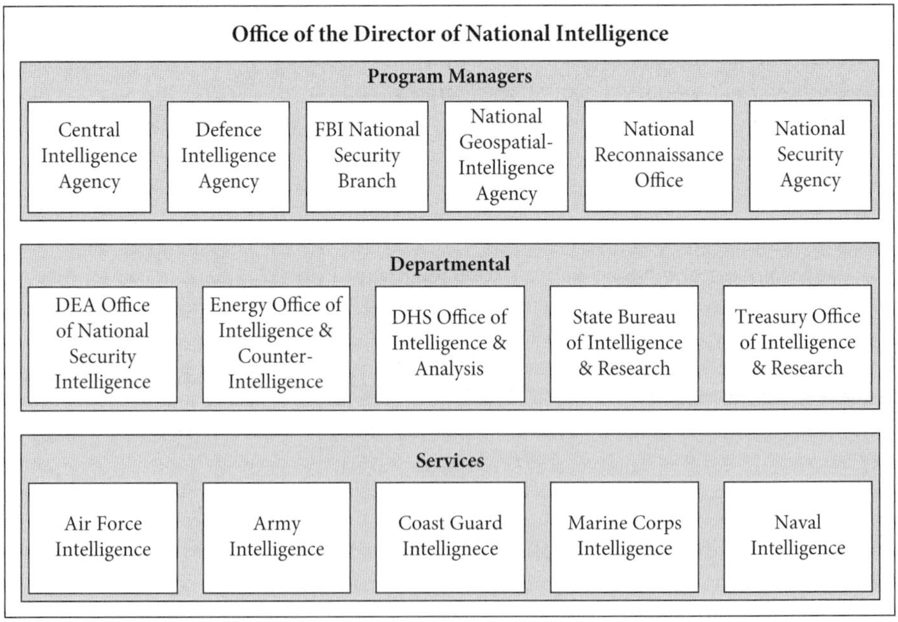

SOURCE: http://www.intelligence.gov/about-the-intelligence-community/structure/

The organizations listed fall within three general categories based on their principal function in the intelligence process. First, the producers are those who analyze and disseminate finished intelligence products to consumers. These products take many forms, from daily summaries to detailed research studies, but it is through these products that the intelligence community primarily interacts with policymakers. Second are the organizations that focus on collection and processing. This is the largest grouping, where most of the growth in the intelligence community has taken place. Third, some organizations also conduct an additional function in the research and development of equipment (or collection platforms). For example, the NRO, while producing imagery products, is also engaged in the development of new, more technologically advanced imagery systems. In addition, some of these organizations may also have counterintelligence and political and paramilitary intervention missions.

For most of the post–World War II period, these agencies were only loosely coordinated—the fourth function—by the Director of Central Intelligence (DCI), who also served as the director of the CIA. Always in a weak position, without the power over budgets, tasking, or hiring and firing in any of the agencies other than the CIA, the DCI rarely succeeded in imposing much order on the intelligence community. In 2004, the Intelligence Reform and Prevention of Terrorism Act (PL-108-458) created the new ODNI, and the Director of National Intelligence (DNI) was provided with increased powers to coordinate the activities of the rest of the intelligence community.

Intelligence Organizations of the Defense Department

Most of the U.S. intelligence organizations, including personnel and budget, are officially a part of the DOD. The Pentagon spends about eighty cents of every intelligence dollar, with the big accounts being those of the NSA and NRO, America's technical collection services.

THE NATIONAL SECURITY AGENCY (NSA) The highly secretive NSA was created in 1952 within the DOD, though its origins go back to World War I and the army's Signal Corps. It has grown to become the largest and, along with the CIA, most important intelligence agency. Until relatively recently, the NSA was so secretive that for decades its acronym was said to stand for "No Such Agency" (Bamford 1982:2001). The major function of the NSA is the collection and exploitation of SIGINT (communication, radar, and telemetry intelligence). NSA maintains "listening posts" located in U.S. governmental facilities abroad, including U.S. embassies and particularly American military bases around the world, equipped with sophisticated electronics for intercepting communications messages. The intercepted messages are relayed to NSA's Fort Meade, Maryland, headquarters (about twenty four miles from the White House), where an extensive and sophisticated array of computers processes the information. It was, for example, the NSA that intercepted a 2010 cell phone call to one of Osama bin Laden's most trusted couriers that enabled the intelligence community to track the courier to the compound in Pakistan where bin Laden was hiding. This key piece of information was essential to the subsequent 2011 raid on the compound that killed bin Laden.

NSA also has special responsibility in **cryptology**, the study of making and breaking codes. The NSA devises the codes for the U.S. government, performing an important counterintelligence function by helping to keep communications secret. Since much of the information that NSA intercepts is in code, efforts are made to break the codes of other countries and decipher the messages, unbeknown to the original source. For example, this proved critical to the success of the Allies in World War II and, more recently, the NSA was able to provide good information on Iran's diplomatic, military, and security plans because it had broken that country's codes; U.S. intelligence suffered when this was revealed to Iran and then made public in 2004 (Wright and Ricks 2004).

THE NATIONAL RECONNAISSANCE OFFICE (NRO) AND THE NATIONAL GEOSPATIAL-INTELLIGENCE AGENCY (NGA) Although the NRO and NGA are not well known to the American public, both are involved in the imagery subfield of intelligence, which since the end of World War II has experienced tremendous growth in the techniques and sophistication of intelligence collection. In the 1960s, the National Photographic Interpretation Center and the Defense Mapping Agency worked on imagery. In 1996, these agencies and others were merged into the National Imagery and Mapping Agency (NIMA), which was then renamed in 2004 to bear its current NGA designation.

The NRO was created during the cold war to help centralize the management of reconnaissance flights. In the late 1950s, the United States developed the U-2 spy plane. A fast high-altitude jet aircraft designed to fly long distances over the Soviet Union, the U2 was equipped with photographic equipment for taking detailed ground pictures and became an important source of early information on Soviet military forces. U-2 flights by the CIA and Air Force intelligence also helped to verify the existence of Soviet intermediate-range missiles in Cuba during the early days of the Cuban Missile Crisis in 1962. After the U-2 pilot Francis Gary Powers was shot down and captured by the Soviet Union in 1960, the NRO was created to better coordinate aerial reconnaissance. Later, as the U-2 and its successor—the Lockheed Blackbird—became increasingly vulnerable to surface-to-air missiles, the NRO began to rely on the use of satellites to obtain military information about the Soviet Union and intelligence for the war on terror.

Today, the NRO is responsible for the development as well as the supervision (via the Air Force and NASA) of high-altitude surveillance mechanisms (e.g., imagery-based intelligence, or IMINT). NGA then processes the raw data acquired from the airborne platforms into imagery products used by the all-source analysts. In recent years, however, reliance on imagery has been called into question. Over the years flight paths and orbits of satellites have been compromised. As a result, it is not too difficult for those wishing to keep their activities secret to limit their activities when imagery assists are known to be overhead.

THE DEFENSE INTELLIGENCE AGENCY (DIA) The DIA was created in 1961 in response to the Bay of Pigs fiasco, where the CIA trained Cuban expatriates to invade Cuba and overthrow Fidel Castro—an operation that failed miserably and led to the condemnation of the United States throughout the globe. The DIA's purpose is to better coordinate the many intelligence activities undertaken by the DOD in the hope of giving the military a single and more influential voice in the government's intelligence process. However, many of the problems that afflict the military establishment also plague the DIA. Staff consists of military and civilian analysts drawn from the individual services and the Office of the Secretary of Defense, requiring that the different subcultures and divided loyalties within the organizations be overcome. The DIA provides the military services and the regional combat commanders (COCOMs) with finished intelligence products focused on their requirements. These requirements are usually tactical in nature, focusing on the composition, disposition, and capabilities of potential military adversaries.

THE MILITARY SERVICES Each of the military services maintains its own intelligence capability. American military intelligence consists primarily of service efforts to collect and process tactical military information, including the force structures, tactics employed, and operational capabilities of other military forces—especially those of the Soviet Union after World War II. These include Army Intelligence (G-2), one of the nation's oldest intelligence operations; Air Force intelligence; the Office of Naval Intelligence; the Intelligence Department of the Marine Corp, and the Coast Guard intelligence. Recently, the Army and Air Force have developed unmanned aerial vehicles (UAVs), which now play a more important role in intelligence collection and have been very active in post-9/11 operations in Afghanistan and Iraq. Army intelligence has also had a counterintelligence function and an extensive history of involvement in preventing treason, espionage, sabotage, gambling, prostitution, and black marketeering at home and abroad. As discussed in Chapter 6, the Goldwater-Nichols Defense Reorganization Act of 1986 forced the services into a joint operational environment. As a result, the primary customers of military intelligence are currently the combat commanders of the various regional and functional commands. Each COCOM has its own joint intelligence center (JIC) that responds to his own needs and makes requests for particular intelligence collection, usually through the DIA.

Non-DOD Organizations

Other cabinet level departments have their own intelligence activities. Although the most important are under the Departments of State (the Bureau of Intelligence and Research, or INR) and Justice (the FBI), other executive branch agencies, such as the Departments of Energy, Treasury, and the Drug Enforcement Agency also conduct intelligence activities related to their own areas of interest and are part of the 17 agencies under ODNI. Other departments and agencies throughout the executive branch, such as the Department of Commerce, have intelligence units and engage in intelligence activities as well in a world of globalization.

THE BUREAU OF INTELLIGENCE AND RESEARCH (INR) The State Department is involved in intelligence work, predominantly in analysis, through its Bureau of Intelligence and Research. INR analyzes the department's cable traffic from abroad and information from other agencies in the intelligence community. As one of the producers of finished intelligence, it is actively involved in the process that produces communitywide intelligence estimates (NIEs) and provides advice to the secretary of state and State Department personnel on intelligence matters. Because the INR is so much smaller than the other two producers of finished intelligence (CIA and DIA), it is often thought to be the weakest. However, INR's influence is often a function of the secretary of state. For example, during the Reagan administration, Secretary of State George Shultz (1982–1989) met regularly with the assistant secretary who ran the bureau, whereas James Baker (1989–1992) rarely did.

THE FEDERAL BUREAU OF INVESTIGATION (FBI) The FBI is a part of the Department of Justice. It began as the Bureau of Investigation in 1908 and is the oldest governmental organization developed for the purpose of intelligence. It is the intelligence organization with primary responsibility for U.S. domestic counterintelligence and internal security. The FBI is unique not only in its geographic focus on the United States, but in its performance of both domestic-oriented and foreign policy functions, including federal law enforcement, foreign counterintelligence, and internal security against threats to the U.S. government. Long driven by a law-enforcement and anticommunist counterintelligence orientation fostered by J. Edgar Hoover, who served as its director from 1924 to 1972 (see Kessler 1994), the FBI underwent a major reorganization after the September 11, 2001, terrorist attacks on the United States to improve its antiterrorism activities. Its intelligence

and terrorism elements were reorganized into a National Security division, answerable to both the ODNI and the FBI director. Moreover, it has been working to streamline and better coordinate its own information sharing procedures, including establishing a unified computer system to collect, manage, and share information on its case files.

THE DEPARTMENTS OF ENERGY AND TREASURY AND DEA   The Departments of Energy and Treasury, and DEA control intelligence activities focused on their needs. The Department of Energy's Office of Intelligence and Counterintelligence (OIC) provides technical intelligence analyses on all aspects of nuclear weapons, nuclear materials, and energy issues worldwide. The Department of Treasury's Office of Intelligence and Analysis (OIA) was created in 2004 to help safeguard the financial system against illicit use and combat rogue nations, terrorist facilitators, weapons of mass destruction (WMD) proliferators, money launderers, drug kingpins, and other national security threats. The DEA's (Drug Enforcement Agency) Office of National Security Intelligence (ONSI) provides intelligence on controlled substances laws and regulations of the United States, focusing on illicit traffic and reducing the availability of illicit controlled substances on the domestic and international markets.

Organizations with Intelligence Coordination Responsibilities since World War II

The CIA is the principal intelligence organization responsible for national or strategic needs. Until 2005, the CIA was also supposed to exert coordinating control over the whole community, including "tasking authority" over the intelligence-collecting assets of the entire community to meet national security needs. These coordination and tasking roles have become the responsibility of the DNI since 2004. The CIA's main customers are the DNI, the National Security Council, and the president, with State, Defense and other agencies as important consumers as well.

THE CIA   Created by the National Security Act of 1947, the CIA soon became the best known and most important agency responsible for intelligence abroad. The CIA has played an important role in the collection and analysis of data, is the primary intelligence organization responsible for counterintelligence outside the United States, and has become the major intelligence organization engaged in political and paramilitary action abroad. Until 2005, in addition to these three intelligence functions, the CIA director was also the DCI—a situation called "dual-hatting"—and thus responsible for coordinating the entire intelligence community for the president of the United States (Turner 2005). Since the 2004 intelligence reform law, the DCI position no longer exists (the former DCI is now merely the director of the CIA) and these coordination and tasking roles have passed to the ODNI and its head, the DNI.

The CIA is *composed of several main divisions or directorates:* intelligence, science and technology, and the national clandestine service, which is responsible for intelligence operations. Most current CIA personnel are involved in data collection and analysis in the intelligence directorate (DI). The DI is responsible for producing the CIA's own intelligence assessments (IAs) for the policymaking community and participating in the development of NIEs, which are a product of the entire intelligence community (coordinated by the ODNI). The Directorate of Science and Technology (DS&T) is responsible for developing mechanisms and gadgets used in the type of intelligence activities made most famous in the 007 James Bond movies (though these have always been more science fiction than reality; Richelson 2002). The personnel within the national clandestine service (NCS; formerly the directorate of operations, DO) are involved in covert operations.

THE OFFICE OF THE DIRECTOR FOR NATIONAL INTELLIGENCE The newest element of the U.S. intelligence community is the **Office of the Director of National Intelligence (ODNI)**, which was established in December 2004 with the passage of the Intelligence Reform and Prevention of Terrorism Act (PL-108-458). Headed up by the **director of national intelligence (DNI)**, this office was created to establish a central authority for coordination of the roughly fifteen agencies that make up the intelligence community.

The DNI replaces the DCI (director for central intelligence) position, whose occupant is no longer "dual-hatted," and serves only as the director of the CIA. The 2004 reform legislation provided the new DNI with increased authority (compared to the DCI) to coordinate the intelligence community, including greater budgetary control (the DNI prepares a community-wide budget) and enhanced authority over personnel. However, the reform stopped short of providing the new office with complete or exclusive authority over the intelligence agencies of the Defense, State, Justice, Energy, and Commerce Departments, and the relationship between the DNI and the CIA is ambiguous and contentious. (Pillar 2010). The ODNI has a staff (which has grown to about 1500 people) and four deputies to oversee policy/plans/requirements, collection, analysis, and acquisition. The DNI also supervises the work of the National Intelligence Council (NIC) and a number of intelligence centers, including the National Counterterrorism (NCTC) and National Counterproliferation (NCPC) centers (Zegart 2005).

HISTORICAL DEVELOPMENT OF A LARGE, COMPLEX COMMUNITY

Most European states developed intelligence functions during the 1920s and 1930s, but in the United States, modern intelligence developed more slowly. Nevertheless, according to Nathan Miller (1989), "although most Americans believe the United States did not become deeply involved in intelligence operations until the creation of the Office of Strategic Services (OSS) during World War II . . . [the U.S. government has] participated in such activities—with varying degrees of success—since the Revolution." The U.S. government had a very limited intelligence capability during the nineteenth century, relying on the Secret Service, the military, and the State Department. American intelligence became more professional and grew during the first half of the twentieth century with the establishment of military intelligence, the FBI, and during World War II, the Office of Strategic Services (OSS), the precursor of the CIA.

With the passage of the National Security Act of 1947 and the advent of the cold war, intelligence expanded into large, complex, modern bureaucracies. After the collapse of the Soviet Union, the intelligence budget and staff experienced some downsizing, followed by a significant increase due to the September 11 attacks and the subsequent war on terrorism. Although the exact amount the United States spends on intelligence remains classified, in 1998 then-DCI George Tenet publicly revealed the intelligence budget at $26.7 billion (Shane 2004), while in 2009 the ODNI estimated it to be about $50 billion in support of around 100,000 people (U.S. ODNI 2009).

PATTERNS IN THE INTELLIGENCE PROCESS

The rise of a large and complex intelligence community has affected both the intelligence cycle and product. Until 2005, the DCI was responsible for coordination of the entire community as well as the direction of the CIA, but in reality had direct control only over a small element of the intelligence agencies. In 2003 congressional hearings were held and a "national commission" was created to examine the workings (and failures) of the intelligence community prior and up to the September 11, 2001, terrorist attacks. The political results of the hearings and the so-called "9/11 commission" report (U.S. National Commission on Terrorist Attacks 2003) was the passage of the **Intelligence Reform and Prevention of Terrorism Act of 2004** (PL-108-458), which restructured the intelligence community. Although the consequences of the relatively recent reforms are still evolving, the newly restructured formal relationships are represented in **Figure 7.3.**

Several elements of the new structure are worth noting. First, the ODNI and its director are more central to the intelligence community, with greater budgetary and tasking authority than was provided to the DCI. Second, the director of the CIA has a diminished role, limited mostly to running a single agency. Additionally, the CIA director no longer participates in the NSC process unless invited by the president; that role now goes to the DNI. Finally, while the 2004 reforms increase the potential for central coordination, the new structure still clearly reveals the continuing challenges of a sprawling intelligence community. In particular, the DNI has continued to face serious challenges in bringing the fragmented intelligence community together (Pillar 2010).

Figure 7.3   Intelligence Community After 2005: An Organizational View

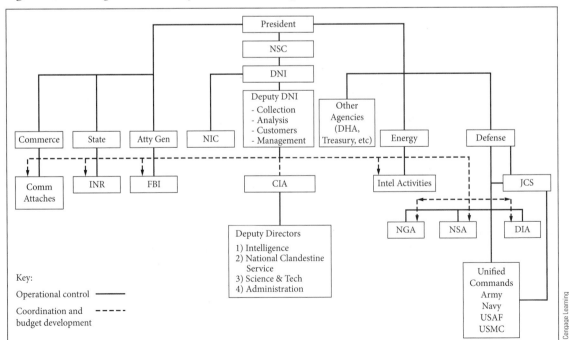

Over time, *three dominant patterns have affected the collection, analysis, and dissemination of intelligence:* (1) difficulties in achieving coordination, (2) producer-consumer problems, and (3) variations in intelligence success. The creation of the ODNI has not eliminated these issues (Pillar 2010).

Coordination Problems

The intelligence community has become so large and complex that *coordinating the work of various intelligence organizations in support of the president's foreign policy is very difficult.* As we have seen, this is a recurring theme in the foreign policy bureaucracy. Indeed, calls for reform—and greater centralization—of the intelligence community go back at least to the Nixon administration (Zegart 2005).

The major problem has been a lack of central authority—despite the existence of a formal DCI after World War II. With so much of the intelligence community operating under the DOD, it was inevitable that the people executing the missions within the intelligence community would be more responsive to the DOD's institutional incentives and pressures. The NSA; Army, Navy and Air Force intelligence; the NRO and NIMA; and the DIA are part of the DOD and most of the personnel operate within the military chain of command. Likewise for many of the other intelligence agencies. The Intelligence and Research Bureau is responsive to the structure and norms of the State Department. And the FBI is a semiautonomous agency within the Department of Justice.

These separate organizations and agencies all have their own reporting lines or channels through their own agency heads, which established **stovepipes** between the agencies and top-level policymakers—direct channels from those involved in collection and analysis to high-level policymakers. Hence, rather than bringing different means of collection together and having a coherent and centralized intelligence cycle, each stovepipe allows intelligence to pass through various agencies, depending on the stage of the intelligence process and the particular means of collecting information. These separate stovepipes demonstrate the "subcommunities" within the larger intelligence community, which have often behaved as competitors in the intelligence process.

The 9/11 attacks changed the context substantially, however, and in 2004 the U.S. Congress enacted legislation to improve centralization and coordination. As we noted earlier, *the principal change instituted by the 2004 reform act was the creation of the ODNI, and the position of the DNI, with greater authority to coordinate the intelligence community.* The first DNI—long-time diplomat John Negroponte, who served as UN ambassador for President George W. Bush in his first term—was confirmed in April 2005. He was followed by former NSA director Admiral Mike McConnell in 2007, Admiral Dennis Blair in 2009, and Lt. General James R. Clapper in 2010. The fact that the position of DNI has changed hands four times since 2005 is indicative that the effort to reform and centralize intelligence has only had limited success (see Kirchick 2010; Pillar 2010).

The DNI has the authority to develop the intelligence budget for most of the community (covering about 80 percent of the spending, including that of the Defense Department elements), as well as to transfer funds among agencies to meet priorities. The DNI was also assigned direct control of the National Intelligence Council and the Community Management Staff (discussed later), which play important roles in the coordination of collection and processing of intelligence. Moreover, new centers on counterterrorism and counterproliferation were established as a consequence of the reforms, both of which are under the DNI's authority, even though they are staffed by representatives of the other agencies. Finally, although the DNI has no role in determining the heads of the other agencies, he or she has the authority to approve or disapprove the hiring of key deputy positions across the intelligence community.

Thus, the fallout from the September 11 attacks prompted key structural and procedural changes. However, ambiguities in the reform legislation, coupled with long-standing bureaucratic practices and the continued fragmentation of separate agencies, make it unclear what effect this reform will produce in real terms. While the new DNI has increased authority and control over some of these subcommunities—especially in wielding budgetary power— early indicators do not suggest dramatic changes (Pillar 2010).

In 2005, John Negroponte took steps to solidify his budget powers, reprogramming some funds, canceling others, and announcing a review designed to shift budgets away from technical collection toward human intelligence (Giorman 2005; Miller 2005). However, because the 2004 intelligence reform act included language confirming the authority of cabinet officials in the intelligence community, for example, the DNI has faced continued challenges. For one, the Defense Secretary's statutory authority continues to include control over the DIA, NSA, NRO, and NGA, and so represents a major challenge for coordination (Fessenden 2005). Additionally, tensions between the DNI and the CIA also exist. Indeed, in 2006, CIA Director Porter Goss was forced out, replaced by Negroponte's deputy, General Michael Hayden, who had previously served as director of the NSA. Among the reasons for Goss's departure was feuding between his office and the DNI as Negroponte sought to move analytical resources from the CIA to his own office (Ackerman 2006). Similarly, in 2009, Barack Obama's DNI Dennis Blair and CIA Director Leon Panetta clashed over who had the authority to appoint "station chiefs" for coordinating intelligence activities in foreign countries (Baer 2009; Mazzetti 2009).

The successful raid that killed Osama bin Laden in 2011 suggests there are times when intelligence coordination does occur. This operation involved coordination across the intelligence community, including intercepts by the NSA, tracking and imagery analysis by the NGA, and aggressive efforts by the CIA. The actual raid on Abbottabad, Pakistan, involved an elite Navy Seals team from the Defense Department's Joint Special Operations Command (JSOC), which carried out the ground operation, under the direction of the CIA. As a former CIA official noted, "the Abbottabad raid amounted to 'a complete incorporation of JSOC into a C.I.A. operation' " (Schmidle 2011). However, ODNI was almost invisible in this effort, which was managed principally by Leon Panetta, who was then director of the CIA.

The Community Management Staff (CMS) and the NIC are the two principal tools through which the DCI, and now the DNI, coordinates the community. The CMS was vastly enlarged in the 1997 intelligence authorization bill by its funding of several new high-level positions (called assistant directors, ADs). Assistant directorships were created over collection and analysis and production, giving the DCI greater ability to manage the community than before. The CMS was transferred to the DNI in the 2004 reform, and makes up the heart of the DNI's staff. By 2009, the DNI's office had expanded to over 1500 staff. Among them, as noted earlier, are deputy directors for collection; analysis; policy, plans, and requirements; and future capabilities.

While the CMS is supposed to help coordinate the collection effort, the National Intelligence Council (NIC) is supposed to assist in the dissemination stage of the intelligence process. The NIC is an interagency organization composed of senior analysts from the various members of the intelligence community. The NIC produces the **National Intelligence Estimates (NIEs)**, intended to be an important product of the intelligence community. The NIEs is one of the few products the intelligence community produces jointly.

Yet policymakers often criticize NIEs because they are said to reflect the lowest common denominators agreed upon by the various members of the community. Such compromised intelligence assessments tend to be the order of the day, given the intelligence agencies' different subcultures and perspectives. Originally, under the direction of the DCI, the NIC was transferred to the DNI's office in the 2004 intelligence reform.

The most significant challenge is that the decentralized bureaucratic nature of the intelligence community means considerable independent action is performed by the various intelligence agencies, regardless of coordination efforts at the top. When they do interact, the policymaking process experiences infighting and compromise. During the Cuban missile crisis, for example, when the president was trying to verify whether intermediate-range strategic missiles capable of delivering nuclear warheads on the United States were stationed in Cuba, the NRO and the CIA were feuding over which bureaucracy had responsibility for the U-2 flights. U-2 flights were deferred for two days until the NRO and the CIA agreed that they would each be responsible for alternate flights. Thus, crucial information was delayed during a period when the United States and the Soviet Union faced their greatest crisis (Allison 1971).

Coordination in counterintelligence has been an area of particular historic contention between the FBI and the CIA (Reibling 2002). The cultures of intelligence and law enforcement are vastly different. For the intelligence-oriented CIA, the purpose is policy. For the law enforcement–oriented FBI, the purpose is to convict criminals. Various spy cases have highlighted the lack of coordination between the two organizations. For example, the lack of coordination probably delayed the detection and arrest of CIA double agent Aldrich Ames for years until 1995. In the aftermath of the Ames case, the FBI and CIA created a jointly staffed counterintelligence office to try to correct the mistakes.

The events of September 11, 2001, however, show there is still much to be worked out. Despite the initial emphasis by the Bush administration and the media on the lack of warning and complete surprise of the terrorist attacks, it is now known that the intelligence community actually had many different pieces of information, but there was very poor communication, coordination, and cooperation among a variety of intelligence organizations, especially within the FBI. Subsequent intelligence failures regarding the prewar assessments of Iraq's WMD capabilities also highlighted serious deficiencies in the intelligence structures and processes. These problems led directly to congressional hearings and to the 2004 intelligence reform legislation (see **A Closer Look** on coordination problems related to the September 11 attacks).

Another consequence of the September 11 attacks was the creation of the Department of Homeland Security. Initially, an Office of Homeland Security (OHS) within the Executive Office of the Presidency was created by President Bush's executive order, with former Pennsylvania governor Tom Ridge as its first director. Planned almost entirely within the White House, "No department heads were asked to join the clique of senior White House aides who planned the redesign. Cabinet secretaries didn't know about the plan until the last minute," including most major foreign policy advisors (Lizza 2002:10–12). The purpose of OHS was to coordinate and centralize intelligence among the numerous organizations involved (which include literally dozens of different governmental departments and agencies, plus their interaction with state and local governments) to prevent and respond to security threats against the United States. Despite the authority given to Director Ridge and his ability to report directly to the president, the OHS struggled in gaining control over the agencies it was to coordinate. As former national security advisor Anthony Lake noted, to do so, it had to "take powers away from various different agencies that now have

Intelligence Community Coordination Problems Before September 11, 2001

The sprawling intelligence community poses many coordination problems. Consider the following two excerpts about recent events before September 11. They demonstrate the impact of diverging departmental missions, policy preferences and cultures, and coordination challenges that led to demands for reform.

> [W]hile the issue of terrorism was rising in importance in every agency with a role to play in guarding against the threat, terrorism remained just one among their many concerns. For the Pentagon, preparing to fight two major theater wars remained the priority—and in the distance loomed the rise of China and the acquisition of long-range missiles by nuclear-armed rogue states. The customs agents searched luggage and shipments coming across borders—to sniff out illegal drug shipments more than germ weapons. Foreign service officers working their first tour of duty in consular sections of U.S. embassies abroad, and Immigration and Naturalization Services personnel at U.S. ports of entry worried more about preventing entry to people who wished to stay for good than keeping out people who wished to do the United States harm. The FBI tracked federal criminals at home and sought to garner evidence that could stand up in U.S. courts against terrorists abroad, but did not take the initiative to track people who might terrorize our nation. And the list goes on. In each and every cast other critical agency functions were, for very understandable reasons, given priority

over countering the terrorism threat. (prepared statement of I. H. Daalder and I. M. Destler before the Committee on Governmental Affairs, U.S. Senate, October 12, 2001)

Looking back on it now, it is difficult to choose the precise moment when U.S. government officials—hobbled by old-fashioned rules, saddled with ancient computers that could not talk to one another and driven by silly bureaucratic rivalries—missed their best chance to thwart the plot by 19 hijackers to take over four airplanes, turn them into flying missiles, and kill almost 3,000 people on September 11, 2001.

Was it in early 1999, when the National Security Agency, eavesdropping on a suspected terrorist facility in the Middle East, first learned (but kept to itself) that a 25-year-old Saudi named Nawaf Alhazmi had links to Osama bin Laden? Or was it in March 2000, when the CIA heard from its spies overseas (but did not tell the FBI) that Alhazmi had flown to Los Angeles a few weeks before? Then there was the bungled meeting between the CIA and the FBI in June 2001, when the CIA hinted at Alhazmi's role but would not put everything it knew on the table. Washington may have had one more chance to change history in late August 2001, when FBI headquarters finally heard that Alhazmi and other bin Laden operatives were loose in the U.S. But against the advice of detectives in the field, agents at FBI headquarters assigned the case a low priority, and nearly two weeks passed before the bureau asked its Los Angeles field office to track down the suspects. That last e-mail was dated Sept. 11, 2001.

Apart from the terrorists, the biggest enemy the government faced before 9/11 was itself. Agents at both the FBI and the CIA had a longtime habit of stovepiping—keeping information to themselves or sharing it with only a handful of people. That made for good secret-keeping but discouraged critical thinking by the people on the front lines. When an FBI agent in Phoenix, Arizona noticed two months before the attacks that Middle Eastern men were taking flying lessons in his backyard and alerted headquarters that something ghastly might be in the offing, agents in Washington took no action. And a month later, when a group of agents in Minnesota warned that a French-born Moroccan named Zacarias Moussaoui was in the area illegally and trying to learn how to fly a commercial jet, officials at FBI headquarters never put the two warnings together. In the culture of the FBI, agents were not champions at imagining crimes that had not been committed; they were simply supposed to investigate crimes after they occurred. (Michael Duffy, "Could it Happen Again?" *Time,* August 4, 2003)

How does the creation of the ODNI, led by the DNI, help to address these coordination problems, and how does it fail to do so, or even make them worse?

SOURCE: Michael Duffy, "Could it Happen Again?" Time, August 4, 2003.

them. There is nothing harder in the federal government than doing that" (quoted in Nakashima and Graham 2001:A1).

In June 2002, President Bush asked Congress (at the urging of many members) to increase the prestige and visibility of OHS by approving its change to a **Department of Homeland Security (DHS)**—giving it cabinet-level status. Ultimately, the White House and Congress consolidated twenty-two federal agencies and 177,000 employees to form a new department—absorbing the independent Federal Emergency Management Agency (FEMA) and transferring the Customs Service from Treasury, most of the Immigration and Naturalization Service (INS) from Justice, the Transportation Security Administration from Transportation, the Coast Guard from Transportation, and the U.S. Secret Service from Treasury (along with smaller agencies from other departments). With a budget request of about $35 billion for 2003, this represented the most ambitious effort to reorganize and expand the federal government in the area of foreign policy since 1947.

Yet, the DHS has been far from successful. Unlike the OHS, which was part of the Executive Office of the Presidency, the DHS is part of the larger executive branch bureaucracy. In one sense, moving out of a White House office actually dampened the new department's ability to persuade other agencies to participate and collaborate in its efforts. Under the legislation, despite some reorganization and transfer of some agencies to the new department, the most important intelligence agencies involved in antiterrorism—the FBI and CIA, as well as those in DOD—maintained their independence and jurisdictional autonomy. By late 2005, observers were calling the DHS experiment a story of "haphazard design, bureaucratic warfare, and unfulfilled promises," and a "bureaucratic Frankenstein" (Crowley 2004; Glasser and Grunwald 2005). Indeed, Michael Chertoff, Ridge's successor as head of DHS, initiated a sweeping review of DHS because of its failures to make progress. Most observers also concluded that the highly inefficient and haphazard response to Hurricane Katrina in the summer of 2005 further exposed the inability of DHS to coordinate a rapid response to a disaster (Grunwald and Glasser 2005).

Furthermore, former national security advisor Condoleezza Rice (with President Bush's approval) also made it very clear that the national security advisor and NSC staff (and interagency process) would not report to the homeland security secretary, and in response to 9/11, she beefed up the NSC's antiterrorism unit and staff. President Obama's first national security advisor Jim Jones further "integrated" homeland security functions into the NSC system (DeYoung 2009). Moreover, the 2004 reform act created a new National Counterterrorism Center under the direction of the DNI, further eroding the reach of the DHS. At the same time, in 2011 the Obama administration strengthened the DHS role and autonomy on cybersecurity issues, providing it with the central responsibility and enhanced authority to protect the country's federal civilian electronic networks. Overall then, although some improvement in cooperation may eventually develop from the creation of the DHS, the reality is that there is now another large bureaucratic organization and layer, and additional (and more complicated) stovepipes within the intelligence process.

In sum, across the intelligence community, decentralization and coordination problems persist in spite of recent reform efforts. Several examples illustrate the continuing problem. First, the new NCTC Center in the ODNI must contend with the CIA's own counterterrorism center, which retains primary responsibility for disrupting terrorist plots and organizations. Second, while the FBI's intelligence and terrorism elements have been reorganized into a National Security division and placed under the authority of the DNI, the new division remains a part of the FBI, and the DNI shares authority with the FBI director, not to mention the Attorney General. Third, control and coordination over human intelligence and covert operations have been placed in the hands of the deputy director of the NCS, within the CIA. This individual not only controls the CIA's intelligence operations, but also coordinates uniform practices, training, and operations of all human intelligence across the community. This deputy director also reports to both the CIA director and the DNI. Fourth, the Defense Department continues to expand its intelligence activities, and has strengthened the role of the secretary of Defense's office in coordinating and directing those activities. Finally, CIA station chiefs in foreign countries are now required to report to both the CIA director and to the new DNI. In short, while the DNI was developed in part to end the practice of "dual-hatting" the CIA director, the new structures and procedures create a number of new "dual-hat" situations that generate additional coordination problems (see Pillar 2010 and **Table 7.1** for an overview of the elaborate bureaucratic war on terrorism).

Producer-Consumer Problems

The vast array of increasingly effective intelligence-gathering methods has resulted in an explosion of data available to the consumer (i.e., the policymaker). The community now has the ability to easily overwhelm consumers with reams of information. The current challenge posed by the technology and information age is to sort through the volumes of information to produce the relevant finished products to be disseminated to policymakers in various forms (see **Table 7.2** for an overview). The problem is not a shortage of assessments but their production and consumption.

Problems have developed between the intelligence "producers"—analysts within the intelligence community—and "consumers"—the policymakers, especially the president and other high-level officials, who use this information to make decisions and justify their policies. *From the perspective of the president and other senior officials*, the problem is that the intelligence community frequently does not provide actionable intelligence. For the members of the intelligence community, the problem is the ambiguous and contradictory guidelines provided by

Table 7.1 Major Federal Agencies Involved in the War on Terrorism

Although the federal government appears monolithic to many, in the area of terrorism prevention and response (as in so many other areas), it has been anything but. Over forty federal agencies are involved in the war on terrorism (and more than twenty federal entities in bioterroism alone). The war on terrorism, especially at home, also involves the role of fifty states and hundreds of local governments as well (and their corresponding officials and agencies). The official list is classified, but here is a partial list of the major national bureaucratic players and their roles:

NATIONAL POLICY

National Security Council (White House)—coordinates foreign strategy

Department of Homeland Security—coordinates domestic defense

Council of Economic Advisers (White House)—coordinates economic recovery

INTELLIGENCE

Office of the Director of National Intelligence—coordinates all foreign intelligence

Central Intelligence Agency—coordinates all human intelligence; deploys spies

National Security Agency—(Defense) intercepts foreign communications

National Reconnaissance Office (Defense)—runs spy satellites

Defense Intelligence Agency (Defense)—coordinates military intelligence

Special Operations Command (Defense)—scouts hostile territory

State Department—negotiates with foreign governments

Federal Bureau of Investigation (Justice)—investigates attacks

Treasury Department—monitors suspicious financial activity

Securities and Exchange Commission—monitors suspicious trades

PREEMPTION AND RETALIATION

Defense Department—stages military strikes

FBI—arrests terrorists

Drug Enforcement Administration (Justice)—attacks, e.g., Afghan opium trade

Treasury Department—freezes terrorist accounts

BORDER SECURITY

Coast Guard (DHS in peacetime, Defense in wartime)—patrols coasts and waterways

Immigration and Naturalization Service (DHS)—monitors people entering U.S.

Customs Service (DHS)—monitors goods entering U.S.

North American Aerospace Defense Command (Defense/Canada)—monitors aircraft and missiles

DISASTER PREPAREDNESS AND RESPONSE

FBI—coordinates crisis response

Office for Domestic Preparedness (Justice)—trains and equips local agencies

Federal Emergency Management Agency—supports, trains, and equips local fire, medical personnel

Bureau of Alcohol, Tobacco, and Firearms (Treasury)—trains locals in explosives handling

National Guard (Defense)—provides disaster relief, security

Joint Task Force, Civil Support (Defense)—coordinates other military assistance

Health and Human Services Department—assists locals with bioterroism, mass casualties

Centers for Disease Control and Prevention (HHS)—detects disease outbreaks

Environmental Protection Agency—responds to chemical attacks

Energy Department—responds to radioactive and nuclear attacks

Agriculture Department—responds to attacks on food supply, crops, and livestock

Food and Drug Administration—monitors food supply

Veterans Affairs Department—provides extra hospital space

Transportation Department—protects transportation infrastructure

National Infrastructure Protection Center (FBI)—protects computer networks

Critical Infrastructure Assurance Office (Commerce)—protects computer networks

SOURCE: Sydney Freedberg, Jr. "Shoring Up America," *National Journal,* October 20, 2001, p. 3243; U.S. General Accounting Office, *Combating Terrorism: Intergovernmental Partnership in a National Strategy to Enhance State and Local Preparedness* (March 22, 2002).

Table 7.2   Selected Products of the Intelligence Community

The following sample of the voluminous amount of information produced by the community provides an overview of the types of products and the major customers that the intelligence community serves.

Current Intelligence Products	*President's Daily Brief (CIA)*
	Secretary's Morning Summary (INR)
	World Intelligence Review (CIA)
	Economic Intelligence Brief (CIA)
	Military Intelligence Digest (DIA)
	Executive Highlights (DIA/NSA)
	Defense Intelligence Terrorism Summary (DIA)
Weeklies/Periodicals/Ad Hoc Publications	*Defense Intelligence Report (DIA)*
	Intelligence Assessment (CIA)
	Terrorist Threat Report (CIA)
	Peacekeeping Perspectives (INR)
Estimative Intelligence Products	*National Intelligence Estimates (ODNINI)*
	Intellignece Community Briefs (ODNI)
	Defense Intelligence Assessment (DIA)
Warning Intelligence	*Warning Watchlist (NIC)*
	Warning Memoranda (NIC)
	Defense Warning System Reports and Watch Condition Changes (DIA)
Research and Scientific and Technological Intelligence	*The World Factbook (CIA)*
	Handbook of Economic Statistics (CIA)

SOURCE: U.S. Director of Central Intelligence, *A Consumer's Guide to Intelligence.*

their superiors and the president. The president and other policymakers and members of the intelligence bureaucracy occupy different roles, and different motivations influence their behavior.

Consequently, it should not be too surprising that a producer-consumer problem has arisen and has become a common part of the intelligence process. Presidents are always sensitive to the domestic political implications of their policies as they try to gain control of the bureaucracy, govern foreign policy, and lead the country. When they have not already made up their minds or when they are not strongly leaning in a particular direction, presidents often want relevant information and honest intelligence appraisals to better understand the issue and arrive at an optimal decision. However, when a course of action has been already decided or if a president is ideologically predisposed, he is likely to want information that reinforces his views. Under either of these circumstances, a president may become frustrated with the intelligence product that comes across his desk, especially if it is a result of infighting and compromise.

In the bureaucratic and political environment in which the intelligence community operates, *it is easy to see how analysts can also become frustrated with the intelligence process.* The ideal mission of intelligence officers involved in data collection and analysis is to provide a comprehensive and honest assessment of available information. Yet, they operate within a bureaucratic setting and must be cognizant of how their work affects their careers. Furthermore, they have to be carefully attuned to the policy inclinations and personal perspectives of higher-level officials, such as the president and his political appointees. While in principle intelligence analysis should provide policymakers with what they need to make good decisions, not what they want to hear, in many ways "the analyst is the modern messenger whose penalty for bringing bad news might not be so severe as in ancient times, but who does risk 'banishment' of sorts if his conclusions fail to serve a policymaker's need to appear in control of events . . . the first commandment for the analyst . . . is (and has to be) 'Thou Shalt Not Lose Thy Audience' " (U.S. National Intelligence Council 2005: xx, xxxvi).

One of the problems analysts face is that they and their consumers may have different priorities as to what issues are important. For example, antiterrorism was not a relatively high foreign policy priority before 9/11 under presidents Reagan, the elder Bush, Clinton, or the younger Bush, despite the warnings of many analysts. Even when producers and consumers share similar priorities, their different perspectives can lead to the **politicization of intelligence**, which occurs when intelligence is slanted to fit the policy preferences of assumptions of key officials. *In practice, politicization can occur in at least two ways:* (1) when policymakers exert pressure on the intelligence community to produce evidence or finished intelligence that suits their preferences; and (2) when policymakers "cherry-pick" from raw intelligence or reports only those pieces of evidence or conclusions with which they agree. In either form, the result is a corruption of intelligence.

As a facet of the producer-consumer problem, politicization has been a long-standing concern, made especially problematic when key intelligence officials such as the DCI are too heavily engaged in policy advocacy, or when policymakers exert too much pressure in favor of policy positions they hold strongly. For example, politicization affected intelligence estimates in Vietnam. According to John Huizenga, chief of intelligence estimates for Soviet affairs during the Lyndon Johnson administration, "In doing estimates about Vietnam, the problem was that if you believed that the policy being pursued was going to be a flat failure, and you said so, you were going to be out of business" (Ranelagh 1986:455).

The same pattern of the politicization of intelligence plagued the process in the Reagan administration. For instance, Reagan officials pressured the CIA to produce studies concluding that El Salvadoran guerrillas and the Nicaraguan government posed a threat to U.S. security, and compelled the CIA to bring its estimates of Soviet military expenditures and production into accordance with the more pessimistic assessments made by military intelligence. DCI William Casey was especially demanding. Not only was Casey given cabinet-rank, he was also a policy advisor with strongly held policy preferences. According to many, the combination led to pressure on the CIA from Casey and others to produce evidence in support of Casey's views.

For example, Casey exerted considerable pressure on intelligence analysts to conclude that the Soviet Union had been behind the assassination attempt on the Pope in 1981 and equally powerful pressure to conclude that the Soviet Union was a major sponsor and coordinator of terrorism. In the latter instance, Casey eventually demanded a report that reviewed only the evidence in favor of that view, and then circulated it as the judgment of his agency (Jeffrey-Jones 1989).

Similar concerns have been expressed about pressure from President Bush's administration on the prewar intelligence on Iraq and its possession of weapons of mass destruction. A leading expert on intelligence, Thomas Powers (2003:12), concludes that "the invasion and conquest of Iraq by the United States" in spring 2002 "was the result of what is probably the least ambiguous case of the misreading of secret intelligence information in American history" by both producers (including the role of DCI George Tenet) and, in particular, by the consumers.

According to Kenneth Pollack (2004:78), who served the U.S in the CIA and on the National Security Council Staff for the Reagan, elder Bush, and Clinton administrations, "The intelligence community did overestimate the scope and progress of Iraq's WMD programs, although not to the extent that many people believe. The administration stretched those estimates to make a case not only for going to war but for doing so at once." As Pollack (2004:78–92), whose account is worthy of quoting at length, described it:

> [M]any administration officials reacted strongly, negatively, and aggressively when presented with information or analyses that contradicted what they already believed about Iraq. . . . Intelligence officers who presented analyses that were at odds with the preexisting views of senior administration officials were subjected to barrages of questions and requests for additional information. They were asked to justify their work sentence by sentence. . . .
>
> Bush administration officials also . . . set up their own shop in the Pentagon, called the Office of Special Plans [OSP], in order to sift through the information on Iraq themselves. To a great extent, OSP personnel "cherry-picked" the intelligence they passed on, selecting reports that supported the administration's preexisting position and ignoring all the rest.
>
> Most problematic of all, the OSP often chose to believe reports that trained intelligence officers considered unreliable or downright false. In particular, it gave great credence to reports from the Iraqi National Congress, whose leader was the administration-backed Ahmed Chalabi. . . .
>
> [Administration officials were also guilty of] distortion of intelligence estimates when making the public case for war. As best as I can tell, these officials were guilty not of lying, but of creative omission. They discussed only those elements of intelligence estimates that served their cause . . . time after time senior administration officials discussed only the worst-case, and least likely, scenario, and failed to mention the intelligence community's most likely scenario.

In effect, in these instances, intense preconceptions of senior administration officials were said to have slanted and tainted the honesty of the process responsible for intelligence information and assessments. Clearly, members of the intelligence community often must respond to cross-cutting pressures, and this affects the intelligence process and often contributes to producer-consumer problems (Goodman 1997).

Variation in Intelligence Success

In an ideal setting, the intelligence community is engaged in a precarious business. Even without problems in the producer-consumer relationship and coordination difficulties due to the intelligence community's large size, bureaucratic nature, and complexity, the success of intelligence is not guaranteed. The world is simply too big, too complex, and constantly evolving for information ever to be complete or adequate, while predictions about future behavior and trends can never be more than probabilities.

In fact, ever since the surprise attack on Pearl Harbor in 1941, scholars and analysts have pointed out that there will always be a major **signal-to-noise problem**—in other words, given the vast amount of stimuli and potential information available, it is difficult to sort out the truly relevant information and signals that need to be highlighted, collected, processed, and analyzed. And the environmental and noise problems have grown tremendously over the years. According to Lt. General Michael V. Hayden, who served as director of NSA before becoming the deputy DNI, and then the CIA director, "Forty years ago there were 5,000 standalone computers, no fax machines and not one cellular phone. Today there are over 180 million computers—most of them networked. There are roughly 14 million fax machines and 40 million cellphones, and those numbers continue to grow" (Bamford 2002:5). Of course, the world today is marked by exponentially greater numbers of all these devices!

When one adds the size and complexity of the intelligence community, difficulties in coordination, and producer-consumer problems, *a considerable amount of intelligence failure is inevitable in actual practice.* The ambiguity of the phenomena to be explained and predicted, the intelligence community's bureaucratic structure, and major policymakers' personalities and beliefs together determine the nature of the intelligence process and the value of the end product. Along with intelligence successes, such as the Cuban missile crisis, there will be intelligence failures (Betts 1978; Westerfield 1995).

Critics of the intelligence community's record argue that there have been many major errors. When North Korea invaded South Korea in 1950, it did so with no warning from the intelligence community. Nor did the community warn of the likelihood of Chinese intervention a short time later. A decade later, no systematic warning of the Soviet's move to place missiles in Cuba came before the U-2 over-flights provided photographic evidence in October. During the Vietnam War, key questions involved the strength of the enemy's forces and the ability of the U.S. military to weaken enemy will by destroying enemy personnel and supplies getting into South Vietnam. As noted in Chapter 6, the military and the CIA constantly fought over these intelligence estimates during the mid-1960s, while President Johnson and his closest military and civilian advisors supported the more optimistic military assessments.

In the 1970s, the intelligence community gave no warning of the Egyptian attack on Israel in 1973. Moreover, the size and scope of the Iranian Revolution against the shah of Iran in 1979, as well as the failure of the shah to repress it, was a surprise to members of the U.S. government. One reason was the dependence of the intelligence community on official Iranian sources and Savak, Iran's intelligence agency, for information about Iran's domestic situation. The information Savak provided portrayed a stable and vibrant shah regime, even though the domestic opposition was slowly building over the years (Sick 1985).

Critics also argue that the intelligence failed to predict the collapse of the Soviet Union in the late 1980s and early 1990s, while Iraq's attack on Kuwait on August 2, 1990, represented both intelligence failure and success. First, the U.S. intelligence community and policymakers showed little foresight concerning any threat that Iraq posed to American interests. On the contrary, after the rise of Ayatollah Khomeini in Iran, the Reagan and elder Bush administrations supported and sided with President Saddam Hussein in the 1980s. Second, as Saddam Hussein's threats against Kuwait increased and he began to mass Iraqi troops along the Kuwaiti border in July of 1990, the CIA warned administration policymakers of a possible invasion and predicted that one was imminent twenty-four to forty-eight hours before it occurred. Third, despite this warning, President Bush and his close advisors chose to discount and ignore the warning as unlikely—a classic example of the producer-consumer problem with intelligence estimates. Hence, when the Iraqi invasion occurred on August 2, President Bush and his advisors were initially shocked and caught by surprise (Wines 1990; 1991).

About a year later, on August 18, 1991, President Bush and other high-level officials of his administration were shocked to learn of the overthrow of Mikhail Gorbachev, the president of the Soviet Union. Yet, according to *Newsweek* (1991:44), "for nearly a year the CIA and the Pentagon's DIA had peppered the Bush administration with a series of increasingly dire warnings that Mikhail Gorbachev's days were numbered. The problem was getting anyone to pay attention." In fact, on August 17, the day before the coup, "the CIA's *National Intelligence Daily* (NID), which circulates among top administration officials, said Kremlin conservatives were prepared to move against the Soviet president." Nevertheless, "until tanks rolled in the streets of Moscow, the White House and the State Department insisted that Gorbachev could weather any challenge." One of the problems was that the State Department's Bureau of Intelligence and Research maintained that Gorbachev's future was safe. More important, however, it appears that President Bush's commitment and reliance on Gorbachev in American-Soviet relations, shared by his senior advisors, colored his optimism. Thus, what could have been a great intelligence success ended in intelligence failure.

Even more recently, the intelligence community's well-publicized failures prior to the 9/11 attacks exposed an unimaginative and uncoordinated counterterrorist program excessively reliant on technical sources. Intelligence and law enforcement officials were tantalizingly close to uncovering the al-Qaeda plot, but failed to share information or act aggressively to pursue leads. At the same time, the president and his senior advisors were largely inattentive to repeated warnings issued by the CIA and the NSC's Counterterrorism Strategy Group (Clarke 2004; Parker and Stern 2005; Eichenwald 2012). Subsequently, the failures to provide accurate and reliable assessments of Iraq's programs and capabilities for WMD further exposed weaknesses in the intelligence process. While senior officials were responsible for politicizing intelligence, and bear some responsibility for the failure, the intelligence community also failed to provide good assessments, basing many of its conclusions on sketchy, controversial evidence. At times, other evidence or points of view were insufficiently weighed or incorporated into the finished products, or raw intelligence was stovepiped into the highest levels without adequate vetting. In the end, as countless postwar reports on the weapons indicate, the prewar claims were almost entirely wrong.

With the advantage of hindsight, it is clear that "the CIA, FBI, and other agencies had significant fragments of information that, under ideal circumstances, could have provided some warning if they had all been pieced together and shared rapidly" (Risen 2001). The **9/11 Commission** investigating the matter details a number of important facts that demonstrate this. Among others these include the following: After tracking two identified terrorists abroad and living in the United States for one year and nine months, the CIA did not notify other government agencies until August 23, 2001; after one of their visas expired, the State Department, not knowing any better, issued a new one; in another instance after being warned by the CIA, the FBI lost track of two suspected terrorists after their arrival in the country and processing by the INS; in January 2001, the Federal Aviation Administration (FAA) issued fifteen memos to the aviation industry warning of possibly imminent hijacking of airliners inside the United States, with two naming Osama bin Laden as a suspect; on July 5 in a White House meeting, counterterrorism officials warned the FBI, FAA, INS, and other agencies that a major attack on the United States was coming soon; on July 10, the FBI's Phoenix office warned that an unusual number of Middle Eastern men were enrolling in U.S. flight schools and speculated that they may have been part of an Osama bin Laden plot—but the report was ignored at FBI headquarters; on August 6, President Bush was warned in a *President's Daily Brief* entitled "Bin Laden Determined to Strike in US" about the possibility of al-Qaeda strikes, including the hijacking of airplanes; on August 17, an

FBI field office in Minnesota warned that Zacarias Moussaoui might be planning to "fly something into the World Trade Center"—he was arrested, but there was no follow-up FBI investigation; on the day before September 11, the NSA intercepted two cryptic communications that referred to a major event scheduled for the next day but analysts at the secret eavesdropping agency did not read the messages until September 12 (U.S. National Commission on Terrorist Attacks 2003).

Whether these general (strategic) warnings could have led to a successful tactical (specific) warning is still unlikely. But there is no doubt that the intelligence community and the intelligence cycle could have performed much better. This realization led to a major shake-up of the intelligence community and other governmental organizations, first in the Homeland Security reorganization, and then in the broader intelligence reforms of 2004. Yet the patterns of coordination problems, producer-consumer problems, and variations in intelligence success are likely to continue, and are not well known or understood among the general public. In fact, the origins of America's vulnerability of the terrorist attacks of 9/11 go back to the failure of the intelligence community to address the rise of the terrorist attacks during the 1970s, the support of the covert war in Afghanistan in the 1980s, and the collapse of the Soviet Union and the end of the cold war in the 1990s.

THE CIA AND COVERT OPERATIONS

The origins of the CIA lie with the operations of the **Office of Strategic Services (OSS)**, which was created on June 13, 1942, under the authority of the armed services chiefs of staff in support of U.S. efforts in World War II. Although the OSS is often remembered for some daring (and usually unsuccessful) covert operations behind enemy lines under Director "Wild Bill" Donovan, the office was also engaged in analyzing the enemy using bright, young minds of all ages and diverse backgrounds. The OSS was disbanded following the war, and many of its intelligence activities and personnel were lodged temporarily with the Central Intelligence Group until the passage of the National Security Act of 1947, which created the CIA.

The National Security Act, which made the CIA the major agency responsible for intelligence abroad, was the product of political compromise. Many perceived a need for a foreign intelligence capability during peacetime and supported an agency that could centralize the intelligence process. However, others argued against the rise of a super spy agency reminiscent of the German Gestapo, and some saw the power of centralization as a threat to those agencies already involved in intelligence. Therefore, a new intelligence agency was created but placed under "civilian leadership." At least one of the two leadership positions, the DCI and deputy director, had to be occupied by a civilian. Both positions had to be confirmed by the Senate, and the DCI reported directly to the president. While the DCI was given the responsibility for coordinating the intelligence process throughout the government and to act as the major advisor to the president on intelligence matters, the other intelligence agencies retained their autonomy. The act also attempted to clarify jurisdictional boundaries and disputes, restricting the FBI to domestic activities and limiting the CIA's legal role to areas outside U.S. borders.

Although the CIA is heavily involved in all three basic intelligence functions and had the additional responsibility of coordinating the intelligence community until 2005, when most people think of the CIA, they think of covert operations and "dirty tricks." The **National Clandestine Service (NCS)**, which was originally called the **Directorate of Operations (DO)** until 2005, is responsible for the CIA's most renowned activities—covert operations. *Operations actually involve two types of activities:* espionage and political and paramilitary covert intervention. **Espionage** involves human intelligence and counterintelligence, such as running spies and double agents abroad in order to access information and preventing foreign intelligence agencies from penetrating the CIA. Political and paramilitary **covert intervention** involves a variety of operations, where so-called dirty tricks and coercive force are most commonly practiced.

The CIA, in other words, is composed of different subcultures. The intelligence directorate (DI) and the DS&T tend to employ analysts and scientists who often hold Ph.Ds and are research and scholarly oriented, paralleling what one might find in a research institute or university. *Operations, in contrast, are composed of two different subcultures* because espionage and political-paramilitary intervention are two different activities and require different kinds of skills. Espionage agents act as spies and tend to be secretive, cautious, and loyal. CIA operatives involved in political and paramilitary activities tend to be much more action oriented, adventuristic, bold, and often flamboyant (Hersh 1992).

Operations and action types—often referred to as "cowboys"—have dominated CIA leadership through most of its history. For a long time, directors of central intelligence, for example, have tended to come from the operations side of intelligence within the government and military (many of the earlier DCIs were originally with the OSS). More importantly, *American policymakers have relied upon CIA covert action as a major U.S. foreign policy instrument since World War II.* While the U.S. government attempted to deter Soviet expansion through the threat of nuclear and conventional war, it also relied on political and paramilitary intervention to fight communism covertly throughout the globe during the cold war. Theodore Shackley (1981), a senior covert operations specialist who spent twenty-eight years with the CIA, has referred to political and paramilitary action as "the third option," superior to diplomacy and war.

Since the 1970s a growing body of information has painted a consistent picture of CIA covert operations in pursuit of American national security (e.g., Godson 2000; Jeffreys-Jones 1989; Johnson 1991; 2000; Prados 1986; Ranelagh 1985). From its creation until the collapse of the Soviet Union, *the CIA and its covert operations evolved through four stages:* (1) the "good ol' days," 1947 through the early 1970s; (2) the "fall" and reform, early 1970s to 1979; (3) the resurgence, during the 1980s; and (4) the adjustment, in the post–cold war and post-9/11 periods (Johnson 2004).

The "Good Ol' Days"

Initially, extensive covert operations were not envisioned. The CIA was created to provide the president with an intelligence capability to engage in data collection and analysis as well as to coordinate the larger intelligence community existing at the time. In fact, "nobody mentioned the Soviet Union or its clandestine services in the congressional debate on the CIA provision of the National Security Act. Congressmen were introspectively concerned with Gestapo-like tendencies at home" (Jeffreys-Jones 1989:41). However, one clause of the CIA charter allowed it to "perform such other functions and duties related to intelligence affecting the national security as the National Security Council may from time to time direct," which provided the later legal justification for involving the CIA in cloak-and-dagger operations. Thus, the CIA soon became the major governmental organization responsible for covert actions abroad in support of the policy of containment.

Soon, presidential directives, such as NSC 5412/I on March 12, 1955, called for covert operations "so planned and executed that any U.S. Government responsibility for them is not evident to unauthorized persons and that if uncovered the U.S. Government can plausibly disclaim any responsibility for them" (Jeffreys-Jones 1989:83). As NSC 5412/I stipulated, everything and anything was allowed:

> Propaganda, political action; economic warfare; escape and evasion and evacuation measures; subversion against hostile states or groups including assistance to underground movements, guerrillas and refugee liberation groups; support of indigenous and anticommunist elements in threatened countries of the free world; deception plans and operations; and all activities compatible with this directive necessary to accomplish the foregoing. (quoted in Jeffreys-Jones 1989:83)

Such measures were justified in terms of an anticommunist philosophy and a power-politics, ends-justify-the-means strategy that became the basis of a **national security ethos** that pervaded American policymakers during the cold war consensus.

As explained by the top secret report of the General James Doolittle Committee to the 1954 Hoover Commission on government organization:

> It is now clear that we are facing an implacable enemy whose avowed objective is world domination by whatever means at whatever cost. There are no rules in such a game. Hitherto acceptable norms of human conduct do not apply. If the U.S. is to survive, long-standing American concepts of "fair play" must be reconsidered. We must develop effective espionage and counterespionage services. We must learn to subvert, sabotage and destroy our enemies by more clever, more sophisticated and more effective methods than those used against us. It may become necessary that the American people will be made acquainted with, understand and support this fundamentally repugnant philosophy. (U.S. Congress 1976:9)

Many of these covert operations were so incompatible with the American political culture of liberal democracy that secrecy was of the essence. Often the goal was not really to maintain secrets from enemies abroad; the existence of an operation was often exposed, sometimes deliberately, on the assumption that knowledge of a CIA operation invoked sufficient fear to promote its success. Instead, it was imperative to maintain secrecy at home for fear that leaks would trigger domestic opposition that would place the future of covert operations at risk.

The heyday of covert operations occurred under Director **Allen Dulles** from 1952 to 1961, a time when his brother, John Foster Dulles, also served as secretary of state (Grose 1995). Even though the president often remained distant from the details of an operation, the DCI responded to presidential initiative and choice. Also, no real oversight existed outside the executive branch, as Congress generally preferred to remain on the sidelines in deference to presidential leadership and the cold war consensus (Barrett 2005). It has been reported that, by 1953, the CIA had major covert operations in progress in forty-eight countries, while three-fourths of the agency's budget and two-thirds of its employees were devoted to espionage and political intervention (Ransom 1983:303). A U.S. Senate select committee investigating foreign and military intelligence in 1975 found that the CIA had "conducted some 900 major or sensitive covert action projects plus several thousand smaller projects since 1961" (U.S. Congress 1976:445). In other words, the CIA, in its heyday, was engaged in covert operations all over the world, with as much as one-third of its interventions taking place in "pro-Western" democracies (Jeffreys-Jones 1989:51). **Table 7.3** highlights some of the major covert operations during the "good ol' days" that have come to light, although much CIA covert activity remains unknown.

Table 7.3   Major CIA Covert Operations During the "Good Ol' Days"

1947–48	Propaganda campaign during the 1948 Italian national elections
1947–48	Propaganda campaign during the 1948 French national elections
1948–52	Partisan resistance movements in Eastern Europe and Soviet Union
1949	Anglo-American effort to overthrow the Albanian government
1950–70s	Propaganda campaigns through Radio Liberty and Radio Free Europe
1952–60	Kuomintang (KMT) Chinese partisan resistance movement on Sino-Burmese border
1953	Anglo-American overthrow of Prime Minister Mohammed Mossadegh of Iran
1953–54	Campaign to support Ramon Magsaysay's presidential candidacy and counter Huk insurgency in Philippines
1954	Overthrow of democratic President Jacobo Arbenz of Guatemala
1950s–70s	Subsidization of domestic and foreign groups and publications
1953–70s	Drug testing and mind-control program
1954–70s	Effort to overthrow leader Ho Chi Minh and the North Vietnamese government
1955	Effort to destabilize President José Figueres's government of Costa Rica
1958	Support of Tibetan partisan resistance movement in China
1958–65	Effort to destabilize President Sukarno of Indonesia
1960	Alleged effort to assassinate General Abdul Kassem, leader of Iraq
1960	Alleged effort to assassinate President Abdul Nasser of Egypt
1960	Alleged effort to assassinate political leader Patrice Lumumba of Congo
1961	Effort to overthrow Fidel Castro, leader of Cuba
1961	Effort to assassinate Rafael Trujillo, leader of Dominican Republic
1961	Effort to destabilize President Kwame Nkrumah of Ghana
1960s	Effort to assassinate Fidel Castro of Cuba
1960s	Fought secret war in Laos
1962–63	Destabilized the Ecuadorean governments of Ibarra and Arosemena
1963	Destabilized Prime Minister Cheddi Jagan's government of British Guiana
1963	Supported overthrow of President Ngo Dinh Diem of South Vietnam
1960s	Conducted pacification and Phoenix programs in Vietnam
1964	Campaign in support of President Eduardo Frei in 1964 Chilean elections
1964	Supported military coup against President Joao Goulart of Brazil
1967	Supported military coup in Greece
1967–70s	Domestic campaign against antiwar movement and political dissent
1970–73	Destabilized democratic Chilean government of President Salvador Allende

SOURCES: Rhodri Jeffreys-Jones, *The CIA and American Democracy* (New Haven: Yale University Press, 1989); Jonathan Kwitny, *Endless Enemies* (New York: Penguin, 1984); Thomas Powers, *The Man Who Kept the Secrets* (New York: Pocket Books, 1979); John Prados, *President's Secret Wars* (New York: William Morrow, 1986); John Ranelagh, *The Agency* (New York: Simon and Schuster, 1986); David Wise and Thomas B. Ross, *The Invisible Government* (New York: Vintage, 1974); U.S. Congress, Senate, *Alleged Assassination Plots Involving Foreign Leaders*, Congressional Report (94th Cong., 1st sess., November 18, 1975); and U.S. Congress, Senate, *Final Report of the Select Committee to Study Governmental Operations with Respect to Intelligence Activities,* Books 1–6, Congressional Report (94th Cong., 2nd sess., April 14, 1976).

The CIA became an important tool of U.S. foreign policy immediately after its creation in 1947. The examples discussed next highlight but a few of the *important types of covert activities:*

1. *Manipulating foreign democratic elections.* In both Italy and France in 1948, for example, the United States worried that the economic and political instability after World War II, which strengthened legal communist parties in those countries, would eventually result in electoral victories for the Communist parties. Consequently, the CIA engaged in a variety of efforts to undermine the communists and strengthen the centrist parties.

2. *Organizing partisan resistance movements.* In the late 1940s and 1950s, the CIA also supported partisan resistance movements in communist countries to promote internal instability and domestic uprisings. For example, the CIA trained emigrés and secretly transported them into Albania, Poland, Yugoslavia, the Baltic states, Soviet Georgia, and the Ukraine.

3. *Overthrowing foreign governments.* Under President Dwight Eisenhower, the CIA became involved in a series of efforts to overthrow foreign governments. Such efforts include the Iranian coup of 1953 to overthrow the Iranian nationalist leader Mohammed Mossadegh and restore the Pahlavi dynasty, headed by the shah (Bill 1988) and the 1954 coup in Guatemala to overthrow democratically elected President Jacobo Arbenz and replace him with a military dictator, General Castillo de Armas (Immerman 1982; Schlesinger and Kinzer 1982).

4. *Participating in foreign assassinations.* During this period, the CIA engaged in plans to assassinate foreign leaders. *Later* investigations revealed efforts to kill such leaders as Patrice Lumumba, prime minister and national leader of the Congo (Zaire), Fidel Castro in Cuba, and the democratically elected socialist president Salvador Allende in Chile. With respect to Castro, for example, most were hair-brained schemes that only James Bond could have pulled off such as attempts to slip Castro the hallucinogen LSD via a cigar, to give him a pen with a poison tip, to explode clamshells while he dove in the Caribbean, and to sprinkle his shoes with an agent to make his beard fall out and with it, according to the psychological warfare experts, his Latin machismo (Jeffreys-Jones 1989:132). The CIA even went so far as to turn to the Mafia for assistance to kill him. Most of these assassination efforts were unsuccessful, although Lumumba was assassinated eventually, clearing a way for the U.S.-backed dictator—Mobuto Sese Seko—who ruled a corrupt regime for thirty years and impoverished the country (Kalb 1981), and Allende was eventually removed from power three years after one of his top supporters in the military, General Rene Schneider, was assassinated. The CIA also conducted the infamous **Phoenix program**, during the Vietnam War, which targeted thousands of suspected Vietcong and communist supporters for "neutralization." Not only were many innocent individuals jailed, but torture, terrorism, and assassination were also used as part of the Phoenix operation.

5. *Supporting friendly, often authoritarian, governments.* The CIA also supported foreign governments allied to the United States in such places as Iran, Cuba (before Fidel), Nicaragua, and elsewhere, often participating in an allied government's violent repression of its own people. For example, in Indonesia, after actively destabilizing President Sukarno (like many Indonesians, he had only one name), a prominent leader of the Third World nonaligned movement beginning in 1958, the CIA then actively supported his successor after Sukarno's ouster. The CIA then assisted the new government of General

Suharto in eliminating Indonesian Communist Party (PKI) members and repressing all internal dissent, which included providing the Indonesian army with lists of people to be arrested and killed—estimated as high as two to three million people (Bleifuss 1990; Smith 1976). In South Africa, the CIA supported the "white" apartheid regime, even provided the regime with a tip from a "deep cover" CIA agent that led to the August 5, 1962, arrest of Nelson Mandela, the underground leader of the African National Congress (ANC), the major force opposing the Afrikaner government and the system of apartheid (Albright and Kunstel 1990).

6. *Training foreign military, intelligence, and police personnel.* The CIA also frequently offered "retainers" to foreign leaders, putting them on the CIA payroll, and the CIA frequently engaged in training of foreign intelligence personnel, including those engaged in covert operations. The armed forces and the national police of many governments allied with the United States also were trained by U.S. military and government personnel.

7. *Pursuing various covert actions at home against American citizens.* The CIA spent millions of dollars funding hundreds of private individuals and groups active in business, labor, journalism, education, philanthropy, religion, and the arts as a means to promote the anticommunist message and stifle dissent against the U.S. policy of containment (U.S. Congress 1976:179–204). The fear of communism was so great that the president and the intelligence agencies often saw any domestic dissent as an internal threat and often acted to repress it. In domestic covert operations the CIA opened the mail of American citizens, kept over 1.5 million names on file, and infiltrated religious, media-related, and academic organizations; the FBI carried out more than 500,000 investigations of so-called subversives without a single court conviction and created files on over 1,000,000 Americans; the NSA monitored cables sent overseas or received by Americans from 1947 to 1975; Army intelligence investigated over 100,000 American citizens during the Vietnam War era; and the Internal Revenue Service allowed tax information to be misused by intelligence agencies for political purposes. Paranoia about threats to security in the late 1950s was so great that Project MKULTRA (pronounced "m-k-ultra") was created. Its purpose was to acquire "brainwashing" techniques that the U.S. intelligence community was convinced were used by the Chinese, North Korean, and Eastern European governments. Project MKULTRA consisted of Frankenstein-like projects that involved mind-control experiments on human beings (Donner 1981; Halperin et al. 1976).

The "Fall" and Reform During the 1970s

The failure of Vietnam politicized segments of American society and contributed to the collapse of the anticommunist consensus. The domestic political environment became even more critical when the revelations of Watergate uncovered abuses of presidential power. A period of intense scrutiny ensued. President Gerald Ford appointed the Rockefeller Commission in 1975 to investigate the intelligence community and recommend reforms. But, as with many presidential commissions, the Rockefeller Commission had little credibility. In fact, while the Rockefeller Commission was operating, President Ford and Secretary of State Henry Kissinger were supervising a major CIA covert operation in Angola. Ford and Kissinger tried to keep the operation secret from Congress at a time when members of Congress were reasserting their authority in foreign affairs. When word of the Angolan operation leaked, Congress voted to abort it and began its own investigation of intelligence (Stockwell 1978).

The House and Senate each conducted major investigations of the intelligence community and covert operations. The **Pike and Church Committee investigations** (named after the chairman of each chamber's Foreign Relations Committee) led to the first public knowledge of the scale of covert operations conducted by the CIA. In this political climate, the intelligence community, especially the CIA and covert operations, experienced a major decline. During this time, over 1800 covert operatives were fired or forced to take early retirement, and most covert operations were cut, including major political and paramilitary programs. Congress also asserted itself in oversight. For example, in the 1980 Intelligence Oversight Act, it established new, permanent **intelligence committees** in both chambers and required the submission to Congress of a **presidential finding**, explaining the need and nature of any covert actions. Presidential executive orders were issued that limited the kinds of covert operations the CIA could conduct, such as forbidding U.S. governmental personnel from becoming involved in political assassinations. The net impact was that the use of covert operations as a tool of U.S. foreign policy, and morale among covert operatives, reached its nadir by the end of the 1970s (Johnson 1989;2005).

Resurgence in the 1980s

Beginning in 1980, the CIA and covert operations got a new lease on life. The resurgence of the CIA began during the last year of the Carter administration, when President Carter approved a major covert operation to send money and arms to the Afghan resistance forces fighting the Soviet occupation through U.S.-controlled sources and agents in Pakistan and Saudi Arabia (Coll 2004). It was under the Reagan administration, however, that the CIA and the use of covert operations became a major force in U.S. foreign policy, reminiscent of the cold war days. Under **William Casey**, a strident anticommunist and former member of the OSS during World War II, the CIA rejuvenated its operations division and rehired many former covert operatives. Although the CIA's budget remained secret, experts believe that it may have grown over 20 percent a year during this time—a faster rate of growth than that experienced by the military in its buildup and at a time when efforts were made to impose domestic spending cuts (Taubman 1983).

Under Casey, the CIA launched over a dozen "major" covert operations (defined by the congressional intelligence committees as an operation costing over $5 million or designed to overthrow a foreign government) in places such as Central America, Angola, Libya, Ethiopia, Mauritius, Cambodia, Afghanistan, and Iran. Major operations included a huge CIA **Afghanistan operation** to support insurgents—known as the *Mujahideen*—against the invading Soviet military, and a campaign to destabilize and overthrow the new Nicaraguan Sandinista regime. In Nicaragua, the **Contra covert war** in Nicaragua was eventually outlawed by Congress in 1985 and 1986. Nevertheless, the Reagan administration circumvented the law by pursuing the Contra operation through the NSC staff and relying on private operatives and groups, triggering a crisis of governance for the Reagan presidency when the true nature of the Contra covert operations became exposed (Kagan 1996; Scott 1996). In Afghanistan, through Pakistan and Saudi Arabia, the CIA provided billions in support for arms and training, and played an important role in helping the insurgents force the Soviets to withdraw and the Taliban regime to take power, although it also inadvertently helped to create the al-Qaeda network that would plague the United States later (Coll 2004; Scott 1996).

Adjusting to the Post–Cold War and 9/11 Era

According to Theodore Draper (1997:18), "Of all the organizations that miss having the Soviet Union as an enemy, the CIA has undoubtedly been hit the hardest. The reason is that the CIA was specifically established in 1947 to struggle with the Soviet enemy. . . . But now the enemy has vanished. Its most dedicated American antagonist has been deprived of its mission. . . . [Now], the CIA wanders about in a wilderness of self-doubt and recrimination." Recent years have not been much kinder, as the spectacular failures of September 11 and Iraq left the CIA reeling. One analysis concluded that the CIA has "lost its place and standing in Washington," while a CIA veteran reacted to the 2004 intelligence reforms by saying "The agency, as we know it, is gone" (Gorman 2005; Risen 2006:220). Yet in late 2005, the CIA's central role in collecting human intelligence and carrying out and coordinating covert operations was confirmed with the strengthening of the "National Clandestine Service," the new name for its directorate of operations. And, since 9/11, the agency's covert antiterrorist programs have grown into the largest covert action program since the height of the cold war.

The cold war's end ushered in a set of challenges for the CIA and its covert action mission, which appeared much less central to U.S. foreign policy without the cold war's context. Consequently, while the CIA sought new missions in the post–cold war context, its budget growth first slowed under George H.W. Bush and then began to decline under Bill Clinton. At the same time, challenges to CIA activities began. Congress attempted to enact tighter controls over covert action, but the elder Bush vetoed the legislation in 1992. Not long after, New York Senator Daniel Patrick Moynihan sponsored legislation to eliminate the CIA entirely. Between 1990 and 2001, a spate of studies—some from Congress, some from special commissions, and some from policy think-tanks—all recommended reforms of the intelligence community (U.S. House 1996; U.S. Commission on the Roles and Capabilities of the United States Intelligence Community 1996; Council on Foreign Relations 1996).

In the midst of this turmoil, the CIA continued some traditional covert operations and added some new actions as well. For example, the CIA applied its traditional instruments in the 1990s against Iraq and Kosovo. In Iraq, starting with a Bush administration finding that authorized efforts to destabilize the Iraqi economy in 1990 (after the Iran-Iraq War), the CIA engaged in a series of efforts to undermine Saddam Hussein, none of which was particularly effective. Under Bill Clinton, for example, the CIA supported the "Iraqi National Congress," spending about $120 million seeking Hussein's assassination or overthrow. These operations collapsed when the resistance was infiltrated by Hussein's forces, although the U.S. committed itself to "regime change" in Iraq again in 1998. In Kosovo in 1999, the CIA launched a campaign against Serbia and **Slobodan Milošević´** that combined propaganda, destabilization, support of opposition groups, and other methods to undermine the regime (Godson 2000; Johnson 2000; Risen 2000).

At the same time, the CIA took up a role in new areas as well, including drug trafficking, economic intelligence, and counterterrorism. On the drug war, the CIA began to cooperate with other agencies, including the FBI and the Drug Enforcement Agency, to break up drug rings. The CIA also increased its activities in the highly controversial arena of economic espionage, not only collecting information on trade practices, but even attempting to steal trade secrets. Finally, with rising concerns about terrorism after the 1993 World Trade Center bombing, the CIA accelerated its counterterrorism operations as well. Osama bin Laden and the al-Qaeda network were especially important targets, and the CIA established a new counterterrorism center and a "bin Laden station" to oversee its efforts. Although some success occurred, the attacks in 1998 on U.S. embassies in Kenya and Tanzania, the 2000 bombing of the *USS Cole* in Yemen, and, of course, the September 11 attacks amply demonstrate the limits of these efforts (Baer 2002: Naftali 2005).

AFTER SEPTEMBER 11, 2001 The attacks of 9/11 initiated a new season for the CIA and its covert operations mission. Just a few days after the attack, George W. Bush signed a presidential finding starting what has grown into the largest covert operation since the heydays of the cold war, dwarfing even the decade-long Afghanistan operations of the 1980s. In addition to activities in advance and support of U.S. operations in Afghanistan and Iraq, the CIA began a host of interrelated programs to break up terror cells, assassinate terrorists, capture and interrogate al-Qaeda suspects, gain access to and disrupt financial networks, eavesdrop, and a variety of other activities (Clarke 2004; Risen 2005; Schroen 2005). As Bob Woodward reported (2001:1), "The gloves are off. The president has given the agency the green light to do whatever is necessary. Lethal operations that were unthinkable pre-September 11 are now underway."

The CIA budget for covert operations was nearly doubled to almost $50 billion. For the first time in a decade, the CIA began to expand its operations directorate as well, and the counterterrorism center at the CIA more than doubled in size, becoming the center of covert actions against terrorism (Pincus 2001). The administration and Congress rushed the Patriot Act through and dramatically expanded the intelligence and investigative powers of the government.

The administration sought and received broad grants of authority to conduct its war on terrorism, and it authorized even broader activities by the intelligence community. Little congressional oversight occurred either, as Congress deferred to the administration in the atmosphere of national security urgency. This began to change in 2003 and 2004 when certain intelligence practices were revealed and became politicized, such as U.S. involvement with torture and the Abu Ghraib scandal (see **The Liberty–Security Dilemma**).

The year 2004 saw renewed concern for democratic norms due to a series of revelations stemming form several highly controversial programs intended to thwart the growing insurgency in Iraq and engage in the war on terror. These revelations included: (1) decisions about the treatment of prisoners, which allowed harsh treatment, even torture, in U.S. facilities in Guantanamo Bay, Iraq, Afghanistan, and elsewhere in violation of both domestic and international laws as described earlier; (2) the establishment and operations of secret CIA-run prisons in other countries; and (3) most controversial of all, spying activities at home that impact American citizens' civil liberties, including intrusive information gathering, "fishing expedition" investigations by the FBI and Army intelligence, and extensive eavesdropping by the NSA (Baker 2005; Gellman and Linzer 2005; Isikoff 2006; Risen 2005).

As the *Washington Post* summarized in late 2005 (Gellman and Linzer 2005:1):

Since October, news accounts have disclosed a burgeoning Pentagon campaign for "detecting, identifying, and engaging" internal enemies that included a database with information on peace protesters. A debate has roiled over the FBI's use of national security letters to obtain secret access to the personal records of tens of thousands of Americans. And now come revelations of the National Security Agency's interception of telephone calls and e-mails from the United States—without notice to the federal court that has held jurisdiction over domestic spying since 1978.

At the same time, however, the CIA came under criticism for its failures to prevent the September 11 attacks and then, later, for its role in the prewar Iraq intelligence fiasco. A number of investigations issued scathing reports of CIA failures. Additionally, as some of the covert actions become public—especially the CIA programs for assassination, capture,

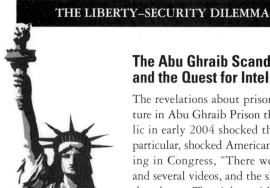

The Abu Ghraib Scandal, Human Rights, Torture, and the Quest for Intelligence

The revelations about prison abuse and torture in Abu Ghraib Prison that became public in early 2004 shocked the world and, in particular, shocked Americans. Before a hearing in Congress, "There were 1,800 slides and several videos, and the show went on for three hours. The nightmarish images showed American soldiers at Abu Ghraib Prison forcing Iraqis to masturbate. American soldiers sexually assaulting Iraqis with chemical sticks. American soldiers laughing over dead Iraqis whose bodies had been abused and mutilated" (Barry, Hirsh and Isikopf 2004:29). According to numerous official governmental and nongovernmental reports, including the International Red Cross, "These methods of physical and psychological coercion *were used in a systematic way to gain confessions and extract information*" (see also Danner 2004).

How could such physical abuse and torture occur? First, interrogation and torture are usually a part of war. Second, "the roots of the Abu Ghraib Prison scandal lie . . . in a decision, approved last year by Secretary of Defense Donald Rumsfeld, to expand a highly secret operation. . . . with blanket advance approval to kill or capture and, if possible interrogate 'high value' [terrorist] targets" (Hersh 2004). Third, with the insurgency in Iraq expanding in 2002, military, intelligence community, and civilian leaders became desperate for acquiring information and intelligence in an effort to counter the insurgency. The U.S. military began to increasingly arrest ("cordon and capture") and detain Iraqis, many of whom were sent to Abu Ghraib. Hard-core special operatives from the intelligence community worked with military intelligence and military police in the prison. Torture and abuse became the norm, despite evidence that 80 to 90 percent of those held at Abu Ghraib were innocent civilians.

Finally, a major part of the purpose of the interrogation programs was to bypass international law and the Geneva Conventions that had been long established during a time of war (especially Geneva III on the rights of "prisoners of war" and Geneva IV on the rights of civilians). President Bush and his closest advisors believed that the global war on terrorism gave the president broad executive prerogative that would allow both domestic and international law to be ignored or circumvented. At the beginning of 2002, President Bush decided to withhold protection of the Geneva Conventions both from al-Qaeda and from Taliban fighters in Afghanistan. In "secret legal opinions drafted by lawyers from the Justice Department's Office of Legal Counsel, and then endorsed by the DOD and ultimately by White House Counsel Alberto Gonzalez," the administration argued that America's enemies were "unlawful" combatants without rights to Geneva protections (Barry, Hirsh and Isikopf 2004:29). The administration also argued that "Any effort by Congress to regulate the interrogation of unlawful combatants would violate the Constitution's sole vesting of the Commander-in-Chief authority in the President"—reflecting the notion of "unitary executive authority" discussed in Chapter 3 (Lewis 2004:4).

What does the Abu Ghraib incident and the Bush administration's justification of "harsh interrogation techniques" in the war on terrorism suggest about the tension between liberty and security in U.S. foreign policymaking. What, if anything, has changed under President Obama?

interrogation, and its secret "rendition" prison system abroad—heightened scrutiny occurred. Hence, by 2006, with major intelligence reform weakening the CIA's role, sagging morale from the failures of the previous five years, leadership turnover and infighting among careerists and appointees, new organizational rivalries between the CIA and the ODNI, and new challenges from the Defense Department for roles in covert operations, the future of CIA activities in this arena was far from certain. Indeed, new revelations surfaced in 2009 of potential torture and a potential assassination program deliberately concealed from Congress and the American people by the Bush administration. These revelations generated new outcries, and calls for full investigations, and further illustrated the ongoing tension between security imperatives and oversight/rule of law (Kane and Pershing 2009) (See **A Different Perspective**).

However, under Barack Obama, the CIA continued a variety of covert actions in the war on terror. As we discussed earlier, aggressive efforts were made to locate Osama bin Laden and other al-Qaeda leaders, including the highly publicized and successful May 2011 raid in Pakistan that resulted in bin Laden's death. Additionally, under CIA director Leon Panetta, and then General David Petraeus, his successor when Panetta moved on to the secretary of defense position in 2011, the CIA expanded its use of unmanned drones to strike terrorist targets. This program was first expanded in Pakistan, and involved what the CIA called "profile" strikes (involving drone attacks on a specific individual) and "signature" strikes (involving more general targeting of groups and suspicious activities). For example, while a profile attack might kill an al-Qaeda leader traveling in a vehicle, a signature attack might target a funeral of a known al-Qaeda leader, "on the grounds that attending an al-Qaeda funeral is evidence of hostile intentions toward the United States. . . . if the US slaughters a particular crowd of people at an al-Qaeda funeral, they are sure to kill men plotting to attack the United States" (Morley 2012). Highly controversial within US interagency discussions, and with US allies such as Pakistan, drone strikes were soon expanded into Yemen as well, first as "profile" strikes. Even in the face of criticism (including a law suit filed by the families of three American victims of a strike in Yemen), right up until his November 2012 resignation, CIA director David Petraeus and his allies were advocating for the escalation of the Yemen program to include signature strikes as well, claiming that such covert actions had resulted in the death of more al-Qaeda operatives than the more limited targeted strikes (Morley 2012).

THE FUTURE OF INTELLIGENCE AND THE DILEMMAS OF DEMOCRATIC GOVERNANCE?

As we have seen, the intelligence community plays a significant role in the formulation and implementation of U.S. foreign policy. At the same time, it remains heavily influenced by powerful bureaucratic functions, structures, and subcultures that have developed over time, and problems of coordination, producer-consumer challenges, and intelligence failures continue to plague it. Moreover, since the cold war spurred the development of the large and complex intelligence community, its proper structures and functions have presented significant dilemmas for democratic governance. As our previous discussion demonstrates, the evolution of the intelligence has resulted in the *existence of an extensive security and secrecy system in government.* This development

Checks and Balances, What Role for Big Brother?

Congresswoman Jane Harman (D-CA), former chair of the House Intelligence Committee, shared what the Bush Administrated selectively communicated to Congress in an article entitled, "What the CIA Hid From Congress":

As ranking member on the House Intelligence Committee from 2003 to 2006, I was part of the so-called Gang of Eight— a group made up of the House and Senate leaders plus the chairs and ranking members of the two chambers' intelligence committees that is required by law to be briefed on the CIA's "covert" action programs.

Those briefings were conducted roughly quarterly at the White House—either in the vice president's office or the Situation Room. Most of the ones I attended concerned a code-named program now known as the Terrorist Surveillance Program. Respectful of the double oath I signed to protect highly classified material, I did not take notes or speak to anyone about the meetings. However, comments by Michael Hayden, former director of the NSA and the CIA, that the Gang of Eight was "fully" briefed on the TSP prompt me to disclose, for the first time, what they were like.

In virtually every meeting, Hayden would present PowerPoint "slides," walking us through the *operational* details of the TSP. The program has since been described, in part, as one that intercepted communications to and from the U.S. in an effort to

uncover terrorist networks and prevent or disrupt attacks. We were told that the program was the centerpiece of our counter-terrorism efforts, legal and yielding impressive results.

Often present were CIA officials (including then-Director George Tenet) and then-White House counsel Alberto R. Gonzales. Missing was any Justice Department presence—a tipoff, in retrospect, to the legal limbo under which the program operated.

Fast-forward to the jaw-dropping inspectors general report released this month, which makes clear that the TSP's legal underpinnings were fatally flawed and its results minimal. Those topics consumed scant time at our briefings. Why?

It is now clear to me that we learned only what the briefers wanted to tell us—even though they were required by law to keep us "fully and currently informed." Absent the ability to do any independent research, it did not occur to me then that the program was operated wholly outside of the framework Congress created as the *exclusive* means to conduct such surveillance: the Foreign Intelligence Surveillance Act.

Nor did I know that the Justice Department was cut out of the process, and that one lawyer, John Yoo, had drafted the internal memo justifying the TSP under the president's Article 2 authorities. A new head of the Office of Legal Counsel repudiated that memo, citing the "shoddiness" of the legal reasoning. Among other things, it even failed to cite the key Supreme Court precedent—the steel-seizure case—which held in 1952 that when Congress has acted on an issue (as it did by passing FISA in 1978), the president's power is at its "lowest ebb."

And I did not know—until I read it in the press—of the 2004 drama at then-Atty. Gen. John Ashcroft's hospital bedside, when Bush officials sought his sign-off on an extension of the program. I recall being told that there was a "glitch" in the approval process. A glitch? More like a near-hijacking of our democracy.

Much has happened since. The Yoo memo was officially discredited and replaced. After considerable resistance, the Bush administration finally briefed the full intelligence committees, and FISA was amended to assure its application to the TSP.

In a July 16 Op-Ed article in the *Wall Street Journal*, Yoo wrote that "it is absurd to think that a law like FISA should inhibit live military operations against potential attacks on the United States." I see it rather differently. While our country had experienced the worst terrorist attack

in our history, the Orwellian solution conjured up by a small group in the Bush administration was to shred our laws and Constitution in order to save us—a false and unnecessary choice.

Security and liberty are not a zero-sum game. Our Constitution protects both. Members of each branch of government take an oath to uphold the Constitution. Bipartisan oversight by Congress to assure that the laws we pass are faithfully executed is an indispensable part of that equation.

The House and Senate intelligence authorization bills would require increased notification, including, in the House bill, information on lawfulness, cost, benefit, and risk. The White House has issued a veto threat, citing constitutional concerns. Surely both sides—and policy—would profit more from a robust partnership.

How much should the U.S. Congress be involved in such intelligence policy matters in order to maintain democratic accountability?

SOURCE: Jane Harman, "What the CIA hid from Congress." *Los Angeles Times,* July 25, 2009.

---

has created a dilemma for the United States and its citizens, for the demands of national security and the demands of democracy are often difficult to reconcile. ***Tensions between national security and democracy are particularly significant in three areas:***

1. independence versus accountability,

2. secrecy versus availability of information, and

3. the legitimacy of covert operations.

On one hand, democracy requires that governmental agencies be held accountable to elected leaders and the public. Since the height of the cold war, the need for oversight of the intelligence community has been a regular item on the foreign policy agenda, and controversial policies such as those enacted during the cold war and since the September 11 attacks clearly demand such scrutiny. The demands of national security, on the other hand, often require a quick and efficient foreign policy response. A premium is placed on the independence and secrecy of governmental operations to keep the enemy at bay. The use of all means available to protect and further national security is considered a necessity in a world where morality is seen to have little relevance. How to reconcile these competing demands continues to be a challenge for American foreign policymakers in both branches, and for the American public as well.

A general pattern can be identified. ***When perceptions of enemy threat*** are high, the demands of national security tend to prevail, resulting in the rise of intelligence activities, particularly covert operations. When threat perceptions decline, democratic considerations tend to rise, and the legitimacy of intelligence functions, especially covert operations, is often questioned. Hence, (1) during the cold war years of high threat perceptions, the demands of national security prevailed over democracy, and a national security ethos grew; (2) after the Vietnam War, low threat perceptions prevailed and democratic norms grew in importance while the demands of national security lost much of their legitimacy outside the government, although the national security ethos continued to prevail within government; and (3) the September 11 attacks and the war on terrorism have so far resulted in a similar pattern, with national security demands ascendant in the immediate post-attack period, and concerns with democratic norms increasing after 2003 when the threat environment appeared less urgent—producing an uneasy coexistence between national security and democracy.

The collapse of the Soviet Union and the end of the cold war in 1989, and the subsequent challenges generated by the post-9/11 war on terrorism, represented a historic opportunity for some serious rethinking of the role of intelligence in American society and U.S. foreign policy. For example, how large and what kind of an intelligence community is required as the United States enters the twenty-first century? What type of intelligence and counterintelligence activities does the government require? How much accountability and independence (and secrecy) should be required or allowed? Will the 2004 reforms and other developments change the ways the intelligence community behaves? As Gregory Treverton (2001) has stated, "September 11 drove home the fact that terrorism is an old world problem but in new world circumstances. . . . The required reshaping of the clandestine service goes well beyond what is imaginable in today's political climate."

As President Barack Obama began his second term, these challenges remained. Adapting the intelligence community and its activity to the demands of the 21st century remains difficult and elusive. Areas of progress and success continue to be matched by shortcomings, as the incomplete and ambiguous intelligence on the September 2012 attack on a U.S. diplomatic facility in Benghazi, Libya indicate. Given the long tension between intelligence needs and intelligence capabilities, these dilemmas are not likely to disappear.

SUGGESTED SOURCES FOR MORE INFORMATION

Bamford, James. (2004) *A Pretext for War: 9/11, Iraq, and the Abuse of America's Intelligence Agencies.* New York: Doubleday. Addresses both the intelligence failures leading to the 9/11 attacks as well as the Iraq invasion.

Berkowitz, Bruce, and Allan Goodman. (2000) *Best Truth: Intelligence in the Information Age.* New Haven, CT: Yale University Press. Addresses the implications of the end of the cold war for the future of intelligence.

Danner, Mark. (2009) *Torture and Terror: America, Agu Ghraib and the War on Terror.* New York: New York Review of Books. Powerful overview of torture on the ground and the torture memos of the Bush administration.

Godson, Roy. (2000) *Dirty Tricks or Trump Cards: U.S. Covert Action and Counterintelligence.* New Brunswick, NJ: Transaction. A useful examination of the evolution and role of covert action.

Jeffreys-Jones, Rhodri. (2003) *The CIA and American Democracy.* New Haven, CT: Yale University Press. A good analytical treatment, emphasizing the impact of politics on the CIA's evolution.

Johnson, Loch, and James Wirtz, eds. (2004) *Strategic Intelligence: Windows into a Secret World.* Los Angeles: Roxbury. Excellent overview of the intelligence community and process.

Lowenthal, Mark M. (2011) *Intelligence: From Secrets to Policy.* Washington, D.C.: Congressional Quarterly Press. Excellent overview of the intelligence community and process.

Pillar Paul L. (2010) "Unintelligent Design," *The National Interest* (September/October). Critical analysis of the so-called restructuring reforms and creation of the DNI by a respected intelligence expert.

Risen, James. (2006) *State of War: The Secret History of the CIA and the Bush Administration.* New York: Free Press. Surveys the range of activities taken in response to 9/11.

The National Commission on Terrorist Attacks upon the United States. (2004) *The 9/11 Commission Report.* New York: W.W. Norton. Examines the nature of the intelligence process relative to the tragedy of the September 11 attacks.

Treverton, Gregory F. (2011) *Intelligence for an Age of Terror.* New York: Cambridge University Press. Provides insights into the post-9/11 context and challenges.

KEY CONCEPTS

all-source analysts	intelligence cycle
counterintelligence (CI)	national security ethos
covert intervention	politicization of intelligence
cryptology	presidential findings
espionage	signal-to-noise problem
finished intelligence	stovepipes
intelligence	torture
intelligence community (IC)	

OTHER KEY TERMS

Abu Ghraib scandal
Afghanistan operation
Allen Dulles
Contra covert war
Department of Homeland Security
    (DHS)
director of central intelligence
    (DCI)
directorate of operations (DO)
director of national intelligence
    (DNI)
intelligence committees
Intelligence Reform and Prevention
    of Terrorism Act of 2004

National Clandestine Service (NCS)
National Intelligence Estimate
    (NIEs)
9/11 Commission Report
Office of the Director of National
    Intelligence (ODNI)
Office of Strategic Services (OSS)
Phoenix program
Pike and Church Committee
    investigations
Project MKULTRA
William Casey

PRESIDENT BARACK OBAMA PARTICIPATES IN A G8 SUMMIT WORKING SESSION FOCUSED ON GLOBAL AND ECONOMIC ISSUES, IN THE DINING ROOM OF LAUREL CABIN AT CAMP DAVID, MD., MAY 19, 2012.

FOREIGN ECONOMICS, THE NATIONAL ECONOMIC COUNCIL, AND THE GREAT RECESSION

Most observers recognize the importance of the presidency and certain executive branch agencies in the making of American national security policy. However, the executive branch includes numerous, less visible agencies that play a vital role in U.S. foreign economic policy—a topic that deserves more attention than it usually receives. As a result of industrialization, the growing role of the United States in the world's political economy since World War II, and the dramatic changes associated with globalization and its impact on the United States, the foreign economic bureaucracy has steadily expanded in size. Likewise, foreign economic policy has increasingly become "high policy" since the collapse of the Bretton Woods system in the early 70s to the present day, best exemplified by the Great Recession (review Chapter 2).

This *chapter provides an overview* of the foreign economic bureaucracy and the president's ability to manage the policymaking process in their historical and contemporary contexts—especially the key governmental institutions involved, presidential efforts at coordination, the prevailing free market economic subculture, and the new role of the National Economic Council. We will also examine the Great Recession and the policy responses to it, as well as its effects on the 2012 elections and future administrations.

U.S. FOREIGN ECONOMIC POLICY IN CONTEXT

Let's begin by discussing: (1) the historical context of U.S. foreign economic policy, (2) the rise of the post–World War II free market ethos, and (3) the contemporary nature of the U.S. economy's increasing interdependence with the global economy.

Historical Context

For most of America's history, foreign and national security policy heavily revolved around foreign economic policy—especially involving trade. In fact, trade policy played an important role in the movement for independence from Britain, and America's first attempts to project military power beyond its shores were motivated by the high costs of sailing the Mediterranean Sea imposed by attacks on commercial shipping by the Barbary pirates. Even after World War I, Americans believed that their interests in the rest of the world were largely commercial. American foreign economic policy since the United States' inception has focused on internal economic development, the protection of domestic industry from foreign competition and investment, and the expansion of American commerce abroad, especially in Latin America and Asia.

This pattern in U.S. foreign economic policy was deeply affected by the collapse of the international economy accompanying the Great Depression and the onset of World War II. After the war with Germany and Japan, Americans realized that "open door" policies, "dollar diplomacy," and world trade depended on global peace and stability, which in turn depended upon America's military strength and determination to maintain international order. With the rise of U.S. power, this eventually resulted in active efforts to restore a new stability and prosperity to the international political economy by the creation of the Bretton Woods system. The Bretton Woods international economic system was founded by the United States and its major allies, including the United Kingdom (the previous hegemonic power), premised on the principles of free trade, fixed exchange rates based on the gold standard, reconstruction and development aid, and the development of international economic organizations (such as the General Agreement on Tariffs and Trade, the International Monetary Fund, and the World Bank; see Chapter 2 for an overview).

Given the preeminence of the American economy in the international political economy *after WWII and during the cold war years, the president was able to subordinate foreign economic policy to the pursuit of national security* and the containment of Soviet communism. In the wake of the Great Depression and World War II, during the 1950s and 1960s the American economy prospered. American business expanded its multinational presence throughout the world while European economies recovered and the international economy grew, with the United States occupying the role of global banker and consumer. Economic sanctions were imposed on the Soviet Union and its close allies in support of the containment strategy. Thus, foreign economic policy was typically considered "low" policy during the cold war, requiring little attention and expertise by most policymakers involved in the "high" policy of national security affairs. This meant that there was much delegation of responsibility to senior and lower-level officials within the bureaucratic agencies involved in foreign economics.

However, such delegation and subordination proved to be an aberration and artifact of the cold war: *Foreign economic policy is now "high" policy once again in the post–Vietnam and post–cold war eras.* Beginning in the 1960s, the international economic system experienced increasing instability, while American economic strength declined dramatically relative to others. By 1971, the Bretton Woods system no longer could be sustained: President Nixon removed a weakened dollar from the gold standard and allowed its value to float relative to other major currencies; a surcharge was placed on Japanese imports to offset growing deficits in the balance of payments and the rise of protectionist sentiment at home; and "wage and price controls" were imposed on the American economy to arrest the growth of domestic inflation. Beginning in 1973, America's energy costs also dramatically increased with the rise of the ability of the Organization of Petroleum Exporting Countries (OPEC) to influence the supply of foreign oil, which the U.S. economy became increasingly dependent.

These changes in the international economic environment intensified many of the problems of inflation, unemployment, and deficits experienced by the U.S. economy and Americans beginning in the late 1960s at all levels—national, state, and local. Such conditions forced international economic issues onto the government and public agendas, making foreign economic policy and the foreign economic bureaucracy part of "high" U.S. foreign policy. The signing and passage of the North American Free Trade Agreement (NAFTA), as well as the creation of the World Trade Organization (WTO) with American participation under the elder Bush and Clinton, are indicative of the high priority of U.S. foreign economic policy in recent years. Then in 2007, the U.S. and global economy experienced a meltdown forcing George W. Bush and Barack Obama (and Americans in general) to devote a level of attention to the "high" policy of economics not seen since the Great Depression (see Madrick 2009; Roubini and Milm 2010; Spero and Hart 2009).

The Post–World War II Free Market Ethos

Throughout its development and integration into the global economy, *an economic culture premised on a strong free market ethos and a classical liberal economic paradigm* has provided common direction in U.S. foreign economic policy since World War II. This **free market ethos** rests on the faith in the power of the private market to promote growth and prosperity with minimal governmental intervention. However, given America's economic nationalist and protectionist past, the free market ethos did not dominate thinking about U.S. foreign economic policy until after World War II—when the United States became the world's economic superpower. Today, these beliefs have become so firmly embedded in American culture that the free market ethos provides the common understanding on which most Americans base their belief in the benefits of "free trade" and the proper path of economic development (see Goddard 1993; Goldstein 1988; Hartz 1955; Mingst 1982; Rohrlich 1987).

The free market ethos is held by most American policymakers. Presidents and other high-level officials may lack knowledge and confidence in matters of international economics in comparison to specialists. However, their understanding of the world, as well as their policy inclinations, tend to be heavily informed by a free market perspective. Officials throughout the foreign economic bureaucracy, such as former Assistant Secretary of International Affairs Gerald L. Parsky in the Treasury Department in the 1980s, consistently proclaimed the free market ethos as the basis of policy: "Although markets do not always operate efficiently, the appropriate remedy is to strengthen their functioning, not intervene, or further impede market operations" (quoted in Mingst 1982:193). This ethos is not without its controversies though (see **The Liberty–Security Dilemma:** Free Trade and Economic Security).

THE LIBERTY–SECURITY DILEMMA

Free Trade and Economic Security

In the foreign economic policy realm, post–World War II American policymakers have long embraced the fundamental principles of liberal economics, with its emphasis on the benefits and advantages of free trade for countries and individuals. A cornerstone of U.S. foreign economic policy since World War II has been to work toward the reduction of trade barriers and increasing engagement and integration of the U.S. and other economies into an open trading zone with very few formal barriers to trade, especially those generated by policy decisions such as tariff and nontariff barriers.

This embrace of liberty and the principles of Adam Smith in the foreign economic policy arena are not without contradictions and controversy. Advocates stress the merits of openness for the *aggregate* economic growth of the United States and its trade partners, as well as the political benefits of international cooperation that economic interdependence and integration fosters. They often point to the historical lessons derived from periods of relatively free trade versus those in which protectionism was more common and aggressive—with the 1920s–1930s interwar experience of the Great Depression and global conflict as key examples. As the undersecretary for commerce for George W. Bush's administration summarized in 2001: " Open markets . . . lead to more jobs, higher revenues, more profits, and overall economic growth. . . . While the United States negotiated and implemented the North American Free Trade Agreement and the Uruguay Round trade agreements, the U.S. economy grew at its fastest rate in a generation" (Luster 2001).

Critics argue that free trade can have important negative consequences for economic security. For one, skeptics point to the harsh impact of free trade on specific sectors of the economy and workforce, with the loss of jobs in sectors such as the auto industry and other manufacturing sectors Moreover, some stress the potential consequences of free trade for strategic industries, arguing that sectors vital to national security must be maintained—the U.S. steel industry and other high-tech sectors vital for the defense industry come to mind. Many critics further highlight that freer markets tend to become more unstable at times and produce gross inequalities, best illustrated by the recent Great Recession. Finally, critics also argue that the expanding reach of economic interactions fostered by globalization and free trade are at the heart of the cultural clashes between the United States and other parts of the world, contributing to the anti-Americanism and hostility that can lead to violence such as terrorism.

The tension between free trade and economic security was on display in the 2012 election cycle. President Obama, for example, sought to expand free trade agreements, but did so slowly, and with efforts to secure policy protection for labor and the environment. Mitt Romney, his Republican challenger in the 2012 election, aggressively advocated a purer form of free trade, without interference from the government. In the spring of 2012, for example, former Florida Republican governor Jeb Bush, with the support of the Romney campaign, criticized the president for failing to pursue free trade: "President Obama missed several opportunities early in his administration to secure quick passage of trade agreements with Colombia and Panama which together will create thousands of jobs here in Florida. Instead, President Obama bowed to political pressure from powerful labor unions to stall these agreements." (quoted at http://economyincrisis.org/content/romney-campaign-criticizes-obama-for-passing-trade-agreements-too-slowly). Meanwhile, the "Occupy Wall Street" movement attacked the president from the opposite position, charging the administration with sacrificing the economic security of the United States and ordinary Americans to wealthy corporate interests.

What do you think is the proper balance between the principles of liberal trade and the need for economic and human security given increasing globalization?

Globalization, Interdependence, and Contemporary Economic Involvement

The U.S. economy has bewcome more intertwined with the workings of the international economy, which helps to explain the significance and impact of the severe Great Recession that began in 2007–2008. American economic transactions have proliferated abroad and continue to have considerable impact on the evolution of the international political economy. At the same time, economic transactions emanating from abroad have increasingly penetrated the American economy. Thus, the American economy has become a larger part of, and more dependent upon, the global political economy.

Let's begin with international trade. In 2011, American exports of merchandise and services exceeded $2 trillion. Likewise foreign imports of goods and services exceeded to over $2.4 trillion (see **Table 8.1 for figures from 1960–2010**). Whereas the United States

Table 8.1   U.S. International Trade (in Billions of Dollars)

Year	Exports	Imports	Trade Balance
1960	25.9	22.4	3.5
1965	35.3	30.6	4.7
1970	56.6	54.4	2.3
1975	132.6	120.2	12.4
1980	271.8	291.2	−19.4
1985	288.8	410.9	−122.1
1990	537.2	618.4	−81.1
1995	794.4	890.8	−96.4
2000	1,065.7	1,441.4	−375.7
2001	1,004.9	1,370.0	−365.1
2002	977.3	1,398.5	−421.2
2003	1,022.6	1,517.4	−494.8
2004	1,151.4	1,769.0	−617.6
2005	1,283.8	1,995.3	−711.6
2006	1,457.0	2,210.3	−753.3
2007	1,645.7	2,346.0	−700.3
2008	1,835.8	2,517.0	−681.1
2009	1,575.0	1,956.3	−381.3
2010	1,837.6	2,337.6	−500.0

SOURCE: U.S. Department of Commerce, Bureau of Economic Analysis, 2012.

typically ran small merchandise "trade surpluses" in the 1950s and 1960s (exporting more than importing), annual "trade deficits" began in 1971 and have been the norm since, as indicated in Table 8.1. The trade deficits have grown quite large since 1985, especially in the areas of merchandise goods, running consistently more than $500 billion over the last few years.

Figure 8.1 shows that the leading countries for U.S. trade exports and imports are in North America, Asia, and Europe. At the same time, billions of dollars' worth of exports and imports involve countries of the developing world as well. The figure shows that the country that the United States trades with the most is Canada. At the same time, it also clearly shows that the large trade deficits that the United States has are with such countries as Canada, Mexico, Japan, England, Germany, and, especially, China. The American economy, obviously, and the standard of living of Americans have become increasingly affected by the flows of international trade.

American international investment has also exploded, while the American economy has similarly become more heavily affected by foreign investment. American (government and private) investment assets abroad have grown from just $86 billion in 1960 to over $20 trillion today. Total foreign investment assets within the United States also surged from $41 billion in 1960 to almost $23 trillion, surpassing U.S. investments abroad in 2000 (see **Table 8.2**). Many of these foreign assets are investments in securities and other liabilities (such as corporate and U.S. government bonds) used to finance U.S. corporate spending and the government deficits that have both ballooned since the 1980s. Most American investment abroad represents private (corporate and individual) assets.

Figure 8.1   U.S. Trade with Leading Countries (in Billions of Dollars)

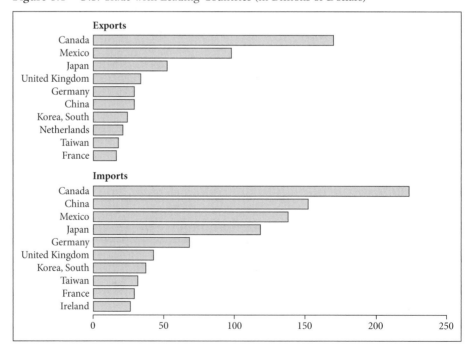

SOURCE: U.S. Census Bureau, *Statistical Abstract of the United States: 2012.*

Table 8.2 Foreign Investment (in Billions of Dollars)

Year	U.S. International Investment	Foreign Investment in the US
1960	86	41
1965	120	59
1970	165	107
1975	295	221
1980	607	501
1985	949	1,061
1990	2,179	2,424
1995	3,452	3,967
2000	6,231	7,620
2001	6,270	8,160
2002	6,413	8,647
2003	7,203	9,633
2004	9,341	11,586
2005	11,962	13,887
2006	14,381	16,607
2007	17,640	20,082
2008	19,465	22,725
2009	18,487	20,883
2010	20,315	22,786

SOURCE: U.S. Census Bureau, *Statistical Abstract of the United States: 2008–2012.*

In 1988, foreign "direct" investment by foreign companies in the United States ($329 billion), such as building a factory, surpassed direct foreign investment by U.S. companies abroad ($327 billion) for the first time. U.S. foreign direct investment today is about $3 trillion, while foreign direct investment in the United States is comparable and growing faster. Where two-thirds of direct American investment abroad is made within developed countries, more than one-third (and growing) is made in developing countries and emerging markets, especially in Latin America and Asia.

During the 1970s and especially during the 1980s, the U.S. government also began to experience huge budget deficits. During the Reagan administration the total national debt of the U.S. government almost tripled, from $900 billion in 1980 to $2.6 trillion in 1988. After reaching over $4 trillion of total debt in the late 1980s and early 1990s, the federal budget began to experience surpluses for the first time in decades during the Clinton administration, some of which went to pay down the total national debt—setting the stage, according to many people, for the economic boom of the 1990s. Under presidents George W. Bush (with tax cuts and consequences of 9/11) and Obama (with the recession) deficits swelled, exceeding a trillion dollars per year (see **Table 8.3**).

Table 8.3   U.S. Government Budget (in Billions of Current Dollars)

Year	Total Budget Outlays	Surplus or Deficit (−)	Gross Federal Debt	% of GDP
1960	92.2	0.3	290.5	56.0
1970	195.6	−2.8	380.9	37.6
1980	590.9	−73.8	909.0	33.4
1985	946.3	−212.3	1,817.4	43.8
1990	1,253.0	−221.0	3,206.3	55.9
1995	1,515.7	−164.0	4,920.6	67.0
1996	1,560.5	−107.4	5,181.5	67.1
1997	1,601.1	−21.9	5,369.2	65.4
1998	1,652.5	69.3	5,478.2	63.2
1999	1,701.8	125.6	5,605.5	60.9
2000	1,789.0	236.2	5,628.7	57.3
2001	1,862.8	128.2	5,769.9	56.4
2002	2,010.9	−157.8	6,198.4	58.8
2003	2,159.9	−377.6	6,760.0	61.6
2004	2,292.8	−412.7	7,354.7	62.9
2005	2,472.0	−318.3	7,905.3	63.5
2006	2,655.0	−248.2	8,451.4	63.9
2007	2,728.7	−160.7	8,950.7	64.4
2008	2,982.5	−458.6	9,986.1	69.4
2009	3,517.7	−1,412.7	11,875.9	84.2
2010	3,456.2	−1,293.5	13,528.8	93.2
2011*	3,818.8	−1,645.1	15,476.2	102.6

* Estimate by U.S. Congressional Budget Office.
SOURCE: U.S. Census Bureau, *Statistical Abstract of the United States: 2012.*

Indeed, the *cost of American military actions in Afghanistan and Iraq since 2001 so far has exceeded $1.4 trillion as of 2011* (surpassing the costs of World War II) and is growing (U.S. CRS 2011). As the size of the debt balloons, the interest that the government has to pay to finance the debt also increases each year (representing anywhere from 8 to 15 percent of the total federal budget). Such budget deficits have an impact on domestic interest rates, currency exchange rates, and international transactions such as the trade balance—eating away, many people argue, the fabric of America's economic strength. Much of the foreign financial investment discussed above is generated by trade deficits, which lead to the purchase of U.S. monetary assets (such as Treasury bills) by foreign countries, individuals, and institutions, who hold about one-third of the total U.S. debt.

Deficits, economic transactions, and currency exchange rates in other countries also impact the United States and the overall international political economy. Recent examples are the collapse of the Mexican peso and economy in 1995, the Asian financial crises during the late 1990s, and the Argentinean–South American crises of the early 2000s. In each case, as the leading international and economic actor, the United States actively intervened in order to prevent the financial instability from spreading to the United States and the rest of the world, as well as restore financial stability to the immediate countries of concern.

What made the Great Recession that began in 2007 so unique was that the meltdown began in the United States and subsequently the European Union—the core capitalist and market-oriented economies of the world. Such economic instability is illustrative of globalization and the growing interdependence among the economies of the world. Moreover, it is likely to intensify in the future as markets grow and technology spreads and accelerates (see Roubini and Milm 2010).

Finally, as we discussed in Chapter 2, while the United States represents 5 percent of the world's population, it consumes roughly 25 percent of the world's energy. The United States remains highly dependent on the importation of foreign oil—the key source of energy in industrialized societies—for almost 70 percent of its oil consumption. American energy dependence on foreign oil plays a critical role in making the Middle East region of great strategic importance, as demonstrated in the Persian Gulf War of 1991, the war on terrorism following September 11, 2001, and Iraq and Afghan (and Libyan) wars (review Table 2.2).

In sum, the trends in trade, investment, governmental spending, and energy show the increasing importance of the international economy to American economic performance, standard of living, and quality of life. They also indicate why foreign economic policy has grown in importance.

RELEVANT GOVERNMENTAL AGENCIES

As the global political economy grew in importance for the national economy, U.S. foreign economic policy broadened and the bureaucratic structures involved in this arena expanded. Since the 1950s, small departmental advisory staffs with international responsibilities have turned into full-fledged bureaus, while agencies within the Executive Office of the Presidency have become more active in international economic matters. Furthermore, the jurisdictional lines between those governmental institutions that have primary responsibility for domestic economic policy, as opposed to foreign economic policy, have become blurred, for domestic and international economics have become much more intertwined.

Now, *numerous governmental institutions and agencies play a role—large or small—in the making of U.S. foreign economic policy.* Several are located within the Executive Office of the Presidency (EOP) and occupy more of a consultative or coordinating role, as indicated in **Table 8.4**. The following review highlights key agencies and their roles and interaction in foreign economic policy, with attention to areas of continuity and change in order to better understand presidential efforts to manage and coordinate them (see Cohen 2000; Destler 2005; Goddard 1993).

Table 8.4   Executive Branch Organizations Shaping Economic Policy Today

Organization	Offices, Bureaus, and Agencies
EOP AGENCIES	
Council of Economic Advisers	
Office of Management and Budget	
Office of U.S. Trade Representative	
National Economic Council	
EXECUTIVE DEPARTMENTS	
Treasury Department	Office of International Economic Affairs, U.S. Customs Service
State Department	Bureaus of Economic, Business, and Agricultural Affairs, International Organizations, and Oceans and International Environmental and Scientific Affairs
Agriculture Department	Office of International Cooperation and Development, Foreign Agriculture Service, and Commodity Credit Corporation
Commerce Department	International Trade Administration, Bureaus of Export Administration, Foreign Commercial Service, and U.S. Travel and Tourism Office
Energy Department	Offices of Assistant Secretary for International Affairs and Energy Emergencies
Labor Department	Bureau of International Labor Affairs
OTHER AGENCIES	
Federal Reserve System	Board of Governors,12 Federal Reserve Banks and Federal Open Market Committee (FOMC)
U.S. Agency for International Development	
U.S. International Trade Commission	
Export-Import Bank	
Overseas Private Investment Corporation	
Trade and Development Agency	
And others such as CFTC, FDIC, SEC, FTC	

SOURCE: *The U.S. Government Manual.*

Executive Departments

TREASURY DEPARTMENT   The Treasury Department *is probably the most important agency* in areas of international economics, such as trade and monetary issues, and it has often taken the lead on questions of foreign economic policy in general. The **secretary of the treasury** acts as a major policy advisor to the president, with responsibilities involving domestic and international financial, economic, and tax policy. The treasury secretary also officially represents the U.S. government in key international economic organizations such as the International Monetary Fund (IMF), the World Bank, the WTO, the Inter-American Development Bank, and the African Development Bank.

The secretary heads a large, complex bureaucratic department of which the undersecretary for international economic affairs and the Office of the Assistant Secretary for International Economic Affairs have primary departmental responsibility over international monetary, financial, commercial, energy, and trade policies and programs. The office plays an important role in diplomatic negotiations concerning international economic matters and oversees U.S. participation in the multilateral development banks such as the World Bank, to which the U.S. government contributes over $9 billion in grants and credits on an annual basis. This helps to explain why the United States has such a major voice in the World Bank and the IMF.

DEPARTMENT OF STATE   The Department of State also plays a prominent role in all areas of U.S. foreign economic policy. Although the State Department has had a long history of managing U.S. external relations, it has declined relative to the Treasury Department in influence on U.S. international economic policy. At the senior official level, the undersecretary for economic growth, energy, and environment acts as principal advisor to the secretary concerning international trade, agriculture, energy, finance, and transportation and relations with developing countries. Further down the hierarchy, the Bureau for Economic and Business Affairs has primary day-to-day departmental responsibility for formulating and implementing policy with regard to foreign economic matters. Other bureaus also share some major responsibilities in international economic issues. As we discussed in Chapter 5, the State Department is also home to the U.S. Agency for International Development (USAID), which is principally responsible for administering economic assistance and supervising economic development policy abroad.

DEPARTMENT OF AGRICULTURE   The Department of Agriculture plays a major role in the area of agricultural trade. The Office of International Cooperation and Development works with international food and agricultural organizations and provides technical assistance and training in agriculture to other countries, particularly in the developing world. The Foreign Agricultural Service was created in 1953 to stimulate overseas markets for U.S. agricultural products, principally through its network of agricultural counselors, attachés, and trade officers stationed overseas and reinforced by a support staff abroad and at home. The Foreign Agricultural Service maintains a worldwide agricultural intelligence and reporting system and plays an active role in U.S. governmental trade policy and trade negotiations. The Foreign Agricultural Service also supervises and participates in the Food for Peace Program (Public Law 480 Program) and the Commodity Credit Corporation, which provides grants and credits to foreign governments and purchasers both as economic assistance and to encourage the development and expansion of overseas markets for U.S. agricultural commodities.

DEPARTMENT OF COMMERCE   The Department of Commerce has important international responsibilities in the area of trade. The department's International Trade Administration has the primary responsibility for the importation of foreign products, international economic policy, and trade promotion, especially nonagricultural. The Foreign Commercial Service is stationed overseas to provide services to the U.S. exporting and international business community. The United States Tourism and Travel Office is the bureaucratic agency within the Commerce Department that attempts to promote foreign **tourism** in the United States, with foreign visitors exceeding 50 million and spending over $100 billion. The Bureau of Export Administration directs the government's export control policy, which includes processing license applications and enforcing U.S. export control laws (including high-technology items).

DEPARTMENT OF ENERGY The Department of Energy has the major responsibility for energy policies, plans, and programs. The Office of the Assistant Secretary for International Affairs and Energy Emergencies manages programs and activities relating to the international aspects of overall energy policy. These activities include energy preparedness and plans in case of national emergency, involvement in international energy negotiations, and coordination of international energy programs with foreign governments and such international organizations as the International Energy Agency and the International Atomic Energy Agency.

DEPARTMENT OF LABOR The Department of Labor handles questions concerning domestic and international labor. The department's Bureau of International Labor Affairs assists in formulating international economic and trade policies that affect American workers; represents the United States in international bodies such as the International Labor Organization; and engages in technical assistance abroad and trade union exchange programs.

Other Agencies

Other agencies have missions that affect U.S. foreign economic policy. We highlight the most important, and briefly discuss them.

THE FED Similar to other agencies with specialized missions, the involvement of the **Federal Reserve Board (the Fed,** located in Washington, D.C.) in the international economic sphere flows from its monetary management within the domestic (and international) economy. The Fed is an independent agency that determines and executes the general monetary, credit, and operating principles of the U.S. Federal Reserve System (consisting of twelve Federal Reserve Banks), serving as the government's central bank. It is headed by a seven-member Board of Governors and twelve-member Federal Open Market Committee (FOMC) that makes the key financial decisions and oversees the Fed system as a whole. Although the president appoints the seven members of the Fed's Board of Governors and most of the members of the FOMC (with the advice and consent of the Senate) and designates the chair, as an independent agency the Fed is not "officially" under presidential control.

The Chair of the Fed is the single most important official as the chair of the Board of Governors and the FOMC. The president of the New York Fed is the vice chair of the FOMC and is the next most consequential official, given his strategic location in the financial center of the United States. By influencing the lending and investing activities of American commercial banks, such as the cost and availability of money and credit, the Fed affects not only the state of the American economy, but the country's international balance-of-payments position and the government's foreign economic policy as well. Fed policies also influence the activities of other major banking systems as well, such as in Europe and Japan—giving it a critical economic role (see Greider 1987).

THE U.S. INTERNATIONAL TRADE COMMISSION The U.S. International Trade Commission (ITC) is an independent agency with broad powers of investigation relating to customs laws, export and import trade, and foreign competition. For example, the commission often adjudicates disputes between American industry and international corporations within the United States over charges of unfair trading practices. The ITC is made up of six commissioners appointed for nine-year terms by the president with the advice and consent of the Senate.

THE EXPORT-IMPORT BANK The **Export-Import Bank (Eximbank)** is a government corporation that subsidizes American company exports abroad. Although established in 1934 to promote trade only with the Soviet Union, during most of its history it has provided grants and credits to aid the export financing of U.S. goods and services abroad in general. However, it is prohibited from competing with private financing. The Eximbank also guarantees the Foreign Credit Insurance Association, an association of U.S. insurance companies organized by the bank in 1961 to ensure export transactions against risk of default.

THE OVERSEAS PRIVATE INVESTMENT CORPORATION The Overseas Private Investment Corporation (OPIC) is an independent agency that stimulates foreign investment, predominantly in developing countries. It offers U.S. exporters assistance in finding investment opportunities, insurance to protect their investments, and loans and loan guarantees to help finance their projects. OPIC insures American companies against the political risks of foreign investment, such as expropriation and damage from war, revolution, insurrection, or civil strife. With the collapse of communist regimes, OPIC began to actively support American investment in the economies of Eastern Europe in the 1990s.

There are other regulatory agencies which play an occasional international role or impact international markets, including the Trade and Development Agency, which became an independent entity in 1992. It was designed to assist in the creation of jobs for Americans by helping U.S. companies export and pursue other overseas business opportunities. It tries to work closely with industrializing and developing countries abroad. Others include the CFTC (Commodity Futures Trading Commission), FDIC (Federal Deposit Insurance Corporation), SEC (Securities and Exchange Commission), FTC (Federal Trade Commission)—some of which have received much more attention since the Great Recession of 2007.

EOP Agencies

Agencies within the EOP also have become more active in the making of U.S. foreign economic policy. The **Council of Economic Advisors (CEA)**, with three members and a small staff, was created in 1946 to assess the state of the American economy and advise the president on economic matters. One of the three CEA members is assigned international responsibilities and participates in official delegations to the Organization for Economic Cooperation and Development (OECD) countries—Western Europe, Canada, and Japan. CEA members are usually academics in economics and often do not have much of a role in day-to-day economic advice, although occasionally they may depend on their particular relationship to the president.

The Office of Management and Budget, the Office of the United States Trade Representative, and the National Economic Council, which are discussed in greater detail later, have major responsibilities concerning budgetary and trade matters and play important roles in the president's effort to coordinate and manage U.S. foreign policy as it affects economic policy.

COORDINATION EFFORTS AND CHALLENGES

So many agencies are involved in U.S. foreign economic policy that a major problem of governmental coordination and presidential management has arisen within the executive branch. Historically, the State Department was the lead agency responsible for coordinating

U.S. foreign economic policy (except during war, when the White House usually became more prominent), while the foreign economic bureaucracy was much smaller and less complex and bureaucratic. This began to change during the twentieth century, especially after World War II and since the 1950s when the foreign economic bureaucracy expanded in size and complexity. The main result is that the Treasury Department has grown in prominence, but not to the point of being powerful enough or able to coordinate foreign economic policy. The department became "a first among equals," with the secretary of treasury usually serving as the president's official economic spokesperson. Power, therefore, is extremely decentralized within the foreign economic bureaucracy, making it very difficult for the president to manage economic aspects of foreign policy.

Presidents have used different strategies to coordinate the foreign economic policymaking process over the years, including relying on:

1. the Office of Management and Budget,

2. the United States Trade Representative, and, most often,

3. interagency committees usually coordinated within the EOP. (See Cohen 2000; Destler 1996, 2005; Dolan 2001; Juster and Lazarus 1997; and Malmgren 1972.)

An early effort at coordination involved the government's budgetary process. The Bureau of the Budget was created in 1921 and placed within the Executive Office of the Presidency by President Franklin Roosevelt in 1939 in order to coordinate and streamline the budgetary process of an expanding government. The Bureau of the Budget was the precursor of the **Office of Management and Budget (OMB)**, created in 1970 to coordinate and supervise the government's budget and fiscal program for the president. The formulation of the budget of the U.S. government is of great importance because it affects the activities of all bureaucratic agencies and represents the fiscal and spending policies of the federal government, currently to the tune of over $3 trillion per year. As one analyst has stated, "Although the politics of the budget is often considered an internal concern, no external issue is as critical to foreign and national security strategy" (Deibel 1991:15). However, even the assistance of the OMB and a sizable staff have not allowed the president to develop a coherent governmental policy with respect to issues involving international monetary matters, trade, investment, energy, and assistance.

The late 1970s witnessed the growing prominence of the **Office of the United States Trade Representative (USTR)** as a coordinator of U.S. trade policy. Created by Congress in 1962 as part of the EOP, beginning under President Carter, the USTR, a cabinet-level official with the rank of ambassador, has acted as a major presidential advisor, public spokesperson, and often the chief representative of the U.S. government on trade matters. Nevertheless, the USTR has had limited success in directing and managing U.S. trade policy for the president. Much depends on the individual trade representative, his or her relationship with the president, and the quality of the USTR staff.

Most presidents have come to rely on the third strategy—the creation of different "interagency committees" at the cabinet and subcabinet levels to promote interaction and coordination of foreign economic policy. These agencies are often coordinated within the EOP or are chaired by a lead agency, most often the Treasury Department. These efforts have had mixed success, and none of the interagency groups has gained the kind of permanence and prestige that the National Security Council (NSC) system has come to enjoy in national security policy. On the whole, U.S. policymakers found it very difficult to pursue a steady economic policy, and presidents failed to establish consistency in their organization of economic issues and the policymaking process. The interagency process has varied under each president and sometimes within the same administration. Foreign and domestic economics were sometimes integrated, sometimes kept distinct.

Presidential Attention and Knowledge

Part of the problem in coordinating the foreign economic bureaucracy involves the lack of presidential attention to and knowledge of international economic affairs. *Since the cold war, most presidents, and their closest foreign policy advisors, have been more knowledgeable and comfortable dealing with traditional political and military issues associated with national security policy.* Paul Volcker, former chair of the Fed, has commented that American presidents "have not in my experience wanted to spend much time on the complexities of international finance" (quoted in Goddard 1993:176). For the most part, during the cold war, foreign economics was not considered "high" policy and, hence, did not attract much presidential attention.

Not surprisingly, the "low" priority of international economics during the cold war left a strong legacy in the making of U.S. foreign policy: a foreign economic bureaucracy expanding in size and power but enjoying considerable freedom from supervision and control despite efforts to do so by different presidents. As I. M. Destler (1994) put it, the net result has been a divided governmental policymaking process with a relatively centralized "security complex" and a decentralized "economic complex." The overall result for the making of foreign economic policy, according to Harald Malmgren (1972:42), a former deputy special representative for trade negotiations for the president, is that "widespread confusion exists as to who is responsible for what. Both policy and daily decisions seem to be aimed in several different directions simultaneously."

For certain policy areas, appropriate lead agencies are readily identifiable: the Department of Treasury for monetary matters, USTR for most trade issues, the Department of Agriculture for food, the Department of Energy for issues within its sphere, and the Department of State for matters concerning assistance and many Third World issues. "But it is much harder, of course, to assure that [these agencies] will keep their parochialism in check. And no single department or cabinet member can exercise effective oversight of overall foreign economic policy" (Destler 1983:215). Many of these agencies have also tended to be more accountable to Congress and economically oriented interest groups.

To promote greater policy coordination and coherence, a number of reforms and reorganization plans of the foreign economic policymaking process were recommended. Little came of these recommendations to better coordinate and centralize the making of U.S. foreign economic policy under the president, until the arrival of Bill Clinton as president and the creation of the National Economic Council.

CLINTON, THE NEC, AND THE HIGH POLITICS OF ECONOMICS

Although Bill Clinton was relatively inexperienced in national security policy, he was deeply interested and knowledgeable about issues of economics, both domestic and international. As one Clinton advisor stated, "Unlike his predecessors, he doesn't see the distinction between economics and politics or between the domestic economy and the international economy" (Stokes 1993:615). This interest led Clinton to better organize and coordinate the (foreign) economic bureaucracy by establishing a new unit within the EOP by executive order in 1993—the **National Economic Council (NEC)** (Destler 1996; Dolan and Rosati 2006; Juster 1997).

The functions of the new organization were as follows:

1. to coordinate the economic policymaking process with respect to domestic and international economic issues,

2. to coordinate economic policy advice to the president,

3. to ensure that economic policy decisions and programs were consistent with the president's stated goals and ensure that those goals are being effectively pursued, and

4. to monitor implementation of the president's economic policy agenda.

The NEC—like the National Security Council, after which it was modeled—is a formal mechanism led by **national economic director (or NEC director)**—and a small staff (of a few dozen people).

During his two terms of office, Bill Clinton relied on three national economic directors to help him manage the bureaucracy and make economic policy at home and abroad. Along with the secretary of the treasury, the new national economic director clearly became one of the president's most prominent advisors in the making of U.S. economic policy (see **Table 8.5**).

The NEC was designed to function as an "honest-broker" coordinating the formation and implementation of economic policy by the major policymakers and the variety of executive agencies involved. It has been described as a "low-profile but powerful institutional mechanism created to coordinate the Administration's Cabinet-level economic policymaking. The goal was to do for economic policy what the National Security Council (NSC) has done for national security policy" (Wildavsky 1996:1417). Much like the 1947 creation of the NSC, *the creation of the NEC was a revolutionary institution change in the making of U.S. economic policy.* Let's consider the origins, development, and operation of the NEC to highlight the challenges of managing the foreign economic policy bureaucracy.

Table 8.5   National Economic Directors

Name	Year	President	Background
Robert Rubin	1993	Clinton	Law and Wall Street
Laura D. Tyson	1995	Clinton	Academia
Gene Sperling	1997	Clinton	Law and Government
Lawrence Lindsey	2001	Bush	Academia
Stephen Friedman	2003	Bush	Business and Wall Street
Allan B. Hubbard	2005	Bush	Business
Keith Hennessey	2007	Bush	Business and Government
Lawrence Summers	2009	Obama	Academia, Business, and Government
Gene Sperling	2011	Obama	Law and Government

© Cengage Learning

Origins

Clinton's NEC was based on a notion that had bounced around Congress, universities, and think tanks for years. His predecessors, especially presidents Nixon and Ford, had also attempted to coordinate economic policy from within the White House. Despite previous presidential efforts and failures at coordination, Clinton was determined to try again. The notion first appeared in the Clinton-Gore campaign tract, *Putting People First*. Clinton (and Gore, Jr. 1992:131–132) wanted to create an "Economic Security Council, similar in status to the NSC, with responsibility for coordinating America's international economic policy."

Despite the misgivings of some advisors, President-elect Bill Clinton pushed his economic team to develop a plan. His team embraced the concept, as reflected in a "Memorandum to the President-Elect":

> [T]he combination of Cold War victory and deep economic difficulties allows—
> and indeed, demands—a shift of priority and resources away from national security
> as traditionally defined, toward the broader problems of making America com-
> petitive in a fiercely competitive world. . . . [T]he Economic Council and its staff
> would be your instrument for assuring that economic policy gets attention equal
> to traditional national security, working extremely closely with the NSC and its
> staff when international economic issues are under consideration, and with the
> domestic policy Council and its staff on domestic policy matters. (Quoted in Juster
> and Lazarus 1997:8)

Reflecting the priority he placed on this issue, Clinton announced his economic team even before his team of national security advisors.

Clinton's choice to head the new council was Wall Street financier Robert Rubin, who he asked to "replicate on the economic side what George Bush had done on the foreign-policy side" (*Economist* 1994:28). Clinton chose Rubin to reassure Wall Street and because of his ability to create an atmosphere of collegiality among a group of smart, aggressive personalities as a partner of Goldman Sachs—Rubin's Wall Street firm. Rubin took the job only after Clinton assured him that the NEC's role would be taken seriously.

Robert Rubin and the Transition

As the first special assistant to the president for economic policy, **Robert Rubin** (who later became treasury secretary) was consequential in defining the initial role of the position and the council operations. He "conceived his role as honest broker, organizing options for the president, but he [was] not . . . hesitant about articulating his own views" as well (Judis 1993:21). For the most part the national economic director and the NEC were able to minimize conflict that its creation engendered with the economic bureaucracy while promoting a relatively open and collegial process, reflecting the teamwork and interaction that President Clinton preferred. Rubin's role demonstrates the importance that individuals and personalities play in impacting the organization and dynamics of the policy process.

Rubin molded the NEC into the center of White House economic policymaking, blending and balancing the roles of the other important economic agencies such as the Office of the U.S. Special Trade Representative (USTR), the OMB, and the Department of Treasury, along with the NSC itself. As his deputies, Rubin chose Gene Sperling, an economic director on the campaign, and W. Bowman Cutter, a former management consultant at OMB under Carter. Rubin also recruited Sylvia Matthews to serve as his chief of staff (though that was not her title). The remainder of the NEC staff—which included lawyers, political activists, professors, Congressional Budget Office analysts, Congressional aides, and former lobbyists—were recruited on the basis of collegiality, teamwork, analytic skills, and physical stamina. Together, this small group—in consultation with Clinton's economic principals—planned the NEC's jurisdiction and modus operandi. For example, they worked with Samuel "Sandy" Berger, deputy assistant to the president for national security affairs, on maintaining a joint international economics staff with the NSC—a strategy that had been worked out by Rubin and Anthony Lake, Clinton's national security advisor, over coffee in late 1992.

As Rubin explained: "We had to define [the NEC], we had to create its acceptance within the government process, and then we had to staff it, all at the same time that we were working on the economic plan" (quoted in Ifill 1993:22). Put another way, "when he [Rubin] was asked to set up the economic council, and superimpose it on an existing bureaucracy, it was as if he were being asked to land an alien spacecraft atop the White House without shattering the fine china" (Ifill 1993:22). Forming a team that reflected Clinton's broad ideology but without "sharp elbows" or big egos was difficult enough; Rubin also faced the challenge of harnessing the numerous departments and agencies into the yoke of a new formal structure responsible for policy coordination.

The NEC had to be powerful enough to enforce policy coordination without stepping on toes. And the most important toes belonged to the new administration's eminences, Treasury Secretary Lloyd Bentsen and Secretary of State Warren Christopher. The State Department was accustomed to policy coordination through the NSC and had steadily become less influential in the making of foreign economic policy. Treasury, however, was a different matter. Not only was Lloyd Bentsen regarded as one of the most prominent and powerful cabinet members, the Treasury Department had little experience with policy coordination and was considered the most resistant to NEC management.

With Bentsen and the other principal participants, Rubin succeeded largely because he had the support of the president, and because he nurtured the view of the NEC as an honest broker of each agency's policy input. Still, the task of integrating a broad range of policy preferences from over sixteen cabinet members with a variety of bureaucratic, constituency, and political agendas was difficult. As Rubin characterized the situation:

> Almost all issues have cross-agency ramifications, so you have to have some mechanism for getting the views of the different agencies, or you wind up with the President making a decision based on the perspective of one agency and not knowing what six other agencies might think about it. . . . You have to make sure that you are dealing with the President—and with everybody else in the economic team and in the Administration—in a totally neutral way . . . that you express the pluses and minuses, and then totally separate that from the expression of your opinion. (quoted in Ifill 1993:22)

The NEC in Operation

The NEC is structured very much like the NSC, with two important exceptions: First, the NEC coordinates domestic, intermestic and international economic policy (with two deputy assistants, one for international economic affairs and the other for domestic economic affairs). Second, the NEC's staff is considerably smaller—a few dozen members within the NEC versus well over 100 within the NSC. Nevertheless, the national economic director was created to serve as "senior economic advisor—chairing senior staff meetings and conferring with the president privately" (Judis 1993:25).

Like the NSC, the NEC consists of three basic interagency committees. First, a "core group" of senior officials—the Principals Committee—met for the most prominent issues, usually led by the national economic director. Second, a Deputies Committee was created of senior subcabinet officials. And finally at the lowest level, other interagency working groups were created on an ad hoc basis, made up of various officials and chaired by key NEC aides. As with national security policymaking, foreign economic policymaking consists of informal interaction among prominent officials and a more formal interagency process usually through the NEC (see **Figure 8.2**).

The NEC operates at various levels. Apart from the role of managing the process, the special assistant to the president for economic policy was responsible for communicating the council's advice to the president. Beginning with Rubin, NEC directors would brief the president on economic policy proposals generated by the NEC vetting the process along with his own views. If the president planned to be involved in the policy debate, as Clinton liked to, the NEC director would set an agenda, gather the NEC principals, and rehearse the discussion before the presidential meeting.

The principals committee was NEC's power base. Here Rubin and subsequent directors utilized their management skills while demonstrating their influence with the president. The principals usually discussed only urgent issues and proposals that were ready for an executive decision. At the deputies committee level, the NEC met two or three times a week to discuss policy. The NEC formed ad hoc interagency issue clusters around international economic policy; regulatory policy, financial institutions, and community development; energy, environment, and natural resources; research-and-development and technology policy; defense conversion and reuse of military bases; and infrastructure and transportation. At this level, the deputies' meeting involved a core group of officials from the NSC, State, Treasury, USTR's office, and Commerce, who worked on "building a policy community" and "bridging jurisdictions." Deputy Assistant for International Economic Affairs Bo Cutter ran deputies' meetings, often in conjunction with Sandy Berger at the NSC. Because the foreign policy deputies "bonded," under Clinton, meetings were freewheeling and involved much brainstorming (Destler 1996:28).

The creation of this new coordinating council had almost immediate effects on "front-burner action issues: the budget, the North American Free Trade Agreement (NAFTA), the Uruguay Round, Japan," as I. M. Destler (1996:28) observed, and it has continued to be important ever since. As the national economic director and the NEC became a significant force in coordinating myriad bureaucratic agencies and officials and providing policy advice for the president, the scope of its activities expanded. It was soon "playing a growing role in shaping the president's political messages, working with the White House's communications and political advisors on events and speeches designed to highlight Clinton's economic views and plans" (Destler 1996:14,18), roles that continued under Rubin's successors Laura Tyson and Gene Sperling for such issues as most favored nation (MFN) status for China. For other economic issues the NEC played a less prominent role, such as in the U.S. response to the Mexican peso crisis and the Asian financial crisis, where Treasury took the lead at a time when Rubin was treasury secretary.

In sum, presidents have a greater ability to coordinate foreign economic policymaking with the NEC, but the process remains more decentralized than national security policymaking because of the critical role of Congress, domestic politics, and the increasing role played by state and local governments. And as Destler (1996:40) has pointed out, the NEC system was not without problems: "Interagency coordination is extraordinarily difficult, particularly on economic issues, and particularly with a president who engages in a freewheeling

Figure 8.2   Organizational Structure of the NEC Policymaking System

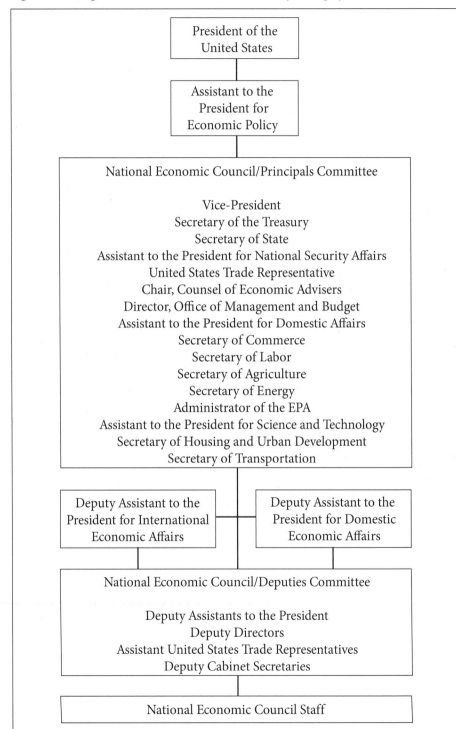

and not always predictable manner." Nevertheless, Destler (1996:61) concluded that *the NEC system was a relative success in helping the president manage the making of U.S. economic policy.* The NEC tended to work well, especially when four criteria were met: (1) the issue was important to the president and the administration, (2) the issue was clearly within NEC jurisdiction, (3) the NEC had firm deadlines and action-forcing events that required central decisions, and (4) there was a natural lead operating agency (Destler 1996:36; see also Dolan and Rosati 2006).

POLICYMAKING UNDER GEORGE W. BUSH

While the NEC became a powerful institutionalized presence in the making of foreign policy, its continued role depended greatly on presidential interest in international economics. *Four major patterns emerged in the making of foreign economic policy under President George W. Bush:* (1) Bush decided to keep and even strengthen the NEC; (2) the president had a difficult time staffing his economic team, especially the national economic director (3) some of the real power behind the President's economic policies came from outside of the NEC (Dolan and Rosati 2006; Sanger 2001); and (4) once the economy collapsed in 2007 and especially 2008, the president deferred to the leadership of the Treasury Department under Secretary Henry Paulsen to respond to the crisis.

First, President Bush continued to rely on and institutionalize the NEC. With respect to the nexus between security and economic issues, Bush enacted some major changes in the relationship between the NSC and NEC in the policymaking process. In particular, Bush ordered the national security advisor and the NEC director to "share a foreign policy desk to more effectively integrate economics with security issues in America's post–cold war foreign policy objectives." Bush stated that the move was designed to make sure the economic people don't run off with foreign policy, and vice versa. He justified his moves by referring to the major role the Treasury Department had in the Clinton administration in setting foreign policy toward East Asia, Latin America, and Russia. "Globalization has altered the dynamics in the White House, as well as between the White House and the Treasury. We have to respond to that" (Sanger 2001).

In addition, Bush enlarged the joint NSC/NEC international economics staff by adding more foreign economics experts to make it more aware of the economic changes that had caused upheaval around the world and by cutting the number of security officials in the office. The staff dealt with two sorts of issues, setting general international economic policy and coordinating White House responses to regional and international financial crises, similar to those that erupted in Mexico, East Asia, and Russia during the Clinton administration. Initially, under Condoleezza Rice, the staff was physically located within the NSC structure, but reported both to her and to the NEC director through a newly created deputy assistant for international economic policy.

Second, the Bush administration had considerable turnover in its senior foreign economic policy officials, especially the Secretary of Treasury and the NEC director. In economic policy, Bush originally appeared to be comfortable with Lawrence Lindsey heading the NEC. Lindsey brought to the NEC years of experience as a member of the Federal Reserve Board of Governors, as a professor of economics at Harvard, and as a staff member on Reagan's CEA. He was chosen to head the NEC over others in part because of his friendship and his ability to explain complex economic issues to Bush in simple terms. For treasury secretary, Bush initially selected Paul O'Neil, former CEO of Alcoa. O'Neil had a reputation as a deficit hawk and had little experience in international economic policymaking. O'Neil was never seen as effective and was often off-message with the White House. Lindsey, in contrast, was a Reagan-style tax cutter and ardent free trader and his role as go-to guy in both domestic and foreign economic policy was seen in Bush's insistence on sticking to the $1.6 trillion tax cut he proposed during the campaign and his willingness to go ahead with American participation in the Free Trade Agreement for the Americas (FTAA).

With the lackluster performance of the American economy, President Bush changed his major economic team following the 2002 congressional elections. Treasury Secretary O'Neil was replaced by business executive Jack Snow and National Economic director Lindsey was replaced by Stephen Friedman. While O'Neil provided a scathing critique of the inner workings of the Bush administration in a book that came out in 2004 (Suskind 2004), Lindsey "took the news more graciously . . . praising the president in private." However, Lindsey was asked to resign because he was seen as an ineffective manager, unable to unify support for the president's economic policies. Moreover, and most damaging to his career, was his public estimate that the war in Iraq might cost over $200 billion, which was seen as an act of disloyalty and drew the ire of Vice President Cheney and the president.

Stephen Friedman, a former partner of Robert Rubin at Goldman Sachs and an advisor to the Clinton administration, replaced Lindsey and was expected to bring more centrist support to the president's economic plans. However, Friedman was staunchly opposed to the ballooning deficit and never really asserted himself on other issues. He was replaced in 2005 by the third NEC director, Allan B. Hubbard, who reinforced the president's policies much more publicly than had his predecessors. Hubbard seemed to align himself well with the president based in part on their past friendship; both Bush and Hubbard were classmates at Harvard business school. Hubbard also served under the elder Bush administration as a campaign fundraiser and as head for the White House Council on Competitiveness (promoting deregulation), as well as working as a campaign fundraiser for the younger Bush in both elections. Being a close friend of the president increased his ability to get the president's economic advisors to work together, something that did not occur smoothly under the two previous NEC directors.

Third, it appears that much of the influence for the president's economic policy came from outside the NEC and the Treasury Department. Of particular importance are the members of the Council of Economic Advisors, who were considered major economic heavyweights (as thinkers), especially in comparison to the Secretary of Treasury and the NEC director. The important role of the CEA was also complimented by some senior White House officials, such as Vice President Cheney and senior advisor Karl Rove.

The Geroge W. Bush administration experienced both positive and negative results of policymaking in the post–cold war era. Several of Bush's staff changes and structural reforms clearly strengthened the NEC, including his move to create a joint desk for both the national economic director and national security advisor in the White House. This insistence on structural cooperation among the NEC and NSC acknowledged that the role of economics in U.S. foreign policy is important, making issues on the international economic agenda high-policy priorities for policymakers in the Bush White House despite the emphasis on the war on terrorism. On the other hand, the heavy turnover in national economic directors and the post-9/11 dominance of the war on terrorism detracted from the NEC role and continued development. During the cold war, the key to exercising strong presidential power rested on national security issues, in particular the use of military force. Bush's insistence on pursuing a global war on terrorism may have been a reflection of his desire to invoke strong presidential leadership and to minimize involvement in issue areas, such as economics, in which the president had strong faith in the free market ethos.

Finally, the economic crisis that hit full force in 2008 put the Bush administration in crisis management mode, which overrode the three patterns discussed above. Very simply, the financial system and the U.S. economy had "derailed" off the tracks of conventional free market thought. President Bush realized that something had to be done to restore "confidence" in the financial, monetary, and banking sector of the economy, which was on the verge of collapse. He turned to Treasury Secretary Henry Paulsen who asked for massive government intervention in the economy, including the $700 billion TARP (Troubled Asset Relief Program) to restore liquidity (i.e., money) and lending to the financial-banking sector. As part of the **Emergency Economic Stabilization Act of 2008,** commonly referred to as a "bailout" of the U.S. financial system, Congress quickly enacted a law proposed by Paulsen in October 2008 for the U.S. government to purchase distressed assets, especially mortgage-backed securities, and make capital injections into banks—both foreign and domestic banks. But it was "too little, too late" at the time due to the intensity of the actual financial and housing crisis (where money and credit were unavailable and frozen), the controversial nature of the initial proposal, and the low approval of President Bush (see **A Different Perspective** on macroeconomic policy).

A DIFFERENT PERSPECTIVE

The Two Dominant Views on Macroeconomic Policy

Differences in policy orientations between and within administrations over international economics have existed and grown over the years, usually involving priorities and tactics of policy as opposed to the basic goals of the free market ethos.

Conservatives (especially Republicans) tend to oppose intervention by governments in the global political economy in favor of free trade and the "magic" of the marketplace. Such **laissez-faire economics** will, it is argued, enhance economic growth and prosperity. Economic downturns, such as recessions, would automatically "correct" without government intervention. The recent popularity of this orientation, especially since the 1980s, was promoted by President Ronald Reagan, and became much stronger during the 1990s, reaching its height during the presidency of George W. Bush.

Liberals (especially Democrats) tend to see markets go through "booms" (growth and prosperity) and "busts" (downturns and recessions). Therefore, they tend to advocate greater governmental involvement (and multilateral management) to minimize economic instability, promote transparency (and information about economic transactions), and maximize economic growth while minimizing recessions in a global economy of growing interdependence—**Keynesian economics**. This orientation grew in popularity during the Great Depression, was promoted by President Franklin Delano Roosevelt and his "New Deal," and continued during the 1950s and 1960s especially under Democratic presidents Truman, Kennedy, and Johnson.

The economic crisis of 2007 and beyond has, if anything, intensified the debate and partisanship about macroeconomic views and policies and the presidential election of 2012 clearly reflected these differing perspectives. (see Roubini and Milm 2010).

Is there a preferred balance between the so-called free market and the role of government in domestic and, especially, international economics?

OBAMA AND THE "GREAT RECESSION"

When Barack Obama was inaugurated in January 2009, he inherited a dramatic economic crisis, what is now referred to as the Great Recession. At the time, it was a crisis and severe—the financial and banking crisis, rapidly increasing housing foreclosures, rising unemployment, huge federal government deficits, and major corporations heading toward bankruptcy were all components of the worst economic situation since the Great Depression of the 1930s. And, as the core economy since World War II, the severity of the economic decline was felt within the United States, impacted the European economy, and together the global economy—feeding each other due to globalization and, once and for all, making it clear that "high" foreign policy consists of both national security and economic policy (see Madrick 2009; Roubini and Milm 2010; Spero and Hart 2009).

The key economic decisions were taken during the transition and the first year of the Obama presidency. Beginning with the presidential transition, the initial emphasis by the newly elected Barack Obama was to take aggressive governmental actions to restore "confidence" in the financial and banking sector of the economy that was on the verge of collapse. The fear was that the measures taken by the Bush administration in late 2008 were inadequate for restoring such confidence, including the $700 billion TARP program. The election of a new president, Obama's charisma and constant public efforts to reassure investors and the American people, the perception of a strong and proactive economic team working together, and changes in the TARP program to increase transparency and accountability all helped to stave off collapse and to restore confidence in the banking and financial system nationally and globally.

The second major emphasis of the Obama administration was to "stimulate" the economy and promote recovery, both in the short-and long-term, by having Congress pass in February 2009 an economic package of nearly $800 billion to invest throughout the economy, hoping to keep and create jobs, increase spending, and spur economic growth. Known as the **American Recovery and Reinvestment Act of 2009**, the stimulus act included federal tax cuts; expansion of unemployment benefits and other social welfare provisions; and domestic spending in education, health care, and infrastructure, including the energy sector. Finally, the third emphasis of the Obama administration was to tackle reform of the health care system and, in the future, to promote new and alternative energy policies.

To head off what appeared to be a looming global catastrophe and promote recovery, Obama enlisted a proactive team of strong personalities with often differing economic philosophies. The members of the President's economic inner circle also had much government experience and strong reputations. *Most of the influence in economic policymaking came from three sources:* (1) the NEC and National Economic Director Lawrence Summers and his successor Gene Sperling, (2) the Treasury Department and Treasury Secretary Timothy Geithner, and (3) the Federal Reserve Board and Fed Chief Ben Bernanke. As Simon Johnson (2009), a former chief economist at the IMF, described the new economic team:

> In the configuration of responsibility for economic strategy in the current administration, the NEC, led by Lawrence Summers, has a broad mandate—covering essentially all issues to some degree. But the Treasury Secretary Timothy F. Geithner has enormous authority and discretion with regard to the financial sector. The CEA plays a supportive analytical role, which can matter on particular points, and other departments or agencies tend to have a more limited scope. For major

economic policy initiatives, the most important drivers within the administration are the views of Mr. Summers, Mr. Geithner and their respective staffs. These obviously interact with—and bump up against—the Federal Reserve on many technical issues and Congress on everything political. There are also increasing indications that Mr. Summers's economic council and Mr. Geithner's Treasury are not exactly on convergent paths.

Obama assembled his first economic team from a group of individuals renowned for their experience, intellect, and ability to deconstruct the most challenging economic problems, while trying to create an atmosphere of consensus through open discussion. One of the most critical hurdles was minimizing the impact of weaknesses, while exploiting the strengths of each of the key team players. Bernanke, Summers, and Geithner maintained a positive working relationship over the years. In fact, Summers often acted as the "mentor" to Geithner who acted as a "protégé" (Hirsh and Thomas 2009; see **Figure 8.3**).

Not surprisingly, there appeared to be tremendous overlap in the minds and thinking of the principal advisors on whom President Obama initially relied. They also appeared to have a complementary working relationship with each other and the president despite differences in personality, temperament, and policy views. *What was particularly unique though was the close and overt working relationship between the Fed Chair Ben Bernanke and the rest of the Obama economic team*—especially given the Fed's traditional independence within the executive branch and from the president. Clearly, the necessity to work together on the very serious crisis over-rode some of the bureaucratic autonomy and protectiveness (see **A Closer Look** on the economic team).

At the same time, there were reports that the forceful and experienced personalities that Obama assembled also clashed under the stress of their work. According to Jackie Calmes (2009):

> Underlying tensions have gripped Mr. Obama's economic advisors as they . . . struggled with the gravest financial crisis since the Depression. By all accounts, much of the tension derive[d] from the president's choice of the brilliant but sometimes supercilious Mr. Summers to be the director of the National Economic Council, making him the policy impresario of the team. . . . Along the way, Mr. Summers . . . forcefully debated the Treasury secretary, his onetime protégé Timothy F. Geithner, over what to do with troubled banks. He . . . clashed with Peter R. Orszag, the budget director, over fiscal and health policy issues. He . . . collided with Austan Goolsbee, an economist on the Council of Economic Advisors, over whether to rescue Chrysler. And he and Mrs. Romer [CEA chair] have squabbled over how best to make the economic case for overhauling health care.

Surprisingly, one might have thought that Fed Chair Bernanke would be the most difficult, given the independent authority of the Fed.

Confident and inexperienced, President Obama had the enthusiasm to transform economic policy as he proposed to do in his 2008 campaign, but he did not exert a proactive "process" role (as opposed to policy) in economic issues given the nature of his economic team. This was reinforced by his limited experience and knowledge of the international economy. Obama understandably wanted "results" and proved more pragmatic in practice that his populist and idealistic rhetoric during the campaign suggested (see Alter 2009; Calmes 2009; Green 2010; Johnson 2009; Lizza 2010; Suskind 2011).

Figure 8.3 Characteristics of Key Obama Team Players

	Title	Background	Experience	Common Ground	Specialty/Strengths
Bernanke, Ben S.	**Federal Reserve Chairman**	**Academia and Government**	**Chairman of the President's Council of Economic Advisors** (2005–2006) **Federal Reserve System Member Board of Governors** (2002–2005) **Federal Reserve Banks—Visiting Scholar** (1987–1991, 1994–1996) **Federal Reserve Bank of New York Academic Advisory Panel** (1990–2002)	—Implemented an intimate working relationship with previous Secretary of Treasury Henry Paulson —Has received high marks for implementing measured to reduce economic damage and speed the pace to recovery —Likely to receive another term as Chairman in 2010	**Responsibility—Accountability to the People** **Demystification of the "Fed"** **Goal Setting and Attainment**
Summers, Larry	**Director National Economic Council**	**Academia**	**Secretary of the Treasury** (1999–2001) **Harvard University President** (2001–2006)	—Appointed Geithner as a special assistant at the Treasury Department —Secretary of the Treasury with Geithner as Under Secretary-(1999) —Close relationship with the President —Primary candidate to succeed Bernanke if his term is not renewed in Jan 2010	**Strategic Economic Management** **"Intellectual Bulldozer"** **"Bad Cop"** **Mentor**
Geithner, Timothy F.	**Secretary of the Treasury**	**Government**	**Federal Reserve Bank**—President (2003–2009) **Policy Development and Review Department at the International Monetary Fund Director** (2001–2003) **Undersecretary of the Treasury for International Affairs** (1999–2001)	—Became Under Secretary of the Treasury to Secretary Summers-(1999) —Worked closely with Summers in the Department of Treasury during Asian Economic Crisis (1997) —Close relationship with the President —Summers was also at the top of the short list to become the current Secretary of Treasury	**Diplomacy—Exerting influence in a non-confrontational manner** **Politically Savvy** **Team/Consensus Builder** **"Good Cop"** **Protégé**

President Obama's First Economic Team

NEC Director **Lawrence Summers** was the only Obama top economic director with a West Wing office. He had daily access to the president and saw the president more than his other advisors, and Summers also controlled the daily economic briefings. "As the Obama team has coalesced, Summers, who leads a daily economic briefing for the president, has seemed to emerge as the strategic mastermind of the administration's macro-economic response to the biggest crisis since the Depression." He outlined his responsibilities as National Economic Director:

"My role is to make sure the president gets access to the best economic thinking he can on everything that touches the economy. That means making sure that no arguments go unscrutinised . . . and it means helping everyone on the president's economic team make the best case for whatever policies they prefer. It is certainly incredible, as intellectually challenging as anything I've ever done . . . What makes it so challenging and exciting, as well as exhausting, is the range of subjects." And Summers was impressed with "Obama's determination to use his presidency to effect long-term change—no matter how pressing the immediate problems" (Freeland 2009).

Timothy Geithner, Obama's secretary of the treasury, was the president of the Federal Reserve Bank of New York and intimately involved during the start of the banking crisis in the fall of 2008. "Mr. Geithner has been the most prominent administration spokesman on all matters financial and fiscal." As he explained it,

Although this crisis in some ways started in the United States, it is a global crisis. . . . The rest of the world needs the U.S. economy and financial system to recover in order for it to re-

vive. We remain at the center of global economic activity with financial and trade ties to every region of the globe. Just as importantly, we need the rest of the world to recover if we are to prosper again here at home. As a consequence, the community of nations must work together . . . to revive economies around the world and to lay the groundwork for a new, more stable and more sustainable pattern of growth in the future. This crisis is not simply a more severe version of the usual business cycle recession, the typical downturn in which economies ultimately adjust and stabilize. Instead, it is an abrupt correction of financial excesses that has overwhelmed economies' and markets' self-correcting mechanisms, and so can only be ended by extraordinary policy responses. (Geithner 2009; Johnson 2009)

Ben Bernanke is the Chairman of the Board of Governors of the United States Federal Reserve, a post he has filled since January 2006.

The Fed has never wielded as much power as it does right now, but the very expansion of its mission has exposed it to more second-guessing and more challenges to its political independence than ever before. The Fed chairman and the central bank are also caught in a political cross fire over how to overhaul the nation's system of financial regulation. President Obama has proposed a sweeping plan that would make the Fed more powerful in some respects and less powerful in others. Mr. Obama's plan would put the Fed in charge of regulating systemic risk, like the buildup of dangerous mortgages during the housing bubble, and would give the Fed power to im-

(Continued)

pose tougher regulation over financial institutions deemed too big to fail. As Bernanke saw it, it was the "perfect storm," of economic misfortune in which "housing, credit and financial problems converged into a major crisis the likes of which haven't been seen since the 1930's." Therefore, we need to think "outside the box" (Andrews 2009; Bernanke 2009).

Richard Wolffe (2010) argues that the economic team saw it as their patriotic duty to govern and save the economy first and foremost. If that meant compromise and bending to Washington's and Wall Street's political realities, that was the cost of doing the country's business. Most importantly, Bernanke set an unprecedented role for working and cooperating with Treasury and the NEC, rather than its more passive or invisible, and definitely independent role historically. In practice, Bernanke minimized the political independence of the FED because of his real fear that the loss in "confidence" and the economic meltdown would snowball into a real global depression.

Does it really matter which individuals occupy the positions of the NEC Director, Treasury Secretary, and Chair of the Fed?

Ultimately, President Obama was successful in restoring confidence in the financial system, getting his stimulus package passed, arresting the economic decline in 2009, and passing his major health care legislation. After this flurry of activity in the first eighteen months of the administration, the president made some changes in his economic team. The most notable of these was the replacement of Larry Summers as NEC director with Gene Sperling—who had previously occupied the same role under President Clinton—in early 2011. Sperling was a central figure in the administration's struggle with the Republican-controlled house over the U.S. budget, and was central to other administration initiatives such as the American Jobs Act, the extension of Transition Adjustment Assistance, the universal dislocated workers, and the small business tax credit, manufacturing policy, housing, and economic assistance for veterans. As NEC director, Sperling continued the central coordinating efforts established by his predecessors.

The policies that began under Bush and were passed in 2009 by Obama became controversial and helped to intensify the partisanship that was already pervasive in Washington, D.C., politics. Criticized on the right for being too liberal, and by the left for falling under Wall Street's spell, Obama managed to make both unhappy. With the significant gains by the Republicans during the 2010 election, especially in Congress, gridlock became the norm in the nation's capitol relative to the economy. President Obama was increasingly vulnerable in the presidential election of 2012 to Mitt Romney, the Republican challenger, as most Americans soon forgot about the economic crisis and focused on what was the most important factor in the outcome of the 2012 presidential election: the current state of the economy and the nature of the recovery.

Nevertheless, amid signs of economic improvement throughout the summer and fall of 2012, President Obama won re-election in a campaign in which economic issues — including the federal budget and debt, jobs and growth, trade and investment — dominated. Immediately after the November election. President Obama and his economic moved to address efforts to sustain and accelerate the slow economic recovery at home and abroad.

FOREIGN ECONOMICS AND THE UNCERTAIN FUTURE OF PRESIDENTIAL POWER

In sum, presidents are not that powerful in the making of economic policy and for deter-mining the future of the U.S. economy. Domestic and international economics are classic intermestic issues, which heighten the paradox of presidential power. The politics and the nature of the U.S. economy often drives much of the life cycle that presidents experience and the frustrations of exercising leadership in a political environment with so many constraints and uncertainties as discussed in Chapter 3.

In addition to the complex politics of U.S. economic policy, the U.S. government also is heavily involved in the "politics of the international political economy." The United States is not all-powerful and is increasingly enmeshed in a global interdependent world. As depicted in **Figure 8.4,** the U.S. president and the foreign economic bureaucracy must also interact with other governments—especially in developed countries such as Canada, Europe, and

Figure 8.4 The U.S. and the International Political Economy

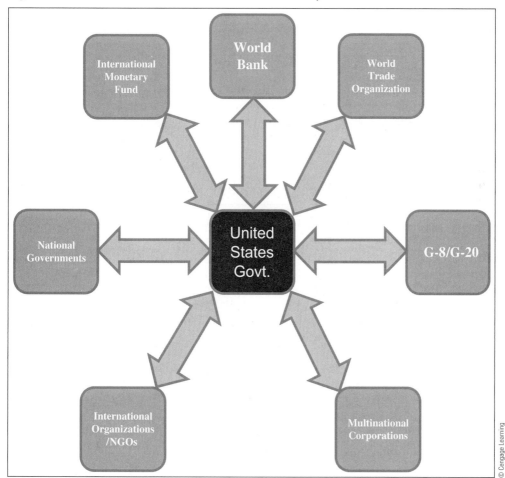

© Cengage Learning

Japan (often referred to as the G-8) and other strongly emerging markets such as Australia, Brazil, China, India, South Korea (the G-20)—in efforts to minimize global economic instability and downturns as well as to promote economic growth and prosperity (see cartoon on page 239). The U.S. foreign economic policy must also contend with other important governmental and nongovernmental organizations, such as the IMF, the World Bank, the WTO, multinational corporations, and private voluntary organizations. The days of hegemonic power abroad and expected frequent economic prosperity at home are probably less likely in the future, regardless who is president—as reflected by the Great Recession (review Chapter 2; see Madrick 2009; Roubini and Milm 2010; Spero and Hart 2009).

The good news is that presidents are finally better able to coordinate economic policymaking process better with the creation and reliance on a NEC, indicating the continued and growing importance of foreign economics. Traditionally, the Treasury Department and the treasury secretary have taken the international lead, but the NEC has become institutionalized and a prominent part of the policymaking landscape. Furthermore, the Fed has demonstrated an unprecedented willingness to be both independent and work closely with the president's economic team.

However, the foreign economic policymaking process remains an incredible challenge for any U.S. president, given the complexity of the domestic and international political economy. It symbolizes the continued trend toward White House–centered policymaking in response to challenging presidential efforts to better manage and govern foreign policy in general.

For current and future administrations, much will depend on the uncertain and often uncontrollable political forces that underlie the relationship between security and economics in U.S. foreign policymaking, the impact of U.S. foreign economic policy on the domestic economy, and the future of the U.S. and global economy. These complex and dynamic forces will determine the degree with which a post–cold war president will be able to exercise, or be perceived to exercise, presidential power in a pluralistic and globalized policymaking environment well into the twenty-first century.

SUGGESTED SOURCES FOR MORE INFORMATION

Alter, Jonathan. (2010) *The Promise: President Obama, Year 1.* New York: Simon and Schuster. Excellent overview and analysis of Obama administration's policymaking process in economics and healthcare.

Destler, I. M. (1996) *The National Economic Council: A Work in Progress.* Washington, D.C.: Institute for International Economics. Good overview of presidential efforts to coordinate foreign economic policymaking and the NEC.

Dolan, Chris J., and Jerel A. Rosati. (2006) "U.S. Foreign Economic Policy and the Significance of the National Economic Council," *International Studies Perspectives* 7 (May): 102–123. On the policy significance of the NEC under presidents Clinton and Bush.

Green, Joshua. (2010) "Inside Man," *The Atlantic*, April. Excellent overview of Timothy Geithner and his critical role within the Obama policymaking process.

Inside Job. (2010). Academy Award–winning best documentary on what brought about the financial meltdown.

Madrick, Jeff. (2009) "How We Were Ruined & What We Can Do," *New York Review of Books* (February 12). Excellent overview of the sources and evolution of the collapse of the U.S. economy.

Rohrich, Paul Egon. (1987) "Economic Culture and Foreign Policy: The Cognitive Analysis of Economic Policy Making," *International Organization* 41(1):61–92. Informative discussion on economic cultures and their foreign policy impact.

Roubini, Nouriel and Stephen Mihm. (2010) *Crisis Economics: A Crash Course in the Future of Finance.* New York: Penguin Press. Superb book on differing American economic perspectives, the rise of the economic bubble and meltdown, and prescriptions for the future.

Spero, Joan Edelman, and Jeffrey A. Hart. (2009) *The Politics of International Economic Relations.* Belmont, CA: Wadsworth. An informative overview of the evolution of U.S. foreign economic policy and the global economy since World War II.

KEY CONCEPTS

economic culture

free market ethos

Keynesian economics

laissez-faire economics

tourism

OTHER KEY TERMS

American Recovery and
 Reinvestment Act of 2009

Ben Bernanke

Council of Economic Advisors
 (CEA)

Emergency Economic Stabilization
 Act of 2008

Export-Import Bank (Eximbank)

Federal Reserve Board (the Fed)

Lawrence Summers

national economic director (NEC
 director)

National Economic Council (NEC)

Office of Management and Budget
 (OMB)

Office of the United States Trade
 Representative (USTR)

Robert Rubin

secretary of the treasury

Timothy Geithner

Treasury Department

PRESIDENT BARACK OBAMA IS BRIEFED BY SENIOR ADVISORS ON THE EVE OF THE G20 SUMMIT, JUNE 17, 2012. CLOCKWISE FROM THE PRESIDENT, ARE: ALICE WELLS, SENIOR DIRECTOR FOR RUSSIAN AFFAIRS, NSC STAFF; NATIONAL SECURITY ADVISOR TOM DONILON; CHIEF OF STAFF JACK LEW; BEN RHODES, DEPUTY NATIONAL SECURITY ADVISOR FOR STRATEGIC COMMUNICATIONS; PRESS SECRETARY JAY CARNEY; LAEL BRAINARD, UNDER SECRETARY OF THE TREASURY FOR INTERNATIONAL AFFAIRS; TREASURY SECRETARY TIM GEITHNER; SECRETARY OF STATE HILLARY RODHAM CLINTON; AND MIKE FROMAN, DEPUTY NATIONAL SECURITY ADVISOR FOR INTERNATIONAL ECONOMICS.

DECISIONMAKING THEORY AND FOREIGN POLICYMAKING

Now that we have examined the role of the president and the executive branch bureaucracy, including the National Security Council (NSC), the State Department, the military establishment, the intelligence community, and foreign economic policymaking and the NEC, it is time to think theoretically about the complex and dynamic patterns of executive branch policymaking. As we have seen, many people assume that foreign policy is made by the president and is based on some type of grand design. Yet as Chapters 1–8 have indicated, far less purpose and grand design go on inside the White House and the executive branch than most people think. In the words of Fred Dutton, former White House advisor to President John Kennedy, "Washington isn't all that thought out. So much of it is improvisation. Too much rationality and planning can be attributed to it. Much of it is trying something, taking a pratfall, and then looking either bad or good when you do" (Smith 1988:56). In fact, as Charles Maechling, Jr. (1976:1) states, usually "the making and implementation of foreign policy is a collective process involving half a dozen agencies and hundreds of anonymous officials. In propagating the delusion of a master hand and only one tiller, both the executive branch and the news media have collaborated as if in a silent conspiracy."

In this chapter, we turn to **decisionmaking theory** to *provide the necessary analytical perspective* to conceptualize, synthesize, and better understand the complexity and dominant patterns of the policymaking process within the executive branch. We first review the context of post–World War II policy patterns and the different stages of policymaking. We then describe four basic models of decisionmaking, highlight two major policymaking levels, and analyze the critical role that individual beliefs, personality, and crises play in policymaking before concluding the chapter.

CONTEXT: PATTERNS AND POLICYMAKING STAGES

To begin, let's review the major patterns revealed in the preceding chapters and describe the policy process. *In the post–World War II period, seven major foreign policy patterns* stand out. First, World War II and the cold war resulted in the globalization of U.S. foreign policy. Second, following World War II and again with the collapse of the cold war, the United States became the preeminent global actor. Third, World War II and the cold war resulted in the rise of presidential power in foreign policy. However, the Vietnam War, the breakdown of the Bretton Woods economic system, and Watergate all helped to restrict that power and were symptomatic of greater global and domestic complexity. Fourth, the NSC system gradually replaced the State Department as the central tool for presidential management of national security policy. Fifth, after World War II the national security bureaucracy expanded, especially in the military establishment and the intelligence community. Sixth, bureaucratic agencies not devoted to traditional national security issues became more visible and important since the Vietnam War, especially the foreign economic bureaucracy and the National Economic Council (NEC). Finally, all of these patterns together—especially the tremendous expansion in the size, scope, and complexity of the foreign policy bureaucracy—have greatly complicated presidential leadership and management of foreign policy.

The policymaking process within which these patterns are embedded is also complex. Although any number of stages can be delineated, most scholars of foreign policy emphasize the involvement of at least *three general stages in the policymaking or decisionmaking process* (Robinsan and Majak 1967; Robinson and Snyder 1965): agenda setting; policy formulation; and policy implementation.

The initial stage of policymaking is **agenda setting**, where an issue must get the attention of governmental officials and organizations if policy is eventually to be produced. Issues become part of the government's agenda in a variety of ways (Kingdon 1984; Rochefort and Cobb 1993). First, issues get on the agenda as a result of initiatives taken by officials, including the president. Hedrick Smith (1988:93) points out in *The Power Game* the importance of defining and manipulating an issue to affect the "power loop"—that is, to affect which participants are involved and the circulation of information in order to control the policymaking process. "Those who are in control of policy, whether the president and his top advisors or bureaucrats buried in the bowels of government, will try desperately to keep the information loop small, no matter what the issue; those who are on the losing side internally will try to widen the circle."

Moreover, issues that the government has considered important in the past tend to remain on the agenda. Continuing agenda status explains much governmental behavior: the hundreds of issues that the bureaucracy considers daily are usually of this type. This also accounts for the difficulty presidents have managing the bureaucracy, since so much of what the government does involves refining and implementing existing policies. Many of these policies become so institutionalized and routinized that careerists can "control policy by keeping the power loop small" (Smith 1988:80).

Finally, issues are placed on the agenda as a result of domestic and international events, such as crises. The terrorist attacks of September 11, Hurricane Katrina demolishing New Orleans and impacting the price of oil, the collapse of the financial markets in 2008, and the the so-called Arab spring and subsequent violence in the Middle East since 2010 are examples of crises that received considerable media coverage and are a common agenda-setting path.

Once an issue makes it on the governmental agenda, the second stage—**policy formulation**—begins. This stage is what most people think of when it comes to policy-making—the process of identifying and weighing goals and options and the interaction of policymakers as they arrive at a decision. Once a policy is identified and selected, the final stage begins: in this **policy implementation** stage the decision is carried out by members or agents of the government. These two stages have been the focus of decisionmaking theory and are the principal focus of the rest of this chapter.

The distinction between agenda setting, policy formulation, and policy implementation is not as clear-cut as described, since policymaking is usually a complex, political, and messy process. For example, once an issue is on the governmental agenda, its level of importance may change due to events at home or abroad. Issues and policies are not formulated solely at one point in time but often involve a series of decisions over time. Furthermore, the implementation of policy does not necessarily end the policymaking process for any one issue, given that its success or failure often affects future agenda-setting and formulation, which may produce changes in policy. In other words, the agenda-setting, policy formulation, and policy implementation stages affect each other, overlap and proceed in cycles. Nevertheless, the three stages serve as useful analytical tools for making sense of the nature of policymaking within the executive branch.

DECISIONMAKING MODELS

Scholars of U.S. foreign policy have developed *four major theoretical models to explain how the policymaking process operates within the executive branch:* (1) rational actor, (2) groupthink, (3) governmental politics, and (4) organizational process. The rational actor, governmental politics, and organizational process models were developed and popularized by political scientist Graham Allison (1971); groupthink was developed by psychologist Irving Janis (1982). These models provide four alternative perspectives on presidential power, the nature of the policymaking process within the executive branch, and the politics of U.S. foreign policy. As "models," they represent simplifications of reality that highlight only the most significant, consequential players and processes to explain why the United States takes particular foreign policy actions.

We begin with the rational actor model because it involves the most simplistic version and "ideal" process that most people assume when they think of foreign policymaking. This model assumes that the president is "the decisionmaker," who arrives at decisions through a very rational process. The alternative three models are presented from the most central-ized to the most decentralized—groupthink, then governmental politics, followed by the organizational process model—and they assume a less rational, more political process in which the beliefs, personalities, and roles of officials within and outside the Oval Office are consequential in affecting the outcomes. Whereas groupthink portrays a centralized policy-making process under presidential control, governmental politics and organizational process

Table 9.1 Decisionmaking Models

The Model	Decision Structure and Process	Key Explanatory Concepts
Rational Actor	Centralized	Presidential goals and beliefs
	Rational	
Groupthink	Centralized	Beliefs of leader(s)
	Irrational	Personality of leader(s)
		Group norms and dynamics
Governmental Politics	Pluralistic	Policymaker beliefs and personality
	Political	Policymaker roles and power
Organizational Process	Decentralized	Organizational structures and roles
	Relatively autonomous bureaucratic	Organizational subcultures
	Dynamics	Organizational programs and routines

© Cengage Learning

portray a decentralized policymaking process with little control exercised by the president. (**Table 9.1** provides an overview of each model.)

The Rational Actor Ideal

On Tuesday, October 16, 1962, the intelligence community informed President John Kennedy that the Soviet Union was transporting and deploying medium- and intermediate-range ballistic missiles with nuclear warheads to Cuba that could strike much of the continental United States. This triggered what became known as the **Cuban missile crisis**. The president assembled a group of his most trusted advisors to consider the American response. The group included Attorney General Robert Kennedy, Secretary of State Dean Rusk, Secretary of Defense Robert McNamara, Director of Central Intelligence John McCone, Secretary of the Treasury Douglas Dillon, Special Assistant for National Security Affairs McGeorge Bundy, Special Counsel Theodore Sorensen, Undersecretary of State George Ball, and Chairman of the Joint Chiefs of Staff Maxwell Taylor. For five days they met secretly and virtually round the clock, discussing and debating the information available, goals, and possible policy options. Then on Saturday, October 20, President Kennedy decided to blockade Cuba, while privately offering Nikita Khrushchev, chairman of the Communist party of the Soviet Union, a political solution (withdrawal of Soviet missiles in Cuba for withdrawal of American missiles in Turkey and a U.S. pledge not to invade Cuba). By the following Sunday, October 28, the Soviet leader had agreed, and the Cuban missile crisis was history.

As Graham Allison suggested in *Essence of Decision: Explaining the Cuban Missile Crisis*, most people assume that the policymaking process operates according to what scholars have referred to as the **rational actor model**. In fact, many scholars have concluded that President Kennedy's decision closely approximated a rational and optimal process under presidential control, contributing to the prompt resolution of the crisis (for other viewpoints, see Lebow 1981; Nathan 1975; Snyder 1978). This is the **ideal type** or model that is consistent with the formal organizational charts that portray the government as extremely hierarchical.

In the rational actor model:

1. problems are identified,

2. goals are listed and ranked,

3. all options are identified and evaluated for their costs and benefits,

4. the optimal policy is chosen based on the available information, and

5. that option is faithfully implemented and its results monitored and evaluated.

This conception rests on several key assumptions: (a) The executive branch operates according to a pyramid of authority; (b) the president is on top and exercises power over foreign policy; (c) advice and information from advisors and the bureaucracy flow to the president; (d) the president makes policy choices based on this advice and information; and (e) the president uses his staff within the Executive Office of the Presidency, such as the NSC or NEC, and his cabinet appointees to manage and coordinate the vast bureaucracy. In this scenario, the president governs foreign policy and the bureaucracy serves and responds to presidential interests—consistent with the popular image of policymaking.

This perspective assumes not only that the president is ultimately in charge, but that the policymaking process proceeds in accordance with a rational or open process responsive to presidential beliefs and wishes. That is, once an issue gets on the governmental agenda, the president relies on formal policymaking channels (such as the NSC interagency process) for information and advice and informally consults governmental policymakers whom he has come to trust. Then, the president determines the foreign policy goals that he wants to achieve, considers a wide assortment of policy options, and selects the policy alternative that will best fulfill his objectives. Once the president makes a decision, the bureaucracy faithfully implements the policy in accordance with his wishes.

For example, in early 2009, President Barack Obama decided to dispatch more than 30,000 additional troops to Afghanistan to address the deteriorating situation in that country in which the Taliban, deposed by the U.S. intervention in 2001, were gaining strength and violence was increasing. A simple explanation of that decision consistent with the rational actor model would depict President Obama as seeking advice and information from several advisors, including Vice President Joe Biden, Secretary of State Hillary Clinton, and Secretary of Defense Robert Gates. After weighing their advice and recommendations, President Obama chose the troop deployment, which was then implemented (Dilanlan 2009; Keating 2009).

Thus, the rational actor model depicts an executive-branch policymaking process that is both centralized and rational. Under presidential management, at times, the policymaking process may in fact operate in a way that approximates the rational actor model. It is possible for the president to manage the policymaking process for those issues in which he has expressed the greatest interest. The policymaking process may approximate a rational process in which a variety of goals, information, and policy alternatives are considered by the president, although much depends on the president's beliefs and personality, the choices a president makes concerning his agenda, level of active involvement concerning issues and policymaking, executive-level appointments of staff and advisors, and organization of the policymaking process. Greater presidential control and management may result from direct personal intervention by the president or, indirectly, through the involvement of his closest personal advisors, such as his chief of staff or the national security advisor. Furthermore, presidential decisions may be implemented through established bureaucratic procedures or, as occurred under President Nixon, by having trusted advisors, such as Henry Kissinger and the NSC staff, take an operational role to impose it on the bureaucracy. In contrast, a rational process may occur because the president and his major foreign policy advisors enjoy a collegial relationship or considerable consensus in foreign policy views—conditions that characterized the early Jimmy Carter and George H.W. Bush administrations.

In any event, whatever the "reality," the result is that the actual process performs "as if" the rational actor model assumptions apply, and the details of what actually occur in the deliberations within the "black-box" of government are just not important enough for attention. This is, in essence, the essential simplification of the model. Many scholars, journalists, and pundits explain diplomatic history and foreign policymaking in terms of a rational actor model. At times the policymaking process within the executive branch does in fact approximate this model, as occurred during the Cuban missile crisis. Nevertheless, the policymaking process often diverges from the centralized and rational process portrayed by the rational actor model.

Groupthink

From 1964 to 1968, President Lyndon Johnson and a small group of advisors agreed to a number of decisions that were responsible for escalating American involvement in the Vietnam War. Once the initial decision was taken to rely on the use of force to defeat North Vietnamese aggression, there was no turning back. At each stage of the Vietnam War policymaking process, decisions centered on force levels and how much force should be used to maintain an independent South Vietnam. Information and policy alternatives that diverged from, or contradicted, the escalatory path were ignored or rejected by the policymaking group. This was primarily because President Johnson was accustomed to getting his way once he had made a decision. Through his strong personality, he dominated the policymaking process on Vietnam. Administration policymakers quickly learned that Johnson was committed to avoiding a loss of South Vietnam to communism and preferred loyalty and support for his Vietnam policy to open discussion. Only the shock of the Tet Offensive and the collapse of the cold war consensus within government and in society forced Johnson to reconsider his policies.

Although some disagree (e.g., Barrett 1988, 1989), the Vietnam War policymaking process under President Johnson did not appear to reflect the rational actor model. Instead, it reflected **groupthink**, a concept developed by Irving Janis (1982) as a result of his work in social psychology. Janis argued that the adage "two minds are better than one" often is not borne out by the dynamics of small-group behavior. Instead, high cohesiveness and *esprit de corps* often develop among members of a group. This is true especially when members have similar backgrounds and beliefs, a strong leader emerges within the group, and the group faces a stressful situation. Under these circumstances, the group develops a strong concurrence-seeking tendency, and members tend to conform to group norms or decisions.

While the rational actor model and groupthink both presume a centralized policymaking structure under presidential control, groupthink describes a different policymaking process. Instead of deliberating the relevant goals, searching for information, considering alternatives, and selecting the policy option that maximizes goals, as the rational actor model depicts, groupthink often results in a nonrational process. *Symptoms of groupthink include*: an overestimation of the competency and inherent morality of the group, a tendency to stereotype out-groups and rationalize decisions, and the tendency to pressure members toward uniformity (usually through self-censorship), providing the illusion of unanimity. Groupthink—having members of a group think alike—is often promoted and maintained because of a strong domineering leader within the group.

Janis predicts that the more groupthink characterizes a policymaking process, the less likely it is that decisions will have a successful outcome. Failure results because the policymaking group is not open to new information and resists considering alternative policy options. These deficiencies prevent adjustments in policy that may maximize the chances of success, as prescribed by the rational actor model. Under groupthink, the group is committed to a particular policy regardless of changes or developments. Groupthink characteristics help to explain the rigidity and ultimate failure of Johnson's Vietnam policy.

A similar situation occurred in the Reagan administration's Iran-Contra affair, especially the Iranian element of the initiative. Throughout 1985 and 1986, a number of decisions were made by President Ronald Reagan that led to selling arms to Iran in exchange for the release of American hostages held in the Middle East, the profits of which were diverted to support the Nicaraguan Contras (in violation of a law prohibiting such assistance). Once it became public, the Iranian initiative led to an outcry against President Reagan and triggered the Iran-Contra affair. The failure of this initiative appears to have been heavily a function of the groupthink process.

While the Reagan administration's foreign policy officials fully supported and actively engaged in efforts to support the Contras and overthrow the Nicaraguan Sandinistas, a major policy split developed within the administration over the Iranian initiative. During the initial policymaking meetings, Secretary of State George Shultz and Secretary of Defense Caspar Weinberger were strongly opposed to the Iranian initiative on both moral and practical grounds. In fact, on two different occasions Shultz and Weinberger believed they had convinced President Reagan to abandon the policy. However, Reagan was personally interested in the fate of the hostages, and the national security advisor (first Robert McFarlane and then John Poindexter) and DCI William Casey were strong advocates of the initiative. With President Reagan committed to the Iranian initiative, the policymaking circle narrowed to include only those who supported the initiative. Thus, dissenters within the administration (i.e., Shultz and Weinberger) were circumvented and a small group of like-minded individuals implemented U.S. foreign policy that was committed to the release of the hostages. Groupthink processes also explain the NSC's operational role in actually carrying out the Iranian initiative, keeping most of the government in the dark (Draper 1991; Tower Commission 1987; Woodward 1987).

The information on the George H.W. Bush administration suggests that the policymaking process during the Persian Gulf crisis may have fallen victim to groupthink, led by the president, who was determined to respond strongly to Iraq's invasion of Kuwait. Initial surprise and indecision soon gave way to the decision to commit over 100,000 American troops to Saudi Arabia and the Persian Gulf. The president apparently made the crucial decision at Camp David with a small circle of his closest advisors, with little debate or discussion about alternative policies once the president's strong views were expressed. Instead, the meeting was devoted almost entirely to military options and how to get Saudi Arabian approval. As Bob Woodward in *The Commanders* (1991; see also J. E. Smith 1992) makes clear, the Joint Chiefs of Staff and in particular CJCS Colin Powell thought that such early reliance on the use of force and subsequent turn to a policy of brinksmanship were ill-advised, yet they were hesitant to challenge the civilian leadership. As David Halberstam observed in *War in a Time of Peace* (2001:69), during the crisis "Bush had been the most hawkish member of his own administration, surprising a number of his closest advisors and the senior people in the Pentagon alike with his singular sense of purpose" (see also Gordon and Trainor 1995). In this case, unlike Janis' predictions, the groupthink process did not lead to a failed policy, but instead in a highly successful military rout by the American and coalition forces.

A similar groupthink process appears to have prevailed following the attacks of September 11, 2001. Like his father, President George W. Bush wanted a strong reaction to the attacks. Unlike the 1991 situation, however, virtually all of President Bush's senior advisors also seemed to favor a relatively strong political and military reaction that quickly became a global war on terrorism from the very beginning. But President Bush was very much the driving force. According to Dan Balz and Bob Woodward of the *Washington Post* (2002:A1), within just thirteen hours after the attacks, President Bush met with his senior foreign policy aides and told them, "This is the time for self-defense. We have made the decision to punish whoever harbors terrorists, not just the perpetrators." Their job, the president said, "was to figure out how to do it." In other words, "the president and his advisors started America on the road to war that night without a map. They had only a vague sense of how to respond, based largely on the visceral reactions of the president." Not surprisingly, within forty-eight to seventy-two hours of September 11, more formal decisions were made and a general strategy was laid out to fight the war on terrorism, beginning with going after al-Qaeda and the Taliban in Afghanistan and then eventually going after Saddam Hussein in Iraq (see also Elliott 2002; Thomas 2002b; Woodward 2002).

After September 11, George W. Bush dominated his meetings with his senior foreign policy advisors. According to Woodward, (2002):

> When the meeting began in the White House Situation Room, Bush decided to let the meeting proceed with its routine presentations and updates before getting to the point. "I just want to make sure that all of us did agree on this plan, right?" he said after the reports. He looked around the table from face to face. There is an aspect of . . . urgency in Bush at such moments. He leans his head forward and holds it still, makes eye contact, maintains it, saying, in effect: You're on board, you're with me, right? Are we right, the president was asking. Are we still confident? He wanted a precise affirmation from each one [of his advisors]. . . . He was almost demanding they take an oath.

National Security Advisor Rice "believed the president would tolerate debate, would listen, but anyone who wanted debate had to have a good argument, and preferably a solution or at least a proposed fix. It was clear that no one at the table had a better idea." However, according to Woodward, "In fact, the president had not really opened the door a crack for anyone to raise concerns or deal with any second thoughts. He was not really listening. He wanted to talk" (Woodward 2002). Even President Bush admitted, "[T]hat is not a good habit at times. It is very important to create an environment in which people feel comfortable about speaking their minds" (quoted Woodward 2002).

The younger Bush also relied on a small group of advisors and process when it came to the critical decision to invade Iraq in 2003. In this case, not only did President Bush play a forceful role, but Secretary of Defense Donald Rumsfeld and Vice President Dick Cheney in particular were very powerful advocates for war. Secretary of State Colin Powell was the major advocate for moving more deliberately, relying on diplomacy, and, most importantly, advocating the building of a strong multilateral coalition and gaining international support before going to war. Powell tended to be the lone voice, with Condoleezza Rice being relatively passive as national security advisor. Over time, Powell found himself more and more isolated, ignored, and even unwelcome in policy discussions. Ultimately, the most hard-line and war prone dominated the proceedings and carried the day, usually led by President Bush himself (see Badie 2010).

Governmental Politics

In a speech before the United Nations on May 20, 1968, the Russians signaled that they were interested in responding to the Johnson administration's overtures to reach an agreement on arms limitations. This was the beginning of the Strategic Arms Limitations Talks, known as **SALT I**. Although President Johnson wanted a U.S. SALT position ready by late summer, he refused to involve the White House in the policymaking process. Instead, he wanted to present the USSR with a consensus SALT position that reflected bureaucratic concerns. "Neither Johnson nor his staff would take part in bureaucracy's epic struggle to produce not just a simple, clear proposal, but one that would actually make a serious matter of SALT. In Johnson's day there was no Henry Kissinger to hold the bureaucracy in line and to force up presidential options, as distinct from the preferences of the various parts of the government. Unlike Nixon, Johnson—as everyone in government knew—wanted agreement, not options. This meant that the Joint Chiefs had to be on board" (Newhouse 1973:108). Accordingly, the national security bureaucracy—the Defense Department, State Department, Arms Control and Disarmament Agency, and the Central Intelligence Agency—was left on its own to interact, bargain, and agree on a consensus SALT position (Newhouse 1973; Rosati 1981).

The formulation of the U.S. government's first SALT position resulted from a policymaking process that did not reflect the rational actor or groupthink models. It reflected a policymaking process that Graham Allison (1971) has called "governmental politics" (see also Halperin 1974; Halperin and Kantor 1973). **Governmental politics** describes a policymaking process that is neither centralized under the president nor rational, but rather is based on a pluralistic policymaking environment where power is diffused and the process revolves around political competition and compromise among the policymakers. This is a very common view of the nature of policymaking in the field of political science.

Under governmental politics, an issue is likely to trigger involvement of individuals from a variety of bureaucratic organizations, each differing in goals and objectives. However, no policymaker or organization is preponderant; the president (or the White House), if involved, is merely one participant, although his influence may be the most powerful. In this "pluralistic structure" within the policymaking process, different policymakers tend to provide information and advocate different policy alternatives. Given the competition and advocacy among the participants, none of whom can dominate the process, decisions emerge from political bargaining, coalition building, and compromise. Nor does the policymaking process necessarily cease once a decision is made. Policymakers and bureaucratic organizations least satisfied by the decision may continue the fight, trying to reverse or modify the decision and its implementation; an old Washington cliché states that the only decision that is final is the one with which you agree. Therefore, policymaking is a pluralistic and political process in which policymakers attempt to advance their personal, organizational, and national interests.

A governmental politics process is likely to prevail for agenda issues that are important enough to trigger the involvement of a number of policymakers and bureaucratic organizations, but not important enough to engage the dominant interest and involvement of the president (or a personal advisor acting in the president's name). *The process is particularly useful for understanding the interagency process for a number of reasons.* First, the president and his closest advisors must be selective as to which issues to emphasize, leaving governmental politics to prevail for most other issues. By 1968, President Johnson and his closest advisors were overwhelmed by the Vietnam War, and thus the bureaucracy dominated the SALT policymaking process.

Second, the president's management style may reinforce the practice of governmental politics. For instance, President Reagan downplayed the role of the national security advisor and staff, preferring to delegate authority and remain removed from most foreign policy issues, as discussed in Chapter 4. This management style intensified the political infighting among policymakers that tends to occur in the foreign policy bureaucracy. As Hedrick Smith describes it in *The Power Game* (1985:561), "the factional strife that plagued the making of Reagan's foreign policy will outlive Reagan—just as it preceded his presidency—because it lies deeply imbedded in our governmental system. Most of the skirmishes of the Reagan period . . . fit a pattern of bureaucratic tribal warfare—institutional conflict fired by the pride, interests, loyalties, and jealousies of large bureaucratic clans, protecting their policy turf and using guile as well as argument to prevail in the battle over policy."

However, Reagan's disengagement exacerbated the situation. A good example is seen in the U.S. intervention in Lebanon in 1982–1983. Policymaking degenerated into a series of political battles with policymakers from State and Defense as rivals determined to shape U.S. policy. The result: a fractured, inconsistent, and contradictory policy that reflected both a tenuous compromise among the key players and poorly coordinated elements, each controlled by a particular part of the bureaucratic landscape (Tanter 1990).

Finally, even when the president, or his closest advisor, becomes heavily involved, he or she may be unable to dominate policymaking. Failure may occur because some of the participants may be quite formidable and the president remains uncommitted to any policy option. Such a situation characterized the Carter administration in its third year during the Iranian Revolution. While President Carter appeared to be uncertain as to what was in the best interests of the United States, National Security Advisor Zbigniew Brzezinski became a major advocate of using force in Iran to support the Shah and lobbied against the more moderate policy recommendations of Secretary of State Cyrus Vance (Rosati 1987).

Governmental politics may be quite prevalent at times, as the following illustrations that were discussed in previous chapters may suggest. Within the State Department, the extensive jurisdictional and clearance process ensures the involvement of numerous bureaus that usually have to agree and sign off on a common position. Before the impact of the Goldwater-Nichols Act, the chair of the JCS was so weak that the joint chiefs often made decisions based on compromise so all the services got part of what they wanted. Within the intelligence community, the weakness of the DCI usually meant that major National Intelligence Estimates were based on compromises between the relevant agencies (with any disagreements hidden in footnotes to the final report). Since 2005, it is not apparent that the new Director of National Intelligence has brought greater centralization of authority and power to the intelligence process, at least in the form of more definitive intelligence estimates.

Recent evidence of the power of governmental politics comes from the Obama administration. From well before he assumed office in January 2009, President Obama welcomed the input of multiple advisors and a variety of perspectives into his administration. In fact, he argued that to avoid the mistakes of the George W. Bush administration, multiple voices would ensure that presidential decisions would be well informed and result from a vigilant and deliberative decision process. As president-elect, Obama argued that he favored strong personalities and strong opinions around him in part to prevent "groupthink." At the same time, Obama desired a collegial approach within his advisory team.

Despite the preference for a collegial inner circle, bureaucratic tensions escalated and strongly impacted the escalation decisions for military operations in Afghanistan-Pakistan. In March 2009 Obama approved a Pentagon request for an additional 30,000 troops that President Bush had deferred to his successor. At the time, Obama relied heavily on the judgment of CJCS Mullins and especially Secretary of Defense Gates (supported by Secretary of State Clinton), in part because of his lack of knowledge about national security, because he was preoccupied with the state of the economy, and because his national security advisor did not play a central role.

Less than half a year later, the Pentagon returned to request an additional 40,000 troops and a broad "counterinsurgency" strategy. General Stanley McChrystal (the U.S. Commander in Afghanistan) released a report initiated by Gates, Mullen, and General David Petraeus (the Combat Commander for CENTCOM). The president and his White House staff reportedly felt manipulated by the Pentagon's public leak of the report and request for additional troops before policy deliberation and the evaluation of the still-incomplete deployment of the previously authorized troops (Alter 2010; Hastings 2010; Woodward 2010).

What followed was a complicated and contentious process that led to a compromise decision (or a "political resultant" in the language of Allison 1971), which was announced in a speech at West Point in December 2009: a "surge" of an additional 40,000 troops, a hybrid "counterinsurgency" strategy with a "covert counter-terrorism" element to pursue the Taliban and al-Qaeda, and an agreement to bolster the Afghan government and train the Afghan military/police. The president and his personal staff had to struggle to persuade the McChrystal Report advocates to agree to a full review in early 2011, and the beginning of the withdrawal of U.S. military forces in July 2011 "depending on the conditions" (as of late 2012, this had not yet begun). Although Vice President Joe Biden and White House staffers opposed the troop escalation, the aggressive efforts of the Defense Department faction and their bureaucratic alliance with Hillary Clinton at State prevailed. Hence, despite the effort by the president to promote a deliberative process with numerous meetings over four months, the process exhibited all the major characteristics of the governmental politics model, with the resulting political compromise producing a tentative consensus for the surge (Alter 2010; Kornblut, Wilson and DeYoung 2009, A1; Woodward 2010).

In sum, governmental politics describes policymaking as extremely political. Unlike the rational actor model or groupthink, governmental politics describes the president as not ultimately controlling the policymaking process. Instead, policymaking is more pluralistic, involving a variety of policymakers and bureaucratic organizations, each exercising some political clout. The actual decisionmaking process is neither as rational as the rational actor model describes nor as conformist as groupthink. When no one actor is able to dominate the policymaking process, competitive politics usually prevail, and decisions become a function of bargaining, infighting, pulling and hauling, coalition building, and possibly compromise.

Organizational Process

On January 28, 1986, the military's ability to place reconnaissance satellites in orbit and the National Aeronautics and Space Administration's (NASA's) space program came to an abrupt halt when the *Challenger* space shuttle exploded shortly after liftoff killing the astronauts. Americans were shocked by the tragedy and tried to understand who was to blame for what went wrong. Governmental investigations were launched. Efforts to locate the responsible parties were based on the assumption that the government operated according to the rational actor model and that particular individuals were in charge. But this is not how the policymaking process for the space shuttle program operated. Nor do the policymaking models of groupthink or governmental politics enlighten us in this case.

To really understand what happened to the *Challenger* and why, one has to look at the organizational routines within the bureaucracies involved, principally NASA, the Department of Defense (DOD), and their corporate suppliers. NASA's major mission by the 1980s had become the space shuttle. Following repeated delays in the *Challenger's* expected launch,

NASA's mission and standard operating procedures resulted in a tendency to deemphasize equipment deficiencies and overlook safety precautions to expedite the launch. The DOD was under pressure to replace aging military reconnaissance satellites with newer, more sophisticated versions. The major mission of Morton Thiokol, Inc., the manufacturer of the rocket boosters, was to make money and maintain its production schedule without damaging the overall reliability of the equipment vital for the space shuttle launchings (including the defective O-rings ultimately found to be at fault). Therefore, the power of the different bureaucratic missions and routines resulted in each of the organizational units, especially within NASA, ignoring warnings about equipment defects and deficiencies. This situation prevailed because all of the organizations involved had played their respective roles for years and enjoyed a string of successful shuttle launches. However, on the day the shuttle exploded, the flaws produced by the organizational routines and standard operating procedures came together, surpassing a critical threshold and resulting in tragedy.

Was any particular individual or set of individuals to blame? Fault actually lay with a bureaucratic system of numerous organizations and with the structures and subcultures prevailing within those organizations. U.S. space policy and the *Challenger* tragedy were a function of the different behaviors produced by the organizations involved in the shuttle program. In *Essence of Decision*, Graham Allison (1971) describes this situation as the **organizational process model** of policymaking. This model emerged from the study of bureaucracy and organizational behavior that has prevailed within the fields of economics and public administration.

The organizational process model depicts a decentralized government in which the key actors are bureaucratic organizations rather than the president or a group of policymakers. Policymaking tends to be feudal, with most bureaucratic organizations relatively autonomous from the political leadership and each other. In this process, U.S. foreign policy consists of the sum of the various foreign policies produced by the organizations comprising the foreign policy bureaucracy. In other words, the bureaucracy has become so large and complex that it is an independent driving force behind policy, and the president, more often than not, is only the symbolic leader.

A policymaking process dominated by the bureaucracy may not only prevent foreign policy coherence, but produce contradictory policies as well. This helps to explain why the State Department can be negotiating peace between warring factions while the CIA is supporting one side or the other at the very same time. It may also help to explain why the CIA's covert national security operations often involve individuals and groups within the criminal underworld, including those involved in the drug trade, even though the government has been fighting a long-standing war on drugs. These contradictions are one of the by-products of the president's limited ability to control the immense bureaucracy and promote a rational policymaking process throughout the executive branch.

Each bureaucracy develops its own organizational missions, occupational roles, and standard operating procedures. As discussed in Chapter 5 and subsequent chapters, each bureaucracy is based on hierarchy, specialization, and routinization. These characteristics are reflected in the bureaucratic structures and subcultures that develop over time. Hence, organizational behavior tends to be "incremental" in nature, where members of organizations act very similarly from one day to the next. Behavior also reflects established bureaucratic repertoires and routines, with standard operating procedures for addressing a set of issue. In other words, much of contemporary policymaking and U.S. foreign policy reflects bureaucratic momentum that has accumulated over the years.

An organizational process model is most helpful in understanding policy formulation for agenda issues that are not important enough to gain presidential attention. Much of the day-to-day policy set by the executive branch involves minor issues that are the domain of bureaucratic organizations. These issues do not move up the bureaucratic hierarchy or, if they do, are routinely rubber-stamped by superiors. Such issues turn bureaucrats into policymakers by allowing them to make and implement policies usually in accordance with their organization's norms and routines.

For those issues that do gain the attention of high-level officials, policymakers are still dependent on the bureaucracy for information, policy alternatives, and policy implementation. These organizational programs and routines often constrain what policymakers can do in the future and determine how their decisions actually will be carried out. For example, intelligence assessments and military requirements heavily influenced President George H.W. Bush's decisions concerning troop levels and strategy that led to war following Iraq's invasion of Kuwait in the following ways. Once the president had decided to send troops to Saudi Arabia, the military pushed for a large force of at least 100,000 troops to ensure they could repel an Iraqi attack should one occur. Yet, the lack of contingency plans for such an emergency forced the military to rely on its all-purpose general deployment plans and resulted in a swelling of the forces sent to the Persian Gulf to over 200,000. Deployment of such a large force required mobilizing the reserves and the National Guard while the military routine of a six-month rotation threatened the maintenance of such a large force abroad, and its abandonment threatened troop morale.

All these bureaucratic imperatives contributed to a presidential decision to abandon economic sanctions, which would have required months to cripple Iraq, in favor of a strategy of brinksmanship based on the threat of war. In fact, military bureaucratic imperatives were such that the presidential decisions to commence war with a large-scale bombing campaign in mid-January followed by a ground campaign late in February were set in motion as early as late October. Ironically, at the time, General "Stormin" Norman Schwarzkopf initially presented a traditional military plan for a direct frontal assault on the Iraqi forces in Kuwait (which was likely to produce thousands of American and allied casualties). He had to be prodded by his superiors to come up with the "left hook" offensive strategy that became quite famous for overwhelming the Iraqi military (Gordon and Trainor 1995; Massing 1991; Woodward 1991).

It is the implementation stage of policymaking that the organizational process model describes most powerfully. For example, although President Reagan made the decision to invade Grenada in 1983, the military bureaucracy was responsible for the bungled operation that eventually succeeded in occupying the island. Likewise, that same military bureaucracy was responsible for the tremendous success of Operation Desert Storm once President Bush officially decided to go to war with Iraq in January 1991.

The bureaucracy, especially the CIA, also appears to have played a crucial role in setting the policy agenda and options for what would become President George W. Bush's war on terrorism in response to the September 11 attacks. According to Balz and Woodward (2002:A1), on the morning of September 13, two days after the attack, President Bush met with his so-called war cabinet in the White House Situation Room. CIA Director George J. Tenet, a holdover from the Clinton administration, "and several other agency officials described in more detail the ideas Tenet had outlined the previous day. This was the second presentation in what became an increasingly detailed set of CIA proposals for expanding its war on terrorism." The CIA plan "called for bringing together expanded intelligence-gathering resources, covert action, sophisticated technology, agency paramilitary teams and opposition forces in

Afghanistan. They would then be combined with U.S. military power and Special Forces into an elaborate and lethal package designed to destroy the shadowy terrorist networks."

As DCI, George J. Tenet had overseen the antiterrorist plans that were developed in response to President Clinton's request after the 1998 bombings of the American embassies in Kenya and Tanzania. These were the plans that Tenet and the CIA put forth before President Bush and his administration. As Balz and Woodward (2002:A1) report, "It was a memorable performance, and it had a huge effect on the president, according to his advisors. For two days Bush had expressed in the most direct way possible his determination to track down and destroy the terrorists responsible for the attacks of Sept. 11. Now, for the first time, he was being told without reservation that there was a way to do this, that he did not have to wait indefinitely, that the agency had a plan. . . . It was a detailed master plan for covert war in Afghanistan and a topsecret 'Worldwide Attack Matrix.'"

Similar bureaucratic factors and momentum—especially the growing troop buildup, presence, and logistical support in the Middle East—made it difficult to *not* invade Iraq in 2003. Such organizational process dynamics probably reinforced the younger Bush's decision and strong inclination to invade Iraq and overthrow Saddam Hussein, even though the inspectors on the ground did not find WMD (weapons of mass destruction) and there were strong concerns by members of the international community, especially France and Russia (who are permanent members of the U.N. Security Council).

As powerful as bureaucracies are, they do not always dominate the implementation process nor are they always devoid of presidential control. In the case of the war in Iraq, the organizational process model did not reflect the final invasion plan. Although conducted by the military, it was not dominated by the military. The actual war plan that the military had "on the shelf" was revised again and again by the civilian leadership, especially within the Office of the Secretary of Defense under Donald Rumsfeld apparently with the president's strong support. The civilian leadership also ignored the many studies and recommendations that were made by various parts of the bureaucracy regarding the difficulty of **Iraq's postwar–reconstruction phase** if the president chose to go to war with Iraq. Furthermore, it also demonstrates that bureaucratic organizations may be better prepared to deal with certain contingencies than a centralized leadership might think (see **A Closer Look**).

SUMMARY   Four ways of making sense of the policymaking process have been presented. *Each model reaches a different conclusion about the decisionmaking structure and process:*

1. The rational actor model sees an open, rational process under the centralized control of the president.

2. Groupthink depicts a centralized structure in which the process is irrational.

3. Governmental politics portrays a pluralistic structure in which the process consists of bargaining and compromise.

4. The organizational process model emphasizes an extremely decentralized structure in which the process is dominated by the norms and routines of organizations.

All four models also highlight different concepts to explain the policymaking process in U.S. foreign policy: the rational actor model emphasizes the beliefs and calculations of the president (and his closest advisors); groupthink focuses on the beliefs and personalities of the leaders within the group and the norms that prevail for the group; governmental politics emphasizes the varying beliefs, personalities, roles, and positions of power that policymakers occupy; and

Bureaucratic Planning for Postwar Reconstruction in Iraq

When President Bush decided to increase the military force presence and troop build-up in the Middle East in order to coerce Saddam Hussein and possibly invade Iraq beginning in the fall of 2002, this triggered considerable bureaucratic involvement. Much of the bureaucracy, in fact, became heavily engaged in postwar reconstruction plans—in particular, the State Department, the Army, the CIA, and the Agency for International Development. See **Table 9.2** for the numerous governmental (and nongovernmental) bureaucratic agencies that became involved and the nature of their involvement before the invasion.

In an exhaustive review entitled "Blind into Baghdad," James Fallows (2004:54) found that "Almost everything good and bad, that has happened in Iraq since the fall of Saddam Hussein's regime was the subject of extensive pre-war discussion and analysis. This is particularly true of what proved to be the harshest realities for the United States since the fall of Baghdad: that occupying the country is much more difficult than conquering it."

The bureaucratic studies and recommendations that were produced were relatively clairvoyant about the difficulty of postwar reconstruction, the importance of establishing immediate security and stability, and the need for a large presence on the ground, including military and civilian components of the government, private voluntary organizations, and international organizations with experience in postwar stability and reconstruction efforts such as in Bosnia and Kosovo. As Fallows (2004:54) summarized, U.S. bureaucratic "predictions about postwar Iraq's problems have proved as accurate as the assessments of pre-war Iraq's strategic threat have proved flawed."

In this case, the DOD and the civilian leadership in the Office of Secretary of Defense (OSD) under Donald Rumsfeld were able to gain control of what the military calls "Phase IV" of the war, ignoring the reports and input of other agencies. Instead Secretary Rumsfeld, Deputy Secretary of Defense Paul Wolfowitz, and Undersecretary of Defense Douglas Feith within OSD, with the strong support of the Office of the Vice President under Dick Cheney and his Chief of Staff Scooter Libby, relied on extremely optimistic assumptions about the postwar environment on the ground in Iraq once the American liberators had arrived and overthrown Saddam Hussein.

The Iraq invasion plan and the subsequent lack of plans or preparedness for postwar reconstruction raise some serious questions about presidential management of the bureaucracy. Why did President Bush not rely on the NSC interagency process for coordinating postwar reconstruction as would normally have been the case? Why did National Security Advisor Rice allow this crucial stage to be delegated outside the White House and to DOD? Why was one part of the bureaucracy—the Office of Secretary of Defense—given so much power and control? Why were other parts of the foreign policy bureaucracy virtually excluded or ignored in the final analysis? As former national security advisors Brent Scowcroft and Samuel R. Berger (2005:51) argue, "Given the stakes, the complexity and the interagency nature of policy decisions associated with stabilization and reconstruction, the National Security Council should have responsibility for overarching policy in this area" (see also Gordon 2004).

James Fallows (2004:73) drew a harsh picture: "None of the government working groups that had seriously looked into the question had simply 'imagined' that occupying Iraq would be more difficult than defeating it. They had presented years' worth of experience suggesting that this would be the central reality of the undertaking." Yet they were ignored and dismissed. Therefore,

James Fallows (2004:73) concluded, "what David Halberstam said of Robert McNamara in *The Best and the Brightest* [for the Vietnam War] is true of those at OSD as well: they were brilliant, and they were fools."

What does the Iraq postwar planning fiasco reveal about the nature of bureaucratic politics and the importance of presidential management?

Table 9.2   Bureaucratic Involvement in Iraq Post-Conflict Reconstruction

1. STATE DEPARTMENT'S "FUTURE OF IRAQ PROJECT"

– Began October 2001

– Seventeen working groups

– Final Report consisted of thirteen volumes, plus a one-volume summary

2. CIA WAR-GAMING EXERCISES

– Began May 2002

– Highlighted risk of civil disorder

3. AGENCY FOR INTERNATIONAL DEVELOPMENT'S (AID) "IRAQ WORKING GROUP"

– Began September 2002

– Heavily involved the NGO and PVO community

4. ARMY WAR COLLEGE, STRATEGIC STUDIES INSTITUTE "POSTWAR PLANNING EXERCISES"

– Began October 2002

– December report titled "Reconstructing Iraq: Insights, Challenges, and Missions for Military Forces in a Post-Conflict Scenario"

5. ARMY AND PENTAGON'S JOINT STAFF "ORIGINAL INVASION PLAN"

– Projected need for very high troop levels, especially for "after" the war

6. SENATE FOREIGN RELATIONS COMMITTEE HEARINGS

– On July 31, 2002

– Emphasized the importance and difficulty of postwar security

7. COUNCIL ON FOREIGN RELATIONS

– Created working group on "Guiding Principles for U.S. Post-Cold War Conflict in Iraq"

– Began on December 2002; report in January 2003

8. DOD'S STUDY BY SAM GARDINER, RETIRED AIR FORCE COLONEL, "NET ASSESSMENT FOR IRAQ"

– January 19, 2003 report

Timeline:

January 29, 2003 – Jay M. Garner, retired three-star Army general appointed to head all postwar efforts in Iraq

– Office in Pentagon

– Started from scratch

March 19, 2003 – IRAQ WAR BEGINS

May 1, 2003 – President Bush declared combat operations were over the organizational process model emphasizes organizational missions, bureaucratic structures and subcultures, roles, and standard operating procedures (review Table 10.1).

The four models have different implications for the possibilities of change in U.S. foreign policy, for **government learning**, and democratic accountability (Etheridge 1985; Levy 1994). The rational actor model suggests that presidents and other government officials are receptive to new information and readily adapt to changes in the environment in order to maximize the opportunity to promote appropriate and successful policies. In other words, such rationality provides optimism about the ability of governments to "learn" and change their foreign policy. It also allows the president to be accountable for the decisions made. This explains why the rational actor model is considered the ideal type (George 1980; George and Stern 2001, Steiner 1983).

The implications of groupthink, governmental politics, and organizational process, in contrast, are much more pessimistic about the government's ability to learn and change its foreign policy. These three models suggest that there are considerable psychological, social, political, and bureaucratic obstacles to governmental learning and that continuity and incrementalism are likely to prevail in U.S. foreign policy over time until crises and failure occur (Krasner 1972; Rosati 1981; Snyder 1978). Moreover, where groupthink allows for democratic accountability given the centralization of power at the top, governmental politics in combination with the insights of the organization process model has significant different implications for policymaking and democratic accountability (see **The Liberty–Security Dilemma**: The Buck Stops Where?).

THE LIBERTY–SECURITY DILEMMA

The Buck Stops Where?

In the post–World War II years, a sprawling foreign policy bureaucracy developed to address the cold war policy context and help devise and carry out policies for the security and prosperity of the United States. Created in part to ensure the security of the United States in a dangerous world, this bureaucratic complex has had a powerful impact on the nature of foreign policymaking, and on the ways that observers have tried to explain it. One implication touches deeply on the democratic values of the United States and the tension between liberty, democratic accountability, and security. As Stephen Krasner (1972:159–160) wrote:

> Who and what shapes foreign policy? In recent years, analyses have increasingly emphasized not rational calculations of the national interest or the

political goals of national leaders, but rather bureaucratic procedures and bureaucratic politics. Starting with Richard Neustadt's *Presidential Power*, a judicious study of leadership published in 1960, this approach has come to portray the American President as trapped by a permanent government more enemy than ally. Bureaucratic theorists imply that it is exceedingly difficult if not impossible for political leaders to control the organizational web which surrounds them. Important decisions result from numerous smaller actions taken by individuals at different levels in the bureaucracy who have partially incompatible national, bureaucratic, political and personal objectives. They are not necessarily a reflection of the aims and values of high officials. . . .

My argument here is that this vision is misleading, dangerous and compelling: misleading because it obscures the power of the President; dangerous because it undermines the assumptions of democratic politics by relieving high officials of responsibility; and compelling because it offers leaders an excuse for their failures and scholars an opportunity for innumerable reinterpretations and publications.

The contention that the Chief Executive is trammeled by the permanent government has disturbing implications for any effort to impute responsibility to public officials. A democratic political philosophy assumes that responsibility for the acts of government can be attributed to elected officials. The charges of these men are embodied in legal statutes. The electorate punishes an erring official by rejecting him at the polls.

Punishment is senseless unless high officials are responsible for the acts of government. Elections have some impact only if government, that most complex of modern organizations, can be controlled. If the bureaucratic machine escapes manipulation and direction even by the highest officials, then punishment is illogical. Elections are a farce not because the people suffer from false consciousness, but because public officials are impotent, enmeshed in a bureaucracy so large that the actions of government are not responsive to their will. What sense to vote a man out of office when his successor, regardless of his values, will be trapped in the same web of only incrementally mutable standard operating procedures?

How does the vast national security and foreign policy bureaucracy affect the tension between liberty and security and complicate democratic accountability in the foreign policy arena?

Clearly, the four models have different implications for the possibilities of change in U.S. foreign policy, for government learning, and for democratic accountability. They also highlight the possibility that different models or processes are likely to occur in different contexts. In the next section, we discuss two major policymaking patterns that are most likely to occur in the actual practice of U.S. foreign policy.

TWO GENERAL POLICYMAKING LEVELS

From the late 1970s to the 1990s, the groupthink, governmental politics, and organizational process models gained popularity relative to the rational actor model as alternative and superior ways of understanding the policymaking process. Yet these three models were also criticized on a number of grounds. Analysts and scholars argued that it was not clear when these models actually explained policymaking. Discussions of the models were often too rigid, for they specified a particular policymaking structure and process, thereby precluding the variety and complexity of political possibilities. The models also were often treated in isolation from one another when, in fact, they overlapped and more than one model was often involved for any particular policymaking process. In other words, it was argued that these models also oversimplified the political messiness and complexity of the policymaking process in U.S. foreign policy.

This point has probably best been made in a volume entitled *Beyond Groupthink: Political Group Dynamics and Foreign Policymaking,* edited by Paul 't Hart, Eric K. Stern, and Bengt Sundelius (1997:5), who contend that most foreign policy decisions are shaped by small groups and are therefore not well explained by rational actor, organizational, or bureaucratic politics models. However, they also argue that group decisionmaking is more varied and complex than just groupthink. As they state:

> It seems eminently reasonable, therefore, to treat groupthink as a contingent phenomenon, rather than as a general property of foreign policy decisionmaking in high-level groups . . . A cursory look at the standard textbooks on foreign policymaking will reveal that if they deal with small group decisionmaking at all, the presentation is likely to be dominated by the groupthink phenomenon, inadvertently equating "group decisionmaking" with "groupthink." This is a gross simplification, betraying the enormous variety of groups and group processes that play a part in foreign policymaking which, ironically had been recognized by early analysts not infatuated with the powerful groupthink heuristic ('t Hart, Stern, and Sundelius 1997:11–12).

Similarly, Thomas Preston and Paul 't Hart (1999; also Preston 2001) argue that bureaucratic politics should also be seen as a variable rather than a constant. These authors contend that "bureaucratic politics manifests itself more and differently in some issues [and] policy domains . . . than in others," and that the key factor accounting for this variance is "the role played by political leaders in shaping the structures and processes involved in governmental decisionmaking." In short, presidential style and attention is a critical determinant of the nature of policymaking.

One particularly fascinating model is referred to as **newgroup syndrome.** Newgroup syndrome refers to that fact that "newly formed groups or groups subjected to drastic changes in membership or in mode of operation may be particularly susceptible to pathologies of group deliberation" (Stern 1997:54). As a new president with his newly appointed foreign policy advisors, John F. Kennedy may have been particularly guilty of this syndrome in approving the poorly planned and poorly executed Bay of Pigs fiasco. It is possible that a type of newgroup system may have played a role in the Bush administration's decisionmaking and groupthink-like process after President George W. Bush appeared to have been radically transformed into a hands-on, war president in response to September 11. The newgroup model suggests that other decisionmaking dynamics may also occur. Ultimately, there needs to be a recognition of a certain amount of decisionmaking variety—"a multilevel approach" that highlights the interplay between individual, group, and institutional factors and takes into consideration complexity and context.

In sum, the four models provide valuable insights concerning some of the key patterns that prevail in policymaking, but as the critics suggest, the models tend to oversimplify the politics and complexity of the policymaking process. Although there are situations in which one of the four models may be particularly applicable, in order to maximize the strengths of the four models and incorporate the criticisms discussed here, it is probably useful to think in terms of *two general types or patterns for understanding policymaking within the executive branch:* (1) presidential politics and (2) bureaucratic politics.

Presidential Politics

Presidential politics operates when the president becomes interested and active in an issue, through direct personal involvement or indirectly when his staff and advisors act in his name. As discussed in Chapter 4, presidents rely both on informal channels of communication with close advisors and on a more formal process, usually under the supervision of the NSC (or NEC) advisor and staff. When an issue is of sufficient importance to gain the attention and interest of the president (or his surrogates), the policymaking process is also likely to involve other high-level policymakers from executive branch bureaucratic organizations and agencies. Such was the case, for example, during the Cuban missile crisis, in decisions leading to the escalation of the war in Vietnam, during the Iran hostage crisis, the Persian Gulf crisis of 1990–1991, and the post–September 11, 2001, terrorist attacks. For example, President Obama clearly embraced a "top-down" approach in responding to so many major issues, such as addressing the severe economic recession and developing the New START nuclear arms treaty with Russia in 2009–2010 among others.

The notion of presidential politics makes it clear that the president's involvement is crucial. Presidential politics also indicates that the policymaking process is very political without precluding any possibilities about the particular dynamics of the process. A relatively open policymaking process may occur in which there is a broad search for information and policy views and alternatives are aired as suggested by the rational actor model. Alternatively, presidential politics may result in a relatively closed process more akin to groupthink. Other patterns may operate, as well, creating situations in which participants may be dissatisfied with presidential decisions and attempt to get them reversed or modified. In all cases, policymaking and politics are inseparable since prominent individuals are likely to be involved, issues in question affect the future of U.S. foreign policy, and the stakes tend to be high. In the final analysis, how the politics of the policymaking process actually proceeds depends on the beliefs, personalities, and roles of the participants and the nature of their interaction.

Bureaucratic Politics

Bureaucratic politics prevail when the president and his closest advisors remain relatively uninvolved or are unable to dominate the policymaking process. Under these circumstances, other policymakers and bureaucratic organizations become the key determinants of policymaking and the interagency process. This perspective is powerfully described by Charles Maechling, Jr. (1976:18):

> The principal actors represent giant departments and agencies, each with its own constellation of vested interests and statutory responsibilities. . . . Behind the confident facade that each actor presents to his colleagues and to the outside world lurks a morbid compulsion to protect himself from the unexpected, to make the weight of one's agency count and to appear effective in the eyes of superiors.

American foreign policy concerning Japan, for example, is often dominated by competing bureaucratic interests. According to Robert Pear (1989:1) "the State Department, the Pentagon, and the NSC emphasize Japan's value as a geopolitical and strategic asset and are seen by officials in other agencies as overly protective of Japan." The Department of Commerce and the Office of the United States Trade Representative usually "worry about the health of the American economy and favor a tougher attitude." The Department of the Treasury, the Office of Management and Budget, and the Council of Economic Advisors usually "adhere to free market principles and have generally opposed any government intervention to help American businesses compete with the Japanese." Not surprisingly, the U.S. government struggles to pursue a coherent policy toward Japan because of the series of turf wars among federal agencies that limit communication and coordination, even with the existence of the NEC.

According to Howard Wiarda, a similar phenomenon occurs in U.S. foreign policy toward Mexico, where dozens of agencies play a role in some aspect of policy. As Wiarda (2000:176) puts it, "not only is there often rivalry and bureaucratic politics between cabinet departments, but there are other rivalries within departments—for instance, between the Army and Navy within Defense, between Customs and INS within Treasury, between FBI and DEA within Justice. To say these agencies are not always on the same wavelength would be an understatement." Similar problems plagued U.S. policy toward China over the past two decades or so as well, as a result of what seem to be competing U.S. national security interests with interests about economic relations and human rights. These illustrations demonstrate the difficulty of making foreign policy when national security and foreign economic (and other) interests intersect.

Such bureaucratic politics may reflect the bargaining, coalition building, and compromise described by the governmental politics model. Or officials may pursue independent policies based on the organizational missions, structures and subcultures, routines, and standard operating procedures as suggested by the organizational process model (Allison and Halperin 1972). Other possibilities, however, cannot be ruled out. For example, bureaucratic and personal infighting could be so intense that compromise among the participants is not possible—instead, political winners and losers result. Regardless of the particular policymaking process, bureaucratic politics always involve a political process reflecting the interactions between the officials, organizations, and the political environment prevailing at the time. The beliefs, personalities, and roles of the individuals involved, often reflecting the bureaucratic structures and subcultures of their respective organizations, determine the nature of bureaucratic policymaking.

Since the president and his closest advisors are involved for only selective issues, bureaucratic politics tends to prevail for most issues in U.S. foreign policy. A minor issue is likely to attract the attention of only very few officials and agencies. Minor issues do not cross over many organization jurisdictions, and the stakes are not high enough to concern many officials (Rosati 1981). More important issues will attract the attention of many more officials and bureaucratic organizations. Ultimately, as Charles Maechling, Jr. (1976:3) states, "For every publicized decision [the president] makes, this second echelon of decision makers makes a hundred equally important ones. And it is this steady stream of less conspicuous decisions, building on and interlocking with their predecessors, that fixes the direction and contours of foreign policy, just as effectively as the few spectacular decisions that are the result of conscious deliberation at the top."

The implementation stage of the policy process is usually dominated by bureaucracy for it usually reflects the bureaucratic structures and subcultures of the organizations involved, thus resembling the organizational process model. Presidential politics may intrude occasionally, as with President Kennedy's efforts to influence policy implementation during the Cuban missile crisis. In some instances, presidential politics may be consequential, as was the case with Kissinger's use of back channels to the People's Republic of China and the Soviet Union under President Nixon. And there is the case of Secretary of Defense Rumsfeld (the civilian leader representing the president) successfully cutting and trimming the military's and CENTCOM's invasion plans for Iraq during 2002 and early

2003. However, most presidential decisions that require implementation are dependent on the bureaucracy.

As Morton Halperin puts it in *Bureaucratic Politics and Foreign Policy* (1974:290), "At one extreme, if an action is a simple one capable of being carried out by a single individual in Washington without detailed technical expertise or training, presidential influence is likely to be overwhelming. To the degree that an action is a complicated one, requiring the cooperation of large numbers of people, many of them stationed outside of Washington, presidential influence on implementation fades." Therefore, the most effective way a president can control the policy implementation stage is to decide against any action or a policy initiative, thereby circumventing the need for bureaucratic implementation altogether.

THE ROLE OF PERSONALITY, BELIEFS, AND CRISES

Presidential politics are heavily a function of the personality and beliefs of the president and his closest advisors, for most of the other policymakers involved take their cues from him and, ultimately, the president makes the decision. Bureaucratic politics are also heavily influenced by the personalities and beliefs of the individuals (and agencies) involved. Both presidential and bureaucratic politics are heavily impacted by the situation or circumstance (such as a crisis).

Therefore, *to understand the four decisionmaking models and politics at both the presidential and bureaucratic levels, we need to understand the role that beliefs, personality, and crises play in policymaking.* First, we will discuss the general patterns and impact of individual cognition and images for the policymaking process. This will be followed by a discussion of the impact of personality on policymaking. We will end with the important role crises have on the policymaking process.

The World of Cognition and Images

It is relatively well known, especially within the study of psychology, that people construct their own reality to a considerable extent. This helps to explain why people often disagree and see different realities. Walter Lippmann (1922:50), one of America's most prominent and insightful journalists, stated in his classic *Public Opinion*: "We do not first see, and then define, we define first and then see." In other words, individuals tend to simplify reality and often are relatively closed minded toward new information. Such is the nature of human **cognition and perception**; that is, how people perceive and process the world around them.

According to John Steinbruner (1974:12–13,112), "The mind of man, for all its marvels, is a limited instrument." Given the complexity of the world and the limitations of the mind, the mind "constantly struggles to impose clear, coherent meaning on events." In other words, "Cognitive theory argues that the mind craves certainty and will work to establish it even when it is unwarranted by objective conditions" (Snyder 1978:553). Therefore, Alexander George (1980:57) concludes:

> Every individual acquires during the course of development a set of beliefs and personal constructs about the physical and social environment. These beliefs provide him with a relatively coherent way of organizing and making sense of what would otherwise be a confusing and overwhelming array of signals and cues picked up from the environment from his senses. . . . These beliefs and constructs necessarily simplify and structure the external world.

Human beings and human thought are not simply random and idiosyncratic. Humans are creatures of habit, and patterns exist in their images and thought processes.

Basically, the mind imposes clarity and tries to make sense of reality through reliance on a *few common cognitive principles* (see Rosati 2000; 2010). These include (1) the principle of cognitive structures of belief (that the human mind tends to consist of a vast assortment of beliefs that are organized and internally structured, especially around more central beliefs); (2) the principle of selective memory (that people tend to remember certain things better than others, especially the general picture or concept, and be loose with the details); (3) the principle of selective attention and perception (that, although the mind can perceive stable, significant features of the environment, it tends to be selective and incomplete in its attention); (4) the principle of causal inference (that people tend to make inferences about what happened and why based on their beliefs); and (5) the principle of cognitive stability (that the mind tends to keep internal belief relationships stable once formed, especially in the core structure of beliefs).

The two dominant theoretical approaches in cognitive psychology—cognitive consistency theory and schema theory—agree that central beliefs are most consequential but differ regarding the level of coherence and interconnectedness between beliefs. During the 1950s and 1960s it was popular to view the individual as a "consistency seeker"—motivated to maintain consistency and reduce discrepancies among beliefs. The assumption behind **cognitive consistency** is that "individuals do not merely subscribe to a random collection of beliefs" but make sense of the world by acquiring and maintaining "coherent systems of beliefs which are internally consistent" (Bem 1970:13). Therefore, individuals attempt to avoid the acquisition of information that is inconsistent or incompatible with their belief systems, especially their central beliefs.

A second generation of scholarship emerged in the 1970s describing a more complex cognitive process based on developments in social cognition and schema theory, viewing the individual as a "cognitive miser"—that is, the minds of individuals are limited in their capacity to process information, so they tend to rely on schemas, shortcuts, or simplifications. **Schemas** are mental constructs that represent different clumps of knowledge (or comprehension) about various facets of the environment. They necessarily simplify and structure the external environment, enabling individuals to absorb new information and intelligibly make sense of the world around them. The more complex and uncertain the environment, the more likely individuals will rely on schemas and cognitive heuristics—shortcuts in information processing—to make sense of the world and the situation at hand.

How do images and cognition matter? How do they impact world politics? Very simply, the mind relies on *common patterns of perception and misperception,* such as a tendency to:

1. categorize and stereotype,

2. simplify causal inferences, and

3. use historical analogies.

As Robert Jervis (1976) stated in *Perception and Misperception in International Politics,* "perceptions of the world and of other actors diverge from reality in patterns that we can detect and for reasons that we can understand."

The human mind perceives the world and processes information by compartmentalizing and sorting things into categories. This necessarily simplifies and often leads to a certain amount of stereotyping. One common tendency in world politics, in this respect, is for the mind to form beliefs and schemas of the "other." The **enemy image**—according to which "we are good" and "they are bad"—may be the most simpleminded image of all. Such is the image of the Soviet Union and communism that most Americans acquired during the cold war. Once formed, such an image of the enemy tends to be very rigid and resistant to change. For example, in a classic work Ole Holsti (1967) found that Secretary of State John Foster Dulles during the 1950s held an enemy image of the Soviet Union and resisted new information inconsistent with this image by engaging in a variety of psychological processes: discrediting (the information), searching (for other consistent information), reinterpreting (the information), differentiating (between different aspects of the information), engaging in wishful thinking, and refusing to think about it.

In fact, it is not uncommon for conflict situations to result in **mirror images**: Each party holds an image that is diametrically opposite the other. In other words, each party has a positive and benevolent self-image, while holding a negative and malevolent image of the enemy. As Ralph White found in *Nobody Wanted War* (1968), an analysis of the two world wars and the Vietnam War revealed that each party tends to hold a "diabolical enemy-image" and a "virile and moral self-image that becomes the source of mutual selective attention, absence of empathy (for the other), and insecurity." Such black-and-white thinking contributes to misperception, escalation, intervention, and war—or a cold war in the case of the United States and the Soviet Union.

Given the mind's need for certainty and clarity and the tendency to categorize and stereotype, there will also be a corresponding tendency to simplify inferences about causality. As Jervis (1976) put it, "People want to be able to explain as much as possible of what goes on around them. To admit that a phenomenon cannot be explained, or at least cannot be explained without adding numerous and complex exceptions to our beliefs, is both psychologically uncomfortable and intellectually unsatisfying."

Four causal inferences likely to be simplified are particularly relevant to foreign policy: (1) a tendency to overestimate or underestimate (internal) dispositional or (external) situational causes of behavior; (2) a tendency to overestimate or underestimate one's importance; (3) a tendency to overestimate the degree to which the behavior of others is planned and centralized; and (4) a tendency to overindulge in pessimistic and wishful thinking.

Such simplifying tendencies heavily reinforce people's perceptions, especially in the case of enemy images. For example, it was virtually inconceivable in the minds of most Americans that the United States could "lose" the war in Vietnam, yet they could not allow South Vietnam to fall to communism given the devastating international and domestic consequences that they feared would result. In fact, American (especially civilian) policymakers constantly fluctuated between optimistic and pessimistic assessments in the early 1960s, immediately preceding the fateful decisions to militarily intervene and Americanize the war.

The third perceptual tendency is to use **historical analogies** in making sense of the present. According to Jervis (1976:217), "Previous international events provide the statesman with a range of imaginable situations and allow him to detect patterns and causal links that can help him understand his world" since "we cannot make sense out of our environment without assuming that, in some sense, the future will resemble the past." But "a too narrow conception of the past and a failure to appreciate the impact of changed circumstances also result in 'the tyranny of the past' upon the imagination."

In his examination of analogies and the Vietnam War, Yuen Foong Khong (1992) concluded that the lessons President Johnson and his advisors drew from Munich, Dien Bien Phu, and most important, the Korean War had a powerful influence on the decisionmaking process The use of these historical analogies helped to reinforce the enemy image and predispose the United States toward military intervention. It also helps to explain how the **domino theory** became a powerful metaphor in the minds of Americans—that the lessons of the past made clear that anything short of a policy of global containment would result in one country after another falling like dominoes to communist expansion.

The enemy image of Soviet communism, and the cognitive dynamics behind it, was the basis of the consensus in the making of U.S. foreign policy during the cold war. It laid the foundation for the rise of the president and the national security state and American intervention (overt and covert) throughout the world. Such an enemy image revolving around Soviet communism would not survive the Vietnam War and the collapse of the Soviet Union. But the enemy image of communism was a powerful cognitive force in the making of U.S. foreign policy following World War II and continues to have a powerful legacy, even as the United States enters the twenty-first century.

As a result of September 11, 2001, such powerful enemy images appear to have heavily influenced President Bush, as he declared and conducted a global war on terrorism. According to the Bush administration, Osama bin Laden, terrorists in general, and Saddam Hussein and other "axis of evil" states supporting terrorism became the new enemy (replacing the Soviet Union and communism). According to Balz and Woodward (2002), "Bush fashioned a war of absolutes: good vs. evil, with us or against us. He brought a black-and-white mind-set" to the problem at hand (see also Kessler 2003; Thomas 2002b).

Such images were reinforced by his national security team. According to George Packer in *The Assassinations' Gate* (2005:64–65), "They entered government in the aftermath of the trauma in Vietnam, and they were forged as cold war hawks. They devoted their career to restoring American military power and its projection around the world." And "when September 11 forced the imagination to grapple with something radically new, the president's foreign policy advisors reached for what they had always known. The threat, as they saw it, lay in well-armed enemy states. The answer, as ever, was military power and the will to use it."

In sum, the cognitive approach and the cognitive patterns of perception and misperception identified above have a profound effect on decisionmaking as some of the examples illustrate. The conceptual baggage, the worldviews, and the cognitive dynamics of policymakers play a powerful role. This means that individuals and policymakers rarely formulate decisions through an open intellectual process where goals (and preferences) are clearly ordered, a strong search is made for relevant information, a variety of different alternatives are considered, and the option that maximizes benefits while minimizing costs is selected. Usually this is simply too demanding and too time-consuming a process for human beings and the human mind (e.g., Tetlock 2006). This increases the likelihood that, rather than a rational actor model, groupthink, governmental politics, organizational process, or other decisionmaking dynamics will prevail at the presidential and bureaucratic levels.

The Impact of Personality

In addition to the study of cognition and images, one must integrate the role of personality and motivation. Increasingly, an individual, including a policymaker, should be viewed as a **motivated tactician**, or "a fully engaged thinker who has multiple cognitive strategies available and chooses among them based on goals, motives, and needs. Sometimes the motivated tactician chooses wisely, in the interests of adaptability and accuracy, and sometimes the motivated tactician chooses defensively, in the interests of speed or self-esteem" (Fiske and Taylor 1999:13).

The role of **personality** and motivation was initially popularized by psychoanalytic theorists such as Sigmund Freud and Harold Lasswell and later culminated in *The Authoritarian Personality*, which argued that beliefs were dependent on ego-defensive needs. Developmental psychologists and other scholars such as Jean Piaget, Eric Erikson, and Abraham Maslow have emphasized that beliefs also fulfill individuals' more positive needs. The classic work highlighting the motivational foundation of political beliefs and behavior is *Woodrow Wilson and Colonel House: A Personality Study* by Alexander George and Juliette George (1956), which distinguished between the "power-seeker" and "power-holder." In Wilson's efforts to gain power in order to overcome his low self-esteem from his childhood days, he conformed to the dominant beliefs of individuals who could significantly influence his rise. However, once Wilson successfully gained a position of power, he would demonstrate incredible rigidity and closed-mindedness after he took a stand.

Ole Holsti (1967:13) also integrated the role of personality in examining John Foster Dulles' rigid enemy image of the Soviet Union, recognizing that "certain personality types can be more easily persuaded than others to change their attitudes." Individuals "also appear to differ in their tolerance for dissonance and tend to use different means to re-establish stable attitudes." As Vamik Volkan (1988) discusses, the need to have enemies and allies appears to be quite powerful among the human species.

The case of Lyndon Johnson, while not unique, demonstrates the impact of an individual's personality and beliefs on the foreign policymaking process and U.S. foreign policy. It demonstrates how prominent individuals are often driven and influenced by basic emotional needs—such as the need for love, power, and control, and the need to do good. According to Doris Kearns Goodwin, in *Lyndon Johnson and the American Dream* (1991), one must delve into Johnson's childhood and personal development in the context of the times to understand his decisions and actions as president.

Lyndon Baines Johnson (LBJ), the eldest of five children, was born in Stonewall, Blanco County, Texas, a small rural community, in 1908. His mother came from a relatively wealthy and well-respected family, but his father was a small-time farmer, heavily involved in local Democratic politics, crude and vulgar, and a hard drinker. According to Goodwin (1991:385), "the picture of Johnson's early life suggests a childhood torn between the irreconcilable demands of his mother—who hoped to find in his intellectual and cultural achievement a recompense of her dead father, unhappy marriage, and thwarted ambition— and those of his father—who considered intellect and culture unmanly pursuits." In this environment, Lyndon did not feel loved for who he was and seemed unable to please his parents. The only time he felt comfortable and secure was with his grandfather, who would reminisce and romanticize about the glory days of the intrepid cowboy and the reformism of the Populist Party. The situation worsened as Lyndon grew older, for when his grandfather died, he drew closer to his father, to the disapproval of his mother.

According to Goodwin's account, to overcome the terrible fear of rejection that resulted from his upbringing, Johnson developed a desperate and insatiable need to be loved. His tremendous drive to "acquire power and achieve good works" was an attempt to fulfill this need. His boundless energy was directed into politics, initially as a staff aide to a congressman, then as a participant in Franklin Roosevelt's New Deal, later as a member of the House of Representatives, then as a senator (becoming the youngest majority leader in history), and finally in the White House, first as vice president and then president. The consummate political animal, Johnson lived and breathed politics, and bargained and compromised to make deals and policy. Yet, given his family and his rural Texan roots during the first half of the twentieth century, he also strived to achieve "great works," to help people as he understood them. This is best embodied in his commitment to eliminate poverty through his Great Society programs, which Goodwin argues acted as a vehicle to attract the admiration and love of Americans, fellow Texans, and ultimately, his parents.

His personality helps to explain his "particular management style" as president. Johnson could not bear to be alone and always had to be in control. He was constantly in motion, on the phone, with the radio or television always on around him. The Johnson White House revolved around his need for people to love, support, and be loyal to him. He often challenged his aides to acts of manhood in order for them to display this loyalty. Once Johnson made up his mind, he wanted consensus and support behind his position. As Johnson himself could so graphically state, "I don't want loyalty. I want *loyalty*. I want him to kiss my ass in Macy's window at high noon and tell me it smells like roses. I want his pecker in my pocket" (Halberstam 1973:434).

Johnson was also overly defensive and sensitive to criticism. Those who were skeptical or didn't go along often received the famous "Johnson treatment"—the use of friendship, intimacy, bargaining, horse-trading, gifts, and anything else it might take to get them on board. Continued criticism or disagreement represented disloyalty and those involved would eventually be completely frozen out of the power loop and Johnson's life. He was so sensitive to what was said about him, for example, "that it was not unusual for him to watch the evening news on all three networks at the same time, all the while paying attention to how they reported 'his' presidency" (Kearns 1991:268).

Although Johnson was primarily interested in and comfortable dealing with domestic issues and politics, "in dealing with foreign policy . . . he was insecure, fearful, his touch unsure. . . . As a result, his greatest anxiety—unlike his attitude toward domestic affairs—was to avoid making a serious error rather than to achieve great things" (Goodwin 1991:268). Johnson tended to be heavily dependent on his advisors for information and understanding about world politics. The experience of World War II and Korea—the need to avoid appeasement at all costs—made a far-reaching and decisive impression on Johnson, as it did for many of the cold war leadership. According to Goodwin (1991:100–101), Johnson believed that "the way to prevent conflict was to stop aggressors at the start—the lesson of Munich. In every war, Johnson believed, the enemy is an alien force that 'invades' the allies' house. . . . America alone, our attitudes and behavior, were the key to war and peace. Nor was this mode of thought unique to Lyndon Johnson. On the contrary, it was deeply rooted in the American experience." These beliefs were the foundation for the global policy of containment that, in failing to discriminate between different situations at different times, led Johnson to Americanize the war in Vietnam.

Although Johnson delegated much authority in foreign policy, he was a domineering leader on those issues in which he was interested. Whereas in domestic affairs Johnson was sophisticated and pragmatic, he operated as much more the "idealist and ideologue" in foreign affairs and for Vietnam. With regard to the deteriorating situation in Vietnam, once the decision to escalate U.S. involvement was made early in his administration, the decision process was then closed. Future decisions never involved a serious consideration of de-escalation or withdrawal—the choices were always between more or less and different types of escalation as a means of finding light at the end of the tunnel. As David Halberstam (1973:456) concluded, "the Presidency is an awesome office, even with a mild inhabitant. It tends by its nature to inhibit dissent and opposition, and with a man like Johnson it was simply too much, too powerful an office occupied by too forceful a man."

The advisors Johnson came to rely on, Walt Rostow and Dean Rusk, shared his anticommunist philosophy and belief in the "utility of force." When one of his advisors, Robert

McNamara, came to reconsider and question the policies in Vietnam, he was shunned and eventually forced to resign. As Goodwin (1991:418) relates, "The President's will, once expressed, was not challenged. . . . Advisors began to anticipate his reactions before they said or did anything. . . . The more Johnson's energies turned to his critics, the more obsessed he became with the need to discredit his opponents, the less anyone tried to stop him." Hence, as the consensus behind Vietnam within his administration and the country began to break, a type of "siege mentality" developed, and the president began to insulate himself, finding comfort in his small group of loyal advisors. Only when many of his advisors and much of the country turned against the American war in Vietnam was Johnson able to realize the tragedy he faced. The Tet offensive and the growing challenges by Eugene McCarthy and Johnson's archrival, Robert Kennedy, in the presidential primaries were clear indicators that Johnson had lost control of his presidency and the country. Although he had risen to the top, the love and admiration he so needed to receive from the American people had been denied him, and he withdrew from public life.

Many additional illustrations can be provided concerning the powerful impact of an individual's personality on decisionmaking. For example, the events of September 11, 2001, had a profound effect on George W. Bush personally and gave him a new national security focus preoccupied with the war on terrorism. According to Woodward (2002), "Reflecting on his own personality, [Bush] described himself at various points as 'fiery,' 'impatient,' 'a gut player' who liked to 'provoke' people around him and someone who likes to talk—perhaps too much—in meetings. He admitted that first lady Laura Bush had told him to tone down the 'tough guy' rhetoric on terrorism."

According to Evan Thomas and Richard Wolfe (2005:33,34,37), "Bush may be the most isolated president in modern history, at least since the late-stage Richard Nixon. It's not that he is a socially awkward loner or a paranoid. He can charm and joke like the frat president he was. Still, beneath a hail-fellow manner, Bush has a defensive edge, a don't-tread-on-me prickliness." In fact, "in the Bush White House, disagreement is often equated with disloyalty. . . . In subtle ways, Bush does not encourage truth-telling or at least a full exploration of all that could go wrong. . . . Bush generally prefers short conversations—long on conclusion, short on reasoning." Clearly, given President Bush's personality, he became much more active and domineering, which contributed to the nature of the national security process over questions of how to respond to September 11 and about going to war with Afghanistan and Iraq (see also Badie 2010).

The forty-fourth president of the United States, Barack Obama, presents interesting contrasts to some of the style and personality characteristics of Johnson and George W. Bush. For one, Obama is more comfortable with argument, disagreement, and complex information than many of his predecessors. Obama's style and personality appear to emphasize collaboration and deliberation, and he enjoys a self-confidence (Drew 2009) that enables him to pay attention to what other people think while being at ease in an environment in which others have a voice. An interesting indicator of this style was his avid embrace of *A Team of Rivals* by Doris Kearns Goodwin (2006), a book about Abraham Lincoln's strong-minded and independent advisors and the way the president selected, worked with, and managed them. Obama's deliberative nature and comfort with debate and disagreement also foster his penchant for good listening, his emphasis on inclusiveness (even with those who disagree), and his self-confidence to serve as a "benevolent referee" by not taking sides in a discussion before a decision is needed. Finally, apparently motivated by achievement rather than power per se (Drew 2009), Obama's preference is to work for consensus while serving as a catalyst (see Drew 2009; Lawrence 2008; Walsh 2008; Yoffe 2008).

In contrast to the previous examples, these traits in Obama produce a less domineering or consensus-forcing president (like Johnson or the younger Bush), and one who does not personalize challenges or challengers (like the elder Bush) or decide rashly, without deliberation (like the younger Bush). Such traits can be linked to Obama's policy preferences as president (e.g., for diplomacy) and the policy-making processes he has fostered (deliberative, open and mostly collegial). These traits have also helped to minimize groupthink, even while they have generated vigorous policy debate and, sometimes, contentious bureaucratic politics.

Following his successful re-election bid in 2012, these links between personality and process promised to take center stage again. As the president shuffled his cabinet and key advisers in his second term, his preference for deliberation and strong advisors continued to be on display. The extent to which his style and preferences continued to generate vigorous, but productive debate or bureaucratic conflict remained to be seen.

In sum, it is certainly fair to say that one must examine the background and upbringing of the individual to better understand their images and personality in order to better understand the policymaking process.

The Role of Crises

Scholars have also found that the decisionmaking "context"—that is, the environment in which decisions are made—has an important influence on individual behavior and the policymaking process. The intensity of an issue or situation may also affect the dynamics of presidential politics. Different issues affect the government's agenda in different ways at different times—the relative importance of any single issue may fall anywhere in a range from extremely significant to very insignificant. Usually, only a few issues are able to dominate the government's agenda and presidential attention.

Crises are times that catapult an issue onto the agenda and trigger intense presidential politics. The media often plays a consequential role in agenda setting during such time, for they affect the information and perceptions formed by people inside and outside the government. Crises such as the 1979 Soviet invasion of Afghanistan, the Iraqi invasion of Kuwait in 1990, and the September 11 terrorist attacks, usually go immediately to the top of the agenda and force policymakers to respond.

President George W. Bush acknowledged how the **crisis of September 11, 2001**, had a profound effect on him personally and gave him a new presidential focus and mission revolving around the threat of terrorism. According to National Security Advisor Condoleezza Rice, "the president really had the sense here that this was a historic moment, that he had been cast into a historic moment" (Balz and Woodward 2002). Or in the words of Brent Scowcroft, National Security Advisor under George W. Bush's father, "It's possible that the transformation came with 9/11, and the current president, who is a very religious person, thought that there was something unique if not divine about a catastrophe like 9/11 happening when he was president. . . . that his mission is to deal with the war on terrorism" (Rothkopf 2005:33; see also Fineman 2003). And after 9/11 Saddam Hussein and Iraq were constantly on his mind. According to Balz and Woodward (2002:A1), "As for Saddam Hussein, his father's nemesis, the president ended a debate that had gone on for six days. 'I believe Iraq was involved, but I'm not going to strike them now,' he said, adding, 'I don't have the evidence at this point.' Bush said that he wanted them [his advisors] to keep working on developing plans for military action in Iraq but indicated there would be plenty of time to do that."

Times of crisis, in fact, tend to produce considerable emotional and psychological stress on policymakers, often intensifying individual images and personalities, which often inhibit an open and rational decisionmaking process. Scholars such as Ole Holsti (1990) have reviewed the literature on the relationship between crisis, **stress**, and decision-making and concluded that situations perceived to be crises produced individual stress and affected the nature of decisionmaking for individuals and policymaking groups (see also Lebow 1981; Oneal 1988; Snyder 1978). *Two patterns, based on experimental work in psychology, were found.* On the one hand, Holsti found that low and moderate levels of stress were often conducive to rational decisionmaking, for individuals became more atten- tive and motivated to find a solution to the problem at hand. In some cases, high levels of stress may increase performance for elementary tasks over limited periods of time.

On the other hand, prolonged periods of high stress tend to result in defective decisionmaking, especially for tasks that are complex, ambiguous, and involve uncer- tainty. A foreign policy **crisis** (commonly defined in terms of surprise, a threat to values, and little time to respond)—Holsti's major concern—involves periods of high **stress** and decisions concerning such complex and ambiguous issues (Hermann 1969). During such crises, "lack of rest and diversion, combined with excessively long working hours, are likely to magnify the stresses in the situation" (Holsti 1990:124). According to Holsti (1990:124), the preponderance of evidence from psychological experiments, psychological field research (e.g., studies of individual behavior during natural disasters and combat), and historical studies of international crises indicated "that intense and protracted stress erodes rather than enhances the ability of individuals to cope with complex problems."

Holsti (1990) further identified *a number of patterns associated with high stress and its impact on individual and group decisionmaking.* Specifically, high stress tends to:

1. heighten the salience of time by distorting judgment, usually leading to a significant overestimation of how fast time is passing,

2. reduce the size of the policymaking group,

3. reduce tolerance for ambiguity and increase the likelihood to stereotype and rationalize,

4. increase cognitive rigidity, reliance on familiar decision rules, and use of basic beliefs and metaphorical thinking,

5. encourage random and selective searches for information,

6. produce concern for the present and immediate future,

7. minimize communication with potential adversaries,

8. increase use of ad hoc communication channels,

9. limit the search and assessment of alternatives, often to one approach,

10. increase the likelihood of a polarized choice, favoring positions of overcautiousness or greater risk-taking, and

11. disrupt complex learning and the reexamination of decisions.

The stress produced by foreign policy crises, in other words, often contributes to poor policymaking performance and maladaptive behavior. Each of the eleven patterns mentioned, with the exception of number 8, tends to contribute to a more closed decisionmaking process.

Stress does not guarantee defective decisionmaking but only increases the likelihood that rational decisionmaking will be constrained or inhibited. This is because "individuals appear to differ rather widely in the ability to tolerate stress, the threshold at which it begins to impair performance, and strategies for coping with various types of stress" (Holsti 1990:127). Ultimately, the policymaking process will be heavily affected by individual personality and perceptions (and misperceptions)—which are usually heightened during periods of crisis and high stress.

Although international crises usually inhibit rational decisionmaking, Holsti (1990:117,127,131) recognizes that "not all crises spin out of control owing to misperceptions, miscalculations, or other cognitive malfunctions." Therefore, "just as we cannot assume that 'good' processes will ensure high-quality decisions, we cannot assume that erratic processes will always result in low-quality decisions" or end up in fiascoes. Nevertheless, theories of deterrence and compellence (and coercive diplomacy), which have been so central to great-power politics and U.S. foreign policy, "presuppose rational and predictable decision processes," and "scholars and policymakers tend to be sanguine about the ability of policymakers to be creative when the situation requires it." In short, periods of intense crisis and stress may inhibit and overwhelm rationality during times when it is most needed.

THE COMPLEX REALITY OF POLICYMAKING

We have examined the complexity of how policymaking operates within the executive branch. We have seen that policymaking involves three stages: agenda setting, policy formulation, and policy implementation. We reviewed four policymaking models and highlighted two general policymaking patterns—presidential politics and bureaucratic politics. We also discussed the important role that beliefs, personality, and crises have on leaders and policymakers in decisionmaking. The reader should now have a better understanding of the president's power and the dynamics of the policymaking process, including the difficulties he encounters in managing the executive branch.

Even our more complicated picture actually oversimplifies policymaking within the executive branch. First, the government does not consider one issue at a time but hundreds of foreign policy issues simultaneously. In other words, numerous policymaking processes operate within the executive branch at the same time. Presidential politics prevails for the more important issues, while bureaucratic politics guides the process for the remainder. Nor are agenda-setting, policy formation, and policy implementation processes clearly separated—they often overlap and have an impact one another. Ultimately, policymaking efforts to address the dozens of issues involve the input of the beliefs, personalities, and bureaucratic roles of hundreds of individuals from numerous organizations throughout the executive branch. In other words, the president, his closest advisors, and bureaucratic officials and organizations throughout the executive branch are constantly initiating and responding to issues, participating in and influencing decisions, and implementing policies. These interactions and dynamic processes represent the complex politics of U.S. foreign policy as it occurs in the executive branch.

At the same time, policymakers operate not in a political vacuum, but in a large governmental, societal, and global context (see, e.g., **A Different Perspective** on the Washington political context in which presidents must operate). This was a dominant theme that most of the early theorists of the U.S. policymaking process, including Neustadt (1960), Schilling, Hammond and Snyder (1962), Hilsman (1964), and Snyder, Bruck, and Sapin (1962), emphasized throughout their work. For example, as Samuel Huntington (1961:x,xi) made clear in his study of the national security process from 1945 to 1960, "If this book has any distinctive message, it is that military policy can only be understood as the responses of the government to conflicting pressures from its foreign and domestic environments. . . . Military policy cannot be separated from foreign policy, fiscal policy, and domestic policy. It is part of the warp and woof of American politics." Or, as Hart, Stern, and Sundelius stated (1997:26), this raises the agency-structure problem noted by international relations scholars by highlighting "the embedded nature of groups in broader organizational, political, and cultural constellations."

A DIFFERENT PERSPECTIVE

The Washington Political Culture

One overlooked source of influence on the policymaking process that warrants some attention is the Washington political culture or what Hedrick Smith, in *The Power Game: How Washington Works* (1988: Chapter 6) calls "life inside the beltway: the folkways of Washington." *At least eight characteristics pervade the Washington political community:*

1. a preoccupation with politics,

2. a quest for power, status, and visibility,

3. networking,

4. pragmatism,

5. workaholism,

6. use of jargon,

7. a lonely existence, and

8. male predominance.

Although some of these norms may be undergoing some change (the increase in ideological dogmatism and political partisanship since the end of the cold war suggesting less pragmatism), the Washington political community is where much of politics and governmental policymaking intersect, affecting agenda setting, policy formulation, and the implementation of policy.

The prevalence and power of the Washington political culture helps to explain why policymaking inside the beltway is often so different from the rational actor model that the public wants to see from outside the beltway and from what presidential candidates realize when governing as opposed to campaigning. Peter Baker (2010) summarizes Obama's "Education as a President": "Most of all, he has learned that, for all his anti-Washington rhetoric, he has to play by Washington rules if he wants to win in Washington" (see also Barry 1989; Greenfield 2001; Mann and Ornstein, 2012).

How does the nature of the Washington political community affect those responsible for foreign policy decisions? Can the Washington political culture be "fixed" or less divisive as so many presidential candidates promise?

We now go beyond the executive branch and turn to the role of Congress, and then to the role of society and domestic politics in the complex politics of U.S. foreign policy. We will explore additional theoretical perspectives—in particular, (1) interbranch politics and (2) domestic politics—in order to have a comprehensive understanding of the making of U.S. foreign policy.

SUGGESTED SOURCES FOR MORE INFORMATION

Allison, Graham T., "Conceptual Models and the Cuban Missile Crisis," *American Political Science Review* 58 (September 1969): 698–718. A summary article of what becomes his classic 1971 book.

Allison, Graham T., and Philip Zelikow. (1999) *Essence of Decision: Explaining the Cuban Missile Crisis.* New York: Longman. Updated version of Allison's 1971 classic analysis of rational actor, governmental politics, and organizational process models.

Badie, Dina. (2010) "Groupthink, Iraq, and the War on Terror: Explaining US Policy Shift toward Iraq," *Foreign Policy Analysis* 6:4 (October): 277–296. An analysis of national security policymaking process under President George W. Bush.

Baker, Peter. (2010) "The Education of a President," *The New York Times Magazine* (October 12). Excellent overview of the difficulty of governing in Washington's political culture as illustrated through President Obama.

Freidman, William. (1994) "Woodrow Wilson and Colonel House and Political Psychobiography," *Political Psychology* 15 (1994):35–59. Good overview of the general role of personality and interpersonal relations on policymaking.

Goodwin, Doris Kearns. (1991) *Lyndon Johnson and the American Dream.* New York: St. Martins. Fascinating psychobiography.

Halperin, Morton H. (1974) *Bureaucratic Politics and Foreign Policy.* Washington, DC: Brookings Institution Press. A classic.

Holsti, Ole R. (1990) "Crisis Management," In *Psychological Dimensions of War,* edited by Betty Glad, pp. 116–142. Newberry Park, CA: Sage. Excellent overview.

Janis, Irving L. (1982) *Groupthink.* New York: Houghton Mifflin.

Jervis, Robert. (1976) *Perception and Misperception in International Politics.* Princeton, NJ: Princeton University Press. Terrific overview.

Khong, Yuen Foong. (1992) *Analogies at War: Korea, Munich, Dien Bien Phu, and the Vietnam Decision of 1965.* Princeton, NJ: Princeton University Press. Highlights the importance of historical analogies used during the Vietnam War.

Paul,'t Hart, Stern, Eric K. and Sundelius, Bengt eds. (1997) *Beyond Groupthink: Political Group Dynamics and Foreign Policy-Making.* Ann Arbor: University of Michigan Press.

Rosati, Jerel A. (1981) "Developing a Systematic Decisionmaking Framework: Bureaucratic Politics in Perspective," *World Politics* 33 (January):234–252. Major critique of bureaucratic politics.

Rosati, Jerel. (2000) "The Power of Human Cognition in the Study of World Politics," *International Studies Review* 2(3):45–75. Overview of the impact of beliefs and cognition on policymaking.

Rosati, Jerel. (2010). "Political Psychology, Cognition and Foreign Policy Analysis," Bob Denmark, ed., *Compendium of International Studies* Volume IX (ISA and Blackwell, 2010), pp. 5732-5755. Explores the power of political psychology and cognition for understanding decisionmaking.

KEY CONCEPTS

agenda setting
bureaucratic politics
cognition and perception
cognitive consistency
crisis
decisionmaking theory
domino theory
enemy image
government learning
governmental politics
groupthink
historical analogies
ideal type

mirror images
motivated tactician
newgroup syndrome
organizational process model
personality
policy formulation
policy implementation
presidential politics
rational actor model
schemas
stress
Washington political community

OTHER KEY TERMS

Challenger
crisis of September 11, 2001
Cuban missile crisis

Iraq's postwar–reconstruction phase
Lyndon Baines Johnson
SALT I

CHAPTER 10

THE SENATE FOREIGN RELATIONS COMMITTEE HEARS TESTIMONY FROM
ACTOR GEORGE CLOONEY DURING HEARINGS ON SUDAN IN 2012.

CONGRESS AND INTERBRANCH POLITICS

Congress plays a significant, often misunderstood, and occasionally controversial role in the making of U.S. foreign policy. Since the U.S. Constitution provides Congress with a seemingly impressive array of foreign policy powers, the institution and its members have the capability of playing a formidable role. However, Congress has, in practice, not been consistent in applying those powers to influence foreign policy. *This chapter considers the context, historical patterns, and policy behavior of Congress in order to examine* the constitutional foundation of Congress's power in foreign policy; the ways the institution and its members influence foreign policy; the patterns of legislative–executive relations and congressional influence since World War II in areas such as the war power, advice and consent, the power of legislation, and the power of investigations; and the prospects for future congressional foreign policy behavior and legislative–executive interaction.

THE CONTEXT OF CONGRESSIONAL FOREIGN POLICYMAKING

Since World War II, Congress has alternatively been characterized as acquiescent, resurgent, deferent, assertive, subservient, coequal, and imperial. As we will see, each of these characterizations has sometimes been accurate. As Rebecca Hersman (2000:105) suggests, "the complex and often troubled relationship between Congress and the executive branch over foreign policy defies simple explanations and convenient caricatures." In fact, *congressional foreign policy behavior is highly context dependent,* which will be readily apparent by the end of this chapter. We begin by discussing the context of interbranch politics in the making of U.S. foreign policy with *a brief overview of three important issues:* (1) the constitutional foundation of foreign policy, (2) the role of the courts in interbranch politics, and (3) congressional actors and avenues of influence in foreign policy.

The Constitutional Foundation of Foreign Policy

Just a few pages in length, and over 200 years old, the Constitution is a short, ambiguous document arrived at by negotiation and compromise. Nowhere is this more evident than with respect to its treatment of foreign affairs: the document does not even mention or refer to "the foreign affairs power." Instead, as we discussed in Chapter 3, *Article II of the Constitution enumerates the powers of the president.* Placing the general executive power in the president, the Constitution also specifies foreign policy powers including commander in chief, treaty-making and the appointment of ambassadors and cabinet heads (with the advice and consent of the Senate), receiving foreign dignitaries, commissioning military officers, the general executive power, and the power of the veto.

Article I of the Constitution enumerates the powers of the legislative branch. It places the general legislative power in the Congress and stipulates important foreign policy powers by stating that Congress shall

> provide for the common Defense and general Welfare; . . . regulate commerce with foreign nations, and among the several States, and with the Indian tribes; . . . define and punish piracies and felonies committed on the high seas, and offenses against the law of nations; . . . declare war, grant letters of marque and reprisal, and make rules concerning captures on land and water; . . . raise and support armies; . . . provide and maintain a navy; . . . make rules for the government and regulation of the land and naval forces; [and] provide for calling forth the militia to execute the laws of the Union, suppress insurrections, and repel invasions.

Further, key diplomatic powers of the president are subject to the advice and consent of the Senate, as noted in the previous paragraph. Finally, Congress has the power "to make all laws which shall be necessary and proper for carrying into execution the foregoing powers, and all other powers vested by this Constitution in the government of the United States, or in any department or officer thereof."

Hence, the Constitution clearly gives the Congress a broad range of powers in the area of foreign policy. There is, in fact, no foreign policy power provided to the president that is not shared by Congress. Although Americans typically understand the distribution of power between Congress and the president as a "separation of powers," the Constitution actually establishes **separate institutions sharing power** (Corwin 1957)—which is what is meant by "checks and balances." For example, while the Congress provides military funding and declares war, the president is the commander in chief. Congress may pass bills, but the president may veto them, and Congress may then override the veto. The president is able to make treaties and appointments, but the Senate must provide its advice and consent. As students of the Constitution such as Edwin Corwin (1957) have indicated, the result is an **invitation to struggle,** which has fostered recurring conflicts between Congress and the president in the making of foreign policy throughout American history (see also Crabb and Holt 1992).

The Courts, the Congress, and the Presidency

Because of the ambiguity in this invitation to struggle, the power of **judicial review** (determining the constitutionality of a law or action) has often required the third branch of the U.S. government to play a role in U.S. foreign policy. Generally speaking, in foreign policy, *the Supreme Court has tended to rule that the office of the president predominates, especially when the use of force abroad is involved* (Fisher 2004a; Henkin 1996). Let us consider a number of key areas in which the courts have shaped the sharing of power among the separate institutions of the U.S. government.

The parameters of the courts' views are nicely summarized in two key cases. In the *United States v. Curtiss-Wright Export Corp.* (299 US 305) of 1936, the Supreme Court not only upheld a congressional grant of authority to the president to prevent the sale of arms to belligerents (which the Curtiss-Wright Corporation had violated in a war involving Bolivia and Paraguay), but ruled generally in favor of national governmental and presidential supremacy in foreign policy. The famous majority opinion by Justice George Sutherland asserted that the president's "very delicate, plenary and exclusive power . . . as the sole organ of the federal government in the field of international relations . . . does not require as a basis for its exercise an act of Congress."

In contrast, the 1952 *Youngstown Sheet & Tube Co. v. Sawyer* case (343 US 579) resulted in the Supreme Court in 1952 invalidating President Harry Truman's attempt to invoke national security emergency powers during the Korean War to seize domestic steel mills that were under nationwide strike. The Supreme Court concluded that the president's steel seizure was not authorized by Congress, so the president had violated Congress's lawmaking authority. The famous concurring opinion by Justice Robert Jackson established a three-tiered hierarchy of legitimate presidential actions. First, "when the President acts pursuant to an express or implied authorization of Congress, his authority is at its maximum, for it includes all that he possesses in his own right plus all that Congress can delegate." Second, "when the President acts in absence of either a congressional grant or denial of authority, he can only rely upon his own independent powers, but there is a **zone of twilight** in which he and Congress may have concurrent authority, or in which its distribution is uncertain." The third level occurs "when the President takes measures incompatible with the express or implied will of Congress, his power is at its lowest ebb, for then he can rely only upon his own constitutional powers minus any constitutional powers of Congress over the matter."

The combination of these cases displays the parameters of the "invitation to struggle." The president is preeminent in some cases—reflecting Justice Jackson's first constitutional level, in which presidential authority is at its maximum. Yet many foreign policy issues are a function of joint participation—Justice Jackson's twilight zone of shared powers. Louis Henkin (1987–88:285) has observed, "Important foreign affairs powers lie in that twilight zone. Indeed, in few other respects is our constitutional system as troubled by uncertainty in principle and by conflict in practice between Congress and the President."

The courts have affected many specific areas of foreign policy. For example, in the area of treaties and executive agreements, the courts have consistently strengthened the power of the president, in part by determining that executive agreements, which are not subject to ratification by Senate as are formal treaties, nevertheless have the same force as treaties (see, e.g., *U.S. v. Belmont, 301 U.S. 324* 1937 and *U.S. v. Pink* 315 U.S 203 1942). With respect to the war power, the courts have struck a delicate balance that also tends to favor the executive branch.

In many instances, the courts have evaded weighing in on such disputes by characterizing them as **political questions**, or relying on doctrines such as "ripeness" and "implied consent." Good examples of this practice include the court's decisions in the 1981 *Crockett v. Reagan* case, in which some members of Congress challenged the Reagan administration's power to send military advisors into El Salvador, and the 1987 *Lowry v. Reagan* case, in which some members of Congress asked the court to require the Reagan administration to comply with the War Powers Act. Similarly, in *Dellums v. Bush* (1990) and again in *Campbell v. Clinton* (1999), the courts rejected claims by some members of Congress that George H. W. Bush and Bill Clinton had violated the Constitution by either not consulting adequately with Congress (Bush) or by using force in Kosovo without a congressional authorization.

In both cases, the courts referred to an **implied consent** doctrine that held that Congress had to try to stop the action before resort to the courts was appropriate. However, in both the Dellums and Campbell cases, the courts rejected broad administration claims that sole authority to determine uses of force rested with the executive branch. In *Dellums v. Bush*, for example, the court ruled that the administration's claim that it had sole power to decide whether to use force "evaded[d] the plain language of the Constitution and it cannot stand" (*Dellums v. Bush*, 752 F. Supp. 1141, 1145 DC Cir. 1990).

Court decisions have affected some congressional foreign policy tools, as well, including the use of the "legislative veto" and access to information. In a 1983 decision, the Supreme Court ruled in *Immigration and Naturalization Service v. Chadha* that the "legislative veto," here involving immigration, was unconstitutional because it violated the separation of powers. The decision called into question Congress's ability to veto presidential decisions—that is, to pass a concurrent resolution without the president's signature—concerning, for example, the use of force abroad under the War Powers Act, sales of major weapons systems to foreign governments under the International Security Assistance and Arms Export Control Act, and the export of nuclear fuel and facilities to foreign countries under the Nonproliferation Act (Destler 1983).

The courts have also ruled on issues related to claims of **executive privilege**, or the right of the executive branch to withhold information from Congress and the public. In the main, the courts have rejected broad claims of this sort and placed restrictions on such privileges. For example, in *New York Times v. United States* (1971) and *U.S. v. Nixon* (1974), the courts denied the executive the power to withhold information or prevent the publication of *The Pentagon Papers* by the press. Similarly, in the 1990s, cases involving Bill Clinton and the Whitewater corruption scandal, the Paula Jones sexual harassment case, and the Monica Lewinsky affair all weakened the president's powers to exert executive privilege and confidentiality. George W. Bush's administration challenged such limits in several instances, including a 2001 case when the U.S. General Accounting Office on behalf of Congress sued Vice President Richard Cheney (who led the energy interagency task force) to release classified information that led to George W. Bush's energy policy. The court ultimately decided for the administration in this case (Fisher 2004b).

Congressional Actors and Avenues of Influence

Congress has been disadvantaged by the combination of the practices and precedents of executive action, the decisions of the courts, and its own structural characteristics. For example, the sheer size of Congress—with its 535 members—makes efficient, coherent foreign policy action difficult. Nevertheless, *the institution is still a formidable player in foreign affairs for several reasons.* First, speaking of Congress as "a player" in foreign policy is inaccurate. In fact, Congress is composed of many players and each is capable of influencing foreign policy. As Rudalevige (2005:428) argues, "Congress is not truly an 'it' but a 'they.'" These multiple actors include the collective institution, each individual chamber, the many committees and subcommittees in which the work of Congress is really done, congressional caucuses, the congressional leadership, the professional staff and support organizations of Congress, and individual members themselves (Carter and Scott 2009). This means that we must be careful to distinguish between "activity" and "influence" when we discuss Congress, as there is more to congressional foreign policy behavior than formal outputs such as legislation (Carter and Scott 2009; Lindsay 1994; Martin 2000).

Members of Congress have a wide range of **congressional avenues of influence** on which to rely. According to Scott (1997), we should *distinguish between two dimensions, along which four congressional avenues of influence can be differentiated* (see **Figure** 10.1). Avenues can be either legislative or nonlegislative. Legislative actions involve those most formal things that Congress does to pass laws, approve treaties, and authorize and appropriate funds. By contrast, nonlegislative actions include congressional activities not related to specific legislative documents. Moreover, there are both direct and indirect avenues. When members take direct action, they target specific foreign policy issues; when they take indirect action, they typically take aim at the broader context, process, or policy climate to signal preferences or condition policy. This distinction helps us to understand that there are many ways other than simply trying to make laws that members can influence foreign policy.

Members of Congress can, if enough votes can be mustered, directly influence policy by legislating action. Also, they can link their efforts across these different paths to maximize their potential impact. Just as important, though, they can also shape decisionmaking by triggering **anticipated reactions**. Essentially, this aspect of congressional influence refers to the threat of congressional legislative action, and the use of that threat as leverage by members to bring administration proposals or actions into line with their preferences. Such congressional signaling or conditioning can play an important role in foreign policy decisions, even without formal legislative actions by the institution (Lindsay 1994; Howell and Pevehouse 2007).

Figure 10.1 Congressional Paths to Foreign Policy Influence

Path	Direct	Indirect
Legislative	(1) Issue-Specific Legislation Treaties (Senate) War Power Appropriations Foreign Commerce	(3) Nonbinding Legislation Appointments (Senate) Procedural Legislation
Nonlegislative	(2) Informal Advice/Letters Consultations Oversight/Hearings Use of Courts	(4) Framing Opinion Foreign Contacts

SOURCE: Adapted from James M. Scott, "In the Loop: Congressional Influence in American Foreign Policy," *Journal of Political and Military Sociology*, 25 (Summer 1997): 61.

Patterns of Interbranch Relations on Foreign Policy

In spite of the opportunities, members of Congress have not always availed themselves of these congressional paths of influence. Historically, the distribution of foreign policymaking power between Congress and the president has fluctuated, sometimes dramatically, with changes in the political environment. ***Interbranch politics in foreign policy have been fluid and dynamic, with neither Congress nor the president always predominant.***

We begin by considering broad patterns of congressional assertiveness on foreign policy, in which we clearly see the dynamic nature of interbranch politics. **Figure 10.2** presents evidence from one analysis of four different types of congressional foreign policy activity and their variance from 1945 to 1997. According to Scott and Carter (2002), when members of Congress accede to the administration's request, their behavior is "compliant." When members modify the administration's request, delivering a result either more or less than the administration desired, their behavior is "resistant." "Rejection" behavior is when Congress flatly refuses to enact the administration's desires. Finally, when members of Congress go beyond reacting to the administration's policy requests and proposals and choose to enact their own foreign policy agenda, their behavior is "independent" (Scott and Carter 2002:128–129). When these activities are separated into cold war, post-Vietnam, and post–cold war periods, they show two characteristics: (1) variance over time and (2) increasingly assertive behavior by Congress across the three time periods.

As Figure 10.2 shows, during the cold war years presidential leadership was common (almost half of congressional action complied with presidential preferences). After Vietnam, congressional compliance with presidential leadership sharply fell, while resistant, rejection, and independent behavior all increased substantially. In the post–cold war period, Congress continued to challenge presidential leadership, becoming more likely to take its own independent foreign policy actions rather than just comply with presidential leadership.

Figure 10.2   Congressional Foreign Policy Assertiveness over Time

Behavior	Time Periods		
	Cold War (1946–67)	**Post-Vietnam (1968–88)**	**Post–Cold War (1989–97)**
Compliant (161)	42.4% (76)	22.6% (18)	23.7%
Resistant (108)	28.4% (129)	38.4% (36)	47.4%
Rejection (31)	8.2% (49)	14.6% (2)	2.6%
Independent	21.1% (80)	24.4% (82)	26.3% (20)
	100.1% (380)	**100% (336)**	**100% (76)**

SOURCE: Adapted from James M. Scott and Ralph G. Carter, "Acting on the Hill: Congressional Assertiveness in U.S. Foreign Policy," *Congress and the Presidency*, 29 (Autumn 2002): 159.

This evidence strongly suggests a cold war period in which presidential dominance and congressional deference prevailed, followed by a post-Vietnam period of congressional reassertiveness. Although this study ends in 1997, the years since 1997 actually displayed a similar pattern, with a period of presidential dominance during the crisis atmosphere during and immediately following the September 11, 2001, attacks giving way to a period of congressional reassertiveness not long after. Let's consider these periods and patterns of behavior in more detail to gain a better understanding of their nature, dynamics, and the factors shaping them.

Presidential Dominance in the Cold War Era

The president and the executive branch dominated the legislative branch in the making of foreign policy during the cold war years. However, presidential dominance neither occurred overnight nor dominated the entire history of the cold war years. *The congressional role in legislative–executive relations evolved through four phases or periods during the cold war:* (1) accommodation, from 1944 to 1950; (2) antagonism, from 1951 to 1955; (3) acquiescence, from 1955 to 1965; and (4) awakening, from 1966 to 1969 (Bax 1977).

CONGRESSIONAL ACCOMMODATION, 1944–1950 Initial signs of reassertiveness by Congress after World War II quickly gave way to accommodation as members of Congress collaborated with the administration to counter the Soviet threat. For example, initial congressional resistance—isolationist sentiment was still strong among members of Congress, especially Republicans—to President Truman's proposal of the Marshall Plan to counter the devastation suffered by Europe in the war gave way to support as Truman convinced Congress and the American public of the grave political instability that most European states faced from their economic situation and from the growing threat of Soviet communism. In fact, during the immediate post–World War II years, bipartisan, collaborative efforts between Congress and the president resulted in American participation in the United Nations, the International Bank for Reconstruction and Development (World Bank), the International Monetary Fund (IMF), and the General Agreement on Tariffs and Trade (GATT). Congress also supported the National Security Act of 1947, foreign assistance to Greece and Turkey as part of the Truman Doctrine, remobilization of the military, and the establishment of the North Atlantic Treaty Organization (NATO) and the permanent stationing of American troops in Europe—a peacetime American military commitment unprecedented in the nation's history.

CONGRESSIONAL ANTAGONISM, 1951–1955 Despite the broad cold war consensus that led to a bipartisan approach to foreign policy, conservative members of Congress, especially in the Republican Party, were increasingly concerned that the United States was not doing enough to "win" the cold war. As the Republican Party gained control of Congress, these concerns and the virulent anticommunism underlying them led to sweeping congressional investigations of communist threats at home, as well as growing political attacks against the Truman administration and the Democratic Party. The political right was motivated by the suspicion that communists and their liberal-left supporters had penetrated the major institutions of American society, including the executive branch, and were aiding and abetting the enemy. According to William Manchester (1975:491–492), "Republicans began referring to their congressional adversaries as members of 'the party of treason'—a slur that [Democratic leader Sam] Rayburn attributed to Nixon, and never forgave." Other conservative members accused the executive branch of knowingly allowing communists to occupy important positions, and attacked high-level administration officials such as Dean Acheson (who served as secretary of state) and General George Marshall (who served as secretary state and secretary defense) as a "criminal crowd of traitors and appeasers." It was in this political climate that Senator Joseph McCarthy of Wisconsin thrived and gave the conservative movement its name—**McCarthyism** (see The **Liberty–Security Dilemma** for more on Joseph McCarthy and McCarthyism).

Such right-wing attacks continued even after the election of Republican Dwight Eisenhower as president who continued the bipartisan foreign policy of containment initiated by President Truman. Perhaps the best illustration was the attempt by Republican Senator John W. Bricker to amend the Constitution in 1953 to provide Congress with the responsibility and authority to approve all international agreements (not just treaties) entered into by the president. However, after a year of intense debate, the **Bricker Amendment** failed by just one vote to achieve the necessary two-thirds majority (60–31), a result that "both symbolized and brought to an end this period of antagonism in legislative–executive relations" (Bax 1977:885).

THE LIBERTY–SECURITY DILEMMA

Joseph McCarthy and McCarthyism

According to Richard H. Rovere (1959:3), "the late **Joseph R. McCarthy,** a United States Senator from Wisconsin, was in many ways the most gifted demagogue ever bred on these shores. No bolder seditionist ever moved among us—not any politician with a surer, swifter access to the dark places of the American mind." McCarthy's political prominence was brief. His rise to power began in 1950, four years after he won a seat in the Senate. Within weeks, he became a major political figure known, loved, hated, and feared throughout the country and the world. By 1954, his career ended when the Senate passed a resolution of censure against him. He died a drunk three years later at age forty-eight. Yet, the impact of Joseph McCarthy and McCarthyism was immense.

During his early years in the Senate, McCarthy was "known as a cheap politician of vulgar, flamboyant ways and a casual approach to the public interest" (Rovere 1959:6). One night in January 1950 in a small restaurant in Washington, D.C., while talking with three dinner companions about his Senate reelection possibilities, he discovered communism as an issue—not out of real concern for American national security, but as an issue that would win him reelection. He tested the issue in a speech he gave on February 9, 1950, in Wheeling, West Virginia, in which he claimed that the Department of State was full of communists and that he and the secretary of state knew their names. To this day, nobody is sure whether he declared that there were 205, 81, 57, or "a lot" of communists; more important was the charge that communists "known to the secretary of state" were "still working and making policy."

Following his Wheeling speech, he accused the Truman administration of conniving with communists: "The Democratic label is now the property of men and women who have . . . bent to the whispered pleas from the lips of traitors" (Rovere 1959:11).

(Continued)

The timing of the charges was impeccable. On January 21, Alger Hiss, a State Department official accused of being a communist, was convicted of perjury, and in June the communist government of North Korea invaded South Korea, vindicating and feeding the anticommunist hysteria that McCarthy represented. Over the next four years, four different congressional committees conducted five major congressional investigations into the threat of communism and alleged treasonous behavior at home. The rise of McCarthy intensified this process and gave it renewed prominence in American politics. He used these committees as his bully pulpits for investigating the government and leveling accusations of communist infiltration in America.

McCarthy was a master of publicity and use of the media to give him power over his senatorial colleagues and throughout American politics. Nothing was immune from attack. He let scarcely a day pass without demanding the resignation of Dean Acheson or the impeachment of Harry Truman. The United Nations, the State Department, the federal government, the Truman administration, the Democratic Party, academia—even the Eisenhower administration after the 1952 elections—were all charged with being infested with communists and traitors who were selling the country down the river. He relied on a secret network of extremely conservative individuals and groups, in government and throughout society, especially his allies J. Edgar Hoover and the FBI to feed him information for his accusations and investigations.

In Rovere's (1959:5) words, McCarthy walked "with a heavy tread over large parts of the Constitution of the United States, and he cloaked his own gross figure in the sovereignty it asserts and the power it distributes. He usurped executive and judicial authority whenever the fancy struck him. It struck him often." McCarthyism led to "the purge

of thousands of government employees, educators, labor leaders, journalists, scientists, writers, and entertainers and, perhaps more important, the intimidation of hundreds of thousands more" (Griffiths 1987:xix). At his height, polls indicated that a majority of the American people had a "favorable opinion" of McCarthy and felt he was serving the country in useful ways. "It was a melancholy time," Rovere has observed (1959:23), "and the Chief Justice of the United States was probably right when he said at the time that if the Bill of Rights was put to a vote, it would lose."

In 1954 McCarthy finally went too far—he attacked and investigated the United States Army for being subversive. The investigation was initiated in order to prevent one of his staffers, David Schine, from being inducted into the Army. However, it quickly ballooned out of control. This turn of events gave his Senate colleagues the courage to vote to censure him. His quick political decline led to more drinking, charges of personal corruption, and death within three years.

There was great irony in the rise and decline of Joseph McCarthy. He was a pragmatist and cynic, a great believer in the promotion of Joseph McCarthy, "a political speculator, a prospector who drilled Communism and saw it come up a gusher" (Rovere 1959:72). Nevertheless, Joseph McCarthy and McCarthyism made their political mark on American history—reflected and promoted the anticommunist climate of the times. He embodied a political force—McCarthyism— that dominated American politics during the early 1950s and was instrumental in pushing the country and U.S. foreign policy to the political right.

What does the McCarthy episode suggest about the nature of the cold war consensus and the role of Congress?

CONGRESSIONAL ACQUIESCENCE, 1955–1965 With the decline of McCarthyism, the ensuing decade constituted the height of **bipartisanship** and congressional compliance with presidential leadership. While pockets and episodes of congressional criticism remained (usually over not doing enough to fight the cold war), this period was the heyday of presidential power and the president's ability to exercise prerogative government in order to fight the cold war in the name of national security. The president's foreign policies were rarely challenged seriously. Although Congress seldom gave the president all that he wanted in important areas such as defense and foreign assistance, members of Congress generally complied with presidential leadership and the growing independence of the executive branch in the making of U.S. foreign policy. Thus, the demands of national security took precedence over all other concerns, and, according to Frans Bax (1977:887), "the chief function of Congress became the legitimizing of presidential decisions."

The cold war consensus and bipartisanship of this period were so strong that, in many cases, foreign policy decisions were made without consulting Congress or getting its formal approval; at best, congressional leaders might be informed after the fact. Presidential supremacy and the assumption of congressional support reached its height under presidents Kennedy and Johnson. Not surprisingly, the fateful decisions to fully Americanize the Vietnam War were made with virtually no input from Congress. The cold war consensus prevented questions from being asked about whether the United States should or should not commit itself to defend South Vietnam from communism. Rather, the questions always revolved only around how much American involvement it would take to contain communist aggression and prevent the downfall of an ally. For example, after the Gulf of Tonkin incidents in August 1964, members of Congress rushed the **Gulf of Tonkin Resolution** through rather than seriously debating the pros and cons of the resolution submitted by President Johnson—the vote was unanimous, 416–0, in the House of Representatives and 88–2 in the Senate. In effect, President Johnson was given what he considered to be a "blank check" for containing communism in Southeast Asia.

CONGRESSIONAL AWAKENING, 1966–1969 Congressional uneasiness with cold war policies and presidential leadership began to emerge even before the escalation of American involvement in Vietnam. According to Carter and Scott (2009), in the early 1960s key individuals in Congress such as J. William Fulbright, Wayne Morse, Ernest Gruening, and Stuart Symington led a "foreign aid revolt" that challenged the amounts, priorities, and purposes of U.S. assistance. These "entrepreneurs" challenged the White House in an effort to recast foreign aid (away from military aid) and place restrictions on it (especially to dictators). Such efforts paid off and, by the mid-1960s, the Johnson administration had been forced to accept a variety of restrictions. As one scholar commented, "The foreign aid revolt had succeeded beyond anything [its initiators] could have imagined. In the process a new era in executive-legislative relations was inaugurated" (Johnson 2006:104).

By 1966, such uneasiness had spread to U.S. foreign policy in Vietnam. Total troop levels were over 550,000 troops, but there still seemed to be no "light at the end of the tunnel." As a result, some members of Congress began to criticize the administration's lack of restraint in and overemphasis on the use of force. Determined to inject a different point of view into the decisionmaking process, the leading critics in Congress began a series of congressional investigations of American policy in Vietnam. These efforts to broaden the debate and scrutinize administration decisions were best symbolized by the hearings convened by the **Senate Foreign Relations Committee** under the chairmanship of **J. William Fulbright** (see **A Different Perspective** on Fulbright and Vietnam).

J. William Fulbright and The Vietnam War

As a member and then chairman of the Senate Foreign Relations Committee from 1944 to 1974, Senator J. William Fulbright, a Democrat from Arkansas, played a leading role in the evolution of U.S. foreign policy (see Carter and Scott 2009). Once a cold warrior in support of administration policy, Fulbright moved steadily from private to public dissent in the 1960s over the Vietnam War.

As President Johnson's perspective narrowed and groupthink among his advisors prevailed (see Chapter 9), Fulbright's moved from private objections to outright dissent by 1965. He was determined to bring a different perspective to the policy debate and he became increasingly public in his efforts. As he characterized it (Fulbright 1966:28–29):

> Since 1961, when the Democrats came back to power, I have made recommendations to the President on a number of occasions through confidential memorandums. In April, 1965, I sent President Johnson a note containing certain recommendations of the war in Vietnam, recommendations which I reiterated thereafter in private conversations with high Administration officials. When it became very clear that the Administration did not find my ideas persuasive, I began to make my views known publicly in the hope, if not of bringing about a change in Administration policy, then at least of opening up a debate on that policy.

On April 5, 1965, Fulbright sent a memorandum to President Johnson laying out six points concerning the Vietnam intervention: (1) it was a costly and grave mistake to engage in a large-scale ground and air war in Vietnam; (2) Chinese imperialism, not Communism, stood as the real threat to Asia; (3) independent Asian nations fearful of Chinese domination would bring about stability and security in the region; (4) the United States should declare a moratorium on bombing and clarify aims; (5) the United States should support an independent, open, and more democratic Vietnam; and (6) it was more advantageous for the United States to have an Asian regime friendly to the Soviet Union than one controlled by the Chinese. Although he was initially optimistic about the effect of the memo on President Johnson's thinking, the escalating U.S. intervention soon persuaded him otherwise (Johnson and Gwertzman 1968:205–206).

Fulbright became more public in 1966 when he began "televised" Foreign Relations Committee hearings to focus on the shortcomings of U.S. policy in Vietnam. He also expanded his public critique of Vietnam policy in his remarks entitled "The Arrogance of Power." First delivered as a 1966 speech to the School of Advanced International Studies at Johns Hopkins University and reprinted elsewhere, he charged, "We are trying to remake Vietnamese society, a task which certainly cannot be accomplished by force and which probably cannot be accomplished by any means available to outsiders. The objective may be desirable, but it is not feasible." In these remarks, he called for peace in Vietnam through the neutralization of both Vietnam and the entire Southeast Asian region under the protection of the great powers, including China.

In 1972, Fulbright held another set of critical hearings. He also took to the floor, speaking forcefully in favor of legislation to cut off all funds for the Vietnam War. Capitalizing on regularly scheduled hearings on foreign aid legislation, Fulbright reoriented the sessions to concentrate on the administration's initiation of a new bombing campaign in North Vietnam, questioning witnesses aggressively and condemning the actions. Then, as war powers legislation wound its way through the Senate, Fulbright gave his support for the strongest versions of the measure, advocating strongly to limit the president to only those war powers available to him from the Constitution or in laws. The War Powers Act was finally passed over a presidential veto in 1973.

What does the example of J. William Fulbright suggest about the efforts and effects of members of Congress to influence foreign policy? To what extent are his criticisms about the Vietnam War similar to the criticisms about the Iraq and Afghan wars?

While members continued to appropriate funds for to support the troops in Vietnam, more and more members became uncomfortable with—and willing to challenge the president over—the lack of progress in the war effort and the administration's failure to consult with them on crucial questions of war and peace. Members also began to question the logic of key foreign policy strategies such as containment, and the cold war consensus that had muted foreign policy competition began to facture. This congressional awakening set the stage for the congressional reassertion in legislative–executive relations that has dominated the post–Vietnam War years.

The Post-Vietnam Congressional Resurgence

In the late 1960s, with the cold war consensus a casualty of the Vietnam War, Congress began to reassert its constitutional authority in the making of U.S. foreign policy. *This reassertion reflected the changes in the political environment abroad and at home, and occurred for a number of complementary reasons, most of which had to do with the Vietnam War.* First, the war was not going well. Over half a million American troops and $30 billion a year were not producing the light at the end of the tunnel that President Johnson and General Westmoreland were proclaiming. In fact, with what became known as the Tet offensive in early 1968, the North Vietnamese successfully contested most of South Vietnam for a short time, occupying major cities and even the American embassy in Saigon before being defeated. Second, growing segments of the American public began to question President Johnson's handling of the unsuccessful war. Third, U.S. policy in Vietnam was increasingly criticized by other countries, including the British, French, and other American allies in Europe. Fourth, Republican Richard Nixon's victory over Democrat Hubert Humphrey in the election of 1968 resulted in divided government in legislative–executive relations and added a more partisan dimension to legislative–executive relations. Finally, although President Nixon began to withdraw U.S. troops as part of a strategy of Vietnamization (to turn the war over to the South Vietnamese), he also escalated the levels of military conflict and bombing to achieve "peace with honor"—which increasingly politicized everything.

A classic struggle between the legislative and the executive branches ensued. Members of Congress became increasingly more active in the making of U.S. foreign policy, demanding from the president and the executive branch more information, consultation, and participation in policymaking. In fact, by 1973, Congress cut off all funding of direct American military involvement in the Vietnam War; and with the end of the war, congressional reassertion intensified. In 1973, the War Powers Act was passed over President Nixon's veto, shortly followed by the Budget and Impoundment Control Act of 1974—both symbolic of congressional reassertion.

Although President Nixon resisted congressional reassertion every step of the way, the end of the Vietnam War and the Watergate affair released a flood of congressional involvement in foreign policy. In addition to efforts to end the Vietnam War, over the ensuing fifteen years or so, Congress inserted itself into practically every corner of U.S. foreign policy. For example, Congress asserted itself in the diplomatic arena, requiring, that executive agreements be reported to Congress for review. Congress also tackled military aid, foreign aid, and arms sales policies and processes, providing itself with greater control in both areas. Substantively, Congress tackled U.S. policies toward many different countries, required human rights and democracy to be considered in U.S. assistance and diplomacy, resisted a variety of arms control and other treaties, and became increasingly involved in defense policy. On intelligence, Congress strengthened legislative oversight in a series of actions between 1975 and 1980, while also establishing new procedures, requirements, and restrictions on nuclear export laws. In the 1980s, Congress continued to assert itself, resisting the Reagan administration's policies on arms control and Central America, and, in the case of South Africa, applying sanctions against apartheid regime over administration resistance and, ultimately, a presidential veto.

Hence, after Vietnam, all presidents have faced a more powerful, less compliant Congress and have had greater difficulty in governing foreign policy. Presidential dominance became the exception rather than the rule as changes in the post-Vietnam political environment resulted in the relative decline of presidential power and the rise of congressional involvement.

There are a number of factors that explain both the efforts to reassert congressional influence, and the success in doing so. First, as Melanson (2005) argues, congressional deference and support was in large part a consequence of the cold war consensus, or shared views about the U.S. role in the world and the strategies to follow to pursue U.S. interests. With Vietnam, Watergate, and other changes in the 1960s and 1970s, the cold war consensus that provided for presidential dominance eroded, or shattered, paving the way for greater congressional activism.

Second, the level of congressional activism on foreign policy depends, at least in part, on the international context, especially the level of threat facing the country, and on the success of presidential policies (Lindsay 2003). As one observer argues, after Vietnam "many Americans became convinced that communist revolutions in the third world posed no direct threat to core U.S. security interests, just as détente persuaded many that Leonid Brezhnev's Soviet Union posed less of a threat to core U.S. security interests" (Lindsay 2003:533). Moreover, Vietnam, intelligence abuses, the excesses of the Nixon administration, and other issues convinced many that cold war policies were anything but successful.

Third, Congress enacted a number of major institutional changes that promoted and have maintained its post-Vietnam reassertion (Crabb and Holt 1992; Ripley 1988). Several of these stand out and discussed in greater depth, contributing to a more diverse, representative, decentralized, open, informed, and independent Congress.

MEMBERSHIP Congress experienced a major turnover in its membership beginning in the 1970s. Changes occurred in region, party, and ideology. Throughout the cold war years of the 1950s and 1960s, both the House and Senate were dominated by southerners, members of the Democratic Party, and political conservatives. The situation changed during the early 1970s. By this time, many of the more powerful **southern Democrats** were replaced by younger members of Congress who still tended to be Democrats but were less conservative. This situation resulted in a new Democratic leadership that was much more liberal, much less southern, and much more willing to be assertive in foreign policy. The rise of the new leadership was reinforced by the 1974 post–Vietnam War and post-Watergate congressional elections, in which Republicans faced major losses, resulting in a large influx of new liberal Democrats into Congress. The new Democratic leadership, in coalition with the new members of Congress, took a more activist congressional role in U.S. foreign policy (Bernstein and Freudenberg 1977). In the late 1970s and early 1980s, when Republicans gained seats in Congress (including a majority in the Senate from 1981 to 1987), the new members tended to be more conservative. The Democrats regained majority control of Congress in 2006 and the Republicans regained majority control of the House of Representatives in 2010. The overall result of these changes in membership has been a more diverse, representative, polarized, and politicized Congress that contained very active liberal and conservative members.

COMMITTEES The change in congressional membership during the 1970s not only produced changes in the distribution and exercise of power within Congress, but the new Democratic liberal leadership changed the congressional committee rules of the game. Power was stripped from committees and in particular from committee chairs. Every committee was now required to have multiple subcommittees, subdividing both issues and committee membership, and no committee member could be chair of more than one of its subcommittees. Thus, power moved from committees and committee chairs to subcommittees and subcommittee chairs. *More committees (and subcommittees) also have gained jurisdiction over foreign policy issues.* For example, new committees covering intelligence and the budget were created and many other committees have become more active in foreign policy. This has been especially the case for other types of international (and intermestic) issues, such as trade, finance, energy, transportation, communications, tourism, technology and space, immigration, and the environment—all of which have grown in importance in foreign policy. These changes have resulted in greater committee and congressional involvement in the making of U.S. foreign policy. (See **Tables 10.1** and **10.2** for a listing of relevant committees and subcommittees, and their membership by party, in the 112th Congress.)

CONGRESSIONAL NORMS AND PROCEDURES Structural and procedural changes reduced (but did not eliminate) the importance of seniority, reciprocity, public collegiality, and other norms, contributing to an increase in the number of members seeking to put their stamp on policy. Moreover, Congressional reforms during the 1970s resulted in a much more open and democratic process instead of occurring behind closed doors. Most formal committee activity is now open to the media and the public. Furthermore, **voice votes** (the option to vote as a group and thus remain unaccountable) have been mostly replaced by **roll call votes**, in which each member must take an independent public stand on the issue. While informal interaction, bargaining, and highly sensitive work such as intelligence continue to occur behind the scenes. Nevertheless, congressional procedures are more open today than in the past (as reflected in **C-Span** television coverage of House and Senate hearings and proceedings in the two chambers).

Table 10.1 Membership of Senate Committees and Subcommittees with Jurisdiction over Foreign Policy in the 112th Congress, 2011–2012

Relevant Committees and Subcommittees	Dems/Reps/Ind
Agriculture, Nutrition, and Forestry (4)	11/10
Appropriations (12)	16/14
State, Foreign Operations, and Related Programs	
Defense	
Military Construction and Veteran Affairs and Related Agencies	
Homeland Security	
Armed Services (6)	14/12
Airland Forces	
Emerging Threats & Capabilities	
Personnel	
Readiness & Management Support	
Seapower	
Strategic Forces	
Banking, Housing & Urban Affairs (5)	12/10
Security and International Trade & Finance	
Budget (0)	12/11
Commerce, Science & Transportation (7)	13/12
Aviation Operations, Safety, and Security	
Oceans, Atmosphere, Fisheries & Coast Guard	
Science & Space	
Surface Transportation & Merchant Marine Infrastructure, Safety, and Security	
Energy & Natural Resources (4)	12/10
Environment & Public Works (4)	10/8
Clean Air & Nuclear Safety	
Finance (5)	13/11
International Trade, Customs, and Global Competitiveness	
Foreign Relations (7)	10/9
African Affairs	
East Asian & Pacific Affairs	
European Affairs	
International Development and Foreign Assistance, Economic Affairs, and International Environment Protection	
International Operations & Organizations, Human Rights, Democracy and Global Women's Issues	
Near Eastern & South and Central Asian Affairs	
Western Hemisphere, Peace Corps, and Global Narcotics Affairs	
Homeland Security and Governmental Affairs	9/8
Intelligence	10/9
Judiciary (6)	11/7
Immigration, Refugees, and Border Security	
Terrorism & Homeland Security	
Veterans' Affairs (0)	8/7
TOTAL SENATE MEMBERSHIP:	53/47

SOURCE: U.S. Senate, http://senate.gov

Table 10.2 Membership of House Committees and Subcommittees with Jurisdiction over Foreign Policy in the 111th Congress, 2009–2011

Relevant Committees and Subcommittees	Dems/Reps/Ind
Agriculture (5)	19/21
Rural Development, Biotechnology, Specialty Crops & Foreign Agriculture	
Appropriations (13)	21/29
Commerce, Justice, Science, and Related Agencies	
Defense	
State, Foreign Operations, and Related Programs	
Financial Services and General Government	
Military Construction and Veterans Affairs	
Homeland Security	
Armed Services (5)	27/35
Air and Land Forces Committee	
Terrorism, Unconventional Threats and Capabilities	
Military Personnel	
Strategic Forces	
Readiness	
Budget (0)	16/21
Education & Labor (5)	17/23
Higher Education, Lifelong Learning, and Competitiveness	
Energy and Commerce (6)	23/31
Commerce, Trade & Consumer Protection	
Communications, Technology & the Internet	
Financial Services (6)	27/34
Domestic Monetary Policy and Technology	
International Monetary Policy and Trade	
Foreign Affairs (6)	18/26
Asia, the Pacific and the Global Environment	
Europe	
Africa and Global Health	
International Organizations, Human Rights, and Oversight	
Middle East & South Asia	
Western Hemisphere	
Terrorism, Nonproliferation, and Trade	
Homeland Security (6)	14/19
Intelligence, Information Sharing, and Terrorism Risk Assessment	
Economic Threats, Cybersecurity, and Science and Technology	
Emergency Communications, Preparedness, and Response	
Management, Investigations, and Oversight	
Intelligence (4)	8/12
Terrorism/HUMINT, Analysis & Counterintelligence	
Intelligence Community Management	
Technical & Tactical Intelligence	
Oversight	
Judiciary (5)	16/23
Immigration, Citizenship, Refugees, Border Security, and International Law	
Crime, Terrorism & Homeland Security	
Natural Resources (5)	21/27
Energy & Mineral Resources	
Oversight and Government Reform (8)	17/22
National Security and Foreign Affairs	
Science and Technology (4)	17/23
Energy and Environment	
Space and Aeronautics	
Small Business (4)	11/15
Finance & Tax	
Transportation & Infrastructure (6)	26/33
Aviation	
Coast Guard & Maritime Transportation	
Veterans' Affairs (3)	11/15
Ways and Means (6)	15/22
Trade	
TOTAL HOUSE MEMBERSHIP:	193/242

SOURCE: U.S. House of Representatives, http://house.gov

STAFFING   Congressional reformers in the 1970s realized that the small legislative support staffs made Congress dependent on the executive branch for information. Consequently, they *expanded congressional staffs tremendously during and after Vietnam*. Individual representatives and senators began to enjoy the presence of large **personal staffs**. **Committee staffs** of both the majority and minority parties, such as for the Senate Committee on Foreign Relations, also expanded tremendously. Congress also increased the size of its support agencies and began using them consistently. For example, the **General Accounting Office (GAO)**, the largest support agency, employing almost twenty thousand people, is the investigative arm of Congress and engages in oversight of the executive branch. The **Congressional Research Service (CRS)**, with almost 15,000 people, provides research and analysis on issues of importance to congressional committees and individual members of Congress. Finally, the **Congressional Budget Office (CBO)**, created in 1974 to provide financial and budgetary information and assessments, gives Congress an alternative to reliance on the executive's Office of Management and Budget. With the increase in staffing, members of Congress were no longer as dependent on the executive branch for information about foreign policy and world affairs.

Overall, these changes provided the foundation for members of Congress to become more active in the making of foreign policy. These changes greatly complicated the president's ability to control the agenda and enact his preferred policies, as they empowered a wider range of members within committees and on the chamber floors. They also made bipartisanship more difficult. Consequently, not only have presidents had greater difficulty enacting their priorities, but the changed issue agenda reflecting the increased importance of intermestic issues has increased the willingness of members of Congress to challenge the president on foreign affairs (Marshall and Prins 2002).

Congress after the Cold War

The end of the cold war in 1989 provided further *incentives for continued congressional reassertion.* The collapse of the Soviet Union and the decline of communism dramatically reduced the level of threat facing the country. As one observer aptly commented, "It's like Las Vegas; when you reduce the size of the ante, more people come to the table" (quoted in *Congressional Quarterly Almanac* 1999:9). Moreover, intermestic issues and increasing constituency pressures have led to greater congressional challenges to presidential leadership on a variety of issues. Also, the cost or risk of challenging the president diminished because of a decline in public interest in international matters (Linday 2000). In short, lack of consensus on foreign policy, more diffuse international security risks, and an interdependent world economy combined to provide greater incentive and opportunity for members of Congress to be less deferential in the post–cold war era.

Several consequences stem from these characteristics. First, **partisanship** on foreign policy increased substantially. Indeed, partisan differences have increased in significance and impact across an array of issues. Partisanship now dramatically affects party leaders, the voting of rank-and-file members on foreign and defense policy issues, and the behavior of individual members of Congress who are especially attentive to foreign policy. In the past several years, for example, President Obama has contended with a poisonous climate of partisanship and polarization that has led to challenges and confrontations from Republicans on many foreign policy issues, a pattern unlikely to change even after his successful reelection campaign in 2012 (see Mann and Ornstein 2012).

Studies show that congressional partisanship has affected general levels of congressional activity and assertiveness in the post–World War II era, and has had an impact on presidential decisions to use force, negotiate executive agreements and treaties, enact economic sanctions, and provide food assistance, among other things (e.g., Carter and Scott 2009; DeLaet and Scott 2006; Howell and Pevehouse 2007; Martin 2000; Scott and Carter 2002; Smith 1994). As David Rohde (1994:99) has argued, "Congress has grown increasingly assertive in foreign and defense policy and . . . conflict over these issues has grown increasingly partisan." Which party controls Congress and the White House is more significant than ever, as both partisanship and the lack of consensus makes foreign policy more like politics as usual.

As in post-Vietnam period, the White House faced a series of challenges across a whole host of foreign policy issue areas, major and minor. For example, in the face of divided government, the Clinton administration watched four major international agreements fall to congressional, often partisan, opposition (the comprehensive test ban, land mines, global warming, and international criminal court agreements). Similarly, its attempts to prioritize democracy promotion and sustainable development as foreign policy goals and its strategy for coping with ethnic conflict and instability were dismantled by Congress. Efforts to strengthen the ability of international organizations such as the United Nations and the International Monetary Fund to respond to global problems were resisted and restricted, and the administration was forced to accept, despite its strenuous opposition, the restructuring of the foreign agencies, increased defense spending, covert assistance to promote regime change in Iraq, strengthened primary and secondary sanctions on Cuba, and a host of other issues driven by Congress (e.g., Scott 1998).

Prior to September 11, 2001, Congress appeared poised to provide the administration of George W. Bush with similar challenges on issues ranging from the United Nations to defense strategy and spending to national missile defense and arms control to trade, especially after Vermont senator Jim Jeffords left the Republican Party and made the Democrats the majority in the Senate. Then terrorists struck New York City and Washington, D.C., and the ensuing state of emergency generated a dramatic shift, and the level of threat and public concern with international affairs surged. Congress almost immediately rallied behind the White House in the face of this crisis. For example, as James Lindsay (2003) describes, members of the president's party dropped their opposition to repaying American dues to the United Nations, while Democrats gave in to the president's position on national missile defense without a fight. Congress also cooperated or acquiesced in granting sweeping new powers for homeland security and intelligence operations and a series of additional issues. Most important, Congress granted broad authorization to the president to use force, first in Afghanistan in 2001, and then, in a 2002 vote, in Iraq as well. These two congressional authorizations were not as sweeping as the original administration requests, but they were as much "blank checks" as the Gulf of Tonkin Resolution had been in 1964 (Kassop 2003). It appeared, at least initially, that the pendulum of legislative–executive power had swung back toward the White House.

However, as the 9/11 attacks receded into the past, and as the costly American military intervention into Iraq ground on with little signs of ending, the state of emergency and concomitant threat context relaxed, and Congress became increasingly restless on a variety of international issues including homeland security, intelligence reform, trade, and others. In 2005 and 2006, congressional Democrats were increasingly bold in their opposition to the administration, and even some Republicans began to join in (e.g., John Warner and Richard Lugar on new strategies and benchmarks for the Iraq war; John McCain on a ban on torture; see Broder 2005; Hulse 2005). Other challenges on issues such as immigration also ensued, leading one observer to flatly declare the "the Bush era . . . isn't over. . . . But the 9-11 era is" (Rozen 2005). Such sentiments grew significantly stronger when the Democratic Party won majorities in both chambers of Congress in the 2006 mid-term elections in what was widely understood as a referendum on the Bush administration's foreign policy (see Chapter 12). Assertiveness across a whole range of foreign policy issues ensued.

The post-Vietnam patterns continued into the Obama administration as well. Divided government and partisanship proved good predictors of legislative–executive relations as Democrats in Congress adopted a more supportive approach to the Obama administration. On the other hand, Republicans, now out of the White House and in the minority for the 111th Congress (2009–2010), seemingly took every opportunity to criticize and attack the democratic administration's foreign policy. Virtually every Republican in both chambers of Congress voted in 2009 against Obama's economic plans for restoring confidence in the financial system (although the original proposal came under President Bush), for stimulating the economy, and for trying to create new regulations to stabilize the financial and economic system. The Republican-led House of Representatives risked an American default on its debt obligations, and downgraded credit status in the international markets when it refused to raise the U.S. debt ceiling (a common step taken by every administration since Jimmy Carter) unless the Obama administration acceded to its budget preferences. Such partisan battles were common in virtually every issue area.

A few other examples illustrate the point. Driven by local economic pressures, Congress defied the president and inserted a "buy American" clause into the 2009 economic stimulus plan, causing controversy among American trade partners. The administration was able only to persuade Congress to water down, not remove the clause. The administration's defense budget was attacked by members from both parties, and even democrats sought to protect a number of weapons systems from being eliminated or have their funding reduced, including the F-22 fighter. Administration plans to revive the Comprehensive Test Ban Treaty and to eliminate trade restrictions to improve relations with Russia also ran afoul of congressional opposition (Sestanovich 2009). And, Obama's efforts to force progress in Israeli–Palestinian negotiations by pressuring Israel to curtail its settlements in the West Bank increasingly drew opposition from concerned members of Congress. Democrats Gary Ackerman and Anthony Wiener of New York and Howard Berman of California publicly cautioned against too much pressure (Richter and Boudreaux 2009).

After the November 2010 elections, the Republican gained the majority in the House of Representatives, and reduced the Democrat majority down to a 53–47 advantage. In the ensuing 112th Congress, foreign policy challenges from Congress, especially the House, ramped up. For example, President Obama was only narrowly able to secure approval of his "New START" nuclear arms control treaty with Russia by a 71–26 vote (67 votes were required) and then only after a lengthy debate and the addition of amendments to placate Republicans. The economy clearly dominated the agenda, to the point where Obama, the democrats, and the republicans fought constant partisan battles and were in constant "gridlock" over such issues as the economic recovery, the budget, and the debt—where the government almost shut down at one point (see Bohan, Sullivan, and Ferraro 2011). The partisanship was intensified by divided government, ideological differences, and political one-upmanship, all reinforced by congressional and presidential primaries and elections that culminated in November 2012.

The 2012 elections returned President Obama to a second term, extended the Democrat majority in the Senate by two seats to 55, and narrowed the Republican majority in the House by 8 seats (234–201). However, given the continuation of a divided Congress, with one chamber controlled by each party, partisan division and conflict continued to have an effect on legislative-executive relations. A good example was the confrontation between the White House and Congress over the raid on U.S. diplomatic facilities in Benghazi, Libya that killed the U.S. ambassador and three others. Republicans in Congress were aggressive in attacking the Obama administration on this matter during and after the election, and the House (which they controlled) initiated hearings on the matter to confront the President.

Summary: From Deference to Assertiveness

Another way to make sense of the complicated patterns our discussion has revealed is to understand that *there are at least two important dimensions that characterize congressional foreign policy behavior:* (1) Congress can be more or less active, engaging in much or little foreign policy-related activity; and (2) Congress can be more or less assertive, supporting or opposing a president's foreign policy and leadership. As Scott and Carter (2002:158–159) show, such a two-dimensional activity-assertiveness model posits *four models of congressional foreign policy behavior,* as shown in **Figure 10.3**:

1. a *"competitive Congress"* whose greater levels of both activity and assertiveness lead it to challenge the president for foreign policy influence, a pattern of behavior reflective of the idea of a resurgent Congress,

2. a *"disengaged Congress"* whose relative inactivity and compliance with presidential preferences reflect the acquiescent Congress more involved in domestic policy than foreign policy and more likely to defer to and support the president,

3. a *"supportive Congress"* whose greater activity is combined with less assertive behavior, indicating a Congress cooperating with the president to achieve foreign policy goals over which there is substantial consensus, and

4. a *"strategic Congress"* whose combination of less activity but greater assertiveness suggest a Congress that selects its battles carefully but is willing to challenge the president when it is interested (less active but more assertive).

Figure 10.3 Models of Congressional Foreign Policy Behavior

ASSERTIVENESS	ACTIVITY	
	More Active	*Less Active*
More Assertive	Co-Equal Congress	Strategic Congress
Less Assertive	Supportive Congress	Disengaged Congress

SOURCE: Adapted from James M. Scott and Ralph G. Carter, "Acting on the Hill: Congressional Assertiveness in U.S. Foreign Policy," *Congress and the Presidency*, 29 (Autumn 2002): 165.

These four models better reflect the range of congressional foreign policy behavior we have summarized in our previous discussion. In the context of the preceding discussion, this two-dimensional conception of congressional foreign policy behavior suggests that Congress has rarely been "disengaged" or acquiescent in the strict sense of being inactive and compliant, nor has it often been "competitive" or resurgent in the strict sense of being both active and assertive after Vietnam and especially in the post–cold war world. Instead, Congress *has shifted from a cold war model of a "supportive Congress" (that is, more active but less assertive) to a post-Vietnam "competitive Congress" (that is, active and assertive) to a post–cold war "strategic Congress" (that is, less active but more assertive)*—for national security and especially economic (and other intermestic) policies.

As Arthur Schlesinger, Jr. (1989) described it in *The Imperial Presidency*, the politics of legislative–executive relations in foreign policy has been characterized by a kind of **pendulum (or cyclical) effect** over the course of American history. In times of national emergency, particularly war, power tends to flow toward the president and the executive branch. During times of peace—that is, when conflict has subsided—power tends to flow back to Congress. In times of conflict the president's roles of commander in chief and chief executive give him control over the conduct of war. This fact is reinforced by the tendency of Congress to delegate extensive emergency powers to the president during wartime. Second, periods of perceived national emergency are also times when most Americans in government and society turn to the president and rally behind him and the exercise of "prerogative power" (see Chapter 3) as the key authority for addressing the gravity of the situation. The end of war and national emergency resulted in congressional reassertion of power. Hence, the president experiences greater constraints on his ability to exercise power in foreign policy.

CONGRESSIONAL BEHAVIOR IN FOUR POLICY AREAS

Now that we have examined the context and overall patterns of legislative–executive relations in foreign policy, we can better assess how the multiple congressional actors and paths of influence contribute to congressional activity and influence. *To do so, we will briefly examine four general issue areas to highlight the range of activity and influence Congress brings to bear on U.S. foreign policy:* (1) the war powers, (2) advice and consent, (3) the power to appropriate funds and to make laws, and (4) the power of oversight and investigation.

The War Powers

The use of American armed forces abroad has been the factor most responsible for the growth of presidential power and the straining of relations between Congress and the president. According to Louis Henkin (1987–1988:290), "There is no evidence that the framers contemplated any significant independent role—or authority—for the President as the Commander in chief when there was no war." Yet Congress has declared war just five times in American history, while presidents have committed military forces abroad in over 200 instances. Therefore, as discussed earlier, the president's power over questions of war has grown remarkably over time, particularly during times of conflict, reaching its peak during World War II and the cold war with military options in Korea, Vietnam, and elsewhere, all without declarations of war by Congress. Only after the bitter experience with the Vietnam War did Congress attempt to redress the imbalance, eventually overriding a veto by President Nixon to enact the War Powers Act.

The WPA was designed "to fulfill the intent of the framers of the Constitution of the United States and insure that the collective judgment of both the Congress and the President will apply to the introduction of United States Armed Forces" into conflict situations abroad. The WPA has three central requirements.

1. Presidential Consultation: According to the War Powers Act, "the President in every possible instance shall consult with Congress before introducing United States Armed Forces" into situations of conflict abroad and "after such introduction shall consult regularly with the Congress until" they have been removed from such situations.

2. Presidential Reporting: According to subsection 4(a) of the WPA, the president shall submit a report to Congress within forty-eight hours if, in the absence of a declaration of war, U.S. armed forces are introduced abroad under the following three situations:

   a. "into hostilities or into situations where imminent involvement in hostilities is clearly indicated by the circumstances,"

   b. "into the territory, airspace or waters of a foreign nation, while equipped for combat, except for deployments which relate solely to supply, replacement, repair, or training of such forces, and"

   c. "in numbers which substantially enlarge United States Armed Forces equipped for combat already located in a foreign nation."

   A report is required to describe the circumstances, the president's constitutional and legislative authority, and the estimated scope and duration of involvement. If U.S. armed forces remain in a situation of hostilities in accordance with subsection 4(a)(1), the president must continue to report to Congress at least every six months.

3. Congressional Action: If U.S. armed forces are introduced into a situation of hostilities as stipulated in subsection 4(a)(1), the president must terminate their involvement within sixty days unless Congress extends the deadline. The president can extend the deadline for an additional thirty days, if deemed necessary for the safe withdrawal of American troops. Congress may pass a "concurrent resolution" to terminate the military intervention earlier; this requires a simple majority in both chambers and is not subject to presidential veto. Second, Congress may pass a "joint resolution," signed by the president, to extend the deadline. Finally, Congress may do nothing, allowing the time limitation to take effect.

The WPA represented a major symbolic effort at congressional reassertion and complicates the president's ability to use force abroad. The War Powers Act does give Congress the potential to influence the president's decision to use troops abroad through the reporting requirement and its ability to terminate, modify, or approve military action if U.S. troops are committed. In this respect, the president must be cautious in deciding when, where, and how U.S. troops are to be committed (Howell and Pevehouse 2007). Indeed, according to David Auerswald and Peter Cowhey (1997:524), "the use of force after the act is significantly different than it was before the act," suggesting that its existence has changed the decisionmaking environment to encourage presidents (by provoking anticipated reactions) to be more selective in their decisions.

However, since 1973 the presidents have used U.S. armed forces abroad in numerous situations involving the WPA. In each case, the president initiated, formulated, and approved the use of the use of force with little or no consultation—only informing members of Congress after a decision has taken place given his role as commander in chief.

The first major test of the War Powers Act occurred when President Reagan deployed 1500 American troops in Beirut from September 1982 to March 1984 to promote stability in **Lebanon**. When Reagan sent U.S. troops (along with British, French, and Italian troops) to Beirut, he reported to Congress in accordance with the WPA. However, he also stated that there is no intention or expectation that U.S. Armed Forces will become involved in hostilities, thereby circumventing the time limitation and Congress's further participation. (U.S. Congress, House Committee on Foreign Affairs 1982). As the conflict in Beirut escalated and American troops were fired upon, a major debate ensued and members of Congress and the president appeared to be heading toward a constitutional crisis over the war-making power. But a legislative–executive compromise was negotiated in which Congress agreed to activate subsection 4(a)(1), indicating a situation of hostilities, by passing a joint resolution that the president would acknowledge by signing; in return the president received congressional support to use military troops in Lebanon for up to eighteen months. However, President Reagan issued a statement to accompany the signing of the resolution that effectively rejected the legitimacy of the War Powers Act (Reagan 1983)—which has become the norm.

The recent cases of Afghanistan and Iraq are also instructive. First, in both cases, the George W. Bush administration made the decision to use force with little involvement or consultation with Congress. In fact, in the Iraq case, the administration made the decision to use force much earlier than it publicly acknowledged, and made a number of efforts to conceal the choice from Congress and the public. Nevertheless, in both cases the president received broad congressional authorization for the use of force (although not as broad as the president wanted), nor was the War Powers Act acknowledged or invoked (Kassop 2003; Packer 2005; Woodward 2004).

Within three days of 9/11, on September 14, the House voted 420–1 and the Senate voted 98–0 in support of a **9/11 military force resolution**, initially submitted by President Bush, "That the president is authorized to use all necessary and appropriate force against those nations, organizations or persons he determines planned, authorized, committed or aided the terrorist attacks that occurred on Sept. 11 or harbored such organizations or persons, in order to prevent any future acts of international terrorism against the United States by such nations, organizations or persons." There was virtually no debate—a situation somewhat analogous to the 416–0 House vote and 88–2 Senate vote in favor of the 1964 Gulf of Tonkin Resolution.

In the more specific **Iraqi resolution**, Congress authorized the president to "use the Armed Forces of the United States as he determines to be necessary and appropriate to (1) defend the national security of the United States against the continuing threat posed by Iraq; and (2) enforce all relevant United Nations Security Council Resolutions." This resolution passed the House 296–133 and the Senate 77–23. Despite some symbolic but ultimately unsuccessful efforts to link these resolutions to the War Powers Act, Congress provided immediate and overwhelming support for the presidential authority to go to war in Afghanistan and Iraq.

In President Obama's decision to use force against Libya in support of the resistance to Moammar Ghaddafi's rule, for example, the administration did not bother to consult prior to the introduction of U.S. forces, and maintained that its briefings of members on the operations were sufficient in his role as commander in chief. In fact, the administration maintained that the WPA did not even apply because "U.S. operations do not involve sustained fighting or active exchanges of fire with hostile forces, nor do they involve U.S. ground troops" (Savage and Landler 2011). Despite complaints and efforts by Congress to force the administration to adhere to the 90-day clock and seek congressional approval, including a bipartisan resolution condemning the action passed by the House of Representatives, the administration continued its use of force. Even a lawsuit by Dennis Kucinich (D-OH) and nine other members did not succeed in persuading the administration to observe the WPA and the furor died down as the U.S. role shifted to less active efforts in the late summer of 2011.

In sum, the War Powers Act has given Congress the potential to play a more active role in the use of force abroad. The War Powers Act has been of major symbolic importance in promoting congressional reassertion in foreign policy and has served as a model for other legislation. The act is indicative of a more assertive Congress and a transformed political environment since Vietnam. It may even have changed the environment and impacted future decisions to use force. However, members of Congress have been extremely cautious in challenging presidential initiatives in so vital a matter even though presidents must be much more cautious today than in the cold war years.

Four factors account for congressional reluctance to challenge presidential freedom when military action is taken. First, the typical response to hostilities by most members of Congress and the public is to "rally round the flag" in support of the president—the September 11 attacks being the most obvious. Second, the lack of congressional "will," reinforced by ambiguity in the language of the War Powers Act, has allowed the president to minimize the reporting requirements and avoid triggering congressional action. Third, the War Powers applies only to the use of U.S. "armed forces" in a "situation of hostilities" or "in the territory of a foreign nation, while equipped for combat." These cases do not include "advisors," "reconnaissance missions," U.S. "military training maneuvers," or U.S. "covert paramilitary action," usually as defined by the president and the executive branch. Finally, as we discussed earlier, in 1983 the U.S. Supreme Court ruling in *Immigration and Naturalization Service v. Chadha* also weakened the WPA, calling the "congressional veto"—a critical means for exercising congressional influence—into question.

Advice on and Consent to Appointments and Treaties

The Senate has the constitutional authority to advise the president on and consent to his appointments and treaties. These are two areas in which senators possess power in foreign policy matters that members of the House of Representatives do not share, helping to account for the Senate's greater prestige and power within the Congress. These powers also give individual members opportunities to shape policy by giving them some influence over personnel, as well as opportunities to link **advice and consent** on appointments and treaties to other policy concerns.

With respect to presidential **appointments**, since World War II members of the Senate have tended to be hesitant to exercise this power aggressively (Franck and Weisband 1979; Johnson 1985, U.S. Congress, House Committee on Foreign Affairs 1982). *Two patterns have prevailed.* First, the Senate has tended to rubberstamp ambassadorships and presidential appointments to the executive branch, especially for lower-level appointments. For example, one recent study examined the ambassadorial appointments for the 100th Congress through the 104th and identified 618 total nominations, of which 564 (or 91 percent) were confirmed (Stack and Campbell 2003:30). However, not only have presidents taken longer to appoint personnel, as explained in Chapter 4, but the Senate confirmation process has become slower and more cumbersome over the years, often taking months (Ornstein and Donilon 2000). Second, partisanship has increasingly impacted the appointment process, so that some appointments (especially to the Supreme Court) result in political and partisan struggles. According to Stack and Campbell (2003:29), "some senators routinely take advantage of their leverage to foil presidential nominations if they consider the nominees are out of step with existing congressional majorities. Others regard advice and consent not as a mere formality but as an important constitutional weapon guarding the independence of Congress from the executive branch."

It is not unusual for at least one major presidential appointment to draw a great deal of attention and political controversy during a president's term of office. For example, President Jimmy Carter's initial appointment as director of central intelligence was Theodore Sorenson, who was heavily criticized by the political right and conservative members of Congress, and President Carter withdrew the nomination. President George H. W. Bush suffered a similar fate when his nomination of John Tower as secretary of defense was denied by a Senate vote. President Clinton appointed his National Security Advisor Anthony Lake to be DCI, only to accept his withdrawal under fierce Republican opposition. And George W. Bush had to resort to an unusual recess appointment to circumvent congressional opposition to John Bolton, his 2005 choice as U.N. ambassador.

Congressional impact can occur at different, and sometimes less visible, levels as well. The late Jesse Helms, a Republican senator from North Carolina was particularly active in the appointment process. As a member of the Committee on Foreign Relations, he held up and criticized many appointments made by presidents Reagan and the elder Bush for holding insufficiently conservative views. When Helms became chair of the Foreign Relations Committee in 1994, he successfully blocked several of President Clinton's appointments, engaging in "hostage-taking" by blocking an appointment "in order to extract concessions from the president" (Stack and Campbell 2003:29; see also Carter and Scott 2009) (see **A Closer Look** on Jesse Helms). Hence, whether members object to a particular individual, or seek to link appointments to other issues to gain leverage, the appointment process ensures the potential for their influence.

The general structure of international agreements has tended to provide advantages to the president. Since World War II, a large number of overseas commitments have been made by the United States—approximately 1,800 such agreements from 1789 to 2000—of which the vast majority came after 1945. However, while almost 2000 such agreements were in the form of formal **treaties,** subject to the advice and consent of the Senate, most of these commitments were **executive agreements**—not requiring Senatorial advice and consent. In fact, by the end of the century, more than 90 percent of the international agreements of the United States were in the form of executive agreements (O'Brien 2003). About the time of the Vietnam War, members of Congress became concerned with the proliferation of executive agreements.

In response, *Congress has tried four techniques in attempting to restore its advice-and-consent role in the agreement-making process.* First, Congress passed 1969 National Commitments Act and the 1972 Case Act, and required the president to report all agreements within sixty days of their completion to ensure that Congress was aware of the commitment and had a chance to review, and even reject it. Second, members of Congress have also tried—mostly unsuccessfully—to force the president to submit executive agreements to the Senate as treaties. Third, Congress has used the power of the purse in some cases, withholding funds necessary to implement executive agreements. Finally, Congress has tried to subject executive agreements to disapproval or approval, with limited success and the likelihood that such requirements may be unconstitutional.

A CLOSER LOOK

Jesse Helms Tackles The Foreign Affairs Agencies

In 1995, Senator **Jesse Helms,** Republican of North Carolina, became chairman of the Foreign Relations Committee and initiated a campaign to restructure the foreign affairs agencies of the United States government. Helms first raised the restructuring initiative in 1994, demanding the abolition of the Agency for International Development, the Arms Control and Disarmament Agency, and the U.S. Information Agency. That same year he also tried to freeze all assistant secretary of state nominations pending reorganization. Helms' campaign centered on a legislative proposal that called for the elimination of the three agencies noted above (whose functions would be merged into the State Department) and changes to streamline and centralize State Department. His committee completed its work on his "Foreign Relations Revitalization Act of 1995" in May and it was ready for the Senate floor in July 1995.

However, Helms' reform initiative met with opposition from the Clinton White House and the foreign policy agencies themselves. Faced with this determined resistance, Helms escalated his efforts. He halted business meetings of the Senate Foreign Relations Committee, blocked more than a dozen treaties and other international agreements, including the second Strategic Arms Reduction Treaty and the Chemical Weapons Convention, so they could not be voted on by the full Senate. Helms also froze State Department promotions and held up thirty ambassadorial nominations and one assistant secretary of state nomination.

A stalemate ensued. Lacking sixty votes to overcome a filibuster, Helms could not take his bill to the floor for a vote. The administration could not get its personnel

confirmed or its international agreements ratified because Helms would not allow them out of his committee. Months of bargaining followed. In August, Helms managed to obtain a personal meeting with the president, and he released a group of the nominees and a handful of minor treaties to the Senate floor in response. In December, a deal was reached in which Helms agreed to release eighteen ambassadorial nominations, several minor tax treaties, and both the START II arms control treaty and the Chemical Weapons Convention in return for action on his restructuring initiative. This deal collapsed in 1996 when the House of Representatives tried to link payment of American UN arrears to international family planning issues, prompting President Clinton to veto the bill in April.

After the 1996 election, Helms revived the initiative, offering the **Foreign Affairs Reform and Restructuring Act of 1997** and informing his colleagues and the administration that ambassadorial appointments and the Chemical Weapons Convention (CWC) would remain locked up in the Foreign Relations Committee until action on his bill was completed. As Helms later described it in a hearing on the initiative:

> I discussed this matter with the distinguished Ranking Member, Senator Biden, who readily agreed that it was essential that this be a bipartisan project. Thereby, we together sent the administration a clear message that there must be no repeat of the unsuccessful battles waged in 1995 and 1996 and to the credit of both the President and the Secretary of State, the administration came forward with a reform plan addressing many, though not all of my key concerns, and in the ensuing months Senator Biden and I,

along with our respective staffs, devoted dozens of hours to hammering out the final package. (U.S. Senate 1997:265–266).

In April 1997, the Senate ratified the CWC and the Clinton administration released a plan supporting the restructuring of the agencies. However, due to the linkage between the restructuring bill, the UN payments, and the family planning issue (driven chiefly by the House of Representatives), the Foreign Affairs Reform and Restructuring Act was placed on the backburner until the fall of 1998. In October of that year, the final version of the legislation

was finally signed by President Clinton. The bill eliminated the ACDA and the USIA, merging their operations into the State Department. USAID survived but was placed under the direct control of the secretary of state. Helms had achieved some but not all of his restructuring.

How do Jesse Helms' efforts illustrate the avenues open to members of Congress to try to influence foreign policy, and what are the consequences of such efforts?

SOURCE: Ralph G. Carter and James M. Scott, *Choosing to Lead: Understanding Congressional Foreign Policy Entrepreneurs* (Durham, NC: Duke University Press 2009).

When international agreements are negotiated as treaties, the Senate's role and influence has been much more significant. For example, President Carter was forced to accept two controversial reservations to the Panama Canal treaties that emphasized American security concerns to protect the canal to gain their passage in 1978. The Senate may also amend a treaty, which requires it to be renegotiated, or it may attach "reservations," "understandings," and "policy declarations" to guide future U.S. practices, both on the treaty and, in increasingly more cases, on other issues. Over time since the Vietnam War and the end of the cold war, members of the Senate have been increasingly likely to use treaty processes to shape policy in these ways (Auerswald and Maltzman 2003). Moreover, Senate opposition can be exercised simply by keeping treaties from ever coming to the floor for a final vote, which has been done repeatedly with international human rights covenants. As well, individual members in key positions can hold treaties hostage just as they do appointments. Presidents are aware of these possibilities, and usually attempt to incorporate congressional preferences during the negotiations to such actions. As Martin (2000) argues, the Senate thus impacts treaties in ways other than up-or-down votes.

Three recent examples provide good illustrations. The Clinton administration gained ratification of the 1997 Chemical Weapons Convention (CWC), but only after a difficult and highly charged political fight within the Senate. First, the treaty was bottled up in the Senate Foreign Relations Committee by Chairman Jesse Helms. Then, the White House had to reach out to Republican Majority Leader Trent Lott of Missouri. In exchange for his support, Lott demanded changes in the Conventional Forces in Europe (CFE) and Anti-Ballistic Missile treaties, while Helms continued to hold the treaty in the Foreign Relations Committee. In order to get the treaty to a vote, the Clinton administration granted virtually everything that Lott and Helms had demanded.

Just two years later, the administration had its Comprehensive Test Ban Treaty (CTBT) rejected outright, with Republicans uniting in opposition to the treaty. As Helms refused to release the treaty from committee, his fellow Republican senators Jon Kyl of Arizona and Paul

Coverdell of Georgia worked to build support against it. By October, confident that he had the votes to defeat the treaty, Lott decided it was time to give supporters a vote. Seeing that they lacked the necessary votes, Democrats, including Clinton, pleaded for a delay but were ignored. On October 13, the treaty was defeated 51–48 (DeLaet, Rowling and Scott 2007).

More recently, Barack Obama had to work hard to secure Senate approval of his "New START" nuclear arms control treaty with Russia. Negotiated over the first sixteen months of his presidency as part of the effort to "reset" U.S.-Russian relations, the treaty, which proposed to slash the two sides' nuclear arsenals by about 30 percent, stalled in the Senate after its completion. Opposition from Republican members blocked ratification until just before Christmas, when the administration and its supporters gained just enough Republican support to ensure ratification by agreeing to two amendments to the ratifying document (not the treaty itself) that stated the administration's support of limited missile-defense program and continued funding of nuclear weapons modernization programs (Sheridan and Branigin 2010).

The Senate has also been very active in the area of foreign economics and trade policy, often through its treaty powers, as these areas are more controversial and often have direct economic implications for their constituents (Destler 1994; Nollen and Quinn 1994). Since the creation of the original Bretton Woods system during World War II, Congress has mostly delegated authority on the regular rounds of negotiations to open trade, including the agreement to create the World Trade Organization in 1994. Another recent set of negotiations between Canada, Mexico, and the United States since the 1980s produced the North American Free Trade Agreement (NAFTA). In both cases, the Senate agreed to provide the executive branch and the president with what is referred to as **fast-track authority** to negotiate such international economic agreements, promising an up-or-down vote on the agreement. However, while Clinton obtained ratification of both of the above treaties, with free trade becoming increasingly controversial in the globalizing economy, he was unsuccessful in getting congressional support for additional fast-track authority for future international economic and trade agreements.

President George W. Bush finally succeeded in 2002—after the 9/11 attacks—in getting compromise legislation giving him fast-track authority, which he used to negotiate the Central American Free Trade Agreement, signed and ratified in August 2005. In October 2011, Barack Obama gained congressional approval of long-delayed free trade agreements with South Korea, Colombia, and Panama, but generated congressional opposition in 2012 to negotiations of further deals with countries in the Pacific Rim over protections for U.S. manufacturers in gaining contracts from the US government.

In sum, the Senate tends to approve most presidential appointments with little difficulty, though some are controversial and can become a political liability for presidents. Also, while Congress lacks influence in the making of executive agreements, the Senate must approve all treaties. Therefore, even though the president is generally preeminent, there are plenty of times when Congress, and even some of its individual members, plays an influential advice-and-consent role. Indeed, this is indicative of a Congress that has become more active in reasserting its role in foreign policy. And given the paradox of presidential power that has developed since the Vietnam War, it does not take many political controversies and failures to weaken the president's ability to govern, even in foreign policy.

The Power of the Purse and the Power to Make Laws

Although Congress has been only somewhat successful in increasing either its war power or its advice-and-consent role relative to the president, it is still a force to be reckoned with, especially given its control of the purse and its ability to make laws. This has always been the greatest strength of the legislative branch, guaranteeing it a role in the policymaking process for most foreign policy issues, especially in economics and other intermestic issues. The tendency has been for the president and executive branch to develop legislation and submit it to Congress, which then approves, modifies, or rejects it. In this respect, Congress reacts to the president's political agenda. Yet members of Congress can also rely on the legislative process and the annual budgetary cycles to initiate action on their preferences as well. Overall, congressional attempts to control policy by these means have intensified since the Vietnam War.

The main vehicles by which members of Congress access their legislative and spending powers are the legislative process and annual budget cycle. These very complex procedures "hard-wire" Congress into policymaking, providing regular opportunities for influence. Ultimately, since presidents cannot do what is not funded, they must eventually come to Congress. This is probably best illustrated by major political battles experienced by President Obama over economics from the time he entered office in 2009, which intensified after the republicans gained control of the House in 2011.

No simplified summary of either the legislative or budget process does justice to the complexity they exhibit. Legislation must wind its way from introduction through (often multiple) committees and subcommittees for hearings and markup, the floors of both chambers, and conference committees to reconcile the differences between House and Senate. While ample access points exist for members to engage in the legislative process, many chokepoints also exist for that reason where legislation can fail or be amended by another member with a different idea. The **legislative process** is also divided between an **authorization process** based in substantive committees that "authorize government programs" and their general amounts, and an **appropriation process** based in the appropriations committees that actually provide "money" for programs. For example, the foreign relations committees play the central role in authorizing the annual foreign aid and foreign operations bills, which fund the foreign affairs agencies and international assistance programs, but the appropriations committees engage in a second process to allocate actual funds to be spent. Both bills must make it through both processes. The legislative process is thus not only incredibly complex but also very political. Ultimately, bargaining and compromise are the keys to legislative success (Oleszek 2003; Sinclair 2000).

A good illustration of the opportunities provided by the legislative and budget processes is foreign assistance. *Congressional involvement in foreign-assistance policy has often been used by members of Congress to influence U.S. foreign policy in at least three ways:* (1) they can "earmark" foreign aid funds for specific countries or purposes (e.g., specifying a certain amount of aid to Pakistan, or to combat the global HIV/AIDS crisis); (2) they can attach conditions that govern the allocation of funds (e.g., progress on human rights); and (3) and they can attach reporting or certification requirements, forcing the executive branch to provide information to Congress. Congress has also leveraged its role in foreign assistance—as well as the broader power of the purse—to make occasional inroads on presidential dominance of the war-making power. For example, Congress cut off all U.S. military assistance to South Vietnam and Cambodia in February 1975, thereby accelerating the end of the war in April of that year. In 1975–1976, Congress halted an intervention into the Angolan Civil War, first rejecting a presidential request for funds and then banning all U.S. assistance for any activities directly or indirectly involving Angola. A third occurred in the 1980s and involved U.S. foreign policy toward Central America, where the administration sought to intervene in a number of indirect and covert ways into the civil wars in both El Salvador and Nicaragua. Congress resisted both initiatives, tying El Salvador aid to human rights progress and restricting, and eventually cutting off, aid to the Nicaraguan contras in 1985–1986. In the Nicaraguan case, President Reagan responded by circumventing Congress, thus triggering the Iran-Contra scandal and its constitutional implications.

At times, Congress has taken the initiative through its power of the purse in setting the public agenda and steering foreign policy. For example, U.S. government **human rights policy** is commonly attributed to the initiative taken by President Jimmy Carter, who was a major advocate of international human rights. However, U.S. support for human rights actually was initiated within Congress following Watergate and was manifested primarily through U.S. foreign assistance policy. Foreign assistance legislation was amended to prohibit security and developmental assistance to any country engaging in a consistent pattern of gross violations of internationally recognized human rights. Likewise, Congress's threatened passage of the 1985 antiapartheid bill over President Reagan's veto forced him to issue an executive order imposing sanctions on South Africa; in 1986, unsatisfied with the half-measures of the administration, Congress enacted the Comprehensive Anti-Apartheid Act over the president's veto.

The terrorist attacks of 9/11 initially increased congressional and bipartisan support for the president's foreign policy in general and antiterrorist policies in particular. Among other things, Congress was quick to pass legislation to authorize wars on terrorism, as discussed earlier, as well as to appropriate funds; to provide additional foreign assistance to countries supporting the antiterrorism war; and to pass an antiterrorism bill—called the USA Patriot Act—that expanded the government's ability to engage in domestic intelligence surveillance, detain suspects, and penetrate the banking and financial systems, Congress also dramatically increased spending on homeland security, defense, and intelligence.

Overall, the same patterns that have evolved with congressional involvement in foreign assistance also operate in other areas of foreign policy, such as national defense, energy, immigration, the environmental, and especially economics. First, members of Congress have taken a renewed interest in foreign policy issues since the Vietnam War. Second, while the president usually initiates policy and proposes legislation, the Congress shapes it. Sometimes major presidential initiatives are rejected outright; more often they are modified or fine-tuned by Congress. Third, Congress occasionally takes the initiative or replaces a presidential initiative with one of its own. Fourth, Congress has become increasingly involved in the details of the defense budget. Fifth, the more an issue is divorced from national security affairs or the use of force—such as economics—the greater the congressional attention, involvement, and influence (Manning 1977).

The Power of Oversight and Investigation

Congress also has the power to oversee and investigate public policy matters. As former House member Lee Hamilton, a Republican from Indiana and his coauthor noted, "Congress must do more than write the laws; it must make sure that the administration is carrying out those laws the way Congress intended" (Hamilton and Tama 2003:56). Linked directly to the legislative process, **congressional oversight** to ensure that the president and executive branch implement policies in accordance with the letter and intent of legislation can powerfully restrain presidential power and the foreign policy bureaucracy. This right represents, in fact, the ultimate means by which Congress may exercise its constitutional role. For if sufficient abuse of power is determined by Congress, the president ultimately may be "removed from office on impeachment for, and on conviction of, treason, bribery, or other high crimes and misdemeanors." *Hence, the power to investigate and engage in oversight is a potent tool that Congress has exercised.*

Since World War II, how has Congress employed its oversight powers? With respect to legislative oversight in foreign policy, *we can identify three main approaches by which Congress oversees the executive branch:* (1) regular oversight tied to the authorization and appropriation cycles, (2) event-driven oversight triggered by policy agendas and issues, and (3) crisis-driven oversight prompted by major policy failures and/or scandals. Together, this may result in a proactive, continuous supervision of the executive branch versus a more reactive, crisis-driven approach (Aberbach 1990; Deering 2003). Over time, members have relied on a mix of each kind, although there has been variation.

With each year's budget cycle, the foreign affairs committees and subcommittees in Congress engage in "regular oversight," holding hearings on agency programs and activities, considering agency budget requests, and collecting information from the executive branch and others. Greatly assisted by personal and committee staff, this oversight provides numerous opportunities for "watchdog" activities, and leads members to support, revise, or oppose policy activities across a wide range of organizations. More episodically, a particular member of Congress in a key position might organize an oversight hearing on an issue of particular interest, or one driven by current developments. In these instances of oversight, Congress gathers information on policy problems and administration responses or policies (or the lack thereof), which may lead to further action. For example, Pennsylvania Senator Arlen Specter, while still a Republican, promised to hold hearings on the controversial issue of domestic spying in 2006 as chair of the Senate Judiciary Committee. Such "event-driven oversight" is especially important to congressional foreign policy agendas.

When policy failures and/or scandals hit, Congress typically responds retrospectively by organizing hearing to investigate the causes of the failures. Such "crisis-driven oversight" occasionally leads to future legislative efforts to correct the problems identified. The most well-known examples of crisis-driven oversight includes the internal security investigations of the late 1940s and early 1950s, when a number of congressional committees were active in investigating communist influence in government, academia and education, the media, Hollywood, and other walks of American life. These increased from four investigations in 1945–1947 to fifty-one in 1953–1955. Following this, during the height of the cold war consensus, oversight lapsed. The general attitude toward oversight of the national security bureaucracy at the time was expressed by Senator Leverett Saltonstall, the ranking Republican on the Armed Services Committee: "It is not a question of reluctance on the part of the CIA officials to speak to us. Instead, it is a question of our reluctance, if you will, to seek information and knowledge on subjects which I personally, as a member of Congress and as a citizen, would rather not have" (quoted in Treverton 1990:74).

With the Vietnam War, crisis-driven investigative oversight increased. A major entry was the **Watergate hearings**—the congressional investigation of Nixon's presidential conduct which eventually produced three impeachment counts by the House Judiciary Committee and forced President Nixon's resignation. Additional investigations included two detailed House and Senate investigations of the intelligence community by the **Pike and Church committees** in 1975, which stimulated the creation of intelligence oversight committees within each chamber and triggered efforts at intelligence reform (Johnson 2005; Smist 1994). A decade later, the Reagan administration's efforts to covertly exchange arms for hostages with Iran and to fight a secret war to overthrow the Sandinista government in Nicaragua produced the Iran-Contra affair, which led to major investigations—the **Tower**

Commission, consisting of John Tower, Brent Scowcroft, and Edmund Muskie; then initial closed-door congressional investigations by the intelligence committees; and then a joint House and Senate congressional investigation that led to the **Iran-Contra hearings** and subsequent report by the joint congressional committee.

After the cold war, Congress investigated the U.S. relationship with Iraq during the 1980s during the elder Bush administration. Later, President Clinton experienced a number of congressional investigations during his term of office, including those of Whitewater, Clinton and Gore's 1996 presidential campaign and fund-raising efforts, and the Monica Lewinsky affair, which resulted in Clinton's impeachment and subsequent trial in the Senate in which the articles of impeachment were voted down. Like investigations of the past, the Clinton investigations were heavily partisan as a result of divided government—led by Republican members of Congress after the 1994 elections to damage a sitting Democrat in the White House.

Most recently, in the aftermath of the 9/11 attacks, the House and Senate intelligence committees held a joint investigation of the intelligence community's mistakes leading to the attacks, releasing a scathing report in December 2002 (U.S. Congress 2002). After it became clear that prewar claims of Iraq's possession of weapons of mass destruction were almost completely wrong, the Senate intelligence committee held another investigation, releasing its highly critical assessment in July 2004 (U.S. Senate Select Committee on Intelligence 2004). Further revelations of controversial activities by the intelligence community as part of the war on terror, including torture and an alleged secret assassination program, led to additional investigations in 2009 (Isenstadt 2009).

Two additional characteristics of oversight bear noting at this point: (1) reporting requirements and (2) the increasingly common use of special commissions to conduct investigations. **Reporting requirements** are a congressional mechanism that fuels oversight. As we noted earlier, such requirements extract information from the executive branch through regular reports and notifications, and special reports. Congress and the president increasingly collaborate to delegate oversight and investigative responsibilities to special, so-called "blue-ribbon" **commissions**, generally drawn from key experts and former policymakers from both political parties (Campbell 2001). Examples include the Rockefeller Commission, appointed by President Gerald Ford to investigate the intelligence community in the mid-1970s; the previously mentioned Tower Commission, the Aspin-Brown Commission, appointed in 1995 to investigate the intelligence community; the Hart-Rudman Commission, appointed in 1999 to study U.S. national security; and the Kean and Silberman-Robb commissions, appointed after 9/11 to investigate the attacks and the intelligence on weapons of mass destruction in Iraq, respectively.

CONGRESS AND THE POLITICS OF FOREIGN POLICY

To what extent is Congress a force to be reckoned with in the making of contemporary U.S. foreign policy? No simple answer or single relationship prevails today between the legislative and executive branches in the making of U.S. foreign policy. Clearly, as we discussed earlier in the chapter, interbranch politics in foreign policy have been fluid and dynamic, with neither Congress nor the president always predominant, especially since the collapse of the cold war consensus. Four patterns or models are likely: a competitive Congress, a disengaged Congress, a supportive Congress, and a strategic Congress (review Figure 10.3). While Congress was more supportive during the cold war years, all four models are likely to operate in the post-Vietnam and post–cold war era, especially a more strategic Congress. *Which model prevails is dependent on four important factors:*

1. the type of issue involved,

2. Congress's tendency to be a reactive body,

3. Congress's nature as the ultimate political institution, and

4. divided government as increasingly the norm.

First, the type of issue affects legislative–executive relations (Rosati 1984). The more an issue involves questions of war, the more likely it is that the president will continue to enjoy disproportionate influence in the making of policy, while the more an issue becomes divorced from the use of force, the more likely it is that Congress will play an active and influential role in the policymaking process. Second, Congress tends to be a reactive body. The president usually initiates foreign policy, and the executive branch actually implements it. Although there are exceptions, when Congress becomes involved in foreign policy, it tends to be in reaction to presidential initiatives and policies pursued by the executive branch. Third, members of Congress are "political animals" who are preoccupied with their institutional status and power, their electoral security, and how they are perceived within and beyond the Washington beltway. They tend to be driven by electoral concerns and are constantly soliciting funds from private contributors for reelection campaigns (Fenno 1978; Mayhew 1974).

Finally, as we discussed in Chapter 3, divided government can be an important factor, especially in light of the increasing role of partisanship and polarization. **Divided government** occurs when the Congress and presidency are controlled by different political parties, increasing the likelihood for interbranch disagreement and conflict (review Table 3.1). The existence of divided government is consequential because members of the party in opposition to the president can exercise greater control within Congress as a result of their majority status. This gives the opposition party the ability to dominate the organization of Congress—in leadership positions (such as Speaker of the House and Senate majority leader), as chairs of committees and subcommittees, and with majority representation on each and every committee and subcommittee.

Hence, President Bill Clinton, a Democrat, had to deal with a Congress that was dominated by Republicans; President George W. Bush had to deal with divided government in the first two and last two years of his presidency; and President Barack Obama faced a partially divided but heavily partisan Congress (with the House of Representatives in Republican hands) after the 2010 midterm elections. Unlike the 1950s and 1960s, which were times of bipartisanship and a cold war consensus—minimizing the impact of divided government in the making of foreign policy—divided government since Vietnam has been much more prone to promote conflict with the collapse of bipartisanship and the anticommunist consensus, reinforced by differing views over the free market ethos (Fiorina 1996; Mann and Ornstein 2012; Mayhew 1991).

How might the complex politics of legislative–executive relations evolve in the future? Three principal elements support the continuation of an active, though sporadic, congressional role in the foreign policymaking process. First, Congress has experienced institutional changes that were instrumental in allowing its reassertion of influence in foreign policy. These changes are not temporary but have been institutionalized in a more bureaucratic environment. Furthermore, major membership turnover—which has the potential to alter Congress as an institution—is difficult to achieve in a short period of time given the high reelection rates of incumbents and the large number of "safe seats." Moreover, the differences in the strength of each major party in each chamber is so small that the switch of only a few seats from one party to another following an election can produce different party control in the House and/or the Senate, creating considerable uncertainty for the future of divided government, presidential power, and majority coalitions. In this sense, the outcome of future congressional elections is both uncertain and likely to be potentially quite significant.

Second, changes in the domestic environment since the cold war have prompted and reinforced congressional activism in foreign affairs. The cold war consensus that fueled bipartisanship and the imperial presidency has been replaced by competing policy perspectives and greater diversity in domestic politics, which constrains presidential power while strengthening Congress's role in foreign policy. The 9/11 attacks and the war on terrorism do not seem to have produced a new foreign policy consensus to replace the anticommunist consensus of the cold war years, nor has the Great Recession reinforced the simple free market and free trade orientation for promoting economic recovery and growth.

Finally, changes in the international environment have affected the foreign policy agenda in ways that should ensure congressional involvement. The international system has become more complex since the 1950s, when most Americans saw the world divided between two superpowers and their opposing forces. A more complex international environment has provided the setting for America's failure in Vietnam and the shattering of the cold war consensus in domestic politics. This has been reinforced by the demise of the Soviet empire and the changes taking place in Eastern Europe. This has elevated what were once considered "low" policy issues, such as international economics, to the top of the contemporary foreign policy agenda—intermestic issues that members of Congress traditionally influence—even with the growing importance of terrorism as an issue.

Although institutional changes in Congress, changes in the domestic environment, and changes in the international environment and foreign policy agenda combine to ensure a prominent role for Congress in the future conduct of U.S. foreign policy, congressional dominance is unlikely. At the same time, however, the days of presidential supremacy in most areas of foreign policy have passed. Unless a global calamity occurs that creates the perception of a chronic state of national emergency for the United States, ushering in a new period of legislative–executive relations, considerable congressional involvement and influence will continue for the foreseeable future regardless of who is president and what party is in power.

SUGGESTED SOURCES FOR MORE INFORMATION

Blechman, Barry. (1990) *The Politics of National Security: Congress and U.S. Defense Policy.* New York: Oxford University Press. A good analysis of the congressional role in both structural and strategic defense policy.

Bohan, Caren, Andy Sullivan, and Thomas Ferraro. (2011) "Special Report: How Washington Took the U.S. to the Brink," *Reuters* (August 4). Detailed analysis of the confrontational politics between President Obama and Congress, democrats and republicans, over the budget battle of 2011.

Campbell, Colton C., Nicol C. Rae, and John F. Stack, Jr. (2003) *Congress and the Politics of Foreign Policy.* Upper Saddle River, N.J.: Prentice Hall, 2003. Good overview of the politics and processes of congressional foreign policymaking.

Carter, Ralph G., and James M. Scott. (2009) *Choosing to Lead: Understanding Congressional Foreign Policy Entrepreneurs.* Durham, NC: Duke University Press.

Fisher, Louis. (2004) *Presidential War Power.* Manhattan: University Press of Kansas. A good, recent discussion of constitutional war powers.

Franck, Thomas M., and Edward Weisband. (1979) *Foreign Policy by Congress.* New York: Oxford University Press. Classic analysis of the resurgent Congress of the 1970s.

Hersman, Rebecca K. C. (2000) *Friends and Foes: How Congress and the President Really Make Foreign Policy.* Washington, D.C.: Brookings Institution. Excellent analysis of the less-formal roles and influence of Congress.

Howell, William G, and Jon C. Pevehouse. (2007) *While Dangers Gather: Congressional Checks on Presidential War Powers.* Princeton: Princeton University Press.

Johnson, Robert David. (2006) *Congress and the Cold War.* New York: Cambridge University Press. An excellent examination of the role and influence of Congress during the height of the cold war.

Lindsay, James M. (1994) *Congress and the Politics of U.S. Foreign Policy.* Baltimore: Johns Hopkins University Press. Good overview of the legislative and nonlegislative activities of Congress.

Mann Thomas E., ed. (1990b) *A Question of Balance: The President, the Congress and Foreign Policy.* Washington, D.C.: Brookings Institution Press. An excellent overview of the contemporary legislative–executive relationship in foreign policy.

Mann, Thomas E., and Norman J. Ornstein. (2012). *It's Even Worse Than It Looks: How the American Constitutional System Collided With the New Politics of Extremism.* New York: Basic Books. Excellent analysis of the increasing polarization and partisanship in both parties in Congress.

Martin, Lisa. (2000) *Democratic Commitments: Legislatures and International Cooperation.* Princeton, NJ: Princeton University Press. An insightful analysis of the foreign policy impact of legislatures in general and the U.S. Congress in particular.

Ripley, Randall B., and James M. Lindsay. (1993) *Congress Resurgent: Foreign and Defense Policy on Capitol Hill.* Ann Arbor: University of Michigan Press. An excellent collection examining the dynamics of congressional foreign policy roles and influence.

KEY CONCEPTS

advice and consent	executive privilege
anticipated reactions	fast-track authority
appointments	implied consent
appropriation process	interbranch politics
authorization process	invitation to struggle
bipartisanship	judicial review
budget cycle	legislative process
congressional avenues of influence	McCarthyism
congressional oversight	partisanship
congressional reassertion	pendulum (or cyclical) effect
Constitution	political questions
divided government	separate institutions sharing power
executive agreements	zone of twilight

OTHER KEY TERMS

9/11 military force resolution	Jesse Helms
Bricker Amendment	Joseph McCarthy
commissions	Lebanon
committee staffs	personal staffs
Congressional Budget Office (CBO)	Pike and Church committees
Congressional Research Service (CRS)	reporting requirements
Foreign Affairs Reform and	roll call votes
Restructuring Act of 1997	Senate Foreign Relations
General Accounting Office (GAO)	Committee
Gulf of Tonkin Resolution	southern Democrats
human rights policy	treaties
Iran-Contra hearings	voice votes
Iraq resolution	War Powers Act
J. William Fulbright	Watergate hearings

THE SOCIETY AND DOMESTIC POLITICS

Part III examines how the larger society and domestic politics affect the government and the policymaking process. Chapter 11 discusses the role of the public and citizens' beliefs in foreign policy. Chapter 12 discusses political participation and group politics. Chapter 13 discusses the role of the media and the communications process.

. . .

Caitlin Mirra/Shutterstock

THE VIETNAM MEMORIAL, WASHINGTON DC. KNOWN AS "THE WALL," IT LISTS THE
NAMES OF THE 58,249 WHO DIED IN CHRONOLOGICAL ORDER.

THE PUBLIC AND ITS BELIEFS

Conventional wisdom tends to dismiss the public and its beliefs when it comes to influence on U.S. foreign policy and policymakers. Ultimately, however, what the American people believe and how they behave sets the social context and domestic political boundaries within which the government and the policymaking process must operate. This chapter focuses on the public's beliefs about the world and its significance in foreign policy, while Chapters 12 and 13 concentrate on the public's participation in the political process through group politics and the role of the media in the politics of foreign policy. *In this chapter we address the following questions:* What is the traditional wisdom and more current understanding about the role of the public in the making of U.S. foreign policy? What are the differences among public opinion, political ideology, and political culture? How does each type of belief impact the making of U.S. foreign policy? Examination of the public and its views provides a crucial foundation for understanding presidential governance, continuity and change, and the tensions between national security and democracy in the making of U.S. foreign policy.

THE IMPACT OF THE PUBLIC

Until relatively recently, policymakers, observers, and academics shared a consensus on the role of public opinion that tended to minimize its importance. However, after the Vietnam War a new consensus began to form that afforded more importance and attention to its role.

The Traditional Wisdom

According to the traditional wisdom, it does not matter what the public thinks about foreign policy issues, because it has little impact on the government and the policymaking process. This provides political leaders, especially the president, a great degree of freedom of action in foreign policymaking. Often characterized as the "Almond-Lippman Consensus," after Gabriel Almond and Walter Lippman, two early advocates of this view, this conventional wisdom allowed most observers of U.S. foreign policy to focus on government policymakers and institutions in explaining how U.S. foreign policy is made, while ignoring the public and much of society (Almond 1960; Cohen 1973; Lippmann 1922).

The **Almond-Lippmann consensus** concluded that public opinion was volatile, unstructured, and of little significance to foreign policy. As Ole Holsti (1992:442) summarized, *the consensus view centered on three major propositions:*

1. public opinion is highly volatile and thus it provides dubious foundations for a sound foreign policy,

2. public attitudes on foreign affairs are so lacking in structure and coherence that they might best be described as "nonattitudes," and

3. public opinion has a very limited impact on the conduct of foreign policy.

Growing out of the height of the cold war, this view continues to be held by many observers of U.S. foreign policy, as well as by much of the general public.

This traditional view leads to a harsh conclusion about American democracy, and about the tension between the demands of national security and democratic practice. If the public role is minimal and the public is responsive to and easily manipulated by political leaders, then U.S. foreign policymaking is not as democratic as it may seem. Many observers and policymakers throughout American history, in fact, have held an **elitist view of the public** and foreign policymaking, arguing that policymakers should be distanced from the public.

As with any stereotype, this traditional picture of the public holds some truth. Much of the public is uninformed, fickle, and responsive to established leaders. These characteristics often have given the president great flexibility in governing foreign policy and have often allowed the demands of national security to prevail over the demands of democracy. However, since the Vietnam War, this conventional wisdom has proven less accurate.

A More Complex and Consequential Public

As Leslie Gelb (1972:461) argued as early as 1972,

> "academicians and public-opinion experts have helped to perpetuate the myth in their own way by 'demonstrating' that foreign policy simply is not a salient issue to the voter and that whatever the president says and does goes, [while] official silence on the subject prevails." [But presidents have] "known better. Citizens may not single out national security affairs as the basis for their votes—although war and peace issues often are so mentioned—but the security area inevitably plays an

important part in determining their overall impression of how the President is doing his job. Moreover, communication leaders and 'elites' judge the President's performance with regard to foreign policy, and the mood which they convey to the public affects public appraisals of the man in the White House."

Hence for Gelb, "American public opinion was the essential domino" affecting U.S. foreign policy in Vietnam.

Spurred by views such as these, a growing number of observers of U.S. foreign policy have challenged the conventional wisdom of the Almond-Lippmann consensus. For example, some studies have indicated that the opinions of the mass public on foreign policy are more stable and structured than the Almond-Lippman consensus suggested, especially when it comes to more general foreign policy opinion (such as preferences for internationalism or opinions on the appropriate uses of force) rather than views on very specific issues that require detailed information. Other studies have concluded that policy generally falls in line with broad public views, and typically shifts in the direction of changes in public views; thus, policy is more responsive to opinion than the Almond-Lippmann consensus indicated. Also, increasingly broad agreement exists that public opinion generates powerful constraints on the range of policy options available to decisionmakers. Finally, studies indicate that greater intensity of opinion leads to tighter links between opinion and specific policy choices (see Holsti, 2004; Jentleson 1992; Page and Shapiro 1992; Popkin 1991).

Unraveling the role of the public and its beliefs in the making of U.S. foreign policy is not a simple task. Nevertheless, ***three major points lend support to the new consensus and indicate that the traditional wisdom is simplistic and incomplete***. First, the public holds different types of beliefs, which include public opinion (the most specific), political ideology (broader values and ideas), and political culture (the broadest orientations about values and norms about society, government, American self-image, and national style abroad). Second, different types of "publics" exist: The most common breakdown is between the elite and mass publics. Finally, the public exercises influence through a number of different behaviors: directly through polls, through participation in elections and group politics, and most indirectly, through **political socialization** (the informal process of human interaction by which Americans acquire their political beliefs, for example, from parents, schools, peers, and media).

The traditional wisdom tends to focus predominantly on public opinion. This emphasis places attention on the level of influence that the specific opinions of the mass public have directly on policymakers, predominantly through the impact of polls. Yet the traditional view typically ignores the important role of the elite public, political ideology and culture, and the other ways in which the public influences national politics and the governmental policymaking process. American political culture sets the broad context within which the politics of U.S. foreign policy operates. The ideological beliefs of Americans further narrow what is possible and probable within domestic politics and the policymaking process. Finally, public opinion affects the foreign policy process as it fluctuates within the confines of American political culture and ideology.

PUBLIC OPINION

To assess the role of public opinion one must be clear concerning the type of beliefs that opinions represent, the type of public most involved, and the type of influence most likely to be expressed. We begin with a discussion of the difference between elite and mass publics.

Elite and Mass Publics

Typically, when people discuss the public, they are referring to all Americans. It is easy to dismiss the public as an inconsequential actor in foreign policy at this level. The traditional wisdom, however, is misleading when it treats the public as a single, homogeneous entity. The United States is a complex and diverse society of over 300 million people. Certainly, not all Americans are inconsequential in American politics and the making of U.S. foreign policy. There are, in fact, *at least two basic types of publics:* (1) the elite public and (2) the mass public.

The **elite public**—a relatively small portion of the population with the means and the interest to participate in and shape politics—*may be distilled further into two general groupings:* opinion leaders and the attentive public. **Opinion leaders** are "all members of the society who occupy positions which enable them regularly to transmit, either locally or nationally, opinions about any issue to unknown persons outside of their occupational field or about more than one class of issues to unknown professional colleagues" (Rosenau 1961:45). Opinion leaders generally are the people who are most informed about national and international affairs and whose ideas and views tend to be communicated broadly. Although a very small percentage (depending on the issue), opinion leaders consist of people in various leadership positions, such as major governmental and business leaders, well-known journalists, established professors and professionals, and other prominent individuals from different walks of life. This is not to say that the information and views they hold are correct; rather, it is that their understanding of the world tends to be more readily communicated to other members of society. In other words, opinion leaders tend to have great visibility in American society, and their views usually are considered more credible and legitimate by other members of society.

The **attentive public** includes people who are also relatively attentive and informed about national and international affairs but whose views are not as widely disseminated as those of opinion leaders. The size of the attentive public varies from issue to issue. For the most visible issues, the attentive public may be as large as one-fourth of the entire public. For most issues that do not receive wide media coverage, the attentive public may represent less than 10 percent of the population. The attentive public tends to be invisible at the national and community levels, but among their peers they may act as opinion leaders. Thus, it is often said that the attentive public acts as local mediators between opinion leaders and the mass public.

Most Americans are not part of the elite public but of the mass public. The **mass public** is the segment of the American population emphasized by the traditional wisdom. Although the number varies, at least two-thirds to three-fourths of Americans form the mass public for most issues. Those within the mass public tend to have little interest in national and international affairs. Only those issues that make it to the front page of the newspaper and receive considerable media play gain the attention of the mass public, and then usually only briefly. Therefore, the mass public tends to be poorly informed about national and international affairs.

Because the mass public includes most Americans, there is obviously tremendous variation in the level of interest and information within this segment of the population. Some Americans, maybe as many as 20 percent, have virtually no interest in public affairs or limited access to information and have been labeled "chronic know-nothings." Others may be more attentive and better informed about foreign policy issues. Within this broad range are most Americans who generally demonstrate little interest but acquire some information about national and international affairs through upbringing, education, and the media (Bennett 1996; Neuman 1986).

Two key characteristics account for the differing levels of interest and information about national and international affairs between the elite and the mass publics: level of education and socioeconomic class. The more educated an individual, the more likely that he or she will be interested in, and informed about, national and international affairs. There is no simple educational threshold beyond which someone within the mass public becomes part of the elite public, for it varies with the times and the individual. Sixty years ago a high school education (as well as life experience) was likely to provide a stronger base of information than an undergraduate degree does today. Now, the elite public are likely to have at least an undergraduate, and often a graduate, university degree.

The second important factor in differentiating among types of publics is socioeconomic class. Although Americans commonly think they are all one large middle class, definite differences exist within American society in wealth, occupation, and status. Individuals raised in upper-middle-class or upper-class families and environments are the people most likely to become interested and informed about national and international affairs. Clearly, socioeconomic class and level of education are closely related. The higher the class background, the more likely one will go to college and pursue a graduate degree; moreover, the higher the level of education achieved, the more likely one will acquire more wealth, a professional occupation, and higher status within society. High levels of socioeconomic status and education not only reinforce each other and produce individuals with high levels of interest and information about national and international affairs but also help to provide the analytical and communication skills that tend to separate the elite public from the mass public.

Major Patterns in Public Opinion

Public opinion refers to the attitudes held by Americans generally toward *specific* issues and topics, expressed primarily through polls and periodically through voting. Hence, we are concerned predominantly with the role of the mass public. Public opinion includes views held by the elite public as well, but it represents no more than a small minority of Americans. *Three major patterns characterize American public opinion.* With respect to particular issues and developments in international affairs, public opinion tends to be (1) inattentive, (2) uninformed, and (3) volatile. These traits support the traditional understanding of the nature of public opinion. However, this fact does not foreclose public opinion from influencing domestic politics and the policymaking process.

First, public opinion represents views expressed by Americans who, for the most part, are inattentive—that is, they have little interest in the details of national and international affairs. Although most Americans are exposed to a great deal of information about national and international affairs through the mass media, few Americans take advantage of the available information. For example, only three of the fifty best-selling magazines— *Time, Newsweek,* and *U.S. News & World Report*—emphasize national and/or international affairs. Clearly, most Americans who try to acquire information beyond television, radio, and the local newspaper by subscribing to magazines are interested in things other than politics: entertainment, travel, household, fashion, sex, sports and recreation, mechanics, family matters, and more. The availability and increasing use of the Internet has reinforced these trends for the most part.

This limited interest in national and international affairs produces and reinforces the second major pattern: most Americans are relatively uninformed about national and international affairs. The mass public acquires little information about the political world and much of the information it does acquire tends to be simplistic and often inaccurate. For example, a poll was taken in 1964 which revealed that 25 percent of all Americans had never heard of the war in Vietnam; 28 percent did not know that mainland China was communist; 29 percent were unaware that another Chinese government existed on the island of Taiwan; and 54 percent had never heard of Mao Zedong, chairman of the Communist party of the People's Republic of China. During the height of the cold war in the early 1960s, barely more than half of Americans polled could describe the meaning of cold war in a reasonably correct fashion. Surveys of American geographical knowledge at the time demonstrated that only 65 percent of people could point out England on a map of Europe and only 60 percent could show Brazil's position in South America, while less than one-third of the respondents could locate most other countries correctly (Erskine 1962, 1963).

Two decades later, little appeared to change. A survey in 1988 found that with regard to U.S. foreign policy in Central America—a salient national security issue when the Reagan administration's secret Contra war was exposed during the Iran-Contra episode—only half of all Americans knew that the Sandinistas and Contras had been fighting. Furthermore, a majority of Americans incorrectly believed that the U.S. government was supporting the guerrillas in El Salvador and the government in Nicaragua. During the same year, one in three Americans could not name a single member of NATO, whereas—it is hard to believe—16 percent thought the Soviet Union was a member of the Western alliance. Americans also had difficulty identifying countries and regions on a world map, as was shown when 75 percent of adult Americans polled were unable to locate the Persian Gulf, 50 percent could not identify Japan and South Africa, and 14 percent could not even correctly locate the United States (Carpini and Keeter 1997).

Not much has changed with the collapse of the Soviet Union, the end of the cold war, and the global war on terrorism. According to a 2002 survey of Americans between the ages of 18 and 24 by the National Geographic Society, one in ten could not locate the United States on a blank map of the world, only one in seven could identify Iraq, one in four could find Saudi Arabia, and 30 percent could not locate the Pacific Ocean, the world's largest body of water (Recer 2002). According to a March 2011 Newsweek survey, an astonishing 73 percent of Americans (of all ages) could not accurately identify the reasons for the cold war.

As recently as the fall of 2011, the Pew Research Center for the People and the Press (2011) found that 43 percent of Americans could not identify the state of Israel—a major U.S. ally and the top recipient of U.S. foreign aid—on a map of the eastern Mediterranean (even when given the names of four countries to choose from). Moreover, almost one in five Americans could not identify Hillary Clinton as the U.S. Secretary of State when pictures of her, Joseph Biden, Bill Richardson, and Condoleezza Rice were provided, despite her prominence. In the same poll, less than half of Americans knew that the Republican Party held a majority of the seats in the U.S. House of Representatives. Meanwhile, in late 2010 the Program on International Policy Attitudes found that the median estimate among Americans was that the United States devoted 25 percent of the budget to foreign aid; their preferred amount was 10 percent. The actual amount is less than 1 percent.

One may argue whether Americans are more or less interested and informed than the citizens of other industrialized countries (the same surveys have placed Americans near the bottom of the rankings, with eighteen- to twenty-four-year-olds usually dead last). Nevertheless, the pattern remains the same—the mass public, whether in the United States or abroad, is minimally interested and poorly informed, especially in comparison to members of the elite public.

Low levels of political interest and information are also quite understandable if one examines the impact of everyday life. Most Americans, like people everywhere, face numerous daily demands and responsibilities that appear to have little to do with politics. While politics impacts their lives, it is often at a distance removed from the individual. The lives of most individuals revolve around work, family, household, and friends. With the increase of divorce and two-income families, adults lead ever busier and more demanding lives. Most want to relax and enjoy life during their leisure time, which is rarely spent reading, talking, or thinking about national and international affairs. It would be a mistake, therefore, to conclude that the ignorance of most Americans is a function of stupidity or lack of common sense—a view often held by the more traditional and elitist perspectives of the mass public. Rather, it is primarily a function of the various pursuits and demands of everyday life, which are reinforced by the existence of few incentives in American society for people to become politically informed and active.

When we consider the historical context of these low levels of interest and information, we can identify three general trends. First, the level of interest and attention accorded to politics by most Americans has probably declined over the past decades. One hundred years ago politics and election campaigns were one of the few major forms of entertainment for many Americans; today, so many things compete with politics for people's attention—such as television, music, professional and college sports, Hollywood and movies, the shopping mall and mass consumerism—that a low level of political interest is only natural. Second, although the mass public tends to be poorly informed overall, Americans today are exposed to more information and are likely to have less simplistic images of the United States and the world than they held during periods such as the cold war. Much of this is due to rising enrollments in higher education over the last three decades and improved news coverage by the mass media and through the Internet. The final trend is that the size of the elite public has grown over time as a result of increases in higher education since the 1960s (Carpini and Keeter 1991).

Low levels of attention and information produce a third pattern in public opinion—its tendency to be volatile and to fluctuate over time. Since most Americans are uninterested and ill informed, their opinions about national and international issues tend to be very "soft" and open to change. Most Americans give little thought to most issues and are not committed to particular positions. Still, they have opinions and readily offer them when solicited by a public opinion poll—no more than a general snapshot of what the mass public may think at that brief moment (Bardes and Oldendick 2002). Not surprisingly, as an issue gets more media coverage, public attention increases for a while, members of the mass public acquire more information, and individual opinions change and harden.

Impact on Foreign Policy

These three public opinion patterns—inattentiveness, low levels of information, and volatility—present problems for American democracy and may limit its impact *Within this context, for foreign policy public opinion has two major paths of influence:* (1) directly on policymakers within the government and (2) much more indirectly by impacting the general domestic political process.

DIRECT AND IMMEDIATE IMPACT   In terms of immediate and direct impact on policymakers within the government, there are two contradictory consequences. The most obvious is that *inattentive, uninformed, and erratic public opinion gives policymakers great* *leeway in acting on most issues*. The content of public opinion serves as a poor guide for policymakers, especially given its fluctuating nature, and political leaders are often able to lead public opinion—that is, educate and manipulate the public—to support and follow their policies. Moreover, during crisis periods, such as when troops are deployed abroad, the public tends to **rally around the flag** by supporting the president and his policies. As the traditional wisdom argues, public opinion often reinforces and strengthens presidential power because the president is the most visible political figure in the United States, especially with respect to foreign policy, in determining which issues are before the public and how they are discussed.

A second consequence, usually ignored by those who hold to the traditional wisdom, is that *for some issues, especially those that are most salient, public opinion may act as an immediate and direct constraint on political officials in the policymaking process*. No matter how inattentive, uninformed, and erratic public opinion is, the public votes political leaders in and out of office, so elected officials are particularly sensitive to public opinion. Within the White House, it is not uncommon to hear people say that "compared with analysts, presidents and potential presidents themselves see a close link between stands in foreign policy and the outcomes of presidential elections" (Halperin 1974:67). Even a casual review of the past two decades reveals extensive efforts by each administration to shape and cultivate public opinion and support (see Heilemann and Halperin 2010 on the 2008 presidential election).

Furthermore, if public feeling becomes intense concerning an issue, it severely constrains the choices available within the policymaking process. As Henry Kissinger (1957:328) once observed, "The acid test of a policy . . . is its ability to obtain domestic support." Once the public was educated and led on the issue of anticommunism, American leaders began to feel constrained by public opinion, as cold war lessons—for instance that the United States should take a hard-line approach and never appease aggressors—were internalized by Americans. The last remnant of this anticommunist legacy in the present era can still be seen in U.S. foreign policy toward North Korea and Cuba.

In addition, public support for a policy may turn rapidly into public disapproval. Although the public tends to rally round the flag and the president during a crisis such as war, public support for presidential policies tends to dwindle over time. Studies, such as John Mueller's (1973) classic, *War, Presidents, and Public Opinion*, demonstrate that the longer a war lasts (and the greater the casualties), the more public support will erode. Quick and successful operations, as in Grenada, Panama, the Persian Gulf, and Kosovo maximize support; lengthy and unsuccessful conflicts, as in Korea, Vietnam, Lebanon, and Iraq bring public disapproval (see Gelpi, Feaver, and Reiffler 2005/06). George W. Bush learned how quickly public approval can pivot as support changed to opposition as time, cost and casualties mounted in Iraq after 2003, and Barack Obama watched public support evaporate for his initial economic policies as well as military action in Afghanistan.

Bruce Jentleson (1992:72) found that public opinion "varies according to the 'principal policy objective' for which force is used." The tendency is for greater public support for the use of force in order to "contain" and "restrain" an aggressor state—such as in the Persian Gulf War—as opposed to using force to "initiate" and "impose" internal political change within another state—such as within Nicaragua, Somalia, or Haiti. Obviously, many cases are likely to be, or be perceived as, somewhat mixed. Nevertheless, Jentleson (1992:72) concludes:

> The American public is less gun shy than during the Vietnam trauma period of the 1970s, but more cautious than during the Cold War consensus of the 1950s and 1960s. . . . Presidents who contemplate getting militarily involved in internal

political conflicts—of which there may well be even more in the post–Cold War world than when bipolarity had its constraining effects—had better get in and out quickly and successfully. Otherwise, the public is strongly disposed to oppose the policy.

Thus the public tends to discriminate over the use of force more than is commonly thought and is "pretty prudent." As can be seen in the war in Iraq, from overwhelming support in early 2003 at the beginning of the invasion, public support dwindled steadily—with temporary interruptions for such events as the capture of Saddam Hussein or the Iraqi elections in 2005—to the point where over half the public regarded the action as a mistake by early 2005. Similarly, the public's preference for withdrawal has also increased steadily as casualties have mounted (Mueller 2005). In late 2005, for example, polls showed that, even while democracy promotion was embraced by most Americans as a foreign policy goal, a majority of Americans opposed the use of military force (either directly or via threats) to promote democracy, and believed that the goal of establishing democracy in Iraq did not warrant going to war.

Finally, the collapse of the cold war consensus has made public opinion somewhat less responsive to the president. During the 1950s, most American leaders and members of the elite public shared a similar cold war view of the world that the mass public tended to follow. Since the Vietnam War, however, differing views of the world and U.S. foreign policy have arisen, leading to greater diversity and volatility in public opinion. This has made it more difficult for the president to rally and maintain public support for particular policies in an environment where opinion leaders with different foreign policy views now compete with each other for public support.

In sum, the influence of public opinion on the foreign policy process has contradictory consequences and is more complex than the traditional wisdom suggests. For many issues, public opinion has limited immediate and direct impact on the policymaking process. However, for other issues high in salience, public opinion has an immediate and direct effect on policymakers within the government, including the president and members of Congress. The common denominators in these two contradictory patterns are (1) the level of salience and the politicization of issues and (2) the level of success or failure perceived among a public that tends to be pragmatic and impatient.

When the public feels things are going well in their lives and for the country and when few issues are salient and controversial, it tends to support the status quo and approve the president's performance. However, if the public perceives problems, such as a foreign policy fiasco or an economic recession, most people will want changes and the president's approval rating will drop. Public perception and satisfaction levels help to explain whether public opinion supports or constrains the president's ability to govern foreign policy. Despite all-time public approval ratings following 9/11, President George W. Bush saw his approval decline steadily in the face of continued violence in Iraq and economic and political troubles at home (review Bush's approval ratings in Figure 3.2).

The impact of public opinion fluctuated even more dramatically for the elder Bush during and after the Persian Gulf Crisis (see **Figure** 11.1). Three stages occurred: public opinion was supportive during August and September 1990—the initial stage of the crisis; became divided from October 1990 to early January 1991as the use of force became more likely; and once the war began, became highly supportive and reinforced presidential power once again. Following the dramatic success of the Persian Gulf War it appeared that President Bush's reelection was assured. Unfortunately and unbelievably for Bush, his high public approval dropped dramatically following the war, especially over economic and

Figure 11.1 President George W. Bush's Public Approval During the 1990–91 Persian Gulf Crisis

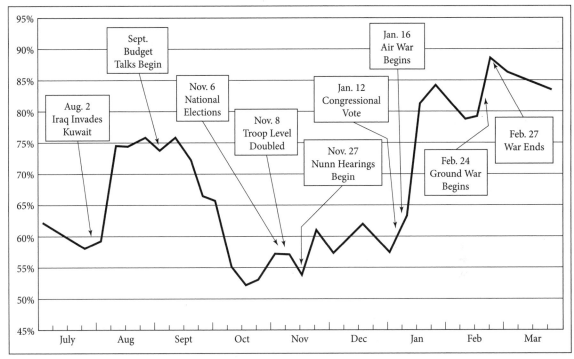

SOURCE: The Gallup Organization.

domestic concerns, and the public voted Bill Clinton in and Bush out in the 1992 presidential election.

Barack Obama faced a similar pattern. As we discussed in Chapter 3, his public approval began in the high 60s and even 70s, but declined steadily in 2009 and early 2010 to reach the mid-40s, where it hovered until the 2012 election (review Figure 3.3) As his successful campaign for re-election unfolded, his approval ratings crept slowly higher, to the point where it exceeded 50 percent in the fall. His handling of national security was a major element of this, as the public consistently approved of his foreign policy leadership (and favored it over his rival, Mitt Romney) throughout the election campaign.

INDIRECT AND LONGER-TERM INFLUENCE The foregoing discussion should help clarify *the more indirect and longer-term influence of public opinion, which is significant in three basic ways.* First, the public elects major governmental officials. Whether or not Americans are interested or informed about foreign policy, the public chooses who becomes president and who runs Congress. Although individuals with high levels of education and socioeconomic class are usually more interested and informed about national and international affairs, members of the elite and the mass public ultimately determine who becomes president and sets the foreign policy direction of the country. This is nicely illustrated by the presidential election of 2012 in **Table 11.1**, which breaks down votes through exit polls for Barack Obama and Mitt Romney by a variety of factors (and compares it to the 2008 election between Obama and John McCain).

Table 11.1   Election Results of 2008 and 2012

Questions	voters '12 %	Obama '12 %	Romney %	Obama '08 %	McCain %
Sex					
Male	47	45	52	49	48
Female	53	55	44	56	43
Age					
18–29	19	60	37	66	32
30–44	27	52	45	52	46
45–64	38	47	51	50	49
65+	16	44	56	45	53
Party					
Democrat	38	92	7	89	10
Republican	32	6	93	9	90
Independent or something else	29	45	50	52	44
Race					
White	72	39	59	43	55
Black	13	93	6	95	4
Hispanic	10	71	27	67	31
Asian	3	73	26	62	35
Other	2	58	38	66	31
Education					
No high school diploma	3	64	35	63	35
High school graduate	21	51	48	52	46
Some college/assoc. degree	29	49	48	51	47
College graduate	29	47	51	50	48
Postgraduate study	18	55	42	58	40
Income					
Under $50k	41	60	38	60	38
$50k – $99,999	31	46	52	49	49
$100k or more	28	44	54	49	49
Sex by marital status					
Married men	29	38	60	46	53
Married women	31	46	53	47	51
Non-married men	18	56	40	58	38
Non-married women	23	67	31	70	29
Ideology					
Liberal	25	86	11	89	10
Moderate	41	56	41	60	39
Conservative	35	17	82	20	78
Religion					
Protestant or other Christian	53	42	57	45	54
Catholic	25	50	48	54	45
Something else	7	74	23	73	22
Jewish	2	69	30	78	21
None	12	70	26	75	23
White evangelical					
White evangelical or white born-again Christian	26	21	78	24	74
All Others	74	60	37	62	36

Second, the ability of political leaders to influence the policymaking process during their tenure is heavily a function of their public prestige. As Figure 3.2 clearly illustrates, public approval of presidential performance over time not only fluctuates dramatically but also tends to decrease for each president. This accounts for the presidential life cycle, during which the president tends to enter office with highly favorable public opinion only to see it diminish with time, weakening his ability to govern.

Finally, public opinion often sets the boundaries of legitimate political discourse and domestic politics, limiting the kinds of issues on the political agenda and politically acceptable options that may be considered by decisionmakers. Although public opinion can be erratic, it tends to fluctuate within a certain range of ideological and cultural beliefs that prevail in American society. It is to these more indirect and longer-term influences of the public to which we now turn by examining the role of, first, political ideology and then political culture.

POLITICAL IDEOLOGY AND FOREIGN POLICY ORIENTATIONS

Political ideology refers to beliefs about the preferred ends and means of a society (e.g., liberty, equality, representative government, market-oriented economy). In this respect, we are also interested in the **foreign policy orientations** permeating American society—that is, how Americans see the world and the preferred role the United States should play in international relations. Together, the ideological and foreign policy orientations prevailing in American society set the broad boundaries of legitimate political discourse and agenda setting within which public opinion operates to influence domestic politics, the policymaking process and country's national interests.

As we review the ideological and foreign policy orientations of Americans, keep *two points about the types of publics and the nature of public beliefs in mind.* First, a discussion of ideological and foreign policy views must focus on the elite public and the extent to which foreign policy is supported by the mass public because the elite public tends to have stronger, less moderate, and more influential ideological and foreign policy beliefs than the mass public. This is consistent with an important distinction that Godfrey Hodgson (1976) makes in America in Our Time between the **moral minority** (the elite public) and the **pragmatic majority** (the mass public). Second, the ideological and foreign policy orientations of Americans tend to be quite stable as compared to their expressions of public opinion. Ideological beliefs do not readily fluctuate; they tend to resist change for they are formed early in life through the process of political socialization. This is especially true among members of the elite public who tend to be more attentive to national and international affairs, and have more knowledge and greater emotional commitment to their views. The pragmatic majority, in contrast, tends to have less sophisticated or consistent views in comparison to the elite public and to occupy more centrist positions while remaining more open and responsive to the ideological and foreign policy appeals of the elite public.

Ideological and foreign policy orientations in American society affect public opinion, influence the electoral process and voters' choices, affect the activity of groups and social movements in domestic politics, and are passed on to newer generations of Americans through the socialization process. In short, they are the field in which public opinion develops and they set the broad boundaries within which the complex politics of U.S. foreign policy operates and the nation's interests are defined.

According to Ole Holsti and James Rosenau (1984), *the ideological and foreign policy orientations of Americans have gone through two major phases since the end of World War II:* (1) an ideological and foreign policy consensus, which prevailed during the cold war years and (2) an increase in ideological and foreign policy diversity, which has occurred since Vietnam and the end of the cold war.

Phase I: The Cold War Years of Anticommunism and the Liberal–Conservative Consensus

Holsti and Rosenau (1984) argue that most Americans in government and society shared a similar foreign policy orientation during the cold war years, which they call **cold war internationalism**. Cold war internationalists saw a conflict-ridden, bipolar world that pitted the Soviet Union and communism against the United States and democracy. The Soviet Union was seen as an ambitious, aggressive, expansionist empire, leading a strong and patient group of Communist allies toward a revolutionary goal: imposing a Moscow-dominated imperial system throughout the world. The United States, in contrast, was seen as the civilized and benevolent leader of democracy and prosperity throughout the so-called "free world." In a world where victory for one side was seen as defeat for the other, the assumed threat to American national security posed by the Soviet Union and communism became the predominant concern of American policymakers. It was this view of the world that laid the basis for the national security ethos to thrive during the cold war years in which U.S. foreign policy revolved around a strategy of containment of Soviet expansionism through the development, threat, and use of force around the world.

The cold war years led to the development of an ideological and foreign policy consensus throughout American society and government, an extraordinary time in American history. As Thomas Mann (1990a:11) explains,

> The bipartisan foreign policy consensus that prevailed for almost two decades after World War II was sustained by a leadership stratum that shared an internationalist and interventionist view of the U.S. role in world affairs, an attentive and educated group of citizens who followed and supported this leadership, and a poorly informed and largely inert mass public that tolerated official policy as long as it appeared to be working.

This societal consensus fostered the rise of presidential power, the expansion of the foreign policy bureaucracy, the development of an acquiescent Congress, and the rise of a national security ethos and free market ethos in government and society. It also set the context for understanding the reinforcing role that public opinion and domestic politics played throughout the cold war years in the making of U.S. foreign policy.

The growing anticommunist foreign policy consensus reflected a larger set of ideological patterns that evolved in American society. During the cold war years, according to Godfrey Hodgson (1976:73), "a strange hybrid, liberal conservatism, blanketed the scene and muffled debate." The two major aspects of the **liberal–conservative consensus** were belief in a democratic-capitalist political economy based on private enterprise and the fear of communism. This was based on a number of basic ideological beliefs.

First, the American free enterprise system is democratic, creates abundance, and has a revolutionary potential for social justice. Second, the key to this potential is economic growth based on private industry and governmental support, which allows the needs of all people to be met. Third, meeting popular needs will produce a more equal society in which conflict between social classes becomes unnecessary and obsolete and workers become members of the middle class. Fourth, social problems can be solved like industrial problems; the economy can be fine-tuned and the welfare state can eradicate poverty. Fifth, the main threat to this beneficent system is communism; therefore, the United States and its free world allies must fight a prolonged struggle against communism while promoting the American free enterprise system throughout the world.

By the mid-1950s, most Americans within both the mass and elite public were part of this liberal–conservative ideological consensus. This consensus became possible during the 1950s because most conservatives accepted the legitimacy of the limited welfare state created by the New Deal under Franklin Roosevelt, while most liberals adopted the anticommunist stance in vogue following World War II. Therefore, the liberal–conservative consensus represented neither liberalism nor conservatism but was a hybrid or amalgamation of the two ideologies.

Differences did exist among members of the consensus. Liberals were more favorable toward welfare and government intervention in the economy, while conservatives generally were opposed to such policies. Conservatives were more prone to rely on force to respond to instability in the Third World, while liberals were more sympathetic to the need to promote Third World economic and political development. However, such differences were overshadowed by agreement on the promise of the American private market system and the threat of communism. According to Hodgson (1976:73), "Since the consensus had made converts on the Right as well as on the Left, only a handful of dissidents were excluded from the Big Tent: southern diehards, rural reactionaries, the more . . . paranoid fringes of the radical Right, and the divided remnants of the old, Marxist, Left."

The cold war anticommunist consensus did not develop overnight but evolved over time. The 1930s and 1940s witnessed the rise of liberalism and the political left and a corresponding decline of conservatism. Then, after World War II, in the late 1940s and 1950s conservatism and the political right experienced a resurgence during which a great debate took place over the future of U.S. foreign policy. By the mid-1950s, the liberal–conservative consensus developed and the cold war internationalist perspective prevailed among most Americans. Although challenged by McCarthyism and the political right, the anticommunist Cold War consensus lasted through the most of the 1960s (see Burns 1989; Goldman 1961; Manchester 1972; Himmelstein 1989; Pells 1985).

During the years of the anticommunist consensus, most liberals became strong advocates of anticommunism and containment during the late 1940s and 1950s, while conservatives increasingly accepted the notion of a limited welfare state in the domestic economy, especially during the Eisenhower administration. Those further to the left, who were critical of an aggressive U.S. policy of global containment abroad and believed in greater restructuring of American society at home, lost credibility and were effectively silenced throughout the cold war with the rise of McCarthyism. But the far right failed to persuade either the Truman or Eisenhower administrations (and most Americans) to reorient foreign policies beyond containment.

In short, a consensus developed within the United States during the 1950s that the world was divided between two hostile forces: communism led by the Soviet Union, and democracy and free markets led by the United States. Despite disagreements over tactics (How much force? Where should it be applied?), most Americans agreed on the source of the threat—communism—and the necessity of using force to counter its expansion throughout the world. Ideological anticommunism thus became the glue that bound the consensus among liberals, moderates, and conservatives, especially within the elite public, and limited political choices available to policymakers. In the words of David Halberstam (1969:108), "It was an ideological and bipartisan movement; it enjoyed the support of the press, of the churches, of Hollywood. There was stunningly little debate or sophistication of the levels of anticommunism. It was totally centrist and politically very safe; anything else was politically dangerous."

The Cold War consensus eventually crumbled under the weight of the U.S. experience in Vietnam. Initially, most Americans were unaware of what was happening in Vietnam (or even where it was located geographically!) and shared the belief that U.S. national security in the cold war necessitated action in Vietnam and elsewhere. Therefore, if the president of the United States, supported by most leaders in government and society (the elite public), contended that Vietnam was vital to American interests and threatened by communism and that the free countries of Southeast Asia would fall if the threat was not contained, the American people stood behind him. Ironically, this domestic political situation prompted greater U.S. intervention in the Vietnam War and eventually led to a crumbling of the foreign policy and ideological consensus (see also Gelb with Betts 1979).

Phase II: The Post-Vietnam Lack of Consensus

Events of the 1960s and early 1970s, such as the civil rights movement, the war on poverty, and Watergate, led many Americans to question the ideological and foreign policy beliefs that were the basis of the consensus during the cold war years. But the Vietnam War had the most traumatic impact on Americans, leading to the collapse of the ideological and foreign policy consensus that prevailed throughout the cold war. The "failure" of Vietnam undermined many of these beliefs. Americans seemed to be dying for a lost cause—over 58,000 Americans died in Vietnam, with over 350,000 other Americans wounded. For what? This tragic loss led people to raise questions about U.S. foreign policy. Members of the mass public, on the one hand, came to critique the Vietnam War and U.S. foreign policy predominantly from a pragmatic perspective—they emphasized the limited importance of Vietnam and questioned U.S. failure to win the war. Members of the elite public, on the other hand, were more likely to debate the goals and virtue of U.S. foreign policy.

By the late 1960s, a substantial number of average Americans had also turned against the government and its policies in Vietnam; some wanted out through victory and military escalation, but most wanted out via withdrawal. For a while, the polarization between the antiwar movement and supporters of the war, between critics and supporters of mainstream society, appeared to verge on civil war.

Ultimately, *polarization gave way to political fragmentation by the 1970s with two major consequences.* First, American society became more ideologically diverse with competing foreign policy orientations. The 1960s and early 1970s resulted in a resurgence of liberalism and the rise of the new left, while the 1970s and 1980s witnessed the rise of modern conservatism and the political right (see **A Different Perspective** on modern American liberalism and conservatism). Second, greater ideological diversity led to competing foreign policy views or schools of thought during the 1970s and 1980s: (1) conservative internationalism, (2) liberal internationalism, and (3) noninternationalism (Schneider 1983; see also Holsti and Rosenau 1984). With the collapse of the Soviet Union, the war on terrorism following the 9/11 attacks, and the global recession, while ideological positions clarified between liberals and conservatives (such as over economics), a great debate prevailed over

Modern American Liberalism and Conservatism

There is considerable confusion over what the terms liberalism and conservatism mean, especially in the modern context. This is understandable given the common roots and their evolution through American history. Several key points help to distinguish between these two perspectives.

First, modern or twentieth- and twenty-first-century liberalism and conservatism in the United States share the same historical roots. They are both derived from **classical liberalism**, which developed in the seventeenth and eighteenth centuries in Europe in reaction to the order and inequality that characterized medieval society and feudalism under the aristocracy and the church. Classical liberals emphasized the importance of individual freedom in economic and political affairs through the promotion of democracy and capitalism and the separation of church and state.

Second, classical liberalism evolved over the course of American history into two modern derivatives developed during the twentieth century: **modern liberalism** and **modern conservatism**. Together, they share a belief in individual freedom and a preference for a democratic/capitalistic political economy. Yet they differ as well. On the one hand, the Great Depression convinced many people—who became known as "liberals"—that the government should take a much more active role in stabilizing, regulating and steering the economy, and should assist the unemployed and the poor, who were frequently victims of the failures and flaws of the market economy. On the other hand, many people—who became known as "conservatives"—opposed such New Deal policies and preferred a minimal, or "laissez-faire," governmental role in the economy, in which people would prosper

through individual work and market forces, while private charities would support the underprivileged. In response to the events of the sixties, liberals also tended to favor greater individualism in social lifestyles, while conservatives promoted more traditional social norms and were concerned with maintaining social stability and order. Within these broad categories, each ideological orientation is made up of many variants.

Finally, although American liberalism and conservatism reflect a rather narrow range of ideological beliefs compared to the politics of European societies, the growth of modern liberalism has been accompanied by the rise of the political left, while the ascendance of modern conservatism has been accompanied by growing strength in the political right. The political left has a long tradition in the history of the United States, and there have been periods when it has grown in popularity and influence: democratic socialism became popular before World War I, communism and pacifism grew during the 1920s and the Depression years, and the new left was prominent during the 1960s and 1970s. The political right, likewise, also has had a long history and has been able to attract support at different times, evident in the rise of McCarthyism during the cold war years and the prominence of the secular and fundamentalist Christian right since Vietnam.

It should be clearer that the popular distinction that most Americans make between liberals as "pro-big government" and conservatives as "anti-big government" is too simplistic. For example, liberals usually prefer greater government involvement in the economy and conservatives less

(continued)

government intervention; however, conservatives usually prefer more government defense spending in support of national security, while liberals prefer less. Likewise, in the area of social policy, liberals emphasize active government in support of the rights of individuals, such as to prevent child abuse, while conservatives emphasize active government to promote certain moral standards, such as school prayer or the prevention of abortion. Regardless of the particular issue and the differences between liberalism and conservatism, however, most Americans have been part of a long (classical) liberal tradition throughout American history. (See Hartz, 1955; Hodgson, 1976; Micklethwait and Woodridge 2004.)

Are you a modern liberal, a modern conservative, or some combination of the two? What about most Americans? How does this impact presidential power, especially for national security and economics?

---

national security policy that created even more conflict and confusion for the politics of U.S. foreign policy (see also Posen and Ross 1996 / 97; Rosati and Creed 1997).

GROWTH OF THE LEFT AND LIBERAL INTERNATIONALISM
The events of the 1960s resulted in the growth of the political left in the United States and an alternative understanding of American society. Although anticommunism and McCarthyism had silenced most liberals and leftists by the early 1950s, the "new left" entered the political scene in the late 1950s with the rise of the civil rights movement and grew dramatically as the Vietnam War intensified. Members of the new left and the counterculture dissented and rebelled against the liberal–conservative ideological and anticommunist consensus of mainstream society, which they held responsible for Vietnam.

With the rise of the new left, liberalism once again began to emphasize the values of freedom and equality and turned away from the importance of anticommunism abroad and at home. Liberals were more likely to promote active governmental intervention in the economy and to support needy individuals. Moreover, the Vietnam War and events of the 1960s prompted most liberals to become supportive of greater individualism in American life. Thus liberalism became quite distinct from conservatism in the post-Vietnam years.

Liberals and those on the political left saw a much more complex and interdependent world, composed of many important countries, global actors, and issues—a position that Schneider (1983) refers to as **liberal internationalism** (and Holsti and Rosenau [1984] refer to as post–cold war internationalism). Liberals now were opposed to anticommunism as the driving force in U.S. foreign policy. They believed it was important to address not only the East–West conflict (and the possibilities for cooperation), but West–West issues (especially economic), involving relations between the United States and its allies, and North–South issues, focusing on the relationship between industrialized nations, international organizations, and the Third World. Such a liberal internationalist orientation tended to have a strong association with members of the Democratic Party, and it has influenced the Democratic administrations of Carter, Clinton, and Obama.

GROWTH OF THE RIGHT AND CONSERVATIVE INTERNATIONALISM
At the same time, many Americans continued to hold a more conservative understanding of America and the world, emphasizing the threat of communism abroad and the importance of

the private market at home—the same values that had once been the basis of the ideological consensus during the cold war. In fact, the late 1970s and 1980s witnessed the resurgence of conservatism and the right, best associated with Ronald Reagan and the Republican Party, in reaction to the perceived excesses of liberalism and the left during the 1960s and 1970s. Conservatives were particularly critical of the insufficient concern with the communist threat abroad and the moral decay they believed prevailed at home. These concerns account for not only the rise of conservatism but the growth of ultraconservatism and the political right as well, including the religious fundamentalist right.

These Americans, especially conservatives and those on the political right, continued to believe in **conservative internationalism** (or cold war internationalism) after the Vietnam War, especially during the 1970s and 1980s. In other words, they believed that the major global threat to the security of the United States and global order was communism directed by the Soviet Union, requiring a strong American military presence in much of the world. Yet disagreement among conservatives existed concerning the severity of the Soviet threat and the appropriate foreign policy strategy.

This also led to the development of another conservative orientation in foreign policy: **neoconservatives**. A strange hybrid of disaffected liberal, cold warriors, "neocons" (as they also came to be known) broke with the Democratic Party over what they perceived as its dovish retreat from assertive foreign policies. However, while Ronald Reagan's "crusade for freedom," the Reagan Doctrine, and other policies met with their approval, the neocons never achieved the influence they sought within the administration. The neocons stressed the preeminence and (benevolent) hegemony of the United States as the world's dominant power, the need to wield American power—especially military power—to promote American democracy and capitalism abroad, unilaterally if necessary. Many of these neocons found a home in George W. Bush's administration and played an instrumental role in shaping the administration's response to the 9/11 attacks, until the Iraq War shifted from what seemed like a success to a failed policy (Ehrmann 1995; Mann 2004).

THE RISE OF NONINTERNATIONALISM Proponents of the third popular orientation, spanning the political spectrum, recognized the increasing complexity of the world and the difficulty the United States had in affecting it and advocated a type of **noninternationalism** (or semi-isolationism). Some noninternationalists argued that the United States needed to limit its involvement to those areas of the world where it really has vital interests—primarily Western Europe and Japan. Other noninternationalists believed that the United States should de-escalate its overseas military commitments and presence—in other words, "strategically disengage"—and concentrate on improving its international commercial and economic position. Whatever the particular position, noninternationalists were likely to believe that the highest priority of American society and the U.S. government should be to avoid entanglements abroad and address domestic issues and problems at home. Noninternationalists also tended to be more supportive of protecting American industry and jobs in the international political economy. Such a noninternationalist perspective was most prevalent among the mass public (in comparison to the elite public), among whom **isolationist sentiment** has historically been strong.

Fragmentation, Confusion, and the Search for Legitimation

The momentous events surrounding the end of the cold war, the collapse of communism in Eastern Europe, and the collapse of the Soviet Union during 1989 to 1991 raised the possibility of profound changes in American foreign policy orientations. The liberal and conservative internationalist orientations became less well defined. In fact, right after the collapse of the Soviet Union, there was an initial outpouring of optimism across the political spectrum that "peace was at hand" and it was "the end of history" in which democratic liberalism would prevail globally (see Fukuyama 1989).

This outlook was short-lived after the September 11, 2001 attacks, the war on terrorism, and the Iraq War. Indeed, another great debate has been generated over the nature of the world and the proper role of the United States abroad during the 1990s to the present that does not fit neatly into liberal, conservative or noninternationalist orientations, especially in the area of national security policy. Foreign economic policy was less affected due to a shared free market ethos, that is until the country was threatened with major economic collapse beginning in 2007. So the net result is that the ideological and foreign policy orientations are more fragmented than ever, there is less consistency and coherence of thought, and presidents find it more difficult to find lasting political support and legitimacy for their policies.

The *movement from cold war consensus to post–Vietnam War diversity to the collapse of the cold war has widened the agenda of domestic politics and political discourse in the making of U.S. foreign policy*. Such changes in ideological and foreign policy beliefs cannot be understated, for this has led to a new era in which public opinion is more volatile, political participation has become more active and diverse, the media are more likely to act independently of the government, Congress is more likely to assert its authority, and the president's ability to govern foreign policy faces both greater constraints and opportunities. As Richard Melanson (1990:17) aptly suggested at the start of these shifts, "In sum, a **fragmentation/swing model** has replaced that of cold war **followership model** as the most accurate depiction of foreign policy attitudes, . . . and its emergence has surely complicated the efforts of presidents to win and keep public support for their foreign policies."

Where once public opinion fluctuated within only a narrow range consistent with the liberal–conservative and cold war internationalist consensus during the cold war years, public opinion is now much more open to greater fluctuation, reflecting the breakdown of the cold war consensus. This is because, unlike the opinions of the elite public, which tend to reflect a greater commitment to a particular ideological and foreign policy view, members of the mass public tend to be more centrist (reflecting a mix of foreign policy orientations, and only a temporary mix at that) and more noninternationalist in their orientations.

Therefore, members of the mass public, since they do not internalize the ideological views of the elite public, are more likely to change their opinion and be open to "populist" appeals. Sometimes they are responsive to a more conservative internationalist position while at other times they are more receptive to a liberal internationalist position or some hybrid orientation. Sometimes they are more responsive to Democratic Party candidates and policies; sometimes they are more receptive to Republican Party candidates and policies (see **Figure** 11.2 for a visual comparison of the cold war versus the post–Vietnam War years).

There has been a general recognition that, with the collapse of the Soviet Union and its Eastern European empire, the structure of the international system has changed—that the United States is the sole global power (or superpower) and is in a more advantageous position than before. But there is great debate about what this means. The post–Vietnam War years have produced a much more complex and messy political process in which public opinion is more volatile than during the cold war years of consensus. As William Schneider (1987:51) pointed out, when a foreign policy issue gets on the political agenda and is framed in terms of security and "military strength," then the conservative internationalist orientation tends to win the political debate—such as immediately following the 9/11 attacks. However, if it is framed in terms of "peace," then the liberal internationalist

Figure 11.2 Comparing American Political Ideology During the Cold War and Since Vietnam

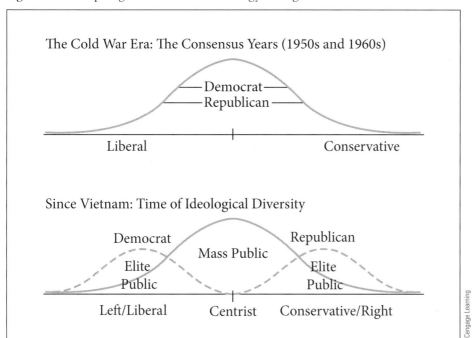

The Cold War Era: The Consensus Years (1950s and 1960s)

— Democrat —
— Republican —

Liberal   Conservative

Since Vietnam: Time of Ideological Diversity

Democrat   Republican
        Mass Public
Elite   Elite
Public   Public

Left/Liberal   Centrist   Conservative/Right

© Cengage Learning

perspective tends to prevail. "Instead of elite consensus and mass followership, what emerged was an unstable system of competing coalitions in which the mass public swings left or right unpredictably in response to its current fears and concerns." There are also times when an issue such as trade may trigger a strong noninternationalist orientation among the public such as over issues concerning jobs and the economy.

Members of the elite public tend to be more committed to some variant of conservative or liberal internationalism, but they usually are opposed to noninternationalism. Members of the mass public tend to be more moderate and pragmatic in their beliefs, demonstrating both liberal and conservative elements, and are more receptive to the noninternationalist orientation (Wittkopf 1990). And now there are differences not only between these internationalist orientations, but increasingly within them reflecting this more complex and confused world reality. Hence, in the area of national security affairs, much remains uncertain and unpredictable for the future, with the potential for much change and disagreement in the foreign policy orientations of Americans about the nature of the world and the most appropriate foreign policy goals and means for the twenty-first century.

Foreign economic policy orientations and the free market ethos were much less affected by the Vietnam War, the collapse of the cold war consensus, the collapse of the Soviet Union, and the 9/11 attacks, but the Great Recession challenged these shared views. Internationalists still tend to sympathize with a free market ethos. Conservative internationalists are the strongest believers and advocates of an unregulated international political economy based on a free market (except for using coercion and embargoes, for example, against perceived enemies such as Cuba). Liberal internationalists, for the most part, also believe in a market-oriented international political economy, but argue for the need for more international multilateral cooperation, management, and regulation. Both conservative and liberal internationalists, for the most part, believe that U.S. foreign policy overall must support, for example, NAFTA, the World Trade Organization (WTO), and trade with China despite different views about its growing great power status. It is the noninternationalists who are the least receptive to the free market ethos and most willing to advocate protectionism for local industry and labor, especially for people who have been, are, or might in the future be directly affected. However, as conservative and liberal internationalists fragment, protectionist sentiments have emerged in both camps.

The consequences of the Great Recession and the activist economic policies of the Obama administration have generated a new debate about the role of the government within the market-oriented economy and the implications of globalization. Although most Americans have become comfortable thinking in terms of less government (and taxes) and greater reliance on market forces within the United States and abroad, most Americans are also sufficiently pragmatic to support policies that prevent an economic collapse, slow the (global) economic recession, and promote economic recovery and prosperity. Nevertheless, the tensions between the more activist and interventionist Obama administration and the free-market purists of the Republican Party have spawned major clashes and much deadlock.

The fragmentation of public ideological and foreign policy beliefs gives a president great opportunities but also creates great risks. Presidents are no longer driven to pursue only an anticommunist containment policy or economic policies that rely principally on market and nongovernmental forces. Yet it is unclear how far a president may go in pursuing any policy before losing public support in either national security or economic affairs. Presidents no longer come to office with automatic majorities behind their policies. No matter what the president and his advisors believe, a substantial number of Americans—in the mass public and especially the elite public—disagree, or are open to disagreement, with presidential policy. Hence, there is a continual presidential search for, and frustration in obtaining, consensus and "policy legitimation" (see Destler, Gelb and Lake 1984; George 1980; Rosati 1997).

All post–Vietnam War presidents have discovered that most Americans expect presidential promises to be fulfilled, but it has become increasingly difficult for presidents to deliver. Differences in the ideological and foreign policy beliefs among the elite public, coupled with a pragmatic but volatile mass public, have provided a new set of domestic boundaries and possibilities for the making of U.S. foreign policy since Vietnam. Although George W. Bush tried his political best to promote a new national security consensus around antiterrorism and unilateral American leadership in world affairs, and Barack Obama sought to promote a post-partisan, pragmatic and multilateral approach to the world, *a new foreign policy consensus appears to be nowhere in the making*. This has all been complicated by an American and global economy that continues to sputter despite the various policy efforts of the Obama administration and other countries.

Indeed, foreign policy orientations continue to be fragmented, the temporary period of consensus immediately after the 9/11 attacks notwithstanding. Increasing isolationism in the general public; growing rifts within both parties about how to contend with terrorism; the ongoing conflict in Iraq, Afghanistan, and Pakistan; a so-called human security agenda involving the global environment and human rights; regional issues such as the Arab Spring uprisings in the Middle East; as well as an increasingly interdependent and globalized political economy have complicated efforts to generate broad agreement. As always, much depends on the extent to which Americans consider their individual and country's security to be threatened, whether by terrorism, global economic crisis, or other countries and issues, Whatever the case, foreign policy orientations are likely to remain highly diverse, especially among members of the elite public, and competitive, particularly for the support of the mass public, making it difficult for any president from either party to govern.

POLITICAL CULTURE AND AMERICAN NATIONAL STYLE

In addition to the role of public opinion and political ideology, political culture plays the broadest, most subtle, role of all. **Political culture** refers to "self-identity" and how people see themselves and their country relative to the rest of the world. The focus in this section is on those cultural assumptions that Americans have about what it means to be an "American." Not only does this suggest the existence of an **American national style**, but such nationalistic beliefs are particularly evident and powerful forces in the politics of U.S. foreign policy in times of crisis and war.

As we consider political culture, our focus is on several things. First, we are most interested in the cultural and national values prevailing in the population; therefore, what the mass public believes plays a predominant role in determining America's national style. Second, cultural values also tend to be the most widely shared, resilient, and consistent set of beliefs held by individuals. Nationalistic views and feelings, in other words, strongly resist change, for people are socialized to acquire them at a very young age. Finally, political culture and national style influence domestic politics and policymaking by coloring how individuals see their country and its special place in the world. Because cultural and national values are deeply held, most people—within both the mass and elite publics—have a somewhat ethnocentric view of the world, thus affecting how foreign policy is made.

Innocence, Benevolence, and Exceptionalism

Studies of American political culture typically portray Americans as a confident and optimistic people who have a special sense of destiny about the future of their country and its place in the world. In *Backfire*, for example, Loren Baritz (1985) argues that *three key characteristics describe how Americans see themselves relative to the rest of the world:* the notion of a "city on a hill," an idealistic and missionary spirit, and the invincibility of American technology. In other words, most Americans tend to believe inherently in (1) American innocence, (2) American benevolence, and (3) American exceptionalism. Together, these beliefs contribute powerfully to the sense of an American "mission" to lead the world, which runs deep within the political culture of the United States. While substantial differences exist over how to do so (e.g., through international engagement or by remaining aloof and setting an example), the sense of purpose and destiny is pervasive (see also Davis and Lynn-Jones 1987).

Americans are raised to believe that the United States is innocent in world affairs as a people and a country. They do not see themselves as manipulative and aggressive but as a benign and defensive people and country. **American innocence** is consistent with the isolationist sentiments that have played such a dominant role in U.S. foreign policy, especially before the cold war. According to this view, Americans have not been an outward-seeking people. Instead, they have been introspective and concerned with nation building and with serving as a "city on a hill" for other people and countries to emulate (promoting and reinforcing the myth of American isolation historically). Over the years, other countries and other ideologies have forced the United States to become actively involved in war and world politics. The German disregard of American neutrality forced the United States to fight in World War I, while the Japanese bombing of Pearl Harbor forced American entry into World War II. The 9/11 attacks have reinforced this, with popular analogies to Pearl Harbor, despite the fact the United States abroad and at home has been a target of terrorists for some time now. Thus, Americans tend to see themselves and their country as the innocent victims of the acts of others.

When the United States does become involved abroad, American behavior is perceived as benevolent. Such benevolence means that Americans do not become involved in war, for example, solely to defend themselves; rather, they enter wars in order to rid the world of evil and promote peace and freedom for all. As Americans have been taught at a very young age, World War I represented the "war to end all wars," in which European realpolitik would be replaced by American idealism, as embodied in President Woodrow Wilson's plan to create a League of Nations. In World War II, the United States and its allies were dedicated to ridding the world of fascism and constructing a world based on a liberal political and economic order as represented by the United Nations. Likewise, the public goal of the war on terrorism is to defeat al-Qaeda and other terrorist networks, while in Iraq and Afghanistan, the United States sought to bring the benefits of freedom and democracy to a region in which they have not flourished.

Finally, Americans have a strong sense of **American exceptionalism** as well. American history is perceived as one success story after another, from westward expansion to economic development to the rise of the United States as a global power. This reflects an American sense of "manifest destiny"—a belief in the superiority of American culture and way of life and the need to Christianize and Americanize the world that goes back to the early nineteenth century. American exceptionalism implies that God is on America's side and that America represents progress and the best social model for the future of the world, "that Americans can do anything they desire, can build nations or rebuild societies, can speed progress, bring freedom and democracy to the world." In other words, as James Oliver Robertson (1980:349) concludes, "America, imperial America, is 'one giant step for mankind.'"

Such American innocence, benevolence, and exceptionalism strongly support the conviction of a uniquely American mission in world affairs such as during the cold war. For most Americans, Soviet aggression forced the United States to take an active global leadership role, build up its military to contain aggression, and intervene throughout the world. Moreover, the cold war was not just a classical struggle for power between two great powers but represented a "messianic" struggle between good and evil—the forces of democracy versus totalitarianism, capitalism versus communism, Christianity versus atheism. Thus, the globe was seen to be divided into two hostile blocs: the "evil" communist world led by the Soviet Union versus the "free world" led by the United States. In addition, the United States had not only rescued Western Europe through its generosity with the Marshall Plan but promoted liberal societies in Third World countries and assisted their nation-building efforts based on the American model. Americans, therefore, saw themselves not as imperialistic or even self-interested during the cold war but as an innocent society composed of benevolent and exceptional people who symbolized progress and a hopeful future for the world.

Anders Stephanson (1995:125) suggests a different connotation—one much more consistent with America's internationalist and historical past:

In the 1840s, the spatial destination of destiny was clearly continental, a westward, horizontal movement; and the agent involved was the United States, separate and alone. In the 1890s the destination was diffusely conceived as a sphere of barbarism where the gradual struggle for civilization and race might occur on the way toward a final victory that was not that urgent; . . . and the agent, though still the United States, was often seen in combination with other Anglophones, even the "West" in general. In the cold war, however, every space could in principle be defined with instantaneous and razor-sharp distinction either as our side or theirs, or as an arena not yet won where destiny would be fought out right now; and the United States was the global agent of freedom in lethal combat everywhere with a single, terrifying antagonist.

Innocence, benevolence, and exceptionalism are not uniquely American beliefs but to some degree are common cultural and national values within all societies. Groups and societies often see themselves as a superior and chosen people. This is typical of all great powers in world history. As Godfrey Hodgson (1976:6) has observed, "All nations live by myths. Any nation is the sum of the consciousness of its people: the chaotic infinitude of the experience and perceptions of millions alive and dead."

Although a strong sense of nationalism is not a uniquely American trait, what may be somewhat unique to the United States is the strong belief in "freedom" (and "liberty")—the key value that unifies and defines Americans as Alexis de Tocqueville (1945) so aptly described it in his masterpiece, *Democracy in America*, in 1835. This may help to explain why phrases such as "the free world," "democracy," "the free market," and "free trade" have been used with great regularity since World War II and resonate throughout the body politic. Furthermore, given America's short history, the rapid changes experienced with industrialization and modernization, and its ethnic diversity, American nationalism is as powerful a cultural force for most Americans as for any people throughout history.

According to Richard Barnet (1971:251), "All nations preach the ethic of national superiority but the United States has made a religion of it." Niall Ferguson (2004:viii)—a very sympathetic observer of the exercise of American power—highlights how the United States acts as an "empire in denial"; that Americans could somehow be a great power without, at the same time, behaving like previous great powers and engaging in imperialism (what he calls the "imperialism of antiimperialism").

Foreign Policy Implications

American culture and national style have at least six important implications for U.S. foreign policy. First, it contributes to the tendency of Americans to oversimplify, with a naive and rose-colored view, the history of the United States and its role in world affairs. Implicit in the previous section, concepts such as "freedom," "democracy," "the free market," and "free trade" have become sacrosanct in the American mind and interwoven with the "United States of America." Westward expansion, for example, is fondly recalled in terms of the frontier spirit, individualism, and ruggedness represented by the farmer and gunslinger (reflected in numerous movies and stars such as John Wayne), ignoring alternative interpretations that emphasize the ruthlessness of westward expansion and the taking of Native American and Mexican land and lives. Such unattractive points of fact are commonly glossed over in the upbringing and education of most Americans at home, in school and American history textbooks, and throughout society, including much of the popular media.

Much "popular folklore and myth" is accepted by Americans as fact and history that helps to unite Americans and makes it easy for them to ignore history and politics, thus reinforcing low levels of attention and information in public opinion. According to Richard Betts (2002:20), with the collapse of the Soviet Union and the cold war's end,

> the novelty of complete primacy may account for the thoughtless, indeed innocently arrogant way in which many Americans took its benefits for granted. Most who gave any thought to foreign policy came implicitly to regard the entire world after 1989 as they had regarded Western Europe and Japan during the past

half-century: partners in principle but vassals in practice. The United States would lead the civilized community of nations in the expansion and consolidation of a liberal world order.

Not only had the United States won the cold war, but it appeared that peace was at hand, and for some, it was "the end of history." However, "September 11 reminded those Americans with a rosy view that not all the world sees U.S. primacy as benign," and yet, also contributed to the oversimplification of good and evil in the world once again. Such simple and naive images make it difficult for Americans to tolerate and accept historical facts or political realities that are inconsistent with their optimistic images.

Second, America's national style has often embodied a nationalist and idealistic yearning that has turned the United States into a **moral crusader**. This is probably best associated with the presidency of Woodrow Wilson and the coining of the term "Wilsonianism." As summed up by Robert Nisbet (1988:32), "From Wilson's day to ours the embedded purpose—sometimes articulated in words, more often not—of American foreign policy, under Democrats and Republics alike oftentimes, has boiled down to America-on-a-Permanent-Mission; a mission to make the rest of the world a little more like America the Beautiful" (see **A Closer Look** on moralism and America's view of the world).

A CLOSER LOOK

Moralism and America's View of the World

The moralization of foreign policy has been a major pattern throughout the twentieth century: from Woodrow Wilson, American cold war policies, President Carter's human rights campaign, President Reagan's battle against the "evil empire," to President George W. Bush's effort to rid the world of all terrorists whether "dead or alive" and a "with-us-or-against-us" approach to international affairs. According to Howard Fineman (2003:25), "Every president invokes God and asks his blessing. Every president promises, though not always in so many words, to lead according to moral principles rooted in biblical tradition." Furthermore, as Stanley Hoffmann (1968:194) has observed,

> There is a parallel here: like the ideological tenets of communism, American principles—those of a deeply Christian, liberal society, a kind of synthesis or smorgasbord of Locke, Paine, and Kant—are universal and equalitarian; all

the nations of the world are seen capable of living in peace under law in an association of equals devoted to harmony. This mixture of universalism, legalism, and equalitarianism diverts Americans from any suggestion that their attempt to spread the gospel might be imperialistic or self-serving; what is being sought is the common good, in the best interest of all. But the proselytizing contradicts the stated purpose, the method clashes with the intended outcome.

In the words of theologian Reinhold Niebuhr (and Heimert 1963:150), "Moral pretensions and political parochialism are the two weaknesses of the life of a messianic nation."

What are the consequences of the tendency to embrace such moralistic positions and rhetoric on U.S. foreign policy choices and the debate over them?

Third, this also produces major contradictions between **principle versus pragmatism**. Despite its moralization, the actual conduct of U.S. foreign policy often involves the pragmatic pursuit of national interests heavily informed by a national security ethos that existed before, and has continued to exist since, the cold war. This means that policymakers engage in diplomacy, secrecy, bargaining, rewards, threats, force, and all of the other instruments associated with power politics in order to successfully promote their national interests as they define them. But such amoral and pragmatic behavior by the superpower, or great power, or hegemonic power of its day is not consistent with notions of American innocence, benevolence, and exceptionalism, to the point that much of U.S. foreign policy has had to remain hidden and disguised from the public.

This contradiction has posed real problems for the leaders and makers of U.S. foreign policy, producing a kind of "American dualism," the necessity to speak two different languages: the language of power and the language of peace and harmony (or democracy and freedom). "Of course," states Stanley Hoffmann (1968:178), "only a symbolic eagle can hold both the arrows and the olive branch easily at the same time." Americans' unwillingness to recognize, and deal with, these contradictions between morality and pragmatism in foreign policy has been a topic of concern for quite some time for such thinkers as George Kennan (1951), Hans Morgenthau (1952), and Reinhold Niebuhr (1944).

Fourth, American leaders often feel the need to oversell their policies in order to legitimate them with the public by simplifying them and infusing them with moral purpose in the process. It matters little whether political leaders themselves share these same cultural and nationalistic values—most do, some do not (at least in varying degrees). The fact is that the pragmatic majority is generally uninterested and uninformed about world affairs, and so political overstatement and oversell is deemed necessary to attract public attention and support, especially when foreign policy changes or the use of force is involved. This compels leaders to speak in terms of power and peace and to rely on the politics of symbolism to legitimize their policies.

To arouse public support, political leaders link issues to moral symbols and values with which most Americans identify. To gain congressional support for military assistance to Greece and Turkey in 1947, Secretary of State Dean Acheson testified what was at stake through use of an analogy for what would become the domino theory, a "Soviet breakthrough [in the Near East] might open three continents to Soviet penetration. Like apples in a barrel infected by the corruption of one rotten one, the corruption of Greece would infect Iran and all to the East . . . Africa . . . Italy and France. . . . Not since Rome and Carthage had there been such a polarization of power on this earth." Senator Arthur Vandenberg, Republican Chairman of the Foreign Relations Committee, literally told senior Truman officials the only way to overcome post–World War II isolationist tendencies and to fully get Congressional and public support was to "scare the hell out of the American people" about the threat of communism to freedom, democracy, and the American way of life. Such was the language of the Truman Doctrine (Yergin 1978:281).

This helps to explain the power of anticommunism, and the free market, in the making of foreign policy since World War II. Likewise, the war on terrorism is sold and legitimized for the American public as necessary to protect democracy, freedom, and the American way of life by exterminating terrorism, ultimately embodied by the most evil and omnipresent figure of first Osama bin Laden and then Saddam Hussein. Phrases such as the war to "end evil" and characterizations of adversaries as an "axis of evil" further illustrate this point.

Fifth, U.S. culture and national style often breeds strong doses of American nationalism and intolerance abroad and at home. Nationalism is often a positive force, for it helps to promote a strong sense of community among members of society in support of a common effort—an essential quality in both war and peace. One of the major problems with a strong sense of nationalism, however, is that patriotism often turns into intolerance and **superpatriotism**. Such attitudes have the tendency to dehumanize adversaries and repress domestic criticism and dissent in the name of national security (see **The Liberty–Security Dilemma** on war, racism, and Japanese internment). Intolerance is particularly evident during periods of national emergency and war, when people feel threats to their values and to their country's security—such as after the 9/11 attacks. Although such emotional responses are quite natural and understandable, strong doses of nationalism heighten the contradictions between the demands of national security and democracy at home, with profound implications for the exercise of individual civil rights and liberties.

THE LIBERTY–SECURITY DILEMMA

The Japanese-American Internment, Race, and the Process of Dehumanization

On February 19, 1942, President Franklin Roosevelt signed Executive Order 9066, authorizing the War Department to remove individuals of Japanese descent living within the continental United States to concentration camps in an effort to ensure the internal security of the country. Those affected had only forty-eight hours to dispose of their homes and businesses, had to forfeit all bank accounts and investments, and were permitted to take only personal belongings that could be carried in hand luggage. Over 110,000 individuals of Japanese descent, including men, women, and children—mostly American citizens on the West Coast—were rounded up and spent the next three years of their lives in eleven camps located in desolate locations throughout the western United States.

General John L. De Witt, commander of the Western Defense Command, expressed the popular sentiment of the times: "A Jap's a Jap! It makes no difference whether he's an American or not." Although the constitutional rights of Japanese-Americans were ruthlessly violated, the U.S. Supreme Court actually upheld the executive order in 1944 in *Korematsu v. United States*, thus reflecting the politics of the war and

the preoccupation with national security over the demands of democracy.

"The wave of antipathy toward Japanese-Americans which engulfed the Pacific Coast in the opening months of World War II had its origin far back in the history of California and the West. It was generated in the climate of indiscriminate antiforeignism which characterized the gold-rush period, and took definite shape during half a century of anti-Chinese activity, during which a hostile image of the 'Oriental' emerged that was subsequently shifted to the Japanese," especially following the attack on Pearl Harbor (TenBroek, Barnhart, and Matson 1954:11).

Yet American fears and paranoia proved to be completely unfounded. The Japanese proved to be very patriotic Americans. The executive order did not apply to the Hawaiian Islands, where over 150,000 Japanese-Americans remained free and where no charges of sabotage were ever reported. The Japanese were model citizens during their stay in the camps. In fact, over 17,000 Japanese-Americans volunteered in the U.S. military to fight in the war, once they were allowed to join in 1944. No Japanese-American soldier ever deserted the U.S. military, even though they were kept in segregated units. Their wartime exploits became legendary.

As John Dower (1986) explained, periods of war usually lead to strong nationalist feelings of self-righteousness, fueled by prejudices of "racial pride, arrogance, and rage on many sides" that dehumanize the enemy. On the home front, it leads to hyper-vigilance against subversives and intolerance of dissent. The **dehumanization process** typically results in simplistic black- and-white views in terms of both one's self-image—as innocent, righteous, superior—and the "image of the enemy" or "others"—as aggressive, evil, inferior.

"The racist code words and imagery that accompanied the war in Asia were often exceedingly graphic and contemptuous" for all parties involved. From the American perspective, the Japanese were portrayed as subhuman and cruel, repeatedly associated with images of apes and vermin in order to convey these traits. Milder images depicted the Japanese as inferior to Westerners and Caucasians, primitive and childish at best, and mentally and emotionally deficient. "Cartoonists, songwriters, filmmakers, war correspondents, and the mass media in general all seized on these images—and so did the social scientists and Asia experts who ventured to analyze the Japanese 'national character' during the war." As Japanese wartime successes mounted early in the war, another stereotype took hold: the Japanese superman, possessed of uncanny discipline and military ferocity. "Subhuman, inhuman, lesser human, superhuman—all that was lacking in the perception of the Japanese enemy was a human like oneself" (Dower 1986:4).

What does the Japanese internment episode suggest about American political culture and the effects of a national security crisis on American values, including freedom of speech and individual rights?

A strong sense of nationalism also has made it difficult for Americans to accept criticism from abroad, including from the country's closest allies, thus reflecting deep-seated isolationist and unilateralist sentiments. As Hoffmann (1968:195) has argued, American foreign policy easily leads to "an activism that others see as imperialistic: for we expect them to join the consensus, we ignore the boundaries and differences between 'them' and 'us,' we prod them out of conviction that we act for their own good, and we do not take resistance gracefully." Americans have such a strong faith in American virtue and progress that it is difficult for them to understand, let alone accept, the value of alternative paths to economic and political development divorced from the American model. Or as was often asked after the 9/11 attacks, how could the United States (and Americans) be so loved and so hated?

A final consequence of American culture and nationalism is its tendency to contribute to major swings in **public moods** or sentiments with respect to U.S. foreign policy. It is commonly argued that "twentieth-century exceptionalism has fueled both interventionism and isolationism" (Davis and Lynn-Jones 1987:24). As Louis Hartz (1955:286) has stated, "Americas seem to oscillate between fleeing from the rest of the world and embracing it with too ardent a passion. An absolute national morality is inspired either to withdraw from 'alien' things or to transform them: it cannot live in comfort constantly by their side." Richard Barnet, in fact (1971:259), has argued that "the internationalist versus isolationist debate is really an argument about little more than military strategy" abroad, in which *both* *competing perspectives ultimately reflect an underlying sense of* unilateralism among the mass public and in America's national style. Or as Stanley Hoffmann (1968:191) has stated, "Both quietism and activism are compensatory assertions of total independence."

Major swings in public opinion have affected U.S. relations with both allies and enemies. This is easily seen in the cycles of American perceptions of U.S.–Russian relations. After the Bolshevik Revolution the United States invaded the Soviet Union during World War I and refused to recognize it until 1933; during World War II the Soviet Union under "Uncle Joe" Stalin was portrayed as a patriotic ally of freedom against fascism; with the rise of the cold war, the Soviet Union represented a monolithic communist threat abroad and at home; the détente years from Nixon to Carter were a time of hope for a cooperative U.S.–Soviet relationship; under Reagan, cooperation was replaced by a new cold war to contain "the evil empire"; and with the collapse of communism Americans hailed Mikhail Gorbachev, Boris Yeltsin, and Vladimir Putin as great leaders in a post–cold war future to be characterized by global peace and prosperity.

Hence, the high hopes and optimism of the immediate post–World War II years were replaced by disillusionment and fear during the cold war. The high hopes of the early post–cold war years have been replaced by the shock and anger of 9/11 that has produced a new global war, but this time on terrorism. Support among elites and the general public for the United States to take an aggressive leadership role in the world surged immediately after September 11, 2001, fueling the Bush administration's assertive policies in the war on terror. As time passed, however, and controversy and cost increased this support eroded, with public sentiment for isolationism surging to what was then its highest level since the start of the cold war—even higher than the immediate post-Vietnam years—by late 2005 (Pew Research Center 2005a). A burst of optimism immediately after Barack Obama's election soon gave way to the opposite, and public sentiment for isolationism continued its climb. Midway into Obama's second year, 49 percent of the American public believed the United States should "mind its own business" and let other nations get along on their own—the highest ever recorded in the Pew polls. Although it receded modestly in 2011, it remained the case that 46 percent of Americans embraced this isolationist perspective (Pew Research Center 2011).

Continuity, Change, and the Vietnam War

This sense of shared nationalism is especially noticeable during war. Thus, despite American fear and apprehension, World War II and the cold war were also times of hope and optimism in America. Not only was the United States innocently thrust onto the world stage to save the world from the tyranny of communism. In the minds of many Americans, especially American leaders, the post–World War II years represented the "American century" and the height of American innocence, benevolence, and, in particular, exceptionalism. As Godfrey Hodgson (1976:12) argues, the United States entered the 1960s in an Augustan mood: "united, confident, conscious of a historical mission, and mobilized for the great task of carrying it out." If Americans were anxious about danger from abroad, "it was because they saw their own society as so essentially just and benevolent that danger could come only from elsewhere. If they found international affairs frustrating, it was because they found it infuriating that foreigners could not always believe that their only ambition was a generous desire to share the abundance of American capitalism and the promise of American democracy with those less fortunate than themselves."

Such a mood of American confidence and mission was best symbolized by **President John F. Kennedy's inaugural address** on January 20, 1961, when he declared:

> Let the word go forth from this time and place, to friend and foe alike, that the torch has been passed to a new generation of Americans—born in this country, tempered by war, disciplined by a hard and bitter peace, proud of our ancient heritage—and unwilling to witness or permit the slow undoing of those human rights to which this Nation has always been committed, and to which we are committed today at home and around the world. Let every nation know, whether it wishes us well or ill, that we shall pay any price, bear any burden, meet any hardship, support any friend, oppose any foe, in order to assure the survival and the success of liberty.

It was this sense of American confidence and exceptionalism—or what J. William Fulbright (1966) called "the arrogance of power"—that ultimately led to war and tragedy in the jungles of Vietnam.

The Vietnam War produced the first major assault on these optimistic assumptions central to American political culture and national style. The Great Depression of the 1930s had precipitated extreme criticism of the innocence and benevolence of American business, capitalism, and free markets. In contrast, the events of the 1960s surrounding civil rights and the Vietnam War led many Americans to question the three assumptions in their entirety. How could the United States be innocent if Vietnam was not vital to American security? How could policies that promoted activities such as the "need to destroy cities in order to save them," carpet bombing and the use of napalm, and the My Lai massacre be justified as acts of American benevolence? How did American failure and withdrawal from the war fit with American exceptionalism? Clearly, Vietnam made clear that Americans were not willing to "pay any price" and "bear any burden." And, especially after Watergate, most members of the public came to lose their trust in public officials, the government, and the political process.

The split between supporters and critics of the war was more than an ideological disagreement over U.S. foreign policy; it represented a fragmentation of American cultural and nationalistic beliefs. The rise of the so-called **Vietnam syndrome** produced different lessons for different segments of the population. Conservatives and the political right saw the Vietnam War as a just cause that was consistent with American innocence, benevolence, and exceptionalism—its failure was explained by the lack of will among the liberal establishment. Liberals and the political left believed that the Vietnam War was an example of the lack of sufficient innocence and benevolence in U.S. foreign policy and that the United States should not and could not impose its will on other people. The mass public emphasized more pragmatic lessons: American troops should be used only for the most vital of interests and for a good cause, where the war would be swift and involve minimal loss of American lives (review A Closer Look on the Weinberger-Powell Doctrine in Chapter 6).

It was the impact of the 1990–91 Persian Gulf War that really was instrumental in renewing American faith in its cultural assumptions and national style. Although many questioned the vital interests at stake, most Americans saw the U.S. role in the Persian Gulf crisis as a just cause. Most important, Americans were able to restore their inherent faith in their exceptionalism with the triumphant and unexpected military rout of Iraq in the war, accounting for the sense of celebration that Americans felt toward the troops who returned from the Persian Gulf and President Bush's historically high public approval ratings following the war. The Persian Gulf War, although it helped restore many of America's cultural assumptions, did not eliminate the memories and shadows of other crucial historical events that have deeply affected the minds of Americans such as World War II, the Korean War, and most important, the Vietnam War.

Events of the last decade in the Middle East have reignited such concerns and contributed to a growing aversion in the American public against aggressive international ventures. In "The Iraq Syndrome," for example, John Mueller (2005:53) argues that, just as the Vietnam syndrome led to a variety of constraints on American foreign policy, so too will an **Iraq syndrome:**

> Among the casualties of the Iraq syndrome could be the Bush doctrine, unilateralism, preemption, preventive war and indispensable nationhood. Indeed, these once-fashionable (and sometimes self-infatuated) concepts are already picking up a patina of quaintness. Specifically, there will likely be a growing skepticism about various key notions: that the United States should take unilateral military action to correct situations or overthrow regimes it considers reprehensible but that present no immediate threat to it, that it can and should forcibly bring democracy to other nations not now so blessed, that it has the duty to rid the world of evil, that having by far the largest defense budget in the world is necessary and broadly beneficial, that international cooperation is of only very limited value, and that Europeans and other well-meaning foreigners are naïve and decadent wimps. The United States may also become more inclined to seek international cooperation, sometimes even showing signs of humility.

The Iraq syndrome appears to have been reinforced by the war in Afghanistan that has been going on for over a decade, and has become not only Obama's war but America's war. Similarly, the violence and unrest associated with the Arab Spring in 2011–2012 have evoked a similar wariness.

Conservatives and liberals possess strong nationalist sentiments and continue to believe in America, but in different ways. Conservatives and the right believe that American innocence, benevolence, and exceptionalism have prevailed throughout American history; in contrast, liberals and the left are more prone to see the good, the bad, and the ugly in American history, while still believing in the possibility of building an America where innocence, benevolence, and exceptionalism reign supreme. As Robertson (1980:348) has put it, "As a New World, many Americans believe their country to be the last, best hope of the world, a place of youth, of new beginnings, of booming. Even those who believe that America is, in reality, no such place of hope or virtue believe it somehow ought to be."

Most members of the mass public, being more pragmatic and centrist, probably entertain both sets of feelings at different times—what they manifest depends upon the salience of the issues and how they are played out politically at the time. A kind of "pessimistic-optimistic dualism," in other words, operates among members of the mass public, since they share a certain cynicism about American politics while still maintaining an optimistic image of American innocence, benevolence, and exceptionalism. This helps to explain how both liberal and conservative views—as embodied, for example, in President Carter's human rights policies, President Reagan's anticommunism, and George W. Bush's war on terrorism—were initially attractive to most members of the public. This may also help to explain why President Obama received so much initial mass support behind his policies to revive the economy despite major governmental activism within the so-called free market system. Such appears to be the contradictory nature of America's culture and national style in the complex politics of U.S. foreign policy.

As the results in Table 11.1 show, in the wake of President Obama's re-election to a second term, the United States remains a narrowly divided nation. Consequently, relatively minor shifts in public opinion can carry larger consequences for how American national style is understood and impacts the politics of U.S. foreign policy. Grappling with this continues to be a major challenge for America's role throughout the world in the second decade of the 21st century.

SUMMARY: PATTERNS IN BELIEFS AND FOREIGN POLICYMAKING

In summary, the public's role in U.S. foreign policymaking depends on three sets of beliefs, providing a more complex view of what makes the public consequential relative to the traditional wisdom. American political culture and national style set the broad context within which the politics of U.S. foreign policy transpire. Then the ideological and foreign policy beliefs of Americans further narrow what is possible and probable within domestic politics and the policymaking process. Finally, public opinion affects the foreign policy process as it fluctuates within the confines of American political culture and ideology.

The rise of a strong sense of American optimism and nationalism, of a foreign policy and ideological consensus, and of a responsive public opinion during the cold war led to increasing presidential power in foreign policy, an expanding national security bureaucracy, the development of a national security and free market ethos, and an acquiescent Congress and domestic environment. In this environment, the president and the executive branch dominated the making of U.S. foreign policy, while the demands of national security took precedence over the demands of democracy.

The challenges of Vietnam and the 1960s led Americans to question the assumptions of American innocence, benevolence, and exceptionalism; produced greater ideological and foreign policy diversity; and contributed to public opinion volatility. These developments led to a reassertive Congress and changes in the domestic environment such as more diverse party politics, new and varied interest groups and social movements, and a more critical media—the topics of the next few chapters. Thus, presidents entering office now face a paradox of presidential power, making it very difficult to successfully govern contemporary foreign policy. Changes in political culture, political ideology, and public opinion since the height of the cold war have meant that the era of extraordinary presidential power in foreign policy has passed and tensions between national security and democracy have increased.

With regard to public opinion, prolonged lack of interest, information, and thought about national and international affairs will not change overnight. Americans, especially members of the mass public, are likely to retain very short attention spans, as well as superficial knowledge and simplistic understandings of national and international affairs despite the rise of globalization. Since the Vietnam War, diversity of ideological and foreign policy beliefs is also likely to continue in the future. While anticommunism was the foundation of the ideological and foreign policy consensus during the cold war, the end of the cold war, 9/11, the Iraq War, and the severe global economic recession have given rise to a new great debate and may impact new interpretations of events. Whatever the case, one thing that can be predicted with great certainty is that the competing foreign policy orientations and the response of public opinion will reflect the moral foundation of American political culture and national style, which together will directly and indirectly impact the making of U.S. foreign policy into the future.

SUGGESTED SOURCES FOR MORE INFORMATION

Davis, Tami R., and Sean M. Lynn-Jones. (1987) "City Upon a Hill," *Foreign Policy* 66 (Spring):3–19. Good overview of American political culture and its foreign policy implications.

Gelpi, Christopher, Peter D. Feaver, and Jason Reifler. (2005/06) "Success Matters: Casualty Sensitivity and the War in Iraq," *International Security* 30 (Winter):7–46. Excellent overview of impact of public opinion.

Heilemann, John, and Mark Halperin. (2010) *Game Change: Obama and the Clintons, McCain and Palin, and the Race of a Lifetime.* New York: Harper. Excellent on the 2008 presidential elections.

Hodgson, Godfrey. (1976) *America in Our Time.* New York: Vintage. Superb historical analysis of the rise and decline of anticommunism and the liberal–conservative consensus.

Holsti, Ole. (2004) *Public Opinion and American Foreign Policy*, rev. ed. Ann Arbor: University of Michigan Press. Provides an excellent overview of the impact of public opinion on foreign policy, including the traditional wisdom and its critique.

Jentleson, Bruce W. (1992) "The Pretty Prudent Public: Post Post-Vietnam American Opinion on the Use of Military Force," *International Studies Quarterly* 36(1):49–74.

Micklethwait, John, and Adrian Woodridge. (2004) *The Right Nation: Conservative Power in America* (Penguin). Excellent on the evolution, contents, and popular appeal of modern conservatism.

Page, Benjamin I., and Robert Y. Shapiro. (1992) *The Rational Public: Fifty Years of Trends in Americans' Policy Preferences.* Chicago: University of Chicago Press. Demonstrates the impact and common sense of an uninterested and uninformed public opinion.

Rosenau, James N. (1961) *Public Opinion and Foreign Policy.* New York: Random House. A classic.

Stephanson, Anders. (1995) *Manifest Destiny: American Expansion and the Empire of Right.* New York: Hill and Wang. Good overview of American exceptionalism.

KEY CONCEPTS

Almond-Lippmann consensus	elite public
American exceptionalism	followership model
American innocence	foreign policy orientations
American national style	fragmentation/swing model
attentive public	Iraq syndrome
classical liberalism	isolationist sentiment
cold war internationalism	liberal–conservative consensus
conservative internationalism	liberal internationalism

mass public
modern liberalism
modern conservatism
moral minority
neoconservatives
noninternationalism
opinion leaders
political culture
political ideology

political socialization
pragmatic majority
principle versus pragmatism
public opinion
rally around the flag
superpatriotism
unilateralism
Vietnam syndrome

OTHER KEY TERMS

dehumanization process
elitist view of the public
moral crusader

President John F. Kennedy's
   inaugural address
public moods

K Street, the center of lobbying in Washington DC — two blocks from the White House

POLITICAL PARTICIPATION AND GROUP POLITICS

Many Americans participate in social movements and in thousands of widely varying groups, such as business, labor, consumer, environmental, religious, ethnic, civic, veterans, and national security groups. To examine the influence of group politics on U.S. foreign policy, *this chapter addresses the following questions:* How do interest groups and social movements influence domestic politics and the policymaking process? What are the origins of groups and how do they develop in American politics? How have group politics evolved since World War II? What has been the nature and impact of the so-called military-industrial complex and the foreign policy establishment? As we will see, group politics have significantly impacted the politics and process of U.S. foreign policy and deeply affect the president's ability to exercise leadership. But let's begin with a general discussion of the public and contemporary political participation, before turning to group politics during the cold war and post–Vietnam eras.

CONTEMPORARY POLITICAL PARTICIPATION

Citizens have many avenues to engage in civic life. They may vote, respond to a public opinion poll, write to their elected representatives, write letters to newspaper or magazine editors, give money for a cause, join an organization or group, work for a candidate or political party, lobby and petition, demonstrate; or become involved in mass movements. While people engage in these activities in elections—by voting and being involved in political parties—they many also actively engage in group politics through interest groups and social movements, which are the focus of this chapter.

Three predominant patterns characterize political participation in the United States. First, most Americans participate infrequently in the political process, and when they do so, it is mainly through voting. Many Americans, in fact, have completely opted out of any form of political participation. Second, American participation in voting declined during the twentieth century, especially after World War II. Since the 1970s, no more than 50 percent of those eligible to vote have cast ballots in presidential general elections and much smaller percentages have voted in presidential primary elections, congressional elections, and state and local elections (the lowest in any developed democracy). Those who do vote are more likely to register as "Independents" as opposed to Democrat or Republican, reflecting "**dealignment**" in which there is no longer a consistent majority party over time. Third, although only a minority participate in interest groups and mass movements, this form of participation actually has increased over time. The rise of interest group and mass movement participation is particularly noticeable if one compares the post–Vietnam War era to the cold war era. In sum, while most Americans do not participate in politics and fewer vote today than in the past, participation in interest groups and social movements has increased since Vietnam.

Who participates? Members of the elite public (and the attentive public) tend to be more likely to vote, join interest groups, and become politically active than members of the mass public. As discussed in Chapter 11, members of the elite public tend to be more interested and better informed about politics and also tend to have greater resources at their disposal—especially information and money—and a greater sense of political efficacy. Members of the mass public also participate, but they do so less frequently than segments of the public who come from the higher socioeconomic classes and who have higher levels of education. Among the mass public, there has been an overall decline in political efficacy and trust in political officials and Washington politics—that is, a sense of powerlessness, mass apathy, and cynicism about the ability to affect change through the political process. Age is another important factor: Older people tend to vote more, younger people less. At the same time, younger people are more likely to become politically active in social movements and group politics than older people.

People participate both to further their own interests and the interests of their country. Interests fluctuate from person to person and depend on how people see the world, which is predominantly a function of their beliefs—that is, of political culture, political ideology, and public opinion (the topics of the previous chapter). While most people who participate do so through voting and, to a lesser extent, through joining groups and giving money, others are more politically "activist"—they give their time and become personally involved (see Conway 2000; Nueman 1986; Verba and Nie 1972; Zurkin, Keeter, Andolina, Jenkins and Karpini 2006).

INTEREST GROUPS AND SOCIAL MOVEMENTS: ORIGINS AND DEVELOPMENT

Interest groups are organizations that possess an overriding concern with the political process and policy outcomes. Interest groups tend to form in waves, usually in reaction to key events often related to political or economic instability or turmoil. For example, large numbers of interest groups formed during the 1930s in response to the Great Depression, during the 1940s and early 1950s in response to World War II and the cold war, and during the late 1960s and 1970s in response to events such as the Vietnam War. These time periods are often characterized by "negative" events—that is, events that hurt people or are perceived to be counterproductive for people's lives. Such events activate people, many of whom previously may have been apathetic and politically passive.

Also, periods of political instability and turmoil often produce **social movements**—large coalitions of individuals and groups that loosely unite around certain issues, usually in opposition to the status quo. Social movements involve thousands, sometimes millions, of people. They usually involve a change in the way people think about an issue, and these changes in attitudes usually remain even after the social movement fades. Social movements involve dozens, sometimes hundreds, of interest groups—both those who have been around for a while and more recent groups that have arisen in reaction to the political climate of the times (Cigler and Loomis 2002; Wilson 1995).

Social movements and groups tend to go through life cycles. Social movements tend to have a relatively short life span. Initially highly visible and potentially influential, they wither away as the issue dies due to either success or failure. Interest groups that survive tend to go through a longer life cycle. Groups in their formative stages tend to be more informally structured and nonbureaucratic. New interest groups, like the social movements of which they are often a part, also tend to be more purposive, as group leaders and members are motivated to accomplish certain goals. They also tend to be **challenging groups** in the sense that group leaders and followers are usually unhappy with things as they currently exist and are change oriented, challenging some aspect of the status quo, such as established groups.

With time, interest groups tend to become more formal and less purposive. The activities of older groups tend to be much more bureaucratic and institutionalized. Members of older, **established groups** also tend to join for material and solidarity (social) reasons—for example, in order to defend certain policies, get certain services, or socialize with others. Older groups, especially those that are accepted or legitimate in society and have been somewhat successful in fulfilling their original purposive goals, also tend to be content with, and supportive of, the status quo. Every political system, according to David Truman (1971:xii) "of course, tends to discriminate in favor of established groups of interests, and it may deny to new groups access to points of decision." Established groups tend to support the status quo and thus promote continuity in the policymaking process.

In sum, *American group politics tends to go through different phases of political stability and instability.* During more stable periods, established groups and the status quo tend to dominate. Challenging groups exist, but they are often few in number, small in size and support, and invisible to most Americans. However, times of greater political instability produce considerable social movement activity and interest group expansion. During these periods, major political challenges of the status quo occur in which efforts are made to change the ideological beliefs and institutions that dominate society and the government. While the forces supporting the status quo usually have a great advantage in resisting challenging groups, it is during these times that political changes have the greatest potential and likelihood of occurring.

Challenging groups, in contrast, attempt to change domestic politics and the policymaking process. *How successful are challenging groups at surviving, being accepted within society, and gaining their original goals?* Sociologist William Gamson performed a classic in-depth study of over fifty major challenging groups throughout American history. As **Figure 12.1** shows, he found that fewer than half of the challenging groups were able to survive and gain minimal acceptance within society. Furthermore, only half of the groups were successful in gaining at least some of their goals. Overall, while roughly 40 percent of the challenging groups were successful in both gaining some legitimacy and achieving some of their goals, over 40 percent collapsed entirely. As Gamson (1975:140) concludes, "The central difference among political actors is captured by the idea of being inside or outside of the polity. Those who are inside are members whose interest is vested—that is, recognized as valid by other members. Those who are outside are challengers. They lack the basic prerogative of members—routine access to decisions that affect them."

Many different factors account for these outcomes. However, challenging groups tend to have their greatest impact on those issues with great salience and visibility in domestic politics. Such issues become politicized and attract the attention of the elite and mass publics throughout society beyond the confines of government policymakers and established groups. However, for issues of low salience—the normal state of affairs for most issues—challenging groups are usually unable to overcome the lack of public attention and penetrate the web of relations that exists between government policymakers and established groups.

Clearly, group politics is demanding and rough. It tends to pit people from new and challenging social groups and movements against people from more established and status quo–oriented groups. Success for new and challenging groups is an uphill battle because more established groups tend to enjoy considerable support from much of society and the government. However, challenging groups that succeed in gaining legitimacy and promoting their goals are able to affect the public and their beliefs, political participation, domestic politics, and the governmental policymaking process.

Figure 12.1 Political Outcomes for Challenging Groups

		LEGITIMACY *Minimal Acceptance*	
		Yes	No
GOALS *Some Achieved*	Yes	Full Response 38% (20)	Preemption 11% (6)
	No	Cooptation 9% (5)	Collapse 42% (22)
		N = 53	

SOURCE: William A. Gamson, *The Strategy of Social Protest* (Homewood, Ill.: Dorsey Press, 1975), p. 37.

INFLUENCE STRATEGIES IN GROUP POLITICS

Interest groups and social movements directly and indirectly influence the domestic political environment and the governmental policymaking process in a number of ways.
First and most well known, groups usually "lobby" policymakers involved in the policy process. This is done by providing information and money, as well as mobilizing followers to provide support or cause political trouble. Second, such techniques are used to influence the political agenda, public beliefs and behavior, and electoral politics. Third, some groups, especially those that are well established and have close relationships with government agencies and personnel, are consulted by and participate in the policy process. Fourth, well-established groups also tend to serve as important sources of political recruitment for official positions within government. Finally, groups that are extremely active internationally, such as multinational corporations, affect U.S. foreign policy and the policymaking process because of their visibility and activities abroad.

As political scientist Chung-in Moon (1988) makes clear, *groups typically engage in four general strategies to influence the politics of foreign policy:*

1. the access-to-power approach,

2. the technocratic approach,

3. the coalition-building approach, and

4. the grassroots mobilization approach.

In the "access-to-power approach," interest groups use high-powered power brokers, law firms, public relations firms, and consultants to gain direct access to top policymakers within the government. The "technocratic approach" is another form of direct lobbying, in which groups retain lawyers and technical consultants who use their expertise and contacts to influence midlevel decisionmakers in government, the media, and other relevant groups in society. The other two **lobbying strategies** used by groups and social movements attempt to affect the policymaking process more indirectly by targeting electoral politics and domestic politics in general. The "coalition-building approach" emphasizes the formation of group alliances based on mutual interests in order to politicize issues, get issues on the political agenda, and place pressure on the government's policymaking process. Finally, "the grassroots mobilization approach" attempts to rally mass support in order to politicize issues, affect electoral and group politics, and increase public pressure on the policymaking process. As Hedrick Smith (1989:ch. 9) points out, the old game of **inside politics** within the Washington community has been supplemented by a new game of **outside politics** since Vietnam.

Social movements and groups are politically active because of their potential impact on domestic politics and, more specifically, on the government's policymaking process. With respect to Congress, for example, a study by the Congressional Research Service (2001:38) concluded:

> Groups come to represent significant allies, or formidable opponents, when they are well organized; when they represent a sizable, well-educated, and middle- to upper-class constituency and when the positions they wish members of Congress to support are viewed as mainstream and respectable, entailing little or no political cost, and some political gains (e.g., support for Israel, Greece, Taiwan, Ireland, etc.); when the groups confront no significant internal counterlobbies in the private sector or can count on the neutral stance of much of the public when an opinion is yet unformed.

As Smith (1989:71) explains, "access is bread and butter. . . . Without it, your case doesn't get heard; you can't be a player in the power game. Obviously that's why corporations, unions, and lobbyists of all sorts pay enormous fees for prestigious Washington lawyers or pump millions into campaigning. They are buying access, if not more."

But outside politics has also been growing among groups, both domestically and transnationally. This has probably become most visible in the economic arena where individuals and a variety of groups concerned with the effects of the globalization of market forces—such as on the environment, over jobs and poverty, and growing national and global inequality—have been building coalitions and engaging in grassroots mobilization against multinational corporations, Western governments, and international organizations, such as the IMF, the World Bank, and the World Trade Organization. This has resulted in major political demonstrations against economic and political leaders, often when they meet to discuss the international economy. Examples include demonstrations at the World Trade Organization meetings in Seattle in 1999 (Aaronson 2002), and the "99%" or "Occupy Wall Street" demonstrations against elitism, corporate greed and the influence of the wealthy over government. So-called Tea Party demonstrations during the Obama administration are also examples of this phenomenon.

In other words, these social movements and interest groups try to influence the political agenda and policymaking by gaining access to policymakers and participating in policymaking, providing information, contributing campaign funds and other money, actively campaigning, engaging in litigation, demonstrating, attracting media coverage, networking with other groups, attempting to gain general public support, having individuals appointed to governmental positions, and by undertaking international activity. Social movements and interest groups have become increasingly active, consequential and complex for the making of U.S. foreign policy since World War II. *Group politics in foreign policy has gone through two major eras: (1) the cold war years and (2) the post–Vietnam years to the present.*

GROUP POLITICS DURING THE COLD WAR

Before World War II, the group process played a vital role in domestic politics and the policy process of U.S. foreign policymaking, especially with respect to economic issues of trade and protectionism. For most social movements and interest groups, however, national security was relatively unimportant and "low" policy compared to economic and domestic issues. Those few groups that were devoted exclusively to foreign policy rarely had much influence over the policymaking process. This situation permanently changed with American intervention in World War II, the rise of the cold war and American hegemonic power abroad.

During the 1940s and 1950s, new and established groups in American society became heavily involved in the foreign policymaking process. Most of these groups were overwhelmingly anticommunist and conservative in their foreign policy orientations, reinforced by the rise of extremely conservative social movements at the time, represented by the forces of McCarthyism. *The results of these developments for group politics and the making of U.S. foreign policy were* (1) the rise of foreign policy– and cold war–oriented groups, (2) the development of a military-industrial-scientific infrastructure, and (3) the rise of a foreign policy establishment. These patterns in group politics during the cold war contributed to a domestic context that led to the rise of presidential power, the expansion of the foreign policy bureaucracy, an acquiescent Congress, a supportive public, and bipartisanship on an anticommunist foreign policy consensus in party politics. Groups and movements that challenged containment policies from the political left did exist during the cold war years. However, they were small in numbers and resources and constantly on the political defensive and remained primarily outside the realm of mainstream domestic politics.

Foreign Policy and Cold War–Oriented Groups

The 1940s and 1950s resulted in the rise of numerous anticommunist groups that became active in the politics of U.S. foreign policy, including (1) national security and public policy groups, (2) veterans and military support groups, (3) political and civic groups, (4) businesses and corporations, (5) labor unions, (6) religious groups, and (7) ethnic groups. There were certainly differences in perceptions among leaders and members of these groups concerning the intensity of the Soviet communist threat and the particulars of U.S. national security policy; some were more anticommunist than others. However, all tended to share a general cold war internationalist orientation that formed the basis of a consensus in the making of U.S. foreign policy.

National security and public policy groups became increasingly active and prominent in the making of U.S. foreign policy during World War II and the cold war. Among others, these groups included the Carnegie Endowment for International Peace, Committee on the Present Danger, Council on Foreign Relations, Ford and Rockefeller Foundations, Foreign Policy Research Institute, and the Rand Corporation. Membership and involvement in most of these groups were limited to proponents of American cold war policies, including select government officials (both current and former), business leaders, academics, journalists, and other opinion leaders within American society. The activities of these groups typically consisted of group seminars on important issues, involvement in policy research and proposals, and the publication and communication of members' work. Not only did these activities affect the beliefs of the attentive and mass publics, but many of these groups became extremely important sources of ideas and personnel for the government during the cold war years, especially the Council on Foreign Relations.

Headquartered in New York City, the **Council on Foreign Relations (CFR)** not only provided a significant forum for generating ideas and policies for opinion leaders and government officials but was a significant source of political recruitment. Many important government positions throughout the foreign policy bureaucracy were often filled by presidential appointment of CFR members, including those at the secretary level and the national security advisor. As Robert Schulzinger (1984) concluded in his history of the Council on Foreign Relations, entitled *The Wise Men of Foreign Affairs*, its members filled the role of a "professional clergy" for the foreign policy community in and out of government.

Veterans and military support organizations were staunchly anticommunist supporters of American cold war policies and emphasized a large defense buildup and reliance on force. These organizations included the major veterans' organizations, such as the American Legion and the Veterans of Foreign Wars, and military support organizations, such as the Navy League and the American Ordnance Association.

Broad-based political and civic organizations also became participants in the anticommunist foreign policy consensus in American politics. Americans for Democratic Action, for example, was launched in the early 1950s by prominent American Democrats and liberals as a means to support the government's cold war policies.

Business and labor groups were also part of the consensus supporting U.S. foreign policy. Business had long played a prominent role in American politics and government, especially since the rise of industrialization and the development of modern corporations. Much of this was because business leaders were regularly recruited into government policymaking positions by political leaders and because of the increasing scale of activities of American business abroad, especially in Latin America.

As historian William Appleman Williams (1962) has argued throughout his work, by the turn of the century U.S. foreign policy became increasingly supportive of a so-called open door policy for American business and investment abroad (see also Lake 1988). Moreover, with World War II and the onset of the cold war, business groups such as the Chamber of Commerce, Committee for Economic Development, and the National Association of Manufacturers became strong supporters of the government's containment policy. Industry involvement in foreign policy was reinforced by the growing role of big business in defense production. As a result, a type of big business and government partnership developed in support of U.S. national security and economic policy during the cold war years.

For example, as American banks and companies became increasingly multinationalized following World War II, they located in countries where there was a strong U.S. governmental presence abroad, such as in Latin America and Europe. One can debate whether the American "flag" led the American "dollar" abroad, or vice versa. Regardless, both business and government were driven to promote an open-door or free market ethos in U.S. foreign policy during the cold war years. The **government–business relationship** was generally interactive and supportive: The increasing global presence of American government and the relocation of American multinational industry abroad led to greater mutual dependency between American business and government abroad. U.S. governmental actions to assist postwar reconstruction of Western Europe through the Marshall Plan also relied on American private investment in the region; in addition, America's military and economy became increasingly dependent on continued access to oil by American petroleum companies, especially in the Middle East. As Michael Stoff (1980:208) concluded, private corporations, not the government, "became the agents of national policy" (see also Ikenberry 1988; Yergin 1990). In turn, American multinational corporations expected the U.S. government to promote American private investment abroad and prevent nationalization by foreign governments.

Organized labor was also a strong supporter of anticommunism at home and abroad. This fact may come as a surprise to many Americans given the popular impression of labor-management conflict and labor's pre–World War II history. However, by the 1930s, as part of Roosevelt's New Deal policies, the government officially recognized the right of workers to form unions, and the often fierce opposition to unions by business and government abated. More important, organized labor's growing legitimacy and moderation in goals, the postwar return of economic prosperity, Republican and McCarthyist attacks against New Deal policies and unionization, and the national security demands of World War II and the cold war produced unions that were much more comfortable and supportive of the status quo.

After World War II, the **American Federation of Labor–Congress of Industrial Organizations(AFL-CIO)**, the umbrella organization to which most American unions belonged during the 1950s, strongly supported the government's cold war policies at home and abroad. The AFL-CIO Institute for Free Labor Development was active, for example, in supporting anticommunist unionization and movements in Latin America (and often worked in conjunction with the CIA). Hence, while many American unions historically were the source of liberalism and the political left, they too became part of the anticommunist consensus during the cold war (Fraser and Gerstle 1989).

Religious and ethnic groups also played prominent anticommunist roles during the cold war. Religious movements and groups have always played a powerful role throughout American history. As Garry Wills (1990:25) argues, "Religion has been at the center of our major political crises, which are always moral crises—the supporting and opposing of wars, of slavery, of corporate power, of civil rights, of sexual codes, of 'the West,' of American separatism and claims to empire." Given this background, it is perhaps not surprising that religion played a prominent role in the rise of the anticommunist consensus during the post–World War II years. For example, the Catholic Church historically was extremely critical of communism and its atheistic views, rallying American Catholics behind the government's cold war policies. The late 1940s and early 1950s also witnessed the rise of Protestant fundamentalism against the secular trends of modern society, a movement that provided support for McCarthyism during the cold war years.

The United States is also a country of great ethnic diversity, and ethnic groups have actively influenced the making of U.S. foreign policy. For example, the Soviet Union's domination of Eastern Europe provoked a strong anticommunist response from ethnic groups with ties to the region. Polish Americans, reinforced by their Catholicism, were particularly vocal over the fate of Poland. Furthermore, they also represented a large bloc of potential voters in a number of key industrial states. This domestic political background helps to explain why Stalin's eventual consolidation of power in Poland was one of the important postwar developments during the late 1940s in hardening attitudes within the Truman administration and throughout society around the issue of anticommunism.

The famed **China lobby**, or Taiwan lobby, gained great prominence during the cold war years. The China lobby consisted of Nationalist Chinese officials and Americans, including government officials, Protestant missionaries, China watchers and journalists, American business leaders, and a broad coalition of diverse anticommunist groups, such as the American China Policy Association, the Committee to Defend America by Aiding Anti-Communist China, and the Committee for One Million (against the admission of Communist China into the United Nations). These groups shared a common concern over the so-called fall of China and identified with the Nationalist Chinese government in Taiwan. Participants within the China lobby tended to emphasize the greater importance of Asia over Europe as a market, for national security reasons as symbolized by the Korean War, and for the future of Christianity. Members of the China lobby attacked the Truman administration for its Eurocentric and inadequate foreign policies, played a prominent role in the rise of McCarthyism, and helped forge an anticommunist consensus throughout society and the government during the cold war years. Their efforts help to explain why American presidents and their advisors were always more concerned about the political threat posed by the right than those on the left (U.S. Congress, House Committee on Foreign Affairs 1982; Bachrack 1976; Koen 1974).

In sum, the prevalent social movements and groups during the cold war together helped to promote and reinforce the development of an anticommunist consensus, a strong national security and free market ethos throughout American society, in electoral and domestic politics, and in the governmental policymaking process. The prominence of these groups and their cold war orientation contributed to the rise of a powerful president in foreign policy, the expansion of the national security and economic bureaucracies, and the development of an acquiescent and bipartisan Congress—all with strong public support throughout society and the domestic political environment. Clearly, the cold war years were a time in which group politics formed a consensus behind a strong anticommunist foreign policy, and most challenging groups remained on the fringes of American politics.

The Military-Industrial-Scientific Infrastructure

Before World War II, few institutions within the government or throughout American society were oriented toward foreign affairs and national security. World War II changed this situation dramatically and permanently. Almost overnight, the U.S. government redirected itself to waging a global war in which the military expanded enormously and civilian agencies grew to assist the president in fighting the conflict. This governmental effort, in turn, put the economy and society on a war footing to provide the necessary personnel, equipment, and services to achieve allied victory. Thus, a military-industrial-scientific infrastructure developed throughout society and government to support the war effort. Unlike the aftermath of previous wars in American history, the U.S. military demobilized for only a short time following World War II. With the rise of anticommunism and the cold war, the United States once more expanded its resources. This not only resulted in the ascendance of the president in foreign policy and the growth of the foreign policy bureaucracy, but it also spurred the growth of the military-industrial-scientific infrastructure, which played a prominent role in defense politics and the making of U.S. foreign policy during the postwar years.

The **military-industrial complex** is a term popularized by President Dwight Eisenhower during his farewell address to the nation to describe the existence of various segments of society with complementary interests that were mutually dependent on one another and together played a vital role in the politics of U.S. foreign policy. Instead of a small collection of individuals within the military and private industry who conspired to dominate American national security policy against the wishes of the American people, Eisenhower argued that a broad complex of private, academic and governmental bureaucratic institutions was an inevitable outcome of a society permanently mobilized for war, necessitated by containment and deterrence policies. Hence, **military-industrial-scientific infrastructure** (or national security infrastructure) is a more accurate term than military-industrial complex (Yarmolinsky 1971).

Four major segments of society comprise this complex: (1) the military establishment within the executive branch, (2) industry and business, (3) Congress, and (4) academia and the scientific community. Each of these organized segments had complementary interests: Members of the military establishment wanted weaponry and equipment to support containment; industry wanted to expand and make money; members of Congress wanted military bases and defense industry in their districts to provide jobs and votes; and scientists wanted the prestige and prominence that came with large grants and direct involvement in government.

As we discussed in Chapter 6, the military establishment within the executive branch, especially the Department of Defense, grew enormously in size and scope as a result of World War II and the onset of the cold war. Demands for personnel, weaponry, and equipment were equally enormous. The government relied on its own production process, supervised by the Atomic Energy Commission and operated by private industry, for building nuclear weapons. However, the military contracted out to private industry to meet its needs in virtually all other areas, from conventional weapons to uniforms to base construction.

Much of American industry became directly involved in equipping the military as a result of the cold war. This transformation began with U.S. entry into World War II, when the production of civilian materials and services changed to military production to defeat Germany and Japan. Large U.S. companies such as General Motors, Chrysler, McDonnell Douglas, and Boeing retooled their assembly lines to produce tanks and bombers rather than cars and commercial airplanes. With the rise of the cold war, these same companies continued working for the government and the Defense Department. By the 1950s, many Fortune 500 companies were **defense contractors** for the U.S. government. Some companies, such as General Dynamics and Rockwell International, became totally dependent on defense production; for other companies, such as General Electric, defense work was only a part of its business. Smaller, local businesses also became involved in defense work through the subcontracting of weapons systems or provision of services at local military bases. Taken together, defense-related industries provided millions of jobs for Americans, gaining the support of organized labor and workers in general. Thus, the permanent cold war economy and a close business–government partnership in defense politics were born (Melman 1970; Barnet 1985).

Congress helped to reinforce the networks of relationships that developed in defense politics. Members of Congress had to approve the defense programs and budget for the government. This role gave them considerable power, especially within the Armed Services and Appropriations committees. In return for political support, members of Congress were able to persuade the Pentagon and defense industry to build military bases and businesses in their states and districts. Not surprisingly, the military came to operate hundreds of bases located in every state, and major weapons systems were typically subcontracted out to dozens of businesses throughout the country. Although many basing and contracting decisions may have been made for sound national security and financial reasons, they also were made in order to win the political support of members of Congress. In this way, members of Congress were able to claim responsibility for economic growth and jobs back home, attracting local constituent support for their reelection.

Although it has typically been deemphasized in discussions of the military-industrial complex, academia and the scientific community represent the final element in the military-industrial-scientific infrastructure. The ties between science and the government date back to the nineteenth century. However, the major drive to bring scientists together to work for the U.S. government began with the **Manhattan Project**, the effort to develop the atomic bomb during World War II (Rhodes 1986). Since that time scientists in physics, chemistry, and other natural sciences have been employed by government, academia, and research and policy institutes to provide the know-how for designing weapons and turning ideas into reality. Led by the more prominent universities, such as Yale University, Massachusetts Institute of Technology, Stanford University, and the University of California at Berkeley, the **militarization of research** occurred as social scientists and other academics provided many of the ideas that became the basis of U.S. national security policy during the cold war years, such as nuclear deterrence theory, the theory of limited war, intelligence analysis and operations, counterinsurgency warfare, and Third World development strategies for nation building and modernization (Kaplan 1983; Latham 2000; Leslie 1994; Packenham 1973; Simpson 1994; Winks 1996). In fact, scholarship in international relations proliferated and graduate programs in international studies grew to become a key source of recruitment and expertise for U.S. government foreign affairs personnel (Hoffman 1977).

In sum, the 1940s and 1950s resulted in the formation of a large military-industrial-scientific infrastructure involving millions of people and the support of most segments of American society. Close and mutually supportive networks of relationships developed between the military establishment, industry, Congress, and the scientific community, particularly among more prominent groups and individuals. These relationships were reinforced by the development of a **revolving door system** through which members of the military were hired by the defense industry upon retirement, defense industry leaders were appointed to important positions within the Department of Defense, and so on (U.S. Congress, GAO 1989).

The net result of these activities was that each organized segment of society could claim that its activities contributed to strengthening American national security while they were enmeshed in the politics of national defense:

> The influence of politics on national defense is so pervasive, so deeply embedded at every level, that it becomes difficult even to identify. Virtually every American is involved, directly or indirectly. Selfish political and economic interests in military affairs are often carefully wrapped in the American flag, and defended with the most elegant, sophisticated, and technically complex rationales. . . . Politics influences literally thousands of decisions that constantly must be made to create the treaties, strategies, forces, bases, and weapons that collectively make up our national defense (Kotz 1988:viii).

The development of a national security infrastructure and the politics of national defense contributed not only to the development of the anticommunist consensus and a permanent large military establishment in support of the requirements of the containment strategy during the cold war era but also to waste, corruption, vested interests, and resistance to any challenges to the status quo. This also had a major impact in exacerbating the tensions between the demands of national security and the requirements of democracy. Aware of this possibility, **Eisenhower's farewell address** to the country warned Americans to be "knowledgeable and alert" concerning the consequences of a military-industrial complex for the functioning of American democracy (see **The Liberty–Security Dilemma**).

THE LIBERTY–SECURITY DILEMMA

Eisenhower Warns of a Military-Industrial Complex

On January 17, 1961, President Dwight Eisenhower, former General and commander of all allied forces in the European theater during World War II, made his farewell address to the American people, imploring them to be knowledgeable citizens alert to the threats and opportunities that the United States faced both abroad and at home. It is in this speech that the term "military-industrial complex" was first used, as Eisenhower warned Americans of the dangers it posed for the workings of democracy. Because he was retiring from public office, **Eisenhower's farewell address** may have represented a public airing of his most personal thoughts and feelings.

In his address, Eisenhower *first warned of a permanent military-industrial complex.* "A vital element in keeping the peace is our military establishment. Our arms must be mighty, ready for instant action, so that no potential aggressor may be tempted to risk his own destruction." Yet as he pointed out, "our military organization today bears little relation to that known by any of my predecessors in peacetime, or

(continued)

indeed by the fighting men of World War II or Korea. Until the latest of our world conflicts, the United States had no armaments industry. American makers of plowshares could, with time and as required, make swords as well." But according to Eisenhower, "we can no longer risk emergency improvisation of national defense; we have been compelled to create a permanent armaments industry of vast proportions. Added to this, three and a half million men and women are directly engaged in the defense establishment. This conjunction of an immense military establishment and a large arms industry is 'new' in the American experience. The total influence—economic, political, even spiritual—is felt in every city, every State house, every office of the Federal government." Although Eisenhower recognized "the imperative need for this development," he also believed that Americans "must not fail to comprehend its grave implications. Our toil, resources and livelihood are all involved; so is the very structure of our society."

Eisenhower, therefore, emphasized the need for vigilance. "In the councils of government, we must guard against the acquisition of unwarranted influence, whether sought or unsought, by the military-industrial complex. The potential for the disastrous rise of misplaced power exists and will persist." Eisenhower continued, *"We must never let the weight of this combination endanger our liberties or democratic processes.* We should take nothing for granted. Only an alert and knowledgeable citizenry can compel the proper meshing of the huge industrial and military machinery of defense with our peaceful methods and goals, so that security and liberty may prosper together" (emphasis added).

The *second new threat that Eisenhower pointed to was the role of technology, science, and academia and the rise of a scientific-technological elite.* "Akin to, and largely responsible for the sweeping changes in our industrial-military posture, has been the technological revolution during the recent decades. In this revolution, research has become central; it also becomes more formalized, complex, and costly. A steadily increasing share is conducted for, by, or at the direction of, the federal government." This technological revolution has changed the nature of academia and the conduct of science. As Eisenhower explained, "Today, the solitary inventor, tinkering in his shop, has been overshadowed by task forces of scientists in laboratories and testing fields. In the same fashion, the free university, historically the fountainhead of free ideas and scientific discovery, has experienced a revolution in the conduct of research." One of the consequences is that "partly because of the huge costs involved, a government contract becomes virtually a substitute for intellectual curiosity." Given these changes, Eisenhower warned that "the prospect of domination of the nation's scholars by federal employment, project allocations, and the power of money is ever present—and is gravely to be regarded. Yet, in holding scientific research and discovery in respect, as we should, we must also be alert to the equal and opposite danger that public policy could itself become the captive of a scientific-technological elite."

Would President Eisenhower argue that a military-industrial complex (along with the rise of a scientific-technological elite) exists today and threatens democratic and civil liberties?

SOURCE: U.S. President Dwight D. Eisenhower, "Farewell Address" (January 17, 1961).

The Foreign Policy Establishment

The cold war years also saw the rise of a **foreign policy establishment**, an informal network of prominent, like-minded individuals who shared an anticommunist consensus and moved in and out of high-level policymaking positions within the executive branch, exerting great influence on the making of U.S. foreign policy. They have been referred to as the "best and the brightest," "national security managers," and the "wise men." By constantly shifting between high-level positions in government and in the private world, they also provided a critical bridge between the president, the national security bureaucracy, and key groups and institutions throughout American society.

According to Godfrey Hodgson (1973), *the foreign policy establishment was defined by commonalities across five areas.* First, they shared a common history. Contrary to popular opinion, this common history was not principally membership in the upper class, although "it may help you to rise in the establishment if you have inherited wealth, or family connections with powerful men in it, or an Ivy League education" (Hodgson 1973:6–7). Nor should the foreign policy establishment be confused with a conspiracy by a small group of individuals to control the government. Rather, they consisted of hundreds of individuals of varying degrees of prominence who came to know each other (or of each other) through governmental service, work outside the government, and through social interaction.

The crucial common experience was World War II. "It was the war which brought together the three groups which make up the modern foreign policy establishment: internationally-minded lawyers, bankers and executives of international corporations in New York; government officials in Washington; and academics" (Hodgson 1973:8). They were initially recruited to staff the war effort in the War Department, State Department, and Office of Strategic Services (OSS). It wasn't long before many of these people began to interact with each other and work together, forming working networks of relationships that continued after the war.

Second, the foreign policy establishment shared common emphases on anti-isolationism and anticommunism in foreign policy. They "felt that appeasement had been a disaster, and that the lesson to be drawn from the struggle against Fascism was that there were those in the world who could only be restrained by force" (Hodgson 1973:9). This approach to foreign policy was heavily conditioned by a "hard" **realpolitik**—or **power politics**—view of the world in which states competed for power, wealth and status, where threats to international stability and order came from unsatisfied and revolutionary great powers, and the threat and use of force (more than diplomacy) were considered the most effective instrument of statecraft. They were particularly concerned with the threat of the Soviet Union and communist expansion in Europe, but had little fear of domestic communism like the political right and McCarthyism.

Third, the foreign policy establishment shared a commitment to global moral and political leadership. They "wanted to succeed Britain as the military and economic guarantor and moral leader of an enlightened, liberal, democratic, and capitalist world order" who felt that the postwar years represented the "American century," and they relished exercising the unprecedented economic, military, and political power of the United States throughout the world (Hodgson 1973:11). This outlook probably reached its height working under President John F. Kennedy, where "they carried with them an exciting sense of American elitism, a sense that the best men had been summoned forth from the country to harness this dream to a new American nationalism, bringing a new, strong, dynamic spirit to our historic role in world affairs, not necessarily to bring the American dream to reality here at home, but to bring it to reality elsewhere in the world" (Halberstam 1969:41,100; see also Isaacson and Thomas 1986). Such an attitude exemplified what many have called "hubris" and what J. William Fulbright (1966) would shortly call an "arrogance of power."

Fourth, the establishment shared a preference for the "political center." As Hodgson (1973:12) put it, "The characteristic men of the establishment—Stimson, McCloy, Acheson, Rusk, Bundy—have always seen themselves as the men of judicious, pragmatic wisdom, avoiding ideology and steering the middle course between the Yahoos of the right and the impractical sentimentality of the left." This reflected a long tradition going back to Teddy Roosevelt, of "an aristocracy come to power, convinced of its own disinterested quality, believing itself above both petty partisan interest and material greed," and viewing their role as service (Halberstam 1969:49)—many neither registered to vote or considered themselves moderate Republicans.

Finally, the establishment's preferred "technique" was to operate out of public view and within the executive branch, especially the White House. Members of the establishment virtually never ran for elective office and they tended to be distrustful and fearful of mass opinion. They were usually appointed by the president to policymaking positions within the foreign policy bureaucracy, constantly revolved from government to the private world and back through membership in prominent foreign policy groups, most notably the CFR.

Thus, the foreign policy establishment consisted of "a self-recruiting group of men (virtually no women) who have shared a bipartisan philosophy towards, and have exercised practical influence on, the course of American defense and foreign policy" (Hodgson 1973:13). They played roles in every post–World War II administration and contributed to a fundamental consistency and consensus through the Vietnam War. Of course, they were not monolithic: differences existed and considerable infighting over U.S. foreign policy took place. With regard to U.S. policy toward Vietnam, for example, debates were limited to when and how to intervene: now or later? With advisors or troops? Therefore, "right up to 1965, the year of decision, the overwhelming consensus of the establishment accepted without moral or intellectual doubt that the war would have to be escalated—if the only alternative was losing it" (Hodgson 1973:13).

THE RISE OF MOVEMENTS OF THE LEFT AND THE RIGHT

The ideological and foreign policy consensus was challenged initially from the political left and then from the political right, changing the nature of group politics since Vietnam. These challenges contributed greatly to the collapse of the anticommunist foreign policy consensus and had dramatic implications for group politics and U.S. foreign policy.

From the Left: The Civil Rights and Antiwar Movements

The rise of liberalism and the new left began in the late 1950s with the **civil rights movement**, led by groups such as the Southern Christian Leadership Conference (SCLC), under the leadership of Martin Luther King, Jr., and the Student Nonviolent Coordinating Committee (SNCC). Many white liberals, especially students from northern schools and groups such as Students for a Democratic Society (SDS), joined the fight for civil rights during the early 1960s as the movement expanded into the North to address issues of racism and poverty (Branch 1988; Halberstam 1998).

The bulk of the civil rights movement represented a nonviolent liberal approach to reforming American society. However, the often violent resistance to the civil rights movement by more extreme segments of the public, established groups, and local governments in the North and the South embittered many of the protesters and radicalized them. Thus, the civil rights movement was accompanied by the growth of black nationalism and black power, represented by Malcolm X and the Black Panthers. Although the Civil Rights Act was passed in 1964 and Johnson initiated the war on poverty, these actions were perceived by many as too little, too late. African-American frustration and despair at local resistance, in fact, reached the boiling point, triggering riots in Los Angeles, Detroit, and other urban areas throughout the country. Therefore, what began as a liberal hope to bring African-Americans into mainstream society ultimately ended with Americans bitterly divided, contributing to the collapse of the liberal–conservative ideological consensus.

The Vietnam War generated the **antiwar movement** during the mid-1960s. The antiwar movement represented a broad coalition of Americans united against the escalation and continuation of the war. Many participants in this movement had been involved in, and heavily influenced by, the civil rights movement. The antiwar movement grew from a few dozen disparate groups during the early 1960s to represent a loose coalition of well over a thousand groups including Quakers, pacifists, students, the old peace movement, Democrats, liberals, and the old left and new left by the late 1960s. At its height, the antiwar movement was supported by a large segment of society and staged peaceful demonstrations involving millions of people throughout the country. Not only did over half a million men refuse to be drafted, but more and more soldiers went AWOL (absent without leave) and service people joined the peace marches as well (Benedetti and Chatfield 1990; Gitlin 1987; Powers 1973).

Like the civil rights movement, the antiwar movement represented the rise of challenging movements and groups reflecting the resurgence of liberalism and the ascendance of the new left. Furthermore, the Johnson administration's continuing escalation of the Vietnam War and the domestic resistance encountered by the antiwar movement led them to question the wisdom of working within the system and relying on nonviolence (Vasquez 1976). Thus, by the late 1960s *opposition to the war took many forms:*

> letters to congressmen and Presidents; advertisements in newspapers; signatures on petitions; vigils in town centers, at government buildings, installations, and other public places; lobbying congressmen; working to elect candidates sympathetic to the cause; tax refusal; draft refusal; desertion from the armed forces; nonviolent civil disobedience resulting in arrest, jailing, and court trials; nonviolent civil disobedience met by tear-gassing and/or violence from police and troops; legal mass marches and rallies of tens and hundreds of thousands of people; strikes on campus or at the workplace; draft board raids to destroy records—burning them or pouring blood on them; illegal, violent acts such as trashing, burning buildings or setting off bombs; suicide. (Zaroulis and Sullivan 1984:xi)

By 1968, the Tet offensive, the assassinations of Martin Luther King, Jr., and Robert F. Kennedy, two powerful advocates for peace, and the results of the **1968 Democratic National Convention** (in Chicago), which produced the nomination of Hubert Humphrey, the endorsement of Lyndon Johnson's Vietnam policies, and dramatic opposition efforts in the streets of Chicago combined to further alienate and radicalize members of the antiwar movement. The domestic conflicts and violence also further splintered an unbelieving public that was watching the war at home on television (the role of the media is the focus of the next chapter). As a result, much of the public—the so-called silent majority—would turn against the demonstrators and toward Richard Nixon, the Republican presidential nominee.

The civil rights and antiwar movements also were responsible for *generating new social movements and politically active groups* in areas such as feminism, native American and Hispanic rights, gay rights, consumer rights (and Ralph Nader), and environmentalism. Many women, for example, were active in the civil rights movement, the antiwar movement, and the new left, an important element in the mobilization of the modern women's movement (Evans 1979). The movements in favor of pro-choice, nuclear freeze, antiapartheid, and human rights that arose in prominence after the 1970s are legacies of the civil rights and antiwar movements as well (Epstein 1991; Waller 1987). Overall, liberalism and the new left became active and influential forces in group and domestic politics since the 1960s.

From the Right: The Resurgence of Conservative Movements

The events and social movements of the 1960s also contributed to the resurgence of movements and groups reflecting conservatism and the **political right**. Conservatives and members of the political right were aghast over the loss of Vietnam to communism, the increasing power of the Soviet Union relative to the United States, the growth of government intervention in the economy and the welfare state represented by President Johnson's Great Society programs, the rise of individualism and sexual promiscuity, and the decline of law and order. Whereas the liberal and new left social movements prevalent during the 1960s had argued that American society and government policies were inconsistent with the moral and cultural values embodied in the Declaration of Independence and the Constitution, many conservatives believed that America was in a state of "moral decline" caused by the rise of liberalism and the left.

Some—including disgruntled liberals and leftists such as Irving Kristol and Norman Podhoretz, eventually known as neoconservatives, or neocons—became concerned by the dovishness of the left and what they characterized as the left's failure to confront and challenge communism. They therefore abandoned the left and pressed for more aggressive and militant foreign policy. In effect, conservatives began to organize and become politically active as well. This activity was reinforced by the election of Nixon to the presidency, which enabled many conservatives to become members of the administration. Hence, social movements representing broad coalitions of conservative-oriented groups within society arose in support of anticommunism, private enterprise, and social issues such as school prayer and antiabortion (Blumenthal 1986; Himmelstein 1991; Nash, 1976).

As with the rise of liberalism and the new left, religious groups and forces played a prominent role in the rise of conservatism and the political right. The **Christian right** and religious fundamentalists, such as Jerry Falwell and Pat Robertson and other televangelists, took to the airwaves. They were dedicated to defeating "secular humanism" through the promotion of anticommunism and religious behavior throughout society. As with the growth of liberalism and the left, the rise of conservatism produced more extremist elements. For example, some religious fundamentalists wanted to change the United States into a theocracy—a religious state; and a few groups on the far right attempted to promote change through violence (Capps 1990; Coates 1987; Wilcox 1991).

Overall, conservatives and the political right posed an effective counter to the left. They gained great influence throughout society and within government, especially with the 1980 electoral victory of Ronald Reagan, and later reinforced by the controversial election of George W. Bush in 2000. The mass public also responded to the symbolic and nationalist appeals of the Republican Party, especially in the South. However, conservatives, like the liberals before them, nevertheless were unable to establish a new consensus behind their ideological view of the world, and clashes between these competing and increasingly fragmented visions continued.

GROUP POLITICS AFTER VIETNAM

As the liberal–conservative ideological consensus that dominated the cold war years collapsed during the 1960s and 1970s, it was replaced by greater ideological, electoral, and group competition in American politics. As David Truman (1971:52) states, "Any considerable increase in the types of such groups, or any major change in the nature of their interrelationships will be reflected subsequently in the operation of the political system." *The breakdown of the foreign policy consensus affected the post–Vietnam role of group politics in the making of U.S. foreign policy in three ways,* with two of the patterns representing change and one representing continuity: (1) the foreign policy establishment collapsed; (2) there was a proliferation of groups, ideological diversity and partisanship, and political activism; yet(3) the military-industrial-scientific infrastructure continued to pervade society. Thus, some cold war patterns continued but were accompanied by new patterns of change. These patterns generally persisted and intensified in the post–cold war and post–September 11, 2001 years, despite the impact of the terrorist attacks and the Great Recession.

Collapse of the Foreign Policy Establishment

The last time individuals within the foreign policy establishment would operate with a consensus and act in unison was in March 1968. The war in Vietnam was going badly and the country was being torn apart at home. As he had in the past, President Johnson convened a meeting of his major advisors and a group of senior policy advisors from outside the government, who were referred to as the "Wise Men." Johnson met with this collection of prominent individuals, many of whom had held high-level government positions in previous administrations under Presidents Truman, Eisenhower, and Kennedy, to discuss what to do about U.S. policy in Vietnam. In effect, the participants represented a who's who of the foreign policy establishment, and they surprised President Johnson by telling him that they no longer supported further escalation of the war. According to Godfrey Hodgson (1973:24) the participants were discouraged by the lack of progress in the war and the relative decline of the United States economically, so they "made a characteristic decision not to put good money after bad."

The consensus in foreign policy views of the establishment had collapsed and splintered, contributing to the ideological and foreign policy diversity that would permeate among the elite and mass publics. By the early 1970s, the establishment was bitterly divided over Vietnam and the future of U.S. foreign policy. Walt Rostow and Dean Rusk, Johnson's national security advisor and secretary of state, continued to believe that the war was justified and that no major avoidable mistakes had been made in the way it was waged. Others, such as McGeorge Bundy, Kennedy's national security advisor, believed that the war was justified but that mistakes were made in its conduct. However, some members of the establishment, such as Clark Clifford, advisor to Truman and secretary of defense under Johnson, believed that the Vietnam War was a mistake. Some such as Paul Warnke and George Ball, high-level Johnson officials in the Defense and State departments, held not only that the Vietnam War was a mistake but that the pursuit of containment in a non-European context was misguided, as well. Finally, people such as Daniel Ellsberg, a prominent Defense Department official, believed that containment and U.S. intervention throughout the world was not only inappropriate but a fundamentally unjust policy as well. These prominent individuals within American society would continue to receive attention and exercise influence, but they would no longer do so as a unified force in support of America's cold war policies. Instead, they would compete with each other for influence in the making of U.S. foreign policy by choosing sides in the group politics since Vietnam.

Expansion of Group Politics

The rise of social movements of the left and right led not only to the collapse of the anticommunist consensus and the foreign policy establishment but to the expansion of group politics as well. Fed by dealignment and the weakening of the two major political parties, *the events and movements of the 1960s and 1970s resulted in three developments:* the proliferation of groups in American politics, increased ideological diversity, competition, and partisanship among groups, and more individual political participation in social movements and group politics. As one former member of Congress has recently characterized the years since 1965, "the last four decades have . . . seen a proliferation of groups outside of government seeking to influence foreign policy: the business community, labor unions, ethnic constituencies, nonprofit organizations, foreign countries, former officials, international organizations, think tanks, universities—and the list goes on. All of these groups and individuals seek to advance their views on Capitol Hill and in the White House . . . " (Hamilton 2006:273). This trend, which began in the wake of Vietnam, accelerated after the end of the cold war.

Let us consider some of the more salient features of this explosion of group activity. Since the 1970s, there has been, first of all, a dramatic expansion in the number of **issue- and cause-oriented groups**—including single-issue groups—seeking to influence U.S. foreign policymakers. For example, liberal and left-leaning groups have actively supported a U.S. foreign policy that promotes human rights and self-determination, arms control and disarmament, the eradication of Third World hunger and poverty, antiapartheid, and global environmentalism. At the same time, more conservative and right-wing groups first emphasized the problems associated with the expansion of Soviet power and communism, the need for a U.S. defense buildup, and support for Third World allies and market economies abroad in the 1970s and 1980s, and then emphasized other security threats, the preservation of American power, sovereignty, and other causes in the 1990s.

After the 9/11 attacks, the left and right bitterly divided over the proper ways to counter the threat of terrorism, the liberty–security trade-offs of domestic measures to reduce the risk of terrorist attacks, and the role of diplomacy and force in U.S. foreign policy. Political, economic and social developments since 2005 produced intense partisan differences over how to address the economic collapse and recession within the U.S. and the global political economy. These differences were probably best seen in sharply diverging visions presented by the Obama-Biden and Romney-Ryan campaigns during the 2012 presidential elections. Hence, the cold war consensus was replaced by considerable national fragmentation, competition, and partisanship, especially among the elite and attentive publics. This prompted more activist Americans and interest groups to attempt to influence American politics and U.S. foreign policy, both in national security and economic affairs.

Another area of expanded group activity is in the efforts of foreign policy organizations. For example, groups such as the Carnegie Endowment for International Peace, CFR, Foreign Policy Research Institute, and Rand Corporation continued to function after Vietnam, and were complemented by new groups such as the Trilateral Commission. However, over the last four decades, these centrist groups were joined by more conservative groups such as the American Enterprise Institute, Heritage Foundation, Hoover Institution, Center for Strategic and International Studies, a new Committee on the Present Danger (formed in the 1970s against the Soviet threat and reborn in 2004 against the threat of Islamic terrorism), and the Joseph Coors and John Scaife Foundations. At the same time, more liberal groups were formed and became prominent as well, including the Arms Control Association, Brookings Institution, Center for Defense Information, Institute for Policy Studies, World Policy Institute, and Worldwatch Institute. These institutions were also joined by those advocating a semi-isolationist orientation, such as the more libertarian Cato Institute.

By the late 1960s and early 1970s, old **think tanks** began to grow and new ones were established, and these were increasingly prone to take independent policy initiatives (as opposed to rely on contract work). Overall, of the more than one hundred or so policy research groups, or think tanks, in Washington, D.C. (some having fewer than a dozen employees, others employing up to 250), two-thirds were set up after 1970. "Every year, these institutes conduct thousands of conferences, luncheons, forums, and seminars, while publishing hundreds of books and innumerable pamphlets, reports, newsletters, backgrounders, and occasional essays. In addition, their members write scores of op-ed articles that appear in dozens of newspapers, and their most articulate fellows perform as commentators on radio and television news programs, often coast-to-coast" (Ricci 1993:208). The foreign policy specialists of these groups increasingly came to wage campaigns in support of or against the policy directions of the administration in power. In fact, many of these think tanks became fertile grounds for administrations of one political stripe or the other to recruit personnel. For example, the Heritage Foundation supplied many people for the Reagan Administration, while the Clinton Administration turned to the Brookings Institution. More recently, the American Enterprise Institute was a key source for the neoconservatives of George W. Bush's Administration, while Barack Obama turned to Brookings, the Carnegie Endowment for International Peace, and the newer Atlantic Council and the Center for American Progress. The net result is that since Vietnam foreign policy expertise and personnel are no longer monopolized by a few old establishment groups, a development that reflects greater ideological diversity, among intellectuals as well (see **Table 12.1** for a list of the most prominent groups or think tanks involved in foreign policy).

A third area for the expansion of group activity involved commercial interests. As the anticommunist and free trade consensus shattered in the aftermath of the Vietnam War and the Bretton Woods international economic system no longer functioned as originally intended, *labor and business (and governmental) interests increasingly splintered.* For instance, the AFL-CIO turned increasingly against free trade (such as the NAFTA negotiations) in order to protect American jobs as foreign economic competition increased. Within the business community, domestic-oriented companies began to push for protectionist measures by the government as large American multinational corporations (MNCs), such as major U.S. banks and other financial institutions, became the champions of free trade and globalization (Barnet and Muller 1976; Milner 1989).

On the question of policy toward China, especially during the debates over trade, sanctions, and normal trade relations in the 1990s, for example, businesses in the aviation and automobile sectors, including Boeing, Ford, General Motors, and others, were advocates of normal trade relations and opponents of sanctions; other businesses such as the music and entertainment industry opposed normal trade relations. Labor, which generally opposed normal trade, also worried about Chinese countersanctions that might cost American jobs (Rourke and Clark 1998). One well-known observer noted this vast array of competing

Table 12.1   Major Foreign Policy Think Tanks

Name Location	Year Began	Issue Orientation	Ideological Orientation
Carnegie Endowment for International Peace Washington, D.C.	1910	Foreign	Liberal
Foreign Policy Association New York	1918	Foreign	Centrist
Hoover Institution Palo Alto, Calif.	1919	Domestic and foreign	Conservative
Council on Foreign Relations New York	1921	Foreign	Centrist
Brookings Institution Washington, D.C.	1927	Domestic and foreign	Liberal
American Enterprise Institution Washington, D.C.	1943	Domestic and foreign	Conservative
Rand Corporation Santa Monica, Calif.	1948	Domestic and foreign	Centrist
Aspen Institute Washington, D.C.	1951	Foreign	Liberal
Foreign Policy Research Institute Philadelphia	1955	Foreign	Conservative
Hudson Institute New York	1961	Domestic and foreign	Conservative
Atlantic Council Washington, D.C.	1961	Foreign	Liberal
Center for Strategies & International Studies Washington, D.C.	1962	Foreign	Conservative
Institute for Policy Studies Washington, D.C.	1963	Domestic and foreign	Liberal
Center for Defense Information Washington, D.C.	1972	Foreign	Liberal
Trilateral Commission New York	1973	Domestic and foreign	Centrist
Heritage Foundation Washington, D.C.	1974	Domestic and foreign	Conservative
World Watch Institute Washington, D.C.	1974	Foreign	Liberal
Cato Institute Washington, D.C.	1977	Domestic and foreign	Noninternationalist
Institute for International Economics Washington, D.C.	1981	Foreign	Liberal
Carter Center Atlanta	1982	Domestic and foreign	Liberal
World Policy Institute New York	1983	Foreign	Liberal
Center for American Progress, Washington, D.C.	2003	Domestic and foreign	Liberal

commercial interests and bemoaned the fragmentation of foreign policy purposes it spawned, worrying that broad strategies and purposes that characterized foreign policy in the cold war were lost to commercial particularism (Huntington 1997).

Not surprisingly, *as commercial interests have multiplied, their presence in Washington, D.C., also has grown substantially.* Before World War II, there weren't a dozen trade associations in town; by the 1960s, however, about one hundred corporations and one thousand trade associations maintained offices in Washington; and by the 1990s, there were over 1300 corporations and 3500 trade associations lobbying government and promoting their special interests. In fact, over eighty thousand people in Washington worked for trade associations alone (Judis 1989:7). These numbers have only increased in the twenty-first century. Thus, commercial interests continue to exert a heavy influence on governmental policies, but in a much more complex and contradictory fashion than prevailed during the cold war. Many of these corporations and interest groups representing them contributed to decreasing governmental regulation and oversight. At the same time they increased their risk-taking in trading and financing complex packages of "derivatives" (such as mortgage loans) in freer markets, which contributed to the economic bubble and eventual collapse in 2007–08 within the United States, throughout Europe, and the entire global economy.

A fourth area of increased group activity and fragmentation involves religious and ethnic groups. With respect to religious groups, one scholar put it this way:

> While religious lobbies were particularly prominent on foreign policy issues during the Vietnam War in the 1960s and 1970s and over El Salvador, Nicaragua and the nuclear freeze issues in the 1980s, these groups have not declined inactivism. Indeed, the end of the cold war has actually sparked renewed activity and involvement to infuse a moral and ethical component into American foreign policy. (McCormick 1998)

Like the issue- and cause-oriented groups we discussed earlier, religious groups run the gamut from conservative to liberal concerns and have actively promoted policies to contend with disease and suffering, promote human rights, fight religious persecution, and oppose family planning and access to abortions overseas (Hertzke 1988; Martin 1999). Over the past ten years, for example, religious groups were heavily active and instrumental in the passage of the International Religious Freedom Act of 1998, the Sudan Peace Act of 2002, the North Korea Human Act of 2004, and a variety of new initiatives in foreign aid designed to alleviate poverty, disease, and suffering in the developing world.

With respect to ethnic groups, since Vietnam "the number of politically active ethnic groups has grown tremendously, and their lobbying techniques have become much more sophisticated. The ethnic groups with the most influence are those that are well funded and have large numbers nationally, heavy concentrations in particular areas of the country, or positions of power in society" (Hamilton 2006:273). Even as the old China lobby declined as a force, especially with the establishment of diplomatic relations with the People's Republic of China in 1978, new ethnic groups grew in prominence. For example, Greek American groups promoted the American embargo of Turkey during the 1970s; African American groups played an important role in the antiapartheid forces leading to U.S. sanctions against South Africa; and Cuban American groups remain very hostile to Fidel Castro and any normalization in American–Cuban relations to the present day. Not only does ethnicity play a role in group politics, but politicians sometimes are very sensitive to the political clout of ethnic groups for electoral politics, especially in key states (see **A Different Perspective** on the clout of the so-called Israeli or Jewish lobby).

How Powerful Is the Israeli or Jewish Lobby?

The so-called Israeli or Jewish lobby, which includes a variety of individuals and groups, such as the American Israel Public Affairs Committee (AIPAC), is widely considered the most powerful of all the ethnic groups. It was not really powerful, well organized, or connected until after the 1967 Arab-Israeli War. A controversial article entitled "Unrestricted Access: What the Israel Lobby Wants, It Too Often Gets" and a subsequent book by John Mearsheimer and Stephen Walt (2006, 2007) credit the Israeli lobby with having gained the backing of members of Congress, as well as the president, to provide unwavering support and assistance to the state of Israel—to the tune of $3 billion of U.S. foreign assistance per year for the state of Israel and its 6 million citizens—as well as being the major provider of military weaponry. This set off a political firestorm, although it has been a recurring controversy over the existence and clout of the Israeli lobby over the years.

While recent years have seen the rise of Arab-American organizations, they have been less successful. For example, Henry Hyde, Republican of Illinois and former chair of the House International Relations Committee, "says he constantly hears from pro-Israel groups on Mideast issues but not so much from Arab or Muslim-American groups. Over the years, the House panel he now chairs has taken such a consistently pro-Israel stance it has been called 'the little Knesset'" (Diamond and Piec 2002).

New York Senator Charles Schumer, a Democrat, described three levels of Israeli political strength in the United States: "The most pro-Israeli group in America is the Congress. Next are the American people. The White House is least of the three because they have to deal with all of the Arab states and the variety of foreign policy factors at work" (Diamond and Piec 2002). Presidents nevertheless have usually been strong supporters of Israel, especially publicly, given the number of Jews in such critical states as California, New York, and Florida. Given this context, presidents have had to manage a difficult balancing act between supporting Israel and trying to act as a third party and evenhanded broker to help resolve the long-standing conflict in the Middle East between Israel and the Arabs.

President Carter was the most successful in beginning the peace process with the Camp David Accords in 1978. President George W. Bush was considerably more pro-Israeli and struggled as conflict has intensified between Israel and the Palestinians (and Arabs), especially after the 9/11 attacks. Early in his first year, Barack Obama strongly signaled a more evenhanded approach, insisting on a viable two-state solution and a cessation in Israeli settlement-building in the West Bank. While pressuring Israeli leaders for concessions, Obama also took a more open and conciliatory tone toward Palestinians and the Arab world, and visited a number of Arab and Muslim countries in an effort to generate early progress toward a peaceful resolution. Such efforts became contentious during the 2012 elections when Republican nominee Mitt Romney accused President Obama of weakening U.S.-Israeli ties. However, the real test will come if and when the Obama administration expands its efforts to include policy actions that require congressional action, such as conditioning U.S. aid to Israel on the end of settlements or other more dramatic steps toward a two-state solution.

How powerful is the Israeli or Jewish lobby? To what extent does it cement U.S. and Israeli ties and constrain U.S. foreign policy efforts to pursue a peaceful settlement to the Arab-Israeli conflict in Palestine and the Middle East?

Another prominent ethnic lobby is the Cuban Americans, whose influence over U.S. policy toward Cuba and Fidel Castro is frequently discussed. This is partly due to their concentration in electorally critical states such as Florida, and partly due to the cohesive message they deliver. As Haney and Vanderbush (1999) describe, the Cuban lobby has been a key player, helping to preserve restrictions, fighting moves toward normalization, and even extending sanctions in the 1990s on Cuba and other countries engaging in relations with Cuba. Moreover, as Vanderbush (2009) documents, the Cuban lobby illustrates an underappreciated aspect of group influence: the role of ethnic groups in marketing administration policies to help the administration shape public opinion and the policy debate. As Vanderbush (2009:291) puts it, "the greatest impact that these groups have is when they cooperate with government officials to sell the public on policies." The Cuban lobby performed this role in many ways, perhaps most recently in the successful passage of the LIBERTAD legislation, also known as the Helms-Burton Act, in the mid-1990s. Iraqi exiles performed a similar function in the run-up to the Iraq War in 2002–03.

Another immigrant group likely to become more active and potentially important is Indians. As one analyst suggests, the growing population of immigrants and families of immigrants from India "are affluent and interested in India, [and] China's rising power and India's decision to move toward a market economy means their calls for a more 'India-Friendly' foreign policy are likely to meet a receptive audience in Washington" (Lindsay 2002:38). Indian-Americans have become significantly more active in politics in recent years, and the Congressional India Caucus now has over 120 members. For example, as Kirk (2008) argues, the aggressive efforts and mobilization of Indian-Americans was a crucial factor behind the generation of congressional support for nuclear trade and cooperation agreements between India and the United States in 2006. This clearly has not helped U.S.–Pakistani relations in general or against terrorism, especially given the ongoing war in Afghanistan. Some of the key factors that contribute to influence by ethnic groups, including the group's size, commitment, resources, skills, whether it seeks to preserve the status quo (as with the Cuban groups) or overturn it, and the range and power of interests who support or oppose the group's preferences (Rubenzer 2008).

The newest forms of interest group gaining prominence in U.S. foreign policy have been consulting firms and foreign lobbies. **Consulting firms** representing different clients, corporations in particular, have proliferated since the 1970s. Henry Kissinger, for example, founded the consulting firm Kissinger Associates in 1982. For annual fees reported to start at $100,000, clients, which include some of the largest multinational corporations in the world, meet with Kissinger and his associates in his New York office overlooking Park Avenue in order to get information about world politics and gain access to policymakers around the world (Feeney 2001). Two of Kissinger's associates, Brent Scowcroft and Lawrence Eagleburger, subsequently became President Bush Sr.'s national security advisor and deputy secretary of state. In another example, Kissinger Associates was a part of the **U.S.–Iraq Business Forum** during the 1980s: a conglomeration of predominantly large American corporations—such as Amoco, Bell Helicopter, Caterpillar, General Motors, Mobil, Westinghouse, Xerox—responsible for increasing business and trade with the Iraqi regime, thus contributing to Saddam Hussein's buildup of his military into a regional threat. With its officers and staff based in Washington, D.C., the Iraqi Business Forum pressured the Reagan and Bush administrations to continue to provide government credits and loan guarantees to Iraq and oppose congressional sanctions, despite Iraq's terrible human rights record. Nevertheless, when Iraq invaded Kuwait in 1990, Henry Kissinger, speaking as a former national security advisor and secretary of state, was a leading proponent to expel Iraq with the use of force (Conason 1990).

Closely related to the rise of consulting firms is the growth of **foreign lobbies** through which foreign governments (and private interests) attempt to influence American domestic politics and the policymaking process. Foreign lobbies rely heavily on American expertise, such as in consulting, law, and advertising firms, and operate in a fashion similar to domestic pressure groups. In fact, foreign lobbies have existed throughout American history and often work closely with their domestic counterparts, such as ethnic groups. The Jewish lobby, for example, has always had strong ties with the state of Israel. By 2007, over 140 countries had secured representation in Washington, D.C., by professional lobbying firms. Among the most prominent contemporary examples of the foreign lobby are Saudi Arabia and Japan. The Japan lobby, for example, is quite multifaceted, ranging from cultural organizations that try to promote favorable American attitudes toward Japan (such as the Japan Foundation) to professional economic organizations (such as the Japanese Economic Institute of America) and direct lobbying activities that represent Japanese business interests. Concerning the latter, according to journalist John Judis (1989:7), "the Japanese alone have hired about 125 former government officials. These include two of the last three special trade representatives, three of the last four Democratic National Committee chairmen, and the last two Republican chairs." More recently, the countries of the former Soviet Union, Eastern Europe, Africa, and every other corner of the world have expanded their presence and lobbying activities as well.

Obviously, the close ties between interest groups and the U.S. government (and foreign officials) raise important questions concerning personal and national **conflicts of interest** and ethical (and legal) behavior. These issues were illustrated clearly when Michael Deaver, deputy chief of staff and close friend to President Reagan, was convicted of perjury in federal court for lying about his lobbying activities in policy areas in which he was previously involved as a government official (an activity prohibited by law for just one year). Upon resigning from public office in 1985, Deaver immediately established his own consulting firm that represented domestic clients, such as Rockwell International, and foreign clients, such as the governments of Canada, South Korea, and Panama. In fact, a 1986 General Accounting Office (GAO) study found seventy-six former high-level federal officials representing foreign interests from fifty-two countries after leaving office during the period from 1980 to 1985—probably a very strong contemporary trend as well (U.S. Congress, GAO 1986).

One final recent development involves the *direct international activities of various groups.* Such direct international activities impact international politics and affect the conduct and making of U.S. foreign policy. Although individuals and groups have long played direct roles in world events (e.g., Doyle 1986), such widespread efforts are a relatively recent phenomenon. Some examples are the missionary activities of American Christian religious organizations, including certain protestant, catholic, and Mormon denominations. Moreover, with gross sales often greater than the gross national product (GNP) of many Third World countries (see **Table 12.2**), the business activities of **American multinational corporations (MNCs)** abroad are extensive and their lobbying efforts can be quite pervasive.

But other types of private groups are active abroad, as well. Many private consulting firms and individuals, for instance, sell their services to foreign governments to provide advice on domestic and foreign policies. Moreover, a number of think tanks are now self-styled "action tanks" engaged in a variety of hands-on work around the world rather than the traditional educational and policy analysis work for which they received their traditional label (Scott 1999). Such activity became particularly noticeable in Eastern Europe with the end of the cold war, a region in which many American firms and individuals (often with the support of the U.S. government and the IMF) instructed Eastern Europeans on transitioning

Table 12.2 Revenues of Largest U.S. Corporations Relative to Various Countries' GNP

Corporation (Rank)/ Country	Revenues/GNP ($Millions)	Corporation (Rank)/ Country	Revenues/GNP ($Millions)
United States	14,645,629	Chevron (3)	163,527
China	5,720,811	General Electric* (4)	156,779
Japan	5,334,370	Algeria	155,683
Germany	3,521,983	Bank of America (5)	150,450
France	2,749,821	ConocoPhillips (6)	139,515
United Kingdom	2,377,244	Ukraine	137,771
Italy	2,159,254	Peru	136,705
Brazil	1,830,384	Hungary	128,611
India	1,553,937	Kazakhstan	123,801
Canada	1,475,865	AT&T (7)	123,018
Spain	1,462,894	Ford Motor (8)	118,308
Russian Federation	1,403,847	J.P. Morgan Chase (9)	115,632
Australia	1,030,268	Hewlett-Packard (10)	114,552
Mexico	1,012,545	Berkshire Hathaway (11)	112,493
Korea, Rep.	972,299	Citigroup (12)	108,785
Netherlands	814,762	Verizon Communications (13)	107,808
Turkey	719,878	McKesson (14)	106,632
Indonesia	599,157	Bangladesh	104,681
Switzerland	559,735	General Motors (15)	104,589
Belgium	499,506	American International Group (16)	103,189
Poland	474,891	Vietnam	101,089
Sweden	469,805	Cardinal Health (17)	99,613
Norway	427,071	CVS Caremark (18)	98,729
Wal-Mart Stores (1)	408,214	Wells Fargo (19)	98,636
Austria	394,575	International Business Machines (20)	95,758
Argentina	348,387	Kroger (23)	76,733
Venezuela	334,055	Iraq	74,885
Denmark	329,507	Boeing* (28)	68,281
Greece	304,963	Home Depot (29)	66,176
South Africa	304,661	State Farm (34)	61,480
Thailand	286,553	Microsoft (36)	58,437
Exxon Mobil (2)	284,650	United Technologies* (37)	52,920
Colombia	255,289	Goldman Sachs (39)	51,673
Finland	255,154	Pfizer (40)	50,009
Portugal	232,648	Lockheed Martin* (44)	45,189
Hong Kong	231,658	Tunisia	43,909
Malaysia	220,362	Guatemala	39,396
Israel	207,195	Apple (56)	36,537
Singapore	203,441	Uzbekistan	36,086
Egypt	196,217	Northrop Grumman* (61)	35,291
Nigeria	194,682	Kenya	32,736
Philippines	192,238	General Dynamics* (69)	31,981
Czech Republic	188,255	Panama	24,509
Ireland	187,138	Honduras	14,225
Pakistan	182,788	Nicaragua	6,417
Chile	173,179	Central African Republic	2,067
Romania	168,208		

* Major defense contractors.

SOURCES: CNN/Money "Fortune 1000," http://money.cnn.com/magazines/fortune/fortune500/2012/full_list/ (June 13, 2012); World Development Indicators database, World Bank, June 13, 2012.

from communist systems to hopefully democracies and market economies. This both eased their entry into an expanding European Union (EU) while also contributing to the rise of the large sovereign (governmental) deficits and debts that played a role in the economic crises in Europe and the United States after 2007. Even private individuals, such as former President Jimmy Carter, through the Carter Center in Atlanta, have pursued their own foreign policy agendas abroad revolving around democratic and economic development (which has increased Carter's public approval since he left the Oval Office and for which he was eventually awarded the Nobel Peace Prize).

The international activities of **private voluntary organizations (PVOs)**, such as CARE, Catholic Relief Services, and Lutheran World Relief—many of them religiously affiliated—have proliferated since Vietnam as well. Although they originated primarily as relief organizations during and immediately after World War II and focused most of their attention on the war-torn countries of Europe, over the past thirty years these and newer PVOs have diversified their activities and geographical focus to emphasize emergency and developmental assistance to Third World countries. In the 1980s, for example, over 125 U.S. PVOs received over $740 million from the United States Agency for International Development (AID) in support of their overseas work—a tenfold increase since the 1960s with this trend of subcontracting out foreign assistance increasing to the present day (Smith 1984:116). In the early twenty-first century, PVOs were dispensing considerably more aid than the United Nations system.

Another facet of this recent development, especially evident in the aftermath of the 2003 Iraq War, is the increasing use of **private military contractors (PMCs)**—a new type of interest group (and also a unique type of defense contractor as part of the military-industrial-scientific infrastructure). At least 30,000 private employees from over 60 different PMCs were under contract to the U.S. government to provide logistical support and security services in Iraq as of 2006. (Another 50,000 to 70,000 unarmed civilians—many from PVOs—are under government contract in Iraq to provide other services, from delivering mail to rebuilding essential infrastructure.) The use of PMCs has grown steadily since the early 1990s. During the 1991 Gulf War, the ratio of soldiers to private security contractors was 50 to 1; today, it is closer to 5-1, and even 3-1, depending on the conflict.

In fact, according to Peter Singer (2005:122), the U.S. military is increasingly "**outsourcing war**" and "[p]rivate military companies are not only supporting a shrinking U.S. force in Iraq; they are also playing critical roles for both state and non-state actors in stabilization, drug interdiction, and humanitarian operations" (see also Singer 2003). The United States has increasingly relied on PMCs in the war in Afghanistan, especially given President Obama's decision to withdraw American combat troops after the surge and the fact that the civilian agencies such as the State Department and the USAID have neither the resources or the personnel to provide sufficient support for the Iraqi and Afghani transitions. Therefore, **corporate warriors** through "private companies are becoming significant players in conflicts around the world, supplying not merely the goods but also the services of war" (Singer 2005:119; Singer 2007).

In sum, *the post–Vietnam War and post–cold war years have been accompanied by the proliferation of interest group and social movement activity in foreign policy.* Older, cold war–oriented groups have been joined by more liberal and more conservative groups. Ideologically motivated groups have been joined by hundreds of other groups representing specialized interests, including business, ethnic, and foreign interests. Such groups have flocked to Washington, D.C., which explains the explosion of lobbyists (365 officially registered in 1961, over 40,000 by 2009), lawyers (the District of Columbia Bar Association listed roughly 12,000 members in 1961 and over 80,000 in 2009), and journalists (1,500 were accredited to congressional press galleries in 1961, over 5,200 in the 1990s), whose numbers continue to grow (Smith 1989:29). According to Thomas Mann (1990:16), a major implication is that "conflict between the President and Congress must be seen as a consequence of a broader set of developments affecting America's place in the world and domestic political interests and processes." The cold war consensus years in group politics have been replaced by group competition for public support and control of the government. Despite the events of 9/11 and with the Great Recession, domestic politics continue to be more divisive, complex, and fluid than during the cold war. Therefore, as Mann concludes, "it is no wonder that the President today occupies a less than dominant position in American foreign policy."

Continuation of the Military-Industrial-Scientific Infrastructure

Although the foreign policy establishment collapsed while groups proliferated and became more diverse, a massive military-industrial-scientific infrastructure still pervades the government and American society. *Four patterns have prevailed since Vietnam*:

1. the military establishment continues to require weaponry and other services, private industry manufactures and supplies weapons and material, Congress approves the programs and appropriates the funds that provide jobs and votes back home, and members of the scientific community still offer national security expertise and advice,

2. from the 1970s to the 1990s, in the absence of an anticommunist consensus, the institutions and activities of the military-industrial-scientific infrastructure no longer operated in a highly supportive domestic political environment and have been more likely to be challenged,

3. there has been a downsizing of the military and, therefore, the national security infrastructure has also been impacted since the collapse of the Soviet Union, and

4. the September 11, 2001, terrorist attacks have resulted in a resurgence of an American military buildup and in the military-industrial-scientific infrastructure.

While defense spending has represented a smaller percentage of the federal government's budget and the domestic economy since Vietnam, and has been more open to criticism, *the national security infrastructure remains huge and remains embedded in American society* (Adams 1982; Goodwin 1985; Gregory 1989; Kotz 1988). According to a *Los Angeles Times* analysis on the U.S. defense establishment during the 1970s and 1980s, "the jobs of one out of ten Americans depend directly or indirectly on defense spending. The Pentagon is the largest single purchaser of goods and services in the nation. Defense industries account for 10 percent of all U.S. manufacturing. In certain states, including California, defense-related employment is the largest single source of personal income. Defense employs more than 25 percent of all the nation's scientists and engineers" (Tempest 1983b:1). Throughout the 1980s, the federal government continued to devote the largest share of its budget to defense spending—roughly 30 percent. Defense products, such as arms, also accounted for over one-third of American exports abroad.

Defense Department domestic spending (which includes procurement contracts, payroll, military pensions, and grants) declined somewhat with the end of the cold war. However, in the wake of the 9/11 attacks, defense spending surged to over $500 billion in base budget for fiscal year 2009 (excluding funds for nuclear weapons research, maintenance and production, veteran's affairs, and other supplemental funding necessary for the wars in Iraq and Afghanistan), an additional $70 billion "emergency allowance" for the war on terrorism. According to the U.S. Census bureau, in fiscal year 2008, the top five states receiving federal defense dollars were California ($46.2 billion), Virginia ($44.6 billion), Texas ($38.1 billion), Florida ($19.6 billion), and Maryland ($14.6 billion). And this does not include domestic spending by other national security–oriented government agencies, such as the Department of Energy, NASA, the Department of Justice, and the Department of Homeland Security.

The **pork barrel politics** of defense spending has become more sophisticated. Known as "**beltway bandits**," hundreds of private defense think tanks, lobbying offices, corporate government-relations offices, and law firms specializing in military contracts have sprung up around Washington, D.C., in order to lobby for defense spending and support the military establishment. According to the Fairfax County Office of Economic Development, during the 1980s, over 620 high-tech firms with 47,000 employees, more than 70 percent of whom work on defense-sponsored projects, were located in the four northern Virginia cities closest to Washington (Tempest 1983b:14). And the revolving door system remains alive and well. As Gordon Adams (1982) documented in *The Iron Triangle*, "Our review of DOD data showed that 1,942 individuals (uniformed and civilian) moved between DOD/NASA and the eight [largest defense] companies between 1970 and 1979. Of these, 1,672 were hired by the companies, while 270 company employees went to work for DOD and NASA."

These types of developments have intensified the mutually supportive networks existing between members of the military establishment, Congress, private industry, and academia at national and local levels. The building and production of the B-1 bomber is a typical illustration of the dynamics of the military-industrial-scientific infrastructure (see **A Closer Look** on the politics of the B-1 bomber and **Figure** 12.2 for the geographic contract spreading of the B-1 bomber).

Nevertheless, according to the GAO, *the dynamics of the weapons procurement process remain problematic at the beginning of the twenty-first century*. Procurement of a new weapons system is so laborious and lengthy—averaging at least eleven years from start to finish—that any sense of program continuity and personal accountability is nearly impossible to maintain. "This means that from drawing board to actual deployment, the average procurement project conceivably could outlast the involvement of four program managers, five program executive officers, eight service-acquisition executives, five chairmen of the Joint Chiefs, seven secretaries or undersecretaries of defense and three presidents." The GAO comptroller general recommended that "trying to reduce the acquisition cycle to no longer than five years from technology development to production (as many private companies do) and slowing the revolving door in key management positions might help reduce the number of major projects that are over budget, behind schedule and without focus" (Paige 2000:47).

Furthermore, despite the government efforts to crack down on fraud and corruption in the defense procurement process, *fraud and corruption have been endemic in defense procurement and military spending (and nation-building)* among all four elements of military-industrial-scientific complex since the initial growth of the modern military establishment during the 1940s and 1950s (see, e.g., U.S. Congress, GAO 1982). For example, in Iraq as of January 2012, the Defense and State departments and the U.S. Agency for International Development had reported 88,380 contracting actions, projects, and grants, totaling $40.31 billion for reconstruction since the beginning of the 2003 war. Currently, there are about 15,000 employees of U.S.-funded contractors and grantees (a decline by 72 percent from the 53,447 registered as of September 2011). And over $2 billion dollars worth of contracts appear to be completely unaccounted for (Isenberg 2012).

This demonstrates the difficulty of reconciling democratic practice and accountability with the existence of a large military establishment and foreign policy presence at home and abroad. However, these types of incestuous and corrupt governmental-private relationships are not unique to the military and the defense procurement process. Corruption and scandal may be found wherever money, power, and prestige are highly valued, and these are certainly important attributes for the people and organizations involved in the military establishment and the U.S. defense process.

A CLOSER LOOK

The Politics of the B-1 Bomber

As David Wood (1983:8–9) explains, "The story of the B-1 bomber provides a case-book example of how the military-industrial complex works, how the personal, professional, political and economic interests of thousands of individuals and institutions in government and the defense industries intertwine to influence what America does in the name of national security." Since the late 1950s, the Air Force had wanted a new bomber to replace the B-52. However, critics emphasized the B-1's cost, limited capabilities, and unclear mission.

For three years beginning in 1975, Air Force and Rockwell International officials planned, coordinated, and executed a major political campaign on behalf of the struggling **B-1 bomber program**, which was on the verge of cancellation. Under President Reagan, Congress finally agreed to the full-scale production of one hundred B-1s at a cost of almost $500 million per plane. The Air Force and its supporters not only finally acquired the B-1 bomber but, to their delight, the B-2 "Stealth" bomber as well (at a cost of over $1 billion per plane). Kotz (1988:22) concluded that over the years "the Air Force and its allies in science, industry, labor, and politics have relentlessly pursued their goals—and other groups have opposed them. On both sides, the motives of patriotism, financial gain, career ambition,

political aggrandizement, and loyalty to an institution or idea were often so mixed that it is hard to tell what was narrow self-interest and what was concern for the national good."

Once approval is given for its production, the geography and politics of production virtually guarantees the future of a weapons system such as the B-1 bomber. Although Rockwell International was awarded the $40 billion–plus contract, as many as fifty-two hundred subcontractors were involved in the forty-eight continental states. These subcontractors included most of the largest defense contractors, such as Boeing, TRW, Westinghouse, General Electric, Goodyear, Singer, Sperry, Bendix, Martin Marietta, Northrop, Litton, Westinghouse, IBM, and others. Unions such as the United Auto Workers and the Machinists were also involved. "Contract spreading" involved as many as 400 of the 435 congressional districts. For many Americans, this meant jobs—good-paying jobs. Thus, thousands of individuals and groups at the local and national level had a vested interest in providing support for B-1 production (see Figure 12.2).

What are the economic and political consequences of these influential networks and weapons programs for the national security policies and economic performance of the United States?

Figure 12.2   The Geography of the B-1 Bomber

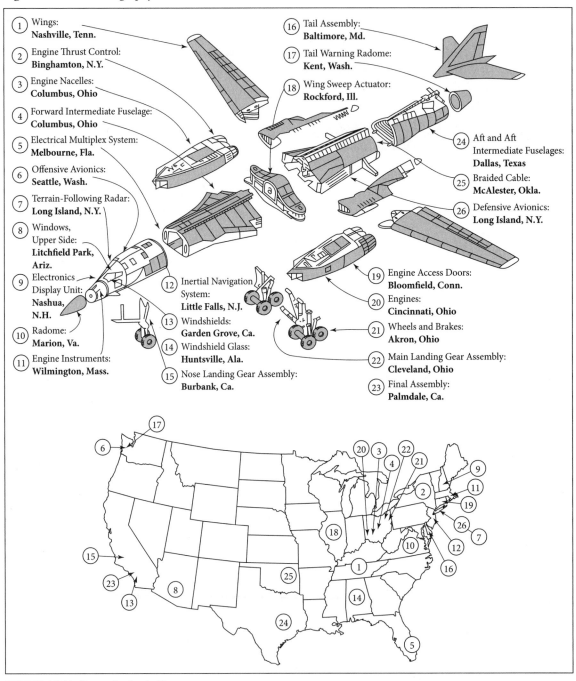

SOURCE: Mickie Garrett, *Los Angeles Times*.

Since the end of the cold war, *there has been a greater concentration of the defense industry,* which has an impact not only on the politics of defense but on people and communities as well. For example, in 1997, Boeing Company (with $20 billion in revenues—about one-third of them military oriented) acquired McDonnell Douglas Corporation (with $15 billion in revenues—about two-thirds military oriented) in a $14 billion deal. Boeing Company replaced Lockheed Martin Corporation (which was formed in 1995 after a merger of Lockheed and Martin Marietta corporations) as the world's largest aerospace company and makes it the only manufacturer of commercial jets in the United States. Although Boeing had 145,000 employees and McDonnell Douglas had 64,000 located in various plants throughout the country, corporate mergers are usually accompanied by considerable streamlining and cutbacks, to minimize overlap and duplication and to cut costs. Such concentration raises serious questions about the future of defense politics. The net result is a few mega-companies with "tremendous political clout" (Korb 1996).

How much is enough? Throughout the 1990s, emphasis was on a "peace dividend," cuts in defense spending, and the need for reform. At the same time, the military triumph in the Persian Gulf War squelched some of the calls for further cuts. Ultimately, how much is enough is dependent on to what extent Americans feel that their country's national security is threatened (and how large a role they think the United States should play abroad). In this respect, 9/11 and George W. Bush's global war on terrorism and military operations in Afghanistan and Iraq have already resulted in a substantial increase in defense spending and a resurgence of the military-industrial-scientific infrastructure. Nevertheless, hard political choices continue to be required concerning the amount and importance of defense spending and the use of force abroad.

With global financial and economic crises that began in 2007 under President Bush and continued into the Obama administration, enormous strains on the federal budget have been generated, with annual deficits skyrocketing and the total U.S. national debt approaching 100 percent of the U.S. GDP (see Table 8.3 in Chapter 8). These choices have serious consequences, not only for the government but for the economy, hundreds of local communities, and the livelihoods of thousands of individuals across many states that have become dependent on the military-industrial-scientific infrastructure. In just one example familiar to the authors, the state of South Carolina and its capital Columbia are heavily dependent on military spending. The Fort Jackson Army base employs 2500 people, trains 50,000 soldiers a year, and has an annual economic impact approaching $2 billion a year. The total economic impact of the three Midlands bases—Jackson Army, Shaw Air Force, and McEntire Joint National Guard Base—is estimated at about $7 billion a year (Wilkinson 2012). Such economic impact produce politicized and difficult choices that are not likely to get any easier as the United States continues to navigate the complex global environment of the twenty-first century.

GROUP POLITICS IN THE FUTURE

As we have seen, group politics, like electoral politics, has experienced considerable change, as well as some important continuities, from the cold war era to the present. Following World War II, the rise of foreign policy and cold war–oriented groups, of a military-industrial-scientific infrastructure, and of a foreign policy establishment provided a significant foundation and domestic context for the politics of anticommunism and the policy of containment. This context made presidents particularly powerful in foreign policy while allowing the demands of national security to prevail.

The rise of the civil rights, new left, and antiwar movements, however, challenged the dominance of presidential power, the liberal–conservative anticommunist consensus, and the national security ethos of the cold war years. Along with the subsequent rise of conservative movements and the right, the foreign policy establishment collapsed while there was a proliferation of new and old groups in American politics, increased ideological diversity and competition among groups, and more individual political participation in social movements and group politics. This contributed to a decline in presidential power in foreign policy and the growth of divided government since Vietnam while the military-industrial-scientific infrastructure continued to operate in a more inhospitable domestic environment. The end of the cold war, the 9/11 attacks, the war on terrorism and the Great Recession appear to have intensified ideological divisions and partisanship, making it even more difficult for any president, regardless of person or party, to lead, govern, or overcome political gridlock in Washington, D.C.

SUGGESTED SOURCES FOR MORE INFORMATION

Ambrosio, Thomas. (2002) *Ethnic Identity Groups and U.S. Foreign Policy.* Westport, CN: Praeger. A discussion of contemporary group politics, including the role of ethnic groups, consulting firms, and foreign lobbies.

Cigler, Allan J., and Burdett A. Loomis, eds. (2002) *Interest Group Politics.* Washington, DC: Congressional Quarterly Press. A good general overview.

Conason, Joe. (1990) "The Iraq Lobby," *New Republic*, October 1, pp. 14–17. Amazing overview of U.S. businesses involved in dealing and helping to arm Iraq and Saddam Hussein before the 1991 Persian Gulf War.

Halberstam, David. (1998) *The Children.* New York: Random House. Excellent on the rise and impact of the civil rights movement, with an emphasis on the role of black students as the new leaders.

Halberstam, David. (1969) *The Best and the Brightest.* New York: Random House. The classic portrayal of the foreign policy establishment and the policymaking process responsible for the Americanization of the war in Vietnam.

Isaacson, Walter, and Evan Thomas. (1986) *The Wise Men: Six Friends and the World They Made.* New York: Touchstone. A good account of key members of the foreign policy establishment and their role and impact.

Kotz, Nick. (1988) *Wild Blue Yonder and the B-1 Bomber.* Princeton, NJ: Princeton University Press. A revealing account of the military-industrial complex at work.

Mearsheimer, John, and Stephen Walt. (2007) *The Israel Lobby and U.S. Foreign Policy.* New York: Farrar, Strauss, and Giroux. A controversial examination of the influence of the Jewish Lobby.

Moon, Chung-in. (1988) "Complex Interdependence and Transnational Lobbying: South Korea in the United States," *International Studies Quarterly* 32:67–89. Conceptual overview with case studies of the four influence strategies in group politics.

Ricci, David M. (1993) *The Transformation of American Politics: The New Washington and the Rise of Think Tanks.* New Haven, CN: Yale University Press. A broad historical context for understanding the expansion of group politics and its implications for the workings of American democracy.

Singer, Peter W. (2007) *Corporate Warriors: The Rise of the Privatized Military Industry.* Ithaca, NY: Cornell University Press. The definitive work of the rise of outsourcing, corporate warriors, and the use of mercenaries.

KEY CONCEPTS

antiwar movement	lobbying strategies
challenging groups	militarization of research
Christian right	military-industrial complex
civil rights movement	military-industrial-scientific
conflicts of interest	infrastructure
dealignment	political right
established groups	pork barrel politics
foreign policy establishment	realpolitik, or power politics,
inside versus outside politics	view
interest groups	revolving door system
issue- and cause-oriented groups	social movements

OTHER KEY TERMS

American Federation of	foreign lobbies
Labor-Congress of Industrial	government–business
Organization (AFL-CIO)	relationship
American multinational	Israeli or Jewish lobby
corporations (MNCs)	Manhattan Project
B-1 bomber program	outsourcing war
beltway bandits	private military contractors (PMCS)
China lobby	private voluntary organizations
consulting firms	(PVOs)
Council on Foreign Relations (CFR)	think tanks
corporate warriors	U.S.–Iraq Business Forum
defense contractors	1968 Democratic National
Eisenhower's farewell address	Convention

CHAPTER 13

Official White House Photo by Chuck Kennedy

PRESIDENT BARACK OBAMA HOLDS A PRESS CONFERENCE IN THE EISENHOWER
EXECUTIVE OFFICE BUILDING OF THE WHITE HOUSE

THE MEDIA AND THE COMMUNICATIONS PROCESS

Much of the information, knowledge, and images that individuals have of the world—whether the mass public, the elite public, or policymakers—comes from the mass media. *This chapter examines the type of mediated reality that Americans tend to acquire through the American mass media and the communications process by addressing the following questions:* What are the conventional images of the media and the complex reality of the news media? How has foreign policy media coverage evolved from World War II to the present? What explains news media coverage? What role, if any, do the entertainment media play? In this respect, examining the role of the mass media and the communications process allows us to better understand the patterns of presidential governance, continuity and change, and tension between national security and democracy that have evolved over time.

CONVENTIONAL WISDOM AND COMPLEX REALITY

The mass media and the communications process have become significant elements in the politics of U.S. foreign policy. As society and the global environment have grown in complexity and in importance in affecting the lives of Americans, people have developed a greater need for information about national and international affairs. Furthermore, during the twentieth century a communications revolution occurred that makes it possible for the mass media to rapidly communicate information anywhere on the planet. Not surprisingly, many people hold strong opinions about the role of the mass media and the news.

Three competing views seem prevalent throughout American society. Conservatives tend to argue that the media play a powerful role in American politics and that there is a "liberal bias" in the American news media. Liberals tend to agree the media play a powerful role, but they believe that there is a "conservative bias" in the news media. Journalists, however, tend to argue that the power of the media has been overblown; the news media are "neutral" and simply attempt to mirror reality, reporting events and the facts as they exist. Very simply, all three views tend to be overly stereotypical and self-serving: the media is not consistently liberal, conservative, or objective.

The complex reality is that *there are contradictory implications of people's dependence on the news media and reliance on the mainstream media.* In many ways, the news media coverage today is better than ever before. The mainstream media are more informative regarding national and international affairs. The quality of journalism has improved and become more professional. More public affairs programs are on television than in the past. Quality newspapers, such as the *New York Times* and the *Wall Street Journal*, are readily available in urban areas throughout the country. And the Internet has made much news accessible to anybody with a computer or smart phone. In sum, members of the public who rely on the mainstream media can gain considerable information about national and international affairs if they are interested, especially if they already possess a good base of information.

At the same time, the news media are highly selective and inconsistent with respect to which events are covered and how they are presented: sometimes being more liberal, other times more conservative, and sometimes more neutral. Many public affairs programs provide soft (as opposed to hard) news. Television news coverage is usually brief and simplistic, appealing to a mass public by emphasizing drama and the least common denominator. Little real investigative reporting is conducted by the mainstream media, while sources of information from alternative media outlets are ignored. Finally, much of the public typically has a short attention span and demonstrates little interest in becoming truly informed. Therefore, the net result of reliance on the mainstream media is often a simplistic understanding of reality: members of the mass public are as much confused as enlightened, while members of the elite public may have a more sophisticated but often narrow understanding because they often lack the historical context or the inclination to rely on diverse sources. As Shanto Iyengar and Donald R. Kinder (1987) demonstrate, the news media provide "news that matters" and this has consequences for the exercise of presidential power and the presidential life cycle.

THE SELECTIVITY OF NEWS COVERAGE BY THE MAINSTREAM-NATIONAL MEDIA

Let's begin by discussing where most Americans get whatever information they have about national and international affairs, followed by the nature of the coverage that is provided to most people by the mass media in the United States—including the revolution in **ICT (information and communications technology)** and especially the Internet. (Use of ICT started to become popular, especially globally, beginning in the 1990s. It emphasizes the integration of information with telecommunication-telephone lines and wireless signals, computers as well as software, storage, and audio-visual systems, which enable users to access, store, transmit, and manipulate information.)

Source of News

Most Americans get their information about national and international affairs from the **mainstream media:** the major newspapers, radio stations, and television stations available in their communities and from the Internet. In the area of news, it could be argued that a **national media**—sometimes referred to as the elite press—has developed and become the primary source of information on national and international affairs for the mainstream media in general and, consequently, for most Americans.

The national media consist of the following organizations: ABC, NBC, CBS, Fox, CNN (Cable News Network), the *New York Times*, *Washington Post*, *Los Angeles Times*, and Associated Press (AP). One could also include *Newsweek*—owned by the *Washington Post*—*Time*, and *U.S. News & World Report* for the attentive public, as well as the *Wall Street Journal*, especially given its unique coverage of economic news. Other large urban media organizations, such as the *Boston Globe*, *Chicago Tribune*, *Miami Herald*, and *Philadelphia Inquirer*, are junior partners of the national media, for they lack national reach beyond their regional market. Each of these media organizations provides its news electronically through its Internet website. The national media, in addition to being the direct source of information for many people, also operate **wire services.** For example, the Associated Press, unknown to most Americans, is a significant part of the national media because it makes available a large number of news stories from its reporters throughout the world to other media organizations (at a cost) through its wire service.

In sum, the mainstream media have become the basic source of national and international news for most television stations, radio stations, and newspapers in the country—the mediums through which most Americans acquire information about the world around them. And this includes the use of **the Internet.** According to a recent study by the *Pew Research Center for the People and the Press* (2011), "In short, instead of replacing traditional news platforms, Americans are increasingly integrating new technologies into their news consumption habits."

The mass public, being relatively uninterested and uninformed about national and international affairs, tends to be most receptive to **headline news** from mainstream sources, such as lead stories on the front page of the newspaper and, in particular, on television. The elite public follows the media's coverage of the news more closely and is most likely to go beyond the headlines and supplement its information beyond television and the local newspaper (especially through use of the Internet), although most still rely on national media sources. In other words, even if they rely on the Internet, most Americans rely on the mainstream and national media for their news, if they pay attention at all (see Bennett 2011; Graber 2009; Stacks 2003/04; Pew Research Center 2010).

Contemporary News Coverage

What do we know about mainstream and national media coverage of contemporary national and international affairs? For one thing, we know that the news media display considerable "selective attention" to the world around them. Most of the American media focus on national and local news, with little attention given to international news. Most studies examining media coverage have found that the percentage of news stories devoted to international affairs by major mainstream media organizations ranged from a low of 10 percent to a high of 40 percent (with the percentage declining over time), representing anywhere from five to fifteen international news stories daily.

Media coverage of international affairs also varies to a considerable extent depending on the "type of medium." The print media, especially newspapers, usually cover more news stories and devote more space to each story than the television media. National news on television has a higher percentage of stories devoted to international affairs, but they are few in number. National television news programs broadcast an average of five to seven international stories (representing a total of seven to eleven minutes) out of fifteen to seventeen stories broadcast daily. At best, national news shown on a major television network, such as ABC, CBS, or NBC, provides only a brief digest of national and international events in less than twenty-one minutes—not much time to cover the world (the regular one-hour news show on CNN provides a longer version of similar coverage). Their Internet sites tend to reflect these patterns as well, although there may be more overall coverage (given its more flexible and dynamic, nonphysical, virtual nature).

International coverage by major newspapers represents a smaller percentage of their total news coverage, but newspapers tend to cover more international stories overall. For example, the *New York Times*—considered the best daily American source of international news—averages thirteen to twenty international news stories per day. Overall, only a limited number of events and issues become news, especially in the media's coverage of the world beyond American shores. Or as H. D. Wu (1998:507) concluded after reviewing and synthesizing fifty-five different media studies of American international news coverage, "One cannot help but realize that the everyday representation of the world via news media is far from a direct reflection of global realities. International news is selected, sifted, edited and mostly discarded through a myriad of processes by the news organizations and professionals."

The type of medium also is important for it affects not only the space available for news coverage, but how the news is presented. Television news stories, in particular, are unique because they are accompanied by video pictures (and sound) that provide the viewer with a greater sense of immediacy—of "being there"—which further affects viewers' perceptions. The **power of television** (and increasingly the Internet with video feeds such as *YouTube*) is particularly noticeable during crisis reporting, when issues and stories that are part of the crisis are highlighted and most vulnerable to being sensationalized. "Television is driven to dramatize the news, to give it plot, theme, and continuity to make it comprehensive to a mass audience. Television needs action and drama. It needs to boil down complexities. It needs identifiable characters. Hence the focus on personality, preferably one personality." Television also has a greater "tendency to present (and understand) politics in terms of demons and friends, good guys and bad guys" (Smith 1988:395).

Overall, television news coverage tends to simplify reality the most for it tends to be more incomplete and provide less depth than the print media, while, at the same time, its visual images make it more compelling and powerful. Television is, nevertheless, the major medium by which most Americans gain their information and understanding of national and international affairs. A Pew Research Center (2005b) survey found that, within a few days after the September 11, 2001, attacks, nine in ten Americans said that they got most of their news from television, some of which was the local TV news. Half the respondents also said that they were reading newspapers more closely, and about a third were checking the Internet more often (but still at very low overall rates at a time when computers, the Internet and social media were becoming very popular). A month later, Americans still relied predominantly on television, but increasingly went back to their regular news sources—especially (local) newspapers, (local) radio, and the Internet (but not magazines)—for coverage of the war on terrorism both at home and abroad, and only about 15 percent said that they followed international news "very closely." In general, older Americans tend to read (local) newspapers more, younger people tend to rely on the Internet more, and the national network news have seen declining audiences (see **Table 13.1** for Americans' news sources following 9/11; see also Pew Research Center 2010).

Given the selectivity and the medium, which international topics actually tend to be covered by the American media? Research has found that, in order to receive mainstream and national media coverage on television or in print as well as the Internet, foreign news in general must be more consequential, especially for Americans; must involve people of higher status; and must entail more violence or disaster than national news. According to *Deciding What's News*, a classic 1979 study of CBS, NBC, *Newsweek*, and *Time* by Herbert Gans (1979), the following international topics tended to receive the most attention by the national media, which has not really changed to the present day (as we discuss below):

1. American activities abroad (especially official visits),

2. foreign events directly affecting the United States (involving especially national security and economic affairs),

3. East–West governmental relations,

4. changes in heads of state (with a special interest in European royalty),

5. dramatic political conflicts (such as wars, coups, revolutions, and terrorism),

6. natural disasters, and

7. excesses of foreign dictators.

Table 13.1   American News Sources Immediately Following September 11 2001, Attacks

News Source	Mid-September %	Mid-November %
Cable News	45	53
Network TV News	30	17
Local TV News	17	18
Radio	14	19
Newspapers	11	34
Magazines	0	2
Internet	5	13
Other	3	3
Don't Know	3	1

The Question: "How have you been getting most of your news about terrorism? From television, newspapers, radio, magazines, or Internet?" (Some cited more than one choice.)

SOURCE: Michael Parks, "Foreign News: What's Next?," *Columbia Journalism Review* 40 (January–February 2002), pp. 54–55.

Not much has changed since the collapse of the Soviet Union and communism in Eastern Europe nor since September 11, 2001, or with the growing popularity of the Internet, with the exception that (if you refer to the list by Gans) attention to East–West governmental relations has been replaced by the war on terrorism, including the war in Iraq and Afghanistan (see also Hess 1996; Pew Research Center 2005b, 2010; Seplow 2002). A typical conclusion is that the American mainstream and national press "pays far greater attention to countries which are economically affluent, politically powerful and culturally similar to the United States" (Semmel 1986:86). And the emphasis is clearly on political and national security affairs among international topics, not on international economics—even with the economic crisis and the Great Recession under Presidents Bush and Obama.

News coverage of events abroad by the U.S. media, in other words, tends to be American- and Western-centric (as opposed to being globally oriented), focuses on government officials (as opposed to nongovernmental groups and publics), emphasizes so-called negative events such as conflict (as opposed to positive stories emphasizing cooperation), and highlights political and national security issues (as opposed to economic or environmental issues). The emphasis on political and national security news remains problematic in informing the public about the workings of the international political economy, especially in light of the 2007 global recession. Not only do issues in the developing world receive little attention; when they do get covered, they often entail more sensational items (military coups, wars, natural disasters, accidents, and crime).

Mainstream media coverage of other countries (and global issues) not only tends to be simplistic and incomplete but often swings back and forth from more positive to more negative coverage. For example, reporting on China over the decades and years has often constantly shifted from "admiration to confrontation." Or as depicted in the title of one study of the media's post–September 11 coverage: "Forgotten Coverage of Afghan 'Freedom Fighters': The Villains of Today's News Were Heroes in the '80s" (Farmer 1999; Gibbs 2002).

This selective and volatile coverage is intensified during times of crisis, whether domestic or international. Crisis coverage is often so great that most other national and international news of consequence disappears entirely. Such was the case during the Bush Administration for months following the September 11 attacks and the launching of the war on terrorism. Crisis coverage by the American news media also tends to be limited to events in which the United States is heavily involved or affected; little or no media coverage would be given to a civil war or a disaster in another country where the United States has little involvement, even though this may clearly be a crisis situation for the people and the region involved (compare coverage of Hurricane Katrina in 2005 or Hurricane Sandy in 2012 with the 2005 earthquake in Pakistan where over 150,000 people died). Even then, where the Afghan War received considerable coverage during the winter of 2001–2002 when the United States militarily intervened, once victory was declared coverage virtually disappeared despite the subsequent "mess in Afghanistan," until it received more attention after the United States withdrew from Iraq (Rashid 2004). Likewise, domestic and international economics received lots of attention in 2007–2009, but once the economic collapse was forestalled the emphasis again became the domestic economy, the recovery, and most stories returned to the business and finance sections or outlets (see **A Closer Look** on crisis coverage).

Crisis Coverage and the News Media Cycle

In order to fully understand the significance of crisis coverage, we must examine patterns in **news media cycle** *coverage as they proceed through three general stages of coverage:* pre-crisis, crisis, and post-crisis. During crisis coverage, the resources of the media are heavily devoted to covering the key issue or event as the lead story. During pre- and post-crisis coverage, however, the bureaucratic and routine nature of media politics prevails, in which any single issue typically receives little and uneven news coverage. James Reston (1967:195) of the *New York Times* explained the reactive nature of media crisis coverage this way: "We are fascinated by events but not by the things that cause the events. We will send 500 correspondents to Vietnam after the war breaks out, and fill the front pages with their reports, meanwhile ignoring the rest of the world, but we will not send five reporters there when the danger of war is developing."

A study conducted for the State Department's Foreign Service Institute by A. Raphael (1981/82), for example, found that the three television networks covered Iran an average of only five minutes each year from 1972 to 1977. Yet, with the fall of the shah of Iran and the taking of American diplomats, the Iran hostage crisis became the ultimate media event throughout 1979 and 1980 for 444 days. Once the international crisis was perceived to be over in Iran—or in Vietnam, Grenada, Panama, Haiti, Somalia, Kosovo, Afghanistan, or Iraq, for example—there is little subsequent attention and follow-up by the media. In addition to the stark contrast between the media attention given to an issue during a crisis in comparison to the little attention devoted both before and after, *crisis coverage is usually incomplete, inflated,* *and often sensationalized,* especially as a result of the immediacy and powerful images provided by television (and its round-the-clock coverage).

Crisis coverage initially strengthens presidential foreign policy power in the short term, primarily because the American media are extremely responsive and vulnerable to becoming overwhelmed with patriotic and nationalistic fervor, typically acting as a medium that promotes the president's views and policies and contributing to a "rally-round-the-flag" phenomenon throughout the country. Kathleen Hall Jamieson (2003) of the Annenberg School of Communication at the University of Pennsylvania made the telling point about the Persian Gulf crisis that "in the early days, the coverage suggested to me that, if you didn't know our television wasn't state-owned, you would have thought it was."

Second, sometimes crisis coverage may actually weaken presidential power. The most obvious examples involved Presidents Richard Nixon and Watergate, Ronald Reagan and Iran-Contra, and Bill Clinton and the Monica Lewinsky affair. Third, the longer the crisis endures, the more likely that news media coverage will weaken presidential power. Although Vietnam contributed to presidential power early on, it ended up being the principal cause of President Johnson's political fall. Such was the pattern with President Bush after 9/11, as he experienced huge approval and then eventual decline of support as the war in Iraq seemed to drag on and on. Although President Obama received more favorable coverage at the beginning of his administration with the focus on overcoming the economic crisis, with time his support declined as the media focused less on the crisis and more on the sputtering economic recovery and slow job growth. Very simply, as the public tires of policies that are not perceived as successful, media coverage is likely to reflect the more critical aspects of the evolving political environment and to constrain the president's power to persuade others to support him and his policies.

To what extent do such patterns in crisis coverage continue in a more electronically-oriented environment? Do social media like "Facebook" and "Twitter" reinforce or change or intensify these patterns?

FOREIGN POLICY COVERAGE SINCE WORLD WAR II

These patterns in American news media coverage can be better understood if we take a closer historical look at the foreign policy coverage of the U.S. mainstream and national media. In the words of Doris Graber (1989:29) in *Mass Media and American Politics*:

> The mass media are more than passive transmission agents for available information. Decisions made by media personnel determine what information becomes available to media audiences and what remains unavailable. By putting stories into perspective and interpreting them, media personnel assign meaning to the information and indicate the values by which it ought to be judged. News shaping is unavoidable because space is limited and because facts do not speak for themselves. Hence the media select and shape much of the raw material needed by political elites and the general public for thinking about the political world and planning political action.

Since the beginning of World War II, there have been three broad patterns in mainstream news media coverage as it has related to the making of U.S. foreign policy: (1) during World War II, coverage by the American news media both reflected and reinforced the U.S. government's war effort, allowing presidents to be supreme; (2) during the cold war, news media coverage reflected and reinforced the anticommunist consensus prevailing in society and the government, strengthening presidential power especially in national security; and (3) since the Vietnam War, news media coverage has had a greater tendency to reflect diverse views and, consequently, has become less consistently supportive of the government's foreign policy, weaken presidential power and requiring greater presidential leadership. Since World War II mainstream media coverage has also emphasized the "high" politics of national security over foreign economics despite the latter's increasing importance and the near economic meltdown in 2007–08.

World War II Coverage

Once the U.S. government declared war on Japan and entered World War II, the American mainstream and national media quickly acted as a medium to rally mass support behind the cause. Times of war are also times of intense nationalism and restrictions on civil liberties. The U.S. government censored the media and conducted a domestic propaganda campaign of vast proportions in order to maximize public support and minimize dissent. The media became the principal means by which pictures of the enemy were portrayed to the American public and acted as an important source for unifying the country against the Axis powers. The media depicted the allied countries as righteous defenders of democracy and freedom against the aggression and evil represented by Germany and Japan. Among other things, this contributed to a West Coast hysteria concerning Japanese sabotage and the internment of Japanese Americans in concentration camps during the war (Roeder 1993; Sweeney 2001).

American leaders also used the media to preach the value of Soviet–American friendship and continued cooperation following the war. The media popularized the Soviet Union as the great ally of the United States, frequently referring to Joseph Stalin as "Uncle Joe." Thus, the media not only played a prominent role during World War II in reflecting the views of the U.S. government and promoting American nationalism but also contributed to creating a set of unrealistic expectations about Soviet–American friendship that would haunt the postwar years.

Cold War Coverage

Immediately following World War II, the American news media began to reflect greater diversity of views, consistent with the great political debate raging over the future of U.S. foreign policy. However, with the rise of the cold war, mainstream and national media coverage again began to narrow and reflect the growing anticommunist political environment. The administrations of Harry Truman and Dwight Eisenhower communicated their fears of communism through the media to both educate the mass public and rally support for the containment policy. Such media coverage both reflected and contributed to the rise of the political right and anticommunism, further narrowing public debate.

As Edwin Bayley (1981) found in *Joe McCarthy and the Press*, charges of internal subversion were news and contributed to the rise of Senator Joseph McCarthy and McCarthyism. Media coverage also eventually led to the downfall of Senator McCarthy. Nevertheless, by the mid-1950s, an anticommunist consensus pervaded American society, including American journalism.

There was no outright government censorship of the news media during the cold war (except for Korean War coverage)—there didn't need to be, given the consensus of thought and McCarthyism. In fact, as Carl Bernstein (1977) of Watergate fame has reported, over 400 American journalists occasionally worked closely for the CIA, and many carried out assignments (not always knowingly). This included major executives and reporters in the field from every major news organization in the country, as well as a few minor ones. As pointed out by the Senate's Church committee investigation in 1975, such cozy relationships between the mainstream **media and the CIA** (and the intelligence community) raised serious concerns about the "potential, inherent in covert media operations, for manipulating or incidentally misleading the American public" and the "damage to the credibility and independence of a free press" (U.S. Congress, Senate, Final Report 1976:197).

Although the national media are credited with being critical of the Vietnam War, it is usually forgotten that in their **Vietnam War coverage** during the late 1950s and early 1960s the media dutifully communicated the government's position and promoted the Americanization of the Vietnam War. As David Halberstam (1979:446) observed, "The great heads of the media were anxious to be good and loyal citizens, and the working reporters had almost without question accepted the word of the White House on foreign policy. . . . The press corps might be congenitally skeptical in assessing the intentions and ambitions of domestic politicians, but it brought no such toughness of mind to the politics of foreign policy." Thus, the media contributed to the growth of presidential power in foreign affairs and the rise of a national security ethos in which the demands of national security often prevailed over the demands of democracy in response to the cold war.

Given the national emergencies represented by World War II and the cold war, it is understandable that the views dominating the executive branch pervaded the mainstream and national news media, and became the orthodoxy by which Americans understood international politics and U.S. foreign policy. As a popular saying goes, "Winners write history."

Post–Vietnam War Coverage

Reflecting the breakdown of the anticommunist consensus, it was not until the mid- and late 1960s that the national news media's coverage of the Vietnam War became more critical of the government. As Daniel Hallin (1986) found, media coverage of U.S. foreign policy in general and Vietnam policy in particular tended to reflect events occurring inside the government. As long as consensus prevailed within the government, national media coverage reflected this consensus and supported government policy. It was only when dissent increased within the government—both in Congress and in the Johnson Administration— that media coverage became more critical of the war and the government's policies.

By the late 1960s and early 1970s, national media coverage increasingly reflected the collapse of the anticommunist consensus in the government and society. The Watergate crisis, in fact, represented the height of a critical and cynical media independent of the administration and engaged in investigative reporting. Still, the American failure in the Vietnam War was one of the few times that the popular interpretation—that Vietnam did not represent a vital interest and that the war was a mistake—became inconsistent with the presidential view.

Clearly, since Vietnam the president no longer monopolizes media coverage as he did during World War II and the cold war. With the collapse of the anticommunist consensus, the national media in particular are more likely to represent a greater diversity of foreign policy thought (especially in the area of national security), rely on more sources of information throughout society and in the policymaking process, and present news in a more critical and cynical fashion. This has contributed to the rise of Congress, the proliferation of group politics in the making of U.S. foreign policy, and the expansion of news programs in the electronic media and the Internet.

Sometimes national news media coverage ends up being more supportive of the president and sometimes it is more critical. Much depends on the nature of the issue, the political environment, and the times. For example, for months following the September 11 attacks in 2001, the media and the country rallied behind President Bush's war on terrorism—giving him the highest presidential approval ratings in modern history. But within months following the president's announcement that the Iraq War was over in spring of 2003, questions and criticisms occasionally began to be raised about the Bush administration's foreign policy toward the Middle East and terrorism and, in particular, relative to the decision to invade and overthrow Iraq. Following the 2004 presidential election and especially in 2005, the mainstream media became much more critical in response to the continued difficulties of the so-called postwar occupation, efforts at nation-building, and increasing casualties of American soldiers—reflecting and promoting the public's growing disapproval of the president's handling of the war. Initially, President Barack Obama received positive coverage based in part on his pledge for "hope and change." However, the positive tone evaporated by the end of 2009 due to the slow pace of the economic recovery and short-term, "what are you doing for me today" aspects of media coverage. These news cycles may have a faster and more intense pace with constant changes in ICT and the Internet. Therefore, the mainstream and national media act as a major, and often unpredictable, source of both presidential power and the paradox of presidential power as explained below.

EXPLAINING NEWS MEDIA COVERAGE

Conservative and liberal critics of the American media agree that the news media must select, simplify, and, consequently, distort reality. Most mainstream journalists, however, have difficulty acknowledging or admitting this, because it contradicts their belief that they are able to mirror reality. Perhaps most important, this admission would damage the news media's credibility with the American public as providers of information and the watchdog of government. Due to the increasing complexity of the world and the changing technology of communications, the news media can provide only a **mediated reality**, yet one that has an important impact on the politics of U.S. foreign policy. *Two general explanations account for the selectivity of American news media coverage:* (1) the characteristics of the news business and (2) the politics of the communications process. Much of this was on display and reflected in the continual news media coverage, which began as early as late 2011, of the presidential elections of 2012.

Characteristics of the News Business

News media coverage is affected by the history, functions, organization, and subculture of the mass media (as with any bureaucratic organization). Therefore, we must examine *a number of important characteristics concerning the nature of the mass media and journalism in American society*—including that the media (1) have become concentrated, (2) are big business, (3) are very competitive, and (4) have become bureaucratic and professionalized.

THE CONCENTRATED MEDIA   The mainstream media is not only led or dominated by the national media when it comes to national and international news, the mainstream and national media are increasingly owned by only a handful of corporations.

Of the 1500 daily newspapers that existed in the 1990s, 99 percent were local monopolies, and about a dozen corporations controlled most of the country's circulation. Independently owned newspapers, once dominant, have been replaced by large media chains, such as Gannett, which operates *USA Today* and over ninety other dailies (representing 10 percent of total circulation in the country); Knight-Ridder, which runs the *Philadelphia Inquirer*, the *Miami Herald*, and over thirty other daily newspapers; the *New York Times Company*, which operates the *New York Times*, the *Boston Globe*, and over thirty other dailies (as well as numerous magazines and television and radio stations); and the *Chicago Tribune*, which merged with Times Mirror and owns the *Los Angeles Times* (as well as other regional newspapers and radio stations and over twenty television stations and national magazines).

The three major broadcasting networks have a majority of the television audience, although it has been declining. This decline in viewership for the major networks is in part due to the existence of thousands of cable systems (and the rise of the Fox network), but each cable system operates local monopolies, and over half of all the cable systems are owned by four companies. Altogether, roughly seven media corporations control the seeming diversity of channels and choice on television. And five companies own over 300 radio stations throughout the country with a few basic formats.

Overall, Ben Bagdikian (2000:xx), in *The Media Monopoly*, found that concentration in the communications industry grew rapidly in the 1980s and 1990s, a time of numerous mergers:

> When the first edition of this book was published in 1983, fifty corporations dominated most of every mass medium and the biggest media merger in history was a $340 million deal. At that time, the strategy of most of the fifty biggest firms was to gain market domination in one medium—to have the largest market share solely in newspapers, for example, or in magazines, or broadcasting, or books, or movies, but not in all of them. By the time the second edition was published

in 1987, the fifty companies had shrunk to twenty-nine. By the third edition in 1990, the twenty-nine had shrunk to twenty-three, by the fourth edition to fourteen. By the fifth edition in 1997, the biggest firms numbered ten and involved the $19 billion Disney-ABC deal, at the time the biggest media merger ever. But the "biggest" of 1983, worth $340 million, would give way seventeen years later to AOL Time Warner's $450 billion merged corporation, more than 1,000 times larger.

Today six firms or conglomerates dominate most American mass media and "those six have more communications power than all the combined fifty leading firms sixteen years earlier" (Bagdikian 2000:xx). The six conglomerates are AOL/Time Warner; The Walt Disney Company; Murdoch's News Corporation, based in Australia; General Electric; Viacom; and Bertelsmann based in Germany (and Clear Channel especially for radio stations; see also Bagdikian 2004). All are among the largest corporations in the world (see **Figure 13.1** on five of the largest media conglomerates).

So the mainstream media and the national media have become the basic source of national and international news through which most Americans acquire information about the world around them, and they are owned by predominantly six global conglomerates. While the existence of so many news sources provides the appearance of considerable diversity, the national media and its overall concentration tend to present **homogeneous news coverage** rather than a diverse picture of the news and the world. Regardless of which of the national television news programs or newspapers one watches or reads, all of these sources usually select the same lead news item, cover the same stories, and provide similar information and interpretations. Differences do exist, but they tend to be minor, concerning detail and nuance regardless of the party and president in power, as both Bush and Obama experienced. What about the revolution in ICT and the Internet? Hasn't it circumvented the concentrated media (see **A Different Perspective** on the alternative media and the Internet)?

THE MEDIA BUSINESS One reason the news media have become concentrated and their coverage so homogenized is that the mass media have increasingly become a big business. Historically, the American press used to consist of small, independent operations that were usually quite partisan. Presses frequently were operated to make money and provide a living for those involved. In addition, many were financed by wealthy patrons who were more interested in providing news and political interpretation, even at a financial loss. With the rise of industrialization, urbanization, and mass society, however, the media have become a big business where the bottom line—financial worth and profit—predominates.

As economics has replaced politics as the basic source of motivation within the news business, "muckraking" journalism has declined and partisan viewpoints have been relegated to the editorial pages. And with revenues in the billions of dollars, the news and communications process has become big, and is becoming bigger, business. This is probably best illustrated when *Time Inc.* merged with *Warner* in 2000 to form *Time Warner* at a cost of $450 billion, becoming the largest multimedia firm in the world. At the same time, with the rise of the Internet and the great recession of 2007–2008, newspapers, in particular, have been losing their readership (especially among younger people), profitability, and are struggling to survive (see **Figure 13.2** Americans changing source of news).

Overall, growing concern with generating revenue and maintaining profitability has led to the mass media's preoccupation with maximizing its appeal to very broad as well as

Figure 13.1 The Concentrated Media

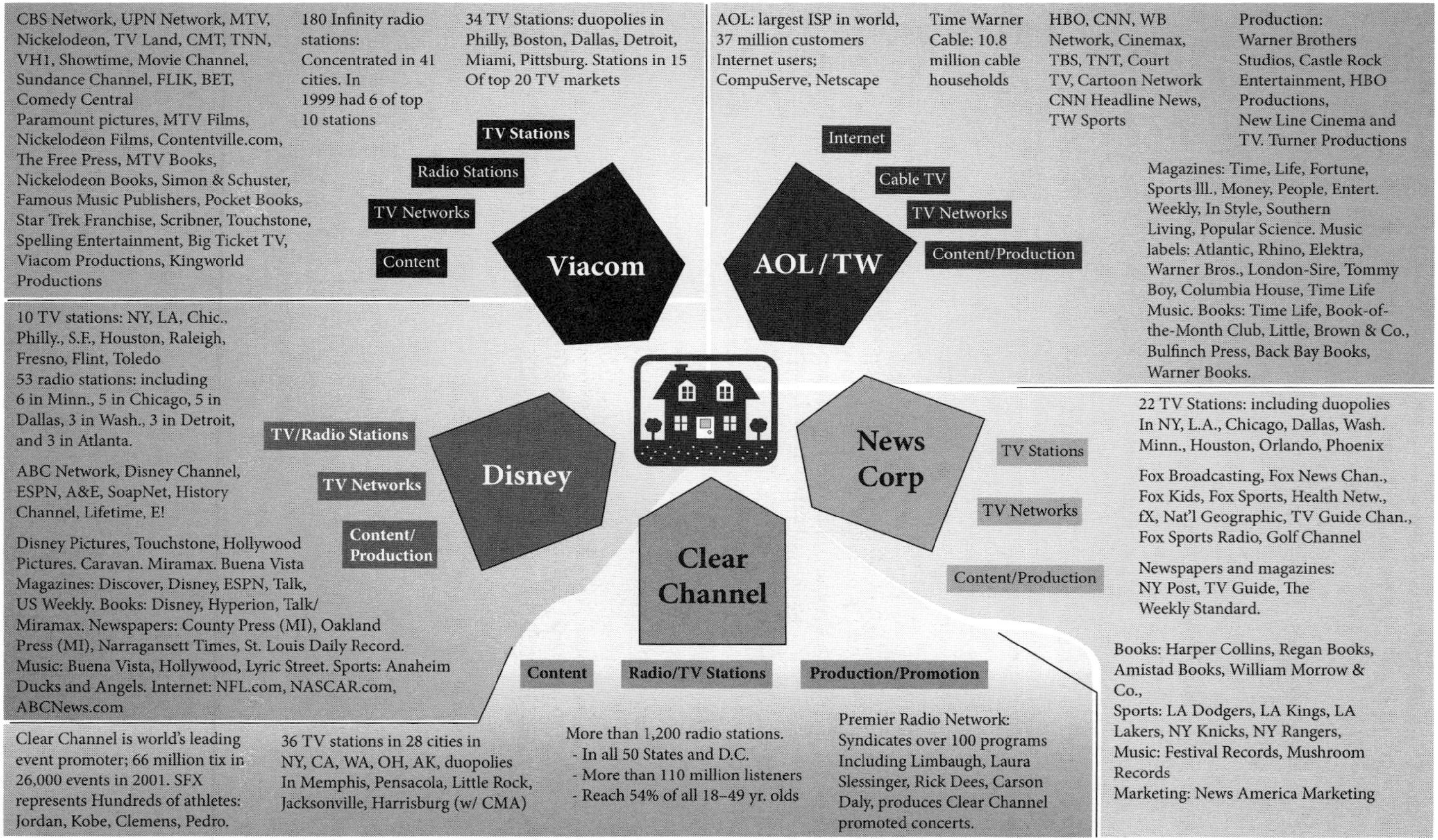

AOL/TW

AOL: largest ISP in world, 37 million customers Internet users; CompuServe, Netscape

Time Warner Cable: 10.8 million cable households

HBO, CNN, WB Network, Cinemax, TBS, TNT, Court TV, Cartoon Network CNN Headline News, TW Sports

Production: Warner Brothers Studios, Castle Rock Entertainment, HBO Productions, New Line Cinema and TV Turner Productions

Magazines: Time, Life, Fortune, Sports Ill., Money, People, Entert. Weekly, In Style, Southern Living, Popular Science, Music labels: Atlantic, Rhino, Elektra, Warner Bros., London-Sire, Tommy Boy, Columbia House, Time Life Music. Books: Time Life, Book-of-the-Month Club, Little, Brown & Co., Bulfinch Press, Back Bay Books, Warner Books.

Internet

Cable TV

TV Networks

Content/Production

News Corp

22 TV Stations: including duopolies In NY, L.A., Chicago, Dallas, Wash. Minn., Houston, Orlando, Phoenix

Fox Broadcasting, Fox News Chan., Fox Kids, Fox Sports, Health Netw., FX, Nat'l Geographic, TV Guide Chan., Fox Sports Radio, Golf Channel

Newspapers and magazines: NY Post, TV Guide, The Weekly Standard

Books: Harper Collins, Regan Books, Amistad Books, William Morrow & Co., Sports: LA Dodgers, LA Kings, LA Lakers, NY Knicks, NY Rangers, Music: Festival Records, Mushroom Records Marketing: News America Marketing

TV Stations

TV Networks

Content/Production

Clear Channel

Production/Promotion

Premier Radio Network. Syndicates over 100 programs Including Limbaugh, Laura Slessinger, Rick Dees, Carson Daly, produces Clear Channel promoted concerts.

Radio/TV Stations

More than 1,200 radio stations.
- In all 50 States and D.C.
- More than 110 million listeners
- Reach 54% of all 18–49 yr. olds

Content

Clear Channel is world's leading event promoter; 66 million tix in 26,000 events in 2001. SFX represents Hundreds of athletes: Jordan, Kobe, Clemens, Pedro.

Disney

36 TV stations in 28 cities in NY, CA, WA, OH, AK, duopolies In Memphis, Pensacola, Little Rock, Jacksonville, Harrisburg (w/ CMA)

ABC Network, Disney Channel, ESPN, A&E, SoapNet, History Channel, Lifetime, E!

Disney Pictures, Touchstone, Hollywood Pictures. Caravan. Miramax. Buena Vista Magazines: Discover, Disney, ESPN, Talk, US Weekly. Books: Disney, Hyperion, Talk/ Miramax. Newspapers: County Press (MI), Oakland Press (MI), Narragansett Times, St. Louis Daily Record. Music: Buena Vista, Hollywood, Lyric Street. Sports: Anaheim Ducks and Angels. Internet: NFL.com, NASCAR.com, ABCNews.com

TV/Radio Stations

TV Networks

Content/ Production

Viacom

34 TV Stations: duopolies in Philly, Boston, Dallas, Detroit, Miami, Pittsburg. Stations in 15 Of top 20 TV markets

180 Infinity radio stations: Concentrated in 41 cities. In 1999 had 6 of top 10 stations

CBS Network, UPN Network, MTV, Nickelodeon, TV Land, CMT, TNN, VH1, Showtime, Movie Channel, Sundance Channel, FLIK, BET, Comedy Central Paramount pictures, MTV Films, Nickelodeon Films, Contentville.com, The Free Press, MTV Books, Nickelodeon Books, Simon & Schuster, Famous Music Publishers, Pocket Books, Star Trek Franchise, Scribner, Touchstone, Spelling Entertainment, Big Ticket TV, Viacom Productions, Kingworld Productions

10 TV stations: NY, LA, Chic., Philly, S.F., Houston, Raleigh, Fresno, Flint, Toledo 53 radio stations: including 6 in Minn., 5 in Chicago, 5 in Dallas, 3 in Wash., 3 in Detroit, and 3 in Atlanta.

TV Stations

Radio Stations

TV Networks

Content

SOURCE: Mark Crispin Miller, "What's Wrong With This Picture?" in The Nation, Jan. 7, 2002. The graphic is an in-house production.

The Alternative Media, Social Media, and an Internet Revolution?

The **alternative media** simply refers to those media outlets—such as television and radio programs, film, books, and magazines, and most recently, the Internet—that tend to address more varied issues, provide additional information, and offer interpretations beyond those available in the mainstream and national media.

Alternative media have existed throughout American history. Numerous and diverse alternative media have proliferated, especially since Vietnam and then with the rise of the Internet, although Americans are generally so dependent on the national media that the alternative media remain relatively invisible and unknown.

There are some alternative sources on television and cable, radio and even film. Some TV programs such as *Frontline* (on PBS) and *60 Minutes* (on CBS) tend to provide information from a more liberal orientation; while other shows such as *Fox News* and *The McLaughlin Group* have a more conservative orientation, as well as a so-called Christian right presence. Comedy news shows, such as *The Daily Show with Jon Stewart*, are overwhelmingly liberal. Radio has become an increasing alternative source of programming and information for more Americans over the last few decades. This would include the rise of public radio, such as National Public Radio (NPR), university radio stations, progressive and community radio, and Christian broadcasting. Probably of greatest visibility since the 1980s has been the rise of "talk radio," usually conservative in orientation and best symbolized by Rush Limbaugh. The rise of independent film and cinema has led to an increase in viewership and is more likely to be associated with more critical and so-called progressive perspectives, especially in the area of documentary film, best embodied

by filmmaker and director Michael Moore.

But historically (since the invention of the printing press), it is in the print mediathat diversity most proliferates. Today, New York's *Village Voice*, San Francisco's *SF Weekly*, and Los Angeles's *LA Weekly* are among the most prominent of the left-oriented free press, while the *Washington Times*, in contrast, reflects the rise of the right. And dozens of opinion journals and magazines exist on the left and the right. Most cities often have free weekly newspapers that emphasize entertainment information around town but usually also include news and alternative commentary. Small publishing houses and large publishing firms also produce thousands of books a year, ranging from the far right to the far left. Hundreds of newsletters also are produced by a variety of private individuals and groups, each with a topic or cause to promote. There is also a rash of alternative publications that are politically oriented and that target women, blacks, Hispanics, labor, environmental groups, and other more specialized audiences and interests, not to mention blogs and lots of other diverse sources on the Internet.

Today, **Internet journalism** *provides the most diverse (and accessible) alternative information and viewpoints.* According to Michael Massing (2009:29), "a remarkable amount of original, exciting, and creative material has appeared on the internet . . . with a variety of fascinating experiments in the gathering, presentation, and delivery of news." It offers a podium to Americans of all ages and backgrounds; opened up topics that have been off-limits to the press; and provides more than "two sides," and only two sides to every debate—the Beltway Democratic (liberal) establishment and the Beltway Republican (conservative) establishment.

(Continued)

"Optimists" believe that Internet journalism and social media can and will have profound effects on news and politics—that there will be greater power exercised from "the bottom up." According to the Pew Project (2009) for Journalism Excellence "State of the News Media" report:"Power is shifting to the individual journalist and away, by degrees, from journalistic institutions. . . . Through search, e-mail, blogs, social media and more, consumers are gravitating to the work of individual writers and voices, and away from institutional brands." As Massing (2009:32) says, "the rise of the internet is loosening the grip of the corporate-owned mass media. A profound if unsettling process of decentralization and democratization is taking place." Optimists are quick to point to the so-called "Arab spring" in which a number of authoritarian regimes, such as President Mubarak in Egypt, collapsed in response to mass demonstrations that were triggered by instantaneous communications through the Internet and social media.

"Pessimists" tend to believe that the potential for informing people and building social networks for change through ICT is possible, but difficult to put into practice. In an article titled "Small Change: Why the Revolution Would Not Be Tweeted," Malcolm Gladwell (2010) states "The world, we are told, is in the midst of a revolution. The new tools of social media have reinvented social activism. With Facebook and Tweeter and the like, the traditional relationship between political authority and popular will has been upended, making it easier for the powerless to collaborate, coordinate, and give voice to their concerns."

Yet, the hopeful but more pessimistic views highlight the repression in Iran and Syria, as well as the uncertainty of who rules in Egypt, as examples of the temporary and illusive impact of social media. That real, permanent change requires well-organized groups and real social movements based on "strong ties" (or networks). However, social media are platforms for quick interaction between strangers, "but weak ties seldom lead to high-risk activism" (Gladwell 2010).

Not only are social networks fleeting, but Internet journalism has troubling features: polemical excesses, exaggerated headlines, source credibility, and just too much information "noise" available. Not surprisingly, most people continue to rely on mainstream and national media sources, now in digital form as opposed to television or print. Furthermore, governments and other powerful actors increasingly are able to exercise some control of communications "from above." Gladwell (2010) concludes that Internet journalism and social media is "simply a form of organizing which favors the weak-tie connections that give us access to information over strong-tie connections that help us persevere in the face of danger. It shifts our energies from organizations that promote strategic and disciplined activity . . . It makes it easier for activists to express themselves, and harder for that expression to have any impact."

To what extent do people seek out alternative media or diverse sources on the Internet? How does alternative and social media complicate President Obama's efforts to govern? Does social media really threaten the status quo and incumbent leaders?

---

very specialized audiences, reinforcing the tendency to provide a selective and homogenized picture of national and international politics if any is provided at all. Sometimes this strengthens a president, sometimes it weakens him, as Bush and Obama know all too well.

Figure 13.2   Trends in News Consumption "Yesterday"

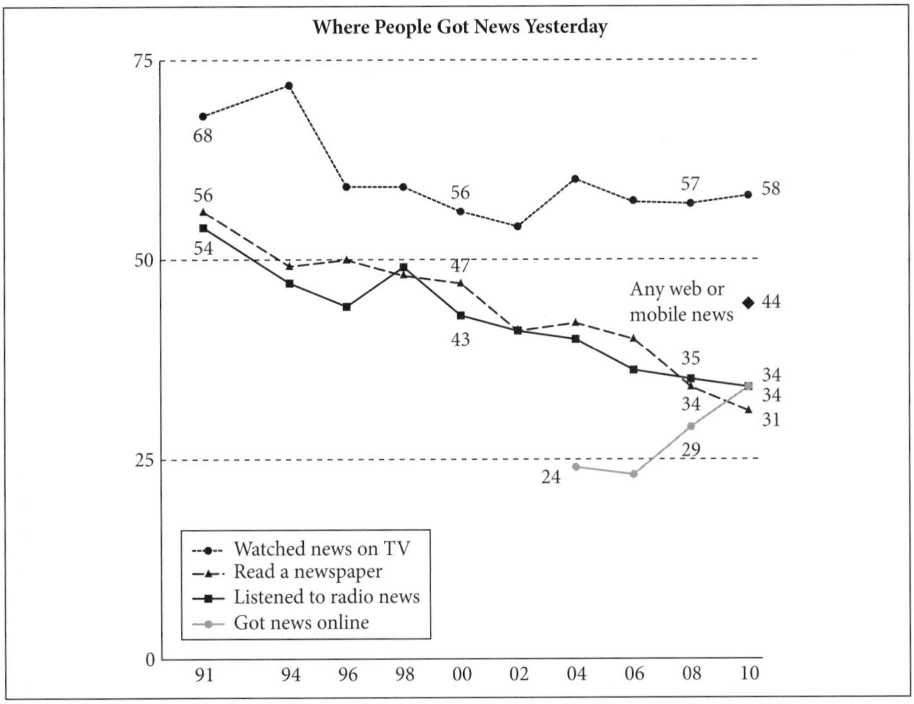

Where People Got News Yesterday

SOURCE: Pew Research Center for the People and the Press, http://www.people-press.org/2010/09/12/
section-1-watching-reading-and-listening-to-the-news/

THE COMPETITIVE MARKET MEDIA The third characteristic is that the news media are also very competitive, but in a narrow sense that reflects their concentrated and big-business orientation. The phrase used by one scholar to describe this situation is that the mass media are "**rivals in conformity**" for audiences and advertisers, which has little to do with improving the quality of media coverage (Bigman 1949). The news media, as in any business, attempt to increase their market share because their revenues are obtained predominantly through advertising. Hence, a key concern of national media organizations is to present news in such a way that attracts, not alienates, audiences and advertisers—that, in other words, takes into consideration the beliefs of the mass and elite publics. This would include not alienating business in particular, since it is the major source of most media advertising.

Television is probably the most competitive and "infotainment-oriented" because the national networks compete for the same viewing audience (and the same national advertisers). Although advertising rates are lower for news than for entertainment programs, it still costs advertisers almost $500,000 a minute for a commercial on one of the nightly network news shows (as opposed to almost $3 million for a thirty-second ad during the Super Bowl professional football championship game). Having a larger or smaller audience means a difference of millions of dollars in yearly revenues. Ironically, the audience for the major networks has been declining, especially with the rise of cable television (Auletta 1991).

This competitiveness, ironically, tends to promote what might be called a "risk-avoidance approach." Their fear of losing viewers and offending corporate sponsors makes the media act with great caution in their programming, usually preferring to emulate the news organization (or the entertainment shows) currently enjoying the greatest amount of success. This is especially true of television, whose news media executives, for example, have become increasingly attuned to the entertainment aspects of the news as a means of attracting the public's attention:

> The impulse to take risks in quality programming, to serve the national interest in public affairs, became weaker all the time. And the enormity of the new profits . . . ironically [made the company] more nervous, more insecure. The race was getting faster and faster and the ice was getting thinner and thinner. . . . Now broadcasting was obsessed with the ratings. (Halberstam 1979:415)

"Soft" public affairs programs that emphasize entertainment and personalities, such as *The Today Show* and *20/20*, have proliferated. Even the nightly network news programs on television have tried numerous gimmicks, such as having the anchorperson report live from abroad, designed not to improve the quality of coverage but to increase popular appeal and viewership. The Internet, with the popularity of *You Tube* and *Facebook*, appears to have reinforced short attention spans and infotainment for most Americans, especially the mass public.

Journalists also are highly motivated, especially at the national level, to excel within their profession. They can command considerable fame, prestige, power, and fortune—strong factors motivating individual journalists. Television anchorpersons and journalists have become well-known celebrities who enjoy annual salaries in the millions of dollars.

In addition to finances, journalists and the major media organizations are preoccupied with getting the story first and being the "number one" source of news. This concern with being the media leader tends to result in the phenomena of **pack journalism**, in which journalists chase the same headline stories. This tendency to congregate while in search of the same story is reinforced by the strong *esprit de corps* that develops among journalists (see also Sabato 1991). Pack journalism is most noticeable, for instance, during crisis coverage or with the media's effort to cover election campaigns (as depicted by Timothy Crouse's 1972 classic *The Boys on the Bus*), such as during the Republican primary which was won by Mitt Romney and then the general presidential election of 2012.

THE MEDIA BUREAUCRACY AND PROFESSIONAL JOURNALISM   The fourth important characteristic of the national media, in addition to its concentration, big-business orientation, and competitiveness, is that it has become extremely bureaucratic and professionalized in the production of the news. National media organizations are large, complex bureaucratic enterprises involving thousands of people organized in terms of hierarchy, specialization, and routines. They are also heavily influenced by a media subculture based on certain norms and standards of professional journalism. This affects how the news media portray contemporary national and international affairs in terms of which issues, places, and events get covered (or do not get covered), how things are reported, which stories are finally run, and how they are presented to the public, including use of the Internet. Presidents and political leaders can try to manage and manipulate the press, as will be discussed in the next section, but this is difficult to do except early in a honeymoon or during a crisis, especially in national security.

Much of the news is a function of the **beat system**, in which reporters are given responsibility for covering a particular issue or institution. Although journalists like to talk about the age of investigative reporting following the Vietnam War and Watergate, *there* *are actually very few investigative reporters* per se who make a concerted effort to uncover as many relevant sources and pieces of information as possible in putting a story together. Instead, "beat reporters" are assigned by their media organizations to cover established political and national security institutions, such as government (including the White House, Pentagon, State Department, Congress, and Supreme Court) and rely on the authorities available as their basic source of information. Naturally, the most prestigious beat is the White House. A lower priority is business and finance which is covered by more economically oriented journalists within its own beat system.

Not surprisingly, much of the news is about what government officials from these institutions have said or done. In the *New York Times* and *Washington Post*, for instance, Leon Sigal (1973), in *Reporters and Officials*, found that stories from regularly covered beats outnumbered offbeat stories two to one, including front-page headlines. Because so many journalists cover the same institutions and issues while operating under the same time constraints, the beat system also sets the stage for pack journalism.

International coverage, likewise, is heavily a function of the **foreign correspondents**, which developed during World War II and the cold war. They tend to be stationed in countries that are allied with the U.S. government and located in major cities. At their peak, of roughly 700 foreign correspondents at least half were routinely stationed in Europe, while fewer than 10 percent were stationed in each of the three regions of Africa, Latin America, and the Middle East. Since the end of the cold war, *most media organizations actually have cut back on the number of their foreign bureaus and foreign correspondents.* The only media organization with extensive global geographic coverage is the Associated Press, the largest American wire service (which submits stories that have to be selected and purchased by news media outlets; see Hess 1996; Hannerz 2004). **Table 13.2** shows, as of the

Table 13.2   Foreign Correspondents and Bureaus of Major Media Organizations (as of September 1, 2001)

Organization	Bureaus	Correspondents
Associated Press	10	150
New York Times	26	40
Los Angeles Times	21	26
Washington Post	20	26
Knight Ridder	4	14
USA Today	4	4
Time	7	19
Newsweek	11	16
CNN	30	55
CBS	4	9
NBC	5	8
ABC	6	7
Fox	6	6

Regional papers with five or more bureaus: *Chicago Tribune* (10), *Dallas News* (5), *Baltimore Sun* (5), and *Boston Globe* (5).
SOURCE: Michael Parks, "Foreign News: What's Next?," *Columbia Journalism Review* 40 (January/February 2002), p. 53.

time of the terrorist attacks on September 1, 2001—the number of bureaus and the approximate number of correspondents for major American news organizations.

After 2001, the number of foreign journalists has declined considerably as a means to cut costs and with the rise of the Internet, with the exception of the Associated Press (see Kumar 2011). The major exception may be the Middle East due to the wars in Afghanistan and Iraq. CNN's number of foreign bureaus and correspondents appears large, but most of their work is predominantly for *CNN International*. According to John Stacks (2003/04:13), "Because it reaches a well-speaking audience, CNN International is tailored to a much more upscale demographic viewership than is the American service the domestic CNN that most Americans are familiar with."

This limited physical presence abroad is reinforced by the fact that most foreign correspondents have **limited language competency** beyond English (or possibly Spanish and French for some), thereby being dependent for their information on local elites who speak English. This is reinforced by the tendency to "embed" reporters with the military during war, such as in Iraq. According to U.S. Army Captain Zachary Miller, who commanded a company of U.S. troops in eastern Baghdad in 2004, "Of the fifty or so Western journalists who went out on patrol with his troops, hardly any spoke Arabic, and few bothered to have interpreters." As a result they were totally dependent on Miller and his fellow soldiers. "Normally, the reporters didn't ask questions of the Iraqis," Miller said, "They asked me" (Massing 2005:44). American reporters often face the additional constraints of government censorship (foreign as well as U.S. during times of war) and extremely unsafe environments such as in Iraq, which makes them more dependent on certain sources and further distances them from the reality on the ground.

Editors and executives at the top of the bureaucratic hierarchy also play an important role, for they supervise and oversee the news production and **editorial process**. They make crucial decisions concerning which journalists are hired, what gets covered and by whom, which stories are published, the length and location of the stories, and their final presentation and wording. The importance of this is evident, for example, by studies that have found a much higher proportion of stories on the Third World in the AP and UPI wire services than appear in the American press (Gerbner and Marvanyi 1971; Stacks, 2002/03). Journalists of major news organizations who work in the field recognize that editors have certain idiosyncrasies and beliefs that make them more receptive to certain kinds of information and news angles than others. In this sense, a type of "self-censorship" actually occurs within the news process, as it does in all professions, given the incentives and disincentives built into the media bureaucracy and the journalistic profession.

The mediated reality that most Americans see and read is not only affected by the bureaucratic nature of the beat system and the editorial process; much of news media coverage is heavily affected by *the subculture of the journalistic "profession"* that prevails as well. First, journalists tend to be generalists, not specialists. What a generalist gains in terms of breadth of information is offset by limited depth of knowledge and understanding relative to any particular issue or area. In fact, most American journalists are not particularly well-versed in economics—domestic or international—in comparison to political and national security affairs despite ever-increasing globalization.

More importantly, the contemporary mainstream media take a so-called nonpartisan approach in their news coverage—often referred to as **objective journalism**. Journalistic norms emphasize independence (acting free of "outside" political pressures), objectivity (presenting the facts without prejudice or distortion), and impartiality (avoiding partisanship and providing balance in representing without favor the views of contending parties).

Although this may result in less personal bias, the emphasis becomes on what is "factual" in a news story from "establishment" sources (the opposite may be true for the political blogs on the Internet). As we will see in the next section, the concept of objective journalism is a misnomer, for journalists do not operate in a political vacuum and they have political values that affect what they see and what they report.

The Role of Culture, Ideology, and Politics

The second general explanation that accounts for the selectivity and content of news media coverage, in addition to the characteristics of the news business, is the impact of the political environment on the communications process. *News coverage by the national media is heavily affected by the political environment in two fundamental ways.* First, journalistic perceptions of the world are shaped by the dominant political ideology and culture of American society. Second, the media are perceived as so important in affecting American politics that individuals and groups in and out of government actively attempt to influence and manipulate news media coverage. These factors not only reinforce the tendency of selective and homogenized news coverage but result in the national and mainstream media usually communicating a politically centrist understanding of reality, within a modern liberal to conservative range, to the American public—sometimes strengthening presidential power and other times constraining it (see Epstein 1973; Graber 2009).

IDEOLOGY, CULTURE, AND THE CENTRIST MEDIA

As Walter Lippmann (in Steel 1980:181), one of America's most prominent twentieth-century journalists, asserted in 1922, "We do not first see, and then define, we define first and then see." This is inevitable and perfectly understandable because journalists hold cultural and ideological beliefs; as Americans they are socialized to see the world in terms of a liberal–conservative orientation. Therefore, it would be more accurate to say that *mainstream members of the mass media tend to operate from a nonpartisan tradition and cover the news from a centrist ideological perspective that ranges within a liberal–conservative understanding of the world.*

No matter how hard American journalists try to be objective, they are influenced by the values of democracy and capitalism they tend to hold dear. Viewpoints that are critical of this classical liberal orientation are rarely heard or communicated within the mainstream American media. The political consequences, as Doris Graber (1989:24) claims in *Mass Media and American Politics*, are that "the media usually support the political system and rarely question its fundamental tenets. They limit their criticism to what they perceive as perversions of fundamental social and political values." And it affects **framing**—how the news and information is presented.

News media coverage sometimes may be more liberal and at other times may be more conservative—it ultimately depends on the issue, the times, and the political environment. The particular ideological slant of the coverage for any issue will normally reflect political thought prevalent throughout the mass and, in particular, elite public in American society at that time. As Stephen Hess (1981:118) argues in *The Washington Reporters*, "Washington news gathering, in other words, is an interaction among elites. One elite reports on another elite." More specifically, the content of national media coverage tends to reflect the beliefs of the individuals within institutions and groups, in and out of government, that prevail in American politics.

A study of the guests on ABC's *Nightline* from 1985 to 1988 found that over 89 percent were men, over 92 percent were white, and over 80 percent were professionals, corporate representatives, or government officials. In the area of foreign policy, the national media rely overwhelmingly on prominent current and former government officials as sources of information and for guests on public affairs programs, with the same faces—such as David Gergen—appearing time and time again. Similar results were found in a recent study for *The NewsHour* on PBS, considered to be the most in-depth news show on TV (Hoynes and Croteau 1989). Watch most news programs, such as the Sunday morning talk shows on ABC, CBS, and NBC, to see not much has changed.

The news media, in other words, tend to practice **source journalism** (versus **investigative journalism**). "Very few newspaper stories are the result of reporters digging through files; poring over documents; or interviewing experts, dissenters, or ordinary people. The overwhelming majority of stories are based on official sources—on information provided by members of Congress, presidential aides, and other political insiders" (Karp 1989:61). As Carl Bernstein (1992:22), who was critical in breaking Watergate has pointed out:

> America's news organizations assigned only fourteen of those 2,000 men and women [reporters working in Washington, D.C.] to cover the Watergate story on a fulltime basis. And of those fourteen, only six were assigned to the story on what might be called an "investigative" basis, that is, to go beyond recording the obvious daily statements and court proceedings, and try to find out exactly what had happened.

And according to Bernstein, not much has changed in post-Watergate journalism.

As Daniel Hallin (1986) concluded in The *Uncensored War: The Media and Vietnam*, *the national media tend to reflect the views of prominent (and therefore legitimate) leaders and government officials:* When they agree, the news media reflect the consensus view (the sphere of consensus); when they disagree, the media reflect their level of diversity (the sphere of legitimate controversy). Topics and viewpoints that do not reflect prominent leaders and the political mainstream tend to be ignored, and not covered, by the national media (the sphere of illegitimate sources and views). In this respect, news media coverage of the world is heavily dependent and conditioned by the national politics of the times that transpire at home (see **Figure** 13.3 on the political boundaries of national media coverage).

In the post–Vietnam War era, for example, the rise of liberalism has resulted in civil rights coverage that often represents a more liberal viewpoint. On the other hand, economic issues tend to be covered from a more conservative perspective, especially since the resurgence of conservatism. To illustrate the point further, economic news in the mainstream media is equated with the coverage of business, finance, and investment (as reflected in the title of that separate section of the newspaper). The *New York Times* has approximately sixty reporters assigned to business coverage, but only one full-time reporter assigned to labor and work-related issues.

Very little has changed despite the near collapse of the U.S. and international economy—the media now focuses on the pace of the current "domestic" recovery as if the "global" economic crisis never occurred and will not reoccur in the future. During the 2012 election campaign, for example, attention to the domestic rate of growth and recovery dominated, with little or no historical context or discussion of the causes. And journalists continue to refer to economics in the U.S. as "domestic economics"—ignoring globalization and the interconnected global economy (with a rare reference to the EU economy and the rise of China).

National security coverage also reflects the greater ideological diversity that grew out of the breakdown of the cold war consensus as well as who is president and from

Figure 13.3   The Political Boundaries of National Media Coverage

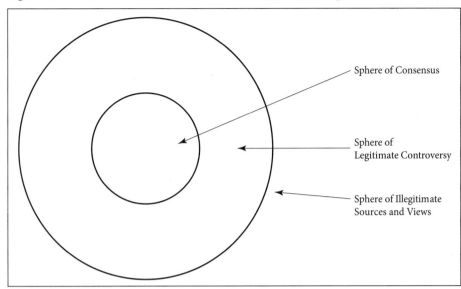

SOURCE: Daniel Hallin, *The Uncensored War: The Media and Vietnam* (Berkeley and Los Angeles: University of California Press, 1986).

what party. *Sometimes foreign policy coverage is more supportive of the president and other times more critical;* sometimes it is more liberal and other times more conservative. During a foreign policy crisis, early coverage tends to be highly supportive of presidential policies, while later coverage is more likely to become diverse and critical. The cultural and ideological foundations of American journalism are also particularly noticeable. *During crises American journalism is extremely vulnerable to becoming consumed by patriotic and nationalistic fervor.* In fact, journalists often lose their non-partisan nature and closely identify with the U.S. government and its policies; this is evident when journalists speak in terms of "we" and "they" as opposed to speaking in a more neutral language that distances them and their reporting from the parties and events, in accordance with the norms of objective journalism.

Sensationalist and nationalistic coverage was evident to a great extent in the months following the September 11, 2001, attacks on the World Trade Center and the Pentagon. This was acknowledged in an article by Matthew Engel (2002) of the *Guardian*, a U.K. daily, entitled "US Media Cowed by Patriotic Fever, Says CBS Star." The star was Dan Rather—the twenty-year anchor for CBS News:

> In the weeks after September 11 Rather wore a Stars and Stripes pin in his lapel during his evening news show in an apparent display of total solidarity with the American cause. However, based on an interview with BBC's [British Broadcasting Corporation] "Newsnight," he graphically described the pressures to conform that built up after the attacks, "It starts with a feeling of patriotism within oneself. It carries through with a certain knowledge that the country as a whole—and for all the right reasons—felt and continues to feel this surge of patriotism within themselves. And one finds oneself saying: 'I know the right question, but you know what? This is not exactly the right time to ask it.'"

Engel found such a view "astonishing" in the way it demonstrated the problem of **self-censorship**. According to Rather,

> There has never been an American war, small or large, in which access has been so limited as this one. Limiting access, limiting information to cover the backsides of those who are in charge of the war, is extremely dangerous and cannot and should not be accepted. And I am sorry to say that, up to and including the moment of this interview [eight months after the attacks], that overwhelmingly it has been accepted by the American people. And the current administration revels in that, they relish that, and they take refuge in that. (Engel 2002)

The BBC interview with Dan Rather was *never* reported within the American mainstream press.

In sum, conservative groups who perceive a liberal bias and liberal groups who perceive a conservative bias both oversimplify the ideological nature of the news media. Liberal, conservative, and other ideological outlets are extensive, especially on radio and the Internet (and *MSNBC* and *Fox News* on cable). But for the mainstream and national media, the personal beliefs of journalists are often moderated by their professional journalistic roles, for they must operate within the constraints of mainstream media that are concentrated, run as a business, competitive, and bureaucratic within a larger cultural and political environment. The net result is a tendency for the national media to present a homogenized view of the news, with coverage reflecting a more centrist ideological and sometimes nationalist orientation, but always within a liberal to conservative orientation.

At the same time, we should not ignore the increasing divide between the more ideologically driven news outlets. In the 2012 election campaign for example, the nature and tone of the coverage of the contest between Barack Obama and Mitt Romney was strikingly different on MSNBC and Fox News, with the latter consistently more critical of the president and more supportive of his rival, and vice versa for the former. While the "average" of the coverage worked out to a centrist balance, viewers relying on one or the other received a very different depiction of issues and events compared to more mainstream news media relied on by most of the mass public—reinforcing partisan politics among the most politically attentive and active.

THE MEDIA AND POLITICS   The news media are also directly affected by the political dynamics of the policymaking process and domestic politics. In fact, *government officials and societal groups attempt to influence and manipulate the media's coverage* of domestic and international affairs because they understand that the images communicated by the media, especially television, have a powerful influence on domestic politics and the policymaking process by impacting the political agenda and the public's climate of opinion. In other words, groups engage in **public relations** (or propaganda) **activities,** attempting to influence the media in order to promote a favorable image and response among the general public—the sphere of consensus or legitimate controversy discussed by Hallin and depicted in Figure 13.3. The president has the initial advantage, especially in national security and during a crisis, but not to the same extent during the cold war years.

Competing groups attempt to take advantage and manipulate the news business. For example, as Doris Graber (1989:92) observes,

> Public relations managers know the deadlines of important publications, such as *The New York Times, The Wall Street Journal, Time, Newsweek,* and network television news. They schedule events and news releases so that stories arrive in gatekeepers' offices precisely when needed. If their releases are attractively presented and meet

newsworthiness criteria, journalists find it hard to resist using them. . . . If news sources want to stifle publicity, they can announce the news just past the deadlines, preferably on weekends when few newscasts are scheduled.

As discussed earlier, established groups and institutions, such as government and business, tend to succeed more often than challenging groups in gaining access to the mainstream media and having their views communicated. Established groups are typically seen as more significant, newsworthy, and credible (i.e., legitimate) sources of information. Challenging groups—more critical of the president, big business, and the status quo in general—have greater difficulty in gaining access to the media, for they are treated as less legitimate, less credible, and less newsworthy sources of information (and depicted in a more negative light if depicted at all; see Gitlin, 1981). It is often through symbolic appeals that individuals and groups attempt to influence and manipulate the media, hence influencing the American public and the politics of U.S. foreign policy.

The **politics of symbolism and legitimacy** has been important in politics throughout history, especially given the role of American political culture as discussed in Chapter 11. Power, for the president or any political actor, depends heavily on the illusion of power and the politics of symbolism. This was a key to the success of Ronald Reagan and the Reagan's "television presidency." As Hedrick Smith (1988:345) explained it, "Reagan is so natural onstage that, unlike most politicians, he creates the illusion of not being onstage." Furthermore, "Reagan has a political genius for selling his message—like the genius of Franklin Roosevelt. His secret is his mastery of political shorthand. He knows how to make ideas accessible and popular."

> Politicians and voters depend on labels, slogans, quickstick, fast-fix clichés immediately recognizable to millions (though vaguely understood): Communists, welfare cheats, bureaucrats, New Right, New Deal, Star Wars, deficit spenders, supply-side, tax reform, evil empire. Reagan has a knack for coining phrases that tap into reservoirs of popular feeling—like his refrain to "get government off your back"—without having to explain what he means in policy terms, what his ideas will cost, or whom they will hurt. He is a master at using symbols that convey broad intention and leave him free to interpret their meaning.

A favorite technique of symbolic politics, especially given the decline in public trust of government officials, is **blame game politics**. When the policymaking process becomes gridlocked, when policies fail, or when they are poorly received by the public—such as been occurring during the Obama administration with the economy—all government and private parties involved rush to disclaim any responsibility and blame others: The president blames Congress, members of Congress blame the president, Republicans blame Democrats, and Democrats blame Republicans. Given this atmosphere, it has become fashionable for politicians to "run against Washington." Yet, everyone involved nonetheless makes a concerted effort to appear to be "above politics." As Timothy Wirth, a Democratic congressman from Colorado, commented while preparing a video news release for the local media back home, "You have to get over the embarrassment of doing [public relations] and feeling it's hokey" (in Smith 1988:129).

The politics of symbolism is particularly prominent *whenever the U.S. government has relied on the use of force abroad.* During the Vietnam War, Daniel Hallin (1986:158), found that:

> Television coverage of Vietnam dehumanized the enemy, drained him of all recognizable emotions and motives and thus banished him not only from the political sphere, but from human society itself. The North Vietnamese and Vietcong

were "fanatical," "suicidal," "savage," "half-crazed." They were lower than mere criminals (there is usually some "human interest" angle in crime reporting): they were vermin. Television reports routinely referred to areas controlled by the NLF [National Liberation Front] as "Communist infested" or "Vietcong infested."

In the post–cold war global environment new pictures of the enemy have to be highlighted and sold to the public. The September 11 terrorist attacks on the United States, as tragic as they were, gave the younger Bush administration the opportunity to declare a war on terrorism and to communicate classic stereotypical images of the enemy, best illustrated by President Bush's State of the Union address on January 29, 2002—better known as his "Axis of Evil" speech. The speech promoted and reinforced evil and negative images of the enemy—which automatically conjured up in the minds of most Americans the names Osama bin Laden or Saddam Hussein or the countries of Iraq, Iran, and North Korea.

The institution most successful in gaining access to the news media and influencing their coverage is the government and, in particular, the presidency. With the president considered the center of foreign policy activity, the national media, with their beat system and norms of objective journalism, have become heavily dependent on the government and especially the executive branch for much of their information concerning U.S. foreign policy and international affairs. As Jon Western (2005:18) argues, "most correspondents are reluctant to challenge executive sources openly" and they tend to accept administration assumptions, definitions, and so on as legitimate. As Bernard Cohen (1963:28) explained in his classic *The Press and Foreign Policy*, "the more 'neutral' the press is . . . the more easily it lends itself to the uses of others, and particularly to public officials whom reporters have come to regard as prime sources of news merely by virtue of their positions in government. This is unquestionably the case at the Presidential level." Or according to Daniel Hallin (1986:8), with the rise of so-called objective journalism, "journalists gave up the right to speak with a political voice of their own, and in turn they were granted a regular right of access to the inner councils of government, a right they had never enjoyed in the era of partisan journalism."

Thus, the president—the top governmental official—has a unique advantage in gaining access to the news media and having them communicate his views and preferences to the American public, most visibly during the early stages of a foreign policy crisis. Whatever and whenever the president speaks or acts, it is newsworthy by definition. President Obama, for example, made numerous public statements, held press conferences, and been interviewed before the media in an effort to communicate and educate the American public (and journalists) about economics and the state of the American and the global economy (somewhat reminiscent of FDR's fireside chats on the radio), which was relatively successful early on in his presidency.

Also, with the rise of the paradox of presidential power since the Vietnam War, the president and government officials have become much more public relations conscious than ever before and strive to promote the kind of media coverage that strengthens their political position. It would not be an overstatement to say that all presidents have been preoccupied with their public images. Not surprisingly, presidents have increasingly institutionalized and expanded their White House press and communications operations, beginning with Richard Nixon (review Figure 4.2 to see the prominent office of some of the communications people within the Obama White House).

The machinery allows presidents to *utilize a number of tools at their disposal to influence media coverage* of national and, in particular, international affairs (Cohen 2004). First, realizing that presidential acts are "newsworthy," presidential appearances in public are often "staged" to maximize positive news coverage and communicate the desired information and message. According to David Gergen, a member of the White House staff to presidents Richard Nixon, Ronald Reagan and Bill Clinton, "We had a rule in the Nixon operation that before any public event was put on his schedule, you had to know what the headline out of that event was going to be, what the picture was going to be, and what the lead paragraph would be. You had to think of it in those terms, and if you couldn't justify it, it didn't go on the [president's] schedule" (in Smith 1988:401).

A second important advantage is that the government is perceived as a "highly credible source" of information. Under the beat system, government officials are able to control the release of information through press releases, briefings, and public statements. During foreign policy crises, the news media are almost exclusively dependent (or allow themselves to become almost exclusively dependent) on the executive branch for their information.

A third way that the executive branch controls information is to take advantage of the "classification of information." This can be done by "denying" or through **leaks** of information. As Hedrick Smith (1988:80) points out, "On Wall Street, passing insider information to others is an indictable offense. In Washington, it is the regular stuff of the power game." Although leaking is widespread throughout the Washington community, it tends to be more frequent within the executive branch, especially the closer one gets to the president (these are, in fact, the primary sources that journalist Bob Woodward, of Bernstein and Woodward Watergate fame, relies on for his insider books).

As did most administrations before it, the Obama administration, especially the White House, routinely leaks information. For example, many believe that the article written by Michael Hastings (2010) *in The Rolling Stone* on "The Runaway General" Stanley McCrystal—the article that led to him being fired as commander of American forces in Afghanistan, that led to a more involved president and deliberative process in fall 2009 about McCrystal's request for a surge in troops, and that ultimately led to his replacement by General Petraus (a demotion from being Combat Commander of CENTCOM; discussed in Chapter 6)—was based on a White House leak countering unauthorized leaks by the Pentagon (Gates, Mullins, and Petraeus) in favor of an Afghan surge. Moreover, in 2012, an uproar occurred over allegations that the Obama administration leaked highly sensitive information about one antiterrorist operation that foiled a planned airline bombing and another that resulted in the death of a high-ranking al-Qaeda leader.

Another technique is the use of **propaganda and censorship.** Members of the executive branch occasionally orchestrate public relations campaigns with propaganda (that is, consciously distorting information and lying), employ disinformation (that is, knowingly manufacture false information), and resort to censorship (based on secret classified information)—to manipulate the media and rally public support for their foreign policy efforts. Ironically, the Obama administration has done everything to make *WikiLeaks* founder Julian Assange a fugitive and to shutdown *WikiLeaks* for releasing classified information, despite a long history of White House and executive branch leaks (see **The Liberty–Security Dilemma** on presidential censorship and propaganda).

Finally, government officials often promote favorable news media coverage by building upon their many contacts and personal relationships within the media. Henry Kissinger was a master, for example, at wooing the media in order to promote his foreign policy purposes. He was a constant source of information, often classified, anonymously provided to the media in general or to selective journalists, which they would then attribute to a "senior government official." As Stanley Hoffmann (1968:308) pointed out long ago:

> The closeness to official Washington of the nation's leading columnists and
> reporters, writing for the main newspapers and television networks, is especially

Presidential Censorship and Propaganda

The Persian Gulf and Iraq Wars serve as excellent illustrations of presidential censorship and propaganda. As an article entitled "The Propaganda War" (1991:28) stated, "In theory, reporters in democratic societies work independent of propaganda. In practice they are treated during war as simply more pieces of military hardware to be deployed," reinforcing the old adage that "truth is the first casualty of war." Clearly, one of the major lessons learned by many within the national security bureaucracy was the need to "control" the news media.

According to one assessment, "one casualty of the Gulf War appears to be the independent, itinerant war correspondent. The press pool system used in the Gulf encouraged the most docile sort of pack journalism" in which members of the national media competed in tandem for whatever censored information and video images that the White House and the Pentagon allowed them to communicate" (Schmeisser 1991:21). The public relations and propaganda strategy was fairly straightforward: "provide a lot of military briefings and high-tech videos to keep the press supplied with images and reports, impose strict censorship on everything you don't want covered (including images of people returning home in 'human-remains pouches'), overemphasize your successes and tell nothing of your failures. Most of all, keep the human dimension [that is, death and casualties] to a minimum" (Douglas 1991:20). According to Michael Deaver, President Reagan's deputy chief of staff and communications chief, "The Department of Defense has done an excellent job of managing the news in an almost classic way. There's plenty of access to some things and at least one visual a day. If you were going to hire a public relations firm to do the media relations for an international event, it couldn't be done any better than this is being done" (in Jones 1991:A9). Despite being fed what became known as "Iraq, the Movie," the American people seemed to like it that way—typical of rallying round the troops and the president during a national crisis and war.

The administration of President George W. Bush and Vice President Richard Cheney has been accused of being among the most secretive in controlling information in modern presidential history. Bush administration officials have been accused of using knowingly false information about weapons of mass destruction (WMD) and al-Qaeda's links with Saddam Hussein in rallying public (and international) support for its invasion of Iraq. Michael Massing (2005:43) highlights how the mainstream media, focusing on the *New York Times,* missed (or buried) the story about Iraq's WMD before the attack— the heart of the president's case for war. "In the period before the war, U.S. journalists were far too reliant on sources sympathetic to the administration. Those with dissenting views—and there were more than a few—were shut out. Reflecting this, the coverage was highly deferential to the White House. . . . Despite abundant evidence of the administration's brazen misuse of intelligence in this matter, the press repeatedly let officials get away with it."

Looking back, former Secretary of State Colin Powell regretted the key United Nations speech in which he publicly made the case in 2003 for going to war with Iraq because many of the assertions he made were false. In a September 7, 2005, interview on *20/20* with host Barbara Walters, Powell said that although he was glad that Saddam Hussein's regime was toppled he felt "terrible" and that his reputation was tarnished, "It's a blot. I'm the one who presented it on behalf of the United States to the world and it will always be a part of my record. It was painful. It's painful now" (ABC News 2005).

Why do most American mainstream journalists allow the executive branch to exercise so much direct and indirect control? Why has *WikiLeaks* been the recipient of U.S. governmental attacks to discredit and destroy it despite the "leak culture" of Washington, D.C.?

responsible for numbing the mass media's capacity to question and challenge. . . . Enjoying the confidence of the great usually kills the urge to investigate. Officials disarm these men by giving them the illusion of being admitted to the mysteries of decisionmaking, and by making them sympathize with their ordeals.

The net result is that *three major patterns exist in the politics of the media.* First, government–media relations are very much a symbiotic process. The nature of the news business and the political environment in American society have made the news media more dependent on the government, especially the president and the executive branch, whereas the president and government have become more dependent on the media. Second, the president and the executive branch have considerable advantages in promoting positive news media coverage, especially early in an administration, over issues of foreign policy and during crises, when presidential legitimacy and support are at their highest. Third, even with all its advantages, the presidency in the post–Vietnam War and post–cold war eras is unable to dominate and influence media coverage to the same extent it did during the cold war, even in the area of foreign policy.

. . .

So what are our *overall conclusions about the nature of the news media in the making of U.S. foreign policy?* First, most Americans are dependent on the news media, especially the national media, for information and understanding of national and international affairs. Second, the national media provide a considerable amount of information regarding national and international affairs. Third, coverage tends to be selective, disjointed, and American-centric as stories come and go with little history or context provided. Fourth, the mainstream and national media are a business and a bureaucratic profession. Fifth, since the collapse of the anticommunist consensus and the cold war, the national media tend to provide a homogenized and centrist picture of national and international news—sometimes reflecting a more liberal orientation, sometimes a more conservative one—consistent with legitimate, mainstream American political ideology and culture. Sixth, media coverage is influenced by politics and political actors (such as the president) and, at the same time, influences domestic politics and the policymaking process. Finally, these patterns are magnified by the revolution in ICT (information communications technology), especially during times of crisis, when certain issues are often inflated and sensationalized and certain actors and institutions are able to have a disproportionate influence on media coverage.

These patterns reinforce the paradox of presidential power in national security and economic affairs making presidents incredibly powerful and incredibly weak, depending on the issue and the times. They contribute to the presidential life cycle and the need for strong presidential leadership. They contribute to the illusions of great presidential power, high expectations during elections and the beginning of an administration, usually followed by growing domestic frustration and partisanship making it increasingly difficult for a president to govern, and to fulfill promises and expectations. Presidents Bush and Obama both experienced these trends over time.

THE ENTERTAINMENT MEDIA

While the foregoing focuses on the influence of the news media on American politics, the role of the **entertainment media** must also be considered. The news, after all, is only a small part of mass media offerings. The mass media's basic orientation is to entertain people: through television, radio, movies, novels, and more, especially the Internet. Americans respond voraciously; most Americans are much more interested in being entertained than in being informed about public affairs and, thus, devote a considerable amount of attention to the entertainment media, especially television and increasingly the Internet. Given the importance of entertainment programming—accompanied by a considerable amount of advertising—for the mass media and the general public, the entertainment media may have an indirect and subtle effect on American political beliefs and behavior. If anything, *the entertainment media appear to reinforce the consequences of the news media on American politics and U.S. foreign policy discussed earlier* (see Gitlin 1985; MacDonald 1990; Parenti 1992).

First, the entertainment media reinforce the pattern of public knowledge and democratic citizenship that prevails for most Americans. For example, watching and listening to entertainment shows (with an occasional newsbreak) on television or social media on the Internet on a daily basis contributes to a public that is uninterested and uninformed concerning national and international affairs. Not only does a preference for entertainment lower the priority for information about the world, the contents of the programs themselves often promote simplistic and stereotypical images of the world.

A study by George Gerbner and the Annenberg School of Communications, for example, found that perceptions of reality concerning American sex roles, age, race, work, health, and crime by "heavy viewers" of television (those who watch more than four hours a day, representing about one-third of the population) closely reflected the misrepresentations and biases of the world found on entertainment television. If entertainment viewing affects Americans' perceptions of their own country, imagine the effect it may have on the image that Americans acquire of the rest of the world. For example, how are Arabs and Muslims commonly depicted? Who do Americans typically believe are terrorists? According to Gerbner, "no other medium reaches into every home or has a comparable, cradle-to-grave influence over what a society learns about itself" (Gerbner, Gross, Morgan, and Signorielli 1982:100).

Second, the content and images of the entertainment media reflect the political environment of the times, reinforcing the evolution of news coverage. During World War II, **Hollywood movies**—one of the major forms of mass entertainment—were overwhelmingly patriotic in nature, depicting the United States as the "land of the free and the home of the brave." In war movies, Americans tended to be portrayed as innocent victims of aggression by ruthless and evil heathens, such as the Nazis and the Japanese. Some of this was a function of an industry that allowed itself to be censored in the name of national security. As explained by Clayton Koppes and Gregory Black (1987:vii) in *Hollywood Goes to War:*

> During the war the government, convinced that movies had extraordinary power to mobilize public opinion for war, carried out an intensive, unprecedented effort to mold the content of Hollywood feature films. Officials of the Office of War Information, the government's propaganda agency, issued a constantly updated manual instructing the studios in how to assist the war effort, sat in on story conferences with Hollywood's top brass, reviewed the screenplays of every major studio (except the recalcitrant Paramount), pressured the movie makers to change scripts and even scrap pictures when they found objectionable material, and sometimes wrote dialogue for key speeches.

This pattern continued into the cold war years. Although government censorship was lifted, its legacy remained with the rise of McCarthyism, the blacklists, and the anticommunist consensus throughout society. "Enemies changed, with wrenching suddenness," observed John Dower (1986:309) in *War Without Mercy*, "but the concept of 'the enemy' remained impressively impervious to drastic alteration, and in its peculiar way provided psychological continuity and stability from the world war to the cold war." Hence, as J. Fred MacDonald (1985) describes in *Television and the Red Menace: The Video Road to Vietnam*, the entertainment media during the cold war years became filled with dehumanized images of the communist bogeyman and the totalitarian threat to the United States and the so-called free world.

It was not until the 1960s that this cold war image of America was finally challenged within the entertainment media, most noticeably by the youth culture and, in part, through the growing popularity of rock music—another form of entertainment media. With the eventual collapse of the anticommunist and ideological consensus following the Vietnam War, the topics and images in the entertainment media—in movies and television dramas, comedies, and docudramas—pertaining to national and international affairs began to reflect the greater diversity of the times. John Wayne's *Green Berets*, for example, reflecting the classic cold warrior view of an overconfident America (inevitably) containing the threat of communism in Vietnam, gave way to interpretations and impressions of the Vietnam War ranging from *Rambo* to *Apocalypse Now* to *Platoon* to *Born on the Fourth of July* (as well as the movie and television hit *M*A*S*H*, despite its Korean War context).

Hollywood has produced successful movies with powerful political messages. This has been reinforced by the rise and increasing popularity of "independent films" (and film festivals such as Sundance and Cannes) that are often much more about real life and are thought provoking. But the bulk of American films (and TV shows), especially from major Hollywood studios, tend to continue to focus on entertainment and maximizing the box office, usually by developing "blockbuster" action-, thriller-, mystery-, romance-, and comedy-oriented films. Since the September 11 attacks, there appears to be a renewed emphasis and popularity of war and spy movies and television shows not seen since the cold war. But it is important to remember that these shows remain entertainment oriented, with relatively simple story lines revolving around a hero's journey. Therefore, given the levels of public interest and information, the entertainment media since Vietnam are likely to reflect, reinforce, as well as promote the beliefs, stereotypical views, and simplistic images of national and international affairs held by most Americans (see King 2002).

Finally, the prevalence of the entertainment media in the lives of most Americans reinforces the politics of symbolism. Much of the entertainment media, especially movies and television, deal with the world of symbols and make-believe. Although Paddy Chayefsky (1976:98) overstates the nature of the entertainment industry in his 1976 screenplay (and movie) *Network*, he nonetheless provides some important insights when he has the protagonist—a former news anchorman—shout out through the television:

> Television is not the truth! Television is a goddamned amusement park, that's what television is! Television is a circus, a carnival, a traveling troupe of acrobats and storytellers, singers and dancers, jugglers, sideshow freaks, lion-tamers and football players! We are in the boredom-killing business. . . . No matter how much trouble the hero is in, don't worry: just look at your watch—at the end of the hour he's going to win. We'll tell you any shit you want to hear! We deal in illusion, man!

SOURCE: Network By Paddy Chayefsky Copyright © 1976 Metro-Goldwyn-Mayer Inc. and United Artists Corporation. All rights reserved. Reprinted with Permission of Applause Theatre & Cinema Books.

There is one other impact of the entertainment media that is often overlooked—its impact on the images that foreigners have of Americans and the United States. Most countries and peoples in the world are highly dependent on foreign imports of entertainment media, especially television and movies made in America. American movies dominate the world market. In fact, most American movies today gross more money from foreign viewership than they do from American viewership and sales (from 30 percent in 1980 to over 50 percent by 2000; see **Table 13.3** on domestic versus international box office revenues). This means that what other people see on TV and in movies, much of which is

Table 13.3   Domestic and International Movie Box Office Revenues (in Millions of U.S. Dollars)

Rank	Domestic	Overseas	World	Titles (1900–2012)
1	$ 760.5	$ 2021.8	$ 2782.3	*Avatar* (2009)
2	$ 658.7	$ 1526.7	$ 2185.4	*Titanic* (1997)
3	$ 617.6	$ 874.0	$ 1491.6	*The Avengers* (2012)
4	$ 381.0	$ 947.1	$ 1328.1	*Harry Potter and the Deathly Hallows: Part 2* (2011)
5	$ 377.0	$ 752.2	$ 1129.2	*The Lord of the Rings: The Return of the King* (2003)
6	$ 352.4	$ 771.4	$ 1123.8	*Transformers: Dark of the Moon* (2011)
7	$ 423.3	$ 642.9	$ 1066.2	*Pirates of the Caribbean: Dead Man's Chest* (2006)
8	$ 415.0	$ 648.0	$ 1063.0	*Toy Story 3* (2010)
9	$ 422.8	$ 632.7	$ 1055.4	*The Lion King* (1994)
10	$ 241.1	$ 802.8	$ 1043.9	*Pirates of the Caribbean: On Stranger Tides* (2011)
11	$ 474.5	$ 552.5	$ 1027.0	*Star Wars: Episode I - The Phantom Menace* (1999)
12	$ 334.2	$ 690.1	$ 1024.3	*Alice in Wonderland* (2010)
13	$ 533.3	$ 468.6	$ 1002.0	*The Dark Knight* (2008)
14	$ 317.6	$ 657.2	$ 974.8	*Harry Potter and the Sorcerer's Stone* (2001)
15	$ 309.4	$ 654.0	$ 963.4	*Pirates of the Caribbean: At World's End* (2007)
16	$ 296.0	$ 660.4	$ 956.4	*Harry Potter and the Deathly Hallows: Part 1* (2010)
17	$ 292.0	$ 646.2	$ 938.2	*Harry Potter and the Order of the Phoenix* (2007)
18	$ 302.0	$ 632.5	$ 934.4	*Harry Potter and the Half-Blood Prince* (2009)
19	$ 341.7	$ 585.6	$ 927.3	*The Lord of the Rings: The Two Towers* (2002)
20	$ 401.9	$ 519.0	$ 920.9	*The Dark Knight Rises* (2012)
21	$ 357.1	$ 563.0	$ 920.1	*Jurassic Park* (1993)
22	$ 436.5	$ 483.4	$ 919.8	*Shrek 2* (2004)
23	$ 290.0	$ 605.9	$ 895.9	*Harry Potter and the Goblet of Fire* (2005)
24	$ 336.5	$ 554.3	$ 890.9	*Spider-Man 3* (2007)
25	$ 196.5	$ 693.9	$ 890.4	*Ice Age: Dawn of the Dinosaurs* (2009)
Total	$ 9868.6	$ 18586.8	$ 28455.3	

SOURCE: World Wide Box Office.

American, may affect their images of the United States and contribute to simplistic and incomplete images of America's complexity. The American media, after all, are huge multinational corporations in an age of increasing globalization (Hermann and McChesney 1997).

According to Michael Medved (2002:5), "The vast majority of people in Pakistan or Peru, Poland, or Papua New Guinea, may never visit the United States or ever meet an American face to face, but they inevitably encounter images of L.A. and New York in the movies, television programs and popular songs exported everywhere by the American entertainment industry." Adventure and action movies and TV shows with good guys versus bad guys are popular not only in the United States but everywhere else and are relatively easy to follow (regardless of dubbing and language problems). They also tend to communicate spectacular American feats of power and technology through increasingly spectacular special effects that may have some basis in reality but are usually dramatic simplifications. This helps to promote and reinforce the simplistic, distorted, and naive images that foreigners are likely to have of the United States, American society, and the politics of its foreign policy.

PROMOTING PUBLIC KNOWLEDGE AND DEMOCRATIC CITIZENSHIP?

Because Americans are dependent on the media as their fundamental source of information concerning national and international affairs, the news media have a major impact on public knowledge and democratic citizenship in the politics of U.S. foreign policy. At best, most Americans acquire a simplistic awareness and familiarity of the world around them. This is because the mass public, as discussed in Chapter 11, tends to be uninterested, inattentive, uninformed, and, therefore, most receptive to media headlines. This simplistic awareness is also due to the public's tendency to be "overnewsed" and "underinformed" by the media, including how the Internet is used: issues appear one day and disappear the next, coverage jumps from one crisis to another, the emphasis is on the immediacy of news rather than history and context, the focus is on established institutions and government officials—especially the president—as opposed to the complexity of society and the world.

This problem is much more severe with respect to international news, for most Americans lack the context to make sense of the information and images being communicated to them about "foreign" places abroad. Not surprisingly, most members of the mass public often find events confusing and usually acquire simplistic images of the world. The net result is a mass public that bears little resemblance to the "alert and knowledgeable citizenry" called for by President Eisenhower in his farewell address. Instead, *the nature of media coverage contributes to a relatively poorly informed public vulnerable to wild fluctuations in public opinion and swings in public mood,* which affect both domestic politics and the policymaking process.

If Eisenhower's alert and knowledgeable citizenry is to be found anywhere, it would most likely be among the elite public in American society. Yet, most members of the elite public also tend to rely heavily on the national mainstream media, and their Internet sites, for their basic sources of information. They become informed but learn little history and are more likely to acquire a stronger set of either liberal or conservative ideological interpretations of national and international affairs, both national security and especially economics.

Furthermore, unless individuals are already knowledgeable about the world and make a concerted effort to use that knowledge when viewing or reading the media, media coverage, especially during crises, will likely determine not only what issues members of the elite public think about but how they go about examining those issues. The information and images communicated by the media, therefore, contributed to the rise of antifascism during World War II and anticommunism during the cold war among the mass and elite publics, and an increase in presidential power.

This promoted a preoccupation with the demands of national security over the demands of democracy, and to the political conformity and passivity of most Americans even though the civil liberties of many citizens were being violated. Although post–Vietnam War media coverage has broadened and reflects a greater concern for the demands of democracy, it has also contributed to greater ideological division and heightened partisanship, and affected the paradox of presidential power and the difficulty all presidents have in governing, especially in economics but also for national security.

Therefore, while most Americans rely on the mainstream and national media for their information and understanding of the world around them, they should be sensitive to, and somewhat cynical about, the limits inherent in mainstream media coverage (whether liberal, centrist, or conservative), as well as the power of the Internet and social media despite their incredible potential. In fact, much of the public probably realizes this at times, contributing to a certain "need–hate" relationship with the news media. Such tension between the public in general and the media may simply be unavoidable in today's world.

SUGGESTED SOURCES FOR MORE INFORMATION

Bennett, W. Lance. (2011) *News: The Politics of Illusion.* New York: Longman. Good overview of the news media.

CBS. *60 Minutes.* America's best news magazine and longest-running program on television.

Gladwell, Malcolm. (2010) "Small Change: "Why the Revolution Will Not be Tweeted,"" *The New Yorker* (October 4). Excellent overview of the impact of social media on politics.

Graber, Doris. (2009) *Mass Media and American Politics.* Washington, D.C.: Congressional Quarterly Press. Good overview of the news media.

Halberstam, David. (1979) *The Powers That Be.* New York: Knopf. Classic narrative history of the growth and power of the national media.

Hallin, Daniel C. (1986) *The Uncensored War: The Media and Vietnam.* Berkeley and Los Angeles: University of California Press. Excellent discussion of major patterns of foreign affairs media coverage and media–government relations.

Hannerz, Ulf. (2004) *Foreign News: Exploring the World of Foreign Correspondents.* Chicago: University of Chicago Press. Excellent overview of the media's international coverage.

Iyengar, Shanto, and Donald R. Kinder. (1987) *News That Matters: Television and American Opinion.* Chicago: University of Chicago Press. Classic study demonstrating the impact of the news media on politics.

Koppes, Clayton, and Gregory Black. (1987) *Hollywood Goes to War: How Politics, Profits, and Propaganda Shaped World War II Movies.* New York: Free Press. Excellent analysis of the role of the entertainment industry and film in American politics during war.

Massing, Michael. (August 13, 2009) "The News about the Internet," *New York Review of Books* Interesting analysis of the rise of Internet journalism versus the decline of print journalism.

Medved, Michael. (2002) "That's Entertainment? Hollywood's Contribution to Anti-Americanism Abroad," *National Interest* 68 (Summer):5–14. Interesting analysis of the impact of Hollywood abroad.

Newsroom, The (2012–) New HBO series with an optimistic and semi-utopian orientation about how "real" news should be produced and aired, created by Aaron Sorkin the creator and producer of *The West Wing* and *The Social Network* among others.

Pew Research Center for the People and the Press. (2010) "Americans Spending More Time Following the News Ideological News Sources: Who Watches and Why," September 12. Superb study on contemporary source of news broken down in many categories.

Public Broadcasting System (PBS). *Frontline.* America's premier investigative journalism and documentary series on television since 1983. Many of their documentaries and reports are available for free viewing at http://www.pbs.org/wgbh/pages/frontline/

Stacks, John F. (2003/2004) "Hard Times for Hard News: A Clinical Look at U.S. Foreign Coverage," *World Policy Journal* 20 (Winter):12–21. Excellent overview of foreign policy coverage since 9/11.

Western, Jon. (2005) *Selling Intervention and War: The Presidency, The Media, and the American Public.* Baltimore: Johns Hopkins University Press. Discusses the propaganda campaigns often waged over decisions to use force.

KEY CONCEPTS

alternative media	mainstream media
beat system	mediated reality
blame game politics	national media
editorial process	news media cycle
entertainment media	objective journalism
framing	pack journalism
homogeneous news coverage	politics of symbolism (and
ICT (information and	legitimacy)
communications technology)	propaganda and censorship
internet journalism	self-censorship
investigative journalism	source journalism
leaks	

OTHER KEY TERMS

foreign correspondents	public relations activities
headline news	rivals in conformity
Hollywood movies	the Internet
limited language competency	Vietnam War coverage
media and the CIA	wire services
power of television	

PART IV

CONCLUSION

In our last chapter, we offer some broad conclusions about the major patterns discussed throughout the book, the nature and likelihood of foreign policy change, and implications for the future politics of U.S. foreign policy.

. . .

U.S PRESIDENT BARACK OBAMA GIVES HIS INAUGURAL ADDRESS ON JANUARY 20, 2009, AS THE 44TH PRESIDENT OF THE UNITED STATES OF AMERICA.

PATTERNS, CHANGE AND THE FUTURE OF U.S. FOREIGN POLICYMAKING

In the preceding chapters of this text, we examined the historical and global context of U.S. foreign policy (Part I); the government and the policymaking process, focusing on the president, the National Security Council (NSC), the foreign policy bureaucracy, decisionmaking within the executive branch, and Congress (Part II); and the role of society and domestic politics, concentrating on public opinion, group politics, and the mass media and communications process (Part III). *Our concluding chapter reviews* the dominant patterns of presidential power and governance, continuity and change, and the national security-democracy dilemma in the politics of U.S. foreign policy since World War II—within the perspective of competing theoretical models and the contexts of the cold war and post-Vietnam eras. We end by addressing how foreign policy changes and consider the implications for the future of the politics of U.S. foreign policy.

We began this text by restating two simple but very significant points about the making of U.S. foreign policy: it is a very complex process, and it is a very political process.

Throughout the preceding chapters, we have examined both the complexity and the political nature of foreign policymaking. Overall, it should be clear at this point that the commonly held view that presidents make foreign policy in the United States is a gross oversimplification at best, and an outright inaccuracy at worst. In fact, there are competing theoretical models about how the entire political system works, including the politics of U.S. foreign policy.

COMPETING THEORETICAL MODELS

Most students of United States politics agree that a simple and ideal **republican model** of democracy in which power is exercised by government officials who are elected and held accountable by a "sovereign" public does not accurately reflect the workings of the American political system. Policymaking in the United States is more complex and more political than this simplistic version suggests.

In recognition of this greater complexity, *three competing interpretations or conceptual models have been developed* to understand and explain the political process: (1) pluralism, (2) elitism, and (3) hyperpluralism. Each interpretation provides a different understanding of the distribution of power and beliefs that exist throughout society and the government. When applied to the making of U.S. foreign policy, each model provides a unique understanding of the foreign policy process (**Table 14.1** provides an overview; see Garson 1978; Janoski, Alford, Schwartz and Hicks 2005).

Pluralism

Beginning in the 1940s, some American scholars and analysts developed a conceptual model based on the premise that power was dispersed among numerous groups throughout society, with each competing for control of the government. According to Arnold Rose (1965:5), **pluralism** "conceives of a society consisting of many elites, each relatively small numerically and operating in different spheres of life, and of the bulk of the population classifiable into organized groups and publics as well as masses." Robert Dahl was one of the most popular proponents of pluralism in American politics during the 1950s and 1960s. Dahl (1967:24) stipulated that "the fundamental axiom in the theory and practice of American pluralism is this: instead of a single center of sovereign power there must be multiple centers of power, none of which is or can be wholly sovereign."

Pluralism did not argue for the existence of a republican form of democratic politics. However, pluralists did argue that the decentralization of power among groups with competing goals represented a different form of democratic practice. Virtually all Americans

Table 14.1   Models of the State and Society

The Model	Power	Views	Implications for Political Change
Pluralism	Diffused	Diverse	Incrementalism
Elitism	Concentrated	Shared	Status quo oriented
Hyperpluralism	Decentralized overall Concentrated networks for each issue	Diverse overall Shared for each issue	Status quo oriented

© Cengage Learning

were part of this democratic practice because of their membership in different groups. Moreover, even if they did not participate, their beliefs were represented by different organized interests throughout society. Therefore, as Dahl (1967:24) stated, a pluralist democracy "will help to tame power, to secure the consent of all, and to settle conflicts peacefully."

A pluralistic political system, it was argued, based on the prevalence of competing groups (and elites) representing diverse views also decreased the likelihood of major change. As Robert Dahl (1967:298) stated, pluralism "encourages incremental change, it discourages comprehensive change." This was important to most pluralists, because the rise of mass society promoted too much freedom and too much potential for change with too little order. "Consequently," stated Dahl (1967:24), "no part of the people, such as a majority, ought to be absolutely sovereign." Competing groups representing diverse interests created the barriers between national leaders and the mass public that pluralists believed were essential to prevent the rise of authoritarianism. Therefore, proponents of pluralist democracy argued that it provided a balance between the demands of freedom and order.

Elitism

In the post–World War II context, other scholars and intellectuals began to view the policymaking process in terms of **elitism**: one in which power was concentrated among elites who represented a small segment of the society, shared similar values and beliefs, and dominated the political and policymaking process. According to Schattschneider (1960:25), "The flaw in the pluralist heaven is that the heavenly chorus sings with a strong upper-class accent. Probably about 90 percent of the people cannot get into the pressure [group] system." Some of these scholars adopted a "class elitist" perspective, which emphasized class differences and the disproportionate amount of power that resided with the upper class in American society and government. Others embraced an "institutional elitist" perspective, emphasizing how elites, not necessarily from the upper class, occupied and dominated positions of power within key institutions throughout society and government. Both approaches agreed that the general public exercised little real influence within a governmental-societal political system.

One influential version of the elitist approach came from C. Wright Mills (1956) in *The Power Elite*. Mills argued that *American politics consisted of a three-tiered system of power:* a large, apathetic mass society at the bottom; a limited pluralist politics involving organized interests active in government and society at the middle levels of power (such as within the legislative process); and an elitist politics dominated by top government officials, military leaders, and corporate executives operating within the confines of a narrow ideological consensus at the highest levels of power.

In effect, according to this perspective, pluralist politics actually operated within a narrow set of parameters determined by the elitist structure of society. Power, in other words, was ultimately exercised from the top down, with only a small cross section of elites dominating domestic politics and policymaking for the most significant issues, especially at the national level, throughout society and the government.

Hyperpluralism, Iron Triangles, and Issue Networks

During the late 1960s and 1970s, pluralism was openly challenged by another perspective, sometimes referred to as **hyperpluralism** and popularized by Grant McConnell's (1966) *Private Power and American Democracy* and Theodore Lowi's (1969) *The End of Liberalism*. Scholars have subsequently referred to the development of hyperpluralist networks of interaction throughout society and government as "iron triangles," "subgovernments," "issue networks," and "policy networks" (see also Barrow 1993; Berry 1987; Dahl 1978; Heclo 1978; Prewitt and Stone 1973).

Blending elements of pluralist and elitist models, hyperpluralists emphasize the rise of bureaucratic institutions and groups throughout government and society and the close ties established between them over issues of public policy. Within this context, a particular issue tends to produce a distinct network of interactive and mutually supportive ties between specific individuals (or elites) and groups throughout society and government that dominate the politics of that issue. The existence of a military-industrial-scientific infrastructure in defense policy is often cited as a classic example of hyperpluralist politics.

Hyperpluralism borrows elements from both pluralism and elitism. Looking at American politics from a distance (or macro perspective), the existence of numerous issue networks dominating hundreds of different issues appears pluralist. Rather than competing for political access and influence, however, groups tend to establish networks of mutually reinforcing relationships that dominate access and influence in their particular area of interest. Issue networks develop among established governmental and private groups that, through their political access and influence, are able to keep challenging groups outside the power loop. Taking a close look (or micro perspective) at any single issue, therefore, the dominance of an issue network leads to concentration of power and is, in fact, quite elitist for that issue. Overall, however, different policy issues result in the dominance of different subgovernments or issue networks—the same coalition of individuals (or elites) and groups do not always dominate, in contrast to the elitist interpretation described earlier.

THE MAKING OF FOREIGN POLICY SINCE WORLD WAR II

To what extent do these competing conceptual models reflect the foreign policy process since World War II? Since then, *different interpretations have dominated in different times:*

1. during the cold war, the prevailing interpretation of the foreign policy process approximated the pluralist interpretation as discussed earlier, and

2. since the end of the Vietnam War to the present, the dominant interpretation has been that the foreign policy process tended to be more elitist during the cold war years but has become more pluralist since Vietnam.

Pluralism and the Cold War Years

During the cold war, the prevalent interpretation viewed the making of U.S. foreign policy as rather pluralist in nature (see Almond 1966; Huntington 1961; Hammond, Schilling and Snyder 1962; Hoffmann, 1968; Snyder 1958; Lindblom 1959; Neustadt 1960 and the first wave of foreign policy theorists discussed by Art 1973). One of the most popular and powerful statements of this interpretation was Roger Hilsman's (1964) *To Move a Nation: The Politics of Foreign Policy in the Administration of John F. Kennedy.*

According to Hilsman (1964:552), "In its broadest meaning, politics concerns the activities and relationships of groups of people as groups." *The group process shares three characteristics:* (1) the political process includes the presence of competing groups or factions; (2) "politics implies a diversity of goals and values that must be reconciled;"

(3) the relative power of the different groups prevents the same groups from dominating the policymaking process time after time. Hence, the politics of U.S. foreign policy is essentially pluralist in nature. "The fact that policy is made through a political process of conflict and consensus-building accounts for much of the untidiness and turmoil on the Washington scene. The issues are important; there are rival policies for dealing with them; and the rival policies are sponsored by different groups of advocates competing for the approval or support of a variety of different constituencies" (Hilsman 1964:532–533).

In this conception, policymaking involves a political process of conflict, compromise, and incrementalism due to the multiplicity of actors attempting to reconcile competing goals. Thus, for Hilsman (1964:13), a nation is moved as a result of "the interaction of the President, the Congress, the press, and special interests" and "the rivalries of the great Executive departments, State, Defense, and the Central Intelligence Agency, as they clash in the actual making of policy." According to Hilsman, the implications of such a political and messy policymaking process are that

> over some of this at certain times, the president may merely preside—if it is a matter of slight interest to him and has little impact on his position. But if he is an advocate or if the outcome affects his position and power, then the president, too, must engage in the politics of policymaking. In the field of foreign affairs, the president's power is immense. . . . But he, too, must build a consensus for his policy if it is to succeed. . . . he must bring along enough of the different factions in Congress to forestall revolt, and he must contend for the support of wider constituencies, the press, interest groups, and "attentive publics." Even within the Executive Branch itself, his policy will not succeed merely at his command, and he must build co-operation and support, obtain approval from some, acquiescence from others, and enthusiasm from enough to carry it to completion. (Hilsman 1964:561–562)

Although Hilsman portrays the politics of U.S. foreign policy in pluralist terms, *upon close examination it is a very restricted or limited form.* First, competing groups are not found throughout society but predominantly within the government. Second, in most cases, members of the executive branch have a disproportionate amount of influence within the policymaking process. Third, the mass public plays virtually no role in the policymaking process at all.

As Hilsman (1964:543) described it, the policymaking process consists of a *series of three concentric circles:* an innermost circle of the president, his chief advisors, and his major appointments throughout the executive branch; a middle circle of the other departments, agencies, and layers of personnel within the executive branch; and an outermost circle consisting of "Congress, the press, interest groups, and—inevitably—the 'attentive publics.'" The first two of these concentric circles involve policymaking solely within the executive branch. Hilsman (1964:542) maintained that some matters never go beyond the innermost circle, "but even here the process is political, the 'closed politics' of highly secret decisionmaking." However, "the longer a policy debate goes on, no matter how delicate the issue is, the more people will become involved until eventually the debate spills over into the public arena."

While this may appear like pluralist politics, it is a type of pluralism that is often limited to only a narrow range of government officials and groups located predominantly within the executive branch. According to this interpretation, Congress, the press, interest groups, and the attentive publics play a peripheral role, becoming involved only when issues become politicized beyond the executive branch. Even when this occurs, for Hilsman (1964:557) the influence of Congress tends to be "indirect or limit-setting rather than direct or initiative-taking. In domestic policy, Congress occasionally can take the initiative and force a new policy according to its tastes, but rarely in foreign policy." Hence, pluralist foreign policymaking is largely a function of executive branch activity, with only a peripheral role for the outermost circle—eventually providing the foundation for the model of "governmental politics" developed by Graham Allison (1971) during the early 1970s as discussed in Chapter 9 (on executive branch decisionmaking theory).

Finally, the outermost circle also seems to exclude virtually any role for the mass public—the bulk of the American people. Hilsman never discusses the mass public—only attentive publics—in terms of the influence or constraints that they place on domestic politics and the policymaking process. Instead, the public is indirectly referred to solely as a political target for different groups in their efforts to gain widespread support. This leads to an inevitable oversimplification of foreign policy debates and the overselling of policies. As Hilsman (1964:546) explains, "If the debate is taking place in front of a variety of audiences whose attention is easily diverted, then the alternatives must be very clear-cut, simple, and dramatic and the arguments painted in colors that are both bold and bright." Thus, a foreign policy process that virtually excludes most Americans raises serious questions concerning the extent to which the political system is truly democratic and pluralist.

From Elitism to Pluralism Since Vietnam

Beginning in the 1970s, scholars and analysts of U.S. foreign policy accepted a new interpretation of the making of U.S. foreign policy: During the cold war, the political process tended to be more elitist; since the Vietnam War it became increasingly pluralist. This emerging consensus concerning the politics of U.S. foreign policy is represented by such works as Richard Barnet's (1972) *Roots of War*; Destler, Gelb, and Lake's (1984) *Our Own Worst Enemy*; John Donovan's (1974) *The Cold-Warriors*; Gelb and Betts' (1974) *The Irony of Vietnam*; David Halberstam's (1972) *The Best and the Brightest*; Godfrey Hodgson's (1974) *America in Our Time*; Isaacson and Thomas' (1986) *The Wise Men*; and Hedrick Smith's (1988, 1996) *The Power Game*. This interpretation is also consistent with the basic understanding of the post–World War II foreign policy process provided by this book.

It is not really a case of disagreement over the particulars of Hilsman's (1964) analysis of the foreign policymaking process during the cold war. In fact, there is a great deal of shared understanding concerning the power of the president and the executive branch in a political process in which national security requirements took precedence over the demands of democracy. *The key dispute involves a different interpretation and conclusion concerning the overall political process: that the foreign policy process during the cold war was, in fact, more elitist in nature, as opposed to pluralist.* In other words, the argument is that, while the politics of any particular decision appears under close inspection to resemble a pluralistic process, the overall general political process was in fact relatively elitist in nature.

An elitist interpretation of the cold war years tends to place great weight on the concentration of power and thought that existed throughout society and government in the making of U.S. foreign policy. The focus is not only on the "immediate" politics of U.S. foreign policy but on the general "setting" and domestic context that molds and constrains the making of U.S. foreign policy. In other words, whereas Hilsman emphasizes the direct (and immediate) influence of the innermost and middle circles—the executive branch—beyond all other concerns, a more elitist interpretation is concerned with both the **direct influence** enjoyed by the innermost and middle circles on day-to-day policy as well as the **indirect** (and underlying and contextual) **influence** that the outermost circle has in terms of the constraints on policy and the limits it sets on the political process (Bachrach and Baratz 1962). In this respect, the pluralist interpretation completely underemphasizes the crucial development and impact of the foreign policy establishment and the ideological consensus on the communications process, electoral and group politics, the overall governmental policymaking process, and the decline of economics to low politics.

Very simply, during the cold war, power became increasingly concentrated within the executive branch—especially in the White House and the national security bureaucracy—and in its linkages to key private groups, especially more prominent corporations, foreign policy groups such as the Council on Foreign Relations, and academic institutions. Furthermore, the politics that permeated society and government operated within a strong liberal–conservative ideological consensus that drove Congress to be more supportive of presidential foreign policy leadership, in part from simple policy agreement. This same consensus also resulted in considerable bipartisanship among the most politically active supported by a largely apathetic and compliant mass public.

To briefly summarize, the new dominant patterns after World War II that prevailed during the cold war years were:

- growth of American power and hegemony (Chapter 2),
- growth of presidential power (Chapter 3),
- ascent of the NSC system (Chapter 4),
- expansion of the national security bureaucracy (Chapters 5, 6, and 7),
- rise of the national security ethos (Chapter 7),
- movement of foreign economics to "low policy" and dominated by a free market ethos (Chapter 8),
- development of bipartisanship and a supportive Congress (and courts) (Chapter 10),
- rise of a liberal–conservative and anticommunist consensus (Chapter 11),
- existence of mass apathy and a decline in the exercise of civil liberties (Chapters 11 and 12),
- prevalence of cold war–oriented groups and movements (Chapter 12),
- growth of a foreign policy establishment (Chapter 12),
- development of a military-industrial-scientific infrastructure (Chapter 12), and
- development of a nonpartisan and cold war–oriented mass media (Chapter 13).

The cold war years thus represented a period when the presidency and the executive branch dominated the foreign policy process at the height of American power, with the involvement and support of mainstream groups and institutions throughout society and government, held together by a foreign policy consensus that pervaded the elite and mass public. Let's discuss the implications of these major cold war patterns for the other major themes or questions that have been addressed throughout this book.

We can debate the extent of presidential and executive branch power as a result of these patterns in the making of U.S. foreign policy. However, the cold war years were clearly the height of presidential power in U.S. foreign policy, when the president faced the fewest constraints within government and throughout society. The development of the foreign policy bureaucracy, military-industrial-scientific infrastructure, cold war–oriented groups, and foreign policy establishment further provided the support and means by which to pursue and implement a cold war policy. The rise of the foreign policy establishment and the military-industrial-scientific infrastructure, in particular, were consequential in the formation of significant ties and networks that developed between society and government in support of a cold war foreign policy. All of these developments were held together by the rise of a cold war consensus in which most Americans—throughout the mass and elite publics—came to believe that a national emergency existed due to the threat posed by Soviet communism. This promoted a supportive Congress and mass media, and responsive public. Altogether, these elitist patterns produced the phenomenon of the "two presidencies," allowing the president and the national security bureaucracy to exercise "prerogative government" in foreign policy abroad and at home in the name of national security, for roughly twenty years.

One can also debate how much, or how little, democratic practice existed in the politics of U.S. foreign policy during the cold war. Yet widespread fear of the Soviet Union and communism, reinforced by McCarthyism at its height, clearly meant that the demands of national security often took precedence over the demands of democracy in the two decades following the end of World War II. Consequently, the development of a national security ethos limited the availability of information to the public; Democratic and Republican candidates for national office were cold warriors and offered voters little political choice; political participation declined, with little room allowed for the exercise of political dissent; and the rise of bureaucracy—in the executive branch and the private sector—minimized political accountability. Therefore, the existence of powerful groups in the government and throughout society operating under a cold war consensus considerably narrowed democratic practice within mainstream American politics.

Such an elitist interpretation suggests three patterns. First, the height of presidential power was reached during the cold war years, especially from the mid-1950s to the mid-1960s. Second, the demands of national security took precedence over the demands of democracy. Finally, elitism notwithstanding, the politics of U.S. foreign policy was quite complex, as this book has attempted to demonstrate throughout. Together, the politics of U.S. foreign policy were mutually reinforcing with, and provided political support in government and throughout society for, American cold war policy abroad and decisions that led, for example, to the Americanization of the war in Vietnam. That war contributed to the political turbulence of the late 1960s and early 1970s that produced important changes in the complex politics of U.S. foreign policy. American intervention in the Vietnam War, therefore, represented the height and decline of elitism in the making of U.S. foreign policy.

The argument that the foreign policy process became more pluralist since the Vietnam War is also consistent with the major patterns discussed within the book. *Since the Vietnam War, a new set of patterns have prevailed:*

- (relative) decline of American power and the exercise of its immense power in a complex global system (Chapter 2),

- decline of presidential power (Chapter 3),

- rise of the foreign economics to "high" policy (Chapter 8),

- reassertiveness of Congress (Chapter 10),

- shattering of the liberal–conservative cold war consensus by greater ideological diversity and partisanship (Chapter 11),

- collapse of the foreign policy establishment (Chapter 12),

- proliferation of diverse social movements/interest groups, along with the expansion of civil liberties (Chapter 12), and

- rise of so-called objective journalism and a centrist and potentially more independent mass media (Chapter 13).

Ultimately, the rise of pluralism has led to a decline in the president's ability to govern foreign policy and an increase in democratic practice relative to the demands of national security. This has been reinforced by the collapse of the Soviet Union and the cold war.

Since the late 1960s, presidents have faced greater obstacles and constraints than during the cold war years. The two-presidencies scenario—weak in domestic policy, strong in foreign policy—has been replaced by a paradox of presidential power, which requires the exercise of strong presidential leadership to govern, even in the making of U.S. foreign policy. The crisis of governance facing most post–Vietnam War presidents, however, is so severe that a president has great difficulty fulfilling the high expectations created among the public and, consequently, is prone to experience failure. Most important, a president can no longer exercise prerogative government with virtual impunity, as occurred during the cold war years. To do so is to risk "overshoot and collapse" or "political backlash"—as President Richard Nixon experienced with the Watergate affair, and President Ronald Reagan suffered with Iran–Contra. President George W. Bush faced a similar problem after 9/11 with the Iraq War, and President Obama experienced backlash to his policies to address the economic crisis that reflects the pluralist politics of intermestic policies.

Presidents have greater difficulty governing U.S. foreign policy because *the political process has become more democratic since the 1960s.* While the demands of national security took precedence during the cold war, the political process since Vietnam has become more responsive to the demands of democracy. The public has greater access to information, a choice between more liberal and conservative presidential candidates, and increased opportunities to actively participate (reflecting more the fragmentation/swing model discussed in Chapter 11). Furthermore, the separation of powers has been renewed, diversity in ideological and foreign policy thought has grown, and group politics have diversified and proliferated.

This is not to say that no elitist elements remain. The president and the executive branch retain significant advantages in the politics of U.S. foreign policy due to the legacy of the cold war and the cloak of the national security ethos, especially during crises. Furthermore, political competition among members of the elite public is heavily circumscribed by ideological thought that reflects the liberal–conservative political spectrum. The 9/11 terrorist attacks and President George W. Bush's war on terrorism increased presidential power in national security affairs and the demands of national security relative to democracy in the short term. Nevertheless, presidents have experienced less support and face considerably stronger constraints in exercising prerogative government in the name of national security or a (economic) crisis since Vietnam.

Continuity in Hyperpluralist Politics and an Apolitical Mass Public

The complex politics of U.S. foreign policy not only has experienced change but also has been characterized by continuity since the 1960s. *Continuity has occurred in two important facets of the foreign policy process:* (1) the hyperpluralist politics of national security policy, and; (2) the continuing withdrawal or apathy of much of the mass public from politics. These are two very important dimensions that are often ignored or downplayed by those who conclude that the political process has become more pluralist since the Vietnam War.

HYPERPLURALIST POLITICS   Since World War II and the cold war, foreign policy has become increasingly bureaucratic, which has led to the development of extensive networks between individuals and groups within the executive branch, Congress, and the private sector. Therefore, as discussed throughout the book, *important elements of hyperpluralism within the foreign policy process "continue" to exist to this day:*

- a large national security and foreign economic bureaucracy (Chapters 5, 6, 7, and 8),

- a national security and free market ethos (Chapters 7 and 8),

- the existence of conservative internationalism among a segment of the public (Chapter 11),

- the military-industrial-scientific infrastructure (Chapter 12), and

- the existence of conservative-oriented national security and economic groups (Chapter 12).

Hyperpluralist politics is most visible in the development of defense politics during the cold war and its continuation since Vietnam, reinforced by 9/11 despite the collapse of the cold war. Hyperpluralism also is quite prevalent for intermestic issues such as economics. This is clearly visible in the Obama administration's attempt to address the Great Recession and to affect change in other foreign policy arenas, as we have seen in the preceding chapters. In fact, wherever established groups and bureaucracies have arisen throughout society and government, issue networks have formed and, subsequently, resist changes to the status quo.

Such hyperpluralist politics *both strengthen and weaken presidential power.* For example, the existence of a large national security bureaucracy and military-industrial-scientific support infrastructure strengthens the power of a president who wants to pursue more of a foreign policy reminiscent of the cold war, much as President George W. Bush did with his war on terrorism after 9/11. At the same time, however, presidential policies remain heavily affected by what the bureaucracy is able and willing to implement as President Bush found out in Iraq and President Obama learned on Afghanistan, Pakistan, and the war on terror. Likewise, the large foreign economic bureaucracy, the existence of powerful economic groups, and especially Americans abiding faith in the so-called free market constrained President Obama's flexibility and choice of policies as he attempted to overcome the economic downturn and promote recovery both nationally and globally. In other words, should a president want to pursue a dramatically different, new, or innovative foreign policy, hyperpluralist politics act as a major constraint on new policy initiatives.

Hyperpluralist politics also has *implications for the tension between national security and democracy* that exists in American politics. The existence of a huge national security bureaucracy and support infrastructure means that a strong constituency continues to exist throughout society and the government that remains sympathetic to the demands of national security. And a national security ethos of independence, secrecy, and realpolitik continues to affect domestic politics and, in particular, pervade the governmental policymaking process, especially after the 9/11 terrorist attacks. Therefore, the rise of pluralism and the continuation of hyperpluralism since the Vietnam War have increased the political contradictions and tensions between the demands of national security and democracy.

AN APOLITICAL MASS PUBLIC   One other important trend of continuity concerns the role of the mass public in the politics of U.S. foreign policy. A large segment of the public has basically withdrawn from American politics, despite the increases in presidential turnout in 2004 and 2008. In fact, the 2012 election saw a downtick in overall participation from the 2008 cycle, although that decline was not evenly distributed across demographic groups. Interestingly, younger voters, minorities and women participated at the same or higher levels, while others did not. Overall though, just a little more than fifty percent of eligible voters cast a ballot—over 90 million eligible voters simply sat out the election. The U.S. continues to have the lowest voter participation in industrialized, democratic world. Such mass apathy has added considerable uncertainty to the president's ability to govern and the contradictions between national security and democracy since Vietnam and the end of the cold war (see **Figure** 14.1).

This continuity in the role of the mass public during a time when there is no consensus throughout society and government *adds considerable uncertainty to the president's ability to govern foreign policy.* On the one hand, the mass public's opinions and cultural beliefs, reflecting the split in elite beliefs, reinforces the dominant patterns that prevail since the Vietnam War. At the same time, because most of the public tends to be tuned out of politics, there is a likelihood of greater mood swings—which can strengthen or weaken the president, depending on their direction. Clearly, there was a nationalistic mood swing in support of President Bush and the war on terrorism after 9/11, followed by a decline in public approval and support over the war in Iraq. President Obama received high initial support in tackling the economy, only to see the presidential life cycle kick in within six months, and his public approval decline dramatically. Ultimately, the political apathy of much of the mass public at a time of great foreign policy disagreement and competition is a source of uncertainty and potential instability in the future politics of U.S. foreign policy.

This has important *implications for the practice of democracy* in American politics. Although the rise of pluralism has resulted in greater democracy and a more responsive political system, the prevalence of a predominantly apolitical mass public is a poor omen for the future of democratic politics. It is shocking how little information many Americans possess concerning national and international affairs. Furthermore, public cynicism toward politics appears to have grown. The political result has been a decline in mass participation in the electoral process, for example, and a mass public that has become increasingly vulnerable to the politics of symbolism. Turnout did increase in the elections of 2004 and 2008 by an impressive 10 percent, but this was only at the presidential level. Forty percent of all eligible voting age population still chose not to participate in these elections (over 80 million Americans;

Figure 14.1   Presidential Electoral Turnout

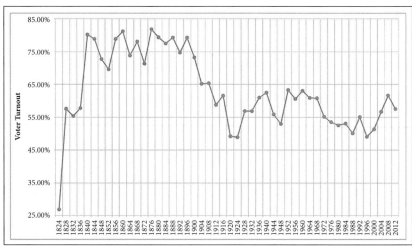

SOURCE: Congressional Quarterly

see Figure 14.1), and the number fell in 2012 back down to around 50% as noted above. This remains a far cry from the "alert and knowledgeable" citizenry that President Eisenhower called for and democratic practice demands. In other words, the increase in democratic politics since the Vietnam War has been paradoxically accompanied by the bulk of the American public tuning out of politics altogether.

In sum, the politics of U.S. foreign policy is too complex for any single model of the political process to capture, for much depends on the time and the issues of concern. Overall, the complex politics of U.S. foreign policy has experienced continuity and change since World War II: A more elitist form of politics dominated the cold war years; after the Vietnam War, elitism was replaced by a more pluralist form of politics; politics during the cold war was also characterized by the rise of hyperpluralism in defense politics and a mass public that remained beyond politics altogether, which continued into the post–Vietnam era. With the collapse of the Soviet Union and the end of the cold war, these post–Vietnam patterns have continued and intensified. Therefore, the cold war years represented the height of the president's ability to govern foreign policy, a time when the demands of national security prevailed over the demands of democracy. In contrast, the years after the Vietnam War represented a decline in presidential power due to growing contradictions between the growth of democracy and the persistence of national security demands. Neither the 9/11 attacks nor the economic crisis that began in 2007 have fundamentally altered theses patterns where the long-term consequences remain quite uncertain in such a volatile global, domestic, and political environment.

As McGowan and Walker (1981:378) have argued, much depends, on the question and the level of generality that one is addressing:

> On the one hand, if one is interested in delineating the outer parameters of change in American policy, an [elitist] perspective identifies the constraints that limit the range of variation and provides insights into the deeper structural changes that appear to be required in order to reshape U.S. foreign economic policy. If, on the other hand, the analyst is interested in short-run, incremental changes in U.S. foreign economic policy, then the [pluralist] perspective sensitizes him to the immediate surface causes of these fluctuations.

The foreign policy process is actually more complex and messy than this summary analysis suggests, because the role of chance or "fortune" (and unintended consequences) in the unfolding of politics has been ignored, often leading to a false sense of clarity about the making of U.S. foreign policy due to the benefit of hindsight.

FOREIGN POLICY CHANGE?

What will the future entail? Why do some patterns remain the same over time? When does **foreign policy change** occur? This is an area that has received only sporadic attention despite its importance in the twenty-first century. Nevertheless, tentative generalizations can be derived from the work that has been done on the study of political change.

Although political systems can proceed down different historical paths, certain patterns of continuity and change tend to prevail in the politics of U.S. foreign policy. As numerous scholars have argued (see Goldmann 1988; Huntington 1981; Hermann 1990; Holsti 1982; Rosenau 1981; Welch 2005; and Rosati, Hagan, and Sampson 1994), American politics normally tends to resist change but is interrupted occasionally by political crises that stimulate change. **Incremental change**—that is, little change over a period of time—tends to be the prevailing norm during times of high political legitimacy and stability—a period of equilibrium in the political system. **Major change** tends to be infrequent and often abrupt, usually triggered by major crises indicative of failed policies and the rise of political instability—a time of disequilibrium in the political system.

As David Truman (1951:44) characterized it, "The moving pattern of a complex society such as the one in which we live is one of changes and disturbances in the habitual subpatterns of interaction, followed by a return to the previous state of equilibrium or, if the disturbances are intense or prolonged, by the emergence of new groups" that establish "a new balance, a new adjustment in the habitual interactions of individuals." In other words, American politics tends to evolve from periods of political stability in which continuity (and incrementalism) prevails to periods of political instability and transition in which change is most likely. These **cyclical patterns of continuity and change** are consistent with those found in this book on the politics of U.S. foreign policy (see **Figure 14.2** for an overview).

Why does status quo politics tend to prevail?   All political systems, whether pluralist, elitist, or hyperpluralist in nature, tend to resist change. This situation prevails because established groups and institutions throughout government and society engage in politics to promote their interests and protect the status quo from challenging groups and ideas. This influence is usually reinforced by the support of the mass public. Although predominantly apolitical, they support mainstream institutions and beliefs, ultimately providing the political system with its legitimacy and political stability. According to V. O. Key, Jr. (1964:70),

> The system—the established way of doing things—constitutes a powerful brake on political change. Those who agitate for a new order invariably encounter the resistance of the old order which exists, in considerable degree at least, in the revered values more or less firmly anchored in group life. These patterns of behavior, traditional modes of action, group norms, or social equilibria—the concept employed in their description may not matter—possess a powerful capacity for their own perpetuation and resist movements that would disturb them.

Figure 14.2   Cycles of Foreign Policy Continuity and Change

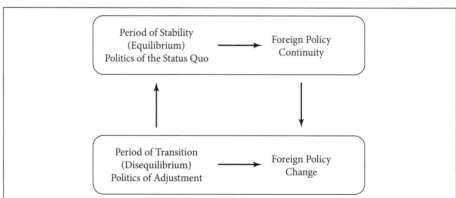

SOURCE: Jerel A. Rosati, "Cycles in Foreign Policy Restructuring: The Politics of Continuity and Change in U.S. Foreign Policy," in *Foreign Policy Restructuring: How Governments Respond to Global Change*, edited by Jerel A. Rosati, Joe D. Hagan, and Martin W. Sampson, p. 227 (Columbia, SC: University of South Carolina Press).

In other words, all political systems with an established set of institutions and beliefs in place throughout the society and government tend to resist change, although with varying degrees of rigidity and success. The implication is that change, if it occurs at all, tends to be incremental in nature.

Although continuity and incrementalism tend to be the norm, major change periodically occurs throughout society and the government. The politics of change and adjustment is most likely to prevail over the politics of the status quo during times of crisis and political instability, when the legitimacy of the political leadership is most likely to be questioned by members of society. This eventually occurs because of the growing gap that develops between the incrementalist policies of the government and the inevitable change experienced throughout the global environment and society. As the politics of the status quo continues to prevail and governmental policies fail to adjust to new developments in the international and domestic environment, the contradictions grow, increasing the likelihood of policy failure abroad and the growth of internal opposition at home.

As Stanley Hoffmann (1968:277) stated, "When rigidity leads to failure—but only then—the policy becomes unstuck and sudden reversals become possible." Should these contradictory developments continue and intensify with time, governmental policy becomes increasingly maladaptive. Eventually, this may lead to major political crises at home that politicize members of society to challenge the legitimacy of the policies and the beliefs held by the individuals and groups that dominate society and the state.

The key to understanding the dynamics of foreign policy, in other words, is the interaction of the state, the society, and the global environment (or context) that produces a political process that usually reinforces governmental resistance to change and the maintenance of foreign policy continuity; sometimes, however, it produces contradictions to the status quo that contribute to foreign policy change. Whatever the causes, public policies that were once considered successful are now increasingly seen as failures and counterproductive. During such periods of political instability, greater numbers of people are likely to question and criticize the status quo, more new issues are placed on the political agenda, challenging groups and ideas gain strength, and the dominant groups and beliefs throughout society and government have less success dominating politics. Therefore, times of major crisis and political instability are often transitional periods that may produce major political change (see **Figure** 14.3 for an overview).

The making of U.S. foreign policy has followed this pattern in which the politics of the status quo tends to be superseded by the politics of transition, producing change and a new politics of the status quo. The political crises faced by the United States in association with World War II, the rise of American power, and the development of the cold war triggered a number of significant changes in government and society, resulting in the more elitist political patterns of U.S. foreign policy during the cold war years that we have identified in this book. These patterns in the foreign policy process prevailed throughout the 1950s and early 1960s until the political crises and instability of the late 1960s and early 1970s, especially over U.S. foreign policy in the Vietnam War, triggered additional political changes in government and society in a more pluralist direction that have prevailed since Vietnam. At the same time, the hyperpluralism of defense politics and the political apathy among the mass public are continuing legacies of the cold war. Thus, the politics of U.S. foreign policy has experienced continuity and change over time, with significant implications for both the president's ability to govern and for the contradictory tension between the demands of national security and of democracy.

Figure 14.3   The Dynamics of Foreign Policy Change

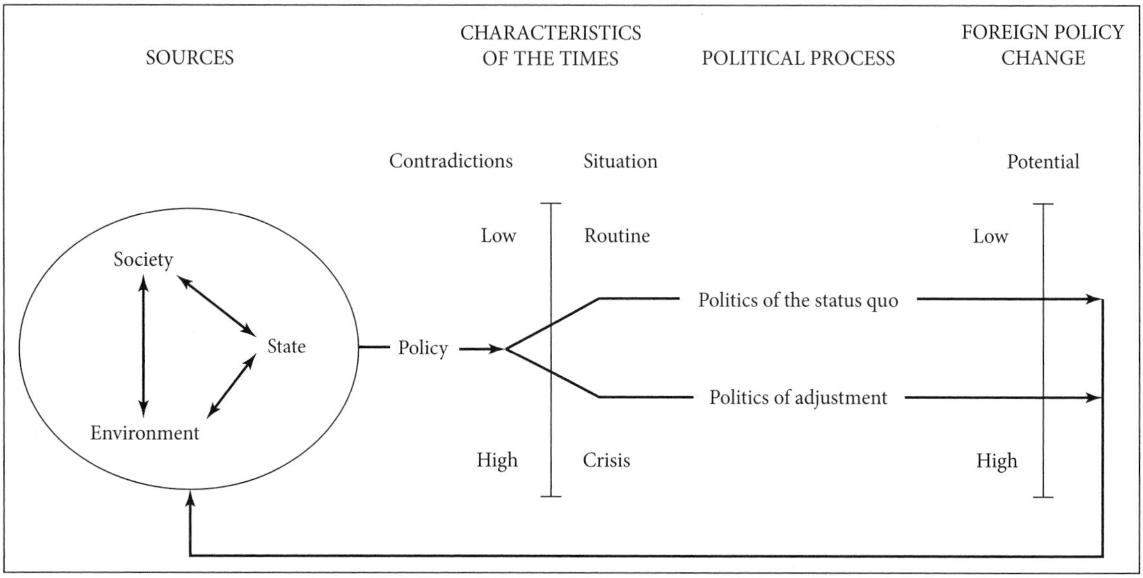

SOURCE: Jerel A. Rosati, "Cycles in Foreign Policy Restructuring: The Politics of Continuity and Change in U.S. Foreign Policy," in *Foreign Policy Restructuring: How Governments Respond to Global Change*, edited by Jerel A. Rosati, Joe D. Hagan, and Martin W. Sampson, p. 237 (Columbia, SC: University of South Carolina Press).

FROM 9/11 AND THE GLOBAL RECESSION TO THE FUTURE

Clearly, the end of the cold war and the evolving post–cold war global environment have contradictory implications for the future politics of U.S. foreign policy. The end of the cold war has created increasing global complexity, posing both greater opportunities and constraints for the evolution and exercise of American power. The collapse of communism, the decline of the Soviet Union, and the rise of new issues on the political agenda suggest the likelihood of more foreign policy change heading away from cold war policies of the past, further weakening the president's ability to govern foreign policy and increasing the demands of democracy. Yet the continued existence of instability and conflict throughout the world, although on a smaller scale than a potential U.S.–Soviet war, reinforces the likelihood of an active United States presence in the world and the continued exercise of presidential power in the name of national security.

Such continuity in the politics of U.S. foreign policy is most open to change and adjustment in response to new global and internal developments that prevail in the post–cold war era, especially if they are accompanied by political crises. *The question now is to what extent will the 9/11 attacks, the war on terrorism, and the global economic crisis be perceived as a time of real and permanent crisis and national emergency?* How long and how much will they resonate in the American political system? To what extent can the president successfully exercise political leadership? Will this be perceived as another time of permanent war or national emergency, or as war (or national emergency) in a time of relative peace?

According to George Packer (2005:385) in *The Assassins' Gate: America in Iraq*, "America in the early twenty-first century seemed politically too partisan, divided, and small to manage something as vast and difficult as Iraq." Following 9/11, "Bush's rhetoric soared and inspired [at home, but not abroad], but his actions showed that his actions had a narrow strategy for fighting the war, which amounted to finding and killing terrorists and their supporters." And when Iraq "looked nothing like the president's soaring vision—when Iraq was visibly deteriorating, and no one in authority would admit it—the speeches produced either illusion or cynicism in the public." And "war, unlike budget forecasts and presidential campaigns, is merciless with untruth. In refusing to look honestly at Iraq, Bush made defeat there more likely (Packer 2005:392)." So despite 9/11 and reelection, President Bush faced a crisis of governance and leadership like his predecessors since the Vietnam War.

A similar situation faced President Obama despite the worst economic crisis since the Great Depression. The political context in Washington—rife with partisanship, divided government and competing ideological visions—contributed substantially to gridlock and inertia. Despite ambitious goals and rhetoric, the Obama administration managed much less dramatic change or progress than was promised.

The slow pace of change and progress was central to his difficulty in securing re-election. In the end, President Obama won a second term, campaigning chiefly on a call to continue his efforts to seek progress rather than return to past policies. However, his margin of victory declined and the narrowness of his win combined with ever-greater partisan divisions promised to make dramatic change even more difficult to accomplish in his second term.

It was the sense of national emergency associated with the cold war during the 1950s and 1960s, after all, that was the ultimate source of presidential power and American global leadership following World War II. Clearly, such a sense of national emergency tremendously declined following Vietnam, reinforced by the end of the cold war. This means that the fragmented and pluralist political environment that has prevailed since Vietnam—resulting in a paradox of presidential power and a strong tension between national security and democracy—is likely to continue in the twenty-first century, posing greater foreign policy opportunities and political risks for presidents and American leadership abroad. And although the 9/11 terrorist attacks and the economic crisis that began in 2007 produced a crisis-like atmosphere, neither lasted long (or was able to replace Soviet communism as a comparable crisis). The Iraq War, rather than promoting a unified sense of national emergency, divided the country, as did President Obama's national security and, especially, economic policies.

In short, the paradox of presidential power and the continuing tensions between democracy and national security appear alive and well into the foreseeable and uncertain future. Ultimately, it is the dynamic and unpredictable interaction of the government, the society, and the environment that will determine the complexity and direction of the future politics of U.S. foreign policy.

SUGGESTED SOURCES FOR MORE INFORMATION

Heclo, Hugh. (1978) "Issue Networks and the Executive Establishment," In *The New American Political System*, edited by Anthony King, pp. 87–124. Washington, DC: American Enterprise Institute. Classic on the rise of hyperpluralism and issue networks.

Hermann, Charles F. (1990) "Changing Course: When Governments Choose to Redirect Foreign Policy," *International Studies Quarterly* 34 (March):3–21. Excellent overview of theories of foreign policy change.

Hilsman, Roger. (1964) *To Move a Nation: The Politics of Foreign Policy in the Administration of John F. Kennedy.* New York: Delta. Chapters 1 and 35, especially, provides the best example of the pluralist perspective applied to the making of U.S. foreign policy for the cold war years.

Huntington, Samuel P. (1981) *American Politics: The Politics of Disharmony.* Cambridge, MA: Harvard University Press. Develops a fascinating theory of continuity and change in American politics.

Miliband, Ralph. (1969) *The State in Capitalist Society: The Analysis of the Western System of Power.* London: Quartet Books. Classic on elitism, with an emphasis on class.

Mills, C. Wright. (1956) *The Power Elite.* London: Oxford University Press. Classic on elitism, with an emphasis on institutions.

Rosati, Jerel A., Joe D. Hagan, and Martin W. Sampson, eds. (1994) *Foreign Policy Restructuring: How Governments Respond to Global Change.* Columbia, SC: University of South Carolina Press. Good overview and application of theories of foreign policy change.

KEY CONCEPTS

cyclical patterns of continuity and change

direct influence

elitism

foreign policy change

hyperpluralism

incremental change

indirect influence

major change

pluralism

republican model

REFERENCES

Aaronson, Susan Ariel. (2002) *Taking Trade to the Streets: The Lost History of Public Efforts to Shape Globalization*. Ann Arbor: University of Michigan Press.

ABC News, 20/20. (2005) *Colin Powell on Iraq, Race, and Hurricane Relief: Former Secretary of State Speaks Out on Being Loyal—And Being Wrong*, September 8.

Aberbach, Joel D. (1990) *Keeping a Watchful Eye: The Politics of Congressional Oversight*. Washington, DC: Brookings Institution Press.

Ackerman, Spender. (2006) Our Myopic Spooks: Under Analysis. *New Republic*.

Adams, Gordon. (1982) *The Politics of Defense Contracting: The Iron Triangle*. New Brunswick, NJ: Transaction Publishers.

Adkin, Mark. (1989) *Urgent Fury: The Battle for Grenada*. Lexington, MA: Lexington Books.

————. (1990) *U.S. Government International Exchange and Training Activities*.

Albright, Joseph, and Marcia Kunstel. (1990) CIA Tip Led to '62 Arrest of Mandela: Ex-Official Tells of U.S. "Coup" to Aid S. Africa. *Atlanta Constitution*, June 10, p. A14.

Aldrich, John H., John L. Sullivan, and Eugene Borgida. (1989) Foreign Affairs and Issue Voting: Do Presidential Candidates "Waltz" before a Blind Audience? *American Political Science Review* 83: 123–41.

Allard, Carl K., Jr. (1990) *Command, Control, and the Common Defense*. New Haven, CT: Yale University Press.

Allen, Mike. (2004) Rice Is Named Secretary of State. *Washington Post*, November 17, p. A1.

Allison, Graham T. (1971) *Essence of Decision: Explaining the Cuban Missile Crisis*. Boston, MA: Little, Brown.

Allison, Graham T., and Morton H. Halperin. (1972) Bureaucratic Politics: A Paradigm and Some Policy Implications. *World Politics* 24: 40–79.

Allison, Graham T., and Philip Zelikow. (1999) *Essence of Decision: Explaining the Cuban Missile Crisis*. New York: Longman.

Allyn, Bruce J., James G. Blight, and David A. Welch. (1989) Essence of Revision: Moscow, Havana, and the Cuban Missile Crisis. *International Security* 14: 136–72.

Almond, Gabriel. (1960) *The American People and Foreign Policy*. New York: Praeger.

Alstyne, Richard W. Van. (1960) *The American Empire: Its Historical Pattern and Evolution*. General Series Pamphlet No. 43. London: Historical Association.

————. (1974) *The Rising American Empire*. New York: W.W. Norton.

Alter, Jonathan. (2010) *The Promise: President Obama, Year 1*. New York: Simon and Schuster.

Ambrosio, Thomas. (2002) *Ethnic Identity Groups and U.S. Foreign Policy*. Westport, CT: Praeger.

Andrews, Edmund L. (2009) Forget Aloof, Bernanke Goes Barnstorming. *New York Times*, July 26, p. A1.

Armstrong, David. (1981) *A Trumpet to Arms: Alternative Media in America*. Los Angeles, CA: J. P. Tarcher.

Art, Robert. (1973) Bureaucratic Politics and American Foreign Policy: A Critique. *Policy Sciences* 4: 467–90.

Auerswald, David P., and Forrest Maltzman. (2003) Policymaking Through Advice and Consent: Treaty Consideration by the United States Senate. *Journal of Politics* 65: 1097–110.

Auerswald, David P., and Peter F. Cowhey. (1997) Ballotbox Diplomacy: The War Powers Resolution and the Use of Force. *International Studies Quarterly* 41: 505–28.

Auletta, Ken. (1991) *Three Blind Mice: How the Networks Lost Their Way*. New York: Random House.

Ayres, B. Drummond, Jr. (1983a) A New Breed of Diplomat. *New York Times Magazine*, September 11, pp. 66–67, 70–73, 105.

Ayres, B. Drummond, Jr. (1983b) Grenada Invasion. *New York Times*, November 14, pp. A1, A6.

Bacchus, William I. (1983) *Staffing for Foreign Affairs: Personnel Systems for the 1980's and 1990's*. Princeton, NJ: Princeton University Press.

Bacevich, Andrew J. (1994) Charles Beard, Properly Understood. *National Interest* 35: 73–83.

Bacevich, Andrew J. (2005) *The New Militarism: How Americans Are Seduced by War*. New York: Oxford University Press.

Bachrach, Peter. (1971) *Political Elites in a Democracy*. New York: Atherton Press.

Bachrach, Peter, and Morton Baratz. (1962) Two Faces of Power. *American Political Science Review* 56: 947–52.

Bachrack, Stanley D. (1976) *The Committee of One Million: "China Lobby" Politics, 1953–1971.* New York: Columbia University Press.

Badie, Dina. (2010) Groupthink, Iraq, and the War on Terror: Explaining US Policy Shift toward Iraq. *Foreign Policy Analysis* 6 (October): 277–96.

Baer, Robert. (2002) *See No Evil: The True Story of a Ground Soldier in the CIA's War on Terror.* New York: Arrow Books.

———. (2009) Independent Intel: High Stakes in a CIA Turf War. *Time,* NP.

Bagdikian, Ben. (2000) *The Media Monopoly.* Boston, MA: Beacon Press.

Bai, Matt. (2010) Democrat in Chief? *New York Times,* June 8.

Bailey, Thomas. (1961) America's Emergence as a World Power: The Myth and the Verity. *Pacific Historical Review* 30: 1–16.

Baker, Peter. (2005) President Acknowledges Approving Secretive Eavesdropping. *Washington Post,* December 18, p. A1.

Baker, Peter. (2010) The Education of a President. *The New York Times Magazine,* October 12.

Baker, Russell. (2008) Condi and the Boys. *The New York Review of Books,* April 3.

Ball, Howard. (1986) *Justice Downwind: America's Atomic Testing Program in the 1950s.* New York: Oxford University Press.

Balz, Dan and Bob Woodward. (2002) Ten Days in September. *Washington Post,* January 27–February 3, p. A1.

Bamford, James. (1982) *The Puzzle Palace: Inside America's Most Secret Intelligence Organization.* New York: Penguin.

———. (2001) *Body of Secrets: Anatomy of the Ultra-Secret National Security Agency.* New York: Doubleday.

———. (2002) Eyes to the Sky, Ears to the War, and Still Wanting. *New York Times,* September 8, p. 5.

Bardes, Barbara A., and Robert W. Oldendick. (2002) *Public Opinion: Measuring the American Mind.* Belmont, CA: Wadsworth.

Baritz, Loren. (1985) *Backfire: A History of How American Culture Led Us into Vietnam and Made Us Fight the Way We Did.* New York: William Morrow.

Barnes, Fred. (1991) All the President's Perks. *New Republic,* September 2, pp. 22–25.

———. (1994) Cabinet Losers. *New Republic,* February 28, pp. 22–29.

Barnet, Richard J. (1972) *Roots of War: Men and Institutions Behind U.S. Foreign Policy.* New York: Penguin.

———. (1983) *The Alliance: America-Europe-Japan, Makers of the Postwar World.* New York: Simon and Schuster.

———. (1985) *The Permanent War Economy: American Capitalism in Decline.* New York: Touchstone.

Barnet, Richard J., and Ronald E. Muller. (1974) *Global Reach: The Power of Multinational Corporations.* New York: Simon and Schuster.

Barrett, David M. (1988) The Mythology Surrounding Lyndon Johnson, His Advisers, and the 1965 Decision to Escalate the Vietnam War. *Political Science Quarterly* 103: 637–64.

———. (2005) *The CIA and Congress: The Untold Story from Truman to Kennedy.* Lawrence: University of Kansas.

Barrow, Clyde W. (1993) *Critical Theories of the State: Marxist, Neo-Marxist, Post-Marxist.* Madison: University of Wisconsin Press.

Barry, John M. (1989) *The Ambition and the Power: The Fall of Jim Wright, a True Story.* New York: Penguin.

Barry, John, Michael Hirsh, and Michael Isikoff. (2004) The Roots of Torture. *Newsweek,* May 24, p. 29.

Bax, Frans R. (1977) The Legislative-Executive Relationship in Foreign Policy: New Partnership or New Competition? *Orbis* 20: 881–904.

Bayley, Edwin R. (1981) *Joe McCarthy and the Press.* Madison: The University of Wisconsin Press.

Benedetti, Charles De, and Charles Chatfield. (1990) *An American Ordeal: The Antiwar Movement of the Vietnam Era.* Syracuse, NY: Syracuse University Press.

Bennett, Stephen Earl. (1996) Know Nothings' Revisited Again. *Political Behavior* 18: 1–22.

Bennett, W. Lance. (2011) *News: The Politics of Illusion.* New York: Longman.

Berman, Larry. (1989) *Lyndon Johnson's War: The Road to Stalemate in Vietnam.* New York: W.W. Norton.

Bern, Daryl J. (1970) *Beliefs, Attitudes, and Human Affairs.* Belmont, CA: Brooks/Cole.

Bernanke, Ben. (2009) I'm as Disgusted as You Are. *CBS News.*

Bernstein, Carl. (1977) The CIA and the Media. *Rolling Stone,* October 20, pp. 55–67.

———. (1992) The Idiot Culture. *New Republic,* June 8, pp. 22–26.

Bernstein, Carl, and Bob Woodward. (1974) *All the President's Men.* New York: Warner.

Bernstein, Paul, and William Freudenberg. (1977) Ending the Vietnam War: Components of Change in Senate Voting on Vietnam War Bills. *American Journal of Sociology* 82: 991–1006.

Berry, Jeffrey M. (1997) *The Interest Group Society.* Glenview, IL: Scott Foresman.

Betts, Richard K. (1977) *Soldiers, Statesmen, and Cold War Crises.* Cambridge, MA: Harvard University Press.

———. (1978) Analysis, War, and Decision: Why Intelligence Failures Are Inevitable. *World Politics* 31: 61–90.

———. (1998) Warning: Old Problems, New Agendas. *Parameters* 28: 26–35.

———. (2002) The Soft Underbelly of American Primacy: Tactical Advantages of Terror. *Political Science Quarterly* 117: 19–36.

Biddle, Stephen. (2003) Afghanistan and the Future of War. *Foreign Affairs* 82: 31–46.

Bigman, Stanley K. (1949) Rivals in Conformity: A Study of Two Competing Dailies. *Journalism Quarterly* 25: 127–31.

Bill, James A. (1988) *The Eagle and the Lion: The Tragedy of American-Iranian Relations.* New Haven, CT: Yale University Press.

Binkin, Martin. (1991) The New Face of the American Military. *Brookings Review* 9: 7–13.

Black, Earl, and Merle Black. (1987) *Politics and Society in the South.* Cambridge, MA: Harvard University Press.

Blechman, Barry M. (1990) *The Politics of National Security: Congress and U.S. Defense Policy.* Ithaca, NY: Cornell University Press.

Blechman, Barry M., and Stephen S. Kaplan. (1978) *Force Without War: U.S. Armed Forces as a Political Instrument.* Washington, DC: Brookings Institution Press.

Bleifuss, Joel. (1990) The First Stone. *In These Times.*

Blight, James G., and David A. Welch. (1989) *On the Brink: Americans and Soviets Reexamine the Cuban Missile Crisis.* New York: Hill and Wang.

Blumenthal, Sidney. (1986) *The Rise of the Counter-Establishment: From Conservative Ideology to Political Power.* New York: Basic Books.

Bohan, Caren, Andy Sullivan, and Thomas Ferraro. (2011) Special Report: How Washington Took the U.S. to the Brink. *Reuters,* August 4.

Bolt, Paul J., Damon V. Coletta, and Collins G. Shackelford, Jr. (2005) *American Defense Policy.* Baltimore, MD: Johns Hopkins University Press.

Boot, Max. (2003) The New American Way of War. *Foreign Affairs* 82: 41–58.

———. (2005) The Struggle to Transform the Military. *Foreign Affairs* 84: 103–18.

Branch, Taylor. (1988) *Parting the Waters: America in the King Years, 1954–1963.* New York: Simon and Schuster.

Braumoeller, Bear F. (2010) The Myth of American Isolationism. *Foreign Policy Analysis* 6 (October): 349–71.

Brinkley, Douglas, and Stephen E. Ambrose. (1998) *Rise to Globalism: American Foreign Policy since 1938.* Middlesex, UK: Penguin Books.

Broder, David. (2005) Finally, Congress Stands Up. *Washington Post,* December 4, p. B7.

Brodie, Bernard. (1973) *War and Politics.* New York: Macmillan.

Brody, Richard A. (1991) *Assessing the President: The Media, Elite Opinion, and Public Support.* Stanford, CA: Stanford University Press.

Bryant, Adam. (1996) Boeing Offering $13 Billion to Buy McDonnell Douglas, Last U.S. Commercial Rival. *New York Times,* December 16, pp. A1, D14.

Burke, John P. (2001) Lessons from Past Presidential Transitions: Organization, Management, and Decision Making. *Presidential Studies Quarterly* 116: 5–24.

———. (2005) The Contemporary Presidency: Condoleezza Rice as NSC Advisor: A Case Study of the Honest Broker Role. *Presidential Studies Quarterly* 35: 554–75.

———. (2009a) The Obama National Security System and Process: At the Six Month Mark. *White House Transition Project Report.* Online Edition.

———. (2009b) *Honest Broker? The National Security Advisor and Presidential Decision Making.* College Station, TX: A&M University Press.

Burnham, Walter Dean. (1970) *Critical Elections and the Mainsprings of American Politics.* New York: W.W. Norton.

———. (2009c) The National Security Advisor and Staff: Transition Studies. *Presidential Studies Quarterly* 39 (June): 2, 282–321.

Burns, James MacGregor. (1965) *Presidential Government: The Crucible of Leadership.* New York: Avon.

———. (1978) *Leadership.* New York: Harper Torchbooks.

———. (1984) *The Power to Lead: The Crisis of the American Presidency.* New York: Simon and Schuster.

———. (1989) *The Crosswinds of Freedom.* New York: Vintage.

Bush, President George W. (2002) *West Point Address*, June 1.

Butler, John S. (1996) *All That We Can Be: Black Leadership and Racial Integration the Army Way*. New York: Basic Books.

Calmes, Jackie. (2009) Obama's Economic Circle Keeps Tensions High. *New York Times*, June 8, p. A1.

Campbell, Colton C. (2001) *Discharging Congress: Government by Commission*. Westport, CT: Praeger.

Campbell, John Franklin. (1971) *The Foreign Affairs Fudge Factory*. New York: Basic Books.

Cannon, Lou. (1991) *President Reagan: The Role of a Lifetime*. New York: Simon and Schuster.

Capps, Walter H. (1990) *The New Religious Right: Piety, Patriotism, and Politics*. Columbia: University of South Carolina Press.

Carpini, Michael X. Delli, and Scott Keeter. (1991) Stability and Change in the U.S. Public's Knowledge of Politics. *Public Opinion Quarterly* 55: 583–612.

———. (1997) *What Americans Know About Politics and Why It Matters*. New Haven, CT: Yale University Press.

Carter, Ralph G., and James M. Scott. (2004) Taking the Lead: Congressional Foreign Policy Entrepreneurs and U.S. Foreign Policy. *Politics and Policy* 32: 34–71.

———. (2009) *Choosing to Lead: Understanding Congressional Foreign Policy Entrepreneurs*. Durham, NC: Duke University Press.

Chafe, William H. (1991) *The Unfinished Journey: America since World War II*. New York: Oxford University Press.

Chambers II, John Whiteclay. (1998) Jimmy Carter's Public Policy Ex-Presidency. *Political Science Quarterly* 112: 405–25.

Chayefsky, Paddy. (1976) *Network*. New York: Pocket Books.

Choate, Pat. (1991) *Agents of Influence: How Japan's Lobbyists in the United States Manipulate America's Political and Economic System*. New York: Knopf.

Chubb, John E., and Paul E. Peterson. (1989) *Can the Government Govern?* Washington, DC: Brookings Institution Press.

Cigler, Allan J., and Burdett A. Loomis. (1998) *Interest Group Politics*. Washington, DC: Congressional Quarterly Press.

Cirincione, Joseph, Jessica Mathews, George Perkovich, and Alexis Orton. (2004) *WMD in Iraq: Evidence and Implications*. Washington, DC: Carnegie Endowment.

Clarke, Duncan. (1987) Why State Can't Lead. *Foreign Policy*, pp. 128–42.

Clarke, Richard. (2004) *Against All Enemies: Inside America's War on Terror*. New York: Free Press.

Clausewitz, Carl von. (1983) *On War*. London: Penguin.

Clinton, Bill, and Al Gore, Jr. (1992) *Putting People First: How We Can All Change America*. New York: Random House.

Clodfelter, Mark. (1989) *The Limits of Air Power: The American Bombing of North Vietnam*. New York: Free Press.

Coates, James. (1987) *Armed and Dangerous: The Rise of the Survivalist Right*. New York: Noonday Press.

Coates, James, and Michael Kilian. (1985) *Heavy Losses: The Dangerous Decline of American Defense*. New York: Penguin Press.

Cochran, Thomas B., William M. Arkin, Robert S. Norris, and Milton M. Hoenig. (1987) *Nuclear Weapons Databook*. Cambridge, MA: Ballinger Press.

Cohen, Bernard C. (1963) *The Press and Foreign Policy*. Princeton, NJ: Princeton University Press.

———. (1973) *The Public's Impact on Foreign Policy*. Boston, MA: Little, Brown.

Cohen, David B., Chris J. Dolan, and Jerel A. Rosati. (2002) A Place at the Table: The Emerging Roles of the White House Chief of Staff. *Congress and the Presidency*.

Cohen, Eliot A. (1984) Constraints on America's Conduct of Small Wars. *International Security* 9: 151–81.

———. (1991) After the Battle. *New Republic*, April 1, pp. 19–26.

Cohen, Jeffrey E. (2008) *The Presidency in the Era of 24-Hour News*. Princeton, NJ: Princeton University Press.

Cohen, Stephen D. (1988) *The Making of United States International Economic Policy: Principles, Problems, and Proposals for Reform* (3rd ed.). New York: Praeger.

Cohen, Stephen D. (2000) *The Making of United States International Economic Policy: Principles, Problems, and Proposals for Reform* (5th ed.). New York: Praeger.

Cohen, William I. (1987) *Empire Without Tears: America's Foreign Relations, 1921–1933*. New York: Knopf.

Cole, Leonard. (1988) *Clouds of Secrecy: The Army's Germ Warfare Tests over Populated Areas*. Totowa, NJ: Rowman and Littlefield.

Coll, Steve. (2004) *Ghost Wars: The Secret History of the CIA, Afghanistan, and Bin Laden, from the Soviet Invasion to September 10, 2001*. New York: Penguin.

Combs, Jerald. (1985) *American Diplomatic History*. Berkeley: University of California Press.

Commission on the Roles and Capabilities of the United States Intelligence Community. (1996) *Preparing for the 21st Century: An Appraisal of U.S. Intelligence* (http://

www.gpo.gov/fdsys/pkg/GPO-INTELLIGENCE/content-detail.html).

Conason, Joe. (1990) The Iraq Lobby. *New Republic*, October 1, pp. 14–17.

Conley, Richard S. (2004) *Transforming the American Polity: George W. Bush and the War on Terrorism*. Upper Saddle River, NJ: Prentice Hall.

Cooper, Matthew, and Melinda Liu. (1997, February 10) Bright Light. *Newsweek*, pp. 22–29.

Cordesman, Anthony H. (2012) Afghanistan: The Death of a Strategy. *CSIS: Center for Strategic & International Studies*, February 27.

Corwin, Edward S. (1957) *The President: Office and Powers, 1787–1957*. New York: New York University Press.

Council on Foreign Relations. (1986) *Annual Report, 1985–1986*. New York: Council on Foreign Relations.

Council on Foreign Relations. (1996) *Making Intelligence Smarter: The Future of U.S. Intelligence*.

Cox, Michael. (2002) September 11th and U.S. Hegemony—Or Will the 21st Century Be American Too? *International Studies Perspectives* 3: 53–70.

Crabb, Cecil V., Jr., and Pat M. Holt. (1992) *Invitation to Struggle: Congress, the President, and Foreign Policy*. Washington, DC: Congressional Quarterly Press.

Crapol, Edward P. (1992) *Women and American Foreign Policy: Lobbyists, Critics, and Insiders*. Wilmington, DE: Scholarly Resources.

Crile, George. (2003) *Charlie Wilson's War*. New York: Atlantic Monthly Press.

Cronin, Thomas E. (1979) Presidential Power Revised and Reappraised. *Western Political Quarterly* 32: 381–95.

Cronin, Thomas E., and Michael A. Genovese. (2004) *The Paradoxes of the American Presidency*. New York: Oxford University Press.

Crosby, Harry. (1991) Too at Home Abroad: Swilling Beer, Licking Boots, and Ignoring the Natives with One of Jim Baker's Finest. *Washington Monthly*, September, pp. 16–20.

Crouse, Timothy. (1972) *The Boys on the Bus*. New York: Ballantine Books.

Crowley, Michael. (2004) Playing Defense: Bush's Disastrous Homeland Security Department. *New Republic*, March 15, pp. 17–21.

Crowley, Michael. (2009) The Reinvention of Robert Gates. *New Republic*, November 19, 2009.

D'Antonio, Michael. (1993) *Atomic Harvest: Hanford and the Lethal Toll of America's Nuclear Arsenal*. New York: Crown.

Daalder, Ivo H., and I. M. Destler. (2009) *In the Shadow of the Oval Office: Profiles of the National Security Advisers and the Presidents They Served—From JFK to George W. Bush*. New York: Simon and Schuster.

Daalder, Ivo H., and James M. Lindsay. (2003) *America Unbound: The Bush Revolution in Foreign Policy*. Washington, DC: Brookings Institution Press.

Dahl, Robert A. (1967) *Pluralist Democracy in the United States: Conflict and Consent*. Chicago, IL: Rand McNally.

———. (1978) Pluralism Revisited. *Comparative Politics* 10: 191–203.

———. (1982) *Dilemmas of Pluralist Democracy: Autonomy vs. Control*. New Haven, CT: Yale University Press.

Dallek, Robert. (1991) *Lone Star Rising: Lyndon Johnson and His Times, 1908–1960*. New York: Oxford University Press.

Danner, Mark. (1997) Marooned in the Cold War: America, the Alliance, and the Quest for a Vanished World. *World Policy Journal* 14: 1–23.

———. (2004a) Abu Ghraib: The Hidden Story. *The New York Review of Books*, October 7, p. 44.

———. (2004b) Torture and Truth. *New York Review of Books*, June 10, p. 47.

Danner, Mark. (2009) *Torture and Terror: America, Abu Ghraib and the War on Terror*. New York: New York Review of Books.

Davidson, Janine A. (2005) *Learning to Lift the Fog of Peace: The U.S. Military in Stability and Reconstruction Operations*. Ph.D. dissertation, University of South Carolina.

Davidson, Janine A. (2010) *Lifting the Fog of Peace: How Americans Learned to Learned to Fight Modern War*. Ann Arbor: University of Michigan Press.

Davis, T. R., and S. M. Lynn-Jones. (1987) City upon a Hill. *Foreign Policy* 66: 20–38.

Davis, Vincent. (1967) *The Admiral's Lobby*. Chapel Hill: University of North Carolina Press.

de Tocqueville, Alexis. (1945) *Democracy in America*. New York: Vintage.

Dean, John. (1977) *Blind Ambition*. New York: Pocket Books.

Deering, Christopher J. (2002) Alarms and Patrols: Legislative Oversight in Foreign and Defense Policy. In *Congress and the Politics of Foreign Policy*, edited by Colton C. Campbell, Nicol C. Rae, and John F. Stack Jr., pp. 112–38. Upper Saddle River, NJ: Prentice Hall.

Deese, David A. (1994) *The New Politics of American Foreign Policy*. New York: St. Martin's Press.

Deibel, Terry L. (1991) Bush's Foreign Policy: Mastery and Inaction. *Foreign Policy* 84: 3–23.

DeLaet, C. James, Charles M. Rowling, and James M. Scott. (2007) Partisanship, Ideology, and Weapons of Mass Destruction in the Post-Cold War Congress: The Chemical Weapons and Comprehensive Test Ban Cases. *Illinois Political Science Review* 11: 2–35.

DeLaet, C. James, and James M. Scott. (2006) Treaty-Making and Partisan Politics: Arms Control and the U.S. Senate, 1960–2001. *Foreign Policy Analysis* 2: 177–200.

Destler, I. M. (1972) *Presidents, Bureaucrats, and Foreign Policy*. Princeton, NJ: Princeton University Press.

———. (1994) A Government Divided: The Security Complex and the Economic Complex. In *The New Politics of American Foreign Policy*, edited by David A. Deese, pp. 132–47. New York: St. Martin's Press.

———. (1996) *The National Economic Council: A Work in Progress*. Washington, DC: Brookings Institution Press.

———. (2005) *American Trade Politics*. Washington, DC: Brookings Institution Press.

Destler, I. M. (2009) Jonestown: Will Obama's National Security Council Be Dramatically Different? *Foreign Affairs*, April 30.

Destler, I. M., Leslie H. Gelb, and Anthony Lake. (1984) *Our Own Worst Enemy: The Unmaking of American Foreign Policy*. New York: Simon and Schuster.

Devine, Robert A. (1974) *Foreign Policy and U.S. Presidential Elections: 1952–1960*. New York: New Viewpoints.

DeYoung, Karen. (2009) Obama's NSC Will Get New Power. *Washington Post*, February 8, p. A1.

Diamond, John, and Brianna B. Piec. (2002) Thousands March in Support of Israel: Pro-Israel Lobby Remains Strong Force in D.C. *Knight Rider/Tribune News Service*, April 15.

Diamond, Larry. (2005) *Squandered Victory: The American Occupation and the Bungled Effort to Bring Democracy to Iraq*. New York: Times Books.

Diehl, Jackson. (2005) The Rice Touch. *Washington Post*, May 9, p. A23.

Dilanian, Ken. (2009) Clinton Adopts Low Key Style at State Dept. *USA Today*, June 10.

Dizard, Wilson P. (2001) *Digital Diplomacy: U.S. Foreign Policy in the Information Age*. Westport, CT: Greenwood Press.

Dolan, Chris J. (2001) *Striking a Balance: Presidential Power and the National Economic Council*. Columbia: University of South Carolina.

Dolan, Chris J., and Jerel A. Rosati. (2006) U.S. Foreign Economic Policy and the Significance of the National Economic Council. *International Studies Perspectives* 7: 102–23.

Donner, Frank M. (1981) *The Age of Surveillance*. New York: Vintage.

Donovan, John C. (1974) *The Cold Warriors: A Policy-Making Elite*. Lexington, MA: D.C. Heath.

Dorman, Shawn, ed. (2005) *Inside a U.S. Embassy: How the Foreign Service Works for America*. Washington, DC: American Foreign Service Association.

Dower, John W. (1986) *War without Mercy: Race and Power in the Pacific War*. New York: Pantheon.

Doyle, Michael W. (1986) *Empires*. Ithaca, NY: Cornell University Press.

———. (1997) *Ways of War and Peace: Realism, Liberalism, and Socialism*. New York: W.W. Norton.

Draper, Theodore. (1997) Is the CIA Still Necessary? *New York Review of Books*, August 14, p. 5.

Drew, Elizabeth. (2009) The Thirty Days of Barack Obama. *New York Review of Books*, March 26 (http://www.nybooks.com/articles/22450).

Drezner, Daniel. (2003) Barely Managing. *New Republic Online*, NP.

Duffy, Michael, and Elaine Shannon. (2005) Condi on the Rise. *Time*, March 20, pp. 36–38.

Dylan, Bob. (1964) *The Times They Are A-Changin'*. Columbia Records.

Eckes, Alfred E., Jr. (1995) *Opening America's Market: U.S. Foreign Trade Policy Since 1776*. Chapel Hill: University of North Carolina.

Edwards III, George C., and Stephen J. Wayne. (2005) *Presidential Leadership: Politics and Policy Making*. New York: Wadsworth Publishing.

Edwards III, James C. (2009) *The Strategic President: Persuasion and Opportunity in Presidential Leadership*. Princeton, NJ: Princeton University Press.

Ehrman, John. (1995) *The Rise of Neoconservatism: Intellectuals and Foreign Affairs 1945–1994*. New Haven, CT: Yale University Press.

Eichenwald, Kurt. (2012) The Deafness before the Storm. *New York Times*. September 10, 2012 (at http://www.nytimes.com/2012/09/11/opinion/the-bush-white-house-was-deaf-to-9-11-warnings.html?_r=1).

Elliott, Kim Andrew. (1990) Too Many Voices of America. *Foreign Policy*, Winter, pp. 113–31.

Elliott, Michael. (2002) They Had a Plan. *Time*, August 12, pp. 28–43.

Elliott, Michael, and Massimo Calabresi. (2004) Is Condi the Problem? *Time*, April 5, pp. 32–37.

Emery, Fred. (1994) *Watergate: The Corruption of American Politics and the Fall of Richard Nixon*. New York: Times Books.

Engel, Matthew. (2002) U.S. Media Cowed by Patriotic Fever, Says CBS Star. *Guardian*, May 17.

Epstein, Barbara. (1991) *Political Protest and Cultural Revolution: Nonviolent Direct Action in the 1970s and 1980s.* Berkeley and Los Angeles: University of California Press.

Epstein, Edward Jay. (1973) *News from Nowhere: Television and the News.* New York: Vintage.

Erikson, Robert S. (2001) The 2000 Presidential Election in Historical Perspective. *Political Science Quarterly* 116: 29–52.

Erskine, H. G. (1962) The Polls: The Informed Public. *Public Opinion Quarterly* 26: 669–77.

———. (1963) The Polls: Textbook Knowledge. *Public Opinion Quarterly* 27: 133–41.

Etheredge, Lloyd S. (1985) *Can Governments Learn? American Foreign Policy and Central American Revolutions.* New York: Pergamon Press.

Evangelista, Matthew. (1989) Issue Area and Foreign Policy Revisited. *International Organization* 43: 147–71.

Evans, Sara. (1979) *Personal Politics: The Roots of Women's Liberation in the Civil Rights Movement & the New Left.* New York: Vintage.

Fallows, James. (1986) *National Defense.* New York: Vintage Press.

———. (2004) Blind into Baghdad. *Atlantic Monthly*, January/February, pp. 52–74.

Farber, Farber, ed. (2008) *Security vs. Liberty: Conflicts Between Civil Liberties and National Security in American History.* New York: Sage Foundation.

Farmer, Edward. (1999) From Admiration to Confrontation. *Media Studies Journal*, 136–45.

Feeney, Mark. (2001) All the World's His Stage Revered or Reviled, Henry Kissinger Remains Diplomatic in Spotlight's Glare. *Boston Globe*, June 21.

Feinberg, Richard E. (1983) *The Intemperate Zone: The Third World Challenge to U.S. Foreign Policy.* New York: W.W. Norton.

Fenno, Richard F., Jr. (1978) *Home Style: House Members in Their Districts.* Boston, MA: Little, Brown.

Ferguson, Niall. (2004) *Colossus: The Rise and Fall of the American Empire.* New York: Penguin.

Fessenden, Helen. (2005) The Limits of Intelligence Reform. *Foreign Affairs* 84: 106–20.

Filkins, Dexter. (2008) *Forever War.* New York: Knopf.

Fineman, Howard. (2002) How Bush Did It. *Newsweek*, November 18, pp. 29–38.

———. (2003) Bush and God. *Newsweek*, March 10, pp. 22–30.

Fineman, Howard, and Martha Brant. (2001) This Is Our Life Now. *Newsweek*, December 2, pp. 21–29.

Finkel, David. (2009) *The Good Soldiers.* New York: Farrar, Straus and Giroux.

Fiorina, Morris P. (1981) *Retrospective Voting in American National Elections.* New Haven, CT: Yale University Press.

———. (1996) *Divided Government.* Boston, MA: Allyn and Bacon.

Fisher, Louis. (2004a) *The Politics of Executive Privilege.* Durham, NC: Carolina Academic Press.

———. (2004b) *Presidential War Power.* Manhattan: University Press of Kansas.

———. (2007) Invoking Inherent Presidential Powers: A Primer. *Presidential Studies Quarterly* 37: 1–22.

Fiske, Susan T., and Shelley E. Taylor. (1999) *Social Cognition.* New York: McGraw-Hill.

Fleisher, Richard, Jon R. Bond, Glen S. Krutz, and Stephen Hanna. (2000) The Demise of the Two Presidencies. *American Politics Quarterly* 28: 3–25.

Flynn, Stephen. (2004) *America the Vulnerable: How Our Government Is Failing to Protect Us from Terrorism.* New York: HarperCollins.

Fordham, Benjamin. (1998) The Politics of Threat Perception and the Use of Force: A Political Economy Model of U.S. Uses of Force, 1949–1994. *International Studies Quarterly* 42: 567–90.

Foreign Policy Analysis in 20/20: A Symposium. (2003). *International Studies Review* 5: 155–202.

Franck, Thomas, and Edward Weisband. (1980) *Foreign Policy by Congress.* New York: Oxford University Press.

Fraser, Steve, and Gary Gerstle, eds. (1989) *The Rise and Fall of the New Deal Order, 1930–1980.* Princeton, NJ: Princeton University Press.

Freedberg, Sydney J., Jr. (2001) Shoring up America. *National Journal* 33: 3238–45.

Freeland, Chrystia. (2009) Lunch with Larry Summers. *Financial Times*, July 10.

Friedman, Matthew J. (2004) Acknowledging the Psychiatric Cost of War. *New England Journal of Medicine* 351: 75–78.

———. (1999) *The Lexus and the Olive Tree.* New York: Farrar, Straus, and Giroux.

Friedman, Thomas L., and Elaine Sciolino. (1993) Clinton and Foreign Issues: Spasms of Attention. *New York Times*, March 22, p. A3.

Fukuyama, Francis. (1989) The End of History? *National Interest* 16: 3–18.

Fulbright, J. William. (1966) *The Arrogance of Power.* New York: Vintage.

Fullilove, Michael. (2008) *Hope or Glory? The Presidential Election and U.S. Foreign Policy.* Washington, DC: Brookings Institution Press.

Gaddis, John Lewis. (1982) *Strategies of Containment: A Critical Appraisal of Postwar American National Security Policy.* New York: Oxford University Press.

———. (2005) Grand Strategy Is the Second Term. *Foreign Affairs* 84: 2–15.

Gallagher, Carole. (1993) *American Ground Zero: The Secret Nuclear War.* Cambridge, MA: MIT Press.

Gamson, William A. (1975) *The Strategy of Social Protest.* Homewood, IL: Dorsey Press.

Gans, Herbert J. (1979) *Deciding What's News: A Study of CBS Evening News, NBC Nightly News, Newsweek, and Time.* New York: Pantheon.

Gardner, Richard N. (1980) *Sterling-Dollar Diplomacy in Current Perspective: The Origins and Prospects of Our International Economic Order.* New York: Columbia University Press.

———. (1983) Selling America in the Marketplace of Ideas. *New York Times Magazine,* March 20, pp. 44, 58–61.

Garrison, Jean, Jerel Rosati, and James Scott. (2012, April) *President Obama and the "Team of Rivals" Model in Foreign Policy Decision Making: Presidential Style, Decision-Making Structure, and Policymaking Consequences.* Paper presented at the 2012 International Studies Association Annual Conference, San Diego, California, April 1–4.

Garson, David G. (1978) *Group Theories of Politics.* Beverly Hills, CA: Sage.

Garthoff, Raymond L. (1989) *Reflections on the Cuban Missile Crisis.* Washington, DC: Brookings Institution Press.

Gates, Robert. (2012) Hillary Clinton: Diplomat. *Time Magazine,* April 18 (http://www.time.com/time/specials/packages/article/0,28804,2111975_2111976_2111951,00.html).

Geithner, Timothy F. (2009) *Remarks Before the Economic Club of Washington,* April 25.

Gelb, Leslie H. (1972) The Essential Domino: American Politics and Vietnam. *Foreign Affairs* 50: 459–75.

Gelb, Leslie H., and Richard K. Betts. (1979) *The Irony of Vietnam: The System Worked.* New York: Warner.

Gellman, Barton. (2008) *Angler: The Cheney Vice Presidency.* New York: Penguin.

Gellman, Barton, and Dafnia Linzer. (2005) Pursuing the Limits of Wartime Powers. *Washington Post,* December 18, p. A1.

Gelpi, Christopher, Peter D. Feaver, and Jason Reifler. (2005/2006) Success Matters: Casualty Sensitivity and the War in Iraq. *International Security* 30: 7–46.

George, Alexander L. (1972) The Case for Multiple Advocacy in Making Foreign Policy. *American Political Science Review* 66: 751–85.

———. (1980a) Domestic Constraints on Regime Change in U.S. Foreign Policy: The Need for Policy Legitimacy. In *Changes in the International System,* edited by Ole R. Holsti, Randolph Siverson, and Alexander L. George, pp. 233–262. Boulder, CO: Westview Press.

———. (1980b) *Presidential Decision Making in Foreign Policy: The Effective Use of Information and Advice.* Boulder, CO: Westview Press.

———. (1993) *Bridging the Gap: Theory and Practice in Foreign Policy.* Washington, DC: U.S. Institute of Peace.

George, Alexander L., and Eric K. Stern. (2001) Harnessing Conflict in Foreign Policy Making: From Devil's Advocate to Multiple Advocacy. *Presidential Studies Quarterly* 31: 484–508.

George, Alexander L., and Juliette L. George. (1956) *Woodrow Wilson and Colonel House: A Personality Study.* New York: Dover.

George, Alexander L., and Richard Smoke. (1974) *Deterrence in American Foreign Policy: Theory and Practice.* New York: Columbia University Press.

Gerbner, George, and George Marvanyi. (1977) The Many Worlds of the World's Press. *Journal of Communication* 27: 52–66.

Gerbner, George, Larry Gross, Michael Morgan, and Nancy Signorielli. (1982) Charting the Mainstream: Television's Contributions to Political Orientations. *Journal of Communication* 32: 100–27.

Gibbs, David N. (2002) Forgotten Coverage of Afghan "Freedom Fighters": The Villains of Today's News Were Heroes in the '80s. *Extra!* January/February, pp. 13–16.

Gibbs, Nancy. (1997) The Many Lives of Madeleine. *Time,* February 17, pp. 52–61.

Gilpin, Robert. (1981) *War and Change in World Politics.* Cambridge, UK: Cambridge University Press.

Ginsberg, Benjamin, and Martin Shefter. (1990) *Politics by Other Means: The Declining Importance of Elections in America.* New York: Basic Books.

Gitlin, Todd. (1985) *Inside Prime Time.* New York: Pantheon.

———. (1987) *The Sixties: Years of Hope, Days of Rage.* New York: Bantam.

Glad, Betty. (1980) *Jimmy Carter*. New York: W.W. Norton.

Gladwell, Malcolm. (2010) Small Change: Why the Revolution Will Not Be Tweeted. *The New Yorker*, October 4.

Glasser, Susan B., and Michael Grunwald. (2005) DHS Undermined from the Start. *Washington Post*, December 22, p. A1.

Glennon, Michael J. (1991) *Constitutional Diplomacy*. Princeton, NJ: Princeton University Press.

Goddard, C. Roe. (1993) *U.S. Foreign Economic Policy and the Latin American Debt Issue*. New York: Garland Publishers.

Godson, Roy. (2000) *Dirty Tricks or Trump Cards: U.S. Covert Action and Counterintelligence*. New Brunswick, NJ: Transaction Publishers.

Goldgeier, James. (2000) *Not Whether but When: The U.S. Decision to Enlarge*. Washington, DC: Brookings Institution Press.

Goldman, Eric F. (1961) *The Crucial Decade—And After: America, 1945–1960*. New York: Random House.

Goldman, Kjell. (1988) *Change and Stability in Foreign Policy: The Problems and Possibilities of Détente*. Princeton, NJ: Princeton University Press.

Goldsmith, Jack L. (2007) *The Terror Presidency: Law and Judgment Inside the Bush Administration*. New York: W.W. Norton.

Goldstein, Judith. (1988) Ideas, Institutions, and American Trade Policy. *International Organization* 42: 179–217.

Goodman, Melvin A. (1997) Ending the CIA's Cold War Legacy. *Foreign Policy* 106: 128–43.

Goodwin, Doris Kearns. (1991) *Lyndon Johnson and the American Dream*. New York: St. Martin's Press.

Goodwin, Jacob. (1985) *Brotherhood of Arms: General Dynamics and Business of Defending America*. New York: Times Books.

Gordon, Michael R. (2004) The Strategy to Secure Iraq Did Not Foresee a 2nd War. *New York Times*, October 19, p. A1.

Gordon, Michael, and Bernard Trainor. (1995) *The General's War: The Inside Story of the Conflict in the Gulf*. Boston, MA: Little, Brown.

Gorman, Siobhan. (2005) Cutbacks Likely Ahead for NSA. *Baltimore Sun*, October 27, p. 1A.

Graber, Doris A. (2009) *Mass Media and American Politics*. Washington, DC: CQ Press.

Green, Joshua. (2010) Inside Man. *The Atlantic*, April.

Greenfield, Meg. (2001) *Washington*. New York: Public Affairs.

Greenstein, Fred I. (1994) The Two Leadership Styles of William Jefferson Clinton. *Political Psychology* 15: 351–62.

———. (2009) *The Presidential Difference: Leadership Style from FDR to Barack Obama*. New York: Free Press.

Gregory, William H. (1989) *The Defense Procurement Mess*. Lexington, MA: Lexington Books.

Greider, William. (1987) *Secrets of the Temple: How the Federal Reserve Runs the Country*. New York: Simon and Schuster.

Griffith, Robert. (1987) *The Politics of Fear: Joseph R. McCarthy and the Senate*. New York: Hayden.

Grinter, Lawrence E. (1974) Bargaining Between Saigon and Washington: Dilemmas of Linkage Politics during War. *Orbis* 18: 837–65.

Grose, Peter. (1995) *Gentleman Spy: The Life of Allen Dulles*. Boston, MA: Houghton Mifflin.

Grunwald, Michael, and Susan Glasser. (2005) Brown's Turf Wars Sapped Fema's Strength. *Washington Post*, December 23, p. A1.

Hadley, Arthur T. (1986) *The Straw Giant—Triumph and Failure: America's Armed Forces*. New York: Random House.

Halberstam, David. (1969) *The Best and the Brightest*. New York: Random House.

———. (1986) *The Reckoning*. New York: Avon.

———. (2000) *The Powers That Be*. Champaign: University of Illinois.

———. (2001) *War in a Time of Peace: Bush, Clinton, and the Generals*. New York: Scribner.

Halberstam, David. (1998) *The Children*. New York: Random House.

Halberstam, David. (2007) *The Coldest Winter: America and the Korean War*. New York: Hyperion.

Hallin, Daniel C. (1986) *The Uncensored War: The Media and Vietnam*. Los Angeles: University of California Press.

Halperin, Morton H. (1974) *Bureaucratic Politics and Foreign Policy*. Washington, DC: Brookings Institution Press.

Halperin, Morton H., and Arnold Kanter. (1973) *Readings in American Foreign Policy: A Bureaucratic Perspective*. Boston, MA: Little, Brown.

Halperin, Morton H., and David Halperin. (1984) The Key West Key. *Foreign Policy* 52: 114–30.

Hamilton, Lee H. (2006) The Making of U.S. Foreign Policy: The Roles of the President and Congress over

Four Decades. In *Rivals for Power: Presidential-Congressional Relations*, edited by Jordan Tama, p. 273. New York: Rowman and Littlefield.

Hamilton, Lee H., and Jordan Tama. (2003) *Creative Tension: The Foreign Policy Roles of the President and Congress.* Washington, DC: Woodrow Wilson Center Press.

Hammer, Joshua. (2004) Uncivil Military. *New Republic*, March 1, pp. 16–18.

Hand, Mark. (2005) State Department Sets up Rapid Response Operation. *PR Week*, November 21, p. 3.

Haney, Patrick J., and Walt Vanderbush. (1999) The Role of Ethnic Interest Groups in U.S. Foreign Policy: The Case of the Cuban American National Foundation. *International Studies Quarterly* 43: 341–61.

Hannerz, Ulf. (2004) *Foreign News: Exploring the World of Foreign Correspondents.* Chicago, IL: University of Chicago Press.

Hansen, Allen C. (1984) *U.S. Information Agency: Public Diplomacy in the Computer Age.* New York: Praeger.

Harman, Jane. (2009) What the CIA Hid from Congress. *Los Angeles Times*, July 25 (http://articles.latimes.com/2009/jul/25/opinion/oe-harman25).

Harris, John F. (2005) *The Survivor: Bill Clinton in the White House.* New York: Random House.

Hartz, Louis. (1955) *The Liberal Tradition in America.* New York: Harcourt Brace and World.

Hastedt, Glenn P., and Anthony J. Eksterowicz. (1993) Presidential Leadership in the Post Cold War Era. *Presidential Studies Quarterly* 23: 445–58.

Hastings, Michael. (2010) The Runaway General. *Rolling Stone*, June 25.

———. (2011) King David's War. *Rolling Stone*, February 11.

Havemann, Judith. (1989) State Department Acknowledges Sex Bias. *Washington Post*, April 20, pp. A1, A20.

Heclo, Hugh. (1977) *A Government of Strangers: Executive Politics in Washington.* Washington, DC: Brookings Institution Press.

———. (1978) Issue Networks and the Executive Establishment. In *The New American Political System*, edited by Anthony King, pp. 90–121. Washington, DC: American Enterprise Institute.

———. (1988) The In-and-Outer System. *Political Science Quarterly* 102: 37–56.

Heilemann, John. (2009) Inside Obama's Brain Trust. *New York Times Magazine*, March 2 (http://nymag.com/news/politics/55511/).

Heilemann, John, and Mark Halperin. (2010) *Game Change: Obama and the Clintons, McCain and Palin, and the Race of a Lifetime.* New York: Harper.

Helms, Jesse. (1995) For a More Effective State Department. *Freedom Review* 26: 8.

Hendrickson, David C. (2004) A Dissenter's Guide to Foreign Policy. *World Policy Journal*, (Spring): 102–13.

Henkin, Louis. (1972) *Foreign Affairs and the Constitution.* Mineola, NY: Foundation Press.

———. (1987) Foreign Affairs and the Constitution. *Foreign Affairs* 66: 284–310.

———. (1990) *Constitutionalism, Democracy, and Foreign Affairs.* New York: Columbia University Press.

———. (1996) *Foreign Affairs and the Constitution.* Mineola, NY: Foundation Press.

Herek, Gregory M., Irving L. Janis, and Paul Huth. (1987) Decision Making during International Crises: Is Quality of Process Related to Outcome? *Journal of Conflict Resolution* 31: 203–26.

Hermann, Charles F. (1969) International Crises as a Situational Variable. In *International Politics and Foreign Policy*, edited by James N. Rosenau, pp. 409–21. New York: Free Press.

———. (1990) Changing Course: When Governments Choose to Redirect Foreign Policy. *International Studies Quarterly* 34: 3–21.

Hermann, Edward S., and Robert W. McChesney. (1997) *Global Reach: The Missionaries of Global Capitalism.* New York: Continuum International Publishing.

Hermann, Margaret G., and Charles F. Hermann. (1989) Who Makes Foreign Policy Decisions and How: An Empirical Inquiry. *International Studies Quarterly* 33: 361–88.

Hermann, Margaret G., and Robert B. Woyach. (1994) Toward Reflection, Evaluation, and Integration in International Studies: An Editorial Perspective. *Mershon International Studies Review* 38: 1–10.

Hersh, Burton. (1992) *The Old Boys: The American Elite and the Origins of the CIA.* New York: Scribner.

Hersh, Seymour H. (1983) *The Price of Power: Kissinger in Nixon White House.* New York: Summit Books.

———. (2004) The Gray Zone: How a Secret Program Came to Abu Ghraib. *New Yorker*, May 24, p. 38.

Hersman, Rebecca K. C. (2000) *Friends and Foes: How Congress and the President Really Make Foreign Policy.* Washington, DC: Brookings Institution Press.

Herspring, Dale R. (1992) Practitioners and Political Scientists. *PS: Political Science & Politics* 25: 554–58.

Hertzke, Allen D. (1988) *Representing God in Washington: The Role of Religious Lobbies in the American Polity*. Knoxville: University of Tennessee Press.

Hess, Stephen. (1981) *The Washington Reporters*. Washington, DC: Brookings Institution Press.

———. (1996) *International News and Foreign Correspondents*. Washington, DC: Brookings Institution Press.

Hess, Stephen, and Michael Nelson. (1985) Foreign Policy: Dominance and Decisiveness in Presidential Elections. In *The Elections of 1984*, edited by Michael Nelson, pp. 141–52. Washington, DC: Congressional Quarterly Press.

Hilsman, Roger. (1964) *To Move a Nation: The Politics of Foreign Policy in the Administration of John F. Kennedy*. New York: Delta.

Himmelstein, Jerome L. (1991) *To the Right: The Transformation of American Conservatism*. Berkeley and Los Angeles: University of California Press.

Hinckley, Barbara. (1994) *Less than Meets the Eye: Congress, the President, and Foreign Policy*. Chicago, IL: University of Chicago Press.

Hirsh, Michael. (2002) Bush and the World. *Foreign Affairs* 81: 18–43.

Hirsh, Michael, and Evan Thomas. (2009) The Reeducation of Larry Summers. *Newsweek*, March 2, pp. 24–27.

Hoagland, Jim. (2009) White House Fault Lines. *Washington Post*, July 12 (http://www.washingtonpost.com/wp-dyn/content/article/2009/07/10/AR2009071002936.html).

Hodgson, Godfrey. (1973) The Establishment. *Foreign Policy*, pp. 3–40.

———. (1976) *America in Our Time*. Princeton, NJ: Princeton University Press.

Hoffmann, Stanley. (1968) *Gulliver's Troubles, or the Setting of American Foreign Policy*. New York: McGraw-Hill.

———. (1977) An American Social Science: International Relations. *Daedalus* 106: 41–60.

Holsti, K. J. (1982) *Why Nations Realign: Foreign Policy Restructuring in the Postwar World*. London: Allen and Unwin.

Holsti, Ole R. (1967) Cognitive Dynamics and Images of the Enemy: Dulles and Russia. In *Image and Reality in World Politics*, edited by John C. Farrell and Asa P. Smith, pp. 16–39. New York: Columbia University Press.

———. (1971) Crisis, Stress and Decision-Making. *International Social Science Journal* 23: 53–67.

———. (1990) Crisis Management. In *Psychological Dimensions of War*, edited by Betty Glad, pp. 116–42. Newberry Park, CA: Sage.

———. (1992) Public Opinion and Foreign Policy: Challenges to the Almond-Lippmann Consensus. *International Studies Quarterly* 36: 439–66.

Holsti, Ole R., and James N. Rosenau. (1984) *American Leadership in World Affairs: Vietnam and the Breakdown of Consensus*. New York: Allen and Unwin.

Honicker, Clifford T. (1989) America's Radiation Victims: The Hidden Files. *New York Times Magazine*, November 19, pp. 38–41, 98–103, 120.

Hook Steven, and James M. Scott, eds. (2012) *U.S. Foreign Policy Today: American Renewal?* Washington, DC: CQ Press.

Hoopes, Townsend. (1973) *The Limits of Intervention: An Inside Account of How the Johnson Policy of Escalation in Vietnam Was Reversed*. New York: David McKay.

Hopkins, Raymond F. (1978) Global Management Networks: The Internationalization of Domestic Bureaucracies. *International Social Science Journal* 30: 31–45.

Hosenball, Mark, Michael Isikoff, and Evan Thomas. (2003) Cheney's Long Path to War. *Newsweek*, November 17, p. 34.

Howe, Russell Warren, and Sarah Hays Trott. (1977) *The Power Peddlers: How Lobbyists Mold America's Foreign Policy*. New York: Doubleday.

Howell, William G., and Jon C. Pevehouse. (2007) *While Dangers Gather: Congressional Checks on Presidential War Powers*. Princeton, NJ: Princeton University Press.

Hoynes, William, and David Croteau. (1989) *Are You on the Nightline Guest List?* January–February, pp. 1–15.

Hrebenar, Ronald J., and Clive S. Thomas. (1995) The Japanese Lobby in Washington: How Different Is It? In *Interest Group Politics*, edited by Allan J. Cigler and Burdett A. Loomis, pp. 349–67. Washington, DC: Congressional Quarterly Press.

Hudson, Valerie M. (2005) Foreign Policy Analysis: Actor-Specific Theory and the Ground of International Relations. *Foreign Policy Analysis* 1: 1–30.

Hudson, Valerie M., and Christopher S. Vore. (1995) Foreign Policy Analysis Yesterday, Today, and Tomorrow. *Mershon International Studies Review* 39: 209–38.

Hulse, Carl. (2005) Senate G.O.P. Push for Plan on Ending War. *New York Times*, November 15, p. A1.

Huntington, Samuel P. (1957) *The Soldier and the State: The Theory and Politics of Civil-Military Relations*. Cambridge, MA: Harvard University Press.

———. (1961) *The Common Defense: Strategic Programs in National Politics*. New York: Columbia University Press.

———. (1981) *American Politics: The Promise of Disharmony*. Cambridge, MA: Harvard University Press.

———. (1988) The U.S.—Decline or Renewal? *Foreign Affairs* 67: 76–96.

———. (1996) *The Clash of Civilizations and the Remaking of World Order*. New York: Simon and Schuster.

———. (1997) The Erosion of American National Interests. *Foreign Affairs* 76: 28–49.

Ifill, Gwen. (1993) The Economic Czar Behind the Economic Czars. *New York Times*, March 22, p. A1.

Ikenberry, G. John. (1988) *Reasons of State: Oil Politics and the Capacities of American Government*. Ithaca, NY: Cornell University Press.

———. (1989) Rethinking the Origins of American Hegemony. *Political Science Quarterly* 104, 375–400.

———. (1992) A World Economy Restored: Expert Consensus and the Anglo-American Post-War Settlement. *International Organization* 46: 289–321.

———. (1996) Myth of Post-Cold War Chaos. *Foreign Affairs*, May/June.

———. (2002a) America's Imperial Ambition. *Foreign Affairs* 81: 2–15.

———. (2002b) Introduction. In *American Unrivaled: The Future of the Balance of Power*, edited by G. John Ikenberry, pp. 1–28. Ithaca, NY: Cornell University Press.

Immerman, Richard H. (1982) *The CIA in Guatemala: The Foreign Policy of Intervention*. Austin: University of Texas Press.

In Bob We Trust. (1994) *Economist*, December 10, p. 28.

Isaacson, Walter. (1999) Madeleine's War. *Time*, May 17, pp. 26–36.

Isaacson, Walter, and Evan Thomas. (1986) *The Wise Men: Six Friends and the World They Made*. New York: Touchstone.

Isenstadt, Alex. (2009) *Committee Will Investigate CIA* (http://www.politico.com/news/stories/0709/25094.html).

Isikoff, Michael. (2006) The Other Big Brother. *Newsweek*, January 30, pp. 32–34.

Issenburg, David. (2012) SIGIR Reports: Hey, Anybody Know What Happened to the $2 Billion? *Huffington Post*, February 6.

Iyengar, Shanto, and Donald R. Kinder. (1987) *News That Matters: Television and American Opinion*. Chicago, IL: University of Chicago Press.

Jacobson, Gary C. (2001) A House and Senate Divided: The Clinton Legacy and the Congressional Elections of 2000. *Political Science Quarterly* 116: 5–27.

Jackson, Michael Gordon Jackson. (2012) *A Dramatically Different NSC: President Obama's Use of the National Security Council*. Paper presented at the 2012 meeting of the Western Political Science Association, March 22–24, 2012.

James, Dorothy Buckman. (1974) *The Contemporary Presidency*. New York: Pegasus.

Jamieson, Kathleen Hall. (2003) *The Press Effect: Politicians, Journalists, and the Stories that Shape the Political World*. New York: Oxford University Press.

Janis, Irving L. (1982) *Groupthink*. New York: Houghton Mifflin.

Janis, Irving L., and Leon Mann. (1977) *Decision Making: A Psychological Analysis of Conflict, Choice, and Commitment*. New York: Free Press.

Jeffrey-Jones, Rhodri. (1989) *The CIA and American Democracy*. New Haven, CT: Yale University Press.

———. (1995) *Changing Differences: Women and the Shaping of American Foreign Policy, 1917–1994*. New Brunswick, NJ: Rutgers University Press.

Jentleson, Bruce W. (1987) American Commitments in the Third World: Theory vs. Practice. *International Organization* 41: 667–704.

———. (1992) The Pretty Prudent Public: Post-Vietnam American Opinion on the Use of Military Force. *International Studies Quarterly* 36: 49–74.

Jervis, Robert. (1976) *Perception and Misperception in International Politics*. Princeton, NJ: Princeton University Press.

Johnson, Haynes, and Bernard Gwertzman. (1968) *Fulbright: The Dissenter*. Garden City, NY: Doubleday and Co.

Johnson, Haynes, and Dan Balz. (2009) *The Battle for America 2008: The Story of an Extraordinary Election*. New York: Viking Books.

Johnson, Loch K. (1985) *The Making of International Agreements: Congress Confronts the Executive*. New York: New York University Press.

———. (1989) Covert Action and Accountability: Decision-Making for America's Foreign Policy. *International Studies Quarterly* 33: 81–109.

———. (1991) *America's Secret Power: The CIA in a Democratic Society*. New York: Oxford University Press.

———. (2000) *Bombs, Bugs, Drugs, and Thugs: Intelligence and America's Quest for Security*. New York: New York University Press.

———. (2004) The Contemporary Presidency: Presidents, Lawmakers, and Spies: Intelligence

Accountability in the United States. *Presidential Studies Quarterly* 34: 828–37.

———. (2005) Accountability and America's Secret Foreign Policy: Keeping a Legislative Eye on the Central Intelligence Agency. *Foreign Policy Analysis* 1: 99–120.

Johnson, Loch K., and James Wirtz. (2004) *Strategic Intelligence: Windows into a Secret World.* Los Angeles, CA: Roxbury Publishing.

Johnson, Simon. (2009) An Emerging Split That Matters: Treasury vs. The National Economic Council. *New York Times*, July 2 (http://economix.blogs.nytimes.com/2009/07/02/an-emerging-split-that-matters-treasury-vs-the-nec/).

Jones, Alex S. (1991) War in the Gulf: The Press; Process of News Reporting on Display. *Washington Post*, February 15, p. A9.

Jones, David C. (1982) What's Wrong with Our Defense Establishment. *New York Times Magazine*, November 7, pp. 38–42, 70–83.

Jordan, Hamilton. (1982) *Crisis: The Last Year of the Carter Presidency.* New York: G.P. Putnam's Sons.

Judis, John. (2010) The Unnecessary Fall. *New Republic*, September 2.

Judis, John B. (1989) K Street's Rise to Power of Special Interests to U.S. *In These Times*, November 1, p. 7.

———. (1990) The Japanese Megaphone. *New Republic*, January 22, pp. 20–25.

———. (1993) Old Master. *New Republic*, December 13, pp. 21–28.

Judt, Tony. (2004) Dreams of Empire. *New York Review of Books*, November 4.

Juster, Kenneth. (2001, December 6) *Globalization, Free Trade, and National Security: Remarks at Scarsdale Town and Village Civic Club.* Scarsdale, NY: BIS Public Affairs (http://www.bis.doc.gov/news/archive2001/globalizationnscarsdaleny.htm).

Juster, Kenneth I., and Simon Lazarus. (1997) *Making Economic Policy: An Assessment of the National Economic Council.* Washington, DC: Brookings Institution Press.

Kagan, Robert. (1996) *A Twilight Struggle: American Power and Nicaragua, 1977–1990.* New York: The Free Press.

Kahn, E. J., Jr. (1972) *The China Hands: America's Foreign Service Officers and What Befell Them.* New York: Viking Press.

Kalb, Madeleine G. (1981) *The Congo Cables: The Cold War in Africa from Eisenhower to Kennedy.* New York: Macmillan.

Kane, Paul, and Ben Pershing. (2009) Secret Program Fuels CIA-Congress Dispute. *Washington Post*, July 10 (www.washingtonpost.com/wp-dyn/content/article/2009/07/09/AR2009070903017.html).

Kaplan, David A. (2001) *The Accidental President.* New York: William Morrow.

Kaplan, Fred. (1983) *The Wizards of Armageddon.* New York: Touchstone.

Kaplan, Fred. (2010) The Transformer. *Foreign Policy*, September/October.

Kaplan, Lawrence F. (2004) State's Rights. *New Republic*, December 7, pp. 16–17.

Kaplan, Robert D. (1994) *The Arabists: The Romance of an American Elite.* New York: Free Press.

———. (2005) *Imperial Grunts: The American Military on the Ground.* New York: Random House.

Karp, Walter. (1989) Who Decides What Is News? (Hint: It's Not Journalists). *Utne Reader*, pp. 60–68.

Kassop, Nancy. (2003) The War Power and Its Limits. *Presidential Studies Quarterly* 33: 509–29.

Kaufman, Natalie Hevener, and David Whiteman. (1988) Opposition to Human Rights Treaties in the United States Senate: The Legacy of the Bricker Amendment. *Human Rights Quarterly* 10: 309–37.

Kearns, Doris. (1976) *Lyndon Johnson and the American Dream.* New York: New American Library.

Keating, Peter. (2009) The Good Soldier: Hillary Clinton as Secretary of State. *New York Magazine*, June 14 (http://nymag.com/daily/intel/2009/06/hillary_clinton_as_secretary_o.html).

Kellner, Douglas. (1991) *The Persian Gulf TV War.* Boulder, CO: Westview Press.

Kennan, George F. (1951) *American Diplomacy, 1900–1950.* New York: Mentor.

Kennedy, Paul. (1987) *The Rise and Fall of the Great Powers: Economic Change and Military Conflict from 1500 to 2000.* New York: Random House.

———. (1993) *Preparing for the Twenty-First Century.* New York: Random House.

———. (1999) The Next American Century? *World Policy Journal* 16: 52–58.

Keohane, Robert, and Joseph Nye, Jr. (2011) *Power and Interdependence* (4th ed.) New York: Longman.

Kessler, Glenn. (2003) U.S. Decision on Iraq Has Puzzling Past. *Washington Post*, January 12, p. A1.

Kessler, Glenn, and Thomas E. Ricks. (2004) Rice's NSC Tenure Complicates New Post: Failure to Manage Agency Infighting Cited. *Washington Post*, November 16, p. A7.

Kessler, Lauren. (1984) *The Dissident Press: Alternative Journalism in American History*. Beverly Hills, CA: Sage.

Kessler, Ronald. (1994) *The FBI: Inside the World's Most Powerful Law Enforcement Agency*. New York: Pocket Books.

Key, V. O., Jr. (1964) *Politics, Parties, and Pressure Groups*. New York: Thomas W. Crowell.

———. (1966) *The Responsible Electorate: Rationality in Presidential Voting, 1936–1960*. New York: Vintage Press.

Khong, Yuen Foong. (1992) *Analogies at War: Korea, Munich, Dien Bien Phu, and the Vietnam Decisions of 1965*. Princeton, NJ: Princeton University Press.

KilCullen, David. (2009) *The Accidental Guerrilla: Fighting Small Wars in the Midst of a Big One*. London: Hurst & Company.

Kindleberger, Charles P. (1977) U.S. Foreign Economic Policy, 1776–1976. *Foreign Affairs* 55: 395–417.

King, Geoff. (2002) *New Hollywood: An Introduction*. New York: Columbia University.

Kingdon, John W. (1984) *Agendas, Alternatives, and Public Policies*. Boston, MA: Little, Brown.

Kinnard, Douglas. (1977) *The War Managers*. Hanover, CT: University of New England.

Kirk, Jason. (2008) Indian-Americans and the U.S.–India Nuclear Agreement: Consolidation of an Ethnic Lobby? *Foreign Policy Analysis* 4: 275–300.

Kirchich, James. (2010) Turf Warrior. *New Republic*, January 25.

Kirschten, Dick. (1993) Rescuing Aid. *National Journal* 25: 2369–72.

Kissinger, Henry. (1957) *A World Restored: Metternich, Castlereagh, and the Problems of Peace*. Boston, MA: Houghton-Mifflin.

Kitfield, James. (1995) *Prodigal Soldiers: How the Generation of Officers Born of Vietnam Revolutionized the American Style of War*. New York: Simon and Schuster.

———. (2001) A Diplomat Handy with a Bayonet. *National Journal* 33: 250.

Knowledge, Power, and International Policy. (1992). *International Organization* 46: 1–390.

Knutsen, Trobjorn L. (1997) *A History of International Relations Theory*. Manchester, UK: Manchester University Press.

———. (1999) *The Rise and Fall of World Orders*. Manchester, UK: Manchester University Press.

Koen, Ross Y. (1974) *The China Lobby in American Politics*. New York: Harper and Row.

Keohane, Robert O., and Joseph S. Nye, Jr. (1977) *Power and Interdependence: World Politics in Transition*. Boston, MA: Little, Brown.

Kohut, Andrew. (1995) *A Content Analysis: International News Coverage Fits Public's Ameri-Centric Mood*. Washington, DC: Pew Research Center.

Kopp, Harry, and Charles Gillespie. (2008) *Career Diplomacy: Life and Work in the Foreign Service*. Washington, DC: Georgetown University Press.

Koppes, Clayton R., and Gregory D. Black. (1987) *Hollywood Goes to War*. New York: Free Press.

Korb, Lawrence J. (1996) A Military Monopoly. *New York Times*, December 21, p. 25.

———. (2004) Fixing the Mix: How to Update the Army's Reserves. *Foreign Affairs* 83: 2–7.

Kornblut, Anne E., Scott Wilson, and Karen DeYoung. (2009) Obama Pressed for Faster Surge: Afghan Review A Marathon. *Washington Post*, December 6.

Kornhauser, William. (1956) *The Politics of Mass Society*. New York: Free Press.

Kotz, Nick. (1988) *Wild Blue Yonder and the B-1 Bomber*. Princeton, NJ: Princeton University Press.

Krasner, Stephen D. (1972) Are Bureaucracies Important? (Or Allison Wonderland) *Foreign Policy* 7: 159–79.

———. (1982) American Policy and Global Economic Stability. In *America in a Changing World Political Economy*, edited by William P. Avery and David P. Rapkin, pp. 29–48. New York: Longman.

Krepinevich, Andrew F. (1986) *The Army and Vietnam*. Baltimore, MD: Johns Hopkins University Press.

Kumar, Pryar. (2011) Foreign Correspondents: Who Covers What. *American Journalism Review*, January.

Kurth, James R. (1971) A Widening Gyre: The Logic of American Weapons Procurement. *Public Policy* 19: 373–404.

———. (1973) Why We Buy the Weapons We Do. *Foreign Policy* 11: 33–56.

Kuttner, Robert. (1991) *The End of Laissez-Faire: National Purpose and the Global Economy After the Cold War*. New York: Knopf.

Kwitny, Jonathan. (1984) *Endless Enemies: The Making of an Unfriendly World*. New York: Penguin.

Lacey, Marc, and Raymond Bonner. (2001) A Mad Scramble by Donors for Plum Ambassadorships. *New York Times*, March 19, p. 19.

Ladd, Everett Carll. (1978) *Where Have All the Voters Gone? The Fracturing of America's Political Parties*. New York: W.W. Norton.

LaFeber, Walter. (1994) *The American Age: United States Foreign Policy at Home and Abroad: 1750 to the Present* (2nd ed.) New York: W.W. Norton.

————. (2006) *America, Russia, and the Cold War 1945–2006*. New York: McGraw-Hill.

LaFranchi, Howard. (2001) In PR War, US Gets Ready to Turn up Volume. *Christian Science Monitor*, November 1, pp. 7–13.

Lake, Anthony. (1989) *Somoza Falling*. Boston, MA: Houghton Mifflin.

Lake, David A. (1988) *Power, Protection, and Free Trade: International Sources of U.S. Commercial Strategy, 1887–1939*. Ithaca, NY: Cornell University Press.

Layne, Christopher. (1997) From Preponderance to Offshore Balancing: America's Future Grand Strategy. *International Security* 22: 86–124.

Larson, Deborah Welch. (1985) *Origins of Containment: A Psychological Explanation*. Princeton, NJ: Princeton University Press.

Lasswell, Harold D. (1938) *Politics: Who Gets What, When and How*. New York: McGraw-Hill.

Latham, Michael E. (2000) *Modernization as Ideology: American Social Science and "Nation-Building" in the Kennedy Era*. Chapel Hill: University of North Carolina Press.

Lawrence, David G., and Richard Fleisher. (1987) Puzzles and Confusions: Political Realignment in the 1980s. *Political Science Quarterly 102,* 79–92.

Lawrence, Jill. (2008) Obama: Keeping Cool, Focusing on "Common Purpose." *USA Today*, October 8, p. A1.

Lebow, Richard Ned. (1981) *Between Peace and War: The Nature of International Crisis*. Baltimore, MD: John Hopkins University Press.

Lee, Carol E., and Gordon Lubold. (2010) Donilon to Replace Jones. *Politico*, October 8.

Leffler, Melvyn P. (2004) Bush's Foreign Policy. *Foreign Policy* 144: 22–28.

Leibovich, Mark. (2012) For a Blunt Biden, an Uneasy Supporting Role. *New York Times*, May 7.

Lemann, Nicholas. (2002a) The Next World Order: The Bush Administration May Have a Brand-New Doctrine of Power. *New Yorker*, April 1, p. 42.

————. (2002b) The War on What? The White House and the Debate About Whom to Fight Next. *New Yorker*, September 16, p. 36.

————. (2003) How It Came to War: When Did Bush Decide That He Had to Fight Saddam? *New Yorker*, March 31, p. 36.

Leslie, Stuart W. (1994) *The Cold War and American Science: The Military-Industrial Complex at MIT and Stanford*. New York: Columbia University Press.

Leuchtenburg, William E. (2009) *In the Shadow of FDR: From Harry Truman to Barack Obama*. Ithaca, NY: Cornell University Press.

Levy, Jack S. (1994) Learning and Foreign Policy: Sweeping a Conceptual Minefield. *International Organization* 48: 279–312.

Lewis, Anthony. (2004) Making Torture Legal. *New York Review of Books*, July 15, p. 4.

Light, Paul C. (1984) *Vice Presidential Power: Advice and Influence in the White House*. Baltimore: John Hopkins University Press.

Lindblom, Charles E. (1959) The Science of "Muddling" Through. *Public Administration Review* 19: 79–88.

Lindsay, James M. (1994) *Congress and the Politics of U.S. Foreign Policy*. Baltimore, MD: Johns Hopkins University Press.

————. (2000) The New Apathy: How an Uninterested Public Is Shaping Foreign Policy. *Foreign Affairs* 79: 2–8.

————. (2002) Getting Uncle Sam's Ear: Will Ethnic Lobbies Cramp America's Foreign Policy Style? *Brookings Review* 20: 37–40.

————. (2003) Deference and Defiance: The Shifting Rhythms of Executive-Legislative Relations in Foreign Policy. *Presidential Studies Quarterly* 33: 530–46.

Lippmann, Walter. (1922) *Public Opinion*. New York: Harcourt Brace.

————. (1925) *The Phantom Public*. New York: Harcourt Brace.

Lizza, Ryan. (2002) White House Watch: Big Deal. *New Republic*, June 24, pp. 10–12.

————. (2008) Battle Plans: How Obama Won. *New Yorker*, November 17, p. 46.

————. (2009) Money Talks. *New Yorker*, May 4, pp. 50–59.

Lizza, Ryan. (2010) Inside the Crisis: Larry Summers and the White House Economic Team. *The New Yorker*, October 19.

————. (2011) The Consequentialist: How the Arab Spring Remade Obama's Foreign Policy. *The New Yorker*, May 2.

————. (2012) The Obama Memos: The Making of a Post-Post-partisan Presidency. *The New Yorker*, January 30, pp. 36–49.

Locker, James R., III. (2002) *Victory on the Potomac: The Goldwater-Nichols Act Unifies the Pentagon*. Bryan, TX: A&M University Press.

Longley, Jeanne, and Dean G. Pruitt. (1980) Groupthink: A Critique of Janis's Theory. *Review of Personality and Social Psychology* 1: 74–93.

Lowenthal, Mark M. (2011) *Intelligence: From Secrets to Policy*. Washington, DC: Congressional Quarterly Press.

Lowi, Theodore J. (1985) *The Personal President: Power Invested, Promise Unfulfilled*. Ithaca, NY: Cornell University Press.

Lukas, J. Anthony. (1971) The Council on Foreign Relations: Is It a Club? Seminar? Presidium? "Invisible Government"? *New York Times Magazine*, November 21, pp. 231–32.

———. (1973) *Nightmare: The Underside of the Nixon Years*. New York: Penguin.

Luttwak, Edward N. (1985) *The Pentagon and the Art of War*. New York: Simon and Schuster.

MacDonald, J. Fred. (1985) *Television and the Red Menace: The Video Road to Vietnam*. New York: Praeger.

———. (1990) *One Nation under Television: The Rise and Decline of Network TV*. New York: Pantheon.

MacPherson, Myra. (1984) *Long Time Passing: Vietnam and the Haunted Generation*. New York: New American Library.

Madrick Jeff. (2009) How We Were Ruined & What We Can Do. *New York Review of Books*, February 12.

Maechling, Charles, Jr. (1976) Foreign Policy Makers: The Weakest Link? *Virginia Quarterly Review* 52: 1–23.

Malmgren, Harald B. (1972) Managing Foreign Economic Policy. *Foreign Policy* 6: 42–63.

Manchester, William. (1972) *The Glory and the Dream: A Narrative History of America, 1933–1972*. New York: John Wiley.

Manley, John F. (1983) Neo-Pluralism: A Class Analysis of Pluralism I and Pluralism II. *American Political Science Review* 77: 368–83.

Mann, James. (2004) *The Rise of the Vulcans: The History of Bush's War Cabinet*. New York: Vikings Press.

Mann, Thomas E. (1990a) Making Foreign Policy: President and Congress. In *A Question of Balance: The President, the Congress, and Foreign Policy*, edited by Thomas E. Mann, pp. 1–34. Washington, DC: Brookings Institution Press.

———. (1990b) *A Question of Balance: The President, the Congress, and Foreign Policy*. Washington, DC: Brookings Institution Press.

Mann, Thomas E., and Norman J. Ornstein. (2012) *It's Even Worse than It Looks: How the American Constitutional System Collided with the New Politics of Extremism*. New York: Basic Books.

Manning, Bayless. (1977) The Congress, the Executive, and Intermestic Affairs: Three Proposals. *Foreign Affairs* 55: 306–22.

Maranis, David. (1995) *First in His Class: A Biography of Bill Clinton*. New York: Simon and Schuster.

Marger, Martin N. (1987) *Elites and Masses: An Introduction to Political Sociology*. Belmont, CA: Wadsworth.

Marshall, Bryan W. (2003) Presidential Success in the Realm of Foreign Affairs: Institutional Reform and the Role of House Committees. *Social Science Quarterly* 84: 685–703.

Marshall, Bryan W., and Brandon C. Prins. (2002) The Pendulum of Congressional Power: Agenda Change, Partisanship and the Demise of the Post-World War II Foreign Policy Consensus. *Congress and the Presidency* 29: 195–212.

Martin, Lisa L. (2000) *Democratic Commitments: Legislatures and International Cooperation*. Princeton, NJ: Princeton University Press.

Martin, William. (1999) The Christian Right and American Foreign Policy. *Foreign Policy 114*, 66–80.

Massing, Michael. (1991) The Way to War. *New York Review of Books*, March 28, pp. 17–20.

———. (2005) The Press: The Enemy Within. *New York Review of Books* 52: 20.

———. (2009a) A New Horizon for the News. *New York Review of Books* 56: 14.

———. (2009b) The News about the Internet. *New York Review of Books*, August 13.

Mastanduno, Michael. (1985) Strategies of Economic Containment: U.S. Trade Relations with the Soviet Union. *World Politics* 37: 503–31.

Mayer, Jane, and Doyle McManus. (1988) *Landslide: The Unmaking of the President, 1985–1988*. Boston, MA: Houghton Mifflin.

Mayhew, David R. (1974) *Congress: The Electoral Connection*. New York: Yale University Press.

———. (1991) *Divided We Govern*. New Haven, CT: Yale University Press.

Mazzetti, Mark. (2009) Five Years After Overhaul, U.S. Spy Chiefs Still Fight Over Turf. *New York Times*, June 9, p. A10.

McConnell, Grant. (1966) *Private Power and American Democracy*. New York: Vintage.

McCormick, James M. (1998) Interest Groups and the Media in Post-Cold War U.S. Foreign Policy. In *After the End: Making U.S. Foreign Policy in the Post-Cold War World*, edited by James M. Scott, pp. 170–98. Durham, NC: Duke University Press.

McGeary, Johanna. (2001) Odd Man Out. *Time*, September 10, pp. 24–32.

McGlen, Nancy, and Meredith Sarkees. (1993) *Women in Foreign Policy: The Insiders*. New York: Routledge.

McGowan, Pat, and Stephen G. Walker. (1981) Radical and Conventional Models of U.S. Foreign Economic Policy Making. *World Politics* 33: 347–82.

McPherson, James M. (1996) Big Little Big Horn. *New Republic*, July 29, pp. 38–41.

Mearsheimer, John, and Stephen Walt. (2006) The Israel Lobby. *London Review of Books* 28: 3–12.

———. (2007) *The Israel Lobby and U.S. Foreign Policy*. New York: Farrar, Strauss, and Giroux.

Medved, Michael. (2002) That's Entertainment? Hollywood's Contribution to Anti-Americanism Abroad. *National Interest*, July 1, pp. 5–15.

Melanson, Richard. (2005) *American Foreign Policy since the Vietnam War*. Armonk, NY: M.E. Sharpe.

Melanson, Richard A. (1983) *Writing History and Making Policy: The Cold War, Vietnam, and Revisionism*. Lanham, MD: University Press of America.

———. (1990) *Reconstructing Consensus: American Foreign Policy Since the Vietnam War*. New York: St. Martin's Press.

Melman, Seymour. (1970) *Pentagon Capitalism*. New York: McGraw-Hill.

Menand, Louis. (1997) Inside the Billway. *New York Review of Books*, August 14, p. 4.

Mickelson, Sig. (1983) *America's Other Voice: The Story of Radio Free Europe and Radio Liberty*. New York: Praeger.

Micklethwait, John, and Adrian Woodridge. (2004) *The Right Nation: Conservative Power in America*. New York: Penguin.

Milbank, Dana. (2001, November 20) In War, It's Power to the President. *Washington Post*, p. A1.

Milbank, Dana, and Bradley Graham. (2001) No Time for "Strategy." *Washington Post, Weekly Edition*, October 15–21, p. 13.

Miliband, Ralph. (1969) *The State in Capitalist Society: The Analysis of the Western System of Power*. London: Quartet Books.

Miller, Greg. (2005) Lawmakers Hear Progress Report on New Spy Chief. *Los Angeles Times*, July 29, p. A13.

Miller, James. (1987) *Democracy Is in the Streets: From Port Huron to the Siege of Chicago*. New York: Simon and Schuster.

Miller, Mark C. (2002) The Big Ten. *Nation*, January 7.

Miller, Nathan. (1989) *Spying for America: The Hidden History of U.S. Intelligence*. New York: Paragon House.

Miller, Robert Hopkins. (1992) *Inside an Embassy: The Political Role of Diplomats Abroad*. Washington, DC: Congressional Quarterly Press.

Millet, Alan R., and Peter Maslowski. (1985) *For the Common Defense: A Military History of the United States of America*. New York: Free Press.

Mills, C. Wright. (1956) *The Power Elite*. London: Oxford University Press.

Milner, Helen V. (1989) *Resisting Protectionism: Global Industries and the Politics of International Trade*. Princeton, NJ: Princeton University Press.

Mingst, Karen. (1982) Process and Policy in U.S. Commodities: The Impact of the Liberal Economic Paradigm. In *America in a Changing World Political Economy*, edited by William P. Avery and David Rapkin, pp. 191–206. New York: Longman.

Minix, Dean A. (1978) *Small Groups and Foreign Policy Decision-Making*. Lanham, MD: University Press of America.

Moens, Alexander. (1990) *Foreign Policy under Carter: Testing Multiple Advocacy Decision Making*. Boulder, CO: Westview Press.

Moon, Chung-in. (1988) Complex Interdependence and Transnational Lobbying: South Korea in the United States. *International Studies Quarterly* 32: 67–89.

Moran, Michael. (2006) Election Will Turn on Foreign Policy. *Star-Ledger*, September 3, p. A1.

Morgenthau, Hans J. (1952) *In Defense of the National Interest: A Critical Examination of American Foreign Policy*. New York: Knopf.

Morley, Jefferson. (2012) David Petraeus and the Signature of US Terror. *Salon*, April 19.

Morris, Roger. (1977) *Uncertain Greatness: Henry Kissinger and American Foreign Policy*. New York: Harper and Row.

Morse, Edward L. (1973) *Foreign Policy and Interdependence in Gaullist France*. Princeton, NJ: Princeton University Press.

Mueller, John E. (1973) *War, Presidents, and Public Opinion*. New York: John Wiley.

———. (1980) The Search for the "Breaking Point" in Vietnam: The Statistics of a Deadly Quarrel. *International Studies Quarterly* 24: 497–519.

———. (2005) The Iraq Syndrome. *Foreign Affairs* 84: 44–54.

Mulcahy, Kevin V. (1991) The Bush Administration and National Security Policy-Making: A Preliminary Assessment. *Governance* 4: 207–20.

Naftali, Timothy. (2005) *Blind Spot: The Secret History of American Counterterrorism.* New York: Basic Books.

Nakashima, Ellen, and Bradley Graham. (2001) Direct Authority Called Key in Homeland Agency. *Washington Post,* September 27, p. A7.

Nardulli, Peter F. (1995) The Concept of a Critical Realignment, Electoral Behavior, and Political Change. *American Political Science Review* 88: 10–22.

Nash, George H. (1976) *The Conservative Intellectual Movement in America.* New York: Basic Books.

Nathan, James A. (1975) The Missile Crisis: His Finest Hour Now. *World Politics* 27: 256–81.

National Commission on Terrorist Attacks upon the United States. (2003) *The 9/11 Commission Report: Final Report of the National Commission on Terrorist Attacks upon the United States.* Washington, DC: U.S. Government Printing Office.

National Security Council Project. (1999a) *The Bush Administration National Security Council.* Washington, DC: Brookings Institution Press.

———. (1999b) *The Role of the National Security Advisor.* Washington, DC: Brookings Institution Press.

———. (2000) *The Clinton Administration National Security Council.* Washington, DC: Brookings Institution Press.

Nau, Henry R. (1990) *The Myth of America's Decline: Leading the World Economy into the 1990s.* New York: Oxford University Press.

Neack, Laura, Jeanne A. K. Hey, and Patrick J. Haney. (1995) Generational Change in Foreign Policy Analysis. In *Foreign Policy Analysis: Continuity and Change in Its Second Generation,* edited by Laura Neack, Jeanne A.K. Hey, and Patrick J. Haney, pp. 1–15. Englewood Cliffs, NJ: Prentice Hall.

Neumann, W. Russell. (1986) *The Paradox of Mass Politics: Knowledge and Opinion in the American Electorate.* Cambridge, MA: Harvard University Press.

Neustadt, Richard A. (1960) *Presidential Power: The Politics of Leadership.* New York: John Wiley.

Newhouse, John. (1973) *Cold Dawn: The Story of Salt.* New York: Holt, Rinehart, and Winston.

Newman, Robert P. (1992) *Owen Lattimore and the "Loss" of China.* Berkeley and Los Angeles: University of California Press.

Nichols, John Spicer. (1984) Wasting the Propaganda Dollar. *Foreign Policy* 56: 129–40.

Niebuhr, Reinhold. (1944) *The Children of Light and the Children of Darkness.* New York: Charles Scribner's Sons.

———. (1953) The Foreign Policy of American Conservatism and Liberalism. In *Christian Realism and Political Problems,* edited by Reinhold Niebuhr, pp. 55–67. New York: Scribner.

Niebuhr, Reinhold, and Alan Heimert. (1963) *A Nation So Conceived.* New York: Charles Scribner's Sons.

Nincic, Miroslav. (1988) The United States, the Soviet Union, and the Politics of Opposites. *World Politics* 40: 452–75.

Nincic, Miroslav, and Barbara Hinckley. (1991) Foreign Policy and the Evaluation of Presidential Candidates. *Journal of Conflict Resolution* 35: 333–55.

Nisbet, Robert A. (1953) *The Quest for Community: The Study in the Ethics of Order and Freedom.* New York: Oxford University Press.

———. (1988) *The Present Age: Progress and Anarchy in Modern America.* New York: Harper and Row.

Nobles, Gregory. (1997) *American Frontiers: Cultural Encounters and Continental Conquest.* New York: Hill and Wang.

Nolan, Cathal J. (1992) The Last Hurrah of Conservative Isolationism: Eisenhower, Congress, and the Bricker Amendment. *Presidential Studies Quarterly* 22: 337–49.

Nollen, Stanley D., and Dennis P. Quinn. (1994) Free Trade, Fair Trade, Strategic Trade, and Protectionism in the U.S. Congress, 1987–1988. *International Organization* 48: 491–525.

Nye, Joseph S., Jr. (1990) Soft Power. *Foreign Policy* 80: 153–71.

———. (2009) Scholars on the Sidelines. *Washington Post,* April 13, p. A15.

Obama, Barack. (2009) *Press Conference.* Hilton Hotel. Port of Spain, Trinidad and Tobago, April 19.

O'Brien, David M. (2002) Presidential and Congressional Relations in Foreign Affairs: The Treaty-Making Power and the Rise of Executive Agreements. In *Congress and the Politics of Foreign Policy,* edited by Colton C. Campbell, Nicol C. Rae, and John F. Stack, Jr., pp. 70–89. Englewood Cliffs, NJ: Prentice Hall.

Oneal, John R. (1988) The Rationality of Decision Making during International Crises. *Polity* 20: 598–622.

Oldfield, Duane M., and Aaron Wildavsky. (1991) Reconsidering the Two Presidencies. In *The Two Presidencies: A Quarter Century Assessment,* edited by Steve A. Shull, pp. 181–90. Chicago, IL: Nelson Hall.

Oleszek, Walter. (2003) *Congressional Procedures and the Policy Process.* Washington, DC: Congressional Quarterly Press.

Olmsted, M. S., B. Baer, J. Joyce, and G. Prince. (1984) *Women at State: An Inquiry into the Status of Women in the United States Department of State.* Washington, DC: Women's Research and Education Institute of the Congressional Caucus for Women's Issues.

Ornstein, Norman, and Thomas Donilon. (2000) The Confirmation Clog. *Foreign Affairs* 79: 87–99.

Ostler, Jeffrey. (2004) *The Plains Sioux and U.S. Colonialism from Lewis and Clark to Wounded Knee.* Cambridge, UK: Cambridge University Press.

Owens, John. (1991) The U.S. Foreign Service: An Institution in Crisis. *Mediterranean Quarterly,* 27–50.

Packenham, Robert A. (1973) *Liberal America and the Third World: Political Development Ideas in Foreign Aid and Social Science.* Princeton, NJ: Princeton University Press.

Packer, George. (2005) *The Assassin's Gate: America in Iraq.* New York: Farrar, Straus, and Giroux.

Page, Benjamin I., and Robert Y. Shapiro. (1992) *The Rational Public: Fifty Years of Trends in Americans' Policy Preferences.* Chicago, IL: University of Chicago Press.

Page, Susan. (2008) Hillary Clinton's Test at State. How'll She'll Work with Obama. *USA Today,* December 1.

Paige, Sean. (2000) Projects Lose Way in Pentagon's Revolving Door. *Insight on the News,* May 29, p. 47.

Parenti, Michael. (1992) *Make Believe Media: The Politics of Entertainment.* New York: St. Martin's Press.

Parker, Charles F., and Eric K. Stern. (2005) Bolt from the Blue or Avoidable Failure? Revisiting September 11 and the Origins of Strategic Surprise. *Foreign Policy Analysis* 1: 301–31.

Parks, Michael. (2002) Foreign News: What's Next? *Columbia Journalism Review* 40: 52–57.

Pastor, Robert A. (1980) *Congress and the Politics of U.S. Foreign Economic Policy, 1929–1976.* Berkeley and Los Angeles: University of California Press.

Patterson, Bradley H., and James P. Pfiffner. (2001) The White House Office of Presidential Personnel. *Presidential Studies Quarterly* 31: 415–38.

Pear, Robert. (1989) Confusion Is Operative Word in U.S. Policy Toward Japan. *New York Times,* March 20, p. 1.

Pells, Richard H. (1985) *The Liberal Mind in a Conservative Age: American Intellectuals in the 1940s and 1950s.* New York: Harper and Row.

Perkins, Dexter. (1968) *The American Approach to Foreign Policy.* New York: Scribner.

Perret, Geoffrey. (1990) *A Country Made by War: From the Revolution to Vietnam—The Story of America's Rise to Power.* New York: Vintage Press.

Perry, Mark. (1989) *Four Stars.* Boston, MA: Houghton Mifflin.

Peterson, Paul. (1994) *The President, the Congress, and the Making of Foreign Policy.* Norman: University of Oklahoma Press.

Pew Research Center. (2011). *Views of Middle East Unchanged by Recent Events,* June 10 (http://www.people-press. org/2011/06/10/views-of-middle-east-unchanged-by-recent-events/).

Pew Research Center for the People and the Press. (2005a) *America's Place in the World, 2005.* New York: Council on Foreign Relations.

———. (2005b) *The State of the News Media 2004: An Annual Report on News Journalism.*

———. (2005c) *The State of the News Media 2005: An Annual Report on News Journalism.*

———. (2008) Biggest Stories of 2008: Economy Tops Campaign, Internet Overtakes Newspapers as News Outlet. *Where Do You Get Most of Your National and International News?*

———. (2009) *The State of the News Media, 2009: An Annual Report on American Journalism.*

———. (2010) *Americans Spending More Time Following the News. Ideological News Sources: Who Watches and Why,* September 12.

———. (2011) *What the Public Knows—In Words and Pictures,* November 07 (http://www.people-press.org/files/legacy-pdf/11-7-11%20Knowledge%20Release.pdf).

Phillips, David L. (2005) *Losing Iraq: Inside the Postwar Reconstruction Fiasco.* Boulder, CO: Westview Press.

Phillips, Kevin P. (1969) *The Emerging Republican Majority.* New Rochelle, NY: Arlington House.

Pillar, Paul R. (2006) Intelligence, Policy, and the War in Iraq. *Foreign Affairs:* 15–27.

Pillar, Paul R. (2010) Unintelligent Design. *The National Interest,* September/October.

Pincus, Walter. (2001) Intelligence Shakeup Would Boost CIA. *Washington Post,* November 8, p. A1.

———. (2005) Rumsfeld Memo on Intelligence Criticized. *Washington Post,* April 8, p. A4.

Pious, Richard M. (1979) *The American Presidency.* New York: Basic Books.

———. (2002) Why Do Presidents Fail? *Presidential Studies Quarterly* 32: 724–42.

Piper, Richard. (1994) Situational Constitutionalism and Presidential Power: The Rise and Fall of the Liberal Presidential Government. *Presidential Studies Quarterly* 24: 577–94.

Pollack, Kenneth M. (2004) Spies, Lies, and Weapons: What Went Wrong. *Atlantic Monthly*, January/February, pp. 78–92.

Polsby, Nelson W. (1981) The Washington Community. In *The New Congress*, edited by Thomas E. Mann and Norman J. Ornstein, pp. 7–31. Washington, DC: American Enterprise Institute for Public Policy Research.

Pomper, Gerald M. (2001) The 2000 Election: Why Gore Lost. *Political Science Quarterly* 116: 201–24.

Popkin, Samuel L. (1991) *The Reasoning Voter: Communication and Persuasion in Presidential Campaigns*. Chicago, IL: University of Chicago Press.

Posen, Barry R., and Andrew L. Ross. (1996) Competing Visions for U.S. Grand Strategy. *International Security* 21: 5–53.

Posner, Richard. (2005) Important Job, Impossible Position. *New York Times*, February 9, p. A23.

Potter, William C. (1980) Issue Area and Foreign Policy Revisited. *International Organization* 33: 405–27.

Powell, Colin. (1993) U.S. Forces: The Challenges Ahead. *Foreign Affairs* 77: 32–45.

———. (2012) *It Worked for Me: In Life and Leadership*. New York: Harper.

Powers, Thomas. (1973) *The War at Home: Vietnam and the American People, 1964–1968*. New York: Grossman.

———. (2003) The Vanishing Case for War. *New York Review of Books*, December 4, p. 12.

Prados, John. (1986) *President's Secret Wars: CIA and Pentagon Operations Since World War II*. New York: William Morrow.

Preston, Thomas. (2001) *The President and His Inner Circle: Leadership Style and Advisory Process in Foreign Policy Making*. New York: Columbia University Press.

Preston, Thomas, and Paul 't Hart. (1999) Understanding and Evaluating Bureaucratic Politics: The Nexus between Political Leaders and Advisory Systems. *Political Psychology* 20: 48–98.

Prewitt, Kenneth, and Alan Stone. (1973) *The Ruling Elites: Elite Theory, Power, and American Democracy*. New York: Harper and Row.

Priest, Dana. (2000) The "Proconsuls." *Washington Post*, September 28, p. A1.

———. (2003) *The Mission: Waging War and Keeping Peace with America's Military*. New York: W.W. Norton.

———. (2005) Covert CIA Program Withstands New Furor. *Washington Post*, December 30, p. A1.

Priest, Dana, and Joe Stephens. (2004) Secret World of U.S. Interrogation. *Washington Post*, May 11, p. A1.

Pringle, Robert. (1977) Creeping Irrelevance at Foggy Bottom. *Foreign Policy*, pp. 128–39.

Puchala, Donald. (1997) International Encounters of Another Kind. *Global Society* 11: 5–29.

Purdum, Todd. (2010) Washington, We Have a Problem. *Vanity Fair*, September.

Quandt, William B. (1986) The Electoral Cycle and the Conduct of Foreign Policy. *Political Science Quarterly* 101: 825–37.

Ranelagh, John. (1986) *The Agency: The Rise and Decline of the CIA*. New York: Simon and Schuster.

Ransom, Harry Howe. (1983) Strategic Intelligence and Intermestic Politics. In *Perspectives on American Foreign Policy: Selected Readings*, edited by Charles W. Kegley, Jr. and Eugene R. Wittkopf, pp. 299–319. New York: St. Martin's Press.

Rashid, Ahmed. (2004) The Mess in Afghanistan. *New York Review of Books*, February 12, pp. 24–27.

Ratnesar, Romesh. (2005) The Condi Doctrine. *Time*, August 15, pp. 36–42.

Recer, Paul. (2002) Geography Knowledge Lacking. *State*, November 21, p. A4.

Reedy, George E. (1970) *The Twilight of the Presidency*. New York: New American Library.

Reich, Robert B. (1991) *The World of Nations: Preparing Ourselves for 21st-Century Capitalism*. New York: Knopf.

Renshon, Stanley A. (2000) After the Fall: The Clinton Presidency in Perspective. *Political Science Quarterly* 115: 41–65.

———. (2004) *In His Father's Shadow: The Transformations of George W. Bush*. New York: Palgrave/Macmillan.

Reston, James. (1967) *The Artillery of the Press*. New York: Harper.

Rhodes, Richard. (1986) *The Making of the Atomic Bomb*. New York: Simon and Schuster.

Ricci, David M. (1993) *The Transformation of American Politics: The New Washington and the Rise of Think Tanks*. New Haven, CT: Yale University Press.

Rice, Condoleezza. (2000) Promoting the National Interest. *Foreign Affairs* 79: 45–62.

Richelson, Jeffrey. (2002) *Wizards of Langley: Inside the CIA's Directorate of Science and Technology*. Boulder, CO: Westview Press.

Richter, Paul, and Richard Boudreaux. (2009) Some in Congress Uneasy with Obama's Mideast Policy. *Los Angeles Times*, June 4 (http://articles.latimes.com/2009/jun/04/world/fg-us-israel4).

Ricks, Thomas E. (2006) *Fiasco*. New York: Penguin Press.

———. (2009) *The Gamble: General David Petraeus and the American Military Adventure in Iraq, 2006–2008*. New York: Penguin.

Riebling, Mark. (2002) *Wedge: From Pearl Harbor to 9/11—How the Secret War between the FBI and CIA Has Endangered National Security*. New York: Simon and Schuster.

Rieff, David. (2003) Blueprint for a Mess. *New York Times Magazine*, November 2, pp. 28–33.

Ripley, Randall B. (1988) *Congress: Process and Policy*. New York: W.W. Norton.

Ripley, Randall B., and James M. Lindsay. (1997) *Congress Resurgent: Foreign and Defense Policy on Capitol Hill*. Ann Arbor: University of Michigan Press.

Risen, James. (2000) The Clinton Administration's See-No-Evil CIA. *New York Times*, September 10, p. 5.

———. (2001) In Hindsight, CIA Sees Flaws That Hindered Efforts on Terror. *New York Times*, October 7, p. A1.

———. (2006) *State of War: The Secret History of the CIA and the Bush Administration*. New York: Free Press.

Robertson, James Oliver. (1980) *American Myth, American Reality*. New York: Hill and Wang.

Robinson, James A. (1967) *Congress and Foreign Policy-Making: A Study in Legislative Influence and Initiative*. Homewood, IL: Dorsey Press.

Robinson, James A., and Richard C. Snyder. (1965) Decision-Making in International Politics. In *International Behavior: A Social-Psychological Analysis*, edited by Herbert C. Kelman, pp. 433–63. New York: Holt, Rinehart, and Winston.

Robinson, James A., and R. Roger Majak. (1967) The Theory of Decision-Making. In *Contemporary Political Analysis*, edited by James C. Charlesworth, pp. 175–88. New York: Free Press.

Rochefort, David A., and Roger W. Cobb. (1993) Problem Definition, Agenda Access, and Policy Choice. *Policy Studies Journal* 21: 56–71.

Rockman, Bert A. (1981) America's Department of State: Irregular and Regular Syndromes of Policy Making. *American Political Science Review* 75: 911–27.

Roeder, George H., Jr. (1993) *The Censored War: American Visual Experience during World War II*. New Haven, CT: Yale University Press.

Rohrich, Paul Egon. (1987) Economic Culture and Foreign Policy: The Cognitive Analysis of Economic Policy Making. *International Organization* 41: 61–92.

Roman, Peter J., and David W. Tarr. (1998) The Joint Chiefs of Staff: From Service Parochialism to Jointness. *Political Science Quarterly* 113: 91–122.

Romano, Luis. (2010) Hillary Clinton Widens Her Circle at the State Department. *Washington Post*, March 11.

Rosati, Jerel. (2010) Political Psychology, Cognition and Foreign Policy Analysis. In *Compendium of International Studies*, edited by Bob Denmark, Vol. IX, pp. 5732–5755. ISA and Blackwell.

Rosati, Jerel A. (1981) Developing a Systematic Decision-Making Framework: Bureaucratic Politics in Perspective. *World Politics* 33: 234–52.

———. (1984) Congressional Influence in American Foreign Policy: Addressing the Controversy. *Journal of Political and Military Sociology* 12: 311–33.

———. (1987) *The Carter Administration's Quest for Global Community: Beliefs and Their Impact on Behavior*. New York: Harper and Row.

———. (1992) The Domestic Environment. In *Intervention into the 1990s: United States Foreign Policy in the Third World*, edited by Peter A. Schraeder, pp. 175–91. Boulder, CO: Lynne Rienner.

———. (1995) A Cognitive Approach to the Study of Foreign Policy. In *Foreign Policy Analysis: Continuity and Change in Its Second Generation*, edited by Laura Neack, Patrick J. Haney, and Jeanne A. K. Hey, pp. 49–70. Englewood Cliffs, NJ: Prentice Hall.

———. (1997) United States Leadership into the Next Millennium: A Question of Politics. *International Affairs* 52: 297–315.

———. (2000) The Power of Human Cognition in the Study of World Politics. *International Studies Review* 2: 45–75.

———. (2010) Ignoring the Essence of Decision. *International Studies Review* 3 (Spring): 178–81.

Rosati, Jerel A., and John Creed. (1997) Extending the Three-Headed and Four-Headed Eagles: The Foreign Policy Operations of American Elites during the 80s and 90s. *Political Psychology* 18: 583–623.

Rosati, Jerel A., Joe D. Hagan, and Martin W. Sampson. (1994) *Foreign Policy Restructuring: How Governments Respond to Global Change*. Columbia: University of South Carolina Press.

Rosenau, James N. (1961) *Public Opinion and Foreign Policy*. New York: Random House.

———. (1976) The Study of Foreign Policy. In *World Politics*, edited by James N. Rosenau, Gavin Boyd, and Kenneth W. Thompson, pp. 15–35. New York: Free Press.

———. (1980) The National Interest. In *The Scientific Study of Foreign Policy*, edited by James N. Rosenau, pp. 283–93. London: Frances Pinter.

———. (1981) *The Study of Political Adaptation*. New York: Nichols Publishing.

Rosenberg, Emily S. (1982) *Spreading the American Dream: American Economic and Cultural Expansion, 1890–1945*. New York: Hill and Wang.

Rosencrance, Richard. (1990) *America's Economic Resurgence: A Bold New Strategy*. New York: Harper and Row.

Rosenstone, Robert A. (1969) "The Times They Are A-Changin": The Music of Protest. *Annals of the American Academy of Political and Social Science* 382 (1): 131–44.

Rossiter, Clinton. (1960) *The American Presidency*. New York: Harcourt, Brace, Jovanovich.

Rothkopf, David J. (2005a) Inside the Committee That Runs the World. *Foreign Policy* 147: 30–40.

———. (2005b) *Running the World: The Inside Story of the National Security Council and the Architects of American Power*. New York: Public Affairs.

———. (2009) It's 3 A.M. Do You Know Where Hillary Clinton Is? *Washington Post*, August 23 (www.washingtonpost.com/wp-dyn/content/article/2009/08/21/AR2009082101772.html).

Roubini, Nouriel, and Stephen Mihm. (2010) *Crisis Economics: A Crash Course in the Future of Finance*. New York: Penguin Press.

Rourke, John, and Richard Clark. (1998) Making U.S. Foreign Policy toward China in the Clinton Administration. In *After the End: Making U.S. Foreign Policy in the Post-Cold War World*, edited by James M. Scott, pp. 201–24. Durham, NC: Duke University Press.

Rovere, Richard H. (1959) *Senator Joe McCarthy*. New York: World Publishing.

Rozell, Mark J. (1993) Carter Rehabilitated. *Presidential Studies Quarterly* 23: 317–30.

Rozen, Laura. (2005) He's Done. *American Prospect*, November 20, pp. 27–32.

———. (2009) Obama's NSC Takes Power. *Cable*, March 3 (http://thecable.foreignpolicy.com/posts/2009/03/03/jones_s_nsc_moves_to_assert_greater_control_over_interagency_process).

Rubenzer, Trevor. (2009) Ethnic Minority Interest Group Attributes and U.S. Foreign Policy Influence: A Qualitative Comparative Analysis. *Foreign Policy Analysis* 4: 169–85.

Rubin, Barry. (1985) *Secrets of State: The State Department and the Struggle over U.S. Foreign Policy*. New York: Oxford University Press.

Rudalevige, Andrew. (2005) The Executive Branch and the Legislative Process. In *The Executive Branch*, edited by Joel D. Aberbach and Martk A. Peterson, pp. 419–51. New York: The Annenberg Foundation Trust at Sunnylands/Oxford University Press.

———. (2009) *Rivals or a Team? Competitive Advisory Institutions and the Obama Administration*. Paper presented at the American Political Science Association Annual Meeting, September 3–6, 2009.

Ruttan, Vernon W. (1996) *United States Development Assistance Policy: The Domestic Politics of Foreign Economic Aid*. Baltimore, MD: Johns Hopkins University Press.

Ryan, Alan. (2008) What Happened to the American Empire? *New York Review of Books*, October 23.

Sabato, Larry. (1991) *Feeding Frenzy: How Attack Journalism Has Transformed American Politics*. New York: Free Press.

Saffer, Thomas H., and Kelly E. Orville. (1982) *Countdown Zero: GI Victims of U.S. Atomic Testing*. Middlesex, UK: Penguin Press.

Said, Edward. (1978) *Orientalism*. New York: Random House.

Sampson, Anthony. (1975) *The Seven Sisters: The Great Oil Companies and the World They Shaped*. New York: Bantam.

Sanger, David E. (2001) Bush Plans to Stress Effects of Economics on Security. *New York Times*, January 18, p. A10.

Sapin, Burton M. (1966) *The Making of United States Foreign Policy*. Washington, DC: Brookings Institution Press.

Savage, Charles, and Mark Landler. (2011) White House Defense Continuing US Role in Libya Operation. *New York Times*, June 15.

Schake, Kori N. (2012) *State of Disrepair: Fixing the Culture and Practices of the State Department*. Stanford, CA: Hoover Institution Press.

Schandler, Herbert Y. (1977) *The Unmaking of the President: Lyndon Johnson and Vietnam*. Princeton, NJ: Princeton University Press.

Schattschneider, E. E. (1960) *The Semisovereign People: A Realist's View of Democracy in America*. New York: Holt, Rinehart, and Winston.

Schilling, Warner R., Paul T. Hammond, and Glenn H. Snyder. (1962) *Strategy, Politics, and Defense Budgets*. New York: Columbia University Press.

Schlesinger, Arthur, Jr. (1989) *The Imperial Presidency*. New York: Houghton Mifflin.

————. (2005) *War and the American Presidency*. New York: W.W. Norton.

Schlesinger, Stephen, and Stephen Kinzer. (1982) *Bitter Fruit: The Untold Story of the American Coup in Guatemala*. New York: Doubleday.

Schmeisser, Peter. (1991) Shooting Pool: How the Press Lost the Gulf War. *New Republic*, March 18, p. 22.

Schmidle, Nicholas. (2011) Getting Bin Laden. *The New Yorker*, August 8.

Schneider, William. (1983) Conservatism, Not Interventionism: Trends in Foreign Policy Opinion. In *Eagle Defiant: United States Foreign Policy in the 1980s*, edited by Kenneth A. Oye, Robert J. Leiber, and Donald Rothchild, pp. 33–64. Boston, MA: Little, Brown.

————. (1984) Public Opinion. In *The Making of America's Foreign Policy*, edited by Joseph S. Nye, pp. 13–14. New Haven, CT: Yale University Press.

————. (1987) "Rambo" and Reality: Having It Both Ways. In *Eagle Resurgent? The Reagan Era in American Foreign Policy*, edited by Kenneth A. Oye, Robert J. Leiber, and Donald Rothchild, pp. 41–74 Boston, MA: Little, Brown.

————. (1989) JFK's Children: The Class of '74. *Atlantic Monthly*, March, pp. 35–58.

Schraeder, Peter J. (1994) Bureaucratic Incrementalism, Crisis, and Change in U.S. Foreign Policy Toward Africa. In *Foreign Policy Restructuring: How Governments Respond to Global Change*, edited by Jerel A. Rosati, Joe D. Hagan, and Martin W. Sampson III, pp. 111–37. Columbia: University of South Carolina Press.

Schroen, Gary. (2005) *First In: An Insider's Account of How the CIA Spearheaded the War on Terror in Afghanistan*. New York: Presidio Press.

Schulzinger, Robert D. (1984) *The Wise Men of Foreign Affairs: The History of the Council on Foreign Relations*. New York: Columbia University Press.

Sciolino, Elaine. (1989) Friends as Ambassadors: How Many Is Too Many? *New York Times*, November 7, pp. 1, 6.

Scott, Andrew M. (1969) The Department of State: Formal Organization and Informal Culture. *International Studies Quarterly* 12: 1–18.

Scott, James M. (1996) *Deciding to Intervene: The Reagan Doctrine and American Foreign Policy*. Durham, NC: Duke University Press.

————. (1997) In the Loop: Congressional Influence in American Foreign Policy. *Journal of Political and Military Sociology* 25: 47–76.

————, ed. (1998) *After the End: Making U.S. Foreign Policy in the Post-Cold War World*. Durham, NC: Duke University Press.

————. (1999) Transnationalizing Democracy Promotion: The Role of Western Political Foundations and Think-Tanks. *Democratization* 6: 146–70.

Scott, James M., and Ralph G. Carter. (2002) Acting on the Hill: Congressional Assertiveness in U.S. Foreign Policy. *Congress and the Presidency* 22: 151–70.

Scott, James M., and Elizabeth A. Rexford. (1997) Finding a Place for Women in the World of Diplomacy: Evidence of Progress toward Gender Equity and Speculation on Policy Outcomes. *Review of Public Personnel Administration* 17: 31–56.

Scowcroft, Brent, and Samuel R. Berger. (2005) In the Wake of War: Getting Serious About Nation-Building. *National Interest* 81: 49–53.

Seidman, Harold. (1980) *Politics, Position, and Power: The Dynamics of Federal Organization*. New York: Oxford University Press.

Semmel, Andrew K. (1976) Foreign News in Four U.S. Elite Dailies: Some Comparisons. *Journalism Quarterly* 53: 732–36.

Seplow, Stephen. (2002) Closer to Home. *American Journalism Review* 14: 6.

Sestanovich, Stephen. (2009) Hostile Territory. *Washington Post*, April 24, p. A19.

Severo, Richard, and Lewis Milford. (1989) *The Wages of War: When America's Soldiers Came Home—From Valley Forge to Vietnam*. New York: Simon and Schuster.

Shackley, Theodore. (1981) *The Third Option: An American View of Counterinsurgency Operations*. New York: Dell.

Shafer, Byron E. (1991) *The End of Realignment? Interpreting American Electoral Eras*. Madison: University of Wisconsin Press.

Shafer, Michael D. (1988) *Deadly Paradigms: The Failure of U.S. Counterinsurgency*. Princeton, NJ: Princeton University Press.

Shane, Scott. (2004) Official Reveals Budget for U.S. Intelligence. *New York Times*, November 8, p. A18.

Shapiro, Robert Y., and Benjamin I. Page. (1988) Foreign Policy and the Rational Public. *Journal of Conflict Resolution* 32: 211–47.

Shenon, Philip. (1990a) F.B.I. to Promote 11 Hispanic Agents in Bias Case. *New York Times*, September 20, p. A11.

————. (1990b) F.B.I. Settles Suit by Black Workers on Discrimination. *New York Times*, January 12, pp. 1, 12.

Sheridan, Mary Beth, and William Branigin. (2010) Senate Ratifies New US-Russia Nuclear Weapons Treaty. *Washington Post*, December 22.

Shilts, Randy. (1993) *Conduct Unbecoming: Lesbians and Gays in the U.S. Military*. New York: St. Martin's Press.

Shull, Steven A. (1991) *The Two Presidencies: A Quarter Century Assessment*. Chicago, IL: Nelson Hall.

Sick, Gary. (1985) *All Fall Down: America's Tragic Encounter with Iran*. New York: Penguin.

Sigal, Leon V. (1973) *Reporters and Officials: The Organization and Politics of Newsmaking*. Lexington, MA: D.C. Heath.

Simpson, Christopher. (1994) *Science of Coercion: Communication Research and Psychological Warfare, 1945–1960*. New York: Oxford University Press.

Sinclair, Barbara. (2000) *Unorthodox Lawmaking: New Legislative Procedures in the U.S. Congress* (2nd ed.). Washington, DC: Congressional Quarterly Press.

Singer, P. W. (2003) *Corporate Warriors: The Rise of the Privatized Military Industry*. Ithaca, NY: Cornell University Press.

———. (2005) Outsourcing War. *Foreign Affairs* 84: 119–33.

———. (2007) *Corporate Warriors: The Rise of the Privatized Military Industry*. Ithaca, NY: Cornell University Press.

Skowronek, Stephen. (1997) *The Politics Presidents Make: Leadership for John Adams to Bill Clinton*. Cambridge, MA: Harvard University Press.

———. (2011) *Presidential Leadership in Political Time: Reprise and Reappraisal*. Lawrence: University of Kansas Press.

Smist, Frank J., Jr. (1994) *Congress Oversees the Intelligence Community*. Knoxville: University of Tennessee Press.

Smith, Bruce H. (1984) U.S. and Canadian PVOs as Transnational Development Institutions. In *Private Voluntary Organizations as Agents of Development*, edited by Robert F. Gorman, pp. 115–64. London: Westview Press.

Smith, Hedrick. (1988) *The Power Game: How Washington Works*. New York: Random House.

Smith, Jean Edward. (1992) *George Bush's War*. New York: Henry Holt.

Smith, Joseph B. (1976) *Portrait of a Cold Warrior*. New York: Ballantine Books.

Smith, Steven. (1994) Congressional Party Leaders. In *The President, the Congress, and the Making of Foreign Policy*, edited by Paul E. Peterson, pp. 129–57. Norman: University of Oklahoma Press.

Snyder, Jack L. (1978) Rationality at the Brink: The Role of Cognitive Processes in Failures of Deterrence. *World Politics* 30: 344–65.

Snyder, Richard C. (1958) A Decision-Making Approach to the Study of Political Phenomena. In *Approaches to the Study of Politics*, edited by R. Young, pp. 3–37. Evanston, IL: Northwestern University Press.

Snyder, Richard C., H. W. Bruck, and Burton Sapin. (1962) *Foreign Policy Decision Making: An Approach to the Study of International Politics*. New York: Free Press of Glencoe.

Sorensen, Thoedore C. (1963) *Decision-Making in the White House: The Olive Branch or the Arrows*. New York: Columbia University Press.

Spero, Joan Edelman, and Jeffrey A. Hart. (2002) *The Politics of International Economic Relations*. New York: St. Martin's Press.

———. (2009) *The Politics of International Economic Relations*. Belmont, CA: Wadsworth.

Sprout, Harold, and Margaret Sprout. (1965) *The Ecological Perspectives on Human Affairs*. Princeton, NJ: Princeton University Press.

Stack, John F., and Colton C. Campbell. (2002) Congress: How Silent a Partner? In *Congress and the Politics of Foreign Policy*, edited by Colton C. Campbell, Nicol C. Rae, and John F. Stack, pp. 22–43. New York: Longman.

Stacks, John F. (2004) Hard Times for Hard News: A Clinical Look at U.S. Foreign Coverage. *World Policy Journal* XX: 12–21.

Statement by Reagan on Resolution. (1983) *New York Times*, October 13, p. A7.

Steel, Ronald. (1988) *Walter Lippmann and the American Century*. New York: Vintage.

Steinbruner, John D. (1974) *The Cybernetic Theory of Decision*. Princeton, NJ: Princeton University Press.

Steiner, Miriam. (1983) The Search for Order in a Disorderly World: Worldviews and Prescriptive Decision Paradigms. *International Organization* 37: 373–413.

Stephanson, Anders. (1995) *Manifest Destiny: American Expansion and the Empire of Right*. New York: Hill and Wang.

Stephens, Joe, and David B. Ottaway. (2005) A Rebuilding Plan Full of Cracks. *Washington Post*, November 20, p. A1.

Stern, Eric K. (1997) Probing the Plausibility of Newgroup Syndrome: Kennedy and the Bay of Pigs. In *Beyond Groupthink*, edited by Paul 't Hart, Eric K. Stern, and Bengt Sundelius, p. 154. Ann Arbor: University of Michigan Press.

Stockwell, John. (1978) *In Search of Enemies: A CIA Story*. New York: W.W. Norton.

Stoff, Michael B. (1980) *Oil, War, and American Security: The Search for a National Policy on Foreign Oil, 1941–1947*. New Haven, CT: Yale University Press.

Stokes, Bruce. (1993) Elevating Economics. *National Journal* (March 13): 615–19.

Stoler, Mark A. (1981) World War II Diplomacy in Historical Writing: Prelude to Cold War. In *American Foreign Relations: A Historiographical Review*, edited by Gerald K. Haines and J. Samuel Walker, pp. 187–206. Westport, CT: Greenwood Press.

Stone, Geoffrey. (2007) *War and Liberty: An American Dilemma: 1790 to the Present*. New York: W.W. Norton.

Strauss, Robert S. (1984) What's Right with U.S. Campaigns. *Foreign Policy* 55: 3–22.

Summers, Harry G., Jr. (1982) *On Strategy*. Novato, CA: Presidio Press.

Sundquist, James L. (1980) The Crisis of Competence in Our National Government. *Political Science Quarterly* 95: 183–208.

———. (1983) *Dynamics of the Party System: Alignment and Realignment of Political Parties in the U.S.* Washington, DC: Brookings Institution Press.

———. (1988) Needed: A Political Theory for the New Era of Coalition Government in the United States. *Political Science Quarterly* 103: 613–35.

Suskind, Ron. (2004) *The Price of Loyalty: George W. Bush, the White House, and the Education of Paul O'Neill*. New York: Simon and Schuster.

Suskind, Ron. (2011) *Confidence Men: Wall Street, Washington, and the Education of a President*. New York: HarperCollins.

Sweeney, Michael S. (2001) *Secrets to Victory: The Office of Censorship and the American Press and Radio in World War II*. New Haven, CT: Yale University Press.

't Hart, Paul, Eric K. Stern, and Bengt Sundelius. (1997) *Beyond Groupthink: Political Group Dynamics and Foreign Policy-Making*. Ann Arbor: University of Michigan Press.

Talbott, Strobe. (1997) Globalization and Diplomacy: A Practitioner's Perspective. *Foreign Policy* 108: 69–83.

Tananbaum, Duane. (1988) *The Bricker Amendment Controversy: A Test of Eisenhower's Political Leadership*. Ithaca, NY: Cornell University Press.

Tanter, Raymond. (1990) *Who Is at the Helm: Lessons from Lebanon*. Boulder, CO: Westview Press.

Taubman, Philip. (1983) Casey and His CIA on the Rebound. *New York Times Magazine*, January 16, p. 20.

Taylor, Stuart, Jr. (1983) In Wake of Invasion, Much Official Misinformation by U.S. Comes to Light. *New York Times*, November 6, p. A20.

Tempest, Rone. (1983a) Beltway Bandits Ring Washington. *Los Angeles Times*, July 10, p. 14.

———. (1983b) U.S. Defense Establishment Wields a Pervasive Power. *Los Angeles Times*, July 10, p. 1.

Tenbroek, Jacobus, Edward N. Barnhart, and Floyd W. Matson. (1954) *Prejudice, War, and the Constitution*. Berkeley and Los Angeles: University of California Press.

Tetlock, Philip. (2006) *Expert Political Judgment: How Good Is It? How Can We Know?* Princeton, NJ: Princeton University Press.

Thomas, Evan. (2002a) Chemistry in the War Cabinet. *Newsweek*, January 28, pp. 26–31.

———. (2002b) He Has Saddam in His Sights. *Newsweek*, March 4, pp. 18–24.

———. (2002c) The Quiet Power of Condi Rice. *Newsweek*, December 16, pp. 24–34.

———. (2002d) Rumsfeld's War. *Newsweek*, September 16, pp. 20–27.

———. (2009) *A Long Time Coming*. New York: Public Affairs.

Thomas, Evan, and Michael Isikoff. (2000) The Truth Behind the Pillars. *Newsweek*, December 25, p. 46.

Thomas, Evan, and Richard Wolfe. (2005) Bush in the Bubble. *Newsweek*, December 19, pp. 33, 34, 37.

Thomson, James C., Jr. (1968) How Could Vietnam Happen? An Autopsy. *Atlantic Monthly*, April, pp. 47–53.

Tower Commission. (1987) *The Tower Commission Report*. New York: Bantam.

Trainor, Bernard E. (1989) Flaws in Panama Attack. *New York Times*, December 31, pp. A1, A6.

Treverton, Gregory F. (2001) *Intelligence Crisis*, edited by GovExec.com

Trubowitz, Peter, and Nicole Mellow. (2003) *Bipartisanship, Foreign Policy, and September 11*. American Political Science Association Annual Convention.

Truman, David B. (1951) *The Government Process: Political Interests and Public Opinion*. New York: Knopf.

Tuchman, Barbara. (1988) *The First Salute: A View of the American Revolution*. New York: Ballantine Books.

Turner, Stansfield. (1991) Intelligence for a New World Order. *Foreign Affairs* 70: 150–66.

———. (2005) *Burn before Reading: Presidents, CIA Directors, and Secret Intelligence*. New York: Hyperion.

Tyler, Patrick. (1986) *Running Critical: The Silent War, Rickover, and General Dynamics*. New York: Harper and Row.

U.S. Census Bureau. (2004) *U.S. Statistical Abstract of the United States*. Washington, DC: U.S. Census Bureau.

———. (2005) *U.S. Statistical Abstract of the United States*. Washington, DC: U.S. Census Bureau.

U.S. Chairman of the Joint Chiefs of Staff. (2011) *The National Military Strategy of the United States: Redefining America's Military Leadership* (February).

U.S. Congress. (1976) Final Report of the Select Committee to Study Governmental Operations with Respect to Intelligence Activities. *Congressional Report* 1: 197–98.

———. (1986) *Foreign Representation: Former High-Level Federal Officials Representing Foreign Interests*. Washington, DC: U.S. Government Printing Office.

———. (1989a) *DOD Revolving Door*. Washington, DC: U.S. Government Printing Office.

———. (1989b) *State Department: Minorities and Women Are Underrepresented in the Foreign Service*. Washington, DC: U.S. Government Printing Office.

———. (1991) *Department of Defense: Professional Military Education at the Four Intermediate Service Schools*. Washington, DC: U.S. Government Printing Office.

———. (1992a) *Foreign Assistance: A Profile of the Agency for International Development*. Washington, DC: U.S. Government Printing Office.

———. (1992b) *The Role of Foreign Aid in Development*. Washington, DC: U.S. Government Printing Office.

———. (1993) *Exchange Programs: Inventory of International Educational, Cultural, and Training Programs*. Washington, DC: U.S. Government Printing Office.

———. (1994) *Cleaning up the Department of Energy's Nuclear Weapons Complex*. Washington, DC: U.S. Government Printing Office.

———. (1997) *The Role of Foreign Aid in Development*. Washington, DC: U.S. Government Printing Office.

———. (1987) *Report of the Congressional Committees Investigating the Iran-Contra Affair*. Washington, DC: U.S. Government Printing Office.

———. (2002) *Joint Inquiry in Intelligence Community Activities before and after the Terrorist Attacks of September 11, 2001*. Washington, DC: U.S. Government Printing Office.

U.S. Congress, General Accounting Office. (1993) *State Department: Survey of Administrative Issues Affecting Embassies*. Washington, DC: U.S. Government Printing Office.

U.S. Congress, House Committee on Foreign Affairs. (1981) *The Ambassador in U.S. Foreign Policy: Changing Patterns in Roles, Selection, and Designations*. Washington, DC: U.S. Government Printing Office.

———. (1982) *Foreign Policy Interest Groups as Information Sources*. Washington, DC: U.S. Government Printing Office.

U.S. Congress, Senate. (1953) *Nomination Hearings before the Committee on Armed Services*. Washington, DC: U.S. Government Printing Office.

———. (1976a) *Final Report, Book 1, Foreign and Military Intelligence*. Washington, DC: U.S. Government Printing Office.

———. (1976b) *Final Report of the Select Committee to Study Government Operations with Respect to Intelligence Activities*. Washington, DC: U.S. Government Printing Office.

———. (1976c) *Final Report of the Select Committee to Study Governmental Operations with Respect to Intelligence Activities, Foreign and Military Intelligence*. Washington, DC: U.S. Government Printing Office.

———. (1982) *The Senate Role in Foreign Affairs Appointments*. Washington, DC: U.S. Government Printing Office.

U.S. Congressional Research Service. (2011) *The Cost of Iraq, Afghanistan, and Other Global War on Terror Operations Since 9/11*, March 29 (*www.crs.gov*).

U.S. Department of Defense. (2009) *The National Defense Strategy FY2008*. Washington, DC: U.S. Government Printing Office.

U.S. Department of Defense. (2010) *Quadrennial Defense Review Report*, February.

U.S. Department of State. (1950) *Foreign Relations of the United States*. Washington, DC: U.S. Government Printing Office.

———. (1992) *State 2000: A New Model for Managing Foreign Affairs*. Washington, DC: U.S. Government Printing Office.

U.S. Department of State, Bureau of Public Affairs. (1982) *Use of U.S. Armed Forces in Lebanon*. Washington, DC: U.S. Government Printing Office.

———. (2005) *Diplomacy: The U.S. State Department at Work*. Washington, DC: U.S. Government Printing Office.

U.S. Department of State and U.S. Agency for International Development. (2007) *Transformational Diplomacy: Strategic Plan for Fiscal Years, 2007–2012*. Washington, DC: U.S. Government Printing Office.

———. (1970) *Diplomacy for the 70's: A Program of Management Reform for the Department of State* (http://searchworks.stanford.edu/view/3483695).

U.S. Director of Central Intelligence. (2001) *A Consumer's Guide to Intelligence.* Washington, DC: CIA.

U.S. House of Representatives, Permanent Select Committee on Intelligence. (1996) *Intelligence Community in the 21st Century.* Washington, DC: U.S. Government Printing Office.

———. (1997) *Legislative Activities Report of the Committee on Foreign Relations.* Washington, DC: U.S. Government Printing Office.

U.S. National Intelligence Council. (2005) *Estimative Products on Vietnam, 1948–1975.* Washington, DC: U.S. Government Printing Office.

U.S. Senate, Committee on Foreign Relations. (1989) *United States Foreign Policy Objectives and Overseas Military Installations.* Washington, DC: U.S. Government Printing Office.

U.S. Senate Select Committee on Intelligence. (2004) *Report on the U.S. Intelligence Community's Prewar Assessments on Iraq.* Washington, DC: U.S. Government Printing Office.

U.S. Supreme Court. (1936) *United States v. Curtiss-Wright Export Corp., 299 U.S. 304.*

U.S., White House. (2002) *The National Security Strategy of the United States of America*, Washington, DC, September (http://www.informationclearinghouse.info/article2320.htm).

Ungar, Sanford J. (2005) Pitch Imperfect: The Trouble at the Voice of America. *Foreign Affairs.*

Unprecedented: The 2000 Presidential Election. (2002) A film by Richard Ray Pérez and Joan Sekler.

USAID. (1997) *USAID's Strategies for Sustainable Development.* Washington, DC: USAID.

———. (2002) *Foreign Aid in the National Interest: Promoting Freedom, Security, and Opportunity.* Washington, DC: USAID.

———. (2004) *U.S. Foreign Aid: Meeting the Challenges of the Twenty-First Century.* Washington, DC: USAID.

Valelly, Richard M. (1990) Vanishing Voters. *American Prospect* 1: 140–50.

Van Creveld, Martin. (1989) *Technology and War: From 2000 B.C. to the Present.* New York: Macmillan.

Vanderbush, Walt. (2009) Exiles and the Marketing of U.S. Policy toward Cuba and Iraq. *Foreign Policy Analysis* 5: 287–306.

Vasquez, John A. (1976) A Learning Theory of the American Anti-Vietnam War Movement. *Journal of Peace Research* 13: 299–314.

Vistica, Gregory. (2002) *Fall from Glory.* New York: Simon and Schuster.

Volkan, Vamik D. (1988) *The Need to Have Enemies and Allies: From Clinical Practice to International Relationships.* Northvale, NJ: Jason Aronson.

von Clausewitz, Carl. (1832) *On War.* London: Penguin Press [reprint 1982].

Walcott, Charles E., and Karen M. Holt. (2003) The Bush Staff and Cabinet System. *Perspectives on Political Science* 32: 150–55.

Walcott, Charles E., Shirley Anne Warshaw, and Stephen J. Wayne. (2001) The Chief of Staff. *Presidential Studies Quarterly* 31: 464–89.

Walker, J. Samuel. (1981) Historians and Cold War Origins: The New Consensus. In *American Foreign Relations: A Historiographical Review*, edited by Gerald K. Haines and J. Samuel Walker, pp. 207–36. Westport, CT: Greenwood Press.

Walker, Stephen G. (1977) The Interface between Beliefs and Behavior: Henry Kissinger's Operational Code and the Vietnam War. *Journal of Conflict Resolution* 21: 129–68.

Waller, Douglas C. (1987) *Congress and the Nuclear Freeze: An Inside Look at the Politics of a Mass Movement.* Amherst: University of Massachusetts Press.

———. (1991) The CIA Called It—But Nobody Listened. *Newsweek*, September 2, p. 44.

Walsh, Kenneth T. (2008) The Leadership Style of the Next President. *U.S. News and World Report*, October 17, p. 35.

Walt, Stephen. (2005) *Taming American Power: The Global Responses to U.S. Primacy.* New York: W.W. Norton.

Waltz, Kenneth N. (1959) *Man, the State, and War.* New York: Columbia University Press.

The Washington Post. (2001) *Deadlock: The Inside Story of America's Closest Election.* New York: Public Affairs.

Watson, Jack H., Jr. (1993) The Clinton White House. *Presidential Studies Quarterly* 23: 431–36.

Wattenberg, Martin P. (1991) *The Rise of Candidate-Centered Politics: Presidential Elections of the 1980s.* Cambridge, MA: Harvard University Press.

———. (1997) The Crisis of Electoral Politics. *Atlantic Monthly*, May, p. 119.

———. (1998) *The Decline of American Political Parties.* Cambridge, MA: Harvard University Press.

Wayne, Stephen J. (2001) *The Road to the White House: The Politics of Presidential Elections.* New York: St. Martin's Press.

Weeks, William Earl. (1996) *Building the Continental Empire: American Expansion from the Revolution to the Civil War.* Chicago, IL: Ivan R. Dee.

Weil, Martin. (1978) *A Pretty Good Club*. New York: W.W. Norton.

Weinberg, Albert. (1940) The Historical Meaning of the American Doctrine of Isolation. *American Political Science Review* 34: 539–47.

Welch, David A. (2005) *Painful Choices: A Theory of Foreign Policy Change*. Princeton, NJ: Princeton University Press.

Welsome, Eileen. (1999) *The Plutonium Files: America's Secret Medical Experiments in the Cold War*. New York: Random House.

Westerfield, H. Bradford. (1995) *Inside the CIA's Private World*. New Haven, CT: Yale University Press.

Western, Jon. (2005) *Selling Intervention and War: The Presidency, the Media, and the American Public*. Baltimore, MD: The Johns Hopkins University Press.

White, Ralph K. (1968) *Nobody Wanted War: Misperception in Vietnam and Other Wars*. Garden City, NY: Doubleday.

Whither the Study of Governmental Politics in Foreign Policymaking? A Symposium. (1998). *Mershon International Studies Review* 42: 205–55.

Whyte, William. (1956) *The Organization Man*. New York: Simon and Schuster.

Wiarda, Howard. (2000) Beyond the Pale: The Bureaucratic Politics of United States Policy in Mexico. *World Affairs* 162: 174–90.

Wilcox, Clyde. (1991) *God's Warriors: The Christian Right in Twentieth-Century America*. Baltimore, MD: Johns Hopkins University Press.

Wildavsky, Aaron. (1966) The Two Presidencies Thesis. *Transaction* 4: 7–14.

Wildavsky, Ben. (1996) Under the Gun. *National Journal* 26: 1417.

Wilkinson, Jeff. (2012) Veterans' New Mission: Find a Job. *The State*, March 18.

Williams, William A. (1988) *The Tragedy of American Diplomacy*. New York: W.W. Norton.

Wills, Garry. (1969) *Nixon Agonistes: The Crisis of the Self-Made Man*. New York: Houghton Mifflin.

———. (1988) *Reagan's America*. New York: Penguin.

———. (1990) *Under God: Religion and American Politics*. New York: Simon and Schuster.

Wilson, James Q. (1989) *Bureaucracy: What Government Agencies Do and Why They Do It*. New York: Basic Books.

———. (1995) *Political Organizations*. Princeton, NJ: Princeton University Press.

Wilson, Scott, and Sewell Chan. (2004) As Insurgency Grew, So Did Prison Abuse. *Washington Post*, May 10, p. A1.

Wines, Michael. (1990) The Iraqi Invasion; U.S. Says Bush Surprised by Iraqi Strike. *New York Times*, August 5, p. 8.

———. (1991) Washington at Work; C.I.A. Sidelines Its Gulf Cassandra. *New York Times*, January 24, p. A13.

Winks, Robin. (1996) *Cloak and Gown Scholars in the Secret War, 1939–1961*. New Haven, CT: Yale University Press.

Wittkopf, Eugene. (1990) *Faces of Internationalism: Public Opinion and American Foreign Policy*. Durham, NC: Duke University Press.

Wolfe, Eric. (1982) *Europe and the People without History*. Berkeley: University of California Press.

Wolffe, Richard. (2010) *Revival: The Struggle for Survival Inside the Obama White House*. New York: Crown Publishers.

Wolfe, Tom. (1965) *The Kandy-Kolored Tangerine-Flake Streamline Baby*. New York: Bantam.

Wood, David. (1983) B-1 Symbolizes Power of Military-Industrial Complex. *Los Angeles Times*, July 10, pp. 8–9.

Woodward, Bob. (1987) *Veil: The Secret Wars of the CIA, 1981–1987*. New York: Simon and Schuster.

———. (1991) *The Commanders*. New York: Simon and Schuster.

———. (2001) CIA Told to Do "Whatever Necessary" to Kill Bin Laden. *Washington Post*, October 21, p. A1.

———. (2002) *Bush at War*. New York: Simon and Schuster.

———. (2004) *Plan of Attack*. New York: Simon and Schuster.

———. (2007) *State of Denial*. New York: Simon and Schuster.

———. (2010) *Obama's Wars*. New York: Simon and Schuster.

Worldwide Box Office. (2009) *Domestic and International Movie Box Office Revenues (in Millions of U.S. Dollars)*. (www.worldwideboxoffice.com/).

Wright, Robin, and Thomas Ricks. (2004) Wider FBI Probe of Pentagon Leaks Includes Chalabi. *Washington Post*, September 3, p. A1.

Wu, H. D. (1998) Investigating the Determinants of International News Flow: A Meta-Analysis. *International Communication Gazette* 60: 493–512.

Wyden, Peter. (1979) *Bay of Pigs: The Untold Story*. London: Jonathan Cape.

Wylie, J. C. (1966) *Military Strategy: A General Theory of Power Control*. New Brunswick, NJ: Rutgers University Press.

Yarmolinsky, Adam. (1971) *The Military Establishment: Its Impact on American Society*. New York: Harper and Row.

Yergin, Daniel. (1983) *Shattered Peace: The Origins of the Cold War and the National Security State*. Boston, MA: Houghton Mifflin.

———. (1991) *The Prize: The Epic Quest for Money, Oil, and Power*. New York: Simon and Schuster.

Yoffe, Emily. (2008) The Supervisor, the Champion, and the Promoter: What Psychological Personality Tests Reveal about Clinton, Obama, and McCain. *Slate* (http://www.slate.com/articles/news_and_politics/ politics/2008/02/the_supervisor_the_champion_and_the_ promoter.html).

Yoo, John C. (1996) The Continuation of Politics by Other Means: The Original Understanding of War Powers. *California Law Review* 84: 170–305.

———. (2005) *The Powers of War and Peace: The Constitution and Foreign Affairs after 9/11*. Chicago, IL: University of Chicago Press.

Zakaria, Fareed. (2008) *The Post-American World*. New York: W.W. Norton.

Zegart, Amy B. (1999) *Flawed by Design: The Evolution of the CIA, JCS, and NSC*. Stanford, CA: Stanford University Press.

———. (2005) September 11 and the Adaptation Failure of the U.S. Intelligence Agencies. *International Security* 29: 78–111.

Zimmerman, Tim. (1997) Twilight of the Diplomats. *U.S. News & World Report*, January 27, pp. 48–50.

INDEX

Note: Page numbers followed by "f" indicate figure; and those followed by "t" indicate table.